SIMPLE
ABUNDANCE

SIMPLE ABUNDANCE

A Daybook of Comfort and Joy

Sarah Ban Breathnach

WARNER BOOKS

A Time Warner Company

I would like to gratefully acknowledge all of the writers I have quoted from in my meditations for their wisdom, comfort and inspiration. An exhaustive search was done to determine whether previously published material included in this book required permission to reprint. If there has been an error, I apologize and a correction will be made in subsequent editions.

The following authors, their agents, and publishers have graciously granted permission to include excerpts from the following:

Loving and Leaving the Good Life by Helen Nearing, published by Chelsea Green Publishing Co., is reprinted by arrangement with Eleanor Friede Books, Inc. © 1992 by Helen Nearing. All rights reserved.

In Search of Balance, copyright © 1991 by John Robbins and Ann Mortifee. Reprinted by permission of H J Kramer Inc. P.O. Box 1082, Tiburon, CA 94920. All rights reserved.

Creating Money, copyright © 1988 by Sanaya Roman and Duane Packer. Reprinted by permission of H J Kramer Inc. P.O. Box 1082, Tiburon, CA 94920. All rights reserved.

A Return to Love by Marianne Williamson. Copyright © 1992 by Marianne Williamson. Reprinted by permission of HarperCollins Publishers, Inc.
Copyright information continued on page 512.

SIMPLE ABUNDANCE™ is a trademark of Sarah Ban Breathnach
Warner Books, Inc., 1271 Avenue of the Americas, New York, NY 10020

Visit our Web site at http://warnerbooks.com

A Time Warner Company

Printed in the United States of America
First Printing: November 1995

40 39 38

Library of Congress-in-Publication Data
Ban Breathnach, Sarah.
Simple abundance : a daybook of comfort and joy / Sarah Ban
Breathnach.
p. cm.
ISBN 0-446-51913-8 (hardcover)
1. Women—Religious life—Meditations. 2. Women—Conduct of life—
Meditations. 3. Simplicity. 4. Self-actualization (Psychology)
5. Devotional calendars. I. Title.
BL625.7.B35 1995
158'.12—dc20   95-32330
CIP

Book design by Giorgetta Bell McRee

Her eye, her ear, were tuning forks, burning glasses, which caught the minutest refraction or echo of a thought or feeling. . . . She heard a deeper vibration, a kind of composite echo, of all that the writer said, and did not say.

—WILLA CATHER

For
Chris Tomasino
with love and gratitude
and
Katie
who is the Deeper Vibration
Always

One moved Heaven for this book,
the other moved earth.

. . . in a time lacking in truth and certainty and filled with anguish and despair, no woman should be shamefaced in attempting to give back to the world, through her work, a portion of its lost heart.

—LOUISE BOGAN

FOREWORD

Often people attempt to live their lives backwards: they try to have more things, or more money, in order to do more of what they want so that they will be happier. The way it actually works is the reverse. You must first be *who you really are, then,* do *what you need to do, in order to* have *what you want.*

—MARGARET YOUNG

Several years ago, after I'd written two books celebrating nineteenth-century domestic life, I was about to begin writing one on Victorian decorative details. But the thought of ruminating on ruffles and flourishes for a year brought dread to my heart. What I wanted to write was a book that would show me how to reconcile my deepest spiritual, authentic, and creative longings with often-overwhelming and conflicting commitments—to my husband and daughter, invalid mother, work at home, work in the world, siblings, friends, and community. I knew I wasn't the only woman hurtling through real life as if it were an out-of-body experience. I knew I wasn't the only woman frazzled, depressed, worn to a raveling. But I also knew I certainly wasn't the woman with the answers. I didn't even know the questions.

I wanted so much—money, success, recognition, genuine creative expression—but had absolutely no clue as to what I truly needed. At times my passionate hungers were so voracious I could deal with them only through denial. I was a workaholic, careaholic, and perfectionist. I couldn't remember the last time I was kind to myself. Was I ever? More often than it feels comfortable to admit, I was an angry, envious woman, constantly comparing myself to others only to become resentful because of what seemed to be missing from my life, although I couldn't have told you what it was. This secret sense of longing contributed to a perpetual state of guilt because I share my life with a marvelous man and our smart, sweet, witty, beautiful child, whom I adore. I had so much. I felt as if I didn't have the right to want more.

Money was an enormous, emotionally charged issue that controlled my ability to be happy because I let it; money was the only way I could measure my success and self-worth. If I couldn't write a check on my accomplishments, they didn't exist. Frustrated and unable to fathom why some women appeared to lead much more fulfilling lives—even though I was conscientiously connecting all the dots—I careened between feeling that I was frittering my life away to feeling that I was sacrificing it on the altar of my own ambitions.

I was a woman in desperate need of *Simple Abundance*.

But before this book could be written, I had to take stock of what was working in my life and what wasn't. Perhaps for the first time, I had to be ruthlessly honest both inwardly and outwardly. During this time of profound introspection, six practical, creative, and spiritual principles—gratitude, simplicity, order, harmony, beauty, and joy—became the catalysts that helped me define a life of my own. One morning I awoke to the realization that, almost imperceptibly, I'd become a happy woman, experiencing more moments of contentment than distress. Feeling confident again, I proposed writing a downshifting lifestyle book for women who want, as I do, to live by their own lights.

But the book you're reading now bears absolutely no resemblance to the book I began or to the book my editor expected. While I wrote for two years, *Simple Abundance* underwent an extraordinary metamorphosis, as did I. On the page every morning, spirituality, authenticity, and creativity converged into an intimate search for Wholeness. I began writing about eliminating clutter and ended up on a safari of the self and Spirit. No one is more astonished by this than I am.

As *Simple Abundance* evolved from creating a manageable lifestyle into living in a state of grace, I began to barely recognize the woman I once was. *Simple Abundance* has enabled me to encounter everyday epiphanies, find the Sacred in the ordinary, the Mystical in the mundane, fully enter into the sacrament of the present moment. I've made the unexpected but thrilling discovery that everything in my life is significant enough to be a continuous source of reflection, revelation, and reconnection: bad hair, mood swings, car pools, excruciating deadlines, overdrawn bank accounts, dirty floors, grocery shopping, exhaustion, illness, nothing to wear, unexpected company, even the final twenty-five pounds. *Simple Abundance* has reminded me what to do with a few loaves and fishes and has shown me how to spin straw into gold. *Simple Abundance* has given me the transcendent awareness that an authentic life is the most personal form of worship. Everyday life has become my prayer.

Writing *Simple Abundance* has brought me to the awareness that the reason I was so unhappy, frustrated, resentful, envious, and angry was because I wasn't living the Real Life for which I was created. An authentic life. I try to, now.

At least I can now recognize boundaries; what's more, I'm gradually starting to set them. For a woman in the 1990s, this is nothing less than miraculous. I don't have a million dollars in the bank, but I now realize that abundance and lack are parallel realities; every day I make the choice of which one to inhabit. Now I understand that all my hours aren't billable; finding a quiet center in which to create and sustain an authentic life has become as essential as breathing. I know all this because at the heart of the *Simple Abundance* journey is an exhilarating and earth-rumbling awakening, one that has utterly changed how I view myself and my daily round. *The authentic self is the Soul made visible.*

This book is organized as a walk through the year, beginning on New Year's Day. But if this book finds its way to you in April, don't think that you can't use it. I would suggest, however, that you go back to read the month of January, in which the six *Simple Abundance* principles and how they work are explained. February is devoted to excavating your authentic self; after that, each month ruminates on finding your authenticity in your daily round: the domestic arts, work, beauty, fashion, and personal pursuits that bring contentment.

Reading books changes lives. So does writing them. May *Simple Abundance*, through its gentle lessons of comfort and joy, help you find the authentic life you were born to live.

—SARAH BAN BREATHNACH
May 1995

SIMPLE
ABUNDANCE

JANUARY

And now let us welcome the New Year
Full of things that have never been.
—RAINER MARIA RILKE

January, the month of new beginnings and cherished memories, beckons. Come, let winter weave her wondrous spell: cold, crisp, woolen-muffler days, long dark evenings of savory suppers, lively conversations, or solitary joys. Outside the temperature drops as the snow falls softly. All of nature is at peace. We should be, too. Draw hearthside. This is the month to dream, to look forward to the year ahead and the journey within.

JANUARY 1

A Transformative Year of Delight and Discovery

There are years that ask questions and years that answer.
—Zora Neale Hurston

New Year's Day. A fresh start. A new chapter in life waiting to be written. New questions to be asked, embraced, and loved. Answers to be discovered and then lived in this transformative year of delight and self-discovery.

Today carve out a quiet interlude for yourself in which to dream, pen in hand. Only dreams give birth to change. What are your hopes for the future as you reflect on the years that have passed? Gradually, as you become curator of your own contentment, you will learn to embrace the gentle yearnings of your heart. But this year, instead of resolutions, write down your most private aspirations. Those longings you have kept tucked away until the time seems right. Trust that now is the time. Ask the questions. The Simple Abundance path brings confidence that the answers will come and we will discover—day by day—how to live them.

Take a leap of faith and begin this wondrous new year by believing. Believe in yourself. And believe that there is a loving Source—a Sower of Dreams—just waiting to be asked to help you make your dreams come true.

JANUARY 2

Loving the Questions

You only live once—but if you work it right, once is enough.
—Joe E. Lewis

How often in the past have you turned away from all that is unresolved in your heart because you feared questioning? But what if you knew that a year from today you could be living the most creative, joyous, and fulfilling life you could imagine? What would it be? What changes would you make?

How and where would you begin? Do you see why the *questions* are so important?

"Be patient toward all that is unsolved in your heart and try to love the questions themselves," the German poet Rainer Maria Rilke urges us. "Do not now seek the answers which cannot be given you because you would not be able to live them and the point is to live everything. Live the questions now. . . ."

The answers to your questions will come, but only after you know which ones are worth asking. Wait. Live your questions. Then ask. Become open to the changes that the answers will inevitably bring. This may take some time, but time is the New Year's bountiful blessing: three hundred sixty-five bright mornings and starlit evenings; fifty-two promising weeks; twelve transformative months full of beautiful possibilities; and four splendid seasons. A simply abundant year to be savored.

JANUARY 3

Simple Abundance: The Inner Journey

simple, adj. 1: without embellishment; 2: clarity of form and thought; 3: fundamental

abundance, n. 1: an ample quantity, profusion; 2: wealth; 3: plentifulness

simple abundance, 1: an inner journey; 2: a spiritual and practical course in creative living; 3: a tapestry of contentment

Today I want you to become *aware* that you already possess all the inner wisdom, strength, and creativity needed to make your dreams come true. This is hard for most of us to realize because the source of this unlimited personal power is buried so deeply beneath the bills, the car pool, the deadlines, the business trip, and the dirty laundry that we have difficulty accessing it in our daily lives. When we can't access our inner resources, we come to the flawed conclusion that happiness and fulfillment come only from external events. That's because external events usually bring with them some sort of change. And so we've learned to rely on circumstances outside ourselves for forward or backward momentum as we hurtle through life. But we don't have to do that any longer. We can learn to be the catalysts for our own change.

At the heart of Simple Abundance is an authentic awakening, one that resonates within your soul: you already possess all you need to be genuinely happy. The way you reach that awareness is through an inner journey that brings about an emotional, psychological, and spiritual transformation. A deep inner shift in your reality occurs, aligning you with the creative energy of the Universe. Such change is possible when you invite Spirit to open up the eyes of your awareness to the abundance that is already yours.

There are six principles that will act as guides as we make our inner journey over the next year. These are the six threads of abundant living which, when woven together, produce a tapestry of contentment that wraps us in inner peace, well-being, happiness, and a sense of security. First there is *gratitude*. When we do a mental and spiritual inventory of all that we have, we realize that we are very rich indeed. Gratitude gives way to *simplicity*—the desire to clear out, pare down, and realize the essentials of what we need to live truly well. Simplicity brings with it *order*, both internally and externally. A sense of order in our life brings us *harmony*. Harmony provides us with the inner peace we need to appreciate the beauty that surrounds us each day, and *beauty* opens us to *joy*. But just as with any beautiful needlepoint tapestry, it is difficult to see where one stitch ends and another begins. So it is with Simple Abundance.

Pick up the needle with me and make the first stitch on the canvas of your life. Invite Spirit to open up the eyes of your inner awareness. Be still and wait expectantly, knowing that in the warp and woof of your daily life as it exists today are the golden threads of a simply abundant tomorrow.

JANUARY 4

This Isn't a Dress Rehearsal

When you perform . . . you are out of yourself—larger and more potent, more beautiful. You are for minutes heroic. This is power. This is glory on earth. And it is yours, nightly.

—AGNES DE MILLE

You've probably heard the expression "life's not a dress rehearsal." Unfortunately, many of us unconsciously act as if it were. Like an actress just going through the motions in order to conserve her creative energy and focus for opening night, we hold back. Perhaps you save the pretty china for when company comes; perhaps you're like me and rarely dress up when you're home alone. If we're not playing to an audience, does it really matter?

That's a good question to ask ourselves as the New Year begins and we examine the quality of our real life journey. It does take more effort to set an inviting table, but it enhances our enjoyment of eating. We all feel better when we take those few extra minutes to fix our hair and put on makeup, but what's more, we *act* different. Every actress knows the magic power of props and costumes to create special moods both onstage and off.

None of us can be expected to perform every minute of our lives. But a lot of us might tap into the power, excitement, and glory of Real Life more frequently if we cast ourselves as the leading ladies in our own lives.

JANUARY 5

The Woman You Were Meant to Be

Many women today feel a sadness we cannot name. Though we accomplish much of what we set out to do, we sense that something is missing in our lives and—fruitlessly—search "out there" for the answers. What's often wrong is that we are disconnected from an authentic sense of self.

—EMILY HANCOCK

Has this ever happened to you? You are washing your face, and suddenly you do not recognize the woman staring back at you. "Who is this?" you ask the mirror on the wall. No reply. She looks vaguely familiar but bears little resemblance to the woman you were expecting to see there. Psychologists call this phenomenon a "displacement of self," and it usually occurs during times of great stress (which for many of us is an everyday occurrence).

But what's wrong? What is this sadness we cannot name? Here is a question that deserves loving meditation. Perhaps the heart of our melancholy is that we miss the woman we were meant to be. We miss our authentic selves. But the good news is that even if you have ignored her overtures for decades ("Wear red . . . Cut your hair . . . Study art in Paris . . . Learn the tango . . ."), your authentic self has not abandoned you. Instead she has been waiting patiently for you to recognize her and reconnect. Turn away from the world this year and begin to listen. Listen to the whispers of your heart. Look within. Your silent companion has lit lanterns of love to illuminate the path to Wholeness. At long last, the journey you were destined to take has begun.

Standing Knee-Deep in a River and Dying of Thirst

The thirst after happiness is never extinguished in the heart of [woman].

—JEAN-JACQUES ROUSSEAU

The first time I heard Kathy Mattea's beautiful rendition of the country song "Standing Knee-Deep in a River (Dying of Thirst)," I was on my way to my daughter's school to pick up the afternoon car pool. Suddenly I had to pull over because I was crying so much I couldn't see the road in front of me. Until then, it had been a busy but good day. I was not consciously aware of being sad or depressed. So why was I crying?

As Kathy sang of friends who had been taken for granted, sweethearts she had known, and a wonderful world full of strangers just waiting to make a connection with us (while we turn our eyes away), something deep within me stirred. There was so much I was taking for granted. I didn't want to continue to live unconsciously.

The revelation that we have everything we need in life to make us happy but simply lack the conscious awareness to appreciate it can be as refreshing as lemonade on a hot afternoon. Or it can be as startling as cold water being thrown in our face. How many of us go through our days parched and empty, thirsting after happiness, when we're really standing knee-deep in the river of abundance? Yet make no mistake about it. The Universe will get our attention one way or another—with a sip or a splash. Let's choose today to quench our thirst for "the good life" we think others lead by acknowledging the good that already exists in our own lives. We can then offer the Universe the gift of our grateful hearts.

JANUARY 7

How Happy Are You Right Now?

Perhaps if one really knew when one was happy one would know the things that were necessary for one's life.

—JOANNA FIELD

How happy are you right now? Do you even know? Most women know what makes their parents, partners, or children happy. But when it comes to an awareness about the little, specific things in life that bring a smile to our faces and contentment to our own hearts, we often come up short.

In 1926 a young Englishwoman, Joanna Field, began to feel that she was not living a truly authentic life, that she did not know what made her truly happy. To remedy this she kept a journal in order to discover what specifically triggered the feeling of delight in her daily life. The journal, *A Life of One's Own*, was published in 1934. It was written, she confided, in the spirit of a detective who searches through the minutiae of the mundane in hopes of finding clues for what was missing in her life.

What is missing from many of our days is a true sense that we are enjoying the lives we are living. It is difficult to experience moments of happiness if we are not aware of what it is we genuinely love. We must learn to savor small, authentic moments that bring us contentment. Experiment with a new cookie recipe. Take the time to slowly arrange a bouquet of flowers in order to appreciate their colors, fragrance, and beauty. Sip a cup of tea on the front stoop in the sunshine. Pause for five minutes to pet a purring cat. Simple pleasures waiting to be enjoyed. Simple pleasures often overlooked.

Joanna Field discovered that she delighted in red shoes, good food, sudden bursts of laughter, reading in French, answering letters, loitering in a crowd at a fair and "a new idea when first it is grasped."

Let us each grasp a new idea this year. Let us grasp the awareness of what it is that makes us truly happy. Let us consider our personal preferences and learn how to recognize, then embrace, moments of happiness that are uniquely our own.

JANUARY 8

The Underrated Duty

There is no duty we so much underrate as the duty of being happy.
By being happy we sow anonymous benefits upon the world.
—ROBERT LOUIS STEVENSON

Perhaps you think you'll be happy when you get a bigger kitchen, or a new job, or the perfect someone with whom to share your life. But don't you want to start making happiness a habit right now? Every morning when we wake up we've been given a wonderful gift—another day of life—so let's make the most of it. No one can do it for us. "Happiness is not a possession to be prized," Daphne du Maurier wrote in *Rebecca*. "It is a quality of thought, a state of mind."

Let's adopt a new state of mind about happiness. Let's stop thinking that things outside our control will bring us happiness.

Admittedly, remodeling the kitchen, landing the job we've been dreaming of, or finding that special someone can make us feel—at least momentarily—happier. But the magic seeds of contentment are planted deep within us. Happiness that the world cannot take away only flourishes in the secret garden of our souls. By tending to our inner garden and uprooting the weeds of external expectations, we can nurture our authentic happiness the way we would nurture something that's beautiful and alive. Happiness is a *living* emotion.

Your happiness is not a frivolous, expendable luxury. The pursuit of happiness is an inalienable right guaranteed by the Declaration of Independence. But we have to be willing to pursue it. Ultimately, genuine happiness can only be realized once we commit to making it a personal priority in our lives. This may be new behavior for some of us and a bit intimidating. Be gentle with yourself. It will all unfold. Today you may not be familiar with the happiness habit. But like any new behavior, happiness can be learned.

What Is It You Truly Need?

In my life's chain of events nothing was accidental. Everything happened according to an inner need.

—HANNAH SENESH

Do you have everything you need right now? What about your wants? Few of us have everything we want, and at times our wants can seem positively all-consuming. Our sensibilities become confused and overstimulated by a mass media that glorifies beautiful people and expensive objects. It's easy to lose clarity about what it is we need to live authentically. Most of us *are* hungering for something more in our lives. But do you really think the answer can be found in a glossy magazine or on the movie screen?

If we are to live happy, creative, and fulfilled lives, it is crucial to distinguish between our wants and our needs. Unfortunately, many women blur the distinction and then wonder why they feel so diminished.

Make peace with the knowledge that you can't have everything you want. Why? Because it's more important for us to get everything we *need*. Like infants, we feel contentment when our essential needs are met.

Be courageous. Ask yourself: what is it I truly need to make me happy? The deeply personal answers to this vital question will be different for each of us. Trust the loving wisdom of your heart. It is only after we acknowledge our inner needs that we can harness the creative energy necessary to manifest them in our lives. "It is inevitable when one has a great need of something, one finds it," Gertrude Stein reminds us. "What you need you attract like a lover."

Until It Is Carved in Stone

It's only when we truly know and understand that we have a limited time on earth—and that we have no way of knowing when our time is up—that we will begin to live each day to the fullest, as if it was the only one we had.

—ELISABETH KÜBLER-ROSS

Visiting old cemeteries can be very illuminating. They are so still and silent. So quiet. Old cemeteries remind us that until it is carved in stone, realizing our heart's desire is possible every day if we recognize what it is that makes us happy.

In Thornton Wilder's play *Our Town* a deeply poignant scene takes place in a graveyard. Ghosts comfort the young heroine, who has recently died in childbirth. Emily, still longing for the life she has just left, wishes to revisit one ordinary, "unimportant" day in her life. When she gets her wish, she realizes how much the living take for granted.

Eventually her visit is too much for her to bear. "I didn't realize," she confesses mournfully, "all that was going on and we never noticed. . . . Good-by, world. Good-by, Grover's Corners . . . Mama and Papa. Good-by to clocks ticking . . . and Mama's sunflowers. And food and coffee. And new-ironed dresses and hot baths . . . and sleeping and waking up. Oh, earth, you're too wonderful for anybody to realize you."

This is the season of Epiphany, when the renewal of light and revelation are celebrated in the liturgy of the Catholic, Episcopal, and Eastern Orthodox churches. On our new path we seek everyday epiphanies—occasions on which we can experience the Sacred in the ordinary—and come to the awakening, as Emily finally does, that we cannot longer afford to throw away even one "unimportant" day by not noticing the wonder of it all. We have to be willing to discover and then appreciate the authentic moments of happiness available to all of us every day.

JANUARY 11

Is It Recession or Depression?

No pessimist ever discovered the secrets of the stars, or sailed to an uncharted land, or opened a new heaven to the human spirit.
—HELEN KELLER

It's a recession when your neighbor loses his job," Harry Truman observed, "and it's a depression when you lose your own." As downturns in the economy disturb more and more households, we begin to question seriously the financial yardstick by which we have been measuring our personal net worth and therefore our happiness.

Perhaps the recession has personally affected you and yours. It's hard to believe there's anybody that it hasn't touched, at least indirectly. Millions of women are scaling down their expectations of what constitutes the good life, redefining their values, reordering their priorities, and accepting the challenge of making a virtue out of necessity. But it's very easy to surrender to an emotional depression when a financial one occurs. It's easy to be pessimistic about tomorrow when today seems so bleak.

It's time we put thoughts of lack behind us. It's time for us to discover the secrets of the stars, to sail to an uncharted land, to open up a new heaven where our spirits can soar. But first we'll have to make changes. And lasting change does not happen overnight. Lasting change happens in infinitesimal increments: a day, an hour, a minute, a heartbeat at a time. And the change I'm encouraging you to make with me is fundamental. Take a deep breath. We're going to learn to become optimists.

Now be reassured. Optimism, like the happiness habit, can be learned. Start today with a little experiment. Smile at everyone you meet. Today expect something good to happen to you no matter what occurred yesterday. Realize the past no longer holds you captive. It can only continue to hurt you if you hold on to it. Let the past go. A simply abundant world awaits.

JANUARY 12

There Is No Scarcity

When money is plenty this is a man's world. When money is scarce it is a woman's world. When all else seems to have failed, the woman's instinct comes in. She gets the job. That is a reason why, in spite of all that happens, we continue to have a world.

—LADIES' HOME JOURNAL, *October 1932*

When you are worried about your health or the health of a loved one, your concentration focuses like a laser. Suddenly there's a clarity about all of life because you realize what is important. Living is important. Every day is a gift. You ask for another chance to get it right. Most of the time you're given it, and you're very grateful.

But worries about money mock you. They steal the joy of living because they follow you around all day like a dark, menacing shadow. At night they hover at the foot of your bed waiting to rob you of sleep. When you're worried about money you dread the days and you agonize at night. Without thinking, you throw away every precious twenty-four hours that come your way. You cease to live, and merely exist.

If you are worried about money today, take heart. You have the power to change your lifestyle and move from a feeling of lack and deprivation to a feeling of abundance and fulfillment. Money ebbs and flows in our lives. What should remain constant is our realization that abundance is our spiritual birthright. American gospel singer Mahalia Jackson once said that "It is easy to be independent when you've got money. But to be independent when you haven't got a thing—that's the Lord's test."

This is what I have learned and share with the seeker in you. The simpler we make our lives, the more abundant they become.

There is no scarity except in our souls.

JANUARY 13

Gratitude: Awakening the Heart

The eyes of my eyes are opened.

—E.E. CUMMINGS

Has this ever happened to you? You pick up a book and a sentence leaps off the page as if it had been written just for you. Or you hear a revelation in the lyrics of a song. Sometimes an angel seems to whisper in your ear.

One ordinary morning I realized I was emotionally and physically exhausted from concentrating on things I wanted to buy but couldn't afford. I felt trapped in a vicious circle. The more I focused on lack and on what I couldn't have, the more depressed I became. The more depressed I became, the more I focused on lack. My soul whispered that what I really yearned for was not financial security but financial serenity. I was still—quiet enough to listen. At that moment I acknowledged the deep longing in my heart. What I hungered for was an inner peace that the world could not take away. I asked for help and committed to following wheresoever Spirit would lead me. For the first time in my life I discarded my five-year goals and became a seeker, a pilgrim, a sojourner.

When I surrendered my desire for security and sought serenity instead, I looked at my life with open eyes. I saw that I had much for which to be grateful. I felt humbled by my riches and regretted that I took for granted the abundance that already existed in my life. How could I expect more from the Universe when I didn't appreciate what I already had?

Immediately I made an inventory of my life's assets: my health, a wonderful husband, a beautiful and happy daughter, their health, our home (small but comfortable), and three precious pets who daily bring me faithful companionship and great joy. There's always plenty of good food on the table and wine in the pantry. We are also blessed with many wonderful friends who care deeply about us and share in our lives.

Once I started, my list grew. I loved my work; it was being sent out into the world and had been well received. Many women had let me know that my first book had enriched their lives. I truly believe that what you give to the world will be returned to you—maybe not all at once or in the way you expect it—but if you give your very best, the very best will come back to you. Now was the moment to live my beliefs.

When I looked at my life's ledger I realized I was a very rich woman. What I was experiencing was merely a temporary cash-flow problem. Finally, I came to an inner awareness that my personal net worth couldn't possibly be determined by the size of my checking account balance. Neither can yours.

It doesn't matter how awareness arrives. What matters is that it comes. My heart began to overflow with gratefulness. I started giving thanks for everything: daisies in a jelly jar on my kitchen windowsill, the sweet fragrance of my daughter's hair, the first sip of tea in the morning, pork roast with apples and cranberries for Sunday supper, hearing the words "I love you" before I went to sleep. Each day began to offer me authentic moments of pleasure and contentment. But hadn't they before? The difference was that I was now noticing and appreciating each day's gifts. The power of gratefulness caught me by surprise.

All I ask you to do today is to open "the eyes of your eyes" and give your life another glance. Are your basic needs met? Do you have a home? Food on the table? Clothes to wear? Is there a regular paycheck coming in? Do you have dreams? Do you have your health? Can you walk, talk, see the beauty that surrounds you, listen to music that stirs your soul or makes your feet want to boogie? Do you have family and friends whom you love and who love you?

Then pause for a moment and give thanks. Let your heart awaken to the transforming power of gratefulness. Be open to exchanging your need for emotional and financial security for serenity. "No trumpets sound when the important decisions of our life are made," Agnes de Mille reminds us. "Destiny is made known silently."

JANUARY 14

The Gratitude Journal

Gratitude unlocks the fullness of life. It turns what we have into enough, and more. It turns denial into acceptance, chaos to order, confusion to clarity. It can turn a meal into a feast, a house into a home, a stranger into a friend. Gratitude makes sense of our past, brings peace for today, and creates a vision for tomorrow.

—MELODY BEATTIE

There are several tools that I'm going to suggest you use as you begin your inner exploration. While all of them will help you become happier and more content and will nurture your creativity, this first tool could change the quality of your life beyond belief: it's what I call a daily gratitude journal. I have a beautiful blank book and each night before I go to bed, I write down five things that I can be grateful about that day. Some days my list will be filled with amazing things, most days just simple joys. "Mikey got lost in a fierce storm but I found him shivering, wet but unharmed. I listened to Puccini while cleaning and remembered how much I love opera."

Other days—rough ones—I might think that I don't have five things to be grateful for, so I'll write down my basics: my health, my husband and daughter, their health, my animals, my home, my friends, and the comfortable bed that I'm about to get into, as well as the fact that the day's over. That's okay. Real life isn't always going to be perfect or go our way, but the recurring acknowledgment of what *is working* in our lives can help us not only survive but surmount our difficulties.

The gratitude journal has to be the first step on the Simple Abundance path or it just won't work for you. Simplicity, order, harmony, beauty, and joy—all the other principles that can transform your life will not blossom and flourish without gratitude. If you want to travel this journey with me, *the gratitude journal is not an option.*

Why? Because you simply will not be the same person two months from now after consciously giving thanks each day for the abundance that exists in your life. And you will have set in motion an ancient spiritual law: the more you have and are grateful for, the more will be given you.

I have told you that the Simple Abundance path is a transformative process. We're going to work on one principle for two months at a time, trying to weave that principle into the fabric of our daily life.

Let's begin today with gratitude. Select the prettiest, most inviting blank book you can find for your gratitude journal. Make a pleasant outing for its selection. Note the fabric or design of the cover. The look and feel of the paper. Do you prefer ruled pages or blank? Perhaps you can find one with a ribbon clasp. One of the most valuable lessons Simple Abundance has taught me is that it is in the smallest details that the flavor of life is savored.

As the months pass and you fill your journal with blessings, an inner shift in your reality will occur. Soon you will be delighted to discover how content and hopeful you are feeling. As you focus on the abundance rather than on the lack in your life, you will be designing a wonderful new blueprint for the future. This sense of fulfillment is gratitude at work, transforming your dreams into reality.

A French proverb reminds us that "Gratitude is the heart's memory." Begin this day to explore and integrate this beautiful, life-affirming principle into your life, and the miracle you have been seeking will unfold to your wonder and amazement.

JANUARY 15

Simple Gifts: Embracing Simplicity

'Tis a gift to be simple,
'Tis a gift to be free,
'Tis a gift to come down
Where we ought to be
And when we find ourselves
In the place that's right
'Twill be in the valley
Of love and delight.

—NINETEENTH-CENTURY SHAKER HYMN

Is there a woman today who does not yearn for a simpler life? But for what do we yearn? To chuck it all in and open up a bed-and-breakfast in Vermont? Or could it be something more fundamental, like the simple pleasure of concentrating on one task at a time?

Once we take stock of our lives and let gratitude begin its transformative work, the next step on the path unfolds naturally. When we appreciate how much we have, we feel the urge to pare down, get back to basics, and learn what is essential for our happiness. We long to realize what's really important. Is it more important for you to work overtime to buy that new dining room set or to attend Little League games? Perhaps you could refinish the table and chairs you now have and add some colorful cushions. These choices are part of simplifying our lives. Welcome them. They are part of the authentic journey.

Many people believe simplicity implies doing without. On the contrary. True simplicity as a conscious life choice illuminates our lives from within. True simplicity is both buoyant and bountiful, able to liberate depressed spirits from the bondage and burden of extravagance and excess. True simplicity can elevate ordinary moments, dreary lives, and even inanimate objects—as anyone who has ever looked at an exquisite piece of Shaker furniture will attest—from the mundane to the transcendent.

Less can mean more for those of us on the Simple Abundance path. Today just think about how appealing simplicity can be. Visualize a bouquet of bright yellow daffodils in a white milk jug on a pine mantel, sunlight streaming through sparkling clean windows, the shine of beautifully varnished wooden floors, the shimmering glow and fragrance of pure beeswax candles. Trust that through the balm of simplicity your frazzled and weary soul can discover the place where you ought to be. Every day offers us simple gifts when we are willing to search our hearts for the place that's right for each of us.

JANUARY 16

A Sense of Order: Cultivating Contentment

Order is the shape upon which beauty depends.

—PEARL BUCK

For years I have suspected that in happy and fulfilled lives domesticity and spirituality are invisibly but inexorably connected—one a golden thread, one a silver filament—which, when woven together, create a tapestry of contentment. The Shakers, a religious communal sect that flourished in America during the mid-nineteenth century, invoked a prayer each morning for the grace that would enable them to express their love of God through their daily tasks—tasks as simple and mundane as making a bed. And the seventeenth-century Carmelite friar, Brother Lawrence, wrote in his devotional classic, *Practicing the Presence of God,* that frequently he felt the spirit of God among the pots, pans, and potatoes in his kitchen as he was preparing a meal for his fellow monks.

Whenever I am feeling overwhelmed by outside circumstances—worries about money, concern over a sick family member, or anxiety over prolonged business negotiations—instinctively I turn to homegrown rituals to restore my equilibrium. There is an immediate emotional and psychological payoff to getting our houses in order. We might not be able to control what's happening externally in our lives but we can learn to look to our own inner resources for a sense of comfort that nurtures and sustains. I have even noticed that there is a direct correlation between the days when I'm feeling depressed and the days when the house is in disarray. I suspect that I'm not alone. "It's not the tragedies that kill us," Dorothy Parker once observed, "it's the messes."

If you feel constantly adrift but don't know why, be willing to explore the role that order—or the lack of it—plays in your life. No woman can think clearly when constantly surrounded by clutter, chaos, and confusion, no matter who is responsible for it. Begin to think of order not as a straitjacket of "shoulds" (make the bed, wash the dishes, take out the garbage) but as a shape—the foundation—for the beautiful new life you are creating. It may be as simple as putting something back that you take out, hanging something up that you take off, or teaching those who live with you that they must do the same for the common good of all.

There is a Divine Order—a Sublime Order—inherent in the Universe. We can tap into this powerful source of creative energy when we are willing to gradually cultivate a sense of order as to how we conduct our daily affairs. Invite Divine Order into your life today and a more serene tomorrow will unfold.

JANUARY 17

Harmony: Achieving Balance in Our Lives

The notes I handle no better than many pianists. But the pauses between the notes—ah, that is where the art resides.
—ARTUR SCHNABEL

A Chopin piano nocturne played by a novice musician and by a virtuoso will not sound the same. That's because one of the two pianists has had a lifetime to practice the music as well as learn when to pause in order to color the notes with passion.

So it is with the concerto of our lives. Individual notes must be learned and played and practiced before we achieve harmony. And above all, we must learn how to pause.

Harmony is the inner cadence of contentment we feel when the melody of life is in tune. When somehow we're able to strike the right chord—to balance the expectations of our families and our responsibilities in the world on the one hand with our inner needs for spiritual growth and personal expression on the other. This is one of the most difficult challenges any woman faces because it requires that we make choices every day. And yet most of us often feel too tired to choose anything more than what to have for dinner! Perhaps this explains why we often hear only a cacophony of dissonant demands that drown out the symphonies our souls long to compose. Usually, when the distractions of daily life deplete our energy, the first thing we eliminate is the thing we need the most: quiet, reflective time. Time to dream, time to think, time to contemplate what's working and what's not, so that we can make changes for the better.

On the Simple Abundance path we begin to learn how to pause. As we bring the principles of gratitude, simplicity, and order into our lives, harmony emerges. We learn to balance demands with pleasures, moments of solitude with a need for companionship, work with play, activity with rest, the inner woman with the outer packaging.

Today, just try slowing down. Approach the day as if it were an adagio—a melody played in an easy, graceful manner. Listen to music that soothes and uplifts your spirit. And while you listen, pause to consider how all the individual notes come together harmoniously to give expression to the entire score.

So it shall be with your world. With harmony as your guide, trust that your everyday moments will soon begin to resonate in a rhapsody of fulfillment.

Beauty: Opening Our Eyes to the Beauty That Surrounds Us

You agree—I'm sure you agree, that beauty is the only thing worth living for.

—AGATHA CHRISTIE

While the Simple Abundance path is gentle, its lessons are powerful. First of all, we learn to be grateful no matter what our circumstances may be. In offering gratitude for our real lives, we discover how to change them for the better. As we embrace simplicity, we learn that less is truly more. This freedom encourages us to bring order to our affairs and cultivate harmony in our inner world. Going at our own pace, learning to recognize our limitations, appreciating our progress, we weave the lessons into the fabric of our daily moments until they become a part of us.

Suddenly one day we feel very much alive and desire more beauty in our personal quest. We come to a deep awareness that creating a beautiful life is our highest calling. "It was as if I had worked for years on the wrong side of a tapestry, learning accurately all its lines and figures, yet always missing its color and sheen," the journalist Anna Louise Strong confessed in 1935. We understand her sentiments as life's color and sheen and beauty call to us.

Today, explore ways to see your world differently. Let your eyes drink in the beauty that surrounds you. Walk to a gallery on your lunch hour and meditate upon a beautiful painting or into your backyard this afternoon to catch that "certain Slant of light" that so enthralled Emily Dickinson. Gaze into the faces of those you love, set the table with care, and relish the preparations you make for dinner, delighting in the presentation of your meal. Light the candles, pour wine or sparkling water in your prettiest goblets, and celebrate this new awareness. It is in the details of life that beauty is revealed, sustained, and nurtured.

Outside, winter's darkness closes in. Inside, you have found your own Light.

Joy: Learning Life's Lessons with a Light Heart

I cannot believe that the inscrutable universe turns on an axis of suffering; surely the strange beauty of the world must somewhere rest on pure joy.

—LOUISE BOGAN

The Simple Abundance journey takes us to undiscovered territory. We learn each day how cultivating gratitude tills the soil of our soul and then how the seeds of simplicity and order send their roots down deep into the earth of our everyday existence. As we progress, harmony inspires us with quiet courage to create an authentic life for ourselves and those we love. With patience, beauty blossoms and our hearts experience not only happiness, which is often fleeting, but a wellspring of joy that refreshes and renews. We have found our true place in the world. "With an eye made quiet by the power of harmony, and the deep power of joy," William Wordsworth wrote, "we see into the life of things."

Seeing into the life of things is what engages us at this point in the transformative process. From deep within there comes a longing to give up the path of struggle as a way to learn life's lessons. Finally we are ready to embrace the path of joy.

Learning to live in the present moment is part of the path of joy. But this requires a profound inner shift in our reality. Many of us unconsciously create dramas in our minds, expecting the worst from a situation only to have our expectations become a self-fulfilling prophecy. Inadvertently, we become authors of our own misfortune. And so we struggle from day to day, from crisis to crisis, bruised and battered by circumstances without realizing that we always have a choice.

But what if you learned how to stop the dramas and started to trust the flow of life and the goodness of Spirit? What if you began to expect the best from any situation? Isn't it possible that you could write new chapters in your life with happy endings? For many of us this is such a radical departure from the way we have been behaving that it seems unbelievable. Yet it is possible. Suspend your disbelief. Take a leap of faith. After all, what have you got to lose but misery and lack?

Begin today. Declare out loud to the Universe that you are willing to let go of struggle and eager to learn through joy. It just may take you at your word. What's more, you'll discover, much to your amazement and delight, that such blessings have been waiting patiently for you to claim them all along.

Acres of Diamonds

Your diamonds are not in far distant mountains or in yonder seas;
they are in your own backyard, if you but dig for them.
—RUSSELL H. CONWELL

Few motivational talks have influenced or inspired as many people as the famous Victorian lecture that was known as "Acres of Diamonds." Russell H. Conwell, a former newspaper correspondent and minister, delivered his speech more than six thousand times between 1877 and 1925. When it was published it became an immediate best-seller and a classic in inspirational literature.

The story Conwell told in his lecture had enormous appeal. It recounted the life of a Persian farmer named Ali Hafed who sold his farm and left his family to travel the world in search of wealth. He looked everywhere but he could not find the diamonds he lusted after. Finally, alone and in despair as a homeless pauper, he ended his own life. His search for riches had consumed him. In the meantime, the man who bought the land from Hafed was grateful for every blade of grass that was now his and lavished love and hard work on his farm. At night, surrounded by his family and eating the fruits of his labor, he was a contented man. Finally one day he made a remarkable discovery. In the backyard that Ali Hafed had abandoned was a diamond mine—literally an acre of diamonds. The simple farmer became wealthy beyond his wildest dreams.

Conwell used this parable to illustrate an extraordinary and wonderful message: within each of us lies a wellspring of abundance and the seeds of opportunity. For each of us there is a deeply personal dream waiting to be discovered and fulfilled. When we cherish our dream and then invest love, creative energy, perseverance, and passion in ourselves, we will achieve an authentic success.

Where is your acre of diamonds? If you could do anything in the world, what would it be? Yes, that very thing right now that you believe is impossible! Would you open a store, nurture a family, design a dress, write a screenplay?

We all have an acre of diamonds waiting to be discovered, cherished, and mined. We all have a place from where to begin. Let your imagination soar, for it is your soul's blueprint for success. On the Simple Abundance path you will discover that your own opportunity for personal success, authentic happiness, and financial serenity is as close as your own backyard.

JANUARY 21

Letting Go of Limiting Illusions

I like living. I have sometimes been wildly, despairingly, acutely miserable, racked with sorrow, but through it all I still know quite certainly that just to be alive is a grand thing.

—AGATHA CHRISTIE

For some of us the thought of trusting a power outside ourselves to help make our dreams come true is definitely a threatening concept, especially if we're used to being in control—or rather, used to the illusion of being in control.

Many more of us go through life trapped by another illusion: that an uncaring, capricious fate determines our destiny. Shellshocked from some of the acutely miserable things that life throws our way, we are deeply afraid to believe that a loving, generous Creative Force supports our endeavors. We are afraid to trust that the same Spirit that created the Universe probably knows how to help us write for the grant, get the promotion, go back to school, start our new business, find the new job. Like mirrors in a carnival fun house that distort appearances, what we see with our eyes is not real. We buy in to the illusion that external events possess the ultimate power to deny our dreams.

And we wonder why we're so unhappy?

Let go of limiting illusions that have held you back from knowing that just to be alive is a grand thing. Suspend disbelief. Experiment with a loving, supportive Universe that embraces even skeptics. Today, be willing to believe that a companion Spirit is leading you every step of the way, and knows the next step.

JANUARY 22

The Prosperity of Living

Woman must be the pioneer in this turning inward for strength. In a sense she has always been the pioneer.

—ANNE MORROW LINDBERGH

These are challenging times in which to live. But we are not the only generation of women to have known difficult days. It is comforting to realize that others before us have persevered and prospered. During the dark days of the Depression an editorial in the October 1932 issue of *Ladies' Home Journal* encouraged readers to remember that "The return of good times is not wholly a matter of money. There is a prosperity of living which is quite as important as prosperity of the pocketbook." But the magazine stressed that "It is not enough to be willing to make the best of things as they are. Resignation will get us nowhere. We must build what amounts to a new country. We must revive the ideals of the founders. We must learn the new values of money. It is a time for pioneering—to create a new security for the home and the family. . . . Where we were specialists in spending, we are becoming specialists in living."

I remember the exact moment when I found that quote. I was mining my acre of diamonds: seated on the floor of an antique shop perusing women's periodicals from the past for hints on how to live successfully today. I had been on the Simple Abundance path for a year and felt like a pioneer. In fact, I felt exactly like a woman who had packed up her family and all her worldly possessions in Boston to start across country in a covered wagon in search of the Promised Land. For two thousand miles I had kept the dream of a better life alive while enduring Indian attacks, epidemics, drought, blizzards, tornadoes, snakes, and salted beef. By this time I was in the Nebraska Territory with a thousand more miles to go, but I had come too far to turn back. Like that pioneer woman, I was discouraged. When I found that magazine I immediately embraced it as a telegraph message to my soul. "Keep going. Don't stop. You're on the right path and you are not alone." From that moment, I have never looked back. I learned firsthand that the Simple Abundance path has the power to transform lives.

Are you ready to become a pioneer? Then it's time to invest your soul with all the creative energy at your disposal. Think of me as your scout, your own personal pathfinder. These past few years I've gone ahead and cleared brush from the trail. This much I'll tell you at the outset. The path spirals and takes time—it will take us a year—but it is comforting and nurturing. It can also be undertaken only one day at a time. Don't be afraid. We are not alone. Like pioneers on the trail, we will learn to live by our own lights and the stars of heaven, for that is all we need. There is no obstacle that true grit and Amazing Grace cannot overcome.

JANUARY 23

Accepting Real Life

Everything in life that we really accept undergoes a change.
—KATHERINE MANSFIELD

Accepting and blessing our circumstances is a powerful tool for transformation. In fact, this potent combination is a spiritual elixir that can work miracles in our lives.

What is acceptance? Acceptance is surrendering to what is: our circumstances, our feelings, our problems, our financial status, our work, our health, our relationships with other people, the delay of our dreams. Before we can change anything in our life we have to recognize that this is the way it's meant to be *right now*. For me, acceptance has become what I call the long sigh of the soul. It's the closed eyes in prayer, perhaps even the quiet tears. It's "all right," as in "All right, You lead, I'll follow." And it's "all right," as in "Everything is going to turn out all right." This is simply part of the journey.

Over the years I have discovered that much of my struggle to be content despite outside circumstances has arisen when I stubbornly resisted what was actually happening in my life at the present moment. But I have also learned that when I surrender to the reality of a particular situation—when I don't continue to resist, but accept—a softening in my soul occurs. Suddenly I am able to open up to receive all the goodness and abundance available to me because acceptance brings with it so much relief and release. It's as if the steam of struggle has been allowed to escape from life's pressure cooker.

What happens when we accept our circumstances? Well, first of all, we relax. Next we change our vibration, our energy pattern, and the rate of our heartbeat. Once again we're able to tap into the boundless positive energy of the Universe. Acceptance also illuminates reality so that we're better able to see the next step.

Whatever situation exists in your life right now, accept it. Natalie Goldberg believes that "Our task is to say a holy yes to the real things of our life as they exist." Cast a glance around and acknowledge what's going on. This is my tiny kitchen with the dirty floor, this is how much I weigh, this is my checking account balance, this is where I work right now. This is what is really happening in my life at the present moment. This is okay. This is real life.

Today, let go of the struggle. Allow the healing process of change to begin.

You're ready to move on.

JANUARY 24

Blessing Our Circumstances

Bless a thing and it will bless you. Curse it and it will curse you. . . . If you bless a situation, it has no power to hurt you, and even if it is troublesome for a time, it will gradually fade out, if you sincerely bless it.

—EMMET FOX

After accepting our present circumstances, no matter what they are, we must learn to bless them.

Right. Bless misery?

Through your gritted teeth if necessary. Usually we don't know why something has occurred and we won't until there's enough distance to take a backward glance. However, blessing whatever vexes us is the spiritual surrender that can change even troublesome situations for the better. Blessing the circumstances in our lives also teaches us to trust. Over the years my easiest and most joyous lessons have been learned through blessing. If you're sick and tired of learning life's lessons through pain and struggle, blessing your difficulties will show you there's a better way.

A powerful set of blessings that I learned from the teachings of Stella Terrill Mann, a Unity minister who wrote during the 1940s, encourages us to greet the morning with the affirmation "Blessed be the morn for me and mine." At noon declare, "Blessed be the day for me and mine," and in the evening, invoke this prayer: "Blessed be the night for me and mine." As you go about your work at home or in the office, affirm, "My work is a prayer for good for me and mine." These affirmations of good will bring many blessings into your daily life, as they have in mine.

Then start to count your blessings. Start today. Make a spiritual inventory of all your blessings. See if you can't get to one hundred. So much good happens to us but in the rush of daily life we fail even to notice or acknowledge it. Writing it down focuses our attention on the abundance already within our grasp and makes it real.

Working with What You've Got

*If your everyday life seems poor, don't
blame it; blame yourself; admit to
yourself that you are not enough of a poet
to call forth its riches; because for the
creator there is no poverty and no poor
indifferent place.*

—RAINER MARIA RILKE

Up until now many of us have secretly believed that we had to wait until things calmed down a bit before we started to get our acts together. Tomorrow we'll begin discovering authentic pleasures. Tomorrow we'll treat ourselves better. Tomorrow we'll take the time to enjoy ourselves. Tomorrow, when everything calms down. This I can report from the front lines: life never calms down long enough for us to wait until tomorrow to start living the lives we deserve. Life is always movement, always change, always unforeseen circumstances. There will always be something trying to grab your attention: the phone call, the child, the fax, the car breaking down, the check that never arrives in the mail. Let's just acknowledge that as far as real life is concerned, we are only one step away from dealing with dysfunction.

So what are we going to do about it? We can stop waiting for life to become perfect and start working with what we've got to make it as satisfying as we can. We can accept, bless, give thanks, and get going. Today, we can begin to call forth the riches from our everyday life. Today we can move from lack to abundance. Procrastination has robbed us of too many precious opportunities. Call a friend for lunch, begin to read or even write that novel, organize your papers, try a new recipe for dinner, smile at everyone you meet, sit and dream before a blazing fire, pick up your needlepoint again, act as if you're grateful to be alive, scatter joy. Think of one thing that would give you a genuine moment of pleasure today and do it. Great! The first steps in the journey are always the most difficult to take. "Life begets life. Energy creates energy," the famous French actress Sarah Bernhardt reminds us. "It is by spending oneself that we become rich."

JANUARY 26

Simple Abundance: The Basic Tools

Take the gentle path.

—George Herbert

There is no companion so companionable as Solitude," Thoreau reminds me as I carry a hot cup of tea back to bed. The house is hushed now after the hustle and bustle of a weekday morning. The cats follow me up the stairs, scurrying for nests in the rumpled bed covers. Everyone here knows that a reassuring ritual is about to take place, a civilized ceremonial for a common day.

Although it is still too early to receive business calls, to avoid interruptions I turn on my telephone answering machine. The next hour is spent going within: working with my illustrated discovery journal, writing my daily dialogue, in prayer, playing with my treasure map collage, embarking on the golden mirror meditation, planning my day, and then just sitting in silence. Listening attentively. Waiting expectantly.

These are the basic tools that have helped me on the Simple Abundance path to authenticity. Use them together as I do, or begin to use whichever one sounds intriguing. See if you can't give yourself the gift of one hour a day to journey within. You need enough breathing space to allow your heart to ponder what is precious. Or perhaps you can let your imagination soar to the twilight where dreams first dwell. If you feel a solid hour is too much of a luxury in the beginning (it isn't, but we'll go gently), break up the time during the day. Start with a half hour in the morning and another half hour before you retire in the evening.

Most days after my inner excursion is over, it appears as if nothing has happened that has dramatically changed my life. I have just spent an hour alone. I am not aware of any new insights, inspiration, or guidance. But sometimes I am able to bring the larger picture into sharper focus. You will, too.

This much I know: if you go deep enough, often enough, something good is bound to come back to you. Very often glimmers of the inspiration I desire or the insights I need will come later in the day when I am driving the car pool or preparing supper. But whether or not revelations have been part of my morning, each day offers its own gift.

The Daily Dialogue

I will write myself into well-being.

—NANCY MAIR

Because I write all day long professionally and work very hard at my craft, most of my adult life I have passionately resisted keeping a personal journal. It just seemed like too much effort and I really didn't have the time. But when I embarked on the Simple Abundance path, I became aware of all the conversations that I continuously carry on with myself. There was rarely a quieting of my mind. Instead, I'd hear: "The cat's acting funny, is she sick? If the Cleveland airport gets snowed in on Thursday, how will I get home? Am I ever going to get paid again? We need new slipcovers in the living room—the old ones are starting to look shabby." And so forth. I discovered that my mind will grab hold of a single thought like a pit bull terrier with a bone and not let it go until I'm exhausted or have lost interest.

One day, desperate to quiet the voice in my head, I took a spiral notebook and began having a conversation with myself on the paper. Everything I was worried about just spilled out in a rapid stream of consciousness. What I was doing was not so much recording the events in my life as much as eliminating the mental minutiae that was depleting my creative energy and driving me crazy. I was then able to let go and get on with my day. "Groan and forget it," the writer Jessamyn West advised. She's right. This ritual became very centering and therapeutic.

I have been doing my daily dialogue for several years now, and while I may sometimes skip a few days, I always look forward to checking in with my consciousness because this inner tool really works. It clears my head and calms my restless spirit. It will do the same for you. Interestingly, after a while, the pages take on a life of their own. I call this ritual the daily dialogue because you are really conversing with someone much wiser and saner as you write: your authentic self.

Try writing a daily dialogue as an experiment for twenty-one days. That's the length of time psychologists tell us we need to perform a new behavior before it becomes habitual. Neither the time of day nor the amount you write seems to matter as much as the repetition. Stressed souls need the reassuring rhythm of self-nurturing rituals. Sometimes, when I have a particularly thorny issue to resolve, I'll write two pages in the morning and come back in the evening to see if there isn't an answer that's forthcoming. Very frequently there is. And until there is, at least there is relief and release.

When you start writing the daily dialogue, you will probably be shocked at how much complaining you do at the beginning. That's okay. Actually, that's a very healthy reaction. You can't moan about a situation for months and not decide to do something about it. You'll get tired of the sound of your own nagging and be inspired to get moving.

Another suggestion: don't use a fancy, pretty journal for your daily dialogue. It's too intimidating, because you'll then want it to be perfect and profound and that's not the point; use a spiral notebook or loose-leaf pages. Just get down on paper whatever's hovering on the horizon of your brain disguised as a dull headache.

Alison Lurie confessed that "With pencil and paper, I could revise the world." Writing a daily dialogue is a sure way of revising yours as you search for your authenticity.

JANUARY 28

The Illustrated Discovery Journal

Knowledge of what you love somehow comes to you; you don't have to read nor analyze nor study. If you love a thing enough, knowledge of it seeps into you, with particulars more real than any chart can furnish.

—JESSAMYN WEST

The key to loving how you live is in knowing what it is you truly love. "To know what you prefer instead of humbly saying Amen to what the world tells you you ought to prefer, is to keep your soul alive," Robert Louis Stevenson reminds us. Keeping our soul alive and nurturing our creativity is what interests us today.

One of the most pleasurable ways to start finding out your personal preferences is by creating an illustrated discovery journal. This is your explorer's log as you begin to make your way into the darkest terra incognita: your authentic inner world. We feed our imaginations and get in touch with our authenticity by gathering together beautiful images that speak to our souls. You didn't know that the sun-drenched colors of Santa Fe called to you? Then why do they keep popping up in your pictures? You thought American country was your style but rose-covered chintz is what you're collecting on paper? Isn't that interesting. Here is an occasion when one picture speaks a thousand words. Meditating on one visual image a day can jump-start your creativity and lead to revealing insights.

Today get a blank, black-bound artist's sketchbook at an art supply store, a pair of sharp scissors, rubber cement, and your favorite magazines. Put them all in a basket and keep it by your bed. At night before you go to bed, when you're in a drowsy, relaxed, and receptive state, flip through the magazines. When you see an image you love, cut it out and paste it in your book. Don't try to arrange the pictures in any specific sort of way. Let the collages you are creating simply evolve. Soon they will give you directions about where your heart wants you to go. I have also added quotes, sketches, greeting cards, and art postcards to my discovery journal, crafting with paper what the poet W. H. Auden calls "a map of my planet."

JANUARY 29

Your Personal Treasure Map

For where your treasure is, there will your heart be also.
—MATTHEW 6:21

No self-respecting, swashbuckling buccaneer would set out in search of buried treasure without a map. Why should you? A personal treasure map is a collage of your ideal life that you create as a visual tool to focus your creative energy in the direction you wish to go.

First of all, you'll have to visualize your ideal life. Take a moment to get quiet and go within. Close your eyes. Now see how you live and who lives with you. What does your dream house look like? What part of the country is it in? Do you have children? How many? What type of garden do you have? Is there a gazebo in the backyard? A swimming pool? Do you have any pets? What kind of car is parked in the driveway? What kind of job do you have? Are you publishing your own newsletter, directing a feature film, or raising thoroughbred horses? Now see if you can't find pictures in magazines to match your ideal ones. Cut them out and create a collage on an eight- by ten-inch piece of posterboard. If you can't find images to match your dreams, tap into the creativity deep within and draw a picture. When you're finished, find a photograph of yourself that you especially like. Make sure it's a picture of you looking radiant and happy. Cut yourself out and place yourself in the center of your treasure map collage.

When making your personal treasure map, think fun. Think delight. Think seven years old. This is not an intellectual exercise in existentialism. This is a wish list to the Universe. Our deepest wishes are whispers of our authentic selves. We must learn to respect them. We must learn to listen. "Put your ear down next to your soul and listen hard," the poet Anne Sexton advises.

Above all, remember that no one needs to be privy to your personal treasure map but you. Our wishes for the future, our hopes, our dreams, our aspirations are our truest treasures. Guard yours in the sanctuary of your heart. Keep your personal treasure map in the back of your illustrated discovery journal and look at it often. When you do, give thanks for the wonderful life you are leading. The greatest secret to living a happy and fulfilled life is the realization that everything is created in our minds before it manifests itself in the outer world. We must believe it before we can see it. You have to know what you're digging for, before X can mark the spot.

JANUARY 30

The Golden Mirror Meditation

Almost always it is the fear of being ourselves that brings us to the mirror.

—ANTONIO PORCHIA

For years I have used a special meditation I call the golden mirror meditation. I visualize in my mind an enormous mirror the size of a room, with an elaborately carved, 24-karat gold frame. This is my materializing mirror. Those dreams I wish to materialize in my life are first viewed here.

Now let me share with you an amazing coincidence that a French proverb would suggest is "God's way of remaining anonymous." After I had been doing the golden mirror meditation for about a year, I was invited on an all-expenses-paid business trip to Dublin, one of my favorite cities. I was to stay at one of Dublin's oldest, most beautiful, and expensive hotels, the Shelbourne, where I had never been before. When I arrived at the hotel and walked into the lounge, what should I see but the physical manifestation of my daily meditation: a beautiful mirror with a gold-leaf frame that was so large it took up an entire wall of the lounge. I laughed with delight when I saw my reflection in it, for here was the Universe's way of demonstrating to me that whatever we visualize in our minds can come to pass in the physical world.

Today, find a few minutes to get quiet and journey within. Close your eyes. Visualize a beautiful, large golden mirror surrounded by shimmering white light. This light is Love and it surrounds you, enfolds you, enwraps you, and protects you as you look into the mirror. See the reflection of an extraordinary woman. She is beautiful and radiant. She possesses a strong, healthy, vibrant aura. Her eyes are sparkling and she is smiling warmly at you. Do you know who this woman is? You feel as if you have known her all your life. And you have. She is your authentic self. Spend a few moments with her now. What is she doing? How is she doing it? Visit her as often as you like. She is waiting to help you find your way as you make the journey of self-discovery.

There are days when we all fear the harsh glare of the looking glass, but there is never a time when you should hesitate to encounter the woman in the golden mirror. She is the highest reflection of your soul, the embodiment of the perfect woman who resides within and she sends you Love to light your path.

JANUARY 31

Embracing Joyful Simplicities

Year by year the complexities of this spinning world grow more bewildering and so each year we need all the more to seek peace and comfort in the joyful simplicities.

—WOMAN'S HOME COMPANION, *December 1935*

As we become curators of our own contentment on the Simple Abundance path, one of the great payoffs is that we start to seek peace and comfort in the joyful simplicities. Little things begin to mean a lot to us. Joyful simplicities nourish body and soul by engaging our senses. They teach us how to live in the present moment. Life comes together when we seek out the Sublime in the ordinary.

We all have days in our lives that are marked by great moments of rejoicing and celebration: the baby is born, the promotion comes through, the book contract is signed. But life is not an endless round of cake and champagne. There's a lot of drudgery to most of our days: sheets to be changed, dry cleaning to pick up, garbage to put out. To keep our daily round from being all drudgery, we've got to savor the art of the small: discovering diminutive delights that bring us peace and pleasure. In 1949, the British playwright J. B. Priestly gathered together such moments in a book of essays entitled *Delight*. Among his favorites: waking in the morning to the smell of coffee, eggs, and bacon; reading detective stories in bed; suddenly doing nothing in the middle of the day; buying books; and enjoying the company of (instead of just tolerating) small children.

It's a winter's day. Can you make a pot of homemade soup for supper tonight? I relish this joyful simplicity once a week during the winter. Chopping, paring, and scraping are very calming activities. Really look at the colors of the vegetables—the orange of the carrots, the bright green celery, the pearly white onion. You have a beautiful still life in front of you.

Don't rush through the process but enjoy the *mindfulness*, or the Zen, of cooking. Isn't the fragrance of homemade soup wonderful? It makes you glad to be alive or at least at your own house for dinner.

Don't you see how we have to seize the essence of life? We have to embrace every moment. "People need joy quite as much as clothing. Some of them need it far more," Margaret Collier Graham wrote in 1906. Today, make discovering those joyful simplicities that bring you personal comfort and a sense of well-being one of your highest priorities.

Joyful Simplicities for January

⋙ Write out the aspirations of your heart as you begin the Simple Abundance path.

⋙ Serve a traditional New Year's Day dinner of Hoppin' John: black-eyed peas (for luck), rice (for health), collard greens (for prosperity), baked ham and cornbread (for delicious eating!). I make a scrumptious winter salad of cooked black-eyed peas, diced green and red peppers, and red onion dressed in a French vinaigrette, which is served at room temperature.

⋙ Go through your personal papers at home and organize your desk to get a fresh start on the new year. Discard as much as you can. Hang your new calendars. Try to make your personal space at home where you do paperwork as inviting as possible.

⋙ Visit a good stationery store or a very large bookstore and search for a beautiful blank book to use as your gratitude journal. At the stationery store, you also might want to look at different colored inks and pens.

⋙ Visit an art supply shop and simply look around. Take in all the different ways that you can begin to express yourself: in vivid color, on paper, canvas, in clay. Sound like fun? While you're there pick up a couple of black-bound artist's sketchbooks to use for the illustrated discovery journal you're going to create. My favorite size is eight-and-a-half inches by eleven inches lengthwise.

⋙ Put up some acrylic magnet picture frames to create a gratitude collage for your refrigerator. Place in it photographs of those you love and are grateful for, such as family, friends, and pets. Also place in it reminders of the little things you're thankful for, like the car repair bill that was less than you had feared. If there's something that you particularly want to come into your life, place a picture of it here and give thanks for it ahead of time.

⋙ Prepare for a winter's idyll. Stock the pantry with real cocoa, tiny marshmallows and a bar of good chocolate (for a shaved-chocolate topping). Get some whipped cream and keep it in the refrigerator. When snow comes and school is canceled, stay home with the kids. Lounge about in your pajamas. If you have a fireplace, have a fire all day. Build a snowman together, go sledding, then have tomato soup in mugs and toasted cheese sandwiches for lunch. Take a nap. Luxuriate in an unexpected day off.

🖎 Pay a visit to a great junk store. If you don't know one, start looking. Every woman needs a great junk store in her repertoire.

🖎 Bake a pan of dense, dark, moist gingerbread for after-school tea with the children or for dessert. Read Laurie Colwin's delightful *More Home Cooking: A Writer Returns to the Kitchen* for the ultimate gingerbread recipes.

🖎 Visit the local library and read some new magazines you don't normally subscribe to. I do this once a month. It's fun and frugal.

🖎 Force some spring bulbs to blossom—miniature daffodils, paper whites, hyacinths, and tulips—to brighten your spirits and home with color and fragrance in midwinter. Visit a local nursery and ask for bulbs specifically bred for this purpose.

🖎 Browse through gardening catalogs this month. Cut out your favorite flowers and create your ideal garden on paper. Indulge your passion for a rose-covered gazebo in a gardening collage and keep it in your illustrated discovery journal. Pretend you're creating a secret garden for solitary sojourns. What does it look like? What gardening accessories and furniture appeal to you? Add them to your collage. Let your fantasies come to life on paper first.

🖎 Send for annual seeds that you can begin planting indoors next month.

FEBRUARY

China tea, the scent of hyacinths, wood fires and bowls of violets—that is my mental picture of an agreeable February afternoon.

—CONSTANCE SPRY

February arrives cold, wet and gray, her gifts disguised for only the most discerning spirits to see. Gentle is our path. Gratitude is the thread we weave into the fabric of our daily lives this month, giving thanks for our simply abundant lives and asking for the gift of one thing more: grateful hearts.

Creative Excursions: The Gift of Time

I celebrate myself, and sing myself
I loafe and invite my soul . . .

—WALT WHITMAN

Now that you've met your authentic self, wouldn't you like to get to know her better? You can when you start going on creative excursions together.

Creative excursions are regular solo rendezvous with your authentic self designed for this purpose. In the beginning of any intimate relationship the best gift you can offer another person is the investment of quality time together. So it is with your authentic self. You have probably been ignoring her for decades; now it's time to make amends.

What will you do? Celebrate yourself, find pastimes that make your heart light and your spirit sing. Take in a movie (one of those English period dramas you love), have an early breakfast before work at a new French café, cruise the aisles at that incredible Italian market, explore a fabulous thrift shop, browse in used-book stores, visit an art supply store and imagine all the wonderful ways in which you can begin expressing yourself. When you embark on creative excursions, your authentic self will lovingly reveal to you the beautiful mystery that is *you*. This occurs spontaneously as you make the pursuit of personal growth a sacred endeavor.

Having encouraged you, now let me warn you. This is not as easy as it sounds. In fact, for me the *hardest* part of the Simple Abundance path was creative excursions. I was simply not used to having *fun* by myself. It seemed too frivolous, too self-indulgent. Be prepared for strong, emotional resistance. Excuses will be plentiful: you're too broke, you're too busy, who will watch the kids, maybe next week when you're not so frazzled. Don't give in. Creative excursions require an investment of time, not money. None of us are too busy to find two hours a week. If we are, we seriously need to reconsider our personal priorities. Hire a babysitter, let your spouse watch the kids, carve out time when they are in school, use your lunch hour at work. There are ways to do it, once we realize that nurturing our imaginations and developing a relationship with our authentic selves is an investment we can no longer afford to put off. This week commit to a weekly creative excursion with your authentic self as you follow the Simple Abundance path. Expect nothing less than signs and wonders to follow.

Knowing What You Love

Perhaps loving something is the only starting place there is for making your life your own.

—ALICE KOLLER

It should be straightforward, this knowing what we love. But it seldom is. After decades of letting other people influence us—the media, the magazines, our mothers, our friends—we're going to have to go cold turkey. The only opinion that counts from now on is your own.

This week, try an experiment. Plan a creative excursion to go browsing in a home furnishings and decorative accessories shop. Go somewhere you've never been before, so that you're looking at everything with fresh eyes. What startles you, calls to you, excites you? Write it down in a small spiral notebook that you can keep in your purse. Is it the shape of a teapot, the colors of a hooked rug, the textures in an exquisite dried flower arrangement? You'll know what you love the moment you see it. It's that familiar "Wow" reaction. Trust the impulse, capture the encounter, record the clues. These will be important later on.

Then next week on another creative excursion, go browsing (not to buy) at a new clothing boutique. You know, that place that always intrigues you but you stay away from because it's too expensive. The spring fashions should be arriving about now. See what's new. See what's you. Your spirit perks at the sight of a goldenrod linen blazer. So why are you always dressed in black? A fabulous flowered georgette pleated skirt and tunic top wows you, but you always wear jeans because it's more practical. Maybe, just maybe, feeling gorgeous outweighs practicality. Be open to authentic aspirations.

Remember this is the year for asking questions. The most essential one we can ask is: what is it I truly love? Be patient. We're not going to overhaul our lives, our homes, or our wardrobes in a week. Trust that your authentic life will unfold naturally and with grace.

Discovering Your Authentic Self

To love oneself is the beginning of a life-long romance.
—OSCAR WILDE

One of the surprises that comes when you catch glimpses of your authentic self is the discovery that she's such a positive, upbeat woman. She's always smiling. She's always calm. She's always reassuring. She exudes confidence. Who is this woman, you might ask, and does she bear any resemblance to you?

Yes and no. This is who you are on the inside. The real you. If you don't act this way all the time, it's simply because you haven't evolved to a higher plane of existence yet. Neither have I. Marianne Williamson believes this will come when we "embrace the Goddess" who resides within. "When a woman falls in love with the magnificent possibilities within herself, the forces that would limit those possibilities hold less and less sway over her," she writes in *A Woman's Worth*.

But occasionally we get glimmers of what it's like on this higher plane: on a good-hair day; when we've had twelve hours of sleep; when we soar through a business meeting, thoroughly prepared; when we fit into last year's clothes; when we throw a great party and everyone enjoys themselves immensely. When moments like these occur, we tend to think that all's right with the world. Everything just fell into place. What we don't realize is that all's right with ourselves. We're in the flow of life and loving it. *We're in place*: that special alignment when authenticity and reality merge into Wholeness.

But how do we tap into this spiritual energy source more often? How do we access the flow of life more frequently? How do we learn to live at full throttle?

Meditation helps. So do long walks, soaks in scented bubble baths, washing our hair a day before it needs it, smiling at everyone we meet, being more gentle with ourselves, watching a sunrise or a sunset, petting an animal, playing with a child, having some small pleasure to look forward to every day, being grateful.

But above all, being open to change. Welcoming it. "Watch. Wait. Time will unfold and fulfill its purpose," Marianne Williamson advises. "While we wait, we must not go unconscious. We must think and grow. Rejoice and dream, but kneel and pray. There is holiness in the air today; we are giving birth to goddesses. They are who we are, for they are us: friends, therapists, artists, businesswomen, teachers, healers, mothers. Start laughing, girls. We have a new calling."

The Authentic Self Is the Soul Made Visible

My business is not to remake myself,
But make the absolute best of what God made.
—ROBERT BROWNING

Making the absolute best of ourselves is not an easy task. It is a pleasurable pursuit, it is the reason we were born, but it requires patience, persistence, and perseverance. For many of us it also requires prayer. That's because we find it far easier to learn to live by our own lights when we access a Higher Source of Power to illuminate our path. The filmmaker and writer Julia Cameron calls this switching on "spiritual electricity" that transcends our own limitations.

In my own journey I have found this to be very true. Usually I limited the times I requested that the Power be turned on to the occasions when I was appearing in public: giving workshops, lecturing, holding business meetings. Then it occurred to me that this was like living in a house with electricity but turning on the lights only for a couple of hours every few months. And I wondered why I was frequently bumping into obstacles. So I started to ask for the Power to be switched on in my daily life: as a mother, a wife, a writer, and a friend. When I asked, it was turned on. When I didn't, I stayed in the dark. You don't have to be a master electrician to understand what's going on here: someone has to turn on the switch. Asking is the way of activating spiritual electricity. When there is Light we see remarkably well. We see with clarity. And what we can see if we look deep within is that *the authentic self is the Soul made visible.*

Do not try to remake yourself into something you're not. Just try making the best of what God made. The sacred art and craft of nurturing our souls and the souls of those we love is Simple Abundance soulcraft. Begin today by turning on the Light.

The World Is Too Much with Us

What I mean by living to one's self is living in the world, as in it, not of it.

—WILLIAM HAZLITT

The world is too much with us," poet William Wordsworth complained over two hundred years ago. "Getting and spending, we lay waste our powers." Today many women would agree with him. We're chronically exhausted from the "getting"—the amount of energy spent earning a living and juggling the demands of home and career. And the reality of the recession means we're paying now for the "spending" of yesterday.

But despite all the doom and gloom that constantly assaults our senses, there is a way for us to ransom our lives and reclaim our futures: it consists in turning away from the world to recognize what in life makes us truly happy. For each of us, what that is will be different. But once we obtain this inner knowledge, we will possess the ability to transform our outer world. "You can live a lifetime and, at the end of it, know more about other people than you know about yourself," the pilot and writer Beryl Markham reminds us. We cannot let this continue to occur.

Today, deliberately turn away from the world. Don't read the newspapers or watch the nightly news for a week—longer if you can stand it. Shun the glossy magazines featuring expensive suits designed for success. Wean yourself away from the opinions of others—however talented, creative, and celebrated they may be—as you continue to journey within. Absorb the shock of becoming aware that many of your preferences and opinions are not truly your own. Begin, instead, to listen for the whisper of your authentic self telling you which way to go. We are always being shown the next step of our uniquely personal journey. It may be as simple as clearing up your desk so that you can find that adult extension course brochure with the watercolor classes.

Only when the clamor of the outside world is silenced will you be able to hear the Deeper Vibration.

Listen carefully.

Spirit's playing your song.

Remaking Your Own World

I have made my world and it is a much better world than I ever saw outside.

—LOUISE NEVELSON

Many creation myths say it took only six days to make the world. It will take us a little longer to remake our own. But we can begin where Spirit did by declaring that there be Light to illuminate our journey of self-discovery.

The Quaker tradition teaches that this Light is within each of us. The Quakers, or members of the Religious Society of Friends, are a perfect example of individuals who manage the delicate balance of living in the world but not belonging to it. This is because they refuse to segment their lives into the Sacred and the secular. Instead, Quakers believe that all of life's daily experiences are spiritual in nature, from preparing a family meal to protesting political policy. The British writer George Gorman has observed that "the essence of Quaker spirituality is the certainty that everything we do has religious significance. It is not cutting ourselves off from life but entering deeply and fully into it."

Simplicity is the common thread that stitches together Quaker lives, homes, and dress. Their weekly worship service, or Meeting, is a silent meditation. Rhythm, reverence, and reflection are their hallmarks. These touchstones can help us as well as we attempt to remake our personal world.

Restoring a sense of rhythm to our lives is the first step. How much rhythm do you have in your personal world? Children are not the only ones who need regular bedtimes, mealtimes, and quiet times. Their mothers do, too. Think of the steady, reassuring rhythm of the natural world—the ebb and flow of the tides, the recurring cycle of the four seasons, the monthly phases of the moon, and the daily progression from day into night. Rhythm needs to be the cornerstone in our personal world as well. All of us lead busy lives, some more frantic and frazzled than others. We need to learn where to draw the line and how to say "no."

Today be willing to reflect quietly on the role that rhythm plays in your daily life. Your heart will always tell you what's working and what's not. Restoring rhythm to the way you conduct your affairs can bring you contentment and a sense of well-being that will nurture and sustain you when the cares of the world can't be left behind.

An Artist Is Someone Who Creates

Living is a form of not being sure, not knowing what next or how. . . . The artist never entirely knows. We guess. We may be wrong, but we take leap after leap in the dark.

—AGNES DE MILLE

Most of us feel more secure when we play it safe. We wear a string of pearls, for example, instead of the hand-painted glass beads we glimpsed and passed up at the crafts fair. Yet it is precisely those red and purple glass beads around the neck of another woman that stop us dead in our tracks. "Wow," we mumble as we pass her on the street, "that looks fantastic." We also wonder how she knew it would.

She probably didn't. She probably just took a leap in the dark and trusted her instincts. She trusted her own sense of style. The necklace whispered "Try me!" and she listened. She played at living—in a small way to be sure, but relevant all the same—by taking a chance.

Every day we're given chances to embrace the new. It could be serving focaccia at dinner tonight instead of garlic bread. It could be choosing a pair of floral socks that make our feet want to dance, instead of the plain pair we automatically reach for. It could be trading in the headband for a short, sleek sophisticated cut that really feels right.

Psychologist Susan Jeffers suggests we "take a risk a day—one small or bold stroke that makes you feel great once you have done it." Today, take a real risk that can change your life: start thinking of yourself as an artist and your life as a work-in-progress. Works-in-progress are never perfect. But changes can be made to the rough draft during rewrites. Another color can be added to the canvas. The film can be tightened during editing. Art evolves. So does life. Art is never stagnant. Neither is life. The beautiful, authentic life you are creating for yourself and those you love is your art. It's the highest art. "Since you are like no other being ever created since the beginning of time, you are incomparable," writer Brenda Ueland reminds you.

Hold that thought.

FEBRUARY 8

You Are an Artist

Inside you there's an artist you don't know about. . . . Say yes quickly, if you know, if you've known it from before the beginning of the universe.

—JALAI UD-DIN RUMI

Most of us feel uncomfortable thinking of ourselves as artists, but we are. We think artists write novels, paint pictures, choreograph ballets, act on Broadway, throw pots, shoot feature films, dress in black, drink absinthe, and line their eyes with kohl.

But each of us is an artist. An artist is merely someone with good listening skills who accesses the creative energy of the Universe to bring forth something on the material plane that wasn't here before. It was a part of Spirit before we could see it as a book, a painting, a ballet, a film.

So it is with creating an authentic life. With every choice, every day, you are creating a unique work of art. Something that only you can do. Something beautiful and ephemeral. The reason you were born was to leave your own indelible mark on your personal world. This is your authenticity.

Today, accept that you are creating a work of art by making big and little choices between playing it safe and risking. Is there something you'd like to do that's new and different? Why not order an espresso at lunch, if you've never tried one? Visit the perfume counter and try on new scents? Stick a small bottle of balsamic vinegar in the shopping cart to drizzle over melon? Switch the dial on the radio station and listen to country and western instead of classical as you drive home?

Each time you experience the new, you become receptive to inspiration. Each time you try something different, you let the Universe know you are listening. Trust your instincts. Believe your yearnings are blessings. Respect your creative urges. If you are willing to step out in faith and take a leap in the dark, you will discover that your choices are as authentic as you are. What is more, you will discover that your life is all it was meant to be: a joyous sonnet of thanksgiving.

A Fresh Canvas Every Twenty-Four Hours

Another real thing! I am not dead yet! I can still call forth a piece of soul and set it down in color, fixed forever.

—KERI HULME

Before a painter begins a new work, she takes preparatory steps to get ready. She has probably made preliminary sketches of the scene she is trying to capture. She mixes her pigments to achieve the right colors. She has also prepared the canvas with a fixative coating so that the paint will adhere. All of this takes time. Of course, we don't see the preparations when we look at her completed work. We only see the entire vision. And as artist Helen Frankenthaler once commented, "A picture that is beautiful or that works looks as if it was all made at one stroke. I don't like to see the trail of a brushstroke or a drip of paint."

Preparatory steps are necessary in all the arts. They are also necessary in life if we want to live authentically. Every twenty-four hours we are given a fresh canvas to prime, to make ready for the vision. Quieting our minds in meditation, carving out time to dream and express ourselves with our daily dialogue and illustrated discovery journal, becoming aware of our true preferences, slowing down to concentrate on completing one task at a time—these are the preparatory steps we need to take if we wish to experience contentment.

But our preparation won't have been in vain. For when we are in the flow of life, savoring the moment, the brush strokes don't show. Today, don't rush through your inner preparations as you get ready to set down a piece of your soul on life's canvas.

Creating an Authentic Lifestyle for Yourself and Those You Love

It's a funny thing about life; if you refuse to accept anything but the best, you very often get it.

—SOMERSET MAUGHAM

It's far easier to live an elegant, beautiful life when you're not on a budget. When cash is readily available, you don't have to learn the lessons that delayed gratification teaches us. But having money does not guarantee that we live authentically. Nor does being surrounded by beautiful things guarantee a lifetime of happiness. If you receive heartbreaking news, it's not more comforting to sob into a damask and silk-tasseled cushion.

When I was beginning the Simple Abundance path and began to wean myself away from worldly distractions for several months by choosing not to read magazines and newspapers, not to watch the news, and especially not to go shopping (except for groceries and essential kid's clothing), the symptoms I experienced were similar to withdrawal pains. At times, I actually felt achy, shaky, and even dizzy. When this occurred, my authentic self would reassure my conscious self (who didn't think much of the new program) that I was undergoing a deep inner shift in reality. I was learning to differentiate between my needs and my wants and this powerful lesson had to be mastered before I could move forward. I had to learn what I could live without. Whatever I needed I could budget for—in other words, I could have—but self-knowledge had to come first.

When you learn what you can live without, you are able to ask life for the very best because you possess the gift of discernment. You develop patience that enables you to wait gracefully and gratefully until the best arrives because you know it will. You are able to create an authentic life for yourself and those you love because you are able to make conscious choices. "Long afterwards, she was to remember that moment when her life changed its direction," Evelyn Anthony writes in *The Avenue of the Dead*. "It was not predestined; she had a choice. Or it seemed she had. To accept or refuse. To take one turning down the crossroads to the future or another." Turning away from the world and toward your own happiness is the path of authenticity.

FEBRUARY 11

Divine Discontent: Learning to Live by Your Own Lights

Grace strikes us when we are in great pain and restlessness. . . . Sometimes at that moment a wave of light breaks into our darkness, and it is as though a voice were saying:"You are accepted."

—PAUL JOHANNES TILLICH

When we practice switching on the "spiritual electricity" that Julia Cameron speaks of in her wonderful book, *The Artist's Way: A Spiritual Path to Higher Creativity*, what should we expect? More energy and inspiration, amazing and delightful coincidences, and the ability to accomplish goals with grace? Yes, certainly. That has, at least, been my experience.

But one thing you might not expect—one thing that might throw you—is how dissatisfied you may feel when the Power is not present, when you are in the dark and left to your own devices because you forgot to turn the switch on. I have learned that asking is the only way to activate spiritual electricity. It is always there for me, but I always have to ask for it.

The dissatisfaction you can feel when the switch is off manifests itself in different ways. Suddenly you don't like any room in your house. Decorating mistakes from past lives haunt you. Your clothes don't fit or look right on you anymore. You're bored with the meals you're cooking. You're sick of opening the front hall closet and covering your head. But worse, that expansive, even giddy hopefulness that came from starting to integrate gratitude into your life gives way to restless discontent. You begin to think that the Simple Abundance path might work for some women, but it's not right for you. Hold on. As the English historian Dame Cicely Veronica Wedgwood points out, "Discontent and disorder [are] signs of energy and hope, not of despair."

What is going on is part of the process. I call it Divine Discontent. It is the grit in the oyster before the pearl. This creative second chance is when we come into our own. When we finally claim our own lives and wrestle our futures from fate. When we learn how to spin straw into gold. When we realize gratefully that we can live by our own lights if we access the Power.

Ask for it. Claim it. Today.

FEBRUARY 12

Once Upon a Time You Trusted Yourself

Just trust yourself, then you will know how to live.
—JOHANN WOLFGANG VON GOETHE

Today, try to find a photograph of yourself when you were about ten. Make sure you're smiling. Put it in a pretty frame and place it on your dressing table, desk, or in your illustrated discovery journal and look at it every day. Send love to that young girl. Try to travel back in time and imagination. See yourself at ten: at home, at school, and at play. Where did you live? Can you see your house or apartment, and the street? Walk through the rooms in your childhood home. What did your bedroom look like? Who were your friends? Did you have a best pal? Who was she? How did you play? What was your favorite color in the Crayola pack? Did you play a musical instrument? Who was your favorite doll? Can you recall the scent of Play-Doh? What were your favorite foods? What subject did you like best in fifth grade? Can you remember? Try to recall yourself at ten in your daily dialogue pages.

Have fun with this exercise because age ten was probably the last time you trusted your instincts. You didn't listen to the opinions of your mother, your sister, or your friends because you had your own.

To watch my ten-year-old daughter in the dressing room of a department store is a revelation. "No, that's not me," she'll frequently say as I show her outfits to try on. With an assurance that I envy, she reaches for a tapestry vest and a black felt slouch hat. "There," she announces with satisfaction, "this looks like me." I remind myself that once upon a time, I trusted my instincts. You did, too. Once upon a time there weren't second and third guesses. It can be that way again.

Try to contact the girl you once were. She's all grown up now. She's your authentic self and she's waiting to remind you how beautiful, accomplished, and extraordinary you really are.

You Have a Unique Point of View: Loving Your Authenticity

A sobering thought: what if, right at this very moment, I am living up to my full potential?

—JANE WAGNER

Take a deep breath and relax. The reassuring news is that you've not completely lived up to your potential or you wouldn't be drawn to this book. You're still striving, still dreaming, still yearning, and now still doing. *I've* not completely lived up to my full potential or I wouldn't be writing this book. We're both on an exhilarating adventure that's sometimes a little scary. One of the most important milestones we'll hit along the way is the moment when we finally own our unique point of view and realize how priceless it is. "I'd gone through life believing in the strength and competence of others; never my own," writer Joan Mills observes. "Now, dazzled, I discovered that *my* capacities were real. It was like finding a fortune in the lining of an old coat."

Today, or as soon as you can, indulge yourself with one of my favorite perk-ups. Get $25 from the bank in $5 notes and place them in the pockets of all your coats and jackets. Now forget about it. The next time you wear a coat and find $5, laugh and let it remind you that each day that you love, honor, and respect your own unique point of view, you're a step closer to finding a fortune.

Now do one thing more. Start to treat yourself more generously. Begin with $5. Buy one beautiful flower for your desk, enjoy a French pastry with your morning coffee, stop in at a fancy salon and get yourself some almond-scented shampoo. Just do something out of the ordinary that you normally wouldn't do that will lift your spirits. "Love yourself first and everything else falls into line," Lucille Ball advised. "You really have to love yourself to get anything done in this world."

FEBRUARY 14

Buried Dreams

Where there is great love there are always miracles.
—WILLA CATHER

It takes great love and courage to excavate buried dreams. Today is the day set aside for love, a perfect occasion for going within and glancing back with affection and understanding at your real life journey so far.

Once we were going to set the world on fire. Remember? Today we all have our share of ashes, along with the memory of a few bright sparks, to show for our efforts. Over the years we've buried many a precious dream under layers of soot and rubble. Layers of naivete, good intentions, relinquishment, bitter failures, detours, disappointments, rejections, wrong choices, bad timing, bungled efforts, stupid mistakes, unforeseen circumstances, whims of fate and missed opportunities. It's no wonder that we'll need courage to retrace our steps. But "courage is the price that Life extracts for granting peace," the pilot Amelia Earhart reminds us.

A wise woman once advised me not to be a "would-be-if-I-could-be or a could-be-if-I-would-be. *Just be.*" And while I have learned that dreams need doing as much as they need being, I have learned that the being always comes first.

Today is a day for being. Be with those you love, be kind to yourself. Be quiet and call forth the dream you buried long ago. The ember is still glowing in your soul. See it in your mind, hold it tenderly in your heart. "The dream was always running ahead of one," Anaïs Nin confessed. "To catch up, to live for a moment in union with it, that was the miracle."

FEBRUARY 15

Meeting the Inner Explorer

There is only one journey. Going inside yourself.
—RAINER MARIA RILKE

I craved to go beyond the garden gate, follow the road that passed it by, and set out for the unknown," Alexandra David-Neel wrote in 1923, recalling her daring journey to the Himalayas in search of spiritual truth and high-spirited adventure. A former actress, the Parisian-born explorer dressed as a pilgrim to make her way into the heart of Tibet—the closed and sacred city of Lhasa. Never before had a woman from the West seen its face.

As I drive the afternoon car pool, I wonder, how does a woman today satisfy such wanderlust? How do I reconcile the dream of visiting the temple of Egypt's Queen Hatshepsut near ancient Thebes with the reality of transporting a station wagon full of children from school to soccer practice?

If you, too, crave scenes beyond the garden gate, do what I do to keep the spark of adventure alive: journey within to meet your authentic explorer. Where is she headed? If you could go anywhere in the world, all expenses paid, baby-sitter at your disposal, where would you go? Why? Who would you be with? How long would you stay? What would you do?

Yes, this is a first-class fantasy, and it's supposed to be fun. To inspire your far-flung creative visualization, stop in at the library and peruse the travel shelves. Let your fingers do the wandering. Read about famous women explorers. Collect their exploits and tuck them into your subconscious mind.

Next, take a creative excursion to a travel agent and collect colorful brochures for your discovery journal. When asked, be noncommittal about the date of departure. No one needs to know that you're traveling in your armchair, indulging your imagination on a cold winter's night as you consider exploration as a personal metaphor.

And why, you might ask? Because, as Alice Walker astutely observes, we're learning day by day that "the most foreign country is within." We are our own dark continent, we are our own savage frontier. Many marvels await discovery as we continue on the path to authenticity.

FEBRUARY 16

At the End of Our Exploring

We shall not cease from exploration
And the end of all our exploring
Will be to arrive where we started
And know the place for the first time.

—T. S. ELIOT

When we live our lives authentically, we discover our true place in the world for the first time. But this self-knowledge is not easily acquired. It takes tenacity and daring to travel to the darkest interior of one's self. Who knows what we might find there? "It does not do to leave a live dragon out of your calculations, if you live near him," the writer J. R. R. Tolkien advises.

Our dragons are our fears: our day stalkers, our night sweats. Fear of the unknown. Fear of failing. Fear of starting something new and not finishing. Again. Or the real fear, the one that sends shivers up our spines: the fear of succeeding, of becoming our authentic selves and facing the changes *that* will inevitably bring. We might not be happy with the way we are living now, but at least it's safely familiar.

We don't know where we are headed and it's very scary. Old dreams are resurrecting, new desires are wooing. Instead of clarity, we feel confused. At moments like this, it is comforting to consider T. S. Eliot's belief that there is really nothing to fear from self-awareness because at the end of all our personal exploration, we will arrive back where we started and know in our hearts that we finally belong there.

Women have always known how to deal with dragons hiding under beds or lurking in closets. We turn on the lights and reassure worried souls with love. We need to slay the dragons in our minds the same way.

Today, if you feel frightened or unsure about the future, pick up the double-edged sword of Light and Love. Always remember, it's simply not an adventure worth telling if there aren't any dragons. But as in the best old tales, at the end of your exploring, you will live happily ever after.

FEBRUARY 17

A Safari of Self and Spirit

The woods were made for the hunters of dreams
The brooks for the fisher of song
To the hunters who hunt for the gunless game
The streams and the woods belong.

—SAM WALTER FOSS

In the summer of 1893, an English woman named Mary Kingsley traveled to the wildest and most dangerous part of the French Congo in search of herself. Both her parents had recently died, and suddenly, at the age of 31, Miss Kingsley found herself "not only desolate with grief but bereft of purpose." Her adventures in West Africa changed all that. Several years later her writings and naturalist discoveries, including the documenting of unknown species of fish and animals, were applauded by the Victorian scientific community.

Mary Kingsley was a hunter of a dream: the knowledge of who she really was and her place in the world. So are you. Yet even without encountering the daily dangers she faced—wild animals, menacing spears, and deadly diseases—you have embarked on an adventure as exciting as that of any explorer. Uncovering the source of the Nile or charting the course of the Amazon are outward parallels to the inner journey you are on today—a safari of the self and the spirit.

In Africa, to go on *safari*—the Swahili word for journey—is to leave the comfort and safety of civilization to venture into the wilderness. Each time you listen to the woman within—your authentic self—you do the same. Remind yourself of this often. "You have to leave the city of your comfort and go into the wilderness of your intuition," Alan Alda advises the inner explorer in you. "What you'll discover will be wonderful. What you'll discover will be yourself."

FEBRUARY 18

Safari Life

The heart is a lonely hunter that hunts on a lonely hill.
—FIONA MACLEOD

Winter is the dry season in Africa, the time of safaris. We can learn from the dry seasons in life, and from life on safari.

"You could expect many things of God at night when the campfire burned before the tents," Beryl Markham wrote about safari life. "You were alone when you sat and talked with the others—and they were alone. . . . What you say has no ready ear but your own, and what you think is nothing except to yourself. The world is there and you are here—and these are the only poles, the only realities. You talk, but who listens? You listen, but who talks?"

A safari of the self and Spirit is at times lonely. But we know we are never alone. It is a comfort to realize that this sense of isolation is necessary if we are to encounter Mystery, and mystery is very much a part of a safari. Each day in the wilderness brings with it the struggle to survive and a heightened awareness of how wonderful it is just to see the sun set and rise again in the morning. Each day on safari is lived to the fullest because it is all that is guaranteed. If only we could learn this lesson as well in our everyday lives.

Today, expect many things as you sit around the campfire of your heart.

Someone is listening. Someone is talking to you, encouraging you to take that next step as you embrace the Mystery of the wilderness within.

Expect to have hope rekindled. Expect your prayers to be answered in wondrous ways. The dry seasons in life do not last. The spring rains will come again.

FEBRUARY 19

Rendezvous with the Authentic Archaeologist

We cannot kindle when we will
The fire that in the heart resides
The spirit bloweth and is still
In mystery our soul abides.

—MATTHEW ARNOLD

Like the inner explorer who seeks adventure and the unknown, the authentic archaeologist knows how to unearth remnants of memory buried deeply in the fertile soil of the subconscious mind. Archaeologists "read" artifacts much the way a detective reads clues. The reason we want to awaken the authentic archaeologist is to excavate the real you.

"How we remember, and what we remember, and why we remember form the most personal map of our individuality," writer Christina Baldwin reminds us. Today, become willing to remember. Prepare yourself for a gentle but authentic dig that will help you discover the Mystery in which your soul abides.

Whether you realize it or not, you have lived many lives, and each one has left an indelible mark on your soul. I'm not referring to reincarnation. I'm referring to the episodic way in which our lives evolve: childhood, adolescence, college years or early career, marriages, motherhood, perhaps life as a single mother, widowhood and onward. At each stage in our lives, we have both laughter and tears. But more important for our interests, we develop personal preferences. Each life experience leaves a layer of memory like a deposit of sediment: things we've loved and moments of contentment we've cherished that when recalled, reveal glimmers of our true selves.

Some women are hesitant to recall their past because they're afraid they'll dredge up painful memories. But just as each illness brings a gift for us if we will look for it, so each painful memory comes bearing a peace offering. There is nothing to fear. The past asks only to be remembered.

FEBRUARY 20

The Authentic Dig

Sometimes a person has to go back, really back—to have a sense, an understanding of all that's gone to make them—before they can go forward.

—PAULE MARSHALL

Unearthing a mosaic is one of the most exciting discoveries on an archaeological dig. Mosaics are pictures or decorative patterns formed by inlaying thousands of small, multicolored chips to create a larger visual representation. Early mosaics tell sacred stories about ancient worlds—how people lived and what was important to them—providing archaeologists with revealing glimpses into the past.

On the authentic dig we shall also go in search of a mosaic: what brought us moments of happiness and contentment in our past lives. When taking a backward glance, always bear in mind that memory is fickle. She must be wooed and courted if she is to succumb to our charms. Sometimes she surprises us with her generosity, and we recall moments with astonishing clarity. Most of the time, however, our memories are fragmented, like small colored chips. When this happens, we need to be patient as we brush away the sediment of the past.

Today, prepare for your personal dig in a thoughtful way. Let your authentic archaeologist gather artifacts that can coax memory: old photographs, letters, mementos. Carve out time when you can be alone and take a leisurely trip back in time. Enjoy a glass of wine or a cup of tea. Listen to your favorite music from yesterday: Elvis, the Beatles, the Bee Gees. Peruse the photographs, flip through your high school yearbook, read the old love letters. Trace your life back to when you were ten, sixteen, twenty-one, twenty-five, thirty, thirty-five, forty, and onward. See what memories are triggered as you reacquaint yourself with the girl and woman you once were. Linger only on the happy times. What you are searching for is a pattern of personal, authentic pleasures and preferences. These are the chips in your mosaic.

"The events in our lives happen in a sequence in time, but in their significance to ourselves they find their own order," writer Eudora Welty confides. With patience and quiet observation, these events will provide the seeker in you with a "continuous thread of revelation."

Excavating the Real You, Part I

Maybe being oneself is always an acquired taste.

—PATRICIA HAMPL

Excavating is not glamorous work on an archaeological dig. It demands painstaking effort in often harsh conditions. Tons of dirt need to be removed carefully from the site if the search to uncover treasures from the past is to be successful. No matter how impatient everyone on the dig is, the excavation process cannot be rushed. But there wouldn't be the thrill of discovery if time weren't invested in slowly digging in the dirt.

We must dig patiently with our pens to excavate our real selves. "As long as one keeps searching, the answers come," Joan Baez tells us. And for what are we searching? Shards of our authentic style.

For centuries women have displayed their innate sense of style to the world through choice: in their personal appearance, in the way they decorated their homes, in how they entertained, in their work, and in the pursuit of their personal passions. The more we learn about ourselves and our preferences, the easier it is to make these choices. And creative choice is at the heart of authenticity.

Choice confers freedom—the freedom to embrace the new because it speaks to your soul and you are listening. Today be willing to consider the choices you have made in the past as you trace your life. Have they been the right ones for you? Do you make choices with your heart, mind, or gut? Are you comfortable with your style of making choices, or do you wish to try a different approach? Was there something you did not choose in the past that, with hindsight, you now wish you had?

Perhaps a long-buried dream still calls to you from a road you chose not to take. If this is true, then stop telling yourself that it's too late. Instead, take comfort in what Faith Baldwin tells us: "Time is a dressmaker specializing in alterations." The delay of our dreams does not mean that they have been denied. Perhaps now you have the wisdom to make alterations in your dream so that it can come true. Perhaps now you have the wisdom to choose differently.

Dig with your pen. Have a dialogue with your authentic self. Ask her about the choices you have made or didn't make. Listen for the wisdom she has to offer.

Excavating the Real You, Part II

*My memory is certainly in my hands. I can remember things only
if I have a pencil and I write with it and I can play with it. I think
your hand concentrates for you. I don't know why it should be so.*
—DAME REBECCA WEST

We're back at the site of your soul this morning for some more digging.
Perhaps you wonder why we are spending so much time excavating. Maybe
you balk at having to search your past for clues as to how to live contentedly in the present. Please be open: the excavation process expands your
sense of the possible because it provides you with inner knowledge. Pick up
your pen to play and in your daily dialogue pages return to the home of
your childhood.

How was it decorated? Do you remember? Take a walk through the
rooms and see them once again. Did you clean your room? Was the door
usually kept closed? What was your favorite spot in the house? Was your
mother a good cook? Do you ever prepare any of her special recipes for
yourself?

How did your mother comfort you when you were sick? When was the
last time you had alphabet soup and saltines for lunch on a tray in bed?

Where did you go on vacation? To your grandmothers' houses? Can you
remember them? Is there a sense memory you associate with childhood
vacations?

Now fast-forward to your teenage years. Where there any girls in your
class that you admired? Envied? Who were they and why? Did you go to a
prom? Describe your gown. How did you fix your hair? Who initiated you
into the feminine rituals of good grooming? Was there an older woman in
your life whose sense of style impressed you?

Let's move ahead to when you set up your first home, either as a young
working woman or when you first got married. Where was it? How was it
furnished? Are you still living with some of your early decorating choices?
Do they reflect who you are now or have you outgrown them? Are you living with things that you've inherited from your family? Do they really suit
you?

Now slowly let your attention return to the room. You have excavated
some more chips to place into your authentic mosaic. "Minor things can
become moments of great revelation when encountered for the first time,"
the great ballerina Margot Fonteyn observed. We tend to think it is the major
events that mark our lives, when really it is the minor moments that resonate
in memory. Lovingly pick one pleasant recollection and think about it today.

Making Your Own Imprint

God is in the details.

—Ludwig Mies van der Rohe

Making your own imprint on life implies that you know exactly how to express "your own inimitable style," as my wonderful Irish father used to say. But do you? Today continue to expand your sense of the possible and find out. Consider the following scenarios strictly for fun.

You move into a completely empty house and start over from scratch—money is not a consideration. Write down twenty specifics for your ideal home from architectural features to furnishings that are "must haves" for you. They can range from a window seat in the upstairs hall to an English club chair with a tufted ottoman beside a fireplace. Let your imagination and creative flair have free rein. Are any of these items from your past? Where did you first encounter them? Do you remember? How long have you been dreaming about having them? Are there any items here from your childhood home?

Next, imagine that your closet and drawers are empty. You need to fill them. What are the first ten things you would either hang up or put away? You may either keep favorites from your present wardrobe or buy entirely new items. Which comes first for you, comfort or career?

Your kitchen cabinets are bare. You need to buy new china, flatware, glasses, and linens for everyday use and for entertaining. Where do you begin? What pattern do you want to see every day? What shape glass do you enjoy drinking from? Have you ever thought about this? Do you prefer a pottery mug or a paper-thin china teacup for your morning brew? These details are your authentic preferences.

"The soap in the bathroom, the flowers in the garden, the book on the bedside table are all strong symbols of a life in progress," notes writer and interior decorator Charlotte Moss in her book *A Passion for Detail*. "You look at these details and a world unfolds." Each day you create yourself anew through choice. By paying attention to the details—your authentic gestures—you give expression to the most personal of all the arts: making your own imprint on life.

FEBRUARY 24

Now That I've Gotten
Your Attention

Sometime in your life you will go on a journey.
It will be the longest journey you have ever taken.
It is the journey to find yourself.

—KATHERINE SHARP

For nearly two months we have contemplated the journey within to authenticity. Perhaps you've started to let gratitude till the soil of your soul, preparing it for the seeds of Simple Abundance: finding the Sacred in the ordinary, realizing that all you have is all you need, welcoming creative choices, and savoring life's small moments. Maybe you've set aside time to begin a daily dialogue in search of your authentic self, indulged in the pleasure of dreaming with the illustrated discovery journal, or embarked on the golden mirror meditation to meet the woman within.

Then again, maybe you haven't . . .

If you wonder why I suspect this, it's because I've been where you are now. I know. I know how days, weeks, months, even years can escape your grasp. I know what it's like to put everyone else's needs before your own so that you can't find a half-hour a day for yourself. I know how easy it is to find heartfelt excuses for why you can't begin something new even if you yearn to, desperately. I know how easily the word "tomorrow" slips out unconsciously. Tomorrow you'll begin. Tomorrow. All this I know.

But what I know most of all is that reading about a journey is not the same thing as taking one.

Now that I've gotten your attention, let me tell you about the rest of the year. Each day from now on we're going to use the daily grist of our real lives as a cause for celebration. That's right, celebration. I have learned many lessons on the Simple Abundance path. Chief among them is that the details of our days do make a difference in our lives, that no experience is ever just for drill, and that everything can be a springboard for inspiration if we are willing to be open to the goodness of life.

How many times in the past have we chosen not to change our lives for the better simply by *not* choosing? Today, make a choice. Choose to continue on the Simple Abundance path or close this book now. If you choose to close the book, my blessings accompany you. May peace and plenty be your portion. Pass this book on to a friend.

If you are still with me, you know what you need to do *today*, not tomorrow. Take another look at your life. Give thanks. Accept your circumstances. Give thanks. Count your blessings. Give thanks. Show up for each day's meditation. Be willing to give the basic tools a fair chance. They can help you find your way. Above all, have faith in yourself and Divine Change. "One does not discover new lands without consenting to lose sight of the shore for a very long time," the French writer André Gide warns us.

Set the sails. Pull anchor. Cast away. Feel the wind at your back. Keep your eyes on the horizon.

Or stay on shore.

But choose.

FEBRUARY 25

Reordering Your Priorities

Learn to get in touch with the silence within yourself
and know that everything in this life has a purpose.
—ELISABETH KÜBLER-ROSS

Most women I know have only one conscious priority: making it through the day. This is a direct result of having been torn in a thousand different directions in any one twenty-four hour period for decades. Writer, pilot, wife, and mother Anne Morrow Lindbergh calls it "the centrifugal forces of today" that pull at women. But acknowledging, recognizing, and reordering our priorities so that they can give purpose to our days is a deeply personal task that we all need to do if we are to learn how to live by our own lights.

A priority is anything that is important to you. Providing for your children's education by starting a systematic plan of saving could be a priority. So could increasing your health and vitality through diet and exercise. Achieving financial serenity is another priority for many of us, as is nurturing a family and sustaining a loving, happy marriage.

Priorities are not written in granite. They need to be flexible and change as we do. I find it helpful to think of priorities as the wooden frame upon which we stretch the canvas of our days so that we may apply color and form to the work of art we are creating without the entire painting collapsing in the middle.

It takes peace of mind and clarity to recognize and reorder meaningful, personal priorities. Maybe that is why so many of us procrastinate. But the more our lives and attention spans are segmented by our children, our careers, our homes, our marriages, and our needs for personal expression, the more we need to identify what is truly important in our lives.

Many of us assume that we can continue to get along just by "winging it" indefinitely. We can't. We need an antidote for the hurried and harried lives that threaten to tear us apart. Follow the advice of Anne Morrow Lindbergh and make carving out a small portion of each day for yourself a personal priority. "Quiet time alone, contemplation, prayer, music, a centering line of thought or reading, of study or work. It can be physical or intellectual or artistic, any creative life proceeding from oneself. It need not be an enormous project or a great work. But it should be something of one's own. Arranging a bowl of flowers in the morning can give a sense of quiet in a crowded day. . . . What matters is that one be for a time inwardly attentive."

Today make getting in touch with the Silence within yourself your first priority. As you do, you will be amazed at how everything else seems to find its own order.

FEBRUARY 26

Real Life Begins with Reverence

Let knowledge grow from more to more
But more of reverence in us dwell;
That mind and soul, according well,
May make one music as before.

—ALFRED, LORD TENNYSON

When my daughter was four years old, I asked my husband if he minded if I went away for a weekend by myself. He didn't. It was the first time since Katie's birth that she and I would be apart and I felt I needed to have some centering time to myself, something I seemed unable to do at home. At that time I didn't realize that solitude had to be woven into the fabric of my daily life. While fantasies of sleeping uninterrupted for twenty-four hours and ordering from room service at a local hotel tempted me briefly, I finally decided to spend a retreat weekend for women at a contemplative convent of Episcopal nuns. I realized that what I really wanted to do was to hear the exquisite sounds of Silence.

There were many wonderful moments about that special weekend that I treasure, but the one thing that has stayed with me is the hush of reverence that enveloped life within the beautiful stone convent walls.

Reverence is that altered state of consciousness when you feel awe and wonder because you know you are in the presence of Spirit. Reverence enwraps you in perfect peace because there is no past or future, only the present moment, and you are one with Heaven and earth. There is no distinction between body and soul. Meditation can sometimes spiritually induce this special moment of Wholeness, as does creating something beautiful, whether it's a meal, a painting, or a flower bed. Concentrating on one task at a time with care and attentiveness can invoke reverence as well.

Unfortunately, most of us do not live behind cloistered walls where reverence resides. But I have learned on the Simple Abundance path that gratitude is the gateway to experiencing more reverence in our daily lives. The thirteenth-century German philosopher Meister Eckhart, whose teachings so influenced the Quaker movement, believed that "If the only prayer you say in your life is 'thank you,' that would be enough."

Real Life—the real life of joy we are meant to be living—begins when we restore a sense of reverence to our daily affairs. Today, search for the Sacred in the ordinary with gratitude in your heart and you will surely find it.

FEBRUARY 27

Committing to Your Spiritual Awakening

I don't believe; I know.

—CARL JUNG

By this time it's no secret that the Simple Abundance path is spiritual as well as creative and practical. But Simple Abundance will work for you even if you're ambivalent about whether God exists. If you consciously work to bring more gratitude, simplicity, order, harmony, beauty, and joy into your daily life, your world will be transformed whether you believe a Higher Power is guiding you or not. But if you commit to your spiritual awakening as the most important part of the process, something marvelous will happen. Life will not feel as fraught, as frazzled, or as fragmented as before because you'll realize that the spiritual, the creative, and the practical can't be separated. They each count. They each mean something. They're all connected.

You think you are only making a meatloaf, when really you're ministering to hungry bodies and weary souls in need of love and nourishment. A friend is hurting, so you spend a lunch hour searching for the perfect card to send her. Months later she tells you how much comfort you conveyed across the miles. A woman calls your small and struggling mail-order business looking for a certain item that you are out of temporarily. She can't wait for you to reorder because she needs it for her daughter's birthday party. Instead of sending her away disappointed, you give her the name and telephone number of a competitor who also carries the item. You set in motion a cycle of good that blesses all concerned.

A year ago you might not have done this, but now you know that there is no competition in the spiritual realm. A year ago you were not aware that every choice you make every day is part of the Sacred Whole. But as Christina Baldwin writes in her inspiring book, *Life's Companion: Journal Writing as a Spiritual Quest*, if we "ready ourselves with spiritual openness," eventually we will come to the awareness that "Spirituality is the sacred center of which all life comes, including Mondays and Tuesdays and rainy Saturday afternoons in all their mundane and glorious details."

A year ago you might not have believed this could be true. But with each day of the journey, you have become more open to the mystery, the magic, and the majesty of the Master Plan because you are committed to your spiritual awakening. You don't have to just believe anymore, because you *know*.

FEBRUARY 28

Creating a Sacred Space

You must have a room or a certain hour of the day or so where you do not know what was in the morning paper . . . a place where you can simply experience and bring forth what you are, and what you might be. . . . At first you may find nothing's happening. . . . But if you have a sacred place and use it, take advantage of it, something will happen.

—JOSEPH CAMPBELL

I resisted creating a sacred space for myself for a very long time. The excuses were: (1) I am not a nun and altars belong only in churches or convents; (2) I live in a very small house and don't really have any space to set aside; and (3) I didn't want my husband, who respects and honors my spiritual quest but doesn't share it, or my daughter, to think I was extremely weird.

But I kept discovering other women writers whom I admire (and whom I don't think are weird at all) such as Joan Borysenko and Julia Cameron have created sacred spaces for themselves, and the concept intrigued me. Then one day in meditation my authentic self suggested that I become open to the idea of creating a sacred space to celebrate, concentrate, and consecrate my inner work. "Okay," I said, "I'll be open to it but I don't know where I'll put it."

The very next morning I was propped up in bed writing my daily dia-logue pages. When I looked up I "saw" with my inner vision a small blue bench up against my bedroom wall surrounded by white light. Flash! It was exactly like the one discarded on our porch. I leaped out of bed in a burst of excited enthusiasm and started gathering meaningful objects that evoke love and gratitude to me from various scattered places around the house. A half-hour later I had created a sacred space that delighted me.

Let me tell you about my "meditation table" as it is now called by the family (and if anyone thinks it's strange, they have kept this opinion to themselves). The dark-blue-enamel bench is only eighteen inches long and eight inches deep and is against my blue bedroom wall. A small, white linen and crocheted lace tablecloth covers it. On the table I have a large golden pillar candle sitting in the center; a beautiful Victorian lithograph of an angel representing the guidance of my guardian angel; a print of the Madonna and Child in an oval gold frame (representing the male and female natures of Divinity); a small gold-framed mirror for my authentic-self meditation; pictures of my family and pets; a small blue-and-white china vase (a wedding present) for fresh flowers; rose quartz crystals rep-resenting the natural world; a rose-patterned incense holder; and a small bowl of rose and jasmine potpourri. Hanging above the table at my eye level (whenever I kneel or sit) is a beautiful print in a gold frame by the artist Michael Podesta that represents the essence of Simple Abundance. The table is only about two feet away from the foot of my bed so that the bed supports my back comfortably when I sit and meditate. This encour-ages me to meditate more often.

After I had pulled everything together I consecrated the table with a small ritual of blessing. Afterwards I was surprised by the powerful sense of positive energy that seemed to surround the table. Of course, now I know that this energy is Love. Love created this space for me once I became open to allowing it in my life. The objects displayed on the table represent all that I love and for which I am so grateful.

You might also like to create a sacred spot to celebrate, concentrate, and consecrate your inner work. You don't have to have a lot of room. Joan Borysenko now has a house large enough for a small meditation room but she has used in the past "the top of a bureau, a corner of the kitchen, a nook in the hall." Julia Cameron encourages the seeker in us to create a small personal place for inner work even if it's just a window ledge. She tells us: "In order to stay easily and happily creative, we need to stay spiritually cen-tered. This is easier to do if we allow ourselves centering rituals. It is important that we devise these ourselves from the elements that feel holy and happy to us."

Don't think it will work for other women but not for you. Today, all I ask is that you be open to allowing a creative, sacred space to come into your world. If you are, Spirit will do the rest.

FEBRUARY 29

A Day of Grace

Sweet February Twenty-Nine!—
This is our grace-year, as I live
Quick, now! this foolish heart of mine;
Seize thy prerogative!

—WALTER DE LA MARE

What a wonderful, unexpected gift is Leap Year's extra day and the realization that this is certainly a wonderful year of grace. Quickly we must seize the moment, for this day won't come again for another four years.

We can begin by asking for just one day's portion of grace to guide us today. I do this every morning even before I get out of bed.

My favorite way to ask for a daily portion of grace is writer Marjorie Holmes's prayer, "Just for Today."

Oh, God, give me grace for this day.
Not for a lifetime, nor for next week, nor
for tomorrow, just for this day.
Direct my thoughts and bless them,
Direct my work and bless it.
Direct the things I say and give them blessing, too.
Direct and bless everything that I think and speak
and do. So that for this one day, just this one
day, I have the gift of grace that comes from
your presence . . .

Now let me share something I've discovered about grace. In my lifetime, I have been on my knees many times. Gratefully, most of my prayers have been answered as I had hoped. Some were not, or at least not as I had expected they would be. Others were delayed until I thought my heart would break. Still others were denied. But *never* have I asked for just one day's portion of grace and not received it.

Grace is available for each of us every day—our spiritual daily bread—but we've got to remember to ask for it with a grateful heart and try not to worry about whether there will be enough for tomorrow. There will be.

Joyful Simplicities for February

᠅ Light candles all over your home on Candlemas Day, February 2. Bask in the glow. Relax and see how different the world seems without electricity to blur the distinction between night and day. Notice how slow your pace becomes. Consider that you might like to live by candlelight more often. Invest in beeswax candles. They come in a rainbow of exquisite colors and reflect the light beautifully. Store them in the freezer and they will burn twice as long without dripping.

᠅ Invite a few friends over the Sunday before Valentine's Day to make hand-crafted paper confections for those you love at a "Cupid's tea." Assemble the prettiest doilies you can find, along with wired silk ribbon, floral fabric, wrapping paper, stickers, and construction paper. Don't forget glue sticks and sharp scissors. Borrow some books of poetry from the library and try your hand at reviving this lost art form. Serve a heart-shaped cake with pink butter frosting, heart-shaped scones with strawberry jam, tea, and sherry. Try this once and it is sure to become a February tradition.

᠅ Write a long, wonderful love letter to yourself from your authentic self. Compliment yourself for everything you are doing right now, just the way you are. Let your authentic self encourage you as you would a young child. Mail the letter and save it for when you're feeling discouraged.

᠅ This month become an incurable romantic. Read Elizabeth Barrett Browning and then delight in "everyday's most quiet need."

᠅ Add a bit of lace to a suit or a pantry shelf.

᠅ Have you found a wonderful picture of yourself when you were ten? If you have, find the perfect frame for it and put it on your bureau or dressing table. If you haven't yet, ask your mother or whoever keeps your family photographs to help you.

᠅ Start forcing fragrant bulbs of hyacinths.

᠅ Wear perfume every day.

᠅ Try a red lipstick.

᠅ Treat yourself to one perfect long-stemmed rose for your desk.

᠅ Listen to the music of Cole Porter.

᠅ Rent *Out of Africa* from the video store. Read Isak Dinesen and Beryl Markham.

᠅ Make a batch of old-fashioned chocolate fudge for Valentine's Day.

᠅ Create a sacred space.

MARCH

It is the first mild day of March.
Each minute sweeter than before . . .
There is a blessing in the air . . .
— WILLIAM WORDSWORTH

March arrives, the last hurrah of winter and the first whisper of spring. Slowly our spirits reawaken, along with the natural world, from a long winter's slumber. Branches that just days ago were bare, now blossom with new growth. Deep within we feel stirrings of hope. Turn over the earth in the inner garden. This month we plant the seeds of the second Simple Abundance principle— Simplicity—in the fertile soil of our souls.

Restoring Serenity to Your Daily Endeavors

*God give us the grace to accept with serenity the things that
    cannot be changed;
Courage to change the things that should be changed;
And the wisdom to distinguish the one from the other.*

—Reinhold Niebuhr

W hen thinking about serenity, many people think of the famous prayer written by Protestant theologian Reinhold Niebuhr. Frequently invoked by members of twelve-step programs, it is popularly known as "The Serenity Prayer."

I believe, however, that the time has come for us to stop associating serenity with things that cannot be changed. For we can dramatically change the quality of our lives when we consciously seek to restore serenity to our daily endeavors.

How exactly can this be accomplished in our lifetime? *When women stop behaving as if they were whirling dervishes.*

If you frequently feel as if you're about to spin off this planet, it's probably because you are. I know of a woman who will begin to brush her teeth only to leave the bathroom to start making her bed while she is still foaming at the mouth. And why? Because out of the corner of her eye she saw the rumpled sheets. Before she could rinse her mouth, she had flung herself into the next task. Needless to say, a day that starts off this frenzied can only go from bad to worse.

This is not how the cool and regal Grace Kelly, beloved as Her Serene Highness the Princess of Monaco, spent her days. Nor is it how we should spend ours. And while I'm sure Princess Grace had somebody else making her bed, the point is still valid. Serene women do not become sidetracked. Sidetracked women, who scatter their energies to the four winds, never achieve serenity. (Nervous breakdowns, to be sure, but not serenity.) It's as simple as that.

Today, we must start to recover our sanity. The way we do this is to concentrate slowly on completing one task at a time, each hour of the day, until the day is over. Like the members of twelve-step programs, we will act "as if" we are serene (think Grace Kelly), by bringing all our attention and conscious awareness to whatever we are doing—from brushing our teeth to putting the children to bed. What we will gain from this exercise is the inner peace that comes from living fully in the present moment.

I realize, of course, that for most of us, accustomed as we are to performing six tricks simultaneously, what I'm proposing sounds ridiculous. You wonder how you'll get everything done if you don't do everything at once. But I assure you that you will accomplish all you set out to do and need to do with much more ease, efficiency, pleasure, and satisfaction when you merge mind, body, and spirit with the task at hand.

And you will experience serenity.

MARCH 2

Meditation:
Many Paths to the Present Moment

Meditation is simply about being yourself and knowing about who that is. It is about coming to realize that you are on a path whether you like it or not, namely the path that is your life.

—JON KABAT-ZINN

If you do not already practice meditation, when you hear the word you probably conjure up the unpleasant image of sitting uncomfortably in a lotus position, back aching, mind racing ahead to all the things you need to be doing, and hyperventilating because now you are concentrating on whether you are breathing or not.

This image is unappealing and incorrect. But it goes a long way toward explaining why many people do not meditate. However, there are compelling physiological, psychological, and spiritual reasons why we should engage in regular meditation. It is the mortar that holds mind, body, and Spirit together.

There are many ways of meditating. Dr. Joan Borysenko, the gifted and inspired psychologist, scientist, and spiritual teacher, explains that meditation is intentional concentration on one thing, which can be either secular or spiritual. "Perhaps you have become so absorbed in gardening, reading or even balancing your checkbook that your breathing slowed and you became as single-pointed as a panther stalking her dinner! In this state creativity flowers, intuition leads to a deeper wisdom, the natural healing system of the body is engaged, our best physical and mental potential manifests itself and we feel psychologically satisfied," she writes. Spiritual meditation, on the other hand, "will help you become aware of the presence of the divine in nature, in yourself and in other people. The love and joy that are inherent in Spirit—that are the very essence of Spirit—will begin to permeate your life."

I have many different ways of meditating, depending on my inner needs: the golden mirror meditation, writing my daily dialogue pages, gazing into the flame of a candle, concentrating on a sacred word in a centering prayer, focusing on a poetic phrase to find deeper personal meaning, or setting out on a walking meditation. There are many paths to the present moment. Joan Borysenko's "all-time favorite meditation is a small, moist piece of chocolate cake eaten with exquisite attention and tremendous gratitude. Any time we are fully present in the moment we are meditating."

Today, retreat to a quiet place where you can sit or even lie down in a comfortable position so that you can relax your body. Now close your eyes and let your breathing become slow and steady. Get in touch with the Silence within. Consider how you might be able to carve out twenty minutes a day to meditate. That is all, merely consider.

MARCH 3

Setting Aside a Personal Sabbath

Anybody can observe the Sabbath but making it holy surely takes the rest of the week.

—ALICE WALKER

It was all right for the Great Creator to rest on the seventh day, but many contemporary women I know assume they just can't take the time. After all, they're not creating the world six days a week, just carrying its weight on their shoulders.

The Greeks had a wonderful word for this attitude: hubris. Hubris is an "exaggerated sense of self-confidence" and it usually comes before a humbling. A heart attack is certainly very humbling, and it does not surprise me in the least that heart disease is now the leading killer of women.

"Some keep the Sabbath going to Church," Emily Dickinson confided, "I keep it, staying at Home." So do I. There are some Sundays, especially in winter or when it rains, that I don't even get out of my pajamas until noon. Long ago, I stopped feeling guilty about this because I've learned how to honor my Sabbath by keeping it holy and happy. Many people look upon the Sabbath as Sunday; others keep the Sabbath from Friday at sundown through Saturday. It doesn't matter what day of the week you set aside as your own personal Sabbath, it just matters that you keep one.

Here is a short guide to what you should not be doing on your Sabbath: strenuous household chores (preparing meals is permitted, but they should either be easy or festive depending on your choice); catching up on work that you didn't complete last week or getting a head start on work you're supposed to start on Monday; shopping at large department stores that insert slick circulars in weekend papers.

This is what the Sabbath is for: reverence, rest, renewal, rejuvenation, reassuring rituals, recreation, rejoicing, revelation, remembering how much you have to be grateful for, and saying "thank you!" You can do this in a church, mosque, temple, or synagogue, on a walk, while antiquing, sitting in bed propped up on pillows reading something wonderful with a breakfast tray, working the crossword puzzle before a roaring fire, attending a marvelous art exhibition or movie matinee, or listening to opera in the kitchen as you sip sherry and prepare a fabulous feast. What matters is that you do something special that speaks to your soul and that you revel in whatever you do. Your activities on the Sabbath should uplift you and provide enough inspiration to sustain you during the week to come.

"Sunday is sort of like a piece of bright golden brocade lying in a pile of white muslin weekdays," Yoshiko Uchida wrote in *A Jar of Dreams*. If this is not what the Great Creator intended when She created the Sabbath, then I have no idea what is Sacred.

MARCH 4

Priming the Pump for Inspiration

The well of Providence is deep. It's the buckets we bring to it that are small.

—MARY WEBB

Whenever I prepare to write, I have a carefully crafted ritual of comfort that eases me into creating. I work from my bed with a fresh pot of tea on my bedside table and a beautiful tape of piano nocturnes playing softly in the background. Next to me is a new spiral notebook and cup full of my favorite pens, along with a revered pile of dog-eared books. You see, I am not alone but in the company of my circle of saints—beloved women writers—each of whom has an authentic voice and a special message for me. I savor the work of their hands, hearts, and minds once again to get my own creative juices flowing.

My writing ritual is what I refer to as "priming the pump for inspiration." When you have to pump water from a well the old-fashioned way, by hand, you need to pour a pitcher of water down the pump to get it going. I prime my personal pump in a very particular way because the repetitiveness of the process activates the right side of my brain where creativity dwells: I use the same Blue Willow mug for the tea, listen to the same music, write with the same type of pens and notebooks, reread the same books. The instantly recognizable ritual informs my brain that I'm now working. Before I realize it, I'm jotting down notes as if I'm taking dictation from Spirit. When I've got a rough draft written in longhand, I head into my office to work on the computer. Then the real writing begins. Once again I have coaxed Inspiration into helping me through the power of ritual.

You need to create a reassuring ritual for yourself to access your inner reservoir—that place deep within you inhabited by imagination. Why not create an inviting one for when you work with your illustrated discovery journal? If you find that you can't work on it every day, pick one night a week that you can devote to searching for the visual images that reveal your authentic preferences. Make the process as appealing as possible. Perhaps, after putting the children to bed, you can take a long, leisurely soak in the bathtub. Then, after you are comfortable and relaxed, bring the basket containing your magazines, scissors, and journal over to your bed. Prepare a special hot drink to enjoy only at this time. Light a pretty candle on your dresser to invoke Inspiration.

This week, think of creating a reassuring ritual that primes your personal pump. Carry a large bucket to the well of Providence with a ceremony of comfort.

MARCH 5

Creating a Hope Chest

"Hope" is the thing with feathers—
that perches in the soul . . .

—EMILY DICKINSON

Hope chests were traditional gifts from mothers to daughters in the days when young women brought household dowries with them when they married. Hope chests contained bed linens, quilts, table linens, crockery, flatware, and dreams of domestic bliss.

I didn't have a hope chest when I got married. Did you? I dreamed of getting one for my sixteenth birthday, but we didn't have the money, so it became a dream deferred. I remember poring over the Lane Furniture ads in *Seventeen* magazine featuring a loving mother and daughter packing hopes for the young woman's future into a beautiful cedar-lined chest.

Why do I remember this? Because I've been excavating my authentic self. If you dig deep enough, it all comes back to you. And you'll often be surprised by what you discover. So here I am, thirty years later, looking once again at hope chest advertisements.

However, since I've established a household without one, my hope chest differs from the traditional version. Instead, I use a wicker picnic hamper filled with projects that I hope to do in the future. A few weeks ago I found a beautiful fabric at a remnant sale that will make a lovely tablecloth and napkins for Thanksgiving Day's dinner. Until I can set aside time to sew them, I'm storing the material in my hope chest.

A friend who recently separated from her husband of thirty years is starting life over again so she's redecorating the house they shared. She found some gorgeous needlepoint squares at a thrift shop that she's going to use to recover her dining room chairs some rainy Saturday afternoon. They'd be perfect in a hope chest until she gets around to it.

Get the idea? Not every one of our desires can be immediately gratified. We've got to learn to wait patiently for our dreams to come true, especially on the path we've chosen. But while we wait, we need to prepare symbolically a place for our hopes and dreams. I've even started a wicker hamper for my daughter which I'm filling up with books by my favorite women authors to give her on her sixteenth birthday. I "hope" to present them to her in a beautiful cedar-lined chest. Then my dream of a loving mother and daughter packing hopes together for a young woman's future will come true.

I believe it will. Faith is the very first thing you should pack in a hope chest.

MARCH 6

Creating a Toy Box

I pray you . . . your play needs no excuse.
Never excuse.

—WILLIAM SHAKESPEARE

When my daughter was born, one of the unheralded joys of motherhood was that I finally had a legitimate excuse for buying toys. As Katie grows older and her gift preferences inevitably evolve from miniature china tea sets to compact discs and clothes, I have to constantly remind myself that I don't need an excuse anymore to make toys a part of my life. If I am to continue to grow as a human being and as an artist, it's imperative for me to respect the power of play. That's why I have my own toy box.

Playing is hard for most women I know. Creating your own toy box symbolically suggests the importance of fun if you're to function at full throttle.

First, find the perfect box. A wicker picnic basket, or a small wooden or fabric-covered box with a lid can do duty as a toy chest. But the lid is the most important feature because what goes in there is your business. These are your toys. Your toy box. Maybe you'll share. Maybe you won't. Take it to your bedroom and put it high on a shelf in your closet. Close the door.

Now this week, plan a creative excursion to begin filling it. Take $10 and go to a well-stocked five-and-dime or a great stationery-and-gift shop. Get some stickers, some colored paper clips, some pretty pencils and whimsical erasers. Now look through the funny cards. Get a few that tickle your fancy. What else do you see? A milk jug in the shape of a cow, a string of chili pepper lights, a magic wand. Store your stickers and cards in your toy box until the right moment comes along to use them, place the paper clips and erasers on your desk at work, hang the chili pepper lights over your spice rack, put the cow milk jug in the refrigerator. Laugh when you see your toys and let them visually remind you to lighten up.

Now think about the toys you yearned for as a child but never had. It's not too late to own a Steiff stuffed teddy bear, build a beautiful dollhouse with real electric lights, or complete a thousand-piece jigsaw puzzle. Start changing your holiday or birthday wish list. You don't have to get a Dustbuster if what you really want is an antique French Jumeau porcelain doll. Tell the people in your life your new preferences.

"Play is the exultation of the possible," Martin Buber reminds us. Now get your toys. Go out and play like a good big girl.

MARCH 7

Outfitting a Comfort Drawer

A little of what you fancy does you good.

—Marie Lloyd

Life requires that we prepare ourselves for the inevitable times that try our souls. This is achieved with a comfort drawer. Comfort drawers are for those nights when you feel as if you'd like to pull the covers over your head and never come out. My refuge is the righthand bottom drawer of my dresser, where I stockpile small indulgences throughout the year. But many of my comforts were originally gifts that I simply saved for whenever a homegrown unhappiness remedy might be required.

Let's see what we find: a box of chocolate truffles; miniature (one-serving size) fruit cordials and after-dinner drinks; an aromatherapy bath treatment to promote serenity; various British decorating magazines (look for them at large cosmopolitan newsstands); a small vial of Bach's "Rescue Remedy," a homeopathic essence available at health food stores; a velvet herbal sleeping pillow to induce pleasant dreams; a satin eye mask to shut out distractions; rose-scented bubble bath and talc; old love letters tied with a silk ribbon; a scrapbook of personal mementos; a tin of fancy biscuits; and an assorted gift sampler of unusual teas.

Notice the simply abundant pattern of pleasure? Here is all that is required for the spoiling and pampering of a world-weary woman: a fabulous bath, something scrumptious to nibble, something sentimental to conjure up happy memories, something lovely to sip, and something delightful to read. Now change your sheets, fill your hot water bottle, and assemble a half-dozen white votive candles on a tray. Place the tray on your dresser in front of a mirror, strike a match, and ceremoniously create your own northern lights. Play some soothing music and put on your favorite pajamas or nightgown. Get into bed and luxuriate. If this doesn't work, take two aspirins and call me in the morning.

When outfitting your comfort drawer, be sure to line it with a lovely floral shelf paper and tuck in some scented sachets so that the drawer will delight your senses. Wrap your comforts in pretty jewel-colored tissue paper and tie them with beautiful ribbons. This way, when you open your drawer, you'll see a dazzling array of wonderful presents—gifts of the heart for the most deserving person you know.

MARCH 8

Taking the Plunge

Until you make peace with who you are, you'll never be content with what you have.

—Doris Mortman

Simplicity gains importance in our lives as we begin to make peace with ourselves. This is because we gradually come to the inner awareness that we don't need to gild the lily. Some of the trappings can be relinquished because the Real Thing is finally ready to be revealed.

I call this point in the Simple Abundance process "taking the plunge" because it involves a courageous leap of faith in the most intimate way: exploring the way we express ourselves to the outside world through our personal appearance. But this is much more than just how we dress or style our hair. It's about the many subtle ways we choose either to celebrate or conceal our authenticity. It's about finally acknowledging and accepting the woman within. It's about learning to become comfortable with who we really are. "We are not born all at once, but by bits. The body first, and the spirit later," Mary Antin wrote in 1912 in *The Promised Land*. "Our mothers are racked with the pains of our physical birth; we ourselves suffer the longer pains of our spiritual growth."

Simone de Beauvoir put it another way: "One is not born a woman, one becomes one." This becoming takes time. We need time to consider, time to reflect, time to make creative choices, time to emerge from the cocoon, time to clean out our closets, and time to clear away psychic cobwebs so that we might pare down to our essence.

Some of us have remained dormant for years—oblivious to our genuine beauty—drugged senseless by our own numbing disapproval, nagging doubts, and benign neglect. Coping strategies that once brought a sense of relief now only offer regret. To undo the damage and reconnect with our authentic selves we need to take the plunge, confident that Spirit is holding the net. Above all, we need to treat ourselves gently with the kindness we would bestow on amnesiacs who need the patient reassurance of their true identities.

MARCH 9

A Radiant Reflection: Projecting Your Authentic Self

So many women just don't know how great they really are. They come to us all vogue outside and vague on the inside.
—MARY KAY ASH

Few women know how great they really are. If truth were told, we'd all probably admit to feeling pretty vague about our personal appearance. Many of us would like to trade ourselves in for a sleeker version. Some of us have been wearing our hair the same way for the last decade—not because it's so flattering but because it feels safe. Still others of us haven't changed our makeup since our twenties even though the face in the mirror does not wear the color fuchsia as well as she once did.

But even when we don't consciously know how to pull together our outside packaging, there is someone who does. As we become more intimate with this wonderful source of style, personal fashion know-how, and comfort, we will begin to awaken to our own radiance. This source, our authentic selves, is waiting to help us evolve into the women we were meant to be.

An easy way to let her begin is to gather different mail-order catalogs. Whenever you have a quiet moment to yourself, sit down and flip through the catalogs. Cut out the pictures of the women you think are attractive and the clothing you'd love to wear. Don't even consider whether you can afford anything you select or whether you can fit into it today. This is a creative brainstorming session. Always remember that dreams—your creative visualizations—must come before their physical manifestations. Play with the pictures in your discovery journal. Create a collage of your ideal woman: find the perfect hairstyle, put together a fantastic wardrobe for home and work. Have fun with this. Pretend you're ten years old and playing with paper dolls. See what you discover. Does anything in your discovery journal collage resemble anything hanging in your closet? Consider this carefully.

Now make yourself a promise. Since you have embarked on this adventure to awaken your authenticity and discover your own sense of style, be willing not to buy another item of clothing unless you absolutely cannot live without it. No more settling for something that's not you or that's second-rate. On the Simple Abundance path you're going to discover the joy of surrounding yourself only with things you love, and the pleasure of wearing only clothes that make you look and feel fabulous and project your authentic sense of style. Let the potent power of simplicity begin to work in your life. If it's not authentically you, live without it.

MARCH 10

You Are Not Your Appearance, but Does the Rest of the World Know That?

The tragedy of our time is that we are so eye centered, so appearance besotted.

—JESSAMYN WEST

All of us can pull ourselves together some of the time. Some of us can pull ourselves together all of the time. But none of us wants to be "pulled together" every single moment of our lives. Let's consider those days when you just don't give a damn or are too exhausted to remember to pick up a brush. Can we find inspiration in dirty jeans, an unwashed face, stringy hair? Can there be incarnational revelations when the skirt is too tight and the pantyhose pulls at your hips?

I hope so. For I know those days and those days know me.

Probably you were taught, as I was, that how we present ourselves to the world is very important. Unfortunately, our outside packaging counts for far more than it really should. Often, when we don't live up to the world's expectations of how we should look or behave, we fall victim to a vicious circle of self-loathing and denial that can be difficult to escape from unscathed. At times like these, it's a comfort to remember that our souls are more dazzling than cellophane. "Beauty is an internal light, a spiritual radiance that all women have but most women hide, unconsciously, denying its existence. What we do not claim remains invisible," Marianne Williamson observes in *A Woman's Worth*.

But as you become more intimate with your authentic self—as you recover your true, incandescent identity—there will come a gradual but undeniable physical transformation. It is absolutely impossible to commit to your spiritual growth, awaken to your own radiant Light and not have it reveal itself on the outside. "It is God's will that we be beautiful, that we love and be loved and prosper in all good things," Marianne Williamson reminds us. "It is God's will that we all become the goddesses we were created to be."

MARCH 11

Sending and Receiving Personal Signals

If you will resolve to work each day for self-realization, your whole world can change. . . . The two women you are, they can make you over.

—POND'S COLD CREAM ADVERTISEMENT,
GOOD HOUSEKEEPING, December 1947

I had not seen my friend in months. At first when she approached through the crowd of strangers, I literally did not recognize her. Her hair, always beautifully styled, was disheveled; her unmadeup face was red and puffy with large dark circles under her eyes, and she was wearing a pair of jeans and a lumpy sweater instead of the attractive Laura Ashley dresses she normally favored. I was absolutely stunned. What was wrong with this picture?

When we sat down together to talk over a cup of coffee, she told me about a serious life crisis she was experiencing. But even before she confided in me, I knew only too well that something was seriously wrong.

Each of us transmits personal signals about our self-esteem every day in myriad ways. Most of them are not as dramatic as my friend's but are rather subtle. When we are feeling on top of the world there's a spring in our step, a smile on our face, and a sparkle in our eyes. Then there are those occasions when, through lack of time, energy, or emotion, we become careless about our attire and our personal grooming. We literally begin to care less—until it looks as though we don't care at all. Of course, deep within, we care very much.

But there is an important reason why we *should* give a second thought to our personal appearance, even when we're alone: the inner joy we experience when we look our best. "Many women feel in their hearts that they have missed full self-realization," another advertisement for Pond's Cold Cream in the March 1949 issue of *Good Housekeeping* advised readers. "Yet they need not accept this—help is within themselves. You can feel it within you—an inner drive for happiness. The close interrelation between this Inner You and this Outer You, the almost uncanny power of each to change the other—can change you from drabness to joyous self-fulfillment."

When I first discovered this "New Age" series of beauty advertisements from the late 1940s, I was amused—and then grateful. For one of the most marvelous lessons you learn on a path of personal transformation is that when your heart is open to change, you're able to recognize the personal signals of encouragement your authentic self is constantly sending, no matter how unlikely the source.

MARCH 12

How Do I Look?

How women look and how their looks change in the course of their lives, is not a frivolous question. . . . "How do I look?" she asks as her eyes meet the eyes in the mirror. She listens carefully for an answer, because it might prove quite illuminating.

—KENNEDY FRASER

How do I look?" is a question all of us have spent our lives asking others. But now that you are on the path toward your authenticity you have reached the point when you need to gently ask *yourself* this loaded question. And, once having asked, you need to listen carefully for the answer. Better yet, when you gaze into the mirror you should ask, "How do I feel?"

because how you feel about yourself on any particular day will influence how you look more than what you are wearing.

After years of concentrating on the glitz of the outside packaging, we need to change our approach to beauty completely. Personal transformation begins with a strong inner life. We need to let Spirit show us the way, whether it's changing our wardrobe, losing weight, or finding the right hairstyle. Twenty minutes of meditation a day, quiet reflection, or a restorative walk seeking your authentic self will do more for your looks than you will believe. But of course, you'll believe it when you see it. So what are you waiting for? Start today. Choose one inner tool and make it part of your daily beauty ritual. "If we go down into ourselves we find that we possess exactly what we desire," the French philosopher and mystic Simone Weil believed. Remember this.

MARCH 13

Accepting Yourself as You Are Today

Seek not outside yourself, heaven is within.

—MARY LOU COOK

Today, we make peace with the past: with the bodies and faces we were born with and those that have evolved. Today, we embrace the lines that stare back at us, the parts that sag in the middle or stick out where they shouldn't, the hair that never keeps a curl or never loses it. We begin when we invoke the Tibetan poet and teacher Saraha's song of praise. "Here in this body are the sacred rivers: here are the sun and moon as well as all the pilgrimage places . . . I have not encountered another temple as blissful as my own body."

It will take a bit of doing, learning to love all our personal pilgrimage places. However, before genuine love can flourish, we must finally accept ourselves exactly as we are today. Not tomorrow or next week or when we lose twenty-five pounds. Remember, acceptance is acknowledging the reality of a situation: that we're heavier than we'd like to be, for example, or that our complexion is ruddy or sallow, or that we've got gray streaks, or that leggings just don't work for us. Most of us think of other women as beauties, never ourselves. But every woman was created by Spirit to be a genuine beauty. We learn how to reveal to the world our unique radiance only after we acknowledge it ourselves. Today, take as your personal mantra: "I am what I am and what I am is wonderful."

Loving Yourself into Wholeness

I did not lose myself all at once. I rubbed out my face over the years washing away my pain, the same way carvings on stone are worn down by water.

—AMY TAN

Life batters us whether we are rich or poor, public or private. The wound we suffer may be an open cut or a slow, silent hemorrhage of the soul. On the outside we may look as if we've got our act together, but each of us encounters those dark stormy days when we feel very small, very fragile, and very frightened, as if we might shatter into a thousand pieces and break into heartrending sobs at something as simple as "How are you?"

When this happens we have to be kind to ourselves, not beat ourselves up. Leave that to the rest of the world. Our feelings are valid, our fears very real, even though they are probably not based on reality. Always remember that the best description of fear is "false evidence appearing real."

When these occasions occur in your life, recall that your first duty is to love yourself into Wholeness. How to do this? By pampering yourself with simple pleasures and small indulgences. By treating yourself like the baby you are right now. Could you bring home something wonderful for dinner tonight from a Chinese or Indian carryout? Could you treat yourself to some of the potted daffodils or tulips that are appearing in the shops about now? Could you take the afternoon off and sneak into a matinee? If not, how about bringing home two or three classics from the video store and enjoying a movie marathon with a big bowl of popcorn? Why not delight in an ice-cream cone for lunch, taking it to a park to bask in the sunshine and hear the birds singing? What about saying "no" to the next request for you to do something?

Yes, you can. You don't have to do everything and be everything for everyone else all the time. If you think you can't possibly do one more thing without screaming or crying, you're probably right. Start by saying, "No, I'm sorry, I've got a prior commitment."

For, of course, you do. Today you need to be there for yourself. Remember, we did not lose ourselves all at once. But we recover our authentic selves one kind gesture at a time.

Self-Nurturing:
The Hardest Task You'll Ever Do

*Any little bit of experimenting in self-nurturance is very frighten-
ing for most of us.*

—JULIA CAMERON

Why should self-nurturance be so frightening for most women? Why is
it for you? If you don't think this is true, how many creative excursions have
you been on in the last month? Have you outfitted a comfort drawer for
yourself? Started a hope chest or a toy box? Have you been working in your
discovery journal or writing your daily dialogue pages? Hmmmmmm . . .

Perhaps we are all Scrooges when it comes to self-nurturing because if
we were kind to ourselves, our creativity might begin to blossom like a
plant moving toward the light. Of course, this would mean we'd want to
make some changes in our lives, and we all know how we feel about
changes, even positive ones. We may be in a rut, but at least our own familiar grooves are comforting in their own insidious fashion.

The way to take giant leaps and strides toward our authenticity, however, is through small changes. Leo Tolstoy believed that "True life is lived
when tiny changes occur." Take an honest look at how good you are to yourself. How much sleep are you getting? Are you walking often or getting
enough exercise? Have you given meditation a fair chance? How much time
do you have every week just to relax? To dream? To engage in personal pursuits that bring you pleasure? When was the last time you laughed? "There
is a connection between self-nurturing and self-respect," Julia Cameron
reminds us.

Self-nurturing has been a struggle for me. But believe me, I have learned
on the Simple Abundance path that if you want your life to come together,
you have to start treating yourself better. No one else can do it for you.
Today, make a list of ten nice things you could do for yourself. Now select
one and do it. You have absolutely nothing to lose from experimenting with
self-nurturing and everything to gain.

MARCH 16

What Do You Like about Yourself?

If you want to find the answers to the Big Questions about your soul, you'd best begin with the Little Answers about your body.
—GEORGE SHEEHAN

Like all of us, you see yourself in the mirror every day. But when was the last time you nodded your head in approval at what you saw? Today, I'd like to ask you to try something radically different: look at yourself lovingly and begin to appreciate what you see.

This exercise is more than just skin deep because I want you to take an inventory of what you like about yourself. Most of us are very quick to criticize ourselves. We're always finding things wrong with the way we look. Today we're going to discover and give thanks for what pleases us.

Tonight, set aside an hour to celebrate how marvelous you really are. Prepare an inviting bath, using scented oil or bubble bath. Bring a candle into the bathroom and bathe by candlelight. Allow yourself at least twenty minutes to soak in the warm water to renew yourself. Ask your authentic self to bring to your conscious mind all the special things you should discover tonight. After you pat yourself dry, gently apply some talc or lotion to your body. Give yourself a slow massage and as you work your way down from your shoulders to your toes, visualize each body part surrounded by the most beautiful white light imaginable. This light is Love and you are sending it to every cell in your being. In your most nurturing voice, tell yourself aloud how wonderful you are.

Now go into your bedroom and before getting dressed for bed, take a compassionate look at yourself in the mirror. Continue to gaze approvingly into the mirror until you find ten things that you absolutely love about your face and your body—maybe a perfect nose, beautiful hands, trim ankles. Start at the top and work your way down. Consider everything. You may not like the way your hair is styled, for instance, but you love its color. Write all ten down in your gratitude journal. Now think about aspects of your personality that you like. You're a gifted improviser, a savvy shopper, an empathetic listener, an inspired cook, a patient and loving mother, a great woman for detail. Write it all down. Do not stop until you have at least ten things about your personality for which to be grateful. Now record them all in your gratitude journal.

And if you think you can't find twenty things to love about yourself, go back to the mirror. Do this exercise every day until you can. "Nature never repeats herself and the possibilities of one human soul will never be found in another," Elizabeth Cady Stanton wrote in *Solitude of the Self* in 1892.

Today, be willing to search genuinely for your glorious possibilities and rejoice in your divine authenticity.

MARCH 17

Accentuating the Positive

If one is a greyhound, why try to look like a Pekingese?
—Dame Edith Sitwell

In an age when a woman's beauty was considered her most prized possession, the famed English poet Dame Edith Sitwell, born in 1887, stood out in a crowd. But not for the reasons you might expect. As a young girl she was so homely, awkward, and thin that her family fretted constantly over the fact that marriage would not be in her future. Needless to say, "poor little E," as she was known, endured a miserable, lonely, and frustrated childhood until her beloved governess introduced her to the world of literature and music. She fell in love with the poetry of Swinburne and the Symbolists and in so doing fell in love with her authentic self.

This authenticity found expression in her poetry and in an eccentric personal style rooted in fantasy and drama. She became famous for her long, flowing Pre-Raphaelite dresses fashioned from brocades or upholstery fabrics, for her furs and for her extraordinary hats that highlighted her strong, bony profile and became her own distinctive trademark. To accentuate her long, slender fingers (of which she was very vain) she grew her nails to Mandarin length, painted them red, and wore massive rings.

Dame Edith's flamboyant sense of style is not for many of us. But her glorious way of celebrating her authentic self and of accentuating the positive can speak to every woman. By now you should have discovered wonderful things about your own face and body. Each of us has at least one special feature that can set us apart. Do you accentuate your assets? Are your eyes your most beautiful feature? Then make them up every day, even if you are staying at home with the children. You're turning gray? Have you thought about letting your head shimmer in silver? You're blessed with a beautiful smile and full, luscious lips? Think about wearing red lipstick to call attention to them.

"I have often wished I had time to cultivate modesty," Dame Edith confessed toward the end of her life, "but I am too busy thinking about myself." Most of us don't spend nearly enough time thinking good things about ourselves. Today, follow Dame Edith's example. Discover, flaunt, and celebrate your authentic assets.

Awakening Sleeping Beauty

We are the hero of our own story.

—MARY MCCARTHY

In every one of us there lies a sleeping beauty waiting to be awakened through love. Because she has slumbered for so long, she must be awakened very gently. But instead of waiting for Prince Charming to storm the palace gates, you must summon the magic powers of your authentic self to break any cruel enchantment that has left you unaware of your own glory.

Let me tell you a story about a pretty girl I knew when I was young. Once upon a time there was a garbage strike in our town. For weeks the garbage piled up in front of trim suburban homes. One day a photographer from a newspaper drove up in front of a house and asked if there were any children present. He wanted to photograph children near the garbage pile to emphasize how much had accumulated. The little girl was shyly standing behind her mother when he came to the door, so she was selected and propped up on piles of garbage for the photograph. After the photograph was printed in the newspaper, some children in the school yard taunted the little girl by calling her "just a pile of garbage." In order to handle this public humiliation, she became numb to her own beauty for a very long time. Sitting on the pile of garbage was the same thing as pricking her finger on a spindle and falling into a deep sleep.

"It's hard to tell our bad luck from our good luck sometimes. Hard to tell sometimes for many years to come," writer Merle Shain gently reminds us. "And most of us have wept copious tears over someone or something when if we'd understood the situation better we might have celebrated our good fortune instead."

If that young girl had not pricked her finger, would she have retreated to her bed every afternoon and sought comfort in the world of books? When she became older would she have studied theater to learn the secrets of make-believe? Would she have traveled to London and Paris to write about fashion in order to learn about style? I think not, and I should know.

What was your spindle? Was there a moment when you pricked yourself and fell into a deep slumber? Or did you just slowly shut down? Perhaps the cruel enchantment was caused by overly critical parents, by a devastating breakup, or by a numbing reliance on food, drugs, or alcohol.

It is time to awaken, sleeping beauty. Your creativity, imagination, and authentic sense of style are far superior to any sorcerer's spell, no matter how strong. "One can never change the past, only the hold it has on you," Merle Shain reassures us, "and while nothing in your life is reversible, you can reverse it nevertheless."

MARCH 19

Repose of the Soul

Repose is a quality too many undervalue. . . . In the clamor one is irresistibly drawn to the woman who sits gracefully relaxed, who keeps her hands still, talks in a low voice and listens with responsive eyes and smiles. She creates a spell around her, charming to the ear, the eye and the mind.

—GOOD HOUSEKEEPING, *November 1947*

We have all met her, that special woman who draws you into her orb with a radiant smile. Her eyes light up as you tell her how you've been. She attracts men, women, children, and animals, for her complete attention is soothing and hypnotic. When you walk away from her you feel as if you have been bathed in a beautiful warm light.

You have. It's called Love, and this ancient beauty secret is available to all of us. When we are genuinely interested in others, a graciousness comes over us that is compelling. "She did not talk to people as if they were strange hard shells she had to crack open to get inside. She talked as if she were already in the shell. In their very shell," Marita Bonner wrote of a soulful woman in 1926. Would that each of us were such a woman. Would that each of us could become one.

We can.

Most of us have more harried moments in our daily lives than tranquil ones. But by taking the time to step outside our own sphere to embrace others, we open ourselves up to the power of Spirit. We are suddenly lit up from inside, and this illumination can transform our looks more effectively than any fancy salon beauty makeover.

Today, act as if you are a woman with repose of the soul. Greet everyone you meet with a warm smile. No matter how busy you are, don't rush your encounters with co-workers, family, and friends. Speak softly. Listen attentively. Act as if every conversation you have is the most important thing on your mind today. Look your children and your partner in the eyes when they talk to you. Stroke the cat, caress the dog. Lavish love on every living being you meet. See how different you feel at the end of the day.

MARCH 20

Inner Beauty, Outward Charm

Don't you love it when some incredibly beautiful woman like Linda Evans or Cindy Crawford tells us that the real beauty secret is finding your inner light? No shit. But I've done the same things these women have done to find my inner light and while it's true I'm happier, I still don't look like them.

—MARIANNE WILLIAMSON

We can't all look like Linda Evans or Cindy Crawford, but we *can* each look our best. Simplicity plays a part in striking the right chord of self. This occurs naturally as we begin to rethink how to put together our best look. Our authentic look. Gradually we learn that the "less is more" approach applies to makeup and fashion as well as to decorating and entertaining.

Ironically, this desire to look our best comes *after* we have committed to our inner work. As we go within, searching for spiritual growth, we begin to blossom on the outside. Time well spent in meditation gives us more serenity, and it shows on our faces. Learning to love ourselves exactly as we are gives us the motivation to move forward, whether in searching for a healthier way of eating or finding the right exercise regime. Perhaps we're starting to wear makeup more frequently and caring how we dress even when we're just doing errands or carpooling. These are subtle changes that have a profound impact on how we feel about ourselves.

Why does working on our inner beauty produce outward charm? Perhaps it is because the two are inexorably connected. A Gnostic axiom teaches "As is the inner, so is the outer." Women who realize their full potential delight the Great Creator with their brilliance. Marianne Williamson tells us that the process of personal transformation—whether it be in our lifestyle or in our appearance—"is the true work of spiritual growth."

What Is Self-Confidence?

My after forty face felt far more comfortable than anything I lived with previously. Self-confidence was a powerful beauty-potion; I looked better because I felt better. Failure and grief as well as success and love had served me well. Finally, I was tapping into that most hard-won of youth dews: wisdom.

—NANCY COLLINS

Many women confuse self-esteem with self-confidence. For me, self-esteem is how we really feel about ourselves in the secret sanctuary of our soul. Do we love, accept, and approve of ourselves unconditionally? Do we believe that we are worthy of the love of others and the best that life has to offer? The quality of our self-esteem is very deeply connected to the relationship with our first and most important critics: our parents. If they unconditionally loved, accepted, and approved of us, then we probably do, too.

But self-confidence is a special elixir that Spirit has prepared to help each of us face and surmount the challenges of life. It's an aromatic blending of invigorating essences: attitude, experience, knowledge, wisdom, optimism, and faith. If we were fortunate enough to grow up in loving, supportive homes and our self-esteem is strong, we learned our own homeopathic formula early. If we did not, then we need to learn how to mix our own custom blend. What's important to realize is that self-confidence is available to all of us.

An optimistic attitude is essential to self-confidence. So is learning from our mistakes and recognizing that everything in life can be used as a lesson once we are willing to be taught. "If you think you can, you can," the American cosmetics entrepreneur Mary Kay Ash tells us. "And if you think you can't, you're right."

Today, tell yourself that you can do anything you want to do. Because you can. Like an expensive perfume, only a smidgen of self-confidence is needed to enhance a woman's authentic aura.

Why Self-Confidence Can't Be Bought but Can Be Borrowed

I was thought to be "stuck up." I wasn't. I was just sure of myself.
This is and always has been an unforgivable quality to the unsure.
—BETTE DAVIS

It would be wonderful if we could simply waltz up to a cosmetic counter and purchase a bottle of self-confidence the way we can buy "revitalizing" or "performance" creams for our faces. Unfortunately this spiritual elixir, like an expensive perfume, is different on every woman because of individual chemistry.

When I was younger, my self-confidence potion was heavily scented with attitude, optimism, and faith; experience, knowledge, and wisdom had to come later. But even today, every new opportunity or challenge requires that I prepare a special batch of moxie for myself. I do this by becoming as thoroughly prepared as possible and by looking the part—wearing an outfit, for example, that exudes self-confidence even when it's hanging in the closet. Next I say my prayers and ask for the Power to be switched on. Then "it's showtime." I *act* as if I'm self-confident and the world takes me as such.

When you're unsure of yourself but life requires you to be otherwise, it is comforting to remember that you can always borrow a self-confident attitude from your authentic self. She knows how terrific you are and can give you that little boost, which is all you really need. Our subconscious mind cannot distinguish between what's real and what's imaginary (which is why creative visualization works). If we act as if we're confident, we become so. At least for a little while. "You must do the thing you think you cannot do," Eleanor Roosevelt once observed, and her life was spent proving the point. When life challenges arise, you can surmount them by calling on Spirit and borrowing the scent of self-confidence from your authentic self.

Always Be a First-Rate Version of Yourself

Always be a first-rate version of yourself, instead of a second-rate version of somebody else.

—JUDY GARLAND

I make a terrible Judy Garland but I do a pretty good Sarah Ban Breathnach. It's taken me nearly my entire lifetime to come to this awareness, but I've not been the same woman since I did. Neither will you be once this truth awakens in your heart.

You see, whether we are consciously aware of it or not, we're constantly programmed by the world to be other women, not ourselves. We're supposed to look like Cindy Crawford, entertain like Martha Stewart, and decorate like Alexandra Stoddard. With this pervasive social schizophrenia, it's no wonder that most women are terribly confused about the issue of authenticity.

According to *Webster's Dictionary*, to be authentic is to be "not imaginary, false or imitation." To be authentic is to be "genuine, veritable, bona fide, being actually and precisely what is claimed." The only thing that we can genuinely claim to be is ourselves. But our best is good enough, even on a bad day. I know a woman who is a high-powered advertising executive in New York. There is no one I know on the planet who is more creative, articulate, accomplished, and funny, but some days she doesn't see it that way. She grew up in a home where performance was always graded, and as a result she's extremely hard on herself. Her personal grade of C- is probably everybody else's A+.

We are all so hard on ourselves. We not only want to be other people, we want to be perfect versions of them.

Let me tell you about another woman I know. When her first book was published, close friends will testify, she acted like a raving lunatic. Instead of congratulating herself on producing such a beautiful book after years of effort, she was about to throw herself off a cliff because she had used the wrong verb tense in one sentence. Instead of celebrating her achievement, she robbed herself of joy.

Now she knows better, thank God. Did you know that Amish quilters will deliberately add a mismatched patch to each quilt to remind themselves that only Spirit can create perfectly? We need to remember that. We should only strive to be first-rate versions of ourselves. And our best is always good enough.

The Secret Saboteur:
When You're Feeling Blue

Listening to your heart is not simple. *Finding out who you are is not simple. It takes a lot of hard work and courage to get to know who you are and what you want.*

—SUE BENDER

After self-nurturance, listening to the whispers of our hearts is probably the hardest task we've ever attempted. Some days the Simple Abundance path comes naturally. You realize that all you have is all you truly need. Other days, it's impossible to quiet down the wants. It seems as if you have too many unfulfilled desires and delayed dreams. You're sick and tired of waiting for inner changes to manifest themselves on the outside.

When the dark days come, we need to remember that even if a secret saboteur—depression—is at work temporarily derailing our progress (or so it seems), each day offers us a gift if we will only look for it. Sometimes we're sad for a very apparent reason—an overwhelming loss, for example, or worries over money or health. Other times we don't know why we feel so bad, which makes us feel even worse. It could be for a million different reasons—an appalling lack of appreciation (by ourselves and by others), exhaustion, the weather, hormones, the advent of the flu, or simply part of the process of personal transformation.

I wish I could tell you that spiritual and creative growth was smooth, predictable, and without pain. "All the best transformations are accompanied by pain," Fay Weldon tells us. "That's the point of them." Personal growth also comes in spasms: three steps forward, two steps back, and then a long plateau when it seems as though nothing is happening. But it's important to realize that this dormant period always seems to precede a growth spurt. Unfortunately, during the dormant period we very often become depressed and decide to give up.

It's on days like these that you can barely get yourself dressed and out the door. You look like hell and couldn't care less. You can't remember if you took a shower yesterday or when the last time was you washed your hair. The children's voices are insistent and yours is shrill. You haven't any patience. Life seems bleak, not bright with promise. It's taking more work than you expected to discover who you really are, and now you're no longer sure you even want to find out.

When dark clouds hover, what should you do besides holding on and riding out the storm? You have two choices. One is simply to give in, stop resisting. You've got the blues, so sing them, baby. But before you do, ask for grace. Then have a good cry. Leave work early. Take a nap and try to sleep it off. Indulge—without guilt—in something purely for medicinal reasons, like a piece of cheesecake or a bowl of Häagen-Dazs, but don't eat it standing in front of the refrigerator. Sit down, eat your treat slowly and savor it. If you have the energy, fix comfort food for dinner tonight. If you don't, fix something simple like soup and sandwiches. Rent a three-hanky movie. Put the kids to bed early. Soak in a hot tub. Raid your comfort drawer. Pull up the covers and snuggle down. Find five things for which to be grateful. Turn out the light.

The alternative blues-kicker is to shift gears. Ask for grace. Call a good friend and talk. Put the kettle on for a fresh pot of tea. Wash your face, comb your hair, put on some lipstick, perfume, and earrings. Smile at yourself in the mirror. Straighten the living room so that you can find a place to sit down. Take a walk around the block and clear your head. If you're working in an office, give yourself permission to put off that new project at work until tomorrow when you can concentrate. Instead, clean your desk and organize your papers. On the way home treat yourself to a bouquet of daffodils. Peruse your cookbooks and prepare something different for dinner.

No matter which route you take, within twenty-four hours the day will be over. Tomorrow should be better. But if it's not, nor the next day, or the next, then know that it's okay to ask for help from friends, a support group, a therapist, a doctor, or your Higher Power. Dark days come to all of us. Yet discouraging days bring with them golden opportunities when we can learn to be kind to ourselves. Believe it or not, today offers you a hidden gift, if you're willing to search for it.

MARCH 25

Real Life: Clothes That Fit Your Lifestyle

"I haven't got a thing to wear" does not, of course, mean that we must resort to nakedness or seclusion; it means that our wardrobes contain nothing that might match our mood or offer a just reflection of our current lives.

—KENNEDY FRASER

Most of us have had the experience of looking at a closet full of clothes and finding nothing wearable that matches our mood. With a sigh of resignation we resort to a well-worn and time-tested "uniform," whether it be a black dress and pearls or a denim skirt, sweater, and boots.

Actually, most of us wear, with few exceptions, the same thing or its incarnation over and over again. The outfits may vary according to the season, but not our dependence on a few staples, which, in their own way, offer a revealing reflection of how we view our current lives. The legendary editor-in-chief of *Vogue*, Diana Vreeland, was famous for favoring the same style black couture skirts and sweaters every workday for many years.

So what do we do with all the clothes we don't wear? Nothing. They just hang there abandoned, because of their size or color or lack of appropriateness, because they itch, or because we had that last terrible fight with our ex-husband in that sorry dress and don't want to be reminded of the pain. Sometimes clothes hang around season after season, phantoms waiting for some unforeseen occasion in the future that never comes.

Spring is the perfect time to take stock of our wardrobes and reconsider our relationship to clothes. The wind of refreshing change is in the air. We long to shed our heavy coats and sweaters for lighter garb. Let's shed our outmoded attitudes about what's fashionable, and replace them with new ideas about what works for us in our real lives and truly reflects our authenticity.

What if everything hanging in your closet were something you loved— something that made you look beautiful or made you feel wonderful when you put it on? Think of how good you would feel every day. Embracing the second Simple Abundance principle of simplicity can spiritually induce such a miracle.

Later you'll clean out your closets and dresser drawers, but not today. Today, I only want you to consider your real life and the clothes you wear every day. Do they really reflect the woman within? What about the clothes that speak to you from the pages of your illustrated discovery journal? What about the clothes that hang abandoned in your closet? Every dress, skirt, pair of slacks or jeans, blouse, sweater, T-shirt and jacket tells a story. "Clothes have a life that is quite independent of their shape and color," Kennedy Fraser reminds us in *The Fashionable Mind*. Get quiet, go within, and be willing to really listen to the tale that the threads of your life have woven.

The Unspoken Language of Authenticity

To choose clothes, either in a store or at home, is to define and describe ourselves.

—ALISON LURIE

Most of us do not think we're carrying on a conversation with our psyches, our families, and the outside world when we get dressed in the morning, but we are. Alison Lurie tells us in her fascinating book *The Language of Clothes* that the vocabulary of our wardrobe conveys much more than we ever dreamed possible. "Long before I am near enough to talk to you on the street, in a meeting, or at a party, you announce your sex, age and class to me through what you are wearing—and very possibly give me important information (or misinformation) as to your occupation, origin, personality, opinions, tastes, sexual desires and current mood. I may not be able to put what I observe into words, but I register the information unconsciously; and you simultaneously do the same for me. By the time we meet and converse we have already spoken to each other in an older and more universal tongue."

After you begin searching for your authentic self, one of your more startling insights will occur when you discover that for years another woman has been carrying on conversations for you—at home, at work, in social situations, even on errands. At first this revelation can be disconcerting, even discouraging. But on reflection, it can be an exciting discovery because now that you're beginning to cherish and channel your authenticity through creative choices, you can learn how to become not only bilingual but fluent in expressing yourself. As the famous French fashion designer Gabrielle "Coco" Chanel confessed, "How many cares one loses when one decides not to be something but to be someone."

Glimmers from the Golden Mirror

It is never too late to be what you might have been.
—GEORGE ELIOT

When I began to embark regularly on the golden mirror meditation to meet with my authentic self, one of my recurring insights didn't seem very spiritual but certainly was uplifting. I delighted in discovering that my authentic self was very well dressed and always managed to look glorious, whether the occasion of my creative visualization called for a cotton sweater from the Gap or a wool crepe Giorgio Armani suit. You've probably also received revealing glimmers from the other side of the golden mirror. By paying attention to the subtle signals the woman within is constantly trying to send us, we can learn how to reflect our own best image, even if our pocketbooks don't match our exquisite taste.

Paying close attention to the nuances, I noticed that simplicity was my authentic self's signature. Simplicity is also the key to pulling together and conveying a personal style with panache. It's a woman of substance's secret weapon. Think of Katharine Hepburn's trousers in the 1930s, Grace Kelly's hair and handbags in the 1950s, Jacqueline Kennedy's pillbox hats in the 1960s, Lauren Hutton's white T-shirts and khakis in the 1990s.

Understated. Elegant. Chic. Classy. Stunning.

Simplicity is a fashion statement every woman today can make no matter what her personal style has been in the past. That's because true simplicity never disappoints. Once you learn that less is more, then enough becomes plenty, and your entire outlook on life—including fashion—is transformed.

Today, I want to ask you to consider clearing away the fashion clutter of past incarnations that lurks in your closets. Just because you bought it once doesn't mean you have to keep it forever. Be willing to let simplicity pare down your wardrobe to your authentic essence: identify the clothes you absolutely love and can't imagine living without. That is all. Merely consider and identify, while remembering that it is never too late for you to become the woman you were meant to be. Today you're one step closer to her.

Clearing: Parting with Fashion Mistakes

It's never too late—in fiction or in life—to revise.
—NANCY THAYER

Revising your wardrobe to reflect your authenticity begins when you ruthlessly part with the fashion mistakes and mismatches that crowd your closets and confuse your cluttered mind. But let's be realistic for a moment. Most women I know have to be psyched up before they can tackle a project like this. Clearing out closets and dresser drawers is daunting to contemplate (all that money, all those bad choices) and hard work once you're at it. But few things are as satisfying as bringing order to a closet in which chaos once reigned. A change of seasons provides the perfect opportunity to get to work because it's time to pack away winter clothes and bring out spring and summer ones. With a plan of attack, you can also clear away the past.

Find two hours for this activity; for many women Saturday afternoon is perfect. Make sure you gather enough boxes and large plastic garbage bags ahead of time so that after you begin, your energy won't be scattered by constantly having to leave the room to find more containers. Play some delightful music; I like Broadway show tunes for clearing chores. Take a deep breath. Now start by taking everything out of your closet and putting it on the bed. There, it's too late to turn back now.

Go through your wardrobe, item by item. Try things on if you're not sure and look at yourself in a full-length mirror honestly but with compassion. Edit your fashion accessories as well: jewelry, scarves, purses, hats, shoes. Keep *only* those things you love—things that make you look beautiful or feel fabulous. This is simplicity at work. What if some of the items don't fit you today but you still love them? Save only one size smaller than you're wearing now, because getting back into it is a realistic goal and something to work toward.

Consider the various real lives you lead and the clothes you need for them: work, dress-up, and comfort. If you haven't worn something in a year, why not? Be willing to part with it, even if it was expensive. Don't save it unless it has tremendous sentimental value. For example, I went through a phase a decade ago where I wore nothing but Laura Ashley. Today the cottage sprig look doesn't suit me. But because I have so many happy memories of dressing alike with my daughter, I can't bear to part with my Laura Ashley past, so it's packed away in the attic for my daughter to consider when she's older. If you have room to pack away sentimental favorites, then do so. If you don't, be willing to pass them on to someone else who will love them as much as you once did.

Now take the plunge and give away the rest to those who will bless your generosity. In return, you'll experience a sense of grateful abundance when you realize how much you can give away. This positive attitude is essential for attracting more prosperity into our lives. One of my friends has come up with a very therapeutic way of dealing with her expensive discards that her frugal conscious self wants to hoard. She donates them to a charity for women on welfare who need nice clothes in order to go on job interviews. This makes it easy for her to edit her wardrobe because she really is helping other women in a wonderfully positive way. I might also add, my friend is extremely well dressed and regularly finds gorgeous clothing at unbelievable markdowns. She thinks she's just lucky. I think it is the Universe's way of rewarding her for keeping a cycle of good going.

Every woman has fashion mistakes that clutter up her sense of style and tempt her to whine about her wardrobe. Clearing our closets of past incarnations provides the space and freedom for us to choose clothing in the future that authentically reflects the women we are becoming.

MARCH 29

Comfort Clothes and What They Mean

I base my fashion taste on what doesn't itch.

—GILDA RADNER

Most women feel passionately about their comfort clothes. I have a beloved pair of paisley cotton knit pajamas that I would wear twenty-four hours a day, seven days a week, if I could only figure out how to get away with it. During the day they wait patiently on a hook in my bedroom closet; at night they whisper my name. Because I wear these pajamas so religiously, I wash them often, which is why they have become as soft as a baby's cheek. Alas, I have searched in vain to find another pair so that I might have more variety in my "at-home wear" but either the style or the fabric doesn't quite match the perfection of my paisley, so the holy quest continues.

I used to own a special sweater that was an incredible silk/cotton blend. I wore it and washed it so often that it began to unravel at the sides. I wore it anyway. I called it my lucky literary sweater because the days I wore it were incredibly productive. This synchronicity occurred because I felt such exquisite pleasure and experienced such divine comfort all day long that I was free to be a creative conduit. Finally, when the book I was writing was completed, my husband beseeched me to discard the ratty old thing. Since I was known to strangers in our town as simply "the mayor's wife," I reluctantly agreed. Now one of our cats makes a nest on my lost love in our basement. Her look of unadulterated bliss at having inherited such a treasure somewhat alleviates the loss. Somewhat, but not quite.

I am convinced that we are our own best selves in comfort clothes. Somehow, through the alchemy of fiber and fit, we are once again restored to Paradise, this time not naked before the Great Creator, but reveling in the clothes She intended for us to wear.

Unfortunately, comfort clothes exist for most of us only as a footnote to our lives, not center stage as they would if a sensible woman were in charge of the earthly scheme of things. Perhaps we feel good for eight hours out of every twenty-four, but that is not nearly good enough. The rest of the time we're squeezed into uncomfortable things that pull, pinch, tug, choke, itch, hike up or down, and make the days of our lives miserable. We wear these creations of torture, we tell ourselves, in order to be agreeable to the rest of the world. But why shouldn't we find a way of making the world agreeable to us instead?

This week, play detective. Examine closely the items in your wardrobe you reach for when in need of comfort. Look for clues to help you bring more comfort into your life. What fabrics feel good against your skin? Make a note of it on the small spiral notebook you're carrying in your purse. What size are you really comfortable in? Be honest, not vain. It has been my experience that comfort clothes are usually our *true* size or even a tad loose. You don't squeeze into comfort, you slip into something that's more comfortable. What collar style suits you? Yes, these details make all the difference. Expand the comfort concept to how you care for your wardrobe. In the future look for clothes that are easy to maintain—limit labels that say "Dry clean only."

Now see if you can't find clothing that matches your personal preferences and be willing to wait until you do. Consider budgeting and saving for quality comfort clothing you can wear all day long and love for years. The Simple Abundance path encourages us to be patient until we find what's perfect for us, rather than continue to waste our money, energy, and emotion settling for second-best or the second-rate.

Developing a Sense of Style

Taste concerns itself with broad, lifetime progress and never makes mistakes; style moves by fits and starts and is occasionally glorious.
—KENNEDY FRASER

Celebrating your authentic style through the clothes you wear is an art form. But like any of the arts, a sense of style is one that needs to be nurtured after it is initially divined and devised. Style begins when you seek and discover your strengths, then bank on them for all they're worth. Personal style flourishes when you realize that you really don't need as much clothing, accessories, jewelry, or makeup as you once thought you did because you've got attitude.

"We all know style when we see it—Bogart and Bacall, Garbo and Jackie O., Audrey Hepburn, Lauren Hutton, Lena Horne—all different, and all synonymous with style," Leah Feldon-Mitchell writes. "Their clothes, however grand or simple, proclaim not simply taste but intelligence, wit—a little daring. What you see is self-definition rather than trendiness. Style is the intersection of what you wear with who you are."

Remind yourself today that you are an artist. In searching for your authenticity you will uncover your own signature look. It may be the great way you wear hats, highlight stunning eyes with smoky gray kohl, showcase a chic short cut with fabulous earrings, show off gorgeous slender legs with sheer stockings and elegant pumps, or have enough pluck to pair a white cotton T-shirt with a tailored wool jacket.

This year, be willing to experiment to find out what works for you and what doesn't. Then stick with what works, no matter what everybody else is wearing. Linda Ellerbee believes "Styles, like everything else, change. Style doesn't." Your own sense of style may come in fits and starts, but trust that it will come and when it does, it will be glorious.

Never Fall for Fashion, Always Be in Style

Fashion fades. Only style remains.

—COCO CHANEL

Women frequently want to have a mad passionate fling with fashion, but given a choice, most of us would marry style. That's because style, like a good man, doesn't let you down. When fashion seduces you, the affair usually burns itself out before the next season.

Fashion is a show-off, concerned with the cutting edge. Style has seen it all before and knows that the classic tenets of simplicity, beauty, and elegance have staying power. Fashion is a cult; style is a philosophy.

Fashion mocks individuality; style celebrates it. Never forget that fashion, while frequently a charmer, is also a self-centered, frivolous bore. Style is high-spirited and generous, given to touting your best features for all the world to see. Fashion is a provocateur; style prefers to soothe. Fashion is self-congratulatory; style waits for the inevitable compliments. "Fashion can be bought," Edna Woolman Chase observed in 1954. "Style must be possessed."

Fashion guesses, so it can only bluff. Style knows. Fashion is impatient and eventually passes away. Style is steadfast and waits for every woman's awakening, because authentic style is born of Spirit.

Joyful Simplicities for March

৺৳ If you don't have them growing in your garden, bring home a bouquet of daffodils, now available in the shops and from street vendors, to brighten your dining room table.

৺৳ Take a spring walk, scout your backyard, or visit a nursery and get some bare branches for forcing: cherry, crabapple, forsythia, birch. Cut the ends sharply on a slant and place them in a variety of attractive containers—large vases, colorful bottles, pottery jugs, even old milk cans—filled with tepid water. Use your imagination! Place your branches in a sunny spot and wait for spring to arrive indoors.

৺৳ Find a five-and-dime. Cruise the aisles. You'd be amazed at what they still make. Buy some old-fashioned terry-cloth dish towels to replace the ratty ones in the kitchen or get yourself the kind of mascara you put on with a brush.

৺৳ Celebrate St. Patrick's Day (March 17). Wear green. Try your hand at baking a loaf of delicious Irish soda bread, along with a supper of corned beef, cabbage, boiled potatoes, and carrots. Serve with hot tea and cold beer. For those who don't imbibe, there are marvelous nonalcoholic brews available that impart the taste but not the buzz of alcohol. Play some traditional Irish music and dance a jig in your living room. (I'm serious!) Get a small pot of Irish shamrocks at the greengrocer's for your desk.

  ~ Observe the Vernal Equinox on March 21 with a springtime dinner of salmon cakes, fresh asparagus, and new potatoes.

  ~ Gather pussy willows, either on a walk or from a florist, and make a seasonal wreath for your front door. Get a circular wire base at a crafts shop and overlap branches of pussy willow, securing with florist wire. Add a festive bow with long streamers to whip in the March winds.

  ~ Collect your favorite affirmations and then record them on your tape recorder in your own voice. After you've recorded your tape, lie down on your bed, close your eyes, and play it back using headphones. Do this several times a week. This is a *very* powerful tool for transformation.

  ~ When the blues—the secret saboteur—strike, my favorite homeopathic defense is to play the original soundtrack to the movie *Boys on the Side* (Arista Records) over and over again until I can pick myself up off the floor and boogie. Whenever I hear Whoopi Goldberg reinvent the Roy Orbison hit, "You Got It," I hear the voice of my authentic self reassuring me to just hang in there; I'm not alone. Neither are you. Listen to The Indigo Girls sing about the "Power of Two" and you'll hear about the nurturing relationship you can cultivate with your authentic self. It's great music that heals on a very deep level.

  ~ If you have space, this is the month to begin sowing flower and vegetable seeds indoors. This is also the time you must get pansies and primroses. Next month, they'll all be gone! Gather them in a basket; let their bright little faces cheer you.

  ~ The last week in March is the time to plant a living Easter basket. Find a pretty pastel-colored Easter basket, line it with pebbles (or a reusable plastic liner available at gardening centers) and add two inches of potting soil. Sprinkle fast-growing rye grass seed on top of the soil and then cover with another quarter inch of soil. Water well and cover with a brown paper sack for a few days until the seeds germinate. When the grass sprouts, place the basket in a warm sunny window and continue to water. In a couple of weeks you'll have a basket of living grass. Add a bow to the handle and tuck in some painted wooden Easter eggs and a small stuffed bunny for a charming springtime centerpiece. This is a delightful hostess gift to make if you're expected somewhere for Easter dinner.

  ~ Have you started a hope chest, created a toy box, or outfitted a comfort drawer this month? If not, why not? If money is the reason, select one pleasure and begin slowly with one small symbolic item. The crucial point is to start self-nurturance in a tangible way.

  ~ How many creative excursions have you gone on this month? Remember, they don't have to cost a dime—just an investment of time.

APRIL

April, the Angel of the Months.
—Vita Sackville-West

Perhaps it's because April is so full of dazzling sunlight. Perhaps it's because the earth seems greener. Perhaps it's because resurrection is this month's signature. Is this why our spirits start to soar? Now the season of darkness diminishes as the season of Light increases in strength. In the garden, primroses, pansies, violets, tulips, and lilacs burst with color. Each flower, plant, and bough bears profound witness to the power of authenticity. This month, on the Simple Abundance path, we continue to grow gracefully, creatively, and joyously into our authentic selves, awakening to our own beauty.

Playing Dress-Up: Empowering Your Authentic Self with Fun

Learn the craft of knowing how to open your heart and to turn on your creativity. There's a light inside of you.

—JUDITH JAMISON

Today—All Fools' Day—is a day that for centuries has been associated with high spirits and merriment. It's a perfect day for us to remember the importance of lightening up. A lighthearted sense of spontaneity is closely aligned with Spirit. Think of the brother who makes you laugh or the friend who will call you up and ask you to meet her on the spur of the moment for an ice-cream cone. Don't you just love to be in their company? Lighthearted people possess the special gift, as dancer Judith Jamison tells us, of being able to open up their hearts to life and turn on their creativity. Perhaps it is because these special people still honor the child within. This sacred craft of Knowing is one that we can gradually learn to nurture on the path we have chosen.

Children love to play dress-up. Think of the excitement of a little boy putting together his costume at Halloween or a little girl lost in the pleasure of exploring her mother's closet and jewelry box on a rainy afternoon. Today we're going to play dress-up, too. I love to indulge in this pastime in the spring and in the fall when I change my seasonal wardrobe. It's fun to play dress-up by yourself or in the company of an accomplice, such as your daughter or a close friend. (Be forewarned, however, that with your daughter, you'll frequently hear enquiries such as, "Do you still want this?" Yes, you do.)

Look at your pared-down wardrobe with fresh eyes. Small changes can have a big impact on your look. Try jackets on with different skirts and pants and see if you can't put together new outfits. Try pairing a lean, tailored crepe jacket with a flounced skirt. Instead of always wearing the burgundy print silk blouse you bought to go with your navy suit, try a white cotton one with a lace jabot and big cuffs. If you normally wear your collars open, try wearing them closed with a pretty pin at the neck. A new you? Why not? Now pull your hair back and see what dangle earrings look like. Get out your shoes. Do you always wear plain pumps with your suits? What about switching to wedge suede sandals? Work with whatever you've got. Have fun with this exercise. Think seven years old. Think "what the heck!" Gail Sheehy tells us that "the delights of self-discovery are always available." All Fools' Day is the perfect day to engrave this wisdom in our hearts.

APRIL 2

Verve: The Secret of Personal Style

The soul should always stand ajar, ready to welcome the ecstatic experience.

—EMILY DICKINSON

French women are famous for their verve. But Princess Diana, who has a penchant for selecting colorful suits and stunning hats, certainly possesses verve. So does Diane Keaton, who introduced women to the marvels of menswear in 1977 with her signature "Annie Hall" look. A century before, Emily Dickinson showed verve by preferring to dress entirely in white, year-round, at a time when most Victorian women dressed in dark, somber colors. Perhaps Miss Dickinson knew that expressing verve through her clothing could jump-start the ecstatic experience she so fervently sought and encouraged others to seek as well.

Verve is the special ability or talent to pull something off with panache, from a fabulous outfit to an exquisite couplet of poetry. Verve comes into our lives when we finally trust our instincts. When we take risks and they pay off. Verve is passion. It's also the secret of personal style. Verve is focused creative energy, a sense of vitality or zest.

And how do we learn to develop a finely honed sense of verve? By paying attention to the details. By accepting each day's attempt to teach us more about our authenticity. By being constantly on the lookout for the ecstatic experience: what excites us or moves us to tears, what makes the blood rush to our head, our hearts skip a beat, our knees shaky, and our souls sigh. "A market stall, a fine Bokhara rug, a scrap of Chinese embroidery—food for the eye is to be found almost everywhere," the writer Jocasta Innes urges us to remember.

Secret Lives: Gleaning Tips from Our Imaginary Selves

Inside myself is a place where I live all alone and that's where you renew your springs that never dry up.

—Pearl Buck

What are you going to be when you grow up? Today, let's think about paths not yet taken—the paths of our secret imaginary selves. Each of us leads many lives vicariously and often simultaneously. By acknowledging our secret lives and tapping into the wisdom of our imaginary alter egos, we can glean tips to help us develop our own personal sense of style.

If you had ten other lives to lead, what would you be doing? Every time I listen to Mary Chapin Carpenter, I'm a country and western song-writer/singer. When I read the mystical monk, Thomas Merton, I'm a contemplative nun.

You might want to be a radio disc jockey, a mountain climber, a Broadway lyricist, a filmmaker, a romance novelist, a brain surgeon, a syndicated newspaper columnist, a psychic, a horticulturist, a holistic veterinarian, or a potter. You get the drift. So first divine who you'd be if not you. Now write down your secret selves. How do they live? How do they dress? What can you do to bring some of the magic of your imaginary lives into your everyday existence? Brainstorm with your authentic self. For example, I absolutely adore the colorful style of today's country and western women singers. I'm drawn to their exuberant extravagance even though my natural inclination as a communicator is more understated. How to reconcile fantasy with reality and bring more pizzazz into my life? Maybe it's as simple as realizing that I'd really love to wear beautiful red leather cowboy boots. Because this is a recurring fantasy, I'm now saving and searching. When I find them (on sale naturally), I'm going to pair them with a power suit.

Look within today and have fun. Maybe red cowboy boots aren't for you. But one of your secret selves might reveal a passionate wish. Your secret imaginary lives are full of surprises. Be open to gleaning their secrets of personal style.

An Elegant Art: Learning That Less Is More

For me, elegance is not to pass unnoticed but to get to the very soul of what one is.

—CHRISTIAN LACROIX

Many people think that Ludwig Mies van der Rohe, one of the founders of the modern architectural movement, was the first to declare that "less is more." Surprisingly, it was the English poet Robert Browning, writing in 1855. But what applies to architecture and poetry applies equally to personal style.

Elegance is the art of restraint. Famous, wealthy women known for their chic sense of style keep their looks uncluttered: comfortable, beautifully tailored suits in neutral palettes for day; simple, graceful dresses for evening; well-bred accessories that never overpower but always strike the right note. What sets an elegant woman apart from the crowd is her quiet self-assurance; she knows that *she* is what's worth focusing on, not an armload of golden bangle bracelets.

While money is helpful, most women assume it is an essential for an elegant style. Gratefully, it's not. "Elegance does not consist in putting on a new dress," the incomparable Coco Chanel assures us. Rather, elegance in personal style requires only that a woman major in the classics: comfort, color, shape, fabric, value, and appropriateness. Elegance means that clothes never eclipse the woman within but permit her inner light to shine. In fashion, as in life, knowledge is currency: you need less when you know more. Here is a fundamental lesson that every woman can learn if she sets her mind to it.

Perhaps the soul of elegance is a simply abundant state of mind. In fact, Diana Vreeland believed that "The only real elegance is in the mind; if you've got that, the rest really comes from it."

Whom Do You Admire?

Undoubtedly, we become what we envisage.

—CLAUDE M. BRISTOL

Whom do you admire? If you tell me whom you admire, I could probably tell you a great deal about your hopes, dreams, and personal style—and I'm not a psychic. "People change and forget to tell each other," Lillian Hellman once observed. Very often, however, it's the inner you who changes and at the speed of light. Problems can arise when your authentic self and your conscious self don't communicate about the new direction you are moving in. And they probably *aren't* communicating if you're not using an introspective tool like the daily dialogue, the illustrated discovery journal, or meditation. It's no wonder if you feel confused and disoriented. Don't panic. This is a healthy sign of new growth.

Here's what I mean. For several years after my first book was published, I gave workshops and lectures. Because I was the author of a book on Victorian family traditions, people expected me to look the part, and I didn't disappoint. However, after I had embarked on the Simple Abundance path and was keeping an illustrated discovery journal, I began to notice that a lot of pictures of Lauren Hutton—fabulous in her simple, chic, uncluttered style—kept popping up on my pages. At the same time, I was wearing flowery, romantic, fussy clothing and my hair was long and curly. Gradually I began to feel uncomfortable in my own body a great deal of the time, as if I were a ghost unable to move on. Without realizing it consciously, I had been changing within, moving away from what others expected of me and toward my own true identity. But I only came to this awareness when simplicity began to show up visually in my journal. Our authentic selves are constantly alerting us through subtle clues, such as images of the people we admire. But authenticity rarely screams at us; it prefers to whisper.

Today you might like to cast your net for inspiration and consider forming a circle of kindred spirits—women whose personal sense of style you admire. Clip pictures of the way they dress, wear their hair, and do their makeup and log them in your discovery journal the way an explorer logs changes en route.

At this point in the process, don't fret about imitation. Besides its being the sincerest form of flattery, if you begin to trust your instincts, you'll always remain true to your own sense of style. Just think of the women you admire as personal tutors. You're not trying to become them, you're trying to become your *authentic self*. After a couple of months, see if you don't notice a pleasing and revealing pattern that inspires you to grow into the stunning woman you are within.

APRIL 6

Classic Chic 101: The Color Story

Adornment is never anything but a reflection of the self.
—COCO CHANEL

When I lived in London during the early 1970s and wrote about fashion, the first thing I learned to do was to cover "the color story." This was because one season the color story would be the "neons," such as "watermelon" (hot pink) and "key lime" (bright green), and the next season it would be "earthtones," such as "aubergine" (blackish purple) and "saffron" (golden yellow). So if you spent a small fortune to be fashionable, nothing in your closet ever matched.

At the European fashion shows two groups of women stood out on either side of the runway: those who worked in or covered the fashion industry who were dressed in black and those the industry was courting—wealthy women dressed in classic colors. Moral of the story: the fly-by-night colors touted on the runway, in the shop windows, and on the magazine pages might dazzle, but the real money knew that style banks on classics.

If you have now begun to rethink your wardrobe and your personal style, consider the role that color plays in your life. To build a wardrobe with staying power, invest in classic colors for the foundation—black, white, navy, gray, beige, camel, tan, khaki, ivory, and the "reds" including wine and russet. Within this palette are literally a hundred hues for you to choose from. Classic colors don't limit; they liberate. You can use color to cultivate and coordinate a chic look with confidence. This means that the beautifully tailored jacket you buy this year in a classic color can be worn with a skirt from last year or with a pair of trousers next year, and so on. With classic colors, your wardrobe gradually grows and never goes out of style. Now punctuate your personal style with accent colors that you absolutely adore and that look best on you.

How do you find your best colors? Experiment and study yourself in the mirror. All of us look better in some colors than we do in others, depending on our complexions. During the 1980s, discovering your best colors became a growth industry. Today, books abound on how to find the colors that flatter, and many adult extension courses feature classes in personal color selection.

Finally, never underestimate the power of love. Years ago I fell passionately in love with a black silk scarf featuring beautiful red cherries, deep golden pears, and dark green foliage. It was so gorgeous it made my heart race. Although it meant economizing in other areas for a month, I invested in that scarf, and it became a personal palette that has never failed to please me. Trust your instincts. If you do, every time you look into the mirror, you'll be rewarded with a vision of your authentic self.

APRIL 7

Come Alive with Color

With color, for the price of a pot of paint, people can express their own style and individuality. But, as with style, a gift for color has to be developed by experiment. If you don't dare, you are doomed to dullness.

—Shirley Conran

My first visceral experience of how color could change my life occurred when I was a teenager. We had moved from New York to a small Massachusetts town and my parents had bought a beautiful New England Colonial house built in 1789. Set back from one of the main roads and surrounded by a stone wall, the exterior of the house was white clapboard with traditional black shutters, like many of the other houses. Shortly after we moved in, my mother painted the living room a vibrant shade of red. This was long before the color red became chic, and my teenage mind could not fathom what had possessed her. Neither could our new neighbors. But from the street the sight of the red living room through the windows framed by the white and black exterior took your breath away with its beauty. Mother never consulted the family beforehand, she just followed her instincts and the result was stunning, which is often the case when we seek and find our authenticity. Even though I had felt unhappy about moving, I always looked forward to walking through the front door of our new home. The red room transformed my attitude.

But today my living room isn't painted red. It's a bright, sunny yellow like Claude Monet's dining room at Giverny, the painter's home for the last half of his life. We don't get a lot of light from our living room windows and I wanted to lift our spirits, especially during the winter. But I never realized how happy I could be surrounded by yellow until I took a creative excursion one day several years ago to a fancy home decorative accessory shop that was new to me. The walls of the shop were painted a fabulous shade of yellow with dark green trim. I felt as if I were standing in a beautiful garden instead of a city shop. I was so delighted by the color scheme that I asked for particulars and immediately went out to get paint chips. My husband was carried away by my enthusiasm and now our entire family loves our yellow living room.

The colors you wear don't have to be the same colors you live with. I love to wear red and black, strong, creative, and dramatic colors, but I need to live with soothing pastels for comfort and joy. There are many facets to your authentic self just as there are many facets to a beautiful diamond, and you can use color to express your many moods.

Today, think about the colors you love. Are you surrounded by them or wearing them? If not, why not? Look for more ways to come alive this spring with color. Too many of us are afraid of experimenting with color. Take a creative excursion this week to a paint store and look at the color spectrum. What are the colors that speak to your soul? Pick up some chips. Next, go to a fabric store and find a pattern that catches your eye. Buy a yard of it. Drape it over a couch or pin it up on a wall. Live with the colors for a month, then make the fabric into a pillow and paint a room or a piece of furniture your new hue. Brighten up your desk with colored files, paper clips, and note pads. Tuck in perky paper napkins when you pack your lunch. Display produce in a bright ceramic bowl on your kitchen counter so that you can see nature's vibrant spectrum. When next at an art museum, collect art postcards to post on a bulletin board or refrigerator, to place on a desk, and to send to friends. Allow yourself to be carried away by colorful impulses.

The English art critic John Ruskin believed that "The purest and most thoughtful minds are those which love colour the most." Let your love of color express the many hues and shades of your vibrant authentic self.

APRIL 8

More Dash Than Cash

Good taste shouldn't have to cost anything extra.

—MICKY DREXLER

Suppose your authentic self reveals that she'd like to be outfitted in a $1,000 cashmere blazer by Giorgio Armani, and all your budget can spring for is the Gap on sale? How do you reconcile great taste and limited money? Micky Drexler, president of the Gap, believes you don't have to, and I agree. But often, especially on the Simple Abundance path, we need to come to grips with the fact that our material wants and our wallets don't match. This poses a delicate dilemma if you've committed emotionally and intellectually to your spiritual growth.

According to one of Jesus's more unpopular instructions, we're not to worry about what we wear. (Remember the lilies of the field, who neither toil nor spin?) But of course, *we* do. Jesus taught his followers that they should first seek a Source of power and insight within themselves and that then everything else would fall into place. Or, as Marianne Williamson puts it, "Seek ye first the kingdom of Heaven, and the Maserati will get here when it's supposed to."

So will the Armani. In the meantime, call on your creativity to compensate. Your creativity is a Spirit-given gift. Perhaps your frustration about not being able to buy what you want will become the catalyst that sends you to sewing classes and eventually has you designing your own clothes. Perhaps you'll learn how to become an educated, sophisticated, savvy shopper. Seek, we are told, and we shall find, be it a suit or our spirituality. Once we search within for our own special gift of Spirit, our material desires will diminish, whether through sewing or savvy seeking. Our souls divest for us rather than our conscious minds.

APRIL 9

Affordable Luxury

Luxury need not have a price—comfort itself is a luxury.
—GEOFFREY BEENE

When some women hear of Simple Abundance they mistakenly believe the path is part of the new and much-heralded frugality movement. This is not true because the frugality movement of the 1990s is based on fear, and fear repels abundance rather than attracting it. Instead of practical wisdom, such as "A penny saved is a penny earned," we are given parsimonious exhortations to transform dryer lint into Halloween costumes.

Simple Abundance is not about deprivation. Nor is it about spending more than you can afford in order to make yourself feel better. For me, Simple Abundance has become a daily meditation on the true comfort and joy of moderation, as well as gentle instruction on how to become open to receiving the goodness of Real Life.

The Universe is not stingy. We are. Some of us have very stingy souls. Perhaps not in how we treat others—our family, friends, and those less fortunate—but in how we treat ourselves. Yet how can Spirit give more to us if our fists, hearts, and minds are clenched tight? Simple Abundance is about finally learning how to release feelings of poverty and lack and replace them with feelings of prosperity and affluence.

One of the ways in which we can start to experience more affluence in our daily lives is through pampering ourselves with affordable luxuries. Investing in a cord of wood for the pleasure of sitting before a blazing fire throughout the winter is one such luxury. Adding real whipped cream and shaved chocolate to a cup of cocoa to be drunk before the fire is another; it transforms a simple pleasure into complete contentment. Affordable luxuries awaken our awareness to the abundance that's readily available to us once we finally "get it."

Many people think that simplicity frowns on luxury. The Shakers led lives of utmost simplicity, but "the Believers," as they were known, also believed in the sublime luxury of eating well and the importance of using only the freshest ingredients, inventive spices, and herbs a century before Nouvelle Cuisine. In 1886 one visitor at a Shaker table pronounced his meal "worthy of Delmonico's," a famous landmark in New York City where the wealthy dined.

Think about affordable luxuries when you think about nurturing your personal style. What simple pleasures could make you feel more abundant? Perhaps wearing cashmere socks while you save for a cashmere sweater twinset; perhaps indulging in the intoxicating pleasure of your favorite coordinated scent—perfume, body talc, and lotion; the sensuous feel of silk underwear and pure cotton pajamas against your skin; investing in a handsome leather bag that goes with everything; trading in paper tissues for white linen handkerchiefs; getting your hair done between regular visits for color and cut; encouraging your nails to grow with a weekly manicure; replacing cheap plastic buttons on clothing with beautiful ones; enjoying a facial or luxuriating in a body massage; wearing "special occasion" jewelry like your prized diamond stud earrings on an everyday basis.

Today, declare to the Universe that you are open to receiving all the abundance it's waiting patiently to bestow. Each day offers us the gift of being a special occasion if we can simply learn that as well as giving, it is blessed to receive with grace and a grateful heart.

Trompe l'oeil: Thrift-Shop Pleasures

Beauty is altogether in the eyes of the beholder.
—MARGARET WOLFE HUNGERFORD

Jennie Jerome Churchill, the famous American beauty and mother of British prime minister Sir Winston Churchill, believed that "thrift and adventure seldom go hand and hand." Alas, poor Jennie, whose extravagant tastes led her to worry constantly about money, did not know where to shop.

Let us speak today of the rapturous joys of recycling. However, I refer not to bottles and cans, but to the white Liz Claiborne lamb's wool sweater that's yours for $1 and a trip to the dry cleaners. Or the gorgeous, genuine Gucci leather handbag that's a steal at $25, the black Yves Saint Laurent blazer they gave away for $5. (Cross my heart.) There are bountiful bargains with your name on them to be foraged from thrift shops, consignment stores, and vintage clothing boutiques.

Every sane woman needs to have tried-and-true new-to-you recyling centers up her sleeve. There are three different kinds for you to cultivate. First, there are the thrift shops, such as Goodwill and Salvation Army. Because thrift shops sell merchandise donated to them, you never know the quality of what you might find, but it's always worth a look. Upscale consignment shops differ from thrift shops because these are the places where wealthy women who aspire to be fashionable discreetly sell off last season's sweethearts. This is where you can find designer suits, coats, dresses, evening wear, and accessories at a fraction of their original price. Vintage clothing boutiques stock one-of-a-kind classics from other decades—from white cotton Victorian petticoats to Carole Lombard salt-and-pepper tweed trousers from the 1930s. I'd recommend that you gradually work your way up to vintage clothing boutiques; they can be intoxicating, rather like drinking port in the middle of the afternoon.

There are a few ground rules to the successful art of trompe l'oeil ("fool the eye") scavenger sorties. First you must be in the right frame of mind: don't go when you're tired or stressed. You can't rush; you need to take your time and you need to keep your wits about you. Go alone so that the experience can take on a meditative quality. Have no expectations of what you're going to find. Just have a happy expectant attitude as if you were embarking on a treasure hunt. A favorite affirmation that I use is "Divine abundance is my only reality and Divine abundance richly manifests for me in the perfect clothing at the perfect price." It always does. Finally, you must haunt these hideaways regularly. New merchandise is always coming in. That black cashmere turtleneck on your wish list may show up next Tuesday.

This week indulge in a new pleasure: thrifting. The thrill of finding thrift and adventure together makes them worth the search.

APRIL 11

Finishing Touches: The Art of Fashion Accessories

Perhaps too much of everything is as bad as too little.

—EDNA FERBER

Elizabeth Taylor punctuates her personal style with priceless gems; Anjelica Huston's signature is an armload of gold bracelets; *Vogue* editor Anna Wintour is never seen without her dark, glamorous shades, even when indoors. Her predecessor, Diana Vreeland, believed that a woman's first fashion accessory should be a pair of perfect black leather shoes to wear with everything, but the exquisite Coco Chanel argued for perfume, the "unseen but unforgettable fashion accessory."

Women may be ambivalent about their clothing but they often form passionate attachments to their accessories: the gold monogrammed pin your best friend gave you for that landmark birthday, the Donna Karan opaque black hose that make you feel so sleek and sophisticated, the silver necklace you got on that fabulous trip to Santa Fe, the brilliant blue silk scarf your sister brought you back from Paris, the bright straw Nairobi bag that's the depository of your life.

Fashion accessories are the artifacts of our authenticity. They can have sentimental value, track our mood swings, endow us with a sense of security, let our personality shine forth, or sabotage our best efforts. Because of the emotion we invest in them, in many respects our personal accessories are even more important than our clothing—they are the finishing touches that define us. Many famous designers like Bill Blass think women overdo it with accessories. I disagree. I think many of us hold ourselves back with our choice of fashion accessories, conforming to what we think is acceptable or safe. It feels more comfortable when we color within the lines.

But when a woman lets Spirit guide her as she seeks to discover and nurture her authentic style, fashion accessories can help her take small but important risks that increase her self-confidence. Clothes and accessories pulled together in unexpected ways can be empowering. Just think of how far Dorothy Gale traveled in blue check gingham and ruby slippers. Your selection of shoes, hosiery, belts, scarves, jewelry, hats, gloves, handbags, and fragrance can make a big difference in helping you announce to the world who you truly are as you unravel this mystery for yourself. Just remember that fashion accessories, like your wardrobe, should distill your personal style to its purest essence. Love wearing it, or leave it off.

Finally, never forget that the most essential fashion accessories, the ones no woman can afford to do without, come from within. A generous heart, a spontaneous smile, and eyes that sparkle with delight can be part of any woman's signature look once she awakens to her authentic beauty.

APRIL 12

Learning to Love and Honor Your Body

The body is a sacred garment. It's your first and last garment; it is what you enter life in and what you depart life with, and it should be treated with honor.

—MARTHA GRAHAM

Which comes first, learning to love our bodies or possessing a positive body image? Either way, it works. If you don't possess a positive body image—and most of us don't—learning to love your body can help you develop one. "If you can learn to like how you look, and not the way you think you look," Gloria Steinem assures us, "it can set you free."

The time has come for us to realize that until we work on increasing our self-esteem by loving ourselves in small ways, we can't begin changing ourselves for the better in big ways. We must start by choosing to break the self-destructive cycle of unrealistic expectations, especially our own.

Starting today, shun the world's ideal of beauty, because it's constantly changing. Cleopatra longed for varicose veins, Middle Age beauties padded their bellies. Don't wait for the world to celebrate you. Carve your own niche. Focus on what's great, forget what's not. Find joy in your own reflection. Instead of obsessing about a body that's impossible to achieve without a personal trainer, begin to discover how you can feel better about living in the one you now inhabit.

Learn firsthand the transforming power of nurture over nature. Nourish your body with healthy food and pure water. Slow down and remember to breathe before taking a bite. Breathe out stress and negativity, breathe in oxygen and positive energy. Rediscover how marvelous it is simply to move: stretch, dance, walk, run, jump, skip, play, embrace. Pamper your body with comfortable clothes, quiet moments, and soothing beauty rituals.

"A woman's relationship with her body is the most important relationship she'll ever have. More important than husband, lover, children, friends, colleagues. This isn't selfishness—it's just fact," health and fitness expert Diana K. Roesch tells us. "The body is, quite literally, our vehicle for being—for giving, for loving, for moving, for feeling—and if it doesn't work, it's fairly certain that nothing else in our lives will work, either."

Today, instead of hating your body, make peace with it. Choose to consciously love and honor the sacred garment Spirit provided for this lifetime's journey.

APRIL 13

The Only Weight-Loss Aid You'll Ever Need

Self-love is the only weight-loss aid that really works in the long run.

—JENNY CRAIG

In the beginning, eating was meant to be one of life's sublime simple pleasures. But then Eve took a bite out of an apple (so much for the low-calorie, low-fat, high-fiber theory), and women have been at war with food ever since.

But food is not our enemy. If we're alive, we're supposed to love to eat. Food is the source of vital fuel our bodies convert to energy in order to survive. Not wanting to eat—as in anorexia or illness—is a signal that something's seriously wrong with us. Don't fight your hunger. Instead, respect it and respond to it with nutritious food that appeals to all your senses—not just taste but sight and smell as well. But trusting our bodies to tell us what they need is scary for most women. We're afraid that if we throw out all the diets and eat when we're hungry, we'll never stop and end up in the *Guinness Book of World Records*.

However, the more we starve ourselves, the more weight we eventually gain, and then we end up hating ourselves. Any woman who has been on more than one diet in her life knows this painful truth. The only way to stop this heartbreaking cycle of self-loathing is to stop dieting and use our common sense. Eat when you're hungry, drink when you're thirsty, sleep when you're tired, get in harmony with your body through regular exercise, and nourish your soul through prayer and meditation. "Be really whole," the Chinese sage Lao-Tzu told his followers, "and all things will come to you." Even how to finally make peace with our weight. Taoism—the Eastern philosophy of Lao-Tzu—teaches that the only way to be made Whole is to yield. Yield to the fact that your body answers to a Wisdom that's higher than wanting to look like the waif on the cover of *Vogue*.

Every woman has a weight that's ideal for her as opposed to an ideal weight. This is the weight at which you feel the most comfortable, have the most energy, can stay well and feel good about how you look. We can achieve that weight when we begin to trust our bodies. Forget size and abandon the scale. Instead of weighing yourself, let your favorite clothes tell you how you are doing. Above all, trust the guidance of your authentic self. Go within and visualize her. See what weight she carries. Ask her to help you achieve your perfect weight through the power of Love. Today, be willing to believe that self-love is the only weight-loss aid you'll ever truly need, because it's the only one that works.

APRIL 14

When You Hunger and Thirst

The body must be nourished, physically, emotionally and spiritually. We're spiritually starved in this culture—not underfed but undernourished.

—CAROL HORNIG

Many women, including myself, swallow life in an attempt to keep it manageable. I mean this literally and figuratively. Whenever we're anxious, worried, nervous, or depressed, without thinking, we instinctively swallow food and drink in order to push away the uncomfortable negative experience we're feeling in our guts. We hunger and thirst, but it's not for a bowl of ice cream or a glass of wine. It's for inner peace and deeper connection.

Carl Jung, the famous Swiss psychiatrist, believed that alcoholism was a sacred disease. M. Scott Peck relates in his book *Further Along the Road Less Traveled* how it occurred to Jung "that it was perhaps no accident that we traditionally referred to alcoholic drinks as spirits, and that perhaps alcoholics were people who had a greater thirst for the spirit than others, that perhaps alcoholism was a spiritual disorder or better yet, a spiritual condition." I believe this is also true about compulsive overeating, which is the addiction of choice for many women. We have such a passionate appetite for life, we just don't know what we truly need to satisfy our insatiable cravings for Wholeness.

When I first became aware that when I "swallowed" life I was really hungry and thirsty for joy and serenity, it was a turning point for me in learning self-nurturance. Finally, I understood that I wasn't underfed but spiritually undernourished. I realized I could go within and ask my soul—my authentic self—what I needed. I learned to stop and ask myself the questions "How can I care for you at this moment? How can I love you? What is it you truly need?"

The next time you reach to put something in your mouth, take one minute to focus your awareness on what you're doing before you do it. Are you eating because you are physically hungry, or anxious? If you're anxious, a walk around the block instead of into the kitchen would be better for you and more loving. At the end of the day, are you pouring yourself a glass of wine out of habit in order to signal that it's time to relax? Instead, why not take a few moments to slip into comfortable clothes, sip a glass of delicious fruit-flavored mineral water as you prepare dinner, and enjoy the wine with your meal? Learn to create ceremonies of personal pleasure that can nourish your deeper longings. As you nurture your spirit with kindness, your physical cravings will loosen their grip.

Realize today that you hunger and thirst for a reason. Ask your authentic self to reveal your deeper needs, so that Spirit can quench and satisfy your parched and ravenous soul.

APRIL 15

Discovering the Momentum of Creative Movement

The body is shaped, disciplined, honored, and in time, trusted.
—MARTHA GRAHAM

The world as I know it is divided into two types of women—those who exercise and those who don't. Those who do exercise seem to have more energy, less stress, fewer weight problems, and generally a more positive and optimistic outlook on life. Women who are fit will tell you that regular exercise is the single most important thing they have ever done to improve their life.

Women who do not exercise don't believe them and have every excuse in the world for why they can't or won't find out for themselves: they don't have the time, they're too out of shape, they're coming down with the flu, it's too cold or too hot, they're too tired, they're too depressed, maybe next week. I know all about the women who don't exercise regularly because until recently I've been one of them, even after being scolded by my doctor and shamed by my family. We are kindred spirits of the writer

Robert Maynard Hutchins who once remarked that "Whenever I feel like exercise, I lie down until the feeling passes."

This is not good. This is not self-nurturing. This is not healthy. We *know* this intellectually. Since we are all brilliant women, there must be a way in which we can slowly convince our brains to take better care of our bodies. But this won't happen by imposing a strict new regime on the stubborn, conscious mind that always manages to outsmart us. It hasn't worked in the past, so why should it now?

We will change by seduction. Don't refer to the activity as exercise or fitness any longer. If you must call it something, call it creative movement. Forget about gyms, jogging, weights, and aerobic classes led by women with no bones. Think about creative movement as a life-enhancing, enjoyable pastime, because it is. Just pause for a moment and imagine all the ways that you could move creatively that might bring you pleasure: dancing (ballet, jazz, or tap), swimming, fencing, horseback riding, racquetball, tennis, golf, riding a bike. What about a mind-body-spirit form of movement such as yoga or the graceful, ancient Chinese martial art Tai Chi. Now think about taking a walk in the beautiful sunlight today. Walking is the best form of creative movement there is, and it doesn't cost a cent. Walking clears your head, fills your lungs with fresh air, lets off steam, builds up strength and centers your spirit. Start moving, a step at a time, step after step. The positive momentum will take it from there.

Trust me, seduction works. Once upon a time I was kicking and screaming all the way to fitness. Now I'm doing deep breathing and stretching with gentle yoga movements and engaging in walking meditations. I feel better and I'm ready to move on. Diana Roesch assures us, "With enlightenment and self-awareness, we can reguide and realign our *whole* selves: our bodies, by finding new ways of moving and celebrating them and by adding good food in amounts they tell us they need; our souls, our sense of ourselves as good and worthwhile, by connecting them to the earth and to each other."

APRIL 16

Walking as Meditation

I will tell you what I learned myself. For me a long, five- or six-mile walk helps. And one must go alone and every day.

—BRENDA UELAND

As long as I approached walking as exercise, I never made it past the front door. But one day I was so anxious I felt as if I would jump out of my skin, and so I bolted out of the house at lunchtime as if I were leaving the scene of a crime. Filled with disappointments, painful memories, and my own unrealistic expectations from the past—terrified of what the future held and the changes that were inevitable—the only safe place for me was the present moment: my foot against the pavement, the wind on my face, my breath entering and leaving my body. Forty minutes later I stopped, discovered to my amazement that I was on the other side of town, and headed back home, calm and centered. I have been walking ever since.

Slowly I am learning what Henry David Thoreau knew: "It requires a direct dispensation from Heaven to become a walker." But I still don't walk for exercise. Instead, I walk regularly for my soul and my body tags along. There are different reasons for walking—to increase the heart rate and build strength, to solve a creative problem, to finish that argument with yourself or someone else, to saunter and wake up to the world around you, and to meditate. I walk for all of them, but most days I go on walks for a "moving meditation"—fitness of the spirit. I try to quiet the voices in my head, take long strides, and concentrate on the slow, steady rhythm of my breath, comforted by the interior silence.

Suddenly my reverie might be broken by the sound of birds singing, a dog barking, or the sight of a pretty garden. Thoreau complained of walking sometimes "without getting there in spirit. . . . The thought of some work will run in my head and I am not where my body is—I am out of my senses." This happens to me as well, but I have learned to train myself to return my awareness slowly to the physical act of walking, for here in the present moment, one step at a time, I have found peace.

If you have had difficulty sitting down to meditate, you might like to give a walking meditation a chance, especially now that the beautiful weather has returned. Take into consideration your preferences—if you are not a morning person, take a walk at midday, in the late afternoon, or after supper under the stars. Even if you work in a city during the day, you can break at lunch and take a walk. No one needs to know that you've shut the world out and are meditating as you stroll down the street. Twenty minutes to a half-hour every day is a good amount of time to restore a sense of serenity. I have found there is no wrong way to do a walking meditation. Sometimes we expect to experience immediate transcendence and are disappointed when it seems as if nothing is happening. Let go of expectations and life will unfold, step-by-step.

Making Peace with Your Hair

Genius is of small use to a woman who does not know how to do her hair.

—EDITH WHARTON

A woman's hair has for centuries been called her "crowning glory," but every woman I know speaks of her intimate relationship with her hair as a nightmare. I don't know any woman personally who really loves her hair, just women who cope. Hair is a living, powerful, mercurial, metaphysical energy force to be respected, reckoned with, and reconciled to, but it cannot be controlled any more than atomic fusion. Occasionally, it can be cajoled into becoming conduct (we refer to these lapses as "good hair days") but it can never be coerced. Think of all the money, time, creative energy, and emotion we invest in our hair. Yet most of the time it insists on expressing *its* authenticity, not necessarily ours. I don't know about you, but I'm exhausted from the mini skirmishes I wage with life every day, and the battle with my hair is not the least of them.

Most of us exist under a collective hallucination Naomi Wolf calls "the beauty myth." We have all been brainwashed into believing that if we can just get the right shampoo, conditioner, perm, color, and cut, our hair will finally behave like that of the women in the display professions—television, film, and fashion—who, by the way, do not style their own hair. We would all have, if not fabulous, then at least presentable heads if we had a professional hair stylist on call every day, or at least whenever we appeared in public or in print. But that's not real life for me, nor probably is it for you.

At home, my hair never looks the way it does when I come from my monthly appointment with the hairdresser. This is because I have yet to learn how to simultaneously hold a blow-dryer and a curling brush in two hands and do whatever it is my stylist does as she swirls about me in the salon. So at home I have given up trying. I wash it, mousse it, let it dry, and then curl it with electric curlers and a curling iron. Some days it looks wonderful; other days it looks woebegone, and yet the process is virtually the same. Hair humbles us, and we need to make peace with it.

The way we do this is to accept it and acknowledge its personality: whether it's thick or thin, coarse or fine, straight or curly; the way it breaks when permed, is getting gray, or insists on parting down the middle. Getting to know your hair and working with it instead of constantly fighting it is the first step toward rapprochement and peace of mind. While my authentic self wears her hair in shoulder-length, Pre-Raphaelite blond waves, I've had to reconcile myself to the fact that I can't have wavy, blond tresses until they invent a perm that doesn't frizz color-treated hair (and they haven't). So I've chosen color over curl. Always it comes down to creative choice.

If you're currently unhappy with your hair, start patiently searching for pictures of hairstyles you like and bring those pictures to a hair stylist recommended by your friends for a consultation first. Have a conversation about the reality of your hair versus your fantasy about your hair. Consider the time you are willing to spend working with it every day. This is very important. See if you can't arrive at some middle ground that will make you happier. If you're thinking of something drastic, such as going from long hair to short, place pictures of the new hairstyle on your mirror for a couple of weeks so that you're familiar with the change before it happens. It won't be so much of a shock then. Above all, try not to give in to impulse. We all have days when we scream, "I've got to *do* something with my hair," but those aren't the days on which to do it. Remember, the hair you know is easier to handle than the hair you don't. But be open to change because there are few joys in life that can equal finally finding a becoming hair style. And if the worst happens, after you dry your eyes, remember it's only hair. It will grow again and you will have become wiser.

Above all, learning to accept your hair is part of the process of learning to love yourself. The poet Marianne Moore believed that "Your thorns are the best part of you," and she was right.

APRIL 18

The Face in the Looking Glass

The most beautiful makeup of a woman is passion. But cosmetics are easier to buy.

—YVES SAINT LAURENT

Who do you see when you look at the face in the looking glass? Are you beginning to see your authentic self? Are you becoming more comfortable with the uniquely beautiful face that stares back at you? I hope so. But this growth of self-acceptance and self-love is slow and very subtle, especially after years of benign neglect.

One of the ways that we can begin to love our faces is to enhance them with makeup. I have gone through many stages with makeup. There was a time during my twenties while I was working in fashion and theater, when I wouldn't have dreamed of walking out the door without my war paint on.

For me, makeup was a sophisticated mask that endowed me with self-confidence. Then, in my thirties, after I had married, had my daughter, and spent so much time at home writing, I stopped wearing makeup except when I went out with my husband in the evening. It was a relief to stop wearing cosmetics because doing so gave me an opportunity to learn to feel comfortable with my features. The world I had come from had been so self-absorbed and obsessed by appearances. Now I was getting in touch with the inner woman and not concentrating on her outer packaging. But gradually, I noticed a difference in the way I felt about myself without makeup. When I put it on, I liked the reflection in the mirror. When I didn't, I rarely looked. I began to become aware of the fact that looking your best, working with what you have, and bringing out your natural beauty with makeup was not as superficial a goal as I had originally thought. Makeup was simply a tool to help me look my best. When I looked my best, I felt better. When I felt better, I had more energy and accomplished more and was more outgoing. When I accomplished more and reached out more to others, they responded positively and my self-esteem grew. Making up my face again began a self-affirming cycle of acceptance. But more important, it began a ceremony of self-nurturing. I began to see that the ten minutes I took in the morning to put my best face forward for myself and not the world was a small but important way of nurturing my authenticity. Even the ritual of putting makeup on, when it comes from the heart, can be spiritual.

Today when you glance in the looking glass, bless the face that stares back at you and put on some lipstick.

APRIL 19

Spring Rituals of Replenishment

Let your mind be quiet, realizing the beauty of the world, and the immense, the boundless treasures that it holds in store.

All that you have within you, all that your heart desires, all that your nature so specially fits you for—that or the counterpart of it waits embedded in the great Whole, for you. It will surely come to you.

Yet equally surely not one moment before its appointed time will it come. All your crying and fever and reaching out of hands will make no difference.

Therefore do not begin that game at all.

—EDWARD CARPENTER

This is the season of renewal and replenishment. What better way to begin than to meditate on English poet Edward Carpenter's assurance that all our needs will be satisfied by the great Whole. Whatever we are waiting for—peace of mind, contentment, grace, the inner awareness of Simple Abundance—it will surely come to us, but only when we are ready to receive it with an open and grateful heart.

While you are waiting patiently, take comfort and joy in simple spring-time rituals of rejuvenation. A favorite of mine is to search for a new sacred space out in the world. This reminds me that we carry our serenity with us. A shady grove of trees in an old cemetery, a beautiful public garden that's new to you, a museum gallery, the stacks of an old library, the hush of a quiet chapel where you can light a candle, even an outdoor café where you can sit basking in the sunshine can help you realize the boundless treasure and spiritual replenishment of a perfect solitary hour. Joseph Campbell tells us that "Sacred space and sacred time and something joyous to do is all we need. Almost anything then becomes a continuous and increasing joy."

APRIL 20

Taking the Cure: Bathing Pleasures

There must be quite a few things a hot bath won't cure, but I don't know many of them.

—SYLVIA PLATH

Every woman should be aware that there is a significant difference between bathing and taking a bath. Bathing is merely cleansing, but you can remove grime and sweat in a shower for heaven's sake! Taking a bath, as the Victorian social critic Ambrose Bierce described it, is "a kind of mystic ceremony substituted for religious worship."

I believe in the rejuvenating power of hydropathy as a positive adjunct to psychotherapy. A century ago water cures were all the rage to combat the "new American nervousness" or "neurasthenia" which began to sweep the country as our great-great-grandparents adjusted to the relentless intrusion of technology into their lives and the resulting disruptions of "hectic modern living" in the form of telephones and electricity. Victorians would flock to spas to drink mineral waters and take medicinal dunks to cure the fidgetiness and racing pulses of anxiety attacks, insomnia, depression, and headaches.

Today, we can "take the cure" in the privacy of our own bathrooms. And being possessed of common sense, we should do it daily. Do not underestimate the blessings of a bath. It can calm your mind, relax your tired, tense body, and soothe your stressed spirit. It can help you drift off to the exquisite relief of sleep or wake you up and help you greet the day with enthusiasm.

My philosophy in life is very simple: when in doubt, take a bath.

Close the door, run the tap, pour in the bath salts or essential oils, lay out the fluffy towels, tie your hair back, and shut out the world by sinking into the tub. To my mind, baths are as necessary for spiritual replenishment and centering as is prayer and meditation. In fact, a proper bath is one of the best ways of meditating, for once you're submerged in delicately scented warm water, where else would you want to be except in the present moment? Try bathing accompanied by candlelight, classical music, a cold drink, or a good book (nothing too strenuous), or just let the soothing silence envelop you as the ripple of more hot water splashes against your toes.

Begin to indulge in collecting accessories to make your bath more sublime: a long-necked scrub brush, an inflatable pillow, a bath tray. When people ask you what you want for your birthday, holiday, or Mother's Day, tell them pampering bath-products; that way you'll always have an assortment on hand. There is a dazzling array of scented salts, oils, powders, bubble baths and milk baths available now. Start to find your favorites and think of them as affordable luxuries. "I can't think of any sorrow in the world that a hot bath wouldn't help, just a little bit," Susan Glaspell wisely wrote in *The Visioning* in 1911 (probably while sitting in a tub), and she knew what she was talking about.

APRIL 21

Aromatherapy: The Restorative Comfort of Fragrance

Smells are surer than sounds and sights to make heartstrings crack.
—RUDYARD KIPLING

Skeptics make the best seekers. I came to this realization when I discovered the restorative comfort and healing properties of fragrance—aromatherapy—on the recommendation of a trusted friend who is a college vice president by day, and a mystic by night. But until I tried it for myself and became a convert to the simple pleasure and power of scent to heal my body, mind, and spirit to enhance my moods and relieve stress, I thought aromatherapy—the ancient therapeutic art of blending essential oils or extracts distilled from aromatic flowers, plants, herbs, and fruit for medicinal purposes—was New Age hocus-pocus. Actually, it has been a part of the medical practices of the world's great civilizations, including those of ancient Egypt and Rome, for thousands of years. Why? Because it works.

I've personally discovered that lavender oil massaged on my temples will rid me of a headache, and that, instead of brewing another cup of caffeine when I need an energy boost, I can diffuse into the air an inhalation of essential oils to pick me up: basil (to stimulate the brain), rosemary (to activate memory), peppermint (to provide mental clarity and sharpness), and sage (to act as a tonic for mental fatigue and strain). As I write this, an invigorating inhalation sits on my desk, pleasing and inspiring me.

Here's how aromatheraphy works. Our sense of smell is our primordial link to our brains. When we inhale a scent, neurotransmitters in our brains trigger the production of biochemical secretions that affect our moods, feelings, and emotions. When an aromatic essential oil permeates our skin through the bath or a massage, the oil penetrates the epidermis, stimulates our sophisticated lymph duct system, and enters the bloodstream, eventually delivering well-being to our frazzled minds.

You can use aromatherapy in many different ways. A body or facial massage will make you feel like a new woman. Alternatively, you may want to infuse the air surrounding you with fragrance. You can place a few drops of essential oil (choosing the oil according to your need) and water in a ceramic diffuser or potpourri pot that is warmed by a candle. You can drop a mixture of essential oils in a tub of hot water for a personalized bath or sprinkle oil on a cotton handkerchief and pull it out as needed, breathing in fully, deeply, and slowly to encourage relaxation during the day. You can also burn incense when you meditate or light a scented candle in your bedroom as you read and relax at night.

Today, allow yourself to become curious about the soothing spiritual replenishment offered by aromatherapy. Helen Keller tells us that "smell is a potent wizard that transports us across thousands of miles and all the years we have lived." The restorative comfort and power of fragrance also has the ability to enhance the days to come.

APRIL 22

Sensory Awakening

Nothing can cure the soul but the senses, just as nothing can cure the senses but the soul.

—OSCAR WILDE

We were created to experience, interpret, and savor the world through our senses—our ability to smell, taste, hear, touch, see, and intuit. Although we are sentient beings with the capability "to perceive the world with all its gushing beauty and terror, right on our pulses," as poet, pilot, author, explorer, and naturalist Diane Ackerman tells us in her exquisite evocation *A Natural History of the Senses*, most of us journey in a dull trance, asleep to the Mystery of everything about us. In order for us to awaken and "to begin to understand the gorgeous fever that is consciousness, we must try to understand the senses," Ackerman urges. "The senses don't just *make sense* of life in bold or subtle acts of clarity, they tear reality apart into vibrant morsels and reassemble them into a meaningful pattern."

For the next week, I'm going to ask you to pause a moment each day with me and marvel at the natural gifts that have been so richly bestowed on us. George Eliot (the pen name of the nineteenth-century writer Mary Ann Evans) believed that "If we had keen vision and feeling for all ordinary human life it would be like hearing the grass grow and the squirrel's heart beat, and we should die of the roar which lies on the other side of silence. As it is, the quickest of us walks about well wadded with stupidity."

Today, look at the blue sky, hear the grass growing beneath your feet, inhale the scent of spring, let the fruits of the earth linger on your tongue, reach out and embrace those you love. Ask Spirit to awaken your awareness to the sacredness of your sensory perceptions.

APRIL 23

The Scent of a Woman

For the sense of smell, almost more than any other, has the power to recall memories and it's a pity that we use it so little.

—RACHEL CARSON

We each have our own scent, as distinctive as our DNA. It's a deeply personal bouquet of diet, hormones, hygiene, and health. Napoleon once wrote his wife, Josephine, and told her "not to bathe" because he was coming home in three days and adored her natural aroma. When my daughter was younger and I went away on business trips she would sleep on my down pillow and underneath my down-filled comforter because they "smell like you, Mommy." After my father died five years ago, my mother gave me his handkerchiefs. I keep one in my bedside table drawer and when I press it up to my nose I am comforted once again by his immediate presence as scent memories convey his love across time, space, and eternity.

Our homes have their own particular scent, too. The aroma of fresh-baked bread, lemon-scented furniture polish, cat dander, damp dogs, mud on the doormat, laundry in the hamper. The scent of coffee, bacon, and ripening fruit in the kitchen; soapsuds in the bathroom; rumpled sheets in the bedrooms; fresh flowers, potpourri, burning logs, and newsprint in the living room.

"Smells spur memories, but they also rouse our dozy senses, pamper and indulge us, help define our self-image, stir the cauldron of our seductiveness, warn us of danger, lead us into temptation, fan our religious fervor, accompany us to heaven, wed us to fashion, steep us in luxury," Diane Ackerman reminds us.

And if we lost our sense of smell, if suddenly we experienced *anosmia*, as do two million Americans? We would find ourselves bereft and cast adrift without the internal sextant of scent.

Today, let us delight in the simple pleasure of our sense of smell. Indulge yourself with comfort aromas. Take a creative excursion to an Italian market; visit a Chinese restaurant for lunch; browse through a used-books store; stop by the perfume counter of a large department store and inhale delight. Lie on the fresh grass in the backyard, turn over the earth in the garden, bury your nose in a bouquet of lily of the valley (which should be blooming about now) and smell the sweetness of spring. Take a walk in the woods, a garden, or your neighborhood after it rains; go to a farmer's market and gather aromatic herb plants—rosemary, sage, lemon verbena, tarragon, mint, bay, and fresh lavender—for a kitchen-shelf garden; put a scented geranium in the bathroom. Cook plum tomatoes, garlic, onions, sausage, and peppers in olive oil to go on fresh pasta for dinner tonight; simmer cloves, orange rind, cinnamon, and apples on the back burner for a delightful fragrance, experiment with blending your own potpourri; enjoy a scented bath and then a dusting of our earliest scent memory, Johnson's Baby Powder.

The world around us possesses exquisite smells that can stir our memories, color our emotions, and transform our feelings and moods. So sacred was the power of scent that God instructed Moses to build an altar of fragrance and to burn sweet incense when he prayed. Today, when you inhale something wonderful, offer a prayer of thanksgiving for this marvelous gift.

APRIL 24

A Taste for Living

I wish you all manner of prosperity, with a little more taste.
—ALAIN-RENÉ LE SAGE

Taste is the younger sister of our sense of smell, dependent on her sibling's guidance for a head start but eager to strike out on her own as soon as she's able. Diane Ackerman tells us in *A Natural History of the Senses* that a child has more taste buds than adults (who have 10,000 taste sensors located in the mouth, primarily on the tongue but also on the palate, pharynx, and tonsils). Amazingly, our taste buds wear out and regenerate every ten days, although, when we enter middle age, they don't regenerate as frequently as we might wish. The idea that our senses become jaded as we get older—requiring new and fresh awakening—is alas, correct.

The word *taste*, from the old English word *tasten*, meaning to touch and test, has always had a double meaning. In exploring and celebrating the simple pleasure of this intensely personal sense, we should look at both interpretations. The primary definition of "taste" describes the sensory faculty that enables us to distinguish substances dissolved in the mouth as sweet, sour, bitter, or salty. But the other definition of "taste" describes the mental faculty by which we discern or appreciate things for the joy they bring us.

Today let us explore ways to increase our capacity for pleasure—our taste for life—by delighting in this simple, yet highly sophisticated sense.

First, hunt out unusual (for you) ethnic grocery stores in your neighborhood (Caribbean, Oriental, Indian or Pakistani, Italian, Cajun, German, Hispanic, kosher, or soul food). Be open and curious. There's a world of delicious morsels out there waiting to be discovered and savored. Inhale the vibrant aromas and bring home something wonderful, new, and different to cook for dinner this week.

Next, clean out your spice cabinet. This is both symbolic and necessary. Variety, after all, is the spice of life, and fresh spices provide our sense of taste with variety. I had not taken the time to clean out my spice cabinet from the time we moved into our home until I embarked on the Simple Abundance path and was trying to introduce more order into my daily affairs. I reveal this pathetic, embarrassing truth in astonishment and wonder, primarily because, when I tackled my spice cabinet, I was flabbergasted to discover that I possessed eleven cans of poultry spice and eleven cans of pumpkin pie spice. Do you have any idea how much space twenty-two spice containers occupy?

Now it does not take Miss Marple to deduce what had occurred in the life of the woman in charge of this kitchen. Every Thanksgiving since 1981 she had purchased new cans of poultry and pumpkin pie spice. Why did she purchase new tins? Was it because, as a renowned gourmet chef, she was extremely fastidious about the pungency of her spices?

I don't think so.

It was because as a frazzled, disorganized homecarer, she hadn't a clue she had spices left over from the previous year and of course didn't want to be caught short.

Learn from this sorry story. Somehow I suspect I am not the only woman in America with numerous souvenirs of Thanksgiving Days past. And the reason we need to clean our spice cabinets is to make room for fresh ones (in case you're wondering, cardamom and coriander seed fossilize after a decade) because we're going to use them to reawaken our sense of taste. Think of Indian curry, rice, and mango chutney for dinner soon or a pan of lasagna redolent of basil, oregano, and garlic, or a pot of Southwestern chili. Supposedly the dying words of the famous nineteenth-century frontiersman Kit Carson were "Wish I had time for one more bowl of chili." Thank God we do.

Bon appetit!

APRIL 25

On a Clear Day You Can See Forever

The greatest thing a human being ever does in this world is to see something. . . . To see clearly is poetry, prophecy and religion, all in one.

—JOHN RUSKIN

I've reached that awkward stage in my life when I can't see with my glasses on or with them off, so I constantly carry them around with me and momentarily panic whenever I've misplaced them. As my middle-aged eyesight changes, I've become acutely aware of how precious our ability to see clearly is.

A friend of mine, Susan Abbott, is an extraordinary artist who creates panoramic watercolors that are breathtaking in their exquisite detail. Her eyes and hands apprehend a visual catalog of a woman's daily life with astonishing attention to the subtle nuances—nothing is too insignificant or uninspired for Susan's attention. Like a brilliant photograph, her still-life arrangements seize a moment in time to dazzling effect. Artists especially hold sacred the sense of sight.

Pablo Picasso once said, "If only we could pull out our brain and use only our eyes" we would be amazed at the world around us. Paul Klee, the Swiss artist, declared, "One eye sees, the other feels." As Paul Cézanne grew older he doubted his powers of perception and worried that the authenticity of his art might be a quirk of nature. Because he had trouble with his eyesight he wondered if the unique way of seeing the world which he captured on canvas in painstaking single brushstrokes might be mere accident instead of genius. But perhaps Georgia O'Keeffe expressed it best when she observed that "In a way nobody sees a flower really, it is so small, we haven't the time—and to see takes time, like to have a friend takes time."

To see takes time. We haven't the time. Here is the unrelenting truth and it's chilling to the soul. Most of us have been given a miraculous gift—the ability to see—but we don't take the time to do more than glance around. We take our sense of sight for granted. A dear friend of mine has been having some serious trouble with her eyesight and as she shares her worries with me about losing it, I feel helpless. What she laments losing is being able to drive the car pool or take her children to the dentist, to do her grocery shopping, try out new recipes, read the newspaper, see the faces of those she loves, put on her makeup. Infinitesimal, precious moments that make up the days of our lives.

Today, really look around at your world—your family, your home, your pets, your co-workers, and the strangers on the street. Smile at everyone you meet because you can *see* them. Never forget that the gift of vision was so important that when God created the world, the first command was for Light in order to see, and after the Great Creator was finished with each day's task, He glanced back on his handiwork and "saw that it was good."

We need to see how good it is, too.

APRIL 26

Major and Minor Chords of Pleasure

With stammering lips and insufficient sounds,
I strive and struggle to deliver right
the music of my nature. . . .
— ELIZABETH BARRETT BROWNING

Most of us who luckily possess all our senses think that if we had to lose one, the most terrible deprivation would be the loss of sight. But Helen Keller, who became blind and deaf after a mysterious fever at nineteen months of age, mourned the loss of her hearing more than her sight. The writer Hannah Merker tells us in her moving meditation on losing the sense of hearing, *Listening,* that "Psychologists say that deafness, or a severe hearing loss, acquired after a human being has known hearing, can be the single greatest trauma a person can experience."

Eleven years ago I was at lunch with my almost-two-year-old daughter in our favorite fast-food restaurant when a large ceiling panel fell and struck me in the head and sent me crashing into the table. I sustained a head injury that left me partially disabled for nearly two years. During the first three months of recuperation I was confined to bed and my senses were all skewed. My eyesight was very blurry, I was extremely sensitive to light, and even seeing the different patterns of the quilt on our bed disturbed my sense of equilibrium so much that we had to turn it over to the plain muslin backing. I couldn't read or comprehend words on a page. But the most disorienting disability was that my sense of hearing was affected. I could not listen to music because it made me dizzy. I couldn't even carry on a telephone conversation because, without visual clues such as reading lips, I could not process the sounds coming through my ears and rearrange them into meaningful patterns in my brain.

These unsettling side effects lasted for quite a while, but over a period of eighteen months my senses gradually returned—for which I'm deeply grateful. I share this story with you because I want you to consider how much we take for granted until we lose it, either temporarily or permanently. It deeply saddens me that many of us need to have pain as a wake-up call. Now I try my best not to stand on the sidelines of life with deadened, dulled, disinterested senses until another shock makes me suddenly aware of the magic, marvel, and the mystery of it all. And so should you.

Kate Chopin wrote in 1900, "I wonder if anyone else has an ear so turned and sharpened as I have, to detect the music, not of the spheres, but of the earth. . . ." Among my own favorites: the reassuring rhythm of my husband's breathing in the middle of the night when I can't sleep; hearing "I love you" and "We're home," along with footsteps on the stairs; the voice of a good friend on the telephone; raindrops on the roof; cats purring; dogs thumping their tails; teakettles whistling; the melody of words strung together to form a sentence that stirs the imagination and illuminates the soul; the exquisite sounds of silence cascading over me when I momentarily let go and allow the Universe to proceed without my assistance or supervision; and music—music to soothe, inspire, and move me in unexpected waves of sublime pleasure. The concerto of Real Life is playing: delight with thanksgiving in the major and minor chords of its beautiful refrain.

APRIL 27

Reach Out and Touch Someone

O world invisible, we view thee,
O world intangible, we touch thee,
O world unknowable, we know thee.

—FRANCIS THOMPSON

Touch is the first physical sense we experience as strange hands pull us from the dark realm of the soul into the cold, harsh light of earth. After the security and warmth of the womb, frigid air assaults our fragile, naked bodies until we find comfort in our mother's arms with the sense of touch guiding our first few conscious moments. For many people touch is also the last sense we experience as we depart this world—the squeeze of a loved one's hand. Sight, smell, hearing, and taste have gone before us. "The first sense to ignite, touch is often the last to burn out," Frederich Sachs tells us, "long after our eyes betray us, our hands remain faithful to the world."

We describe our mood swings as "feelings" and when something strikes a deep, sentimental chord in us we say we were "touched." When we feel alienated, fragmented, and adrift, we often refer to this estrangement as "losing touch with reality." Bumper stickers ask, "Did you hug your child today?" And did you? Because we all need to be hugged and touched, not just to thrive but to survive.

A good friend of mine, a hardworking single mother of two boys, regularly treats herself to a therapeutic aromatherapy facial and body massage. She budgets for it in her monthly expenses and thinks of it as preventive medicine—not covered by her health insurance but vital to her peace of mind and sense of well-being. She once explained to me that as her life is now—barren of intimacy—she's rarely touched and she often felt overwrought, ill, and deprived until she realized that what she needed was therapeutic touching. Since she started her monthly massage treatments she's hardly been sick and has enormous amounts of energy which she needs for the extremely busy and demanding life she leads. She says that the healing effects of a massage can last up to three weeks and then it's time for another session. "You should try it," she urged me, but being practical and sensible (so I thought), I didn't, until she gave me a body and facial massage as a gift for my birthday several years ago.

Here's how I became a complete "sensuist" (someone who delights in sensory experiences, as opposed to a "sensualist," someone who is excessively concerned with physical gratification). Take one stressed-out woman and isolate her in a tranquil massage room for one hour. Now, awaken her physical senses with the scent of the aromatic essential oils; the hypnotic stroking of her face and body (especially the massaging of her feet and toes); the beautiful strains of Pachelbel's "Canon" playing softly in the background; the sight of shafts of sunlight dancing on the wooden floors; and the refreshing taste of sparkling mineral water and lemon in her mouth after the sublime massage session is over.

My first massage was a mesmerizing way to encounter the passage of time: when it was over I felt such peace, joy, and relaxation it was as if I had been drinking champagne for breakfast or having a transcendental experience. This naturally produced euphoria lasted for many hours and that night I enjoyed the sleep of the innocent. The next day I felt ready to take on the world.

During the 1980s, a popular advertising campaign for AT&T urged us to "reach out and touch someone." Today, reacquaint yourself with this powerful, life-enhancing physical sense so often disregarded. Embrace your children, stroke their hair, cradle them in your arms (no matter how big or squirmy they are), kiss your lover, caress your pets, experience the feel of different fabrics against your skin—do you prefer silk or fur or lamb's wool? Enjoy a sensuous, warm, scented bath, then sleep in the nude on fresh cotton sheets. (And if you don't sleep alone be prepared for what might follow.) Think about treating yourself to a therapeutic body or facial massage. Call up a salon and find out the cost (the average session is about $50), and save $5 a week until you can afford it. Don't feel guilty! Think of a massage the way you would think of getting your teeth cleaned, your hair styled, or a new pair of eyeglasses—occasional but necessary outlays to maintain your physical well-being.

The English poet William Wordsworth wrote, "She seemed a thing that could not feel / The touch of earthly years." Let us become women who embrace our portion of earthly years with a passion by delighting in our sense of touch.

The Intuitive Sense

Intuition is a spiritual faculty, and does not explain, but simply points the way.

—FLORENCE SCOVEL SHINN

Intuition has been called our "sixth sense" and is often an ability ascribed to women. The English writer D. H. Lawrence believed that the intelligence that "arises out of sex and beauty is intuition," while anthropologist Margaret Mead concluded that feminine intuition was a result of our "age-long training in human relations." I'm not here to debate the existence of an intuitive power—the capacity to know something without rational evidence that proves it to be so—because I *know* that it exists. So do you. The question that interests me today is: do you use your intuition? Have you learned how to fine-tune the inner instinct that is constantly transmitting signals to you? Think of yourself as a radio. Is your dial set clearly on the intuitive station so that you can receive the information you need when you need it, or are you just picking up static?

Intuition is the subliminal sense Spirit endowed us with to maneuver safely through the maze that is real life. Wild animals rely on their intuition to stay alive; we should rely on ours to thrive. "It is only by following your deepest instinct that you can lead a rich life and if you let your fear of consequence prevent you from following your deepest instinct then your life will be safe, expedient and thin," Katharine Butler Hathaway wrote in 1946.

Intuition tries to communicate with us in inventive ways. One way is through what my friend, a script consultant, Dona Cooper, calls "the educated gut," which frequently slaps us to pay attention by triggering a visceral, physical reaction in our bodies. One such intuitive signal is the emotional trembling that accompanies creative discovery or warns us not to take a certain action. Another intuitive message breaks through when we suddenly grasp that to try something new might be delightful; we do so and are surprised by joy. A third intuitive nudge occurs through revelation; the inner *knowing* that helps us arrive at the right place at the right time so that we can be swept away by the benevolent flow of synchronicity that gets us where we're meant to be as easily as the Universe can arrange it.

Today, go within and seek the wisdom and guidance of your authentic self. She steadfastly waits to speak to you through the whispers of your imagination and the glimmers of your intuition. But if you want to learn to develop this marvelous power, you must first be willing to take a leap of faith and trust it. Put it to use in little ways. Use it every day, and eventually your sixth sense will flourish and enhance your life the way the other five senses do. William Wordsworth believed that we could all become "one in whom persuasion and belief/Had ripened into faith, and faith become/A passionate intuition."

And we can.

APRIL 29

Allure: The Feminine Mystique

Taking joy in life is a woman's best cosmetic.
—ROSALIND RUSSELL

Ingrid Bergman had it in *Casablanca*. Fifty years later, Michelle Pfeiffer epitomized it as Edith Wharton's heroine, Countess Ellen Olenska, in the film version of *The Age of Innocence*. It is allure, the mesmerizing power to entice or attract through personal charm and mystery.

We're not much into mystery these days, which is a pity. These are the times of tell-all talk shows, tattletale books, and tabloid truths. Ntozake Shange believes that "Where there is a woman there is magic," and I agree. But I also believe that where there is a woman, there should be mystery. What intrigues me most is the mystery—the allure—of how some women seem to pull it all together so effortlessly. This is the aspect of the feminine mystique that compels and invites investigation. Who are these women and how did they evolve into these higher beings?

You see them in business meetings—confident, assured, and in command—or smiling serenely in the hallway at school while waiting patiently to pick up the afternoon car pool, a baby over one shoulder, a toddler in tow. These women don't look frazzled, fatigued, or fed up; they look fabulous. They do not simply juggle; they fly through the air with the greatest of ease. You wonder: what is their secret? Are they all on Prozac? Is it plenty of money, being well organized, positive thinking, or the favorable alignment of celestial bodies? Perhaps it is something more profound: a deep spiritual connection.

Does the computer ever break down when these women are on deadline, do the kids ever whine, does the car ever need to be towed, have they ever taken a dog who's just wrestled with a porcupine to the vet? You and I have, which is why occasionally Rio de Janeiro sounds appealing. Then, without missing a beat, you wipe a snotty nose, change a dirty diaper, defrost the hamburger in the microwave, start the spaghetti sauce, sew a button on a coat, help someone with her homework. You pause for a moment, wondering what they would do if you weren't here and realize in the same breath that you're awfully glad you are. Much to your astonishment, it occurs to you that you must also possess some aspect of allure because everybody in the house gravitates to you. In the middle of the night they call your name.

And there's certainly enough of mystery to ponder—such as the mystery of what will happen next. But instead of worrying or obsessing, you decide to just let go and see what occurs. You choose to take joy in your real life as it unfolds day by day, hour by hour, a heartbeat at a time. Emily Dickinson confessed that "To live is so startling, it leaves little time for anything else." Your face may never end up on the silver screen. Nor will mine. But we can arrive at an inner awareness that just living and loving it all is alluring enough.

APRIL 30

When Did You Feel Most Beautiful?

I don't believe makeup and the right hairstyle alone can make a woman beautiful. The most radiant woman in the room is the one full of life and experience.

—SHARON STONE

Today, think back over your life to the times when you felt most beautiful. I have, and I was surprised to discover that my real moments of beauty resulted from something more powerful than just the combination of the right hairstyle, makeup, and clothing.

The times I felt most beautiful were on my wedding day, the day I gave birth to our daughter, and the first time I taught Simple Abundance in a workshop setting. But on the day I got married I couldn't get my hair to look right. While my future husband stood waiting uncomfortably in a room full of curious and bemused guests, I fussed with my hair so much that I was twenty minutes late for my own wedding. Since we were being married in the home of friends and I was upstairs in a second-floor bedroom, he had every reason to wonder why I couldn't get to the ceremony on time. Finally, I just put my veiled hat on and went downstairs with a smile to start my new life. When friends see my wedding picture today they never comment on my hair; instead they mention the jubilant happiness showing on my face.

The next time I felt like the most beautiful woman in the world was the day our daughter was born. In these pictures I look like a beached beluga whale sitting up in a hospital bed, but I'm still beaming. The beams are what I notice now.

After I taught my first Simple Abundance workshop and came back to my hotel room, I accidentally caught a glimpse of a beautiful woman and I was genuinely astonished. "Who are you?" I asked the face in the mirror and my authentic self smiled back at me. The workshop had been so fulfilling, exciting, and inspiring, and I had experienced such rapport with the women who attended, that I was caught up in the exhilarating flow of life and it showed.

Here's the secret I stumbled upon when trying to solve the beauty puzzle. The situations in my life in which I felt beautiful were all different, but Love was the common denominator that transformed me, not the outer trappings: love for my husband, love for our child, love for my work. This is perhaps the most important beauty lesson any of us can ever learn. Love has the power to transcend our physical limitations. "The more I wonder," Alice Walker confesses, "the more I love." Let us continuously search for the wonder of it all. If we do, we can't help but notice the love bubbling up from deep within. When wonder and love become as indispensible to you as foundation and blush, you will become the most radiant woman in the world.

Joyful Simplicities for April

≈§ Remind yourself what it's like to have fun on All Fools' Day. Surprise your loved ones and co-workers with whimsy—not practical jokes that embarrass. Instead, devise comical, absurd, and amusing surprises. At home, turn everything topsy-turvy: serve bagel or English muffin pizzas for breakfast, pancakes or waffles for supper. After school tell them you've got to take them to a doctor or dentist appointment and then head for the ice cream parlor.

≈§ Pick up a copy of Diane Ackerman's marvelous exploration *A Natural History of the Senses* and revel in an exhilarating reading romp that will intrigue and inspire you to become a sensuist.

≈§ April is a wonderful month for all kinds of walks, whether in warm spring showers or balmy sunshine. The scent of the earth reawakening and the sight of Mother Nature's brilliant display of color will rouse and remind you how wonderful it is simply to be alive.

≈§ Visit a hat store and try on a variety of chapeaux. You're dashing in a black felt fedora, but perhaps the broad-brimmed straw with the cabbage rose has captured your fancy? Play around with the many different possibilities. You might just catch a glimpse of your authentic self in the mirror.

≈§ Find a large fabric store for a creative excursion, even if you don't sew. Browse through the upholstery remnants. They make great inexpensive tablecloths or covers for furniture. Flip through the pattern book. Visualize the possibilities. Is there something you'd like to make for yourself? For the house? Then why not consider the possibilities? Search out sewing classes at adult extension courses.

❧ Sort through your lingerie drawer. Discard ratty, old bras and panties and delight in pretty new undergarments. Lay down scented paper and tuck in lavender-scented sachets.

❧ Go through your makeup and discard what's old and dried out. Replace darker colors with a paler palette for spring. Learn the secret of applying foundation lightly so that it seems natural by blending with cosmetic sponges and brushes instead of your fingers. Visit the cosmetic counters of a large department store and discover who's offering free makeovers. (Many cosmetic companies introduce their new spring line of makeup at this time of year.) You don't have to buy anything! When the beauty consultant is finished, thank her enthusiastically and tell her you want to walk around with your new face and see how it feels before investing in new makeup.

❧ Visit a large record store for half an hour and simply browse. Discover all the different types of music available: classical, country, soft rock, New Age instrumental, gospel, opera, jazz, rhythm and blues, and soul. Flip the radio dial and give something completely different a fair chance. Visit a large library to check out new tapes and compact discs to enjoy sound bites before you buy. Spend a few hours in silence (when you're at home by yourself) and discover how restorative it can be.

❧ Collect rainwater to wash your hair. Victorian women believed rainwater made their hair softer.

❧ Find a refreshing new scent for spring—try rose water, lilac, or lily of the valley. Wear a scent you love every day.

❧ Dye Easter eggs and hide them for children of all ages to hunt.

❧ Resume the restorative pastime of weekend roaming; be on the lookout for vintage linens at estate sales and for plants and herbs at farmers' markets.

❧ When it showers, curl up under a blanket in the afternoon and listen to the raindrops on the roof.

❧ Bake a batch of hot cross buns. Eat jelly beans.

❧ Find the perfect new hat or trim an old-fashioned bonnet.

❧ You can learn all about the healing and beauty benefits of aromatherapy in *The Art of Aromatherapy* by Robert B. Tisserand. One thing you must be aware of: essential oils are not to be swallowed because they can be toxic, even fatal. *They are for external use only.* If your skin is sensitive, test a spot on your arm before submerging your body in a bath. Keep all essential oils out of the reach of children the way you would any medicine, and treat them with the same respect. Mugwort, for example, should not be used by pregnant women. Essential oils should also not be used on the body undiluted; they need to be blended with a neutral base, such as almond oil, wheat-germ oil, or jojoba oil. Read up on the subject and check with a knowledgeable aromatherapist. You can also locate an aromatherapist through health food stores, herbal shops, natural cosmetic shops, therapeutic massage centers, or word-of-mouth. Seek and you shall find.

MAY

Let all thy joys be as the month of May.
—FRANCIS QUARLES

The month of May casts her magic spell as spring's promise is finally fulfilled. This month we turn our attention homeward, as we continue to weave simplicity into our daily round while reacquainting ourselves with the transformative power of the third Simple Abundance principle—Order. With fresh eyes and a loving, appreciative heart, we reconsider our daily rounds. As we learn to savor everyday epiphanies, we encounter the Sacred in the ordinary.

MAY 1

Everday Epiphanies

*Today a new sun rises for me; everything lives, everything is ani-
mated, everything seems to speak to me of my passion, everything
invites me to cherish it.*

—ANNE DE LENCLOS

One of the most famous elegies ever written was "Elegy in a Country
Churchyard" by the English poet Thomas Gray. As the poet wandered
through a graveyard at twilight in 1750, he ruminated on the meaning of
life, the toil of those who achieve and those who don't, the mockery of
ambition, the struggle of both the poor and the rich to be happy, and, eventually, what difference it all makes for those whose heads rest "upon the lap
of Earth." Not much, Gray decided: simple joys are forever gone, destiny is
obscured. "For them no more the blazing hearth shall burn/Or busy housewife ply her evening care . . . the paths of glory lead but to the grave."

We should write an elegy for every day that has slipped through our lives
unnoticed and unappreciated. Better still, we should write a song of
thanksgiving for all the days that remain.

Sometimes we are aware of the poet who dwells within us and registers
every precious moment of our lives. More often, however, we move
through our days in a fog or a frenzy—until we're startled into consciousness by an unforeseen threat to something that we hold dear and have been
taking for granted. I call these luminous moments "everday epiphanies,"
because they jar us into a profound awareness of how much we have, and
how much we have escaped, and how much there is to be grateful for.
Through the mystical alchemy of Grace and thanksgiving, what might have
become an elegy is transformed into exultation: our own recovery or that
of a loved one who has been seriously ill; the overwhelming relief after a
child who has wandered off, even for a few minutes, is found, safe and
unharmed; a reconciliation after a painful breach; the realization of how
lucky we are if we are doing work that we love; the rejoicing that surrounds
a long-awaited rite of passage; the enormous satisfaction that comes after
completing an overwhelming task; the serenity that awaits us after struggle
is abandoned.

Everyday epiphanies encourage us to cherish everything. Today a new
sun has risen. Everything lives. Everything can speak to your soul passionately if you will be still enough to listen. "You have to count on living every
single day in a way you believe will make you feel good about your life,"
actress Jane Seymour suggests, "so that if it were over tomorrow, you'd be
content."

Living in the House of Spirit

How to be happy when you are miserable. Plant Japanese poppies with cornflowers and mignonette, and bed out the petunias among the sweet-peas so that they shall scent each other. See the sweet-peas coming up.

Drink very good tea out of a thin Worcester cup of a colour between apricot and pink . . .

—RUMER GODDEN

It was the small things that helped, taken one by one and savoured," English writer Rumer Godden recalls in her mesmerizing memoir of an authentic life, *A House with Four Rooms.* "Make yourself savour them," she told herself when life was not tidy.

Life is not tidy around here today: schedules are colliding, needs are conflicting, and the house is strewn with real-life refuse, reflecting outwardly the disarray of my mind at this moment. My natural inclination—which I am thwarting with a tremendous act of will—is to start cleaning. But if I stop to clean, I'll interrupt the rhythm of the day. I really only have a few precious hours to work uninterrupted while my daughter is in school. A few precious hours to hold one thought in my head and follow it word by word to its completion, even if it takes all morning.

One of the reasons I love Rumer Godden's writing is that she stitches the colorful threads of her extraordinary life—domestic, creative, and spiritual—with such deftness; the hem that seems to hold her life together rarely pulls or gapes the way mine does more often than I care to admit. She began her career in 1936 and in nearly sixty years has written fifty-seven books: novels for both children and adults, nonfiction, short story collections, and poetry. Many of her renowned novels, which are very mystical, celebrate the fruitfulness of Real Life: the magic, the Mystery, and the mundane. *The New York Times* noted that she was a writer who "belongs in that small exclusive club of women—it includes Isak Dinesen and Beryl Markham—who could do pretty well anything they set their minds to, hunting tigers, bewitching men, throwing elegant dinner parties, winning literary fame." Of all her books, however, it is her memoirs that are my favorites. I am captivated by how she lived, nurtured a family, and created many homes out of shells of houses all over the world, while writing almost continuously. She is a glorious storyteller, but no story is as riveting as real life.

The soulcraft of creating and sustaining safe havens, set apart from the world, in which to seek and savor small authentic joys, is a recurring theme in her work, whether the haven is behind convent walls or in the nursery at the top of the stairs. Rumer Godden's secret to living an authentic life seems to have been dwelling, no matter where she actually kept house, in the House of Spirit. "There is an Indian proverb or axiom that says that everyone is a house with four rooms, a physical, a mental, an emotional and a spiritual. Most of us tend to live in one room most of the time, but unless we go into every room every day, even if only to keep it aired, we are not a complete person."

MAY 3

A Welcome Retreat:
Home as a Haven in a Hectic World

Every spirit builds itself a house, and beyond its house a world, and beyond its world a heaven. Know then that world exists for you.
—RALPH WALDO EMERSON

During the nineteenth century the home was viewed as "heaven on earth," a hallowed haven in an uncertain world. When man, woman, or child crossed the threshold they were safe, "not only from injury," wrote John Ruskin, "but from all terror, doubt and division." Today many of us cast a nostalgic glance backward. The Victorian era seems so calm, gentle, and gracious—so completely opposite from our own. Yet the four decades spanning the Civil War to the turn of the century were among the most politically, socially, and economically turbulent years in our history. Why, then, should a period of such profound upheaval come down to us not only as an age of innocence but as one of stability and tranquillity?

I believe, in large part, it is because of a legacy of love left to us by our great-grandmothers who reigned over their hearths as surely as Victoria did over her empire. Victorian women may not have had the vote or the trappings of power (including personal disposable income and independence) but they were the moral, spiritual, and physical center of the home, responsible for creating a welcome retreat of beauty, comfort, and contentment that would protect, nurture, and sustain those they loved. To achieve this, ordinary middle-class women elevated the pursuit of domestic bliss to an extraordinary art form, from white-linen Sunday dinners to blue-checked-gingham Independence Day picnics. Women approached the domestic arts—cooking, decorating, gardening, handicrafts, and entertaining—not as burdens but as a form of personal expression and a means of persuasion.

Traditions that celebrated the joys of home and family life acted as the mystical mortar that held bodies and souls together in a tumultuous society that was changing at the speed of light.

"Home is where we start from," T. S. Eliot observed. Today, a century after he was born, "home" is the place where many women are longing to return, if not literally, then figuratively. Begin believing that the time, energy, and emotion you invest daily in the soulcraft of *homecaring*—carving out a haven for yourself and those dear to you—is a sacred endeavor. Life holds no more guarantees for us than it did for our Victorian foremothers. Yet they faced the future with full hearts, determined to create a lasting work of art: a happy, secure, and beautiful retreat of love and laughter.

We can, too.

MAY 4

The Personality of Your Home

A house is who you are, not who you ought to be.

—JILL ROBINSON

Like it or not, the personalities of our homes are accurate barometers that reflect, through our surroundings, where we have been, what's going on in our lives, and who we are—today, this moment—though not necessarily where we're heading.

Admittedly, this is not the most reassuring thought for a meditation, especially if you could see the state of my home as I write. Nevertheless, it's true. "You will express yourself in your house whether you want to or not," said the mother of modern style, Elsie de Wolfe, who transformed the way America decorated for half a century with her book *The House in Good Taste*, written in 1913.

Your response is probably: "If I had the money to redecorate, you'd see the real me." No doubt. I don't entirely disagree. But we can't afford to put our lives and creativity on hold until there's more cash, because we only end up shortchanging ourselves and those we love. Today we can use the Simple Abundance steps—acceptance, blessing our circumstances, and discovering our personal preferences—to jump-start the expression of our authenticity through the way we care for and decorate our homes. When we do, the principles of gratitude, simplicity, and order will begin to transform the places where we live into hallowed havens of comfort and contentment—with or without the new slipcovers.

After my first book was published, a sleek, glossy magazine known for its lush pictorials (which I adore) wanted to pay me a visit for an intimate glimpse of "the woman behind the book." So successfully, it seemed, had I evoked the Victorian era in my writing that the magazine assumed I lived in a perfectly restored nineteenth-century home. How could I not?

Alas, I don't. And I panicked.

"Calm down," a longtime friend who works in Hollywood consoled me. "Pull focus and take another look." In the movie business, "pulling focus" occurs when a cinematographer slowly adjusts the camera lens for the sharpest clarity of image. "Your home is warm, charming, cozy, interesting, inviting. There are fabulous shots all around you. Don't be so hard on yourself." But as a journalist, I knew what this magazine expected, and I didn't live in it. If my home was going to be on public display, I wanted it to be perfect; I desperately wanted to live up to the expectations of others instead of realizing that living up to my own was difficult enough. Instead, my publicist arranged for the interview to take place over afternoon tea in a hotel.

While money certainly helps us express ourselves through our surroundings, creating a warm, inviting home that reflects our own personality doesn't have to begin by hiring a decorator or pulling out our credit cards or checkbook.

Today, no matter where or how you live, look upon your home through the eyes of Love. Walk around the rooms and offer thanks for the walls and roof that safely enclose you and yours. Pause for a moment to consider all the women who have lost their homes through death, divorce, debt, or disaster. Be grateful for the home you have, knowing that, at this moment, all you have is all you truly need.

MAY 5

Eminent Domain: Whose Home Is It, Anyway?

Your house is your home only *when you feel you have* jurisdiction *over the space.*

—JOAN KRON

Unless you live alone, is your home your own? Yes, eminent domain prevails to a certain extent. But it also belongs to or is being borrowed by other people as well. This is why your small city apartment living room is also your writer-husband's study during the day. Or why your dining room table and chairs do double duty as a castle fortress. This is why your sewing and crafts snuggery is once again a bedroom for a grown child who has returned home. Or why your guest room has been transformed into Grandma's room; your mother-in-law is ill but unwilling to move into a nursing home. Or perhaps why your basement family room has been revamped into a hideaway to suit teenagers who crave their own eminent domain. Recognizing and acknowledging the needs of those you live with as well as your own is the first step toward making everybody's habitat happy and harmonious, the way a home is meant to be.

For nearly four years after our daughter, Katie, was born, the tables in our home were bare (if you don't count crayons or Legos) until she became old enough to appreciate looking at beautiful objects without playing with them. This was for her safety and my sanity. Gradually Waterford crystal wedding presents started to coexist cozily with her toys as our belongings became intertwined, reflecting the personalities of everyone who resides here. But recently a young male kitten named Mikey, who isn't bound by the laws of eminent domain or gravity, came to live with us (thanks to Katie) and some of our cherished breakables were once again packed away until he learns not to climb onto the mantel.

Because space is not an affordable luxury for many women in the 1990s, does this mean we have to put off the transformative work of authentic homecaring indefinitely? Can we continue to procrastinate if we truly value our peace of mind? A home's tranquillity always comes from within no matter what the circumstances. The space one's soul requires cannot be measured in inches, feet, or dollars.

Don't let your practical considerations discourage you, even if right now they might defer your dream of truly expressing yourself through your surroundings. Begin to work with, instead of fighting against, your real life limitations. Never forget that your life and decorating styles are works-of-art-in-progress. Interior decorator and writer Alexandra Stoddard believes that "where we are in our lives and our relationship *with others*" must take precedence over our decorating choices, and she's right. "Sometimes what *we* want just isn't practical or right for us now. A home with small children *should* be set up differently than one with grown children. If you're divorced or remarried and stepchildren visit you often, you'll have to make appropriate arrangements for them. These are not so much questions of lifestyle as of life *passages*. . . . An honest home that rings true to the lives of the people who occupy it will always be disarmingly refreshing to visitors." And with the right perspective, it can be for those who live there as well.

After the Fact: The Art of Decorative Detection

When friends enter a home, they sense its personality and charac-
ter, the family's style of living—these elements make a house come
alive with a sense of identity, a sense of energy, enthusiasm, and
warmth, declaring, "This is who we are; this is how we live."

—RALPH LAUREN

Shortly after my husband and I were married, my parents moved to a smaller home in a different state and began divesting themselves of furniture and belongings. Because of my love of Victoriana, my mother gave me my grandmother's nineteenth-century front parlor suite—a love seat and two chairs—which she had purchased at an auction in 1921 at the Ritz Hotel in New York City. She also gave me a pair of turn-of-the-century china lamps. Shaped like urns, the lamps (which sat on brass pedestal bases and were nearly four feet high) were forest-green with gold leaf trim and featured a huge pink calla lily in the center.

The lamps were hideous. But it took me years to open my eyes and realize it.

This authentic awareness came as I was attempting to bring order, the third Simple Abundance principle, into our lives. I began to do this by wandering through the rooms of our house dispassionately observing our patterns of living: how we stored things (or didn't), what areas became catchalls, where we succumbed to the tendency to take things out but not put them back because it wasn't convenient. During the course of this investigation I turned my attention, like a detective perusing a crime scene, to examining decorative objects that surrounded me daily, especially noting their presence and validity. "Who lives here?" I asked as I began searching for myself. Every time I came into the living room, I found myself recoiling from those lamps. "God, they're horrible," I would mutter under my breath and move on. Finally one day, God's interior decorator said in desperation, "Well, get rid of the damn things and stop whining."

"What are you doing?" my husband asked as I was removing the objects of revulsion. "I hate these lamps and can't stand living with them for another moment," I told him.

"I've hated these lamps for fifteen years but never said anything because I thought you loved them."

"I thought I had to because I grew up with them and my mother gave them to me. But I don't and I won't."

"Help me understand," he said incredulously. "It's taken you fifteen years to discover this? *Fifteen years?*"

What can I say? Some of us are heavy sleepers and rouse very slowly. Twenty years can go by before you realize one bright sunny morning that your mother's grand piano doesn't fit into your city co-op or lifestyle, especially since you don't play the piano. Or perhaps you've outgrown the veneer bedroom set that you got from a thrift shop for your first apartment and have repainted three times. If the thought of picking up the brush again makes you want to cry, don't do it, even if it's practical. Instead, look for another bargain that you'd like to live with.

During the 1870s and 1880s, a philosophy known as the Aesthetic Movement sprang up on both sides of the Atlantic and began to focus on beautifying every aspect of Victorian life. The heart of the movement was realizing the importance of nurturing the soul through beautiful surroundings. This week I'd like you to wander slowly through your home and glance at the objects that surround you daily. Are you really comfortable with them and what they whisper about you? Do you love them or just live with them? It doesn't matter how you acquired these objects. No immediate decisions need to be made as to whether or not you should keep them. Awareness is all we're seeking. Above all, don't be embarrassed by how long you may have waited to start searching for your authenticity. "To one who waits, all things reveal themselves," the nineteenth-century English poet Coventry Patmore reassures us, "so long as you have the courage not to deny in the darkness what you have seen in the light."

MAY 7

Everyday Edens: Spending Another Day in Paradise

Home is the definition of God.

—EMILY DICKINSON

Eden is that old-fashioned House we dwell in every day," Emily Dickinson reminds me as I wander around my living room picking up a purple hairband, colored markers, a young artist's sketchbook, a tennis racket, minutes from last week's city council meeting, a stack of *Beckett's Baseball Card Monthly*, assorted compact discs, one viola, various mail-order catalogs, three days' worth of newspapers, two pairs of shoes, an empty Doritos bag crumpled up next to the couch, and a hairbrush (mine, but probably used by the owner of the purple hairband).

This is Eden?

Poets, it seems, have waxed lyrical about the joys of domesticity for centuries, no doubt because they lived with loving, patient, and nurturing women who created havens of tranquil order in which they could work in peace and comfort.

But did you know that the spinster Emily Dickinson—who rarely left her home after she was thirty-four—was also very domesticated? In fact, her greatest ecstasies were said to be cooking and writing poetry. And since the bulk of her poems were only published after her death in 1886, it was her cooking skills that first won the belle of Amherst, Massachusetts, her fame for (among other culinary delights) a moist, dense black fruitcake served at afternoon tea and scrumptious parcels of gingerbread lowered in a basket from her second-floor bedroom sanctuary to hungry neighborhood children. Separated from us now by the chasm of more than a century, her contented and self-contained confinement seems to me to be the perfect antidote to late-twentieth-century existence. "I don't go from home unless emergency leads me by the hand," she wrote to a friend in 1854, "and then I do it obstinately and draw back if I can."

How I long to draw back, too. To simply sit still for twenty minutes in the backyard basking in the sunshine, watching the birds build their new nests, watching the cats watching the birds, greeting the new blossoms in the garden, and enjoying a fresh cup of tea and Miss Dickinson's letters.

However, before this idyllic reverie can commence, I must clean. I must pick up the debris of our daily life and bring order to this room, for I cannot stand the chaos, clutter, and confusion here for another single moment. There is simply no time for poetic musings.

Or is there?

Perhaps now—of all times—when I am nearly bowed under physically, emotionally, and psychologically by the minutiae of the mundane, is the very moment I need the reverence of poets who bear witness to the sacredness of the ordinary. Then perhaps I shall see, not just other people's belongings, but all the beauty, joy, and abundance that literally lies at my feet. If I can be still for a moment and fully enter into the experience of bringing order and harmony to my home, perhaps I can discover that the poetry of this afternoon is to be found in the perception of my tasks.

For what is the purpose of cleaning this room? Is it simply to pick up trash and dispose of yesterday's newspaper? Or is some inspired action at work here? In the process of transforming this room into a safe and serene haven where my family can come together to enjoy the comfort of each other's company, am I not changing the perception of my work?

We are all given a choice each day. We can react negatively to the demands made on us or we can choose to live abundantly, to transform the negative into the meaningful. Attitude is all. If I do not endow my life and my work with meaning, no one will ever be able to do it for me. If I don't recognize the value of what I am doing here in this living room, certainly no one else can. And if homecaring is not sacred, then forgive me, for I truly have no conception of the Divine.

And so, to lift my spirits and celebrate my choice, I listen to a Bach concerto as I clean. I put on the kettle to make myself a fresh pot of tea. I throw open the windows to catch a spring breeze. Soon my family will return to this lovely and inviting room.

However, before then, I will carve out a precious interlude of time for myself. I will sit still for twenty minutes in the backyard basking in the sunshine, with the birds, the cats, and the new blossoms and contemplate the blessing of having spent another day in Paradise.

MAY 8

Rediscovering the Sacred Soulcraft of Homecaring

The ordinary arts we practice every day at home are of more importance to the soul than their simplicity might suggest.

—THOMAS MOORE

For centuries young women have learned how to run a home, how to cook, and how to raise a family by tying themselves to their mother's or grandmother's apron strings. George Eliot tells us in her novel *The Mill on the Floss*: "There were particular ways of doing things in the Dodson family—particular ways of bleaching the linen, of making the cowslip wine, curing the hams and keeping the bottled gooseberries, so that no daughter of that house could be indifferent to the privilege of having been born a Dodson, rather than a Gibson or a Watson."

Unfortunately, I wasn't born a Dodson. Nevertheless, when I was a senior in high school I won a "Homemaker of Tomorrow" award. This greatly amused and perplexed the nuns who taught me, considering that home economics was not even part of their curriculum. It also absolutely stunned my mother, who knew the state of my bedroom and her continuing struggle to get me to clean it. But I had won the contest—which was based on an essay and not on a bake-off—by writing about the importance of homemaking as an endangered calling. This was in 1965, when the rumblings of the feminist movement were starting to be heard across the land. In the mid-1960s you didn't prepare your daughter for life as an adult by teaching her how to make a bed, sort white from colored laundry, organize a closet, or make a meat loaf. Instead, many mothers handed out copies of *The Feminine Mystique* after they had finished reading it themselves.

Now, three decades later, women know how to start successful mail-order companies, launch banks and new magazines, walk in space, trade securities on Wall Street, close million dollar movie deals, get elected to national office, anchor the nightly news, write Supreme Court decisions, and win Nobel Prizes. We can secure financing, create, innovate, delegate, and negotiate. But we're also running to the grocery store on our way home from work with tired, cranky children in tow, washing the laundry when everyone in the family has run out of clothes to wear, and searching for a place to sit down comfortably at the end of a long day in the midst of overwhelming pandemonium. Many women today run businesses but don't have a clue how to run their own households competently, which is one of the reasons we are run ragged.

The time has come for us to look deep within. Reconsider how caring for our homes can be an expression of our authenticity. We may not know how to bleach linen, make cowslip wine, cure ham, or bottle gooseberries. But it's not too late for us to rediscover the sacred soulcraft of homecaring. Creating a comfortable, beautiful, well-run home can be among our most satisfying accomplishments as well as an illuminating spiritual experience. Like sweat equity, channeling your time and creative energy closer to home will produce a big emotional return for yourself and those you love.

MAY 9

Getting Your House in Order

My life will always have dirty dishes.
If this sink can become
a place of contemplation,
let me learn constancy here.

—GUNILLA NORRIS

Because we dread it, we put it off for as long as possible until we have to dig ourselves out. Many women approach the unrelenting, repetitive, exhausting, and unproductive work known as housekeeping like the torture of Sisyphus. After offending the Greek god Zeus, Sisyphus was punished by having to roll an enormous stone to the top of a steep hill. Every time he managed to pull off this feat, the stone would slide back down and the poor soul would have to start over again. Women do the same thing, Simone de Beauvoir observed in her book *The Second Sex*: "The clean becomes soiled, the soiled is made clean, over and over, day after day."

That is, of course, assuming we get around to it daily. For two-thirds of American women who also work outside their home, this means tackling household chores between the hours of seven P.M. and seven A.M.

And you wonder why the soiled stays soiled until you can't stand it?

When I discovered—to my dismay—that order was the third principle that needed to be gently explored and embraced on the Simple Abundance path, I balked. Although I frequently felt frazzled and adrift, especially when trying to find something or ignore the disarray around me, the virtue of order seemed very old-fashioned, unimaginative, and uninspired—as dreary and cheerless, in fact, as the word *chore*. What I longed to bring into my life was something more uplifting.

But as I reflected on the simple, uncluttered, *serene* lives of the Amish, the Quakers, and especially the Shakers, I became struck by their seamless stitching together of life, work, and art through the thread of divine order.

Order shaped every part and nurtured every nuance of Shaker life, from their daily schedule of tasks to the way they expressed themselves authentically through their surroundings. Mother Ann Lee, who founded the United Society of Believers in the First and Second Appearance of Christ in 1774, instructed her followers to remember that order was heaven's first law. "There is no dirt in heaven," she counseled her charges. Members of the Shaker "Family" were to keep their personal belongings and tools in such perfect order that they could be found at a moment's notice, day or night. To accomplish this, the Shakers elevated order to a sacred art: just to gaze at the exquisite beauty and brilliance of Shaker built-in drawers and cupboards is to know that in the House of Spirit a sublime pine cubbyhole awaits with your name on it. The Shakers believed that their daily work, including housekeeping, was a personal expression of worship.

"Prayer and housekeeping—they go together. They have always gone together. We simply know that our daily round *is* how we live. When we clean and order our homes, we are somehow also cleaning and ordering ourselves," Gunilla Norris tells us in her modern book of hours, *Being Home*. How we care for our home is a subtle but significant expression of self-esteem.

A Place for Everything: Preserving Your Sanity with a Personal Plan

If a home doesn't make sense, nothing does.
—HENRIETTA RIPPERGER

We long to make sense of the work we do in our home. To master the sacred art and craft of doing it and to create a microcosm of serenity, security, and sanity for ourselves and those we love. But how and where do we begin, especially if we never were taught to put our things away so that we might find them on another day? And if we did not learn the rudimentary lessons ourselves, how can we possibly teach our children the life-sustaining skills they need, from cooperation to cooking? Getting our houses in order and endowing our children with a respect for, and appreciation of, order is one of the most precious gifts we can give them and ourselves.

After searching a century's worth of housekeeping advice found in domestic manuals, from Mrs. Isabella Beeton's classic *Book of Household Management*, published in 1861, to Shirley Conran's *Superwoman: For Every Woman Who Hates Housework*, one thing is clear: sanity is preserved with planning. Always remember that "plan" comes before "work" in the dictionary and with good reason. But before planning, you're going to have to *think* your way through housework, just as you'd approach an overwhelming project at work.

Now none of us would dream of plunging in without thinking when working at a job for which we're paid a salary. Why should we do any less for a job that compensates us with room, board, love, and contentment? By thinking first, instead of just reacting to the chores, interruptions, and demands that are made on us, we can reclaim control over our daily lives. We need to learn to run our homes instead of letting the housework run roughshod over us.

First, figure out what your standard of ideal housekeeping is. Remember, it *doesn't* have to be the same as your mother's or the Dodsons'. Close your eyes for a moment and imagine that you are walking through your front door. In your ideal version, what does the room look like? Your personal standard of ideal homecaring is the minimum you can live with and still feel content. For example, I can personally live with dust (though I do draw the line when I can write my name on the bedroom bureau), but clutter drives me crazy. It's more important for me to have the common rooms of our home and my bedroom tidy than to have them pass a white-glove test. So, given the demands on my time, I will be content if the house can, on a consistent basis, remain reasonably straight instead of being ready for a magazine pictorial. Determine your livability quotient. It's the first step toward devising a personal plan that will work for you.

Next, you need to figure out what needs to be done, who can do it, and when. The simplest way is to break your housekeeping demands into categories: daily duties, weekly chores, monthly jobs, and seasonal tasks. See on paper how much you really do. You will be astounded. Now, who lives with you and can share the load? Once you've identified the jobs for your home and the workers available, write it down. What you're creating is a Simple Abundance strategy that brings order and harmony to your home, while providing you with enough time and space to savor the journey. We have only recently begun focusing our energies and imagination on preserving Mother Earth. (The same need exists for perserving the lives of mortal mothers, but why wait until we are on the brink of emotional extinction to begin this conservation effort?)

To jump-start the bringing of order into your home, here are four old-fashioned rules that can change the quality of your daily life beginning today. Repeat this recipe for contentment out loud every morning and evening for twenty-one days. Let it become your personal mantra to maintain serenity. Write these instructions on index cards and post one in every room of your home. Teach these words of wisdom to your children, whisper them into your partner's ear:

1. If you take it out, put it back.
2. If you open it, close it.
3. If you throw it down, pick it up.
4. If you take it off, hang it up.

The Tao of Homecaring

Time to dust again.
Time to caress my house,
to stroke all its surfaces.
I want to think of it as a kind of lovemaking
. . . the chance to appreciate by touch
what I live with and cherish.

—GUNILLA NORRIS

As the story goes, the Chinese sage Lao-Tzu (who was born five hundred years before Christ) decided to leave the province where he lived because he became disillusioned with the corrupt and decaying dynasty that ruled it. When he arrived at the border, a guard asked the wise old man if he would write a book before he left, instructing seekers in "the art of living." Lao-Tzu willingly agreed. He called his book the *Tao Te Ching*. When it was completed, he departed China, never to be seen again.

The *Tao Te Ching* is the sacred text of the Chinese religion known as Taoism and one of the most widely translated books of all time. Its followers strive to live according to the principles of the Tao (pronounced Dow) which they believe governs the order of the Universe. Like Zen, Tao, or the Way, is a spiritual path; it must be intimately experienced instead of intellectually comprehended if insights are to be discovered. One of its main themes is unity, based on yielding rather than resisting. ("Tao is eternal without doing, and yet nothing remains undone.") When a seeker commits to the Way she sheds her expectations, becoming an empty vessel to be filled to the brim with both the yin and yang, the opposite male and female energies of life—career and home, dark and light, sorrow and joy, intimacy and solitude, aggression and passivity.

How can the enigmatic advice of an ancient Chinese philosopher help us get our houses in order? If our souls are so preoccupied with undoing, how does anything ever get done?

Inexplicably, it gets done by pausing. By reflecting on the way in which our life proceeds day in, day out. What works, what doesn't. As we pause to reflect before doing, we come to an awareness of how the nature of all things—even the minutiae of the domestic sphere—contributes to the harmony of the Whole. One of Lao-Tzu's illuminating lessons is that "naming is the origin of all particular things" and that "mystery and manifestation arise from the same source."

I have taken this wisdom to heart, especially in how I perceive the work I do in our home. Drudgery can be transformed, through a willing and open heart, into labors of love. Begin with the words that describe, or name, your creative efforts. Let "chores" become "tasks." Stop calling your daily round "housework" and begin to call it "homecaring." Redefining our work casts a subtle but powerful spell over the subconscious mind. And after all, *caring*—for yourself, your loved ones, your pets, and your home—is truly what you are doing when you dust, change the kitty litter, sort the laundry, drive the car pool, prepare the meals, and work in the garden.

Domestic theophanies are visible manifestations of Spirit in the home. We find them by looking for Mystery in the mundane, seeing the Sacred in the ordinary. For me, this is the heart of the Way, the Tao of homecaring. Lao-Tzu urged seekers to "regard the small as important" and "to make much of the little." Today, try to glimpse everything you do in your home, no matter how insignificant it may seem, as part of your authentic path to Wholeness and it shall become so.

MAY 12

Restoring a Sense of Harmony to Your Habitat

I am told that when the Chinese, who know everything, build a house, they consult the precepts of an ancient science, Feng Shui, which tells them exactly how, when, and where the work must be done, and so brings good fortune to the home forever.

—JAN MORRIS

Thousands of years ago in ancient China, practioners of the mysterious art of placement known as *feng shui* (pronounced "fung shway") advised emperors and nobles on how to bring more harmony, health, prosperity, and good fortune into their lives through inspired interior design.

Based on allowing the cosmic breath or essential earth energy known as *ch'i*, which the Chinese believe infuses all life, to flow freely in harmony with nature, the esoteric seers of feng shui offered advice on everything from auspicious burial sites (for a comfortable afterlife) to the planning of entire imperial cities. Today this profound and pragmatic Eastern art has been transplanted to the West as more of us become open to living new lives through ancient wisdom. American banks, corporations, and restaurants setting up operations in Asian cities like Hong Kong recognize the importance of hiring feng shui consultants to advise them on every aspect of the design process, from the architectural blueprints to the propitious placement of desks, in order to insure success for their businesses and the well-being of their employees.

Katherine Metz, a contemporary feng shui practitioner, believes that "all of us can make simple and affordable changes in our homes and workplaces that will spark our natural potential to be as alive, receptive and as focused as possible. In these rapidly changing times, simple feng shui adjustments can help bring clarity, peace, joy and prosperity."

Some of her suggestions on how to transcend the mundane through the mystical include hanging a brass wind chime inside your front door for clarity; having books in plain view as you enter your home to increase insight; hanging a round mirror in your bedroom to bring more love, compassion, and understanding to an intimate relationship; placing flowers in your bedroom, kitchen, and study to cultivate good luck; and hanging a mirror on the wall adjacent to or behind your stove to reflect the burners, which are symbols of wealth and prosperity. If you are stuck in a rut or an unpleasant situation (such as sloth) Metz advises moving "twenty-seven objects in your home that have not been moved in the last year" which will "enhance your ability to move forward in life." While we're attempting to bring more order in our lives, this week offers us the perfect opportunity to experiment with feng shui to bring more harmony to our habitats: clear closets and junk drawers or move furniture around to dust behind it. Trust me, you will literally feel the "ch'i" begin to swirl about you as positive energy is released throughout your surroundings.

It may seem illogical and inexplicable to rigid Western minds that good fortune can become ours by hanging mirrors or positioning our bed and desk in a certain way. But it can't hurt to be curious and experimental. After all, if we don't seek, we'll never find.

MAY 13

Honoring the Great Mother

Mothering myself has become a way of listening to my deepest needs, and of responding to them while I respond to my inner child.
—MELINDA BURNS

There's a great flurry of activity downstairs this morning, which I am forbidden to observe. "Big doings going on . . . I can't possibly tell," my husband whispers as he closes our bedroom door with a collaborator's grin. I can hear the clanging of pots and pans, drawers being opened and closed, mixers whirling. Now it sounds as though a breakfast tray is being prepared as the clattering of my best china reverberates through the house. I don't normally eat breakfast. But I will today. As I write, it's Mother's Day.

Later, delicious, daughter-made strawberry muffins, buttery golden, warm from the oven, miraculously appear. I am amazed, proud, perplexed, teary, profoundly grateful. Who is this remarkable young woman with the beautiful, beaming smile bearing gifts from the heart to nourish my body and soul? I believe there has been some spiritual intervention at work here because I have never made strawberry muffins in my life and have no idea how Katie divined the recipe. It's a perfect moment to quietly meditate on the cosmic Great Mother who can inspire us all; the divine, feminine Spirit of nurturance known as The Goddess, so revered in ancient times and being rediscovered by women today.

Many women I know share a seldom-expressed yearning to be comforted. To be mothered. This voracious need is deep, palpable—and often unrequited. Instead, we are the ones who usually provide comfort, caught between the pressing needs of our children, our elderly parents, our partners, our friends, even our colleagues.

Though we are grown, we never outgrow the need for someone special to hold us close, stroke our hair, tuck us into bed, and reassure us that tomorrow all will be well. Perhaps we need to reacquaint ourselves consciously with the maternal and deeply comforting dimension of Divinity in order to learn how to mother ourselves. The best way to start is to create— as an act of worship—a comfortable home that protects, nurtures, and sustains all who seek refuge within its walls.

Gloria Steinem has written movingly of the need to reparent herself after she began exploring, in midlife, the issue of self-esteem. Because her parents divorced when she was ten and her mother suffered from a debilitating depression, the legendary editor of *Ms.* magazine assumed the role of family caregiver. Decades later, as a leader of the feminist movement, she organized, traveled, lectured, campaigned, and successfully raised money for causes, but she didn't know how to take care of herself—emotionally, psychologically, physically—even though she had spent her life taking care of others. Nowhere was this truth more apparent than in her home. She reveals in her book *Revolution from Within: A Book of Self-Esteem* that her apartment was little more than "a closet where I changed clothes and dumped papers into cardboard boxes." Gradually she came to the belated awareness that one's home was "a symbol of the self" and in her fifties created and began to enjoy her first real home.

Today, as you walk through your own home, think about ways that you can start to mother yourself—every day, not just once a year—in small but tangible ways. There should be comfortable places from the living room to the bedroom that invite you to sit, sleep, relax, and reflect. There should be small indulgences from the kitchen to the bathroom that pamper and please. There should be sources of beauty throughout that inspire, order that restores, and the quiet grace of simplicity that soothes. The poet Ntozake Shange writes, "i found god in myself & i loved her/i loved her fiercely." There is no more beautiful way of honoring the love of the feminine divinity waiting to mother us than by celebrating the temple where her Spirit dwells on earth.

MAY 14

A Sense of Charm

Why do we love certain houses, and why do they seem to love us? It is the warmth of our individual hearts reflected in our surroundings.

—T. H. ROBSJOHN-GIBBINGS

The minute we walk into a home, we know whether or not it has charm. There's a coziness that attracts us with cheerful hospitality. The warm resonance of a charming room beckons us to sink into comfort to our heart's content. Simple beauty delights. Serenity, harmony, and order soothe. Touches of whimsy amuse. Personal memory reacquaints the present with the past. All's right with the world in such an engaging and inviting home. Think of the homey settings in the wonderful three-hanky movies of the 1940s, such as *The Best Years of Our Lives* or *The Enchanted Cottage*. In the latter, a handsome, battle-scarred veteran falls in love with a plain servant girl, and charm plays Cupid by casting an intimate spell through lovely surroundings that transform two lonely lives. "If you have it," the English playwright Sir James M. Barrie wrote about charm in 1907, "you don't need to have anything else; and if you don't have it, it doesn't much matter what else you have."

Money can purchase beautiful furnishings and decorative accessories, but it cannot ensure that charm abides with us. I believe this is because charm seems to be a quality of the soul that cannot be bought or sold. But charm can be channeled from Creative Spirit. It is accessed through our authenticity, expressed in our personal flair. "Beauty doesn't lie in the expenditure of much money, but in the artistic disposition of little," says a reassuring article entitled "The Charm of the Unexpected" published in the August 1917 issue of *The Mother's Magazine* during World War I, when making do with less was a necessity. Today, realize that "the desire to make the home dearer and sweeter to those who live in it" is still the enduring secret of endowing our homes with charm.

Progress, Not Perfection

Perfectionism is self-abuse of the highest order.
—ANNE WILSON SCHAEF

It was a beautiful Sunday afternoon in May—sunny and warm with a refreshing breeze. Just perfect. The kind of day you dream about in the depths of winter. That morning my daughter and I had enjoyed a pleasant outing at the farmers' market where we purchased baby lettuces, basil, tomato plants, nasturtiums, and marigolds. The week before we had successfully searched for a lovely terra-cotta urn in which to plant a French salad *potager*. I had discovered this marvelous idea for a container garden in a glossy lifestyle magazine article and thought it sounded like fun. So did Katie. We plotted, planned, and planted with great enthusiasm and pleasure.

When we had finished planting, we had trouble getting some loose, wet potting soil off the sides of the potager. I used a sponge and smeared it with mud; Katie doused it with a watering can, getting better results, but it still wasn't picture-perfect. I'm embarrassed to tell you how long we fussed with perfection but finally, I'd had enough. "Okay, we're done. It's beautiful."

"But it doesn't look like hers," an exasperated voice whined.

"No, it doesn't. It looks like ours. Ours is great. Fine. *Close enough.*"

"But hers is perfect. Everything she does is perfect. I want ours to be perfect, too," a determined young lady of eleven fumed in frustration.

Time out. Serenity 102: Progress, Not Perfection. First of all, I explained, the glamorous lifestyle gurus in the books, magazines, and television have full-time professionals working for them, including stylists— stylists who wave magic paintbrushes dipped in burnt sienna over mud smears on terra-cotta potagers before the flash pops or the tape rolls. "It's image, illusion, make-believe. It's a million-dollar industry. What we're seeing isn't always the real McCoy. Now this," I pointed out with satisfaction, "is real, mud and all. It's Real and it's wonderful."

Eventually I convinced my skeptic to wait and see (Mother Nature did not fail me, and spring showers became our stylist). We spent the rest of the afternoon happily turning over earth as hard as granite for an old-fashioned fragrant cottage garden with English roses, lavender, hollyhocks, and delphiniums. Nearby the cats were delirious over the newly-installed catnip plot.

How much of our lives is frittered away—spoiled, spent, or sullied—by our neurotic insistence on perfection? Perhaps our parents expected us to live up to a standard they knew they themselves could never achieve. Certainly they wanted more for us. But more of what? Misery? Haven't you had enough? Today, accept that perfection is unattainable. In real life we should strive to be our best—not the world's. Still, there will always be a misspelled word, a stain on the carpet, a terra-cotta potager with streaks of mud.

Perfect women do not manifest on this plane of existence. Celebrities who sell perfection are more to be pitied than censured, envied, or emulated. Why? Because, despite their fame and bank accounts, they rarely know a moment's peace; the whole world is watching, waiting for a misstep.

Thank you, no. I'll pass. Won't you? Perfection leaves so little room for improvement. So little space for acceptance—or joy. On the path we have chosen, progress is the simple pleasure to be savored. Daily. Of course, perfect *moments* are sure to be ours, such as spending a sunny afternoon in May gardening with a daughter. Life and potagers don't have to be perfect to be pleasing.

MAY 16

Clearing Out What Isn't Useful or Beautiful

Have nothing in your homes that you do not know to be useful and believe to be beautiful.

—WILLIAM MORRIS

In England during the 1880s, a breath of fresh air blew through stuffy Victorian parlors when poet, craftsman, and designer William Morris founded the influential Arts and Crafts movement. Morris and his associates crusaded against the cheap and shoddy furniture and decorative accessories that were then being mass-produced and crammed into middle-class homes in a frenzy of excess.

In particular, Morris urged Victorians to rid themselves of the ugly, the useless, and the uncomfortable in favor of simple and "honest" furnishings. The Irish poet W. B. Yeats termed Morris's call for the aesthetic alchemy of beauty and function in the home "the long-waited-for deliverance of the decorative arts."

On the Simple Abundance path, our authentic decorative deliverance arrives when we begin to appreciate and put to use the Morris rule—ridding ourselves of anything we do not believe to be beautiful or useful—as we restore order to our homes and simplify our lives.

Begin this week with a pad and pen. Browse through the rooms of your home meditatively. Let the Divine spirits of simplicity, order, harmony, and beauty accompany you. Really look at your surroundings—your furniture and decorative accessories. Give thanks for your home exactly as it exists today. Now begin the inquiry. Ask each possession, are you beautiful? Useful? Is it time for you to move on? You will undoubtedly come to an object that is neither beautiful nor useful but has sentimental qualities. Create a new category (sorry, Mr. Morris) on your clearing list. But use restraint. Does it really tug at your heartstrings? Would you mourn if it disappeared? Be truthful. No one is privy to this exercise except your authentic self and she's trying to tell you something. Listen. (If it tugs at someone else's heartstrings send it to his or her room.) Write all this information down. Always allow yourself time to think on paper before you act.

The next step in the process is to make a commitment *in writing*, on your calendar to do one room a month. On the appointed day, plan to spend a few hours (as you did when you weeded out your wardrobe, remember?). Be sure you have plenty of boxes available. Now, start to sort: if it's not beautiful, useful, or sentimental, it goes. One pile is for items to give away to thrift shop charities—items such as great Aunt Gladys's vase with the nymphs or the Japanese sake set you received as a wedding present and hated on sight. The other pile is for perfectly good objects of previous infatuations that no longer make your heart beat faster. This pile can be recycled as future gifts.

There is an ancient metaphysical law that says if we desire more abundance in our lives we must create a vacuum to allow ourselves to receive the good we seek. How can more good come into our lives if there is no room for it? The way we create the vacuum is by giving away what we no longer need or desire but what can serve others.

We all change as we grow (that's how we know we're growing). This includes our personal style. If you no longer love your Fiesta cereal bowls and now want to collect Blue Willow, or if the Limoges luncheon plates left you by your grandmother don't really suit your casual country style of entertaining, give them away. It is a wonderfully abundant but simple pleasure to bring a friend a hostess gift of homemade banana bread beautifully wrapped up on a platter that never really suited you but is one that she's admired.

Deciding to simplify our lives and bring order to our homes by sending on the objects we no longer love to new, happier incarnations with people who will genuinely appreciate them is the way to open ourselves up to receiving an abundance that will perfectly suit us.

The Ruskin Spring Ritual of Restoration

In order that people may be happy in their work, these three things are needed: They must be fit for it. They must not do too much of it. And they must have a sense of success in it.

—JOHN RUSKIN

The sun is shining, the windows are streaked, the white lace curtains seem more than just a tad dingy. Could this house need a spring cleaning? But the windows and curtains can wait because the sofa and a new book beckon.

So do the junk drawers. You know, those black holes lurking beneath the tidy surfaces harboring clutter and God only knows what else. Lost objects. Found objects. Objects somebody in the family might use in another lifetime. Or the unrecognizable. You name it, it's in there.

Now I don't know about you, but I had (have—life ebbs and flows around here) junk drawers in every room of my house. It got so bad that I never voluntarily opened them except to throw in another item with my eyes shut. I am addicted to junk drawers. But as I've been learning the lessons of Simple Abundance, I have faced my compulsion. I was becoming orderly on the surface, but seething underneath was absolute domestic anarchy. I knew it. My authentic self knew it. So did my husband and daughter. It made me very uncomfortable. "To be buried in lava and not turn a hair, it is then a man shows what stuff he is made of," Samuel Beckett wrote in *Malone Dies*. For grown women the same challenge comes when we rally enough courage to face up to clearing out the junk drawers. Take a deep breath. I'll hold your hand.

It's best to approach clearing out the clutter of a lifetime in manageable increments, following John Ruskin's sage advice. Don't do too much of it at once; that way, you can feel successful about your efforts. Each month, tackle just one room or storage space in your home. Then break the room down: the first week, clean out the junk drawers, then the closets, then any other specific storage areas such as under the beds, the linen closet, the medicine chest, the sewing basket. Above all, don't attempt to do too much at once or you'll sabotage yourself. The family room game closet hasn't been organized in five years? Don't worry, it can wait another two months or however long it takes you to get to it. Carefully consider the areas of your home that are causing you the most frustration today and then prioritize them in order of annoyance.

Although I believe very firmly in sharing work around our home, I have come to the reluctant conclusion that clearing out clutter has to be a solitary occupation. *You must do this alone.* I cannot stress this point enough.

Spouses or partners and children will never let you throw anything away. "Oh, that's where *that* was," they will say picking up virtually every object you're trying to throw out (including the fossilized Silly Putty), then leaving the stuff somewhere else in the house for you to trip over. Forget it. If they've lived without it for five or ten years, they can do without it forever. Trust me, you must clear away clutter alone or you will lose your mind in the attempt.

One last clutter clearing caveat: what to do with the "I don't know what this is and I don't know where it belongs" box. If any item can't be identified by a member of the family, it gets tossed. Here is the only aspect of clearing out where I invite consultation. But remember, you must be ruthless. When in doubt, throw it away. You don't need it. You don't want it. You forgot you even had it, so don't keep it. No, it will not come in handy someday. Furthermore, you do not, under any circumstance, want the contents of your junk drawers ending up being thrown into "junk boxes" (a very real possibility for chronic hoarders) which will then only disappear down to that subterranean landfill known in the common vernacular as the basement. But that is, as they say, another story for another day.

Every cleared junk drawer, each closet, each successful attempt at organizing only reinforces your feelings of taking back control of your life. I had never really considered how being disorganized beneath the surface had weighed upon my mind. But once I cleared away the clutter, I felt a wonderful sense of renewal, joy, and inner peace. Here was the essence of Simple Abundance and it had cost me only time (to plan), courage (to show up for work), and creative energy (to do it).

Don't be surprised if one fine spring day you suddenly feel the urge to wash the curtains and clean the windows. The Light is beautiful and you can see clearly now.

MAY 18

Simplify, Simplify, Simplify

Out of clutter, find simplicity.

—ALBERT EINSTEIN

After a morning spent sifting and sorting through the beautiful, the useful, and the useless, I glanced around our living room floor. It resembled an archaeological dig with small stacks of artifacts all separated according to their domestic categories. I wondered what a late-twentieth-century anthropologist considering the juxtaposition of junk and precious mementos (such as my daughter's last pacifier) would tell the world about the woman whose life was now reduced to a series of neat and pleasing bundles.

Soon it became time to return everything to where it belonged. This, believe it or not, was a source of great contentment. As I wandered through the rooms of the house I began to search for the common thread in the lives of the world's great spiritual teachers and traditions: Jesus Christ, Mohammed, Buddha, Lao-Tzu, The Hebrew prophets, The Moslem Sufis, The Catholic saints, The Hindu rishis, The Shakers, The Quakers, The Amish. *None of them had junk drawers.* That's because all embraced simplicity. Spirituality, simplicity, and serenity seem to be a sacred trinity; three divine qualities of the orderly soul. Henry David Thoreau believed "our life is frittered away by detail." I disagree. I think our lives are frittered away by lack of focus. But how can we focus our attention on what's truly important when we're half-crazed because we can never find anything? However, Thoreau's remedy for the frittering frets still works today: "Simplify, simplify, simplify."

This week, consider that with a little bit of courage and creativity you can find the breathing space you crave. You may think you're only clearing clutter from a junk drawer or juggling commitments to find a few hours to get your house in order. But your soul knows better.

MAY 19

Order Within

What a gift of grace to be able to take the chaos from within and from it create some semblance of order.

—KATHERINE PATERSON

While spring is the traditional season for bringing order to our homes, it is also the perfect opportunity for seeking order within. "Spring cleaning can also be psychological, a time-out to confront the emotional clutter that has accumulated in your mental closet," writer Abigail Trafford recommends. "It's a pause for introspection—a midcourse correction for ordinary people in ordinarily stressful lives."

One way to begin seeking order within is to come to grips with what drives you crazy but what you've been too distracted to do anything about. Run a video of your typical day through your mind and view the woman hanging on at the end of her rope with compassion. What makes you cringe? It could be anything from rushing off to work convinced that you've forgotten something you need for the day, to never finding anything to wear that's unwrinkled, to discovering as you're cooking dinner that you're out of a necessary ingredient. All these situations cry out for order, just as your fragmented soul does.

There is a better way to live. It begins when we establish order within so that order will become a visible reality in our daily round. Start seeking order within by book-ending your day with reflection first thing in the morning and last thing at night. This quietude will remind you that you *can* make the choice every morning to live in the world but not be caught up in the frenzy of it, especially a frenzy of your own devising. Your bookends can be as little as fifteen minutes long. I know I've suggested private interludes before (and will continue doing so). You just don't think you have the time. You may not today. But snatch time tomorrow. Start to allow yourself a quarter of an hour before anyone else is up and after everyone else is settled in.

What to do when you first awaken or before drifting off to sleep? Quiet your mind, lift up your heart, muse, mull over, make discoveries. Consider, conceive, create, connect, *concede that it all starts within*. Pray, read the Scriptures, sacred poetry, or a meditation from an inspirational book. Think about the day ahead and how it might unfold more smoothly. Invoke Divine Order, asking Spirit to take charge of your life today and every day. Visualize yourself at the end of a happy, stress-free, productive day, relaxing and enjoying the well-deserved leisure of the evening. Stroll into the backyard garden, onto a balcony, sit on the front porch or front stoop with a cup of coffee and wait for the sun to rise. Observe how gently but surely the natural world renews itself daily. You may not believe this, but Mother Time does not rush; seven o'clock does not tell six o'clock, "Get a move on, there are places to go, people to see, faxes to send!"

If you have children, have to commute ninety minutes to work, or need to reach European clients on the telephone (as do three very good friends of mine), what I am suggesting probably seems impossible, recommended by a woman who obviously hasn't a clue as to how you really live. Book-ending your day by nurturing your Spirit means rousing your body earlier when you're so exhausted from yesterday that you can barely crawl out of bed, or spending an extra moment with yourself at night when you're ready to fall asleep like a stone. Here's what I do many mornings and evenings: a half-hour before I have to rise and just before I go to sleep, I lie snuggled in bed and listen in the dark to Gregorian chants—the sublime, ancient Latin invocations sung by Benedictine monks for the last 1,500 years. It's a pity I don't understand every word the monks are singing but it doesn't really matter. All I know is that the soft, rhythmic chants reassure and soothe me on a very deep level. Sometimes I pray with the monks, other times I like to imagine they are praying *for me*. It's a gentle, centering, and comforting reminder that another, truer Reality exists, something I'm apt to forget in the middle of a busy day—as you probably are, too. Today, seek order within, so that Divine Order may be manifest outwardly in your daily round.

MAY 20

The Art of Puttering

Puttering is really a time to be alone, to dream and to get in touch with yourself. . . . To putter is to discover.

—ALEXANDRA STODDARD

In my mind there is a significant distinction between straightening, cleaning, and "puttering." The first two homecaring tasks are the underpinnings, providing the order necessary for ritual. Puttering is the intersection of introspection and inspiration. It's not on our "to-do" list, therefore it charms, centers, and cajoles stressed spirits. But I can't begin to enjoy rearranging personal mementos or a beautiful vase of flowers with clutter all around me and cobwebs in the corners. (Surely I'm not the only woman in the world who has ever glanced up at a corner of her living room and found a masterpiece worthy of *Charlotte's Web*?) So I usually set aside late Saturday afternoon for puttering after the house is a fresh canvas inviting me to create.

Unlike cleaning, which can be a group activity, puttering is a solitary pursuit, to be approached with an unhurried pace for maximum metaphysical benefits. The essence of puttering is rearranging, although I also consider polishing silver, washing china and crystal, displaying flowers, even moving furniture to be part of the puttering genus. Part of the pleasure of puttering is free association. Think of puttering as a domestic Rorschach test. Instead of interpreting inkblots, we muse on the hidden meaning of personal possessions until we flow on to dreams, choices, risks, pleasures, authentic preferences. You only think you're rearranging favorite things on a mantel, bookcase, or tabletop when you're really creating a fresh interior lifescape. "Creative puttering" is actually one of my favorite things to do at home," writer and interior designer Alexandra Stoddard reveals. "It helps us to become aware of what's still important to us, what continues to have meaning. This quiet, private act can . . . bring the different aspects of your life into sharp focus—and identify your needs."

Music plays an important part in my puttering ritual. I love to listen to music while homecaring, and my selections, depending on mood and task, range from Bach to Broadway. But for the most introspective puttering, I'll choose a movie sound track, such as *Out of Africa*. As I listen to John Barry's haunting score while rearranging family pictures or my small collection of Irish cut glass, or while replacing winter's dried boughs with fresh flowers, I can't help thinking of Isak Dinesen packing up her silver, crystal goblets, and Limoges china when she emigrated to Africa from Denmark just before World War I. She could not imagine living anywhere without her cherished personal possessions around her. Judith Thurman tells us, in *Isak Dinesen: The Life of a Storyteller*, that "the ambition [was] to make her home an oasis of civilization." This is my heart's ambition as well, even if my wilderness is a small city in Maryland and not the plains of Kenya.

Whether your home is in the city, country, or suburbia, each in its own way offers fertile ground upon which to sow your dreams. Puttering scatters the seeds. In due time we shall reap an abundant harvest of contentment.

MAY 21

A Nest of Comforts

Ah! There's nothing like staying home for real comfort.
—JANE AUSTEN

Jane Austen's novels are known for their witty, ironic, and perceptive slices of eighteenth-century English family life. But they also reveal, between the lines, their author's love of cozy "nest[s] of comforts." Miss Austen, who wrote at a little desk drawn close to her hearth, describes such a haven in her novel *Mansfield Park*, in which her heroine, Fanny Price, can retreat "after anything unpleasant . . . and find immediate consolation in some pursuit, or some train of thought. Her plants, her books . . . her writing desk, and her works of charity and ingenuity, were all within her reach . . . she could scarcely see an object in the room which had not an interesting remembrance connected with it."

No matter what our decorating style—realized or aspired to—the essential spiritual grace our homes should possess is the solace of comfort. As we discover and express our authenticity through our surroundings, comfort becomes our first priority. After I began the Simple Abundance path, it shocked me to discover that there were very few places around my home where I felt truly comfortable. The search for authenticity is like living on a fault line; you never know when the earth is going to move beneath your feet. One day I realized that I spent much of my free time reading in my bedroom, unintentionally away from my husband and daughter, not because of a need for privacy, but because I didn't have a comfortable chair to snuggle into in the living room. My husband had his place on the sofa, my daughter claimed the love seat, while I often ended up in the bedroom by default, when I would have much preferred to be sharing time with them. When I became aware of this, we had a family discussion about how to make ourselves feel more comfortable at home. Now we're saving while patiently searching for what we need to create a nest of comfort that will cradle all our bodies and souls.

Today, think about your own nest. Is it so cozy that you never want to leave? It should be. Do you have the comforts that you crave? Do you even know what they are? When was the last time you gave *your comfort* the thought it richly deserves? Today, make a wish list: soft, snug places to sit; plump pillows to support or encourage you to take a nap; a place to put your feet up; proper reading lamps; plenty of bookcases; something always on hand that's interesting, illuminating, or irresistible to read; places to display favorite things; convenient tables for refreshments; a well-organized and well-stocked desk from which to run your life; as decent a sound system as you can afford and a personal music collection that reflects your many moods; a good coffeemaker, a pretty teapot or juice squeezer; plants and flowers to delight; backyard furniture that beckons you to linger and a pretty garden or terrace to linger in. Everyone's list will be different. Take the time to figure out what you need. Think about rooms in which you have felt instantly at home throughout your life, even if they weren't yours. What appealed to you and made you want to stay? Comfort was probably the key. Today, consider what you need to create a personal nest that comforts body and soul.

MAY 22

The Home of Your Dreams

If I were asked to name the chief benefit of the house, I should say:
the house shelters daydreaming.

—GASTON BACHELARD

Did you ever see the witty and winsome 1948 movie classic, *Mr. Blandings Builds His Dream House*, starring Cary Grant and Myrna Loy? This charming cautionary tale is about a successful New York advertising executive and his family, who live in a cramped city apartment and long for their own home in the suburbs. They embark on an expensive adventure to build the perfect rose-covered cottage in Connecticut. Each day the modest house grows larger and so do their bills. It's a saga anyone who has ever bought a house knows only too well. But at the end of all the Blandings' tribulations their dream comes true, even if their nerves are frayed and their bank account is overdrawn. I hope they lived happily ever after; it turned out to be a wonderful house.

It takes literally years to birth a dream, whether it's a family, a career, a home, or a lifestyle. Dreams also extract a price. An ancient proverb puts it this way: "Take what you want, says the good God, but be prepared to pay for it." Dreams cost money, sweat, frustration, tears, courage, choices, perseverance, and extraordinary patience. But birthing a dream requires one more thing. Love. Only love can transform a houseful of needy, self-centered individuals into a loving, close-knit family, a passion into a livelihood, or a mere dwelling into a home that perfectly expresses your authenticity.

Even when money is not a consideration, love and time are still necessary to turn a house into a home. Samuel Clemens moved into his dream house with his beloved wife Livy and their three daughters in 1874. It was an imposing, nineteen-room, red-brick Gothic Victorian mansion in Hartford, Connecticut. Over the next thirty-five years Mr. Clemens devotedly decorated, renovated, and lavished so much expense on his house that his passion drove him into bankruptcy. (Which he resolved by writing books as "Mark Twain.") Because of all the love he and his family bestowed on their home, "it had a heart and a soul, and eyes to see with; and approvals and solicitudes and deep sympathies; it was of us, and we were in its confidence and lived in its grace and in the peace of its benedictions. We never came home from an absence that its face did not light up and speak out in eloquent welcome—and we could not enter it unmoved."

Is there a woman here who doesn't long to live in such a home? A home that embraces, nurtures, sustains, and inspires? Still, many of us think this will only happen when we've got the money to move someplace else. Surely, it can't happen here. I mean, just look at this place! But let's take another look. "I dwell in possibility," Emily Dickinson confided. We can, too. Don't look at the problems. Search for the possibilities. It doesn't matter where you live at this moment. You may be in a trailer, an apartment, or a house. You may even be rooming in a motel. It may not be your dream but it does shelter your dreams. Those dreams can transform it into the home for which you long. Love knows how to paint, refinish, plaster, wallpaper, stencil, plant, sew, and build, even on a budget. Love knows that whatever you lack in your checking account can be made up by investing time, creative energy, and emotion. We need to learn Love's decorating secrets.

But before we pick up a hammer, a paintbrush, or the real estate ads, we need to daydream. Walk through the different rooms where you eat, sleep, and live. Bless the walls, the roof, the windows, and the foundation. Give thanks as you sift and sort, simplify, and bring order to the home you have. Realize that the home of your dreams dwells within. You must find it in the secret sanctuary of your heart today before you can cross the threshold of tomorrow.

Nurturing Your Authentic Flair

An interior is the natural projection of the soul.
— Coco Chanel

Many of us think of discovering our authentic decorating style as a destination when really it's a point of departure. I am—as I write—completely reconsidering my *entire* house. Not to move from, but to continue to live in and love. How it works, how it looks, who it looks like. Today it certainly doesn't look like anyone I recognize.

As you awaken to your authenticity, you may notice that bare walls, windows, and floors beckon invitingly like a new lover, while the stuff you've accumulated over a lifetime doesn't seem to even notice that you're in the room. It would be fun to eat dinner tonight with my husband and daughter on a wooden crate by candlelight eagerly awaiting a new interior—the authentic projection of my soul—to be delivered tomorrow morning. However, my bank account, probably like yours, won't permit this fantasy and so I have to proceed slowly. We need to view this as an opportunity instead of a stumbling block. Our real life budgets may delay the process longer than our conscious minds might wish—especially when flipping through glossy magazines—but it's the perfect pace to nurture our authentic flair.

To be honest with you, this morning I'm not exactly sure of how I want to express myself through my surroundings. Are you? I thought I knew. I've loved some things passionately that have brought me great pleasure for twenty-five years. But I've also lived with other things I hated so intensely I became psychically numb to their presence. The Simple Abundance path is about transformation. But transformation cannot occur without transition. This is a transitional period of liminality when things are barely perceptible—a personal rite of passage, from sleepwalking to awakening. The process is the reality and it cannot be rushed.

So we learn to wait patiently. To consider. Save. Reflect. Simplify. Embrace order. Get ready. Experiment. Observe. Embark on creative window-shopping excursions to antique and craft shows, auctions, renovator supply companies, thrift stores, flea markets, yard, tag, and estate sales, museums, interior design expositions, elegant decorative accessory shops, furniture showrooms, museums, and galleries. If you see something you like, ask if there is to be a sale in the near future. Take detailed notes. See how other people live or have lived by taking jaunts to decorator showcases, historic homes, and all the wonderful house-and-garden tours that take place in the spring. Read books, clip magazines and catalogs. Continue to prime the well with visual images, collecting everything that you can on paper, from fabulous table settings to beautiful curtain treatments.

Mary Emmerling—a woman I absolutely love, with an incredible authentic style that's grounded in common sense—has a wonderful suggestion for creating a personalized decorating notebook to help us keep track of our meditative musings. She uses a zippered, canvas, looseleaf notebook (seven by nine inches) with plenty of pockets for such tools as a tape measure, scissors, pens, pencils, paper clips, sharpener, and calculator. She gives each room a section of its own, complete with a wish list, photographs charting changes, a floor plan, and an envelope for paint chips, fabric swatches, and receipts. In the back of the book she keeps a year's calendar noting sales and special events and a personalized resource guide with the names and phone numbers of stores, showrooms, dealers, contractors, and material suppliers. It's a dream archive that she can carry around with her so that she can catch inspiration as it floats by instead of letting it dissolve into the ether.

If you follow some of these suggestions, you'll be well on your way to developing and nurturing your authentic flair. Instead of being frustrated, you'll be grateful that you've been given the extraordinary gift of time—time to know what you love so you can love how you live.

MAY 24

The Fullness of Nothing

Since we cannot change reality, let us change the eyes which see reality.

—NIKOS KAZANTZAKIS

My husband came home from work last night and appeared puzzled. "Why's the mantel bare? And where are all the pictures?" As I poured each of us a glass of wine, I told him I was experimenting with positive and negative space.

"Positive and negative what?"

"Space, Dad," the artist in the family explained, looking up from her homework which was spread across the dining room table. "Artists use it to achieve harmony in their work."

"So do the Japanese . . ." I added.

"Fine—artists, Japanese, whatever—but what does it mean and how does it explain where everything's gone?"

Never assume that the people in your life, especially those closest to you, won't innocently meddle in your internal affairs while you're on the path to authenticity. Always remember, the predictable woman they know is more familiar than the woman they don't know, even if she's the Real you.

When an artist prepares to draw or paint, she carefully considers the balance between both "positive shapes" and "negative spaces." Positive shapes are the instantly recognizable objects that are rendered on paper or canvas, such as a bowl of fruit in a still life. The negative spaces surround the objects and define them with a boundary. As many artists will tell you, it is far easier to draw the negative spaces between the positive shapes before anything else. That's because, to the eye trained to see beauty, nothing is invisible. What looks empty to the rest of us appears to the artist's eye as full, a complete mystery in its own right. The space surrounding the bowl of fruit is as important as the bowl itself if Wholeness is to emerge.

In the Japanese culture, the negative spaces in art, philosophy, religion, design, business, and life are not thought of as empty but rather as "full of nothing." Richard Tanner Pascale explains in *Zen and the Art of Management* that the empty spaces, or the "shroud of the unknown surrounding certain events," is referred to in Japanese as *ma*, a word for which there is no English translation. To the Western mind this concept is a little hard to grasp. But to the Oriental mind, the empty space is pregnant with possibility, shrouded by the unknown until the time is right for it to be revealed. As the enigmatic Irish playwright Samuel Beckett (who was more Zen than Celtic) put it, "Nothing is more real than nothing."

Which explains why my mantel is bare at this moment. Gradually, through Simple Abundance, I have discovered that I've outgrown the objects that lived there for years, and my authentic self has yet to reveal what should now take their place, if anything. So, at least for a little while, I am enjoying the fullness of nothing. It's difficult for many of us to accept that emptiness—in life or in a living room—can have a positive influence. I think we need to learn how to tolerate more empty spaces. We need either to become more comfortable with *waiting* to fill what's empty with what's authentic or become just willing to accept the exquisite fullness of nothing. Life's landscape becomes a lot more interesting when we realize there's an entire dimension we've never considered before simply because we couldn't see it.

There is an uncluttered elegance to my bare mantel, a refreshing restraint in the room, that feels new and inviting. What I'm inviting is my authenticity to express itself through my surroundings, maybe one object at a time. Today you might like to create some empty spaces in your home to jump-start your ability to see things in a new light. Move some furniture out of a room. Take pictures off a wall. Clear off tabletops. Experience the fullness of nothing for a week. Then pretend you have just moved into a new home. Don't be surprised if the woman you are becoming reveals that she needs more space in which to grow.

Passion: The Authentic Muse

What is passion? It is surely the becoming of a person.

—JOHN BOORMAN

Many women long to live passionate lives, to be swept away—but at a safe distance and in small doses. That's why we are drawn to juicy novels, three-hanky movies, soap operas, platonic flirtations, and personality journalism that glorifies lives larger than our own. Passion, after all, means the abandonment of reason in the reckless pursuit of pleasure: rushing off with an Argentine polo-playing paramour instead of picking up the afternoon car pool.

Passion is wild, chaotic, unpredictable. Permissive. Excessive. Obsessive. Glenn Close in *Fatal Attraction*. Passionate women can't help but exult in their emotions, revel in their desires, howl at the moon, act out their fantasies, boil a pet rabbit.

The rest of us have real life responsibilities that leave little room (or so we think) for giving in to passionate impulses: runny noses to wipe, dogs to walk, FedEx pickup deadlines to meet, Brownie snacks to prepare, sales conferences to attend, orthodontist appointments to make, summer camp forms to fill out, trains to catch, supper to put on the table. There goes the day. There goes a life, and not with a bang, but a whimper and a whine.

What we don't realize is that passion is the muse of authenticity. It's the primordial, pulsating energy that infuses all of life, the numinous presence made known with every beat of our hearts. Passion does not reveal herself only in clandestine, romantic, bodice-ripping clichés. Passion's nature is also cloaked in the deep, subtle, quiet, and committed: nursing a baby, planting a rose garden, preparing a special meal, caring for a loved one who is ill, remembering a friend's birthday, persevering in a dream. Every day offers us another opportunity to live passionate lives rather than passive ones, if we will bear witness to passion's immutable presence in the prosaic. If we will stop denying ourselves pleasure. If, as James Joyce's heroine Molly Bloom whispered, we can only learn to say ". . . and yes I said yes I will Yes."

Passion is holy—a profound Mystery that transcends and transforms through rapture. We need to accept that a sacred fire burns within, whether we're comfortable with this truth or not. Passion is part of Real Life's package because we were created by Love, for Love, to Love. If we do not give outward expression to our passions, we will experience self-immolation — the spontaneous combustion of our souls.

Did you know that both the Koran, the sacred book of Islam, and the Jewish Talmud teach that we will be called to account for every permissible pleasure life offered us but which we refused to enjoy while on earth? Dorothy L. Sayers, the deeply spiritual English writer, believed, "The only sin passion can commit is to be joyless."

Go now. Depart in peace and sin no more.

MAY 26

Let Passion Be Your Decorator

Passion is what you need to be good, an unforgiving passion.
—David Easton

One of my favorite pastimes is reading novels that celebrate domestic delights. The pages of Kathleen Norris, Laurie Colwin, and Rosamund Pilcher reveal, not only passionate love affairs, but delectable descriptions of food and furnishings that capture my imagination even more than the plots. Another favorite literary domestic is Daphne du Maurier. Here is her rendering of the first Mrs. de Winter's study from her novel *Rebecca*: "This was a woman's room, graceful, fragile, the room of someone who had chosen every particle of furniture with great care, so that each chair, each vase, each small infinitesimal thing should be in harmony with one another and with her own personality. It was as though she who had arranged this room had said: 'This I will have, and this, and this,' taking piece by piece from the treasures in Manderley each object that pleased her best, ignoring the second-rate, the mediocre, laying her hand with sure and certain instinct only upon the best."

Achieving authentic harmony through our surroundings—laying our hands with sure and certain instinct on that which best expresses our sense of self—begins to occur as order is gradually restored to our lives and our homes. But even if you have not yet found the time to clear closets and drawers of clutter, or sift and sort through your belongings and decided what is beautiful, useful, or sentimental, don't be discouraged. Important inner work is taking place that will soon become visible.

Probably because I am a writer, I think discovering your authentic decorating style is very similar to the creative stages of writing a book. A book may look inanimate, but like a home, it lives, breathes, and expresses your being.

As a writer, the gleam of inspiration comes first; your decorating discoveries might begin with a picture of a living room that makes you sigh.

To flesh out the initial idea, I then need to do research; that's what you're doing on your creative excursions and with your decorating archive. Next, I need an outline; you would develop a plan or budget. At this point, I'm usually overwhelmed by the enormity of the project; you may be, too. For me, this feeling only subsides after I plunge in and start to write my rough draft; perhaps you're now pulling up the old carpet to refinish your floors, or you've begun stripping wallpaper or painting. Usually after I've finished the rough draft, there's an initial sigh of relief followed by another wave of panic. (Does this really work?) However, once I step back and begin to edit, a sense of calm is restored. Ideas come fast as the book—or the room— begins to take shape. Now the real fun starts: revising. This is the stage in which you make the room come alive with personal flourishes, adding the decorative details and accessories that have special meaning. I love the flourish of revising because you get to fix what doesn't work, making what does work even better. But we're still not finished: the first draft is always followed by another and another, with more revising until my editor tells me it's time to stop.

However, when you're creating a visual memoir through your surroundings, it's a never-ending story. You don't have to stop. What's more, you really can't. You'll always be revealing a new aspect of your personality as you discover it. You'll constantly be editing, weeding out what you outgrow, making both subtle and significant decorating changes as the chapters of your life allow for, or demand, rewrites.

But whether we're writing a book or creating a home, we need to bring a sense of passion to our work. Let passion be your muse, the authentic decorator. Let her guide and teach you to trust your instincts. Aspire to live surrounded only by those things that you passionately love. Be patient: a magnum opus can take a lifetime to create.

The famous interior decorator Elsie de Wolfe admitted, "I can't paint. I can't write. I can't sing. But I can decorate and run a house, and light it, and heat it, and have it like a living thing . . ." With passion as your authentic decorator, every room in your home can tell a riveting tale about the extraordinary woman who graces it with her presence.

An Interior Vision Inventory

We shape our dwellings, and afterwards our dwellings shape us.
—WINSTON CHURCHILL

The fantasy is that you simply start with a color, a couch, or a pine cupboard that you absolutely adore. So far, so good. What next? Now you effortlessly pull the room together, expressing through your dazzling creative choices—the carpet, the curtains, the crockery, the coffee table—the woman who loves Art Deco or cozy English cottages.

But what if *today* you suddenly don't know what you want to hang over the couch, lay on the floor, or put on the shelves? What if the couch came from your husband's first marriage, the carpet from your mother, the coffee table from Goodwill? What if you know what you want, but have to choose between that pine cupboard and a much-needed new car?

Then it's time for an interior vision inventory. One of the benefits of sorting through your belongings and identifying what's beautiful, useful, or sentimental is that clarity emerges. You will probably be surprised by how much you already own that is simply waiting to be reconsidered, rearranged, reupholstered, refinished. Just don't be surprised to discover that even if what you live with is beautiful, it might no longer suit you.

A dear friend of mine collected kilim pillows with a passion for years. But one day it occurred to her that she hadn't been spending as much time in the living room as in the past, even though she'd invested lots of money and energy to decorate it and loved the look. She finally realized that the patterns were too busy to come home to after the rigors of a long day and that the dark colors, while dramatic, depressed her.

Torn between being practical—just letting the room stay the way it was—and discovering what truly pleased her now, she opted for pleasure. She not only wanted to bring the room to life, she needed to be able to live in it. Her new passion became peace of mind. The first step was to empty the room, leaving only the couches, which she recovered with plain white slipcovers. She painted the walls and bookcases white and eliminated the pillows. But since the pillows are still beautiful, she's storing them until another setting invites their presence. The only color in the room comes from her beloved books. Her new personal flourish is restraint. Now when she comes home she feels contented instead of uncomfortable, which, after all, is what authentic decorating should be about.

Decorating shouldn't be about how a room looks in a magazine as much as how you *feel* in that room. If you are to create rooms with an authentic view, self-exploration must come before paint chips and fabric swatches.

Personal flourishes can bridge the gap while we wait for our interior vision to find outward expression in our surroundings. Maybe you can't afford a new sofa just yet, but could afford new throw pillows to give it a lift. Maybe you could give a lamp a new look with a different shade, arrange flowers in a teapot instead of a vase, find a pretty porcelain cup to hold pens, position a picture on a small easel instead of a wall, hook a rug of your own design, take the doors off the kitchen cabinets, learn what you can live without.

Personal flourishes can be had for little or no money if you are willing to invest passion, perseverance, patience, and a fresh perspective.

MAY 28

By Love Possessed

Your possessions express your personality. Few things, including clothes, are more personal than your cherished ornaments. The pioneer women, who crossed a wild continent clutching their treasures to them, knew that a clock, a picture, a pair of candlesticks, meant home, even in the wilderness.

—GOOD HOUSEKEEPING, *August 1952*

In July 1846, Margaret Reed reluctantly left her beloved home in Springfield, Illinois, with her husband James, their four children, and her ailing mother and set off for California. Margaret had stubbornly resisted her husband's entreaties to move for months, begging him not to abandon the charmed life of comfort and culture they enjoyed. But her Victorian husband, who was a wealthy furniture manufacturer, sought even more wealth, as well as adventure, and in the end, his will prevailed.

Much of James Reed's success in persuading Margaret lay in his promise that she would travel in unsurpassed luxury and style, with all her prized personal possessions. He kept his word. Never before had a covered wagon been built like the Reeds' and never would one be built like it again. Two stories high, with a sleeping loft, it was outfitted with spring seats just like the best stagecoaches, an iron stove, velvet curtains, and her cherished organ. It was stocked with six months' supply of the best food and wine money could buy. As the wagon pulled into formation with the rest of the Donner Party to head west, it was difficult not to stare and gasp.

The tragic saga of the Donner Party is the most indelible tale of triumph and despair ever written in the history of the American West. Twenty-five hundred miles away from home and only two days from safety, thirty-one men, women, and children were stranded for an entire winter in the Sierra Nevada mountains by a succession of the worst blizzards on record. Out of provisions and starving, some members resorted to cannibalism in order to survive. Margaret and her children were not among them. She kept them all alive on snow, bark, and leather broth until James, who had left the group to ride on ahead to California seeking a rescue party, returned. The fact that her family did not perish—physically or spiritually—had absolutely nothing to do with the worldly goods she had counted on, for the wagon and all it carried had to be abandoned along the way because it was too heavy and cumbersome to travel through the mountains. The possessions that saved Margaret and those she loved were of Spirit—her wits, her faith, and her courage.

My daughter's godmother lives in Hollywood. In the terrible Los Angeles earthquake of 1994 she lost nearly all her personal possessions. She and her husband were not hurt, thank heavens, nor was their home structurally damaged, but she learned a valuable lesson about loss. So many things went at once: her home as she knew it, her basic assumptions about safety, and the tangible proofs of her existence, which is what our prized belongings visibly demonstrate. In a few minutes, everything from valuable antiques to sentimental souvenirs became pieces of jagged glass, shards of china, and splinters of wood on the floor waiting to be swept up and thrown in the trash.

Once the initial shock wore off, she said that the loss of her possessions actually became very liberating. After the sharp pain came peace. All sorts of things she thought she couldn't live without, all the things she believed were crucial to expressing her personality became what they really are, just things. Now as she re-creates a nest of comfort, she's surrounding herself only with objects that she really needs or loves—the useful and the beautiful—but fewer than before. Her eye is more discriminating now. She has learned what she can live without and feels lighter. She admits to enjoying her new possessions with a sense of detachment because she knows that with another jolt they could be gone tomorrow.

While I've been on the Simple Abundance path, I've consulted a century's worth of decorating books and women's magazines, searching for simple pleasures to share. They all express the commonly held belief that possessions define a person. During the Victorian period, worldly goods were viewed as evidence of God's favor, and I think that attitude is still very much part of the American consciousness. Certainly I believed it until I began the journey to authenticity. But as I meditated, ruminated, mulled over, and tried to write about how our possessions define us, the Spirit within balked. Reared up and refused to cooperate. Shut down so that I would shut up perpetuating such nonsense. If a writer has a block, it's usually because she doesn't believe in what she's writing.

Here's what I believe. I believe our possessions can be very revealing, offering insights into our personalities in intimate and illuminating ways. I believe surrounding ourselves with objects that speak to our souls can bring us authentic moments of pleasure. *But I do not believe our possessions define us.*

Instead, I believe it's what you *love* that expresses the authentic woman you are, not what you own.

When Jacqueline Kennedy Onassis died, much was written about her style and strength, her grace and beauty. If ever there was a woman who lived by her own lights it was Jackie. Yet here was a woman who could have had virtually anything she wanted in the world, and yet her most prized possession was her privacy, a gift you probably don't think about very much.

But what struck even a deeper chord in me was her son's recollection of what meant the most to her: "The love of words, the bonds of home and family, and her spirit of adventure." Her passions defined this extraordinary woman.

Today I wish for you, as I wish for myself, that when our authentic adventure comes to a close, we can also be remembered as being by love possessed.

MAY 29

Favorite Things: Enjoying Cherished Collections

Each item in a collection *has its own story, its own memory—the search, the day you bought it, who you were with, the vacation...*
—TRICIA GUILD AND ELIZABETH WILHIDE

My husband collects baseball movies and political campaign literature, Katie adores Hollywood memorabilia, and I love teapots, blue-and-white-patterned china, the sparkle of Waterford crystal, and books. This year, however, instead of objects, I have been collecting other women's thoughts, weaving them into the fabric of my daily life. It is probably the most marvelous collection I've ever pursued, and it has cost me nothing but time and creative energy.

What do you collect? What favorite things have you accumulated over the years that you now lovingly display around your home? I hope you collect something that you love with a passion, for there are few pleasures that can compare to browsing in little, out-of-the-way shops and flea markets, searching for that mysterious object of desire, the value of which you alone know in this world. The thrill of the hunt is only equaled by the discovery. You see it—over there—its beauty beckoning you to come closer for a better look. Quietly it whispers, "Take me home." Heart pounding, you turn it over for its price, to see whether you can. Success! Casually, for you would not want to give away your secret, you pay for it, exchanging pleasantries, then slowly walk out the door smiling. (Gloating is considered bad form.) The shopkeeper has no idea what a treasure he gave away. What's important is that *you* do.

Then comes the joy of bringing it to its new home, rearranging its companions to show off your prize. You stand back. It's perfect: the moment and your collection.

For several years I collected Victorian motto cups. The first time I found one of these nineteenth-century china mugs (declaring "Think of Me"), Katie and I were roaming through the antique shops in Saratoga Springs, New York, with one of our favorite people in all the world, my sister-in-law, Karen. It was a wonderful summer afternoon full of good company and great cheer. Suddenly, there it was, just sitting quietly on a table, a white china mug with burgundy and gold-leaf flowers and embossed lettering. I had never seen one before and was immediately charmed. I picked it up and put it down. Walked around the store and came back to it. Put it down again. Finally Katie convinced me that for $10, how could I be without it? (There's nothing like shopping with an accomplice.)

I was so pleased with my purchase that right then I decided I would collect these cups, and over the next couple of years searched for them across the country. But the ones that followed never quite matched the delight I felt when I purchased the first. So I gradually lost interest in them.

Then one Memorial Day weekend at the beach I was rereading Anne Morrow Lindbergh's *Gift from the Sea*, an annual ritual of renewal—especially satisfying if I can dig my toes into wet sand while I'm doing it. Earlier that morning I'd been foraging and had passed up another cup. I was actually a bit puzzled by this phenomenon. Mrs. Lindbergh told me: "The collector walks with blinders on, he sees nothing but the prize. In fact, the acquisitive instinct is incompatible with the appreciation of beauty." This certainly explained my disappointment with the cups that followed the first one. I was less beguiled by their individual beauty than I was compelled to collect them. Actually, what I really wanted to do was to re-create the wonderful memory of that summer day spent with Karen and Katie. Now I have that first cup—that tangible memory—sitting on my desk holding pens. Its singular beauty never fails to please me. I've started to give away the other cups as gifts, receiving more pleasure in sharing them than I ever did in buying them.

I still delight in bringing home treasures—but now, when something catches my eye, I stop for a moment to remember Mrs. Lindbergh's advice: "To ask how little, not how much, can I get along with. To say—is it necessary?—when I am tempted to add one more accumulation to my life." If I think I can't live without the object of desire and I can afford it, I'll collect it. But now I pause first. Simple Abundance is not about saying "no" to our creative impulses, whether in collecting, dressing, or decorating. It's about knowing when to say "enough" because we know that all we have is all we really need. "One cannot collect all the beautiful shells on the beach. One can collect only a few, and they are more beautiful if they are few."

MAY 30

Finders, Keepers: The Fun of Foraging

The whole thrill of junking is that you just know the next table will have what you've been looking for all your life.
—MARY RANDOLPH CARTER

This time of the year you can usually find me foraging on weekends. Rambling and roaming, I rummage, following handwritten signs posted on telephone poles. Searching for nothing in particular and everything in general. Why should I limit myself with expectation? The sun is shining, I've got a full tank of gas, ice-cold lemonade in a thermos, money in my pocket. Sometimes a sidekick rides along, other times I'm footloose and fancy free, just a thrill away from finding what I've been looking for all my life, though Heaven only knows what that is. Maybe today I'll find out.

Now is the season of yard, garage, tag sales and weekend flea markets. It's time to trade in mall shopping for the lure of outdoor tables. Foraging is good for the soul. Often after we've made a major change in our lifestyle by tightening the purse strings—whether it's voluntary or necessary—a deprivation detox is required. The world hasn't stopped selling, we've just stopped buying. It's easy to start feeling a little self-pitying, especially when we are bombarded on all sides with the kind of slick advertising that pushes all our emotional buttons in an effort to convince us that more is what we need, not less. You may intellectually want to divest yourself of the desire for worldly goods, but the material girl in all of us still suffers from the "gimmies." The best way I've discovered to hush her up is to take her out more often to outdoor stalls and sales.

I lump all outdoor shopping under the heading of flea market finds, but there are a few distinctions worth noting. Yard, tag, and garage sales mean someone else hopes their trash will become your treasure. It might, but you've often got to sort through old Tupperware to find it. Still it can't hurt to look. Estate and moving sales offer the best assortment of recycled furniture, household goods, even clothing. Estate sales are often run by professional dealers, so they're more organized and usually start on a Friday running through the weekend; check newspapers for times and locations.

Plan on getting there early for the best selection, but at the end of the day or on Sunday afternoon you'll get the best deals. Weekend flea markets are where professional dealers—many from hundreds of miles away—gather to sell their wares outdoors. You can find virtually anything, from antiques to junk, and the prices will reflect this.

"The strategy of flea market shopping is simple, yet complex," reveals interior designer Charlotte Moss in her book *A Passion for Detail*. "If you go in search of a particular object your eye will "edit out" other very suitable objects. This method sets you up for disappointment. However, if you go for the pleasure of it, for the mere hunt, you are bound to see something to come home with. . . . Don't forget that objects are not the only benefit to shopping a flea market. Your curiosity will be rewarded and you may come home with some great ideas—and the exhilaration is free!"

I have four Simple Abundance suggestions to share that can help make your outings more pleasurable:

1. *Always* remember and *claim* that Divine abundance is your *only* reality and that Divine abundance will richly manifest itself for you in the perfect purchase at the perfect price if it is for your highest good.

2. *Always* ask, "Is this the best you can do?" It's a friendly way of bargaining and you *never* know.

3. *Always* know what you're going to do with the item when you get it home. I know a woman who had a yard sale to get rid of all the things she'd accumulated in a decade of compulsive yard sale bingeing. Just because it's cheap doesn't mean it's your bargain.

4. *Always* set yourself a fixed limit of what you're going to spend for guilt-free shopping. I usually allow myself $10–20 per weekend in the summer for foraging. (Anything over this amount is not a creative impulse but a choice requiring careful consideration.) Always bring cash; it helps to control your spending, and most outdoor sales don't take checks or credit cards anyway. The amount you set doesn't matter as much as your psychological limit. Many weekends I end up not buying anything at all. I just enjoy the chase. And since, of course, you've decided to buy only what's useful or beautiful (preferably both), you're not wasting money; you're investing in your creativity. After all, you can experiment with a new painting technique, such as sponging, stippling, or spattering on a $10 bureau, and if it doesn't work, you can try again.

"It's not about cost or provenance," writer and photographer Mary Randolph Carter reminds us about the beauty of found objects. "You make a connection with something. You want to give it a home and a new life." Foraging gives us the ability to view the old and abandoned in a new light—reclaiming them from oblivion with creativity and choice, just as we do the days of our lives—and redeeming them with love.

Child's Play: Introducing a Touch of Whimsy and Wit to Your Surroundings

Oh, the fun of arriving at a house and feeling the spark that tells you that you are going to have a good time.

—MARK HAMPTON

Many women approach decorating very seriously. But often the homes that best express their owner's authentic sense of style are decorated with a lighthearted touch. They possess that spark of high spirits that tells you good times are part of this home's personal history. "I like houses to be cozy, comfortable, and personal," Candice Bergen confesses. "Not cluttered, but filled with interesting objects and toys and as many jokes as I can get away with." Our sense of humor doesn't have to be communicated through sight gags so much as expressed through the subtle charm of the unexpected through whimsy and wit. From one family's fascinating collection of Niagara Falls souvenir kitsch displayed on their dining room sideboard to another's amusing salt and pepper assortment playfully lining the shelves in their sunny kitchen, a spirit of spontaneity can fill your home with fun.

The whimsical world of Mary Engelbreit's home—like her delightful Engelbreit designs and illustrations that grace everything from greeting cards to wall coverings today—is one that many of us are drawn to instinctively. Mary's warmhearted blending of cozy nostalgia and wry wit is both touchingly familiar and disarmingly fresh. A constant source of inspiration to her are the classic children's storybooks that belonged to her mother and grandmother. In Mary's own home, her personal decorating look includes an exuberant alchemy of bright, colorful patterns mixed with the crisp black-and-white checked borders and bold red cherries that have become her signature. Hand-painted touches abound on stair railings, furniture, and floors. Across her living room hearth she's painted her personal philosophy of life and decorating: "Be Warm Inside and Out."

The golden age of childhood captured in the children's illustrations of yesteryear can be a rich archive of decorating inspiration for you as well. One way to begin is to scour used-book stores looking for children's books from the turn of the century to the 1950s. Some of my favorite illustrators who incorporate enchanting decorating details in their work include Jessie Willcox Smith, Eloise Wilkin, Margaret Tarrant, Harriet Bennett, and Sarah Stilwell. By revisiting your first decorating influences once again, you might reawaken a long-forgotten desire to hear the soft ticking of a mantel clock or be inspired to build yourself a window seat for rainy day retreats; refurbish an overstuffed, flea market footstool with a vintage fabric; cover your kitchen table with a fruit-laden tablecloth; or add a row of ball fringe to a curtain.

"It don't mean a thing," Duke Ellington reminds us, "if it ain't got that swing"—whether it be music or our homes. Today, jazz up your decorating ideas with a sense of playfulness drawn from rooms of enduring charm that spoke to you in the past.

Joyful Simplicities for May

&⸱ On May Day, hang a basket of flowers on your front door and your next-door neighbor's. A breathtaking May bouquet that is the essence of Simple Abundance can be created with small stems of pink dogwood blossoms, lilacs, and white peony tulips. Share a bouquet with someone who works with you. Wear a small posy on your jacket lapel.

&⸱ For Mother's Day, give yourself a small token of esteem (*you* know what you really want) to honor the Great Mother within. See if it can be something from your comfort wish list. Do this whether you have children or not. If you do have children, forgive yourself for not living up to your own expectations (who could?), mentally toss out last year's accumulation of guilt, and start off fresh. If your own mother is still alive, take the time this year to write her the long letter you've often thought about writing, sharing all the loving things you want her to know. If your mother is not in this world, talk to her in your heart. She'll hear you.

&⸱ Learn about the ancient Chinese art of feng shui. A good place to start: *Feng Shui: The Chinese Art of Placement* and *Interior Design with Feng Shui*, both by Sarah Rossback. Move twenty-seven belongings as you begin to bring order to your house.

&⸱ Tackle just *one* junk drawer.

&⸱ One Saturday afternoon after cleaning, putter for an hour to your favorite music. Rearrange your favorite collection of personal mementos and pictures. Savor the sweet memories. Enjoy traveling back in time in your mind.

&⸱ Rent old movies from the 1930s and 1940s or flip through the cable channels looking for old-fashioned treasures. Look for domestic details, the trim of upholstery, the curtains, the knickknacks in the kitchen. Consider why these charming, cozy sets draw us in to stay a while.

&⸱ Take pictures off a wall and clear tabletops and mantels for one week to experience "the fullness of nothing." What do you want to put back?

&⸱ If you have a cherished collection, do you display it? Think of new ways to surround yourself with the things you love.

~∽ Start regular foraging forays to keep "the material girl" distracted. Check newspapers for estate and moving sales, scan grocery store bulletin boards for flea market announcements.

~∽ Books you might enjoy reading for decorating ideas include *Mary Engelbreit's Home Companion: The Mary Engelbreit Look and How to Get It* by Mary Engelbreit and *American Junk* by Mary Randolph Carter.

~∽ Dust off the grill, make potato salad, and get out your white shoes for Memorial Day weekend.

~∽ Be happy.

~∽ Be grateful.

JUNE

*I wonder what it would be like to live in a world
where it was always June.*

—L. M. MONTGOMERY

June is generous with her authentic gifts. Once again the days are sunny and hot. The roses and peonies are in bloom, and it's time to feast on strawberries and cream. School is over, summer camp begins, and visions of vacations dance in our heads. Our smiles deepen, our laughter increases, our hearts open. This month we rediscover that it is life's enrichments rather than the riches of life that bring us true contentment.

JUNE 1

Encountering Hestia

House ordering is my prayer, and when I have finished my prayer is answered. And bending, stooping, scrubbing, purifies my body as prayer doesn't.

—JESSAMYN WEST

You clean a cluttered closet, slowly sorting through clothing, considering what is to be saved, stored, or shared with others. She is there. You gather together the fruits of the earth on the altar of your kitchen counter, baking not a blackberry pie but a benediction, invoking an unspoken blessing for those who will partake of your love offering. She is there. You ready the guest room to welcome friends to your home, dressing the bed with your best linens, laying fluffy towels on the chair, arranging a bouquet of flowers next to the reading lamp along with a few of your favorite books. She is there. You polish the silver, fold the laundry, iron the tablecloth, wash the dishes, replace the candles. She is there. Hestia, the venerable domestic spirit. We may not have known her name, but we have felt her move through us when we experience pleasure in our daily round.

Three thousand years ago in ancient Greece, Hestia was the goddess of the hearth, guardian of family life and the temple. It was to Hestia that women turned for protection and inspiration so that they might, as an act of worship, transform their dwelling places into homes of beauty and comfort. Hestia was one of the twelve Olympians in classical Greek mythology. But she is the least known of all the deities, and there are no legends about her, even though Zeus bestowed on her the privilege of sitting in the center of their celestial home so that she might receive the best offerings from mortals. While the other gods and goddesses were personified in sculpture and paintings, Hestia was not rendered in human form. Instead, her spiritual presence was honored as an eternal flame burning on a round hearth. Jungian analyst and author Jean Shinola Bolen tells us in her book, *Goddess in Everywoman*, that Hestia's sacred fire provided illumination, warmth, and the heat necessary for food. Despite her anonymity through the ages, "The goddess Hestia's presence in house and temple was central to everyday life" in ancient Greece.

Today, as in ancient times, reflecting on Hestia "focuses attention inward, to the spiritual center of a woman's personality," according to Dr. Bolen, enabling us to tap into an inner harmony as we go about our daily round. Hestia is not frazzled, hanging on by a thread. Instead, Hestia is "grounded in the midst of outer chaos, disorder, or ordinary, everyday bustle." Everything that needs to get done in the home is accomplished with ease and grace. By knowingly seeking encounters with Hestia in our daily life, by letting her quiet, calm, orderly presence influence our behavior, we can come to the awakening that there is sacred Mystery in the mundane.

And just how do we do this? Sometimes I'll invoke Hestia's help as I work around my home. Or I'll ask myself, is this how Hestia would approach this task? Of course, if I have to ask that question, I know it's not, but the question brings my awareness back to the contemplative nature of homecaring.

Most of all, Hestia gently reminds me, as Dr. Bolen points out, "tending to household details is a centering activity equivalent to meditation," if we want to make it so. If you feel you have no time to sit down to meditate, that you have a valid excuse for not seeking communion with Spirit because the floor has to be swept, realize that if you approach your tasks with reverence, it won't only be your home that will be transformed. The Goddess knows what it takes to run a household and She has deemed it holy. So should you.

JUNE 2

In Praise of Modesty

Style is to see beauty in modesty.

—ANDRÉE PUTMAN

Modesty isn't a very exciting virtue. A sparse or stark style can be sophisticated and dramatic, but modesty seems dull, too often confused with the girl dressed in muslin sitting on the side of the gymnasium who's never asked to dance. But the French designer, Andrée Putman, who has reinterpreted everything from hotel interiors to pencils, believes "unless you have a feeling for that secret knowledge that modest things can be more beautiful than anything expensive, you will never have style."

Perhaps as a child you were told not to toot your own horn, even when you accomplished something amazing. Or maybe you were told to stop dreaming of setting the world on fire, and "have more modest aspirations, so you won't be disappointed." Maybe when you try to express your authentic self you hear an old voice berating you for "being a show-off."

Yet at the same time, out of the corner of your eye you could see it was the *big* gestures that got all the attention in life. Glamour. Fame. Wealth. The trinity of what's considered good taste worshiped by the world. Or at least that's the way it looks from here. It's always the wealthy women who make it on the international best-dressed lists, the movie stars' mansions that are glorified in glossy layouts. It's not enough to write a finely honed first novel, it has to be a best-seller or you'll have difficulty publishing a second one. You can't just be a talented actress, you have to win an Academy Award to be considered a success. Tell me, when was the last time you knew of a bronze medalist signing a $1 million endorsement deal?

Most of us can't see our name in lights on Broadway, so we give up, sorry we even tried, our sense of self diminished. Being a modest success just doesn't make it. We hear "modest" and think "mediocre."

Meditate on modesty for a moment. What if she isn't the self-effacing, shy, retiring, nerdy virtue we've thought she is? What if Modesty is really passion restrained? What if modesty is a virtue so full of her own smoldering sense of self that she isn't distracted by the glitz? The American writer and illustrator Oliver Herford believed that modesty was "the gentle art of enhancing your charm by pretending not to be aware of it." People with an authentic style know what they are, but even more important, *they know what they are not*. They don't care about labels. They care about personal expression. Frank Lloyd Wright would never have asked Laura Ashley to decorate his house, even though both of them showcased the beauty of modesty in their work. The trick is to go deep enough to mine the core of your authenticity. First, find out what you love, whether it's a coat, a couch, or a career. Worry about the packaging and the tags later.

I leave this thought with you today. Goldilocks was a modest little lady who didn't want very much. She knew what was "just right," what was perfect for her—be it porridge, chair or bed—and she made confident, creative choices. Now *there's* the girl I'd like to be when I grow up!

JUNE 3

Ask, Ask, Ask

Ask, and it shall be given to you; seek, and ye shall find; knock, and it shall be opened unto you.

—MATTHEW 7:7

When was the last time you felt comfortable asking anybody for anything—for advice, for help, or even for directions? I've spent the last twenty years asking questions as a journalist so you'd think that asking on my own behalf would come easy.

It doesn't. Nevertheless, I've recently discovered something that's brought a sense of adventure to my daily round. It's so simple, it's scary.

It's *asking* for what we want. Help. Advice. Wisdom. Guidance.

Information—especially information. Information is what led me to a delightful new coffee bar. As I write, I'm enjoying a delicious glass of iced café latté at an outdoor table, shaded by a bright red-and-white striped umbrella, surrounded by charming white pots of geraniums. Every few minutes I peek with pleasure into the shopping bag at my feet to look at my new summer linen separates. They pass the Simple Abundance test: they look great, feel wonderful, and were on sale. After clearing closets and drawers, I was down to one outfit I could wear on the street (you think I'm kidding?). But everything I saw at the stores was too expensive, didn't look or feel right. So for months I avoided buying. Then I ran into a woman I know who possesses a sure sense of style. Her wardrobe is terrific, but she could pull off wearing a burlap sack with panache. When I've seen her in the past, I usually ended up sighing wistfully. This time I cut to the chase. Where does she shop? She graciously detailed not only the stores but the different fashion lines she prefers. Then she recommended I visit one great shop soon; they were having a fabulous sale. *Ask* to get on their mailing list, she advised, because they'll let you in on unadvertised specials.

"It is a long time since I have asked heaven for anything, but still my arms will not come down," Spanish poet Antonio Porchia mused, giving voice to the profound paradox of asking. We want, we need, we desire, we yearn, but we don't ask. Still our arms stay up in the air. Longings cross our mind, but we don't really commit ourselves. We don't lay it on the line. We don't ask because we're afraid somebody will say "no." Who? It doesn't matter. It could be Spirit, our spouse, or our supervisor. But when wishful thinking doesn't magically manifest what we want, we feel we've been denied. So, in future, we choose not to ask, but continue to wish, existing in a constant state of deprivation.

Asking comes with no guarantees. "I ask for things that do not come. I urge you for things that do not happen," writer Marjorie Holmes confides in her wonderful book of prayers, *I've Got to Talk to Somebody, God.* "Though my knuckles are bloody from knocking, and my voice is hoarse from asking," she writes, the door remains fast and there is only the Great Silence. In the Great Silence of unfulfillment all that you can hear are your own sobs. I know. But I also know if we don't ask, we haven't got a prayer.

Today, start asking. You see a woman with a great haircut? Ask where she got it. Ask for the name of a great paint color in a home accessory shop, a fabulous recipe from a hostess, the name of a piece of music you hear playing in the record store. Ask your husband to take the kids for the afternoon to give you some time to yourself. Ask the kids to pick up their toys so that you don't have to do it. Ask for a deadline extension. Ask for the day off. Ask for a raise. Ask when the next sale will be. Ask Spirit for a daily portion of grace. Ask Divine Wisdom for operating instructions. Ask your guardian angel to manifest holy assistance. While you're at it, ask for a miracle.

Ask for what you need and want. Ask to be taught the right questions.

Ask to be answered. Ask for the Divine Plan of your life to unfold through joy. Ask politely. Ask with passion. Ask with a grateful heart and you will be heard. Just ask.

JUNE 4

Classic Chic 102

Style has nothing to do with money. Anybody can do it with money. The true art is to do it on a shoestring.

—TOM HOGAN

Since the world, with very few enlightened exceptions, does not celebrate thrift shop chic, why don't we? There are five Simple Abundance strategies that are essential to elevating secondhand skills to new-to-you savvy (they apply to both fashion and decorating): (1) Save. Seek. Find; (2) Understand scale and proportion; (3) Trust your instincts; (4) Train your eye; and (5) Take your time.

1. *Save. Seek. Find.* Or, as the ancient Vulcan sages put it, "Live well and prosper." If you save while seeking what you really love, you will eventually find it and have the money to pay for it. (This *is* how the Universe dresses and decorates.) It may take longer than a week, but it will happen. Years from now, we'll meet, probably in a thrift shop, and we'll know each other by the gleam in our eyes. We'll acknowledge each other with the secret slogan, "Save. Seek. Find." I just hope your hand isn't on the mirror I've been eyeing for over my mantel! Oh, go ahead and take it, if it's perfect for you. I know that my authentic good is on its way.

2. *Scale and proportion.* The real reason that your room or outfit doesn't look like the pictures in a magazine has less to do with your choice of fabric, color, or style than with scale and proportion. Tom Hogan, co-owner of the sassy, thrift-shop-chic home furnishings shop Chartreuse in New York, believes the secret to a great-looking room (or outfit) comes down to striving for balance. Not symmetry, so much, as the visual weight of scale and proportion. For example, if you have one big, heavy piece at one end of a room, you need to balance it with another bulky shape at the other end. If you want to mix modern and rustic for an eclectic look, go ahead, just make sure each style is represented in the same proportion.

3. *Trust your instincts.* You know what you love. Don't be guided by "friends, fads and fashion," advises Tom Hogan. If you do, six months from now you'll be so tired of the item, you won't want to walk into the room or your closet. "That is money wasted."

4. *Train your eye.* "Your eye is used to a certain look, so anything differ-ent is going to look funny," says Tom. Before you order twenty yards of a new fabric, live with a sample draped over the furniture for a couple of weeks. If your eyes don't adjust, you know it's not for you. In the same way, your eye may not be used to seeing a piece of furniture, so give it a chance to fit in. After a week you might realize that the table that doesn't work in the living room would be perfect for the bedroom if you painted it white.

5. *Take your time.* "Don't be in a hurry to pull it all together. People make the mistake of doing it too fast and then they end up hating it," Tom coun-sels. The best rooms and wardrobes seem to evolve gradually. They don't spring from your head or a store in finished form. And always leave room for inspiration. You may never know what "find du jour" you'll discover tomorrow.

Next time you head out the door on a shopping expedition, just remem-ber: authentic style has nothing to do with money and everything to do with trusting your instincts.

Class dismissed.

JUNE 5

Your Bedroom: Cradle of Civilization

All one really needs is a divinely attractive bed.
—MRS. WINSTON GUEST

James Joyce might have been able to describe Dublin from his desk in Paris and Willa Cather successfully evoke the prairie from New York City, but if I have any hope of honoring the cradle of civilization—our bedrooms—I need to be in bed. Actually, most of this book has been written in bed, a fact that I find astonishing—as does my family. The English poet John Donne was obviously describing me when he wrote, "This bed, thy centre is/These walls, thy sphere."

You look at a room in a different light when it's your personal domain. You probably don't spend as much time in your bedroom as I do, but yours should be your domain as well. Over the next week, I thought we would take a walk through the rooms that most of us share in common, so that we might reflect on the roles they play in our lives and how we can let them provide us more abundantly with simple pleasures.

As far as I am concerned, bedrooms were created for only two reasons: comfort and joy. Keeping that in mind, are you happy with your bedroom? You will know if you rarely want to leave. Start with the focal point of your room, the bed. Is it large enough for you, and do you have a good mattress that provides you with enough support?

After that you need wonderful sheets. I prefer to sleep on cool, 100 percent cotton sheets in the spring and summer and cozy flannel sheets in the late fall and winter. Next, instead of blankets and quilts, I recommend using a down comforter, or duvet, stuffed with duck or goose feathers and covered with the equivalent of a large cotton pillowcase (removable for washing) to take the place of a top sheet. It turns making the bed into a dream sequence. You've never been caressed until you sleep cuddled in down. The same goes for down-filled pillows to sleep on and assorted pillows to prop yourself up on comfortably. Finding the perfect pillow combination for yourself is not frivolous if you want to be happy in life. If you are simply making do with any old foam rubber block, we need to have a serious talk. Put the comfort level of your pillows on your list of personal preference priorities.

How does your bedroom look? Do you experience a sense of delight when you walk in? Here's where joy enters the scheme of things through visual charm. Your walls should be painted a soothing color—white, blue, a dusty rose, sage green. Make sure you select a color you won't grow tired of. You might think you want to be cheered when you walk into your bedroom, but this is not place for brights. Save yellow, melon, and red for your more active rooms. I prefer the walls of my bedroom plain, with the exception of one picture over my meditation table that complements my smoky blue walls; it is more serene. If you do hang pictures, make sure that you love what you're looking at. It will be the first thing you see in the morning and the last thing at night.

Your bedding should be as inviting to look at as it is comfortable to lie on. I'm convinced that a woman should love her bedcovers with a mad passion. This isn't just aesthetics; it encourages you to keep your bedroom tidy because the bed looks so pretty when it's all made up. And since the bed is made, you might as well hang up your clothes and straighten the dresser. You can see this leads to Sublime Order, at least in one room of your home.

Now add the personal flourishes that can make all the difference: good reading lamps, a flowering plant, small personal mementos, treasured photographs, and a place for books. Keep clutter under control with assorted fabric-covered boxes that are pretty to look at. If you have room in which to put a dressing table, how marvelous! Indulge yourself with this luxury.

Even though I write from my bedroom, one thing I never do is conduct business there. It just doesn't feel right. If I have a business telephone call to make or one I expect to receive, I'll take it in my office. I don't want the world intruding into my private space. When you retreat to your bedroom at night, turn on the answering machine. If you have a fax at home, don't have it here. You need one place of your own where you can stop the world from spinning by getting off.

In our bedrooms we have the ability to not just decorate a room, but to create a sacred space for self-nurturance. If we do, we will be heeding Emily Dickinson's wisdom: "Ample make this bed/Make this bed with Awe."

JUNE 6

The Bath: Secret Haven of Self-Absorption

If I were a psychiatrist, I think I would like to inspect my patients' bathrooms before investigating any other area of their lives.
—MARK HAMPTON

This morning I was mulling over the potential pleasures the bathroom can bring while I was waiting to get in there. We have only one bathroom in our home, and my husband and daughter, who must both leave the house early, have priority in the morning. However, according to a recent national poll conducted by a large manufacturer of bathroom products, we have not fully exploited the room's potential. The survey revealed that for many people, the bathroom is the preferred place for telephone conversations, eating, sleeping, smoking, lovemaking, homework, and dancing!

Not in *my* bathroom. My bathroom is the size of the *Oxford Latin Dictionary* when it's closed. This is a hefty sized book to be sure, but its dimensions leave much to be desired for the most popular room in the house.

The interior decorator Mark Hampton admits that of all the remodeling and redecorating projects that one undertakes in one's life, the prospect of redoing the bathroom is most "numbing." I agree, but not for the reasons he gives, which have to do with considering the input of so many people—architects, decorators, contractors, tilesmen, electricians, and plumbers. The exorbitant cost of hiring all these people to perform their magic for my bathroom, and the fact that there's not one square inch of space surrounding the three fundamental fixtures already in there are what numb *me*.

Still, the importance of the bathroom is irrefutable. As Mark Hampton rightly points out, bathrooms "provide a place for private pampering, for a sybaritic mood that might otherwise be frowned on. Hidden from the scrutiny of others, these rooms are secret havens of self-absorption."

Hold that thought. *Secret havens of self-absorption.* Attitude adjustment in progress. Just because the bathroom is small and the budget even smaller doesn't mean it can't be transformed into a secret haven of self-absorption. I can do that. So can you.

Here's how.

One of my favorite fantasies is to go someday to a luxury spa for a week. Like the armchair traveler, I am collecting spa information and tucking it into my discovery journal. This way, when Real Life presents me with the opportunity, I can be out the door and know where I'm headed. In the meantime, I've created a Simple Abundance spa—seven nights of home-grown indulgence. I think of it as happy hour for the psyche. You might find it fun as well. Every night for a week, experiment with a new kind of bath product: aromatherapy, bath salts, gels, foam, milk, bubble baths, and Vita baths. See which you really prefer. Many bath products come in small sizes, so you can experiment inexpensively. Around the holidays, they're often available as gift freebies. Keep them in your comfort drawer until you need a spa week.

After a leisurely soak in a room illuminated only by scented candles, while listening to fabulous music and sipping a glass of wine or sparkling fruited mineral water (ice-cold blackberry or peach is divine), treat your-self to one beauty treatment per night. How about a mud-pack facial; hot-oil hair conditioning treatment; manicure and pedicure; exfoliation and waxing; cellulite body massage; seaweed body smoother. The final night, play with makeup and hair styling.

Spa toys for your wish list can include a handheld shower attachment with different speeds; natural sponges and scrub mitts; an oversized terry-cloth robe with hood; oversized bath towels; a magnifying mirror so that you can really see what you're doing; and, if you don't already have one, a bath tray to hold everything. An inflatable pillow is lovely to rest your head upon and with a long-necked scrub brush you can scratch your own back. The self-sufficient spa is best.

Today, don't look at the shortcomings of your bathroom. If it's got hot and cold running water, a handle that flushes, and a tub to lie down in, all you have is all you need. Once you experiment with one homegrown spa week, you'll want to make it a seasonal ritual. Seven days of self-nurturing is heady stuff, but believe me, you can get used to it.

JUNE 7

The Joy of Living Rooms

Some of the living-rooms we see have really no right to the name; they are so unattractive they ought, instead, to be called existing rooms. I like to think of the word "living-rooms" being short for the joy-of-living rooms. That is what they ought to be—full of life and happiness and beauty.

—LUCY ABBOT THROOP

Last week I went over to a friend's house for lunch and when I walked into her foyer and glanced at her living room, I was taken aback with surprise and delight. It had been about six months since I'd last visited, and the entire room had been transformed. Everything looked so pulled together. I immediately told her how fabulous the room looked and felt. After a closer look, I realized that she hadn't redecorated; she had just added decorative details that made the room come alive: moving some paintings around, changing the mantel, and dressing up her couches with striking new tapestry pillows that highlighted the subtle colors of her upholstery. What's more, she revealed that she'd found the pillows on sale and that the entire freshening up was accomplished for under $50.

The end result was that her living room—which had always been elegant, beautiful, and quiet—now possessed pizzazz. The room was cozy without being cluttered; it was visually charming and comfortable. It was so inviting I didn't want to leave. Every corner beckoned my attention: her cherished family photos, her stack of well-loved books, her simply stunning arrangement of white hydrangeas picked that morning from her garden, and her artful collection of porcelain eggs displayed on a tiny mirror-topped side table.

But there was something more at work here. I was intrigued, so I gently kept probing. "Well, the room is certainly lived in," she confessed with a laugh, admitting that she now spent more time here than before. Her creative energy was palpable, her authentic flair was visible, and her new enthusiasms, including her second book which she was just beginning to write, were evident. Her living room perfectly expressed her joy of living. It always inspires me to see Simple Abundance at work.

For a lot of us the thought of decorating, like almost everything else in our lives, seems overwhelming. In our minds we don't just tackle one corner of a room until it pleases us, but try to revamp an entire house in a day. The prospect is so exhausting we don't even start. Instead of thinking of decorating as one more burden to deal with, we need to lighten up—to view it as a continuing source of personal expression and contentment.

There are no prizes being awarded here, just finding what brings you pleasure.

When searching for ways to make your living room come alive, first consider its many functions in your family's daily round. Now, if your home is large enough for a family space that's separate from your living room, I think at this moment you should stop and give thanks. Many women would call you blessed. The biggest stumbling block for me when I began to bring more order into the daily fabric of our lives—and I began in the living room—was acceptance, even though I knew this was the crucial first step. I'm embarassed to admit how much time, energy, and emotion (precious natural resources) I squandered hating the fact that our house wasn't more spacious. But hating my house only bound me psychologically and blinded me creatively to its many positive qualities. An ancient metaphysical law says that we can never leave any situation that causes us discomfort until we learn to love it or at least to see love at work in it. I had many lessons to learn about order. Now I know in my heart that my small house is the perfect teacher. What good would a larger house do me if I couldn't keep a small one tidy?

"A beautiful home is an education in itself, but it is not made in a day; it must slowly grow," Lucy Abbot Throop, who wrote on decorating in the early decades of this century, reassured her readers in 1910. Today, look for the lessons your home is waiting to teach you through love. Begin with your living room. Make it as cozy, charming, and comfortable as you can with the resources you now have, and it will become a joy to live in.

JUNE 8

In Praise of Real-Life Dining Rooms

When we are authentic, when we keep our spaces simple, simply beautiful living takes place.

—ALEXANDRA STODDARD

We all long to feel that our presence is welcome in the world. Usually we think of this only when we're invited into the homes of others. But I've come to believe that what we want and need most of all is to experience a sense of welcome in our own homes.

I'm sitting at my dining room table as I write, waiting for a batch of brownies to come out of the oven. The handsome, round oak table on which they will cool is the hub of our family life. From its sturdy center, soulful spokes of food, drink, conversation, conviviality, tradition, and memory sprout, finding outward expression in our daily round.

Much more than eating takes place here. Newspapers are read, mail is sorted, conversations are started, homework is completed, bills are paid, cakes are iced, income tax is computed, flowers are arranged, games are played, confidences are shared, family and friends are gathered. Here, at this replica of the Greek goddess Hestia's round hearth, rites of passage are commemorated, holidays are celebrated, daily grace is offered, minds, bodies, and spirits are nourished.

We entertain in this dear little room a few times a year. But we live and love in it every day.

It's very fashionable at the moment to recommend that families don't really need the separate dining rooms so revered by our parents and grandparents because we lead such different lives today. Progress comes at a price, and we need to be practical, especially in tiny city apartments and modest suburban condominiums. Instead, trendsetters tell us to let the real demands of our lives take precedence over an ideal that's only an illusion. If we're short of space, we should transform the dining room into a library or a playroom or a den.

I really don't know why this suggestion seems so chic, especially since our dining room already provides these functions. My library of cookbooks fills one corner, cats and children play here, a mini television propped on a dining room chair pulled over to the kitchen door lets me catch the evening news as I cook dinner. Our dining room is an all-purpose room; it anchors us all in the morning, in the evening, and in between. The passionate reality of this room—the simply beautiful *living* that takes place here every day—invokes reverence and begs for preservation.

Here, generations of families are tangibly linked as china, crystal, and silver passed from parents to children are lovingly removed from open-shelved cupboards and placed on the table in a comforting reenactment of a timeless ritual of hospitality, homecoming, and Wholeness. The Victorian English novelist and Jewish scholar Grace Aquilar wrote in 1847 that "The Real is the sole foundation of the Ideal." As I prepare this place and my heart to gratefully receive another authentic blessing, I have often wondered if she divined this profound awakening in her dining room.

JUNE 9

Bringing a Sense of Order to the Kitchen

A confused mind cannot direct deft hands and what is more con-
fusing than a cluttered, disorderly place to work? What is more
uninviting, too? The grateful appearance of order—this is the one
important way women judge each other's housekeeping. And every
efficient housekeeper knows that in no room does it count for more
than in the kitchen.

—WOMAN'S HOME COMPANION, August 1924

I couldn't sleep at night if I gave you the impression that cleaning the kitchen is my idea of a great time. The very thought reminds me of a newspaper interview I did with two delightful, funny women who were the authors of a popular series of homemaking books.

I nearly choked when they revealed that they didn't do their own housecleaning anymore because their success had enabled each of them to afford a cleaning woman. It was as if I had wandered behind a curtain and met up with the affable old man the munchkins believed was the Wizard of Oz. Sharing this delicious morsel with my readers would be going for the jugular, and bloodletting has never been my sport. Besides, the practical information they conveyed in their books made sense and was fun to read. Still, I had a difficult time writing the feature (which by the way, the two women and their publisher loved).

So let me be the first to confess from the heart that I have not yet found the way to turn cleaning kitchens into a simple pleasure. Being flesh, blood, and bone, I need a little more time to evolve. This probably explains why, when our homecaring tasks were divided up, I opted for cooking, which I do enjoy, while my dearly beloved volunteered to clean the kitchen on the nights he doesn't have meetings. (One of the many reasons he is dearly beloved.) On the nights he's out, you'll find me at the kitchen sink attempting to learn from the Vietnamese Buddhist monk, poet, and writer Thich Nhat Hanh the spiritual way to wash the dishes. In his book, *The Miracle of Mindfulness: A Manual on Meditation*, he suggests we approach washing the dishes as if it were the most important thing in life. We are to consider each dirty bowl as sacred. I have not gotten to that point of transcendence, but I try my best to approach washing the dishes as if it were the most important thing I could be doing *at that moment*.

Much of our daily round takes place in the kitchen. Cooking and cleaning can be contemplative pursuits but not if you're surrounded by clutter. Still, I dreaded getting in there. I procrastinated for months, always finding something more urgent that needed my rapt attention. But the Amazing

Grace of the Simple Abundance process prevailed. With the other rooms in my house slowly becoming organized, the state of the kitchen didn't just irritate me, it drove me stark raving mad, especially every time I opened a cupboard door. "Back! Back! Back!" I'd yell at the hundreds of used margarine tubs tumbling out at me. Finally, I faced the truth: if this room were truly the heart of my home, it was no wonder I was experiencing palpitations every time I went in there to work.

Like the clearing-out process in the living room, I sorted and organized my kitchen as best I could according to function. We have a small, narrow kitchen the size of a galley in a boat, and space is at a premium. When you organize your kitchen, regardless of its size, keep in mind that there are several different kitchen activities that take place there: the preparation, cooking, and serving of food, clearing up after the meal, and dishwashing.

Once I got in there, I cleared and tossed clutter without a moment's hesitation, and you will, too. As in the other rooms, what I could not identify, I kept in a box for my husband to ponder. This is a most illuminating encounter between a man and a woman. You'll discover why they call men "the opposite sex" when you have your spouse or partner identify such objects. The moment of truth occurs when he tries to retrieve objects from the trash bag: the disgusting, chipped Teflon frying pan from his college days that is "seasoned" just perfectly now. The wine-making apparatus from a previous lifetime. Or the Crock-Pot that can never be washed out properly because of the dangling electrical cord. Just make sure you dispose of these sentimental treasures on the sly. As I've recommended before, clearing out clutter is, in my opinion, a solitary occupation.

The next time you're searching for the kitchen scissors, cleaning out the refrigerator, or scouring a greasy casserole dish, remember that the Sacred can be found in the ordinary when we seek it. I can't promise you that it works every time, but if it works even once, it's worth engraving on your heart.

JUNE 10

A Nook of Your Own

In solitude we give passionate attention to our lives, to our memories, to the details around us.

—VIRGINIA WOOLF

In October 1928, the British novelist and literary critic Virginia Woolf gave two lectures on women and fiction at Cambridge University in England. In her talks she publicly voiced for the first time what women had quietly shared among themselves for centuries: in order for women to create, they needed privacy, peace, and personal incomes. The following year these lectures were published as *A Room of One's Own*, which was Woolf's recommendation if women were to honor and hone their creativity and not become "crazed with the torture" of silence.

Tillie Olsen has exquisitely explored the creative voice when it is muffled, muzzled, and mute—"the unnatural thwarting of what struggles to come into being, but cannot"—in her book *Silences*. Olsen herself was silenced for twenty years while she raised and supported four children through menial jobs that left her no energy to write; she was nearly fifty when she published her acclaimed first novel, *Tell Me a Riddle*.

Many of us today experience creative silence. Not the hush of the heart necessary to bring forth the unexpressed from Spirit, but the creative silence brought about by circumstances we feel are beyond our control: lack of time, and/or lack of space or a place to create. Perhaps we also suffer from a lack of clarity, a failure to realize how necessary it is to nurture our sacred creativity daily.

To begin with, many of us, unless we live alone, don't have a room entirely our own. But that does not mean we cannot carve out a small psychic space—even a nook—to call ours alone. I have a friend who created a personal space in the corner of a city apartment with a floral folding screen from the 1930s that she found at a flea market. Behind it she angled a small desk and a chair near a sunny window for a restorative retreat.

No room for a screen, a desk, and a chair? Then start with a bookcase all your own. The important thing is that the bookcase be yours: a psychic space that offers passionate reminders to attend to your private, artistic impulses, a place to encourage you to reclaim your creativity.

JUNE 11

Creating a Plan for Personal Papers

Tidied all my papers. Tore up and ruthlessly destroyed much. This is always a great satisfaction.

—KATHERINE MANSFIELD

This morning let's mull over how much of our precious natural resources—our time, creative energy, and emotion—we squander looking for the orphans of disorder: the overdue bill, the misplaced party invitation (with directions), the registration form for the swimming lessons that begin this afternoon.

If you don't have a plan for keeping track of your personal papers, take two hours this week to establish one that will. Unless of course, you feel like Winnie the Pooh's creator, A. A. Milne, who believed that "One of the advantages of being disorderly is that one is constantly making exciting discoveries." But my life is exciting enough without tracking down recalcitrant receipts when I need to return something to the store. So is yours.

I've got a very simple version of paper order. In fact, it almost relieves me of the need to think, which can be very handy! Like children who like to store their toys in separate boxes, I store my papers in the same way: different fabric-covered boxes and square baskets sit on shelves above my desk. One box is for unpaid bills and financial records; as soon as they arrive in the mail they're deposited here; after they're paid, the receipts go into a file. Other boxes keep personal correspondence separate from business correspondence. Another box keeps my publishing papers separate from my workshop materials, and still another box is for my business receipts (as soon as I'm home from an errand or a trip, receipts are deposited here until tax time). There's a box for family papers we'll need in the near future: lesson forms, party invitations, directions for visits to my daughter's friends. I know approximately which box to look for something in. Believe me, this helps.

Once a month—usually the afternoon of the last Saturday—I follow Katherine Mansfield's advice and ruthlessly toss and refile. When I get in there monthly, it only takes an hour, and the feeling of being in control of my personal papers is very reassuring. Today, start a paper chase around your home, searching for every stray piece of paper you can find. Gather them all into one large cardboard box. Pour yourself a refreshing drink. Put on some lively music. Go through each paper and separate them into categories. If you don't have boxes or baskets handy for stowing them, put them in large labeled manila envelopes until you do. Throw away whatever you can.

Think of all the time you waste when you don't know where something is when you need it. Now reflect on all the time that you'll be able to ransom simply because you *do*.

JUNE 12

Secret Passions: Scented Linen Closets

And still she slept an azure-lidded sleep / In blanched linen, smooth, and lavender'd.

—JOHN KEATS

Close your eyes for a moment and let an azure-lidded fantasy flood your mind's eye. You open a white door. There, on lace-edged, deep wooden shelves, you find row after row of neat and tidy willow baskets piled high with perfectly folded sheets; fleecy blankets; fluffy terry cloth; crisp, starched, white damask tablecloths; pristine napkins, monogrammed linen tea towels; pillow slips with the patina of the past edged in cotton crochet. Around the bountiful bundles are pale French silk ribbons tied in perfect bows. You stand transfixed before this eighth wonder of the world, a treasure worthy of traders' tales from "silken Samarcand to cedar'd Lebanon." The air is perfumed with an intoxicating fragrance. A sigh of exquisite pleasure escapes your lips. It will be yours. It will.

The delightful writer Mary Cantwell mused about the elegant lives lived in print by today's domestic gurus, who naturally have scented linen closets. She recalled that once she, too, was tempted to create a proper linen closet for herself, but alas, did not succumb because "I am a lazy woman and bad at tying bows."

Still, the pull of perfection is profound. "Ordering my linens into ranks would have been a form of defense in a world I found disorderly," Mary confides wistfully. "There was not, is not, a thing to be done about pestilence, death and the bad dreams that sneak up on us when we're not sleeping. But I would have had that cupboard, that proof positive that I could make tidy my minuscule corner of the universe. Seeing Wamsutta, Martex and Cannon neat and cozy in their ribbons might even have afforded me a Fantin-Latour moment."

Ignace Henri Jean Théodore Fantin-Latour was a nineteenth-century French artist famous for his beautiful paintings of flowers. He remains a recurring source of inspiration to contemporary hearth goddesses. Mea culpa! Even Fantin-Latour could not render a Fantin-Latour moment out of the cupboard in my upstairs hall. Here there are no silk ribbons. Here, on five shelves, sheets fight for space with towels and facecloths, while cold remedies, toilet paper, tissues, and soap battle it out with lightbulbs, extension cords, and hair dryers, and curlers jocky for position with Lysol and Bon Ami.

But where there is life, there is hope. And while there is hope, there is life. It will be mine. It will.

Perhaps you share the secret dream of someday living with a scented linen closet. Here is my plan to make this dream come true this year. Baskets can keep closet chaos confined. A clear vinyl over-the-door hanging shoe bag can hold the medicines, first aid supplies, beauty and personal care products now crowding our shelves. You want only a *clear* shoe bag so you can see what you're looking for. But they can be difficult to find, so start looking today.

I find the best vintage table linens at estate sales and consignment shops. At flea markets and thrift stores, the linens are usually badly picked over and threadbare; at antique shops they are gorgeous, but too pricey (unless, of course, you know a fabulous place to forage; in that case, drop me a line).

White sales for sheets and towels are held in January and June; mark these sales on your calendar. Even if you don't buy, large department store white sales are great sources of inspiration. I spent a pleasant half hour yesterday browsing through a Ralph Lauren bedroom and bath display and got some great ideas.

Now for the scented part. Measure the side of the walls of your linen closet shelves. There should be three horizontal partitions for each shelf. Cut out two identical pieces of white muslin to fit each wall partition and add an inch of fabric on each side. Layer one thickness of cotton batting between the layers of muslin. Sprinkle liberally with dried lavender flowers (available at herb shops and farmers' markets). Sew the two partition pieces together. Tack or use a staple gun to secure each partition onto the walls of the closet. Hang branches of dried lavender above the top shelf. Stand back and revel in your simply abundant creation.

About ribbons: we lust for them, but unless you live alone, you should emotionally and psychologically let go of the idea of living with sheets tied with silk ribbons. I know. It's not that you can't find them. Great vintage ribbons can be found at flea markets and exquisite wired ribbons (which make perfect bows) can be located at good fabric stores and upscale home accessory shops. But who else in your home will *ever* retie a bow except you? Why break your heart? Still, the thrill of rendering reality perfect before you die makes doing it once worth the effort. Take a photograph. After all, as Keats knew: "A thing of beauty is a joy forever."

JUNE 13

Secret Passions: The Fancy Pantry

The array of pots rather amazed her at first, but John was so fond of jelly, and the nice little jars would look so well on the top shelf.
—Louisa May Alcott

Today we shall indulge in the perfect summer fantasy: the time-honored tradition of "putting by" elegant edibles. What would summer be without the contemplation of the preserved, the pickled, the potted, the candied, the brandied—the fabulous foodstuffs of fancy pantries?

Like scented linen closets, well-stocked pantries have long been a feminine passion. Were there shelves carved out of stone in the prehistoric caves at Gargas? Undoubtedly. Where else to store the shanks of salted wild boar? Twenty thousand years later, Victorian women elevated the stocking of a pantry to an esoteric art, inspired by nineteenth-century literary domestics' luminous descriptions of deep drawers, cubbies, and bins big enough to hold cornmeal and graham flour; of spacious shelves on which to store turkey platters; and of row upon row of the prettily packaged and deliciously displayed.

Every woman should know the sublime pleasure of gazing on glistening jars wearing tiny floral scarves and white crochet caps. But how to begin? Look no further than Helen Witty's indispensable, irreplaceable, irresistible primer, *Fancy Pantry*. Written for all those who believe that genuinely delicious food is an affordable luxury, *Fancy Pantry* shows you how. I can't even browse through this delightful book without wanting to jump up and start playing in the kitchen.

No, I do not mean to suggest you should put up a hundred jars of zucchini marmalade in a sweltering kitchen the size of a shoebox (in between summer camp carpooling, finishing next year's projected office budget, attending your child's baseball or softball championship game, and packing for a week at the beach).

I *am* suggesting that you might find as much delight as I do in creating your own caraway rusks, essence of sun-dried tomatoes (which are worth a queen's ransom in fine food shops), spiced blueberries, fruit-flavored vinegars, and my favorite, fruit honeys, which aren't honeys at all but a beguiling cross between syrups and preserves and are scrumptious over pancakes, desserts, or by the spoonful.

Now if after reading Helen Witty's treasure trove of inspiration and information, you are still hesitant to start stocking the larder with the fruits of your own labors, don't be discouraged. Some summers I preserve more in spirit than in substance, but I always have a fancy pantry.

So, take yourself to a farmers' market and stock up on comestibles that other enterprising women with homegrown businesses have preserved especially for souls such as ours. Get pretty, small-patterned fabric and cut out circles to fit on top of your jams, jellies, and chutney, tying with ribbon, raffia, or twine. Pretty labels are available in kitchen and stationery stores. I also like to pick up preserves from other parts of the country when we go away on vacation.

Still, perusing *Fancy Pantry* might be enough to convince you to try your hand at your own put-ups. Helen Witty believes that all "souls should have a pantry, however modest" and I heartily agree.

JUNE 14

Decorating with the Seasons: Summer Houses

The English rose greets the summer garden with a profusion of colour and perfume and our doors and windows are thrown open to allow the season's intoxicating atmosphere to envelop us and our homes.

—SYDNEY A. SYKES

Mother Nature's palette is a rich resource of inspiration for decorating your home. By bringing the seasons indoors with inexpensive personal flourishes, you will rarely grow tired of where you live.

"Change is an excellent remedy for that tired feeling. And by 'change' I do not necessarily mean taking a trip," Elsie King Moreland wrote in *American Home* in 1934. "Changing the furniture around is to a woman what taking a vacation is to a man. . . . Nothing seems to refresh me quite so much, to give me a new 'lease on life' as seeing my piano in another corner, the sideboard under the windows, my bed facing another wall."

Traditionally women have prepared their homes for summer by getting rid of anything that was hot or heavy-looking. Take a look around your home. Roll up the hooked and dhurrie rugs; stow the needlepoint pillows or cover them with ruffled denim or white linen pillowcases. Wealthy women used to slipcover their upholstered pieces during the summer months. Not many of us can do that, but we can cover the furniture with white throws. Fabric remnants are great buys (usually $2 to

$5 a yard) and fabulous cover-ups. So are white cotton *matelasse* (raised appliqué) bedspreads draped over couches and chairs. Even large white damask tablecloths, found at estate sales, can be fetching as summer frocks for furniture. Cover side tables with white muslin; drape voluminous lengths of fine mosquito netting from a wooden pole; hang white lace panels, simple café curtains, or bamboo shades at the windows.

Leave your floors bare or put down sisal or sea grass matting over wall-to-wall carpeting. Clear the mantels and tables. Decorate with seasonal flowers gathered from roadside stands, farmers' markets, or your own garden. Simple but abundant arrangements of one type of flower for each container are especially eye-catching.

Pack away anything that needs to be polished: brass, pewter, copper, silver. Replace heavy stoneware pottery with raffia, wicker, and straw baskets. Place a large basket with dried flowers in the opening of your fireplace, if you have one. Move the furniture away from the hearth and back against the walls for a more open feeling.

Seashells and natural decorations set the mood for a summer house even if you don't live at the seashore. Drape fisherman's netting over the mantel and prop up large starfishes. Add pieces of driftwood, twig picture frames, a bird's nest (after the birds have abandoned it), or a bird's house for charm.

Red, white, and blue accents in the form of American flags, denim, and sailcloth, are appealing in the summer. Brightly striped bath toweling or colorful chenille bedspreads make terrific covers for weather-faded outdoor furniture cushions. Summertime meals seem to taste even better on red-and-white or blue-and-white checked tablecloths. Masses of white beeswax candles in hurricane globes and lanterns cast a moonlit glow over summer rooms.

Not all of us can afford a month in the country or a sojourn at a beach house, but we can transform our homes into refreshing warm-weather retreats by taking a cue from the calendar. Like every other Simple Abundance blessing, creating "a summer house" starts with a state of mind.

JUNE 15

The Secret Anniversaries of the Heart

The holiest of all holidays are those
Kept by ourselves in silence and apart,
The secret anniversaries of the heart . . .
—HENRY WADSWORTH LONGFELLOW

This is the traditional month for orange blossoms, lace, and rice, but wedding anniversaries aren't on my mind. Today I am thinking of singular rites of passage, the secret anniversaries of the heart. These are the anniversaries we never talk about, kept in silence and apart. You might remember a first kiss, while I can't forget the last time I held my father's hand.

I was speaking to a good friend this morning on the telephone. She was enjoying the preparation of a special dinner for a marvelous new man in her life. Last year her marriage of twenty years ended and she says she's grateful her husband told her he was leaving in late summer, when everything was withering on the vine. She says that she never would have gotten over it if he had left during the holidays. I think I know what she means, but I pray I never find out for sure. As she reminds me, it's the "feel" of the year that can trigger a secret anniversary of the heart. Another friend recalls the ritual of her mother braiding her hair whenever she walks out into her backyard in the spring and the first lilacs are in bloom. There was always a bouquet of lilacs on her mother's dressing table.

Every June when I wade into the swimming pool of my former roommate, Dawne, I am once again standing in the pool of my Aunt Mary and Uncle Joe, who were my parents' best friends. Forty years have vanished: I hear children laughing, the clink of lemonade glasses, feel the hot summer sun on my shoulders, the splash of refreshing water on my face. It all rushes back—the cool, leafy places in their yard, the flagstone path, the musty smell of the wooden playhouse where my "cousins" Mary Anne and Diane, my sister Maureen, and I used to plot adventures. The barbecues, the picnics, the sleepovers, the adults' cocktail parties upstairs, the children's parties in the basement recreation room, the plays performed on the patio, the feelings of love, security, delight, excitement, and wonder—all the sudden joys of childhood captured forever in the feel of June. My daughter now has her own secret anniversaries of times spent in the homes of her Aunt Dawne and Uncle Tom—beach vacations, Christmas dinners, Easter-egg rolls. These cherished friends, their lovely daughters, and the good times our families have spent together over the years are beautiful threads in the tapestry of my life.

Secret anniversaries of the heart are not restricted by the passage of the years. "I am," Thomas Wolfe recalled in *Look Homeward Angel*, "a part of all that I have touched and that has touched me." We all are. Although I had not planned it, this afternoon I want to send Dawne a note. And I really must write to Aunt Mary to thank her for the precious memories. I need to share what I've held in my heart for so many decades but have never expressed. Today would be the perfect moment to let two wonderful women I love know how much I love them. I had forgotten. It took a secret anniversary of the heart to remind me that there is always time enough to remember. But there is never time enough to commemorate what we cherish, unless we pause to observe, when they occur, the holiest of all holidays.

JUNE 16

The Fragrant Home

I wish that life should not be cheap, but sacred,
I wish the days to be as centuries, loaded, fragrant.
—RALPH WALDO EMERSON

From the moment man, woman, and child first began to follow their noses, scent has been an irresistible magnet drawing the heart and imagination home. "There's no place like home," John Howard Payne wrote in 1823, recalling the woodsy fragrance from the cheerful hearth of an old, shingled cottage in East Hampton, Long Island, where he spent his early childhood. Perhaps there's no place like home because no place else on earth smells quite like home.

As I write, the delicious aroma of baked chicken smothered in teriyaki sauce fills the house. Be it ever so humble, there's no other place I would rather be tonight. Soon my two "returnees"—she from summer camp and he from his city office—burst through the front door. "Welcome home!" I call from the kitchen. "Welcome home!" they echo in our ritual greeting, dropping gym bags, briefcases, and backpacks, shedding the day. "Something smells great!" "When's dinner?" There's time enough for an antipasto of anticipation, a bike ride around the block, a stroll in the garden, a glass of wine, a homecoming.

A fragrant home is a simple pleasure, but one rich in the resonance of reassurance. Subtly layering scents throughout the rooms in your home imparts a feeling of luxury to your living spaces. Here are some ways to make your home smell heavenly.

Regularly air your rooms out, even in winter, by opening the windows wide and letting fresh air circulate. In the sultry summer months, when the windows are closed to keep in the air conditioning, wait until the evening when it cools down. Be sure to open the windows after a summer shower for a delightful scent.

If you have animals, use a baking soda carpet freshener every time you vacuum to eliminate objectionable odors. We become accustomed to the smell of our pets, but it can be overpowering to unsuspecting visitors.

Add scented powder to your vacuum cleaner bag to diffuse fragrance as you clean the carpets. Clean with pine cleansers for an invigorating scent. Trade in aerosol furniture sprays for rich lemon-scented polish. You'll get a better shine *and* scented surroundings.

Simmer apple cider, cinnamon, and cloves in water. This is a trick realtors suggest to create a cozy, inviting atmosphere when prospective home buyers come to call. It will evoke such an inviting environment you might even stop wanting to move.

Gently rub environmental fragrance oils onto unfinished or unpainted wood, such as the undersides of tables and chairs, doorjambs and windowsills, the interiors of wooden drawers, closet rods, and shelves. These oils can also be added to the metal or terra-cotta rings that sit on lightbulbs (only add oil to a ring when the bulb is cold); whenever you turn on the lights, fragrance will waft through the room. Scented candles and incense bring romance to room settings.

Hang scented padded hangers and sachets in closets; line drawers with scented paper.

Burn aromatic woods and grasses in the fireplace. Collect driftwood at the beach and bring it home; burn pinecones sprinkled with essential oil (balsam, lavender, or cinnamon) and dried rosemary bundles; throw in some cedar chips, mesquite, and piñon with your logs. At Irish specialty shops you can sometimes find small blocks of turf from Ireland (well worth the search)—my favorite sentimental scent, especially in winter. Native Americans burn sage bundles to purify their surroundings and to invoke a blessing on the sacred space of their dwellings. You can do the same.

Set bowls of potpourri throughout your home, but use only one type so that the fragrances won't compete. I like to use florals in the spring and summer and spicy potpourri in fall and winter. Making your own potpourri is an enjoyable, relaxing pastime, as is making sachets, pomanders, fragrant pillows, and floral waters. Easy, inspiring recipes can be found in Barbara Milo Ohrbach's delightful book, *The Scented Room*. There's also nothing like coming in from the heat, dipping a cotton handkerchief in a bottle of cool lavender water, and patting your face and neck just as your great-grandmother did to refresh herself after an episode of the vapors.

"In today's world I find it not just nice but necessary to surround myself and my family with things that are familiar, warm, and reassuring," Barbara Milo Ohrbach believes. Our days at home can also be heady and full of fragrant moments once we start to savor the romance of scented rooms.

JUNE 17

Affordable Splendor

There never has been a house so bad that it couldn't be made over into something worthwhile.

—ELSIE DE WOLFE

In 1972 I moved to London to find my fortune on the stage. I didn't, so for a while I ended up working as a secretary for $100 a week. Of necessity, I lived in a dreary, cheerless cell euphemistically known as a "bed-sitter." It had a hot plate to cook on, a sink, a two-shelf "fridge," and about ten feet of space. Basically it was just four badly plastered walls and an exposed lightbulb on the ceiling. The bathroom was down the hall, and every time I wanted to take a hot bath I had to put a shilling into a meter to fire up the furnace for five minutes. But my cell was located at the top of a stately old Victorian building on a picturesque English side street overlooking a handsome park. It had granite steps, a heavy wooden black door with a lion's head for a brass knocker, pristine white woodwork surrounding tall, elegant windows, and black wrought-iron window boxes overflowing with flowers. From the outside, it looked regal, and I loved walking up to it because I felt "to the manor born." Turning the key was another matter, for after I shut the door and trudged up four flights of stairs, I was Cinderella after midnight. But I was also a dreamer, and I dreamed of living in splendor someday.

One Friday afternoon on my way home from work, I passed the window of a large department store. A huge remnant sale was advertised and the fabrics displayed in the window were dazzling. Curious, I went in, took one glance and visions of grandeur came into view. Mind you, I didn't own a sewing machine; I barely knew how to sew by hand. It didn't matter. The sight of table after table of the most beautiful bolts of fabrics I had ever seen was intoxicating, inspiring, irresistible. Here was splendor, and it was affordable. At only about $2 a yard, I splurged on an entire bolt—thirty-five yards—of rust, hunter green, and saffron Indian paisley print. Almost an entire week's salary spent, but it was worth every penny.

That weekend I cut, glued, stapled, draped, and hung fabric. I covered the walls with it, created a tented ceiling, sewed curtains by hand, covered my box spring, fashioned a bedspread, covered pillows, and draped a canopied alcove to sleep in. By late Sunday night, both the room and I had been transformed. I was exhilarated by my beautiful surroundings and my creative risk-taking.

Years later, when I spotted Diana Phipps's indispensable primer on interior design improvization, *Affordable Splendor*, I knew we were kindred spirits. Diana Phipps's authentic gift is resourcefulness. She uses whatever she has, from cardboard boxes to horsehair mattresses. She camouflages just about everything and has never seen an old shawl, a frayed carpet, or a pair of tattered curtains beyond redemption. The results are luxurious, comfortable, creative settings that are the essence of thrift shop chic via Buckingham Palace. This is no coincidence, since Diana was born a Czechoslovakian countess and spent her childhood living in a castle. Then came the German occupation and the Communist takeover, and her family emigrated to the United States where they lived in freedom but "reduced circumstances." However, her surroundings never gave her away once she hit Woolworth's and walked out with forty yards of blue gingham.

I adore this book because Diana Phipps's spirit of decorating is infectious. She's never listened to any expert in her life but her authentic self, and it shows. She confesses, "By nature I am both lazy and untidy. A professional carpenter, upholsterer or painter could, with reason, find a great deal to criticize in my work. I know neither the orthodox way of doing things nor the correct terminology. In fact, I don't want to. I know what the professionals charge, the intimidating mystery they exude and above all, how long they take." Instead, she does it all herself and the stunning shortcuts she has devised are aimed for people "whose purse, like mine, falls short of realizing their ideal setting."

This may sound presumptuous, but I believe we're all just as clever as Diana. We just haven't accessed our authenticity to the extent that she has, because she *trusts* her eye and creative impulses. She acts on her instincts. We hold back, hesitate, halt—and end by snuffing out the spark. Today I would love to convince you that there is no room in your home that cannot be transformed by using fabric, paints, a saw, a hammer, nails, needle and thread, a sewing machine, glue, the amazing staple gun, and your own imagination, time, and energy.

"The most important thing about decoration," Diana Phipps reassures us, is "the fun of it. The fun of discovering a broken-down nothing and turning it into something. . . . Best is to just charge ahead with confidence, enjoyment and a sharp pair of scissors for cutting corners."

JUNE 18

Choosing to Blossom

And the day came when the risk [it took] to remain tight in the bud was more painful than the risk it took to blossom.

—ANAÏS NIN

How much time, creative energy, and emotion do we expend resisting change because we assume growth must always be painful? Much personal growth is uncomfortable, especially learning to set boundaries in relationships. When we commit to nurturing our authentic selves, people close to us are going to start noticing that changes are taking place. This is the season when growth in the garden, which had been gradual, now accelerates. It's that season for us as well, now that we're six months into the journey toward Wholeness.

For it can be difficult to express your authentic needs by saying "Sorry, I can't" when everybody else assumes you can. But it's worse to thwart the ascent of your authenticity. The day comes—maybe it's today—when "remaining tight in the bud" is more painful than blossoming. "Garden-making is creative work, just as much as painting or writing a poem," the Victorian writer Hanna Rion tells us. "It is a personal expression of self, an individual conception of beauty." Gardening is also a wonderful way to gently explore some of the personal growth issues raised by authenticity. Mother Nature is a patient mentor.

Can you find one perfect rosebud, either in your garden or at a flower shop? Place it on your desk or night table. The Talmud tells us that "Each blade of grass has its Angel that bends over it and whispers, 'Grow, grow.'" So do we.

JUNE 19

Onward and Upward in the Garden

Gardening is an instrument of grace.

—MAY SARTON

Gardening was one of the first gifts Simple Abundance bestowed on me after I embarked on the authentic journey. I had never really gardened before because it seemed like too much mind-numbing, back-breaking work. (Notice that no one ever says *playing* in the garden. It's always *working* in the garden.) I was already working too hard in the house and at my writing to work in a garden as well. But several autumns ago, when authentic longings began surging to the surface, I was seized with the determination not to greet another spring without daffodils and tulips in our yard. Since I knew absolutely nothing about gardening, I sought the advice of famous women gardeners: Gertrude Jeykll, Vita Sackville-West, Celia Thaxter, and Katharine S. White.

Katharine White was an editor at *The New Yorker* from its early days, in 1925, until her retirement in 1958. She was also an avid gardener. Her husband, the writer E. B. White, recalls in the introduction to his wife's book *Onward and Upward in the Garden*, "She simply accepted the act of gardening as the natural thing to be occupied with in one's spare time, no matter where one was or how deeply involved in other affairs." Katharine White also adored shopping in mail-order catalogs. "Hour after hour, she studied, sifted, pondered, rejected, sorted in the delirium of future blooming and fruiting," writes E. B. White. This insatiable passion for gardening catalogs prompted her to take up writing after decades of editing. Her first feature was a critical review of seed catalogs and nurserymen that launched her famous garden writing series "Onward and Upward."

To my mind, there are two types of lady gardeners. There are those extraordinary women who not only know every flower, but know every flower by its Latin name. These women look as beautiful as the flora they nurture, gardening in wide-brimmed straw hats and pearls, trailing chiffon, and wearing Ferragamo shoes. They keep meticulous gardening journals, plot plant placements on graph paper, and never break into a sweat when wielding a trowel and a spade. Katharine White belonged to this gardening genus.

"Grunge" accurately describes the other group. We are always hot, smelly, and sweaty in the garden, boasting not so much a green thumb as dirty fingernails because we forgot where we put our gardening gloves. We speak of "that little yellow flower" and point. We also tend to be manic about gardening, seized not only by visions of earthly Paradise but also

Kubla Khan's Xanadu. How else to explain why it never occurred to me when I ordered fourteen rosebushes in April, that they would all arrive on the same May morning, necessitating two days of frenzied labor? Before rosebushes can go into the ground, very deep holes must be dug. Still, into the ground they all went. Miraculously, the gardener did not accompany them. Now they are the love children of my middle-age, conceived during passionate afternoon perusals of glossy gardening catalogs.

Gardening came easily to Katharine White, but writing was "slow and tortuous going," her husband noted. Phrases are far easier for me than double-ditching a flower bed. Still, I think of my adventures in the garden as a trajectory of forward motion, an evolution of soul. Gardening has become an unexpected instrument of grace, for I've discovered hours of inner peace on my knees, digging in the dirt. Here is the one place I don't think about work or worry about whatever it is that I can't control. The complete absorption, the sacrament of the present moment I experience when planting or weeding brings exquisite contentment. My mind is stilled and my heart expands. Now I know why the Great Creator intended for woman to flourish in a garden. So much for second-guessing the wisdom of Spirit.

A beautiful dusty rose named "Pleasure" beckons me. Onward and upward. It's time to play.

JUNE 20

Secret Gardens

Within your heart, keep one still, secret spot where dreams may go.
—LOUISE DRISCOLL

In 1898, Frances Hodgson Burnett, the bestselling author of *Little Lord Fauntleroy* and an international celebrity on both sides of the Atlantic, rented a manor house in the English countryside known as Maytham Hall. Depressed over the public outcry concerning her divorce and hounded by the press because of her scandalous relationship with her business manager, a handsome man young enough to be her son, Mrs. Burnett sought a quiet refuge in which to gather her thoughts and rebuild her life.

Her favorite sanctuary was an outdoor space surrounded by brick walls which she transformed into a rose garden, planting three hundred coral-pink rosebushes. She referred to her rose garden as her private study. Here she would spend the days alternating between gardening and writing, shaded by a large floral Japanese parasol on sunny days. On chilly days she would wrap herself in a lap rug, only retreating to the house when she had to. Over the next nine years, Mrs. Burnett wrote three books and a play, but it was not until 1907, when she was forced to leave Maytham Hall because her lease had expired, that she returned to America. While she created a new garden at her Long Island, New York home, she also began work on what would become her most renowned accomplishment, *The Secret Garden*, which was published in 1911.

The Secret Garden is the story of the redemption of two miserable children who are nurtured by Mother Nature. As the children bring back to life an abandoned and overgrown garden hidden behind stone walls, its revival becomes an inspiring metaphor for their own restoration.

Toward the end of her life, Frances Hodgson Burnett recalled how working in the garden at Maytham Hall had restored her own sense of self. The fond memories of "a softly rainy spring in Kent when I spent nearly three weeks kneeling on a small rubber mat on the grass edge of a heavenly old herbaceous border bed" remained vivid in her imagination, as well as "the plants which were to bloom in loveliness for me in the summer."

Shortly after I began exploring and experimenting with the principles of Simple Abundance as a creative conduit for contentment, I had a wonderful dream. I was led to an old walled garden and shown a golden key that was lying on the path. As I turned the key, a heavy wooden door easily swung open to reveal a dark, dismal wasteland of dead and overgrown plants. Everything was dark. But once inside, I could see an archway leading to the most beautiful garden I had ever seen, bathed in warm sunlight. Yet I was unwilling to leave the desolate garden behind to step into Paradise. Something invisible held me back, tangled in the underbrush. Finally I struggled through the archway. When I did, the wasteland disappeared. I was surrounded only by beauty and abundance and experienced great joy and serenity.

When I reluctantly awoke, I knew exactly what the dream meant. The lush garden was the awareness of abundance in my life, and the wasteland was the manifestation of my thoughts of lack.

Both abundance and lack exist simultaneously in our lives, as parallel realities. It is always our conscious choice which secret garden we shall tend. The invisible underbrush holding us back is our own thoughts. When we choose not to focus on what is missing from our lives but on the abundance that's present—love, health, family, friends, work, and personal pursuits that bring us pleasure—the wasteland falls away and we experience joy in the real lives we live each day.

It would be wonderful to have a real secret garden, as Frances Hodgson Burnett did, but that's not possible for most of us. Still, we can try to create an outdoor sanctuary. If you have a backyard, could you place a comfortable chair and a small table in a shady nook? Hang a hammock? Arrange some furniture at the end of the front porch or on a patio where you might beat a retreat when you need a respite?

And while you're at it, don't forget to tend your interior secret garden, because the seeds that will blossom in outward expression are always first scattered within. Weed out disappointments, frustrations, diminished ambitions, unfulfilled expectations, and anger about what has gone before or what has not yet come. These emotional weeds only choke your creativity. Let an unfettered imagination sow the seeds of possibility in the rich soil of your soul. Then let passion tend the garden with patience and perseverance. For, as Frances Hodgson Burnett discovered, "When you have a Garden, you have a Future and when you have a Future, you are Alive."

JUNE 21

Bloom Where You're Planted

Bloom where you're planted.

—MARY ENGELBREIT

I am a late bloomer. I married at thirty-two, became a mother at thirty-five, published my first book at forty-three, and planted my first real garden when I was forty-five. I feel shy about admitting all this, as if it's a cosmic flaw, but May Sarton, who wrote, gardened, and lived each day with a passion I envy, reassures me that "Gardening is one of the rewards of middle age, when one is ready for an impersonal passion, a passion that demands patience, acute awareness of a world outside oneself, and the power to keep on growing through all the times of drought, through the cold snows, towards those moments of pure joy when all failures are forgotten and the plum tree flowers."

The plum tree did not flower this morning, but a regal pink lily did, in my cottage garden. How did she get here? I planted her, obviously, but I know as much about lilies as I do about life. There she stands before me, majestic in her mature mystery. She is so ephemeral, so exquisite, her beauty should grace the Taj Mahal, but here she is, blooming in Takoma Park.

There is much to recommend late blooming, but when was the last time this subject was the cover story of a glossy women's magazine? Yet the great Victorian gardener and writer, Gertrude Jeykll, who is considered the first lady of modern garden design, was also a late bloomer. Miss Jeykll spent the first half of her life as an artist, but failing eyesight forced her to lay down the paintbrush and pick up the spade. In her fifties she turned to gardening as her creative outlet. Over the next three decades she designed more than fifty stunning English gardens, and wrote fourteen books and numerous articles. We should all bloom so abundantly.

Being a late bloomer means that you have the time and the opportunity to revise and revamp if you experiment with life and fall short of your dreams. We late bloomers can risk more because at this point nobody really expects anything spectacular from us anymore. We can reinvent ourselves or give birth to our authentic selves as we rediscover and reclaim our essence.

As I have tried and failed and tried again, I have discovered that if we are to flourish as creative beings, if we are to grow into Wholeness, we *must* bloom wherever we are planted. Right now, you might not have the perfect career, home, or relationship. Few of us do. But if you have the gift of today, you've got another chance to re-create your circumstances and make them as perfect as it's possible to do with the resources you have. Today, you get another chance to get it as right as you can make it. What more could you desire?

I have a little climbing rosebush. Her name is Blaze. I really planted her in too small a spot, where she is dwarfed by a profuse old lady of a peony. But I have always dreamed of living in a house covered with climbing roses. Since I have stopped waiting for tomorrow's pleasure, I ordered her. When she arrived, wrapped and demure like a mail-order bride, I gave her a kiss, stuffed her in, said a prayer, and hoped for the best.

For a couple of weeks, nothing happened, even though I misted her canes daily, whispered encouragement and invocations to "grow and flourish abundantly." Finally, a month after her arrival, she sprouted leaves and began her ascent. Today she greeted me with tiny buds. Climbers don't normally blossom their first year, but no one told this to Blaze, who chose to bloom where she was planted.

"The people who get on in this world are the people who get up and look for the circumstances they want," observed the English playwright George Bernard Shaw, who believed he got his best ideas after working in his garden. "And if they can't find them, make them."

JUNE 22

The Gourmet Victory Garden

It's difficult to think anything but pleasant thoughts while eating a home-grown tomato.

—Lewis Grizzard

The 1930s and 1940s were lean and hungry years in America. People hungered in the 1930s because of the Depression: debt, drought, dust storms, displacement, and heartbreaking breadlines and unemployment lines. From 1942 to 1945, people were hungry for peace, order, safety, security, and homecomings, as well as meat, cheese, sugar, butter, coffee, and oil, which were strictly rationed because they were being shipped to American troops fighting around the world.

Home gardening took on new meaning during these decades as women had to "make do" with whatever they had. In the 1930s, women's magazines encouraged their readers to grow "kitchen gardens" for reasons of thrift. In the 1940s, President Franklin Roosevelt ordered "victory gardens" as part of the war effort. Domestic propaganda exhorted women to remember that "waste during war is sabotage," and American women answered the patriotic call by growing more than a million tons of vegetables a year—half of what the home front annually consumed—in backyard plots.

The victory garden is a concept whose time has come again, not so much for reasons of thrift as for thrifty pleasure. Probably the most convincing argument for a personal victory garden is a homegrown tomato, just now beginning to turn pink on the vine. In a couple of weeks, the quintessential summer repast will brighten up my midday, as it should yours, a tomato sandwich and lemonade. Slice thick slices of red beauties, slather mayonnaise on Wonder Bread, season with sea salt and freshly ground pepper. My mouth is watering in anticipation as I write.

Now consider Ronde de Nice squash, cornichon French cucumbers, leaf spinach, sugar snap peas—all growing in your plot or potager. It's time to completely rethink growing vegetables. The victory garden in the 1990s has gone gourmet, and it's an affordable luxury. Food is grown not just for economy but for delight.

Today's gourmet gardens are cooks' gardens. That's because gardening and cooking are complementary creative pastimes. If you've never thought of the marriage of these two simply abundant pleasures before, one glance at Geraldene Holt's delectable *The Gourmet Garden* will make gardeners out of gourmets and gourmets out of gardeners. And if you're neither, you'll discover two new aspirations.

You may not have a gourmet vegetable garden this summer. Gardens need to be plotted, planned, and planted before they yield their harvest. But you can sow the seeds of this simple pleasure into your imagination for next year. "The first gathering . . . of salads, radishes and herbs made me feel like a mother about her baby—how could anything so beautiful be mine?" Alice B. Toklas reminisced. "And this emotion of wonder filled me for each vegetable as it was gathered every year. There is nothing that is comparable to it, as satisfactory or as thrilling, as gathering the vegetables one has grown."

Midsummer Night's Dreams

Now is the high-tide of the year,
And whatever of life hath ebbed away
Comes flooding back with ripply cheer
Now the heart is so full that a drop overfills it,
We are happy now, because God wills it.

—JAMES RUSSELL LOWELL

For centuries, wise women have known that a bit of midsummer madness and magic are good for the soul. This probably explains why in Europe, Midsummer's Eve (June 23) has traditionally been set aside as the night for high-spirited merrymaking and lighthearted bewitchment.

Midsummer's Night is also the high holy feast of the "Stillwaters," the mock New England sect imagined by author and illustrator Tasha Tudor. Stillwater followers—originally Tasha Tudor's family and friends—believe that life's simple pleasures are meant to be savored and that Nature is to be revered.

The Stillwater religion, which combines the best beliefs of the Shakers, Quakers, and Amish, is a state of mind, according to its creator. "Stillwater connotes something very peaceful," Eldress Tudor explains, "Life without stress. Nowadays, people are so jeezled up. If they took some chamomile tea and spent more time rocking on the porch in the evening . . . they might enjoy life more."

On Midsummer's Eve, the Stillwaters have a Great Party—plenty of music, dancing in the barn, and a sumptuous summer supper. "Stillwater believers are very hedonistic. Life is to be enjoyed, not saddled with," Tasha Tudor insists. The first commandment of the Stillwater religion, is to "Take joy" from each day. This is a catechism we should all embrace to experience Heaven on earth. Unfortunately, the Stillwaters don't proselytize door to door, so we are all on our own. Nonetheless, this credo invites personal investigation.

I love Midsummer's Day (June 24). For me, it's a personal midcourse correction for the year. I wander out into the backyard very early in the morning and pluck a blossom from the garden heavy with dew. With my fingers, I'll pat the dew upon my face, for legend has it that any woman who washes her face in the dew of Midsummer's Day will grow more lovely with the passing year. Fairy cakes are made for tea, midsummer's syllabub (a delightful concoction of cider, lemon, berries, and whipped cream) is prepared for a moonlit picnic, and personal dreams are renewed. Being Irish, I don't dismiss the belief in love charms, magic herbs, and divination, for I know there's more to this world than we'll ever hope to understand. But these days I'm not so much interested in what the future holds as I am in the present.

"I believe the nicest and sweetest days are not those on which anything very splendid or wonderful or exciting happens, but just those that bring simple little pleasures, following one another softly, like pearls slipping off a string," the Canadian writer Lucy Maud Montgomery reveals through her heroine, Anne Shirley. When Midsummer arrives, it's a time to look ahead and dream. Perhaps, if one is lucky, the days ahead will unfold as a "never-to-be-forgotten summer—one of those summers which come seldom into any life, but leave a rich heritage of beautiful memories in their going—one of those summers which, in a fortunate combination of delightful weather, delightful friends and delightful doings, come as near to perfection as anything can come in the world."

May this potent Midsummer spell never be broken for you and those you love.

JUNE 24

Splendor in the Vase: Living with Flowers

I'd rather have roses on my table, than diamonds on my neck.
—EMMA GOLDMAN

The famous English gardener and writer Vita Sackville-West believed that gardening was like painting: "One has the illusion of being an artist painting—putting a dash of color here, taking out another dash of color there, until the whole composition is to one's liking." I am still too much of a novice gardener to have experienced her observation firsthand. I only discover what dash of color I've put somewhere after it blooms. But I do feel like an artist when I arrange a beautiful bouquet of flowers.

Now is the season for splendor in the vase. Let's make the most of it. Living with flowers is an exquisite simple pleasure, and in the spring, summer, and fall, it's an affordable luxury. Come the winter months, flowers are too expensive for my budget. Like Emma Goldman, I'd choose roses on my table over diamonds any day. This is a real possibility if you grow your own, which is why I splurged on rosebushes this spring. In my heart and imagination blooms a fragrant English cottage and cutting garden, but it is materializing very slowly. Cutting gardens can take years of nurturing before they reward you with bouquets of flowers. So I weed and water and wait.

But while I'm waiting I head to the farmers' market on the weekends and stop off at roadside stands whenever I spot them to smell the flowers and indulge by spending a few dollars. I've also tried to think of ways to live with flowers year-round. One way is to begin surrounding myself with "botanicals," a bountiful description that includes flowers, fruits, foliage, twigs, and grasses. "Botanicals" also refers to decorative furniture, wall coverings, textiles, and china that feature floral patterns.

People have been decorating their homes with botanicals for over 4,500 years, as evidenced by an Egyptian wall painting of geese grazing on grass and red flowers. Interior florals can make a garden bloom indoors, while abundant natural accents available year-round impart not only visual charm but a sense of comforting continuity. A wonderful way to begin exploring decorating with flowers is Cynthia Gibson's *A Botanical Touch* and *The Floral Home* by Leslie Geddes-Brown.

During the summer months, when flowers are plentiful and inexpensive, I love to fill the house with these heavenly tokens of Simple Abundance. But as I arrange bouquets not only for the living room, but also the dining room, kitchen (remember feng shui!), bathroom and desk, I know I am in good company. "Flowers really do intoxicate me," Vita Sackville-West confesses. She's not the only one.

JUNE 25

Getting Started

Plant it with the green side up.
—MARY ANN AND FREDERICK MCGOURTY

How does your garden grow? Does it grow at all? If you're having a hard time realizing the garden that lives inside your heart, there's a way, if there's a desire. Perhaps you don't have a backyard because you live in a city apartment. That doesn't have to stop you. Some of the prettiest gardens I've ever seen have been on front stoops. If you have a balcony or a patio, you can create breathtaking container gardens that bloom with roses, annuals, herbs, tomatoes, and vegetables.

If you don't have a balcony or a patio, interior window boxes can provide you with blooming miniature gardens of seasonal plants all year long. One of the most charming examples comes to us from the 1930s: place white lattice in front of a window that receives plenty of light and sow morning glory seeds in an interior window box. Train the flowers up the lattice to form a delightful and unusual summer curtain.

If you're fortunate enough to have a bit of earth to call your own, make the most of it. Go back to your discovery journal and see what types of flowers you're longing to see in your backyard. If you're not sure, browse among the gardening shelves at a library and bring home an assortment of books to peruse. Write down the names of the flowers and where to order them if you can't get them locally. Decide to concentrate on just *one* spot this year.

Now get yourself a copy of Barbara Damrosch's *The Garden Primer*. Any book that begins by telling you to "keep the green side up" is my kind of gardening book. I may drool and dream over other gardening tomes, but *The Garden Primer* bears the muddy stains of my devotion because I literally carry the hefty paperback outside whenever I'm gardening. "Good gardening is very simple, really. You just have to learn to think like a plant," confides Barbara, and with her indispensable guide, you will.

A wonderful way to actually start gardening is to send for spring bulb catalogs now. Bulbs need to be planted in the fall, either in late October or early November before the first frost, so the summer is the right time to start stockpiling visions of grandeur. E. B. White, who after his wife Katharine's death edited her *New Yorker* gardening columns into a book, ends his remembrance of her gardening years with a glimpse of her last autumn bulb planting and "her studied absorption in the implausible notion that there would be yet another spring, oblivious to the ending of her own days, which she knew perfectly well was near at hand, sitting there with her detailed chart under those dark skies in the dying October, calmly plotting the resurrection."

I cried when I read that passage for the first time. Now I silently thank Katharine White every spring when my bulbs bloom. After closing her book, I headed to our local nursery and bought a hundred daffodil and tulip bulbs for the resurrection of my own contentment.

Here's a bulb-planting tip that's made all the difference for me. Pay little heed to the accepted wisdom that instructs you to space the bulbs apart. I did that when we first moved into our home and ended up with the most pathetic border ever grown. The sight of it was so depressing I gave up the dream of a garden for a decade. Finally, having lusted for years after the flower beds surrounding the Library of Congress, I asked a gardener his secret for abundant blooming. He told me to plant at least six bulbs in each hole (create a circle of bulbs in the hole with one bulb in the center) and space your holes close together. The result was stunning.

I wish I could convey the feeling of immense delight and contentment as I watched those bulbs push their way through the frozen ground, reach toward the sky and turn their beautiful faces toward the sun. Every spring morning while Katie and I waited for the car pool to arrive, we would converse with "the ladies," as they were known, greeting the new arrivals daily and thanking them for their gift of beauty.

Finally, I leave you today with some comforting advice from Gertrude

Jeykll, who changed the face of gardening a century ago. "Let no one be discouraged by the thought of how much there is to learn," Aunt Bumps (as she was known by intimates) reassures us. "Each new step becomes a little surer, and each new grasp a little firmer."

JUNE 26

Everywoman's Essence of Paradise

All the year round she kept racks full of plants in pots standing on green painted wooden steps. There were rare geraniums, dwarf rose-bushes, spiraeas with misty white and pink plumes . . .

—COLETTE

Many women have backyards in which to make their gardening dreams come true, but not all of us do. If you live in the city, without a patio or balcony, don't skip over these gardening meditations. It doesn't matter where you live, every woman can delight in this simply abundant pastime. A wonderful way to begin is by bringing the outdoors in with plants that bloom all year long.

But not just any plants. Please leave the spiny spider ferns or rubber plants in the office reception area where they belong. Instead, consider fragrant plants redolent of romance: camellias, freesias, narcissus, hyacinths, heliotrope, jasmine, violets, scented geraniums.

I discovered the comfort of an aromatic indoor garden when I couldn't afford fresh bouquets of flowers year round. As I got more in touch with my authentic preferences and sought joyful simplicities to brighten up my daily round, I realized how much I loved, longed for, and needed to be surrounded by the visual beauty of Spirit expressed in Nature. The newly discovered sensuist in me wanted feasts for the eyes and sweet scents for my home. The inspiration that pushed me out the door and toward the nursery was Tovah Martin's *The Essence of Paradise: Fragrant Plants for Indoor Gardens*. Her marvelous book is a seductive walk through the seasons, tending fragrant plants from January through December and detailing how to find them, buy them, and care for them.

I started by forcing bulbs and flowering branches in the winter and spring, because one can rarely fail with them and novice gardeners need constant verdant victories. Then, gradually, I moved on to green growing entities that can actually be called plants. Gardeners who creatively toil in the rich soil of imagination, like myself, often end up surrounded by plants that look as if they had been tended by Morticia Addams. We are not known so much for our horticultural skills as for the triumph of our enthusiasm over our prior experience.

Still, one of my favorite creative excursions is to visit a large greenhouse monthly, just to see what's blooming. Now that my nose knows that this beauty and fragrance can be brought home, I'm becoming quite intoxicated with growing an indoor scented garden.

"Gardening really has no beginning and no end. In particular, pleasures of the sense of smell really know no seasons," Tovah Martin encourages us. "Bottled under glass, blooming at your elbow, the indoor garden has an immediacy that gardens outside cannot match. The aromas impart an intensity that will not be ignored. . . . Deliciously distilled, delectably varied— that is the essence of paradise."

JUNE 27

Rosemary for Remembrance: Sowing Herbal Hopes and Wishes

Balm brings you sympathy and Marjoram joy
Sage is long life . . . Sweet Woodruff augurs well for health—
A blessing richer far than wealth.
While Lavender means deep devotion,
Herb of sweet omen, Rosemary conveys
Affection and remembrance all your days.
May Heaven and Earth and Man combine
To keep these blessings ever thine.

—RACHEL PAGE ELLIOTT

For centuries in Benedictine cloisters, gardening—particularly herb gardening—has been considered an important ritual in the daily round of religious life. But the devotion to growing herbs can be traced back nearly six thousand years before the Christian era began. In ancient civilizations like those of Egypt, China, and Assyria, herbalists were revered, and their teachings about the medicinal properties of herbs were passed down in sacred texts. During the Middle Ages, the herbal tradition was honored and preserved by wise women and midwives, who shared recipes and medicinals made from herbs collected in the wild and cultivated in cottage gardens.

There is probably more mystery and lore to herbs than any other plants. Each herb has its own history, significance, and use for either cooking or remedies. King Charlemagne of France, the first emperor of the Holy Roman Empire, believed that herbs were "the friend of the physician and the pride of cooks" and ordered the planting of a royal herb garden in the ninth century. Herbs were considered essential for a long, happy, and healthy life.

Herbs are another avenue of creative expression for the apartment dweller, because a marvelous windowsill garden of herbs can be grown year-round. If you don't have one, there is still time enough this week to visit a farmers' market and pick up a few plants. Herbs adapt beautifully to container gardens because they don't need much space and are very gardener-friendly. A delightful kitchen herb garden of basil, dill, parsley, sweet marjoram, thyme, and rosemary can be cultivated in a large terra-cotta bowl or *catino*, a staple in Italian kitchens. The fragrance will perk you up every time you walk into the room, and fresh herbs will encourage you to be more adventurous in your cooking.

A friend of mine is an herbalist who manages to keep one foot in the sixteenth century and the other in the twenty-first without ever missing a beat. Jeri knows, respects, and honors the mystery, magic, and the wonder of nature, which she refers to as "Mother." When she collects herbs in the wild to create medicinals for herself, gathering the good that Mother has so generously bestowed on her, she becomes a willing participant in her own healing, her search for Wholeness. When she chooses dill, tarragon, or rosemary to flavor a meal she's cooking, she contributes to her own nourishment, well-being, and pleasure. Her love of herbs is a tangible expression of self-nurturance.

Jeri performs a Native American ritual as she collects herbs. She wears a sacred pouch that carries wheat seeds. As she gathers from the earth, she personally returns an offering by scattering seeds. And even if the seeds don't sprout, at least she is feeding the earth's creatures. "The Native Americans have a chant that they invoke when they gather," Jeri says. "The Earth is my Mother, She takes care of me. The Earth is my Mother, I take care of Her."

Today, sow some symbolic seeds, even if you don't have a garden, as a gesture to ritualize the new life you are creating within. Ask for the blessing of Spirit and the nurturing of the Great Mother and know that in due time there will be an abundant harvest for yourself and those you love.

"In search of my mother's garden I found my own," Alice Walker tells us. Today, may this be your discovery as well as mine.

JUNE 28

Repotting: Giving Roots and Yourself Room to Grow

Little flower—but if I could understand
What you are, root and all, and all in all
I should know what God and [woman] is.

—ALFRED, LORD TENNYSON

Uh-oh. Dropping leaves. Whatever can be the matter? The plant has been watered; it basks in the light; it's neither too hot nor too cold. I pick up the pot and look at the small drainage hole in its underbelly. Tiny white roots are frantically pushing through in a futile attempt to escape confinement or at least find a little more breathing space.

Pot-bound. Did you know that plants need to be repotted at least every two years? This has not been a problem for me in the past, since plants rarely made it that long around here. But as I become a better caretaker of myself, I care better for everything. However, even if the roots don't need more room to grow, the old soil should be replaced because all the nutrients have been consumed. The interior of the pot is a wasteland.

"I don't know when I myself am too pot-bound," Gunilla Norris confesses in her numinous devotional, *Being Home*, "lacking courage to be replanted, to take the shock of the new soil, to feel into the unknown and take root in it."

We, too, need to consider repotting for growth. But when? When we wilt even before the day begins. When we can't seem to visualize or dream. When we can't remember the last time we laughed. When we have absolutely nothing in the next twenty-four hours to look forward to. When this happens, week in, week out, we need to realize that we're pot-bound. We need to gently loosen the soil around our souls, find something that sparks our imagination, quickens our pulse, brings a smile or a giddy lilt to our conversations.

But repotting doesn't mean we have to leave the marriage or quit the job. It just means we need something *new*. Why is it too late to go back to college if you do it one course at a time? Maybe this is the summer to learn to speak French or to start your own gift basket business? Perhaps you can get the sewing machine fixed, try making blackberry cordial, or take up fencing. What's stopping you from writing for that grant, applying for the fellowship, pulling together that one-woman show, attending that lecture series, publishing your own newsletter, or just sending for that intriguing mail-order catalog?

As I work with my plants, I see that the roots are just stunted. Gently, with my fingers, I untangle them.

Leaf. Stem. Root.

Mind. Body. Soul.

Three in one. Spirit's seamless thread of mystery. I have often thought that if I could just discover where one strand left off and another began, I could understand it all. As it is, I understand little, yet somehow I know.

I set the plant into a slightly larger pot. Not too large; we must not overwhelm but encourage. So too, I must not take on the world but simply each task before me. Now I add rich potting soil. Water. Slowly I take the plant to a shady spot for a day so that it can become adjusted to its new environment. But even at this moment, the stem seems straighter, the leaves uplifted. "Speak to Him thou for He hears," Tennyson urges. "Spirit with Spirit can meet—closer is He than breathing, and nearer than hands and feet."

Root and bud bear silent witness to the restoration.

JUNE 29

Pruning Back, Plowing Ahead

My soul is a broken field, plowed by pain.

—SARA TEASDALE

Suddenly, inexplicably, life accidents strike without warning. A long-distance runner discovers that the tingling in her muscles is multiple sclerosis. A beautiful actress, frequently described as a Hollywood siren, undergoes a double mastectomy. The domestic bliss of a popular lifestyle author, so often celebrated in her books, disintegrates in public view. The face of a stunning young model is slashed by assailants. A gifted musician is pushed beneath a subway train and loses a hand.

If life accidents of this kind seem particularly cruel, it's because they are—prima facie evidence of fate's maliciousness. More often than any of us would like to admit, life has a way of hitting us where it hurts most.

The term "life accident" was first coined by Gail Sheehy in her book *Pathfinders*. In this book she delved into the life accidents we are powerless to predict or prevent.

"To paraphrase John Lennon," says Sheehy, "life's accidents are what happen to us while we are making other plans." But life's accidents don't have to be fodder for the six o'clock news. The more familiar ones—

divorce, debts, or drug addiction—can sideswipe us with equal devastation.

Unfortunately, Sheehy discovered in the course of writing her books, "Most people do not negotiate either predictable passages, especially the later ones, or life accidents successfully." However, those individuals who *will* themselves to benefit from adversity become what Sheehy calls "pathfinders": real-life champions who, "by refusing to go under in the onslaught of a life accident," emerge victorious.

Life accidents prune us back. Our souls become broken fields, plowed by pain.

Because I am a novice gardener, the task of pruning seems daunting, formidable. Eleanor Perenyi tells me in *Green Thoughts: A Writer in the Garden* that "Plants know you are there, and when you approach them knife in hand, they utter tiny shrieks; on the other hand, if you talk to them kindly or pray over them, they reward you with better than average growth." I am more a gardener of the praying and cooing persuasion, which is why I always hold my breath when I prune. I am also perplexed by the notion of cutting away what appears to be thriving in order to promote abundant blooming in the future. To my linear logic, this seems backward.

Yes, I understand intellectually that pruning strengthens rather than weakens, but that doesn't mean I have to like it. As I look at the roses, however, I realize that pruning is necessary for complete growth. So, I have come to realize, is a certain amount of pain in our lives. Pain prunes the unessential emotions, ambitions, and illusions, teaching us the lessons we either consciously or unconsciously refuse to be taught by joy. Pain prunes the insignificant details that distract us from what is really important, sapping our days, energies, and spirits.

When we don't prune in the garden, Nature does it for us through wind, ice, hail, fire, and flood. One way or another, the boughs will be shaped and strengthened. If we don't prune away the stress and plow under the useless in our lives, pain will do it for us.

Make no mistake, I think pain is a wretched gardener. Her cuts stun and sting. But after pruning, preferably voluntary, we're able to discern what's real, what's important, and what's essential for our happiness.

Be of good cheer. Study your plants and study your lifestyle. When the right time arrives, go into the garden with sharp shears. Speak kindly. Pray softly. Prune back. Now plow ahead.

JUNE 30

Being There: Lessons from the Garden

All you need is deep within you waiting to unfold and reveal itself.
All you have to do is be still and take time to seek for what is with-
in, and you will surely find it.

—EILEEN CADDY

Thirty years ago, Eileen and Peter Caddy, their three sons, and their friend Dorothy Maclean followed an inner spiritual directive to move to an area on the northernmost coast of Scotland. There, beside a garbage dump bordered by sand dunes, they created a garden following only spiritual guidance. Through prayer and meditation, Eileen and Dorothy contacted the spiritual essence, or "deva" of every plant species, which Dorothy described as "angels, great Beings whose lives infuse and create all of Nature." Each plant imparted spiritual direction of what it needed to flourish despite the wretched circumstances. Within a few years, The Findhorn Community, as their settlement was known, became internationally famous for growing an abundance of large plants, vegetables, fruits, and herbs in the worst possible conditions—a spiritual manifestation of an oasis in the center of a wasteland. "Expect your every need to be met, expect the answer to every problem, expect abundance on every level, expect to grow spiritually," Eileen Caddy tells me as I turn over the earth, sow, weed, water, and wait. These are the lessons she learned in her garden. Lessons I long to learn.

Study the cycles of Mother Nature, the garden whispers, for they correspond with the cycles of your soul's growth. Quiet your mind. Rope in the restlessness. Be here. Learn to labor. Learn to wait. Learn to wait expectantly.

Another important lesson the garden teaches is sowing and reaping, as well as seedtime and harvest. Whatever you sow, you will reap. If I plant lettuce, I will not harvest tomatoes. If I sow only positive seeds in my subconscious—thoughts of plenty and not of lack—abundance will sprout in the garden. As for seedtime and harvest, be forewarned. The spiritual time continuum is not the same as time experienced on the earthly plane. A year for us is a second in the spiritual dimension. This explains why an artist who has toiled for twenty years *suddenly* becomes an overnight success. I have learned this the hard way. By sowing and waiting. Then waiting some more. This doesn't mean that the seeds have fallen on stony ground. I refuse to believe this, for I have worked the soil, dug the double ditch, added the compost, peat, sand, and lime. The soil is rich. Some crops—raspberries, asparagus, grapes—require an investment of years before there is a harvest.

If my harvest is to be a simply abundant lifestyle rooted not in the world but in Spirit, I must be patient.

"You are not living by human laws but by divine laws," Eileen Caddy reminds us. "Expect miracles and see them take place. Hold ever before you the thought of prosperity and abundance, and know that doing so sets in motion forces that will bring it into being."

Joyful Simplicities for June

≈§ Take a trip down memory lane by catching lightning bugs or fireflies on the lawn at twilight. Prepare a comfy hotel for them in a clean mayonnaise jar with holes punched in the lid and layered with grass (remember?). Be sure to let them fly away home after a brief visit!

≈§ Enjoy a frosty pitcher of lemonade and conversation when you come home from work. While the frozen variety is fine for most days, why not treat yourself to an old-fashioned nectar made from fresh lemons and sugar syrup? Here's how. Boil two cups of granulated sugar and one cup of water with the rinds of three lemons cut into thin strips for five minutes. Let the syrup cool and add the juice of eight lemons. Strain and store in a covered container in the refrigerator. Use two tablespoons of the syrup for every glass of ice or carbonated water to make lemonade.

≈§ Be on the lookout for a strawberry festival or hold your own. The Victorians called these homegrown events "Strawberry Regales," and the menu included every strawberry confection imaginable. Turn this into a potluck dessert party and invite friends to bring their favorite strawberry sensation. Indulge!

≈§ Remember that ice cream is good for the soul. Freeze a homemade batch, treat yourself to a cone for lunch, make friends with the Good Humor man.

≈§ One June weekend, buy a whole watermelon and keep it in the refrigerator for at least a day so that it gets ice-cold. Cut it in large pieces and sit on the porch, back deck or front stoop eating watermelon with family or friends, spitting out the seeds. Have a contest to see who can shoot the farthest.

≈§ Hang a hammock. Lie in it.

≈§ Celebrate the Summer Solstice on June 21 by camping out in the backyard. Pitch a tent, bring out the sleeping bags, build a campfire in the grill. Serve hot dogs and S'mores for dessert. (Remember S'mores? Take two graham crackers and sandwich a thin chocolate bar with a toasted marshmallow. Eat one. Eat somemore!) Tell ghost stories, then sleep in the moonlight.

≈§ Hold "The Great Party" on Midsummer's Night Eve (June 23) like Tasha Tudor's Stillwater sect. If you are a fan of Tasha Tudor (and who isn't?), have you seen a copy of the Tasha Tudor gift catalog from the Jenny Wren Press? It features stationery products, artwork, reproductions of Tasha's collection of eighteenth-century furniture, Corgi Cottage Preserves, and much more. A one-year subscription can be ordered by calling 1-800-552-WREN, or by writing the Jenny Wren Press, P.O. Box 505, Mooresville, Indiana 46158.

❧ While dreaming of creating a fancy pantry, call for Allison Kyle Leopold's Victorian Cupboard catalog to savor an authentic taste of the past. Allison, who is the author of many beautiful books on Victoriana, has gathered together nostalgic food specialties from here and abroad, as well as vintage tabletop and home accessories. A catalog can be ordered by calling 1-800-653-8033.

❧ Treat your authentic self to the most fetching straw hat you can find.

❧ Paint your toenails red.

❧ You might not be able to create a real secret garden, but a secret spot in which to sit can be yours by building a tepee in the backyard with a wooden stake and string, then planting scarlet runner beans, morning glories, or sweet peas. When the vines appear, guide them up the strings. Retreat to your "tepee" frequently to contemplate the meaning of life. Everyone needs a refuge where there's no phone and no fax.

❧ Even if you're convinced that you can't have a garden because there's no space, Malcolm Hillier's marvelous *Book of Container Gardening* will inspire you to get in there with a spade and a pot. It's filled with fabulous suggestions and instructions for planting window boxes, barrels, tubs, urns, and baskets, and much more. A sensational idea for spring bulbs is to grow two different types of tulips layered in one pot for a dazzling display of indoor beauty.

❧ Plant rosemary for remembrance, and while you're at it, a little lavender, sage, and thyme. Emelie Tolley's enchanting series of books about herbs (written with Chris Mead) will inspire you to become your own herbalist. *Herbs: Gardens, Decorations, and Recipes* will start you off in the right direction; *Cooking with Herbs*, *Gifts from the Herb Garden*, and *The Herbal Pantry* all provide delightful suggestions for what to do with the herbs after you've cultivated and harvested them.

❧ Call for the comprehensive, inspirational catalog of books for gardeners from Capability's Books. It lists over one thousand books and is a wonderful demonstration of just how much delight can be found in the backyard. Capability's number is 1-800-247-8154.

JULY

Lovely July . . . with the evocative murmur of honey bees on the wing and the smell of sun tan cream.

—CYNTHIA WICKHAM

Sultry, steaming, sweltering. July. Slow down. Or stop. It's time to shed ambition and expectation, along with commutes, clothing, cellular phones, calendars. Now our wants seem to diminish. Is it because our needs are met? A shady nook, a cold drink, a cool breeze—whether indoors or out. A respite from the rigors of the day. Time off for good behavior. Summer is not so much a season as a melody, that tune of contentment we hum as the days begin to beautifully blur. The pursuit of happiness becomes our personal priority this month, as the sweet strains of the fourth Simple Abundance principle—Harmony—start to be heard in our hearts.

JULY 1

Constant Craving

I have learned, in whatsoever state I am, therewith to be content.
—St. Paul

In my twenties, I thought fame would do it. In my thirties, I became convinced that a comma in my checking account balance was the answer. Now that I'm in my forties, I know that all my seeking can be summed up in one word: contentment.

In my forties I realize—gratefully—that fame comes at too high a price. Being considered an "accomplished" woman who shepherds successful creative projects from conception to completion is much more appealing than being famous. And in the deepest recesses of my soul, I know that money cannot guarantee happiness. I realized this with certitude the summer morning I read that a famous and wealthy author, whose books hover on the best-seller lists for months, had lost a beloved child to a freak accident. While washing the breakfast dishes, I glanced out the kitchen window to see Katie bouncing a tennis ball against the back of the house—happy, safe, alive. I knew that famous author would trade all her worldly success in a heartbeat to know again the blessing bestowed on me that morning. After I prayed for her, I prayed for myself. Please let me never forget how rich my wonderful life is right at this moment. Please let me never forget that all I have is all I need. Please let me never forget to give thanks.

But I know that I am a much happier woman when I can pay my bills with ease, take care of all my needs, indulge a few of my wants, and have a comfortable cushion of savings. It would also be wonderful—and I hope to have the experience once before I die—to see something fabulous and just say, "I'll take it," without asking the price.

Still, these days contentment is my constant craving. So much so that I have begun asking each twenty-four golden hours stretching before me, luminous in their potential for pleasure, what might be mine for the taking. Sometimes it's as simple as making a delicious tuna fish sandwich with celery and tarragon mayonnaise on buttermilk honey bread for lunch—the way I do for guests and for my family but rarely take time to do for myself. Or as easy as sitting on the beach, not with work in my lap (even when a deadline looms), but a great book.

Just as negative addictions sneak up on us a day at a time, so do positive cravings. Meditation, creative movement, moments of self-nurturance that bring contentment—all can become positive habits of well-being. I find that when I take twenty minutes to get quiet and go within, work with the visual images in my discovery journal, take a walk, or ask how can I make the next task more pleasurable, my wants diminish.

Today, consider the desires that really count—what you really need to be content. Then make sure there's at least three moments today that fulfill mind, spirit, and body with what you alone must have.

JULY 2

The Simplest of Pleasures: One Good Thing That Is

Redeem
The time. Redeem
The unread vision in the higher dream . . .

—T. S. ELIOT

Some days are shaped by simple pleasures, others are redeemed by them. Today—a beautiful summer's day at the beach—was shaped by joyful simplicities. Idylls on a screened porch, roaming in interesting shops, an afternoon on the shore with family and friends, irresistible reading, confidences exchanged while the waves lap at ankles, an ice-cream cone for lunch, strolling the boardwalk, playing amusement park games, winning a prize. Then back to the house, a refreshing outdoor shower, cocktails and conversation, the conviviality of cooking dinner with a dear friend, an abundance of delicious food, delightful wine, laughter, and good cheer—and so to bed, happily.

An Irish proverb tells us "Better one good thing that is, rather than two good things that were, or three good things that might never come to pass." Today there was no need to glance wistfully at the past or project anxiously into the future because the present was fully lived and simply abundant. Today was rich with one good thing after another until it literally overflowed with pleasure.

But not all my days are beach sojourns. Not too long ago, an eight A.M. phone call announcing a major change in plans sent my day careening out of control. I hung up the telephone, my heartbeat accelerating. In one stroke, my carefully arranged coping strategy was out the window and my host of commitments had been made almost unmeetable. This was too much, I thought, as I paced back and forth, muttering and moaning under my breath. I had three choices before me, but only one real-life solution:

scream with rage at the top of my lungs, put my head in the toilet, or take a deep breath and redeem the day with Plan B.

Since I have an understanding in my home not to do anything that might alarm children or animals, screaming was out. The toilet bowl was out as well. If you're really going to drown yourself, you can't do it in a bucket of water. So I poured myself a cup of tea and recalled the Hasidic prayer, "I know the Lord will help—but help me Lord, until You help."

The reality was that the day would be as hard as I made it. Or as pleasant. There was nothing I could do about my circumstances but accept them. "It's always my choice," I reminded myself. Not necessarily *to like* whatever life throws at me, but to try to catch the ball. After all, success in life is not how well we execute Plan A; it's how smoothly we cope with Plan B. And for most of us, that's 99 percent of the time.

I considered Plan B: redeem the day with simple pleasures, some good things to look forward to. At first, learning to smoothly shift gears to Plan B takes some attitude adjustment, but, like driving a car, it becomes an automatic reflex with practice.

First I took my tea out into the garden to calm down. I pulled a few weeds, picked some flowers. After arranging them, I looked at cookbooks. Should I prepare something new for dinner tonight or a comforting favorite? I decided to stop off at the farmers' stand for fresh produce on my way home and see what appealed to me. Why not pick up a good movie as a treat after supper? The peaches on my table were perfectly ripe, so I decided to make dumplings when I got home. In the meantime, I had an hour to work uninterrupted before I had to leave the house and decided to make the most of it. Better a golden hour that is, than two that were, or three that obviously will not come to pass today.

The day stretched before me—not as I had hoped. But not, thank heaven, beyond redemption.

JULY 3

The Hungry Soul

I cannot count the good people I know who to my mind would be even better if they bent their spirits to the study of their own hungers.

—M. F. K. FISHER

When Eve bit into the apple, she gave us the world as we know the world—beautiful, flawed, dangerous, full of being. She gave us smallpox and Somalia, polio vaccine and wheat and Windsor roses," Barbara Grizzuti Harrison tells us in the illuminating and provocative collection of essays, *Out of the Garden: Women Writers on the Bible.* "Eve's act of radical curiosity" also gave us desire, appetite, and hunger.

Without Eve, I wouldn't be wondering what to cook for dinner tonight. Nor would you. Without Eve, I wouldn't be cooking up creative projects that often have me stewing in my own juices until they are completed. But I also wouldn't know the earthly pleasures that I love, as well as the intense desire for mystical morsels that only Spirit can provide: inner peace, joy, harmony.

Most of us eat three times a day (at least) but how often is our hunger really satisfied? A bacon, egg, and cheese biscuit does more for me than a half grapefruit, but unfortunately, unless I'd like to be the size of the golden arches, I feel I can't indulge that often. Many of us constantly hold ourselves in check—about food, relationships, careers—stuffing our desires down deep into the self, as if sheer determination can keep the lid on longing. But I am gradually coming to an awareness that hunger is holy. We're meant to be hungry every day and to satisfy that hunger every day. Why else would the first petition in the Lord's Prayer be for daily bread, even before divine assistance?

Our souls know many different kinds of hunger: physical, psychic, emotional, creative, and spiritual. But the Great Creator gave us the gifts of reason, imagination, curiosity, discernment; we possess the ability to distinguish between our hungers. Are you really hungry this morning for a breakfast biscuit or a break? Is it passionate kisses you desire or pasta? Or a good night's sleep? Then don't sit up watching reruns with that third glass of wine. Turn the television off and tuck yourself in and if you're not alone, invite someone to join you.

"When I write of hunger, I am really writing about love and the hunger for it, and the warmth and the love of it," the great gastronome and poetic food writer M. F. K. Fisher confessed in 1943. "And then the warmth and richness and fine reality of hunger satisfied . . . and it is all one."

Don't despise desire, daughter of Eve. Within your desire is the spark of the Divine. Spirit desired to be loved. A woman with a lusty appetite was created to satisfy that longing.

Love. Hunger. Appetite. Desire. Holiness. Wholeness.

It is all One.

JULY 4

Getting Real and Personal in the Pursuit of Happiness

Expect nothing; live frugally on surprise.

—ALICE WALKER

We've just come back from watching a wonderful, old-fashioned parade. There's been an Independence Day parade in our town for one hundred and six years; it's the oldest consecutive parade on the East Coast. We take the pursuit of happiness very seriously around here. This year, I hope you do, too.

In 1890, philosopher-psychologist and spiritual pioneer William James, the brother of the famous American novelist Henry James, set off his own fireworks with the publication of a landmark exploration on human happiness, *The Principles of Psychology*. Twelve years in the writing, two volumes and fourteen hundred pages long, it boldly went where no book had ever gone before, investigating the mind-body connection, the impact of our emotions on behavior, and the importance of nurturing an inner life instead of concentrating on the outer trappings to achieve personal harmony. With this book, Dr. James became the father of the American self-help movement.

William James was also an eloquent and persuasive champion of a philosophical school of thought known as Pragmatism. He argued that the world already exists when we are born, and we have to accept it as it is. But our ability to create our own inner reality can determine if we view the Universe as friendly or hostile. "Be willing to have it so," he urged, because ". . . Acceptance of what has happened is the first step in overcoming the consequences of any misfortune."

Being a pragmatist, Dr. James believed that personal happiness hinges on a practicality: if your reality lives up to your expectations, you're happy. If it doesn't, you're depressed. This is as real, personal, and simple as philosophy and psychology get, and it makes perfect sense.

Of course, this means we have a creative choice to make if we want to be happy. Do we consciously and continually strive for more accomplishments and accumulations? Or do we lower our expectations, live with what we have, and learn to be content?

Many of us mistakenly think that lowering our expectations means we must surrender our dreams. As one friend put it, "Sorry, Sarah, but this sounds like giving up to me."

Absolutely not. Dreams and expectations are two very different things. Dreams call for a leap of faith, trusting that Spirit is holding the net, so that you can continue in the re-creation of the world with your energy, soul gifts, and vision. Expectations are the emotional investment the ego makes in a *particular outcome*: what needs to happen to make that dream come true. The ego's expectations are never vague: Oscars, magazine covers, the *New York Times* best-seller list. Your dreams must manifest *exactly* as the ego imagines or someone isn't going to be very happy. And guess who that is? The ego! Since none of us can always predict either the future or the best outcome for our authentic path, this kind of thinking is self-destructive. Because if we don't live up to the ego's expectations, we've failed again. And at some point we really *do* give up.

The passionate pursuit of dreams sets your soul soaring; expectations that measure the dream's success tie stones around your soul. I don't think we should just lower our expectations; I believe if we truly want to live a joyous and adventurous life, we should relinquish them.

Living your life as a dreamer and not as an "expector" is a personal declaration of independence. You're able to pursue happiness more directly when you don't get caught up in the delivery details. Dreaming, not expecting, allows Spirit to step in and surprise you with connection, completion, consummation, celebration. You dream. Show up for work. Then let Spirit deliver your dream to the world.

After a lifetime of setting myself up for heartache, the way I now approach the delicate balance of dreams versus expectations is very Jamesian: dream, do, and detach. "When once a decision is reached and execution is the order of the day, dismiss absolutely all responsibility and care about the outcome," Dr. James tells me. I approach my work with a passionate intensity, acting as if its success depends entirely on me. But once I've done my best, I try to let go as much as possible and have no expectations about how my work will be received by the world. I have consciously chosen to be surprised by joy. It's a choice you can make as well.

Today, try to get real and personal about the pursuit of happiness. Oprah Winfrey once said that God's dreams for her were much more than she could ever have dreamed for herself. I don't think any of our dreams begin to come close to the dreams Spirit has waiting with our names on them. I also believe we'll only find out once we start investing our emotions in authentic expression, and not in specific outcomes.

Cooking Companions

No one who cooks cooks alone. Even at her most solitary, a cook in the kitchen is surrounded by generations of cooks past, the advice and menus of cooks present, the wisdom of cookbook writers.
—LAURIE COLWIN

My mother taught me some of her recipes, but Mary Cantwell taught me how to cook. In the early 1970s, when I started out on my own, Mary wrote a cooking column for *Mademoiselle* and I learned about the glories of macaroni and cheese and the personal triumphs of Christmas puddings. I also learned about her various homes and two daughters, her delights, and her disappointments, all of which were somehow seamlessly connected to good food and good eating.

We became close, Mary Cantwell and I, even though we never met, through that intimate, mystical bond that grows stronger over the years between writer and reader. This occurs when the reader's grateful heart realizes to her astonishment that the writer knows her in a way that even her family and close friends do not.

Then, in the 1980s, I became best friends—again through the printed word—with Laurie Colwin, who captured the ups and downs of domestic bliss with a pen and a fork. Laurie taught me that gingerbread revisited can hold rapture, and that sweet butter, really good olive oil, and organic chickens are affordable luxuries. Our lives were very similar: we were close in age, each had one child, and each wrote for a living. But most of all, we were both dedicated homebodies who did not have to wander farther than our own four walls for adventure and fulfillment. Both our days were structured around pages, after-school pickups, pot roasts, and the shared belief that cooking is a high art.

And while I loved Laurie's novels and short stories, I adored her cooking essays. (Now they are gathered in two delectable collections, *Home Cooking: A Writer in the Kitchen* and *More Home Cooking: A Writer Returns to the Kitchen*.) The day was always richer when I had Laurie to read and a new recipe to try. It was as if a close pal had dropped in for a cup of coffee, a chat, and, of course, a big piece of cake.

Another thing Laurie and I shared was an infatuation with cookbooks. Regular cookbook adventures are a perennial pleasure, and I can't recommend them enough. I read cookbooks the way many women read fiction—in bed at night or while watching the potatoes boil. This probably explains why my favorite fiction is always stronger on the domestic details than the sex. I can imagine how two people make love, but I want to *know* what they ate before and afterwards!

Of course, I haven't actually cooked from all my cookbooks. Yet. I simply love to flip through them and stick little yellow Post-it notes scribbled with "sounds good" on their pages for "tomorrow." Cookbooks aren't so much about what's for dinner as they are about a world of abundant and creative choices. With cookbooks our options are always open; we may not be able to ride the Concorde, but we can open a book and rustle up a Gratin de Poulet au Fromage if we're so inclined.

One terrible October morning several years ago, I came downstairs to make breakfast and get Katie off to school. In between packing lunch and urging her to get a move on, I glanced at the newspaper and was stunned to learn that Laurie had died in her slumber of a heart attack at the age of 48. How could the buddy who urged me not just to make the most of each meal, but each day, be gone? I didn't start crying until everyone left, and have never really stopped. I spent that morning making—and eating—an entire pan of gingerbread, in between blowing my nose, rereading her reminiscences, praying, and mourning the loss of an extraordinary woman and writer who celebrated the Sacred in the ordinary. "I know that young children will wander away from the table, and that family life is never smooth, and that life itself is full," Laurie tells us, "not only of charm and warmth and comfort but of sorrow and tears. But whether we are happy or sad, we must be fed."

This is why I love cookbooks, especially hers.

JULY 6

The Good Life

The one fact that I would cry from every housetop is this: the Good Life is waiting for us—here and now.

—B. F. SKINNER

In 1932, during the darkest days of the Great Depression, Scott and Helen Nearing abandoned life in New York City to become twentieth-century pioneers in the Green Mountains of Vermont. They were socialists, pacifists, and vegetarians; they were also inventive visionaries determined to create a completely self-sufficient lifestyle that was solely dependent on their wits, hard work, and perseverance.

The Nearings went in search of the good life: "simplicity, freedom from anxiety . . . an opportunity to be useful and live harmoniously." Two decades later they had succeeded and wrote a homesteading handbook, *Living the Good Life: How to Live Sanely and Simply in a Troubled World*. This book barely caused a ripple when it was published in 1954; those were the affluent postwar years when a television in every living room, a barbecue grill in every backyard, and a station wagon in every suburban driveway was considered the good life. But in 1970, when the book was published as a paperback, it became a best-seller and the bible of alienated barefoot baby boomers in search of flower power, love, peace, and communal nirvana.

When I began the Simple Abundance journey, I was eager to discover all the advice, encouragement, and wisdom I could find to point me toward the good life. However, the Nearings' grueling saga, which included wresting Utopia from the earth twice (they moved from Vermont to Maine when the area surrounding their farm was being developed as a ski resort), is mythological in scope. Their daunting exploits don't just inspire, they exhaust. I certainly can't identify with a woman who could build a stone house by hand when she was in her seventies and her husband was in his nineties.

And as for the life they led after the house was built, "good" doesn't begin to do it justice. Try saintly. *Living the Good Life* is often described as this century's *Walden*, but the Nearings' asceticism makes Thoreau, who loved his salt pork, look like a sybarite. They drank only water, juices, and herbal brews and consumed little more than raw fruits, vegetables, nuts and seeds "that have finished their life cycle," and copious quantities of popcorn. There was no salt, sugar, tea, coffee, dairy products, or eggs in their pantry, and naturally they did not smoke or drink alcohol. Honey was used only sparingly because it "exploited the bees," and maple syrup—which they tapped and sold for cash or bartered—was swallowed with a smidgen of guilt because it sucked "the life blood of noble maple trees." Of course, this explains why Scott lived to be 100 and why Helen, who is now 91, is still going strong. Perhaps the secret to the "good life" is revealed in the Nearings' simply abundant suggestions for living less stressfully, which Helen shared in her moving memoir, *Loving and Leaving the Good Life*:

- Do the best you can, whatever arises.
- Be at peace with yourself.
- Find a job you enjoy.
- Live in simple conditions; housing, food, clothing; get rid of clutter.
- Contact nature every day; feel the earth under your feet.
- Take physical exercise through hard work; through gardening or walking.
- Don't worry; live one day at a time.
- Share something every day with someone else; if you live alone, write someone; give something away; help someone else somehow.

- Take time to wonder at life and the world; see some humor in life where you can.
- Observe the one life in all things.
- Be kind to the creatures.

I've no doubt that if we lived these suggestions every day, not just thought about them, we would realize as the Nearings did, that the good life is truly here and now.

JULY 7

Cooking for Comfort

It seems to me that our three basic needs, for food and security and love, are so entwined that we cannot think of one without the other.

—M. F. K. FISHER

For Nora Ephron, it's mashed potatoes eaten in bed, for Judith Viorst it's a package of Mallomars. The cookbook author Marion Cunningham chooses spaghetti with garlic and good olive oil. Southern chef Nathalie Dupree craves greens cooked "a long time with fatback," while food critic Mimi Sheraton finds restoration in "almost burned rye bread toast covered with salted butter." As for me, fettucine alfredo never fails.

Comfort food: quirky, quaint, quixotic. Personal patterns of consolation, encoded on our taste buds past all forgetting, as unmistakable as greasy fingerprints. When the miseries strike and you're down in the dumps, food transformed by love and memory becomes therapy.

Today let's celebrate the curative powers of the six basic food groups: haute cuisine, lean cuisine, comfort food, soul food, nursery fare, and chocolate. Now there are some who lump the last four into the same category. However, pilgrims such as ourselves, in search of the sublime, appreciate the subtle nuances of succor.

Comfort food is hearty. When hearts are heavy, they need gravitational and emotional equilibrium: meat loaf and mashed potatoes, macaroni and cheese, chicken pot pie, red beans and rice, creamy risotto. Food that reassures us that we will survive. With such sustenance we can keep on going and going, especially when we don't want to take another step. Soul food takes us back to our roots, nursery fare tucks us into bed, and chocolate alters consciousness. Different foods for different moods.

It's important to realize that comfort food is not haute cuisine. You won't find it in a four-star restaurant, but you might get lucky in a diner. Actually, the more you pay for your meal, the less likely it is to bring you comfort. Pleasure can be bought, but comfort must be given. Even if you give it to yourself.

Comfort food is also not lean cuisine. Perhaps you've wondered why lettuce—even radicchio drenched in balsamic vinegar—doesn't satisfy the way lasagna does. There is a pefectly wonderful scientific reason for this physical phenomenon. Consider this: certain delicious foods—carbohydrates—make us feel calm and content because they literally change our brain chemistry by increasing the levels of serotonin, the *natural* feel-good enzyme recently celebrated on the cover of news magazines. In other words, pasta and potatoes are Mother Nature's Prozac. Are you starting to feel better already?

Here is a Simple Abundance plan for making cooking for comfort a joyful simplicity: start a file just for comfort food recipes. When you prepare hearty comfort foods, double your pleasure by doubling the recipe to freeze another meal. On your refrigerator door keep track of what you've frozen, so that you know what's available when black clouds hover. It's such a simple pleasure knowing that there's something delicious and comforting in the freezer for dinner, especially when you've been working hard all day long and no one appreciates it.

"Since we're forced to nourish ourselves, why not do it with all possible skill . . . and ever-increasing enjoyment," the marvelous M. F. K. Fisher asks. And when we sit down not only to eat, but to be cheered and comforted, let us do so "with grace and gusto" and a grateful heart.

JULY 8

In Search of Soul Food

Soul food is just what the name implies. It is soulfully cooked food or richly flavored food, good for your ever-loving soul.
—SHEILA FERGUSON

In 1900, a Kentucky mountain woman walked fifty miles to seek a place for her granddaughter at Berea College high school. "Hit's a lot worse to be soul-hungry than to be body-hungry," she explained. Now I know why every year I travel a thousand miles for a plate of pinto beans.

Soul food is our personal passport to the past. It is much more about heritage than it is about hominy. It's Grandma's beaten biscuits or Nana's borscht. Sheila Ferguson tells us in her cookbook *Soul Food: Classic Cuisine from the Deep South* that it's "a legacy clearly steeped in tradition; a way of life that has been handed down from generation to generation." And while the expression "soul food" is usually used to describe traditional African-American cooking, this emotionally evocative cuisine is color-blind. Real soul food only knows the borders of the heart. Soul food is universal culinary memories, stories, and recipes. It's how to fry the chicken or the wonton, shape the noodles, simmer the brisket, roll the tortilla, sweeten the iced tea.

Whenever I've gone home to visit my parents, over the last twenty-five years, the first and last meal my mother has always prepared for me is my favorite: soup beans, a tangible time transporter to her old Kentucky home and mine. Soup beans are pinto beans that have simmered slowly for hours, until they create their own soup. Ladle soup beans over mashed potatoes. Serve with coleslaw, hot cornbread slathered with real butter, and an ice-cold beer. This summer my mother is gravely ill and my sister, brothers, and I are struggling with the traumatic reality of saying good-bye. In a few days, Katie and I will travel north for a family reunion of all my mother's children and grandchildren; there will be conversation, cooking, comfort, closure. Although I know intellectually how to prepare my favorite meal, I don't emotionally. I don't think about my mother dying, I think about my last helping of *her* soup beans. There are many ways to grieve.

When preparing soul food, we can't cook by the book but rather by instinct, by using our senses. "You learn to hear by the crackling sound when it's time to turn over the fried chicken, to smell when a pan of biscuits is just about to finish baking, and to feel when a pastry's just right to the touch," Sheila Ferguson tells us. "You taste, rather than measure, the seasoning you treasure; and you use your eyes, not a clock to judge when that cherry pie has bubbled sweet and nice. These skills are hard to teach quickly. They must be felt . . . and come straight from the heart and soul." As I write, I have just come to the heartwrenching awareness that I need at least another lifetime to learn how to cook like my mother but that I only have today, if I'm lucky.

This summer, collect soulful recipes, or have someone you love but don't see very often cook for you. Better still, try taking a personal cooking lesson. You might think you know how to make jam cake with caramel icing, but do you?

JULY 9

Nursery Fare for Children of All Ages

Animal crackers, and cocoa to drink,
That is the finest of suppers, I think;
When I'm grown up and can have what I please
I think I shall always insist upon these.

—CHRISTOPHER MORLEY

The first Christmas I spent away from home was in London in 1972. A few days before December 25, a big box arrived with gifts from home. Among them, from my mother, was a pair of red flannel pajamas-with-feet. Where she ever found them in my size I can't imagine, but now that I know about these things, I'm sure she spent hours planning and searching for my surprise. At the time, though, I didn't appreciate either the gift or the gesture. I was twenty-five, thought I was sophisticated, and was insulted that she still thought of me as a baby—which, of course, is exactly what I was. My mother, who had been stationed in England during World War II as an army nurse, knew that London could be cold, damp, dismal, and, at its worst, numbing. Since I knew zip, I promptly discarded the pajamas, preferring to shiver in a black silk kimono.

What I wouldn't give for those pajamas now! They would perfectly set the mood for a nursery supper, which is what grown women, like you and me, sometimes need in order to "make it all better," at least for a little while.

When you're cranky and cry easily, when you are so tired that your eyes burn from keeping them open, when you need hugs and someone to pat the top of your head and whisper "Shh . . . There, there . . ." and no one is around, you need nursery fare. Nursery foods are the well-loved recipes from childhood that conjure up the happy, innocent moments when all was right with the world because we knew our place in it. The times when, dressed in our flannel pajamas, we sat down for supper before a story and bed . . .

Once, at the end of a delicious sophisticated dinner party attended by smart, successful fortysomethings, the witty banter came to an abrupt halt when our hostess brought out dessert. In front of each guest, she put a bowl of rice pudding, covered with warm cream and sprinkled with cinnamon and nutmeg. After the first tentative mouthfuls came squeals of delight and, in unison, "I haven't had this in years!" The pleasure at that table was palpable.

"Nursery food is the supreme comfort. No wonder, because however abysmal it really was, childhood looks so appealing the farther away it gets," say Jane and Michael Stern, authors of a wonderful collection of yesterday's taste thrills, *Square Meals*. "You remember warm farina served in a bowl decorated with dancing bunnies, or the ritual cup of cocoa after school."

Now that we've grown up and can have what we please, we shouldn't forget that we're never too old for nursery fare: welsh rarebit, milk toast, beef tea, coddled eggs, French toast fingers, porridge with warm apple sauce, baked bananas, custard with caramel sauce, junket, tapioca, and chocolate pudding with a dollop of whipped cream. If you can't remember when you last indulged in something smooth, comforting, and delectable, something that made you smack your lips, then it's been too long. To refresh your memory, the Sterns have devoted an entire chapter to nursery food in *Square Meals*.

The next time you're on edge, or need to be talked down off one, stop for a moment to concoct something bland and creamy to soothe your jaded palate and jangled nerves. And if that doesn't work, there's always teddy and your thumb. So wash your hands and pull up a chair.

> The kitchen's the cosiest place that I know;
> The kettle is singing, the stove's aglow,
> And there in the twilight, how jolly to see
> The cocoa and animals waiting for me.

Don't worry, there's enough for both of us. I'm a big girl now. I know how to share.

JULY 10

Kitchen Mysticism

After all, it is those who have a deep and real inner life who are best able to deal with the irritating details of outer life.
—EVELYN UNDERHILL

Woman's normal occupations in general run counter to creative life, or contemplative life, or saintly life," Anne Morrow Lindbergh consoles me as I fling myself from summer camp dropoff to computer, to summer camp pickup, to computer, to kitchen, and back to computer at eight in the evening. This summer my life is broken up into two-hour increments, which is not the most conducive way to create or contemplate. I have another five weeks of this insanity.

It is a subtle irony, but one not lost on my authentic self, that while writing a book of meditations—a work that you might imagine springs from the author's deep spiritual reservoir of calm—I seem to be in perpetual motion. This is either a cosmic joke or a cosmic lesson, which I can learn the easy way or the hard way. I can't just write about Simple Abundance; I have to live it, or I might as well be writing science fiction.

I desperately need to restore harmony in my life, to find balance again between the inner and the outer, the visible and the invisible. The writing doesn't seem to be coming *from* me as much as *through* me, almost *in spite* of me. Today the strings on this instrument are very taut. I've got to loosen them so that they don't snap. Maybe you feel the same way. Maybe the pitch of pressure is too high, the tone in your voice too sharp, the decibels of the demands on you deafening.

We need to explore the fourth Simple Abundance principle—harmony—most deeply when life is out of tune. I recently read a lovely book, a spiritual journey written by a gifted woman writer, who actually went to a monastery in order to concentrate, create with clarity, and complete her book on time. You can imagine what part of her journey made the strongest impression. Since I obviously cannot follow her example without abandoning husband, child, and animals, all of whom are waiting, at this very moment, to be fed, I'll stop and head into the kitchen. I might not be able to say Mass or meditate today, but I can make a meal.

"The home is a sacred place where you can communicate with the four elements of the universe: earth, water, air and fire," says writer and kitchen mystic Laura Esquivel, author of the luminous novel *Like Water for Chocolate*. "You mix it with your love and emotions to create magic. Through cooking, you raise your spiritual level and balance yourself in a world that is materialistic." In a world that is frequently out of kilter, the kitchen is as mystical as a monastery.

Slice red and yellow bell peppers, tiny eggplants, and zucchini into strips. Chop red onions, fresh basil, oregano, and Italian plum tomatoes. Sauté slowly in good olive oil and minced garlic until the vegetables are soft. Take a sip of wine. Add penne pasta to boiling water for six minutes. Grate fresh Parmigiano-Reggiano cheese. Warm store-bought rosemary and ricotta focaccia in the oven. Toss the pasta and vegetables together. Sprinkle with cheese. Call everyone to the table. Stop to give thanks. Offer a toast and a thanksgiving for good health, love, companionship, delicious food, and a moment of contentment. A day fully lived, simply abundant.

Evelyn Underhill, an English mystic and writer of the early twentieth century, believed that women mystics with worldly responsibilities often became "visionaries, prophetesses" because they were able to combine "spiritual transcendence with great practical ability." Be they poets, saints or cooks, they "remained all their lives the devout lovers of reality" while seeking Spirit.

Now *that* is music to my ears. Want to hum along?

JULY 11

Cooking as Art: Creative Discoveries in the Kitchen

The discovery of a new dish does more for the happiness of the human race than the discovery of a star.
—JEAN ANTHELME BRILLAT-SAVARIN

Few of us have enjoyed the thrill of mounting a one-woman show of our art. But all of us can put on an apron. Tonight, instead of thinking of dinner as just another obligation, think of it as an opportunity for jump-starting your creativity. Cooking is one of best ways for your authentic self to remind your conscious self that you are an artist. Like the union of canvas and pigment, cooking is alchemy, a work of Wholeness-in-progress.

A paring knife can be as creative as a paintbrush. Scraping, slicing, shredding, stirring, simmering, sautéing are all sleights of hand that switch your conscious mind onto artistic, automatic pilot. Once the conscious mind is distracted, the creative mind takes over, even if you aren't aware of it. Whenever I don't know what to do—whether it's writing or living, I seek discoveries in the kitchen, such as trying to re-create a great dish I enjoyed somewhere else. The worst that can happen is that the experiment's a flop and we end up eating sandwiches before bed. The best is that my pleasant brainstorming and the supper that results provide a new taste sensation, reminding me that nothing need be taken for granted—especially moments of doubt, frustration, and hunger.

"If your regrets linger, if you cannot find inspiration in solitude, then you still have much to learn from the writers and the poets and the cooks on becoming the artist of your own life," Jacqueline Deval reflects in her tantalizing novel *Reckless Appetite: A Culinary Romance*. ". . . you can never re-create the past. But you can shape your own future. And you can make a cake."

This week, try making a cake from scratch as a meditation. Think of the most luscious cake you can imagine, the cake of your dreams, the cake you've always wanted to eat but never had the time to make. The cake that has always seemed too daunting. Take time, make time, make your cake.

Declare the kitchen off-limits. The artist is at work. Slowly, carefully, and mindfully gather together the raw materials for your creation: flour, eggs, milk, baking powder, baking soda, salt, spices, and sugar.

If something is perplexing you at the moment, see the situation as simply an ingredient in the great recipe that's Real Life. Each ingredient makes its own authentic contribution to the whole, yet each ingredient changes— the salt and the sugar become one—transformed by the four elements of the Universe: fire in the oven, water from the tap, earth in the grain, the air embracing all. Do not discount the fire that burns in your soul, the water of your sweat and tears, the earthiness of perseverance, and every breath you take as you struggle to master the art and unravel the mystery of an authentic life.

And when your cake emerges from the oven, fragrant and full of flavor, consider for a moment the difference between creating a cake—or a life— from scratch and one that's thrown together with a ready-made mix. Convenience foods may save us time in the kitchen, but the cook always knows, just as the artist does, what is the genuine article and what merely passes for real.

JULY 12

How to Cook a Wolf

There's a whining at the threshold—
There's a scratching at the floor—
To work! To work! In Heaven's name!
The wolf is at the door!

—CHARLOTTE PERKINS GILMAN

Who's afraid of the big, bad wolf? We all are. Because sooner or later he's whining and scratching at everybody's door.

Having money in the bank isn't necessarily insurance against huffing and puffing. Recently more than one hundred of America's wealthiest men and women who invested in the prestigious but now insolvent insurance company, Lloyd's of London, lost all their personal assets when their promissory notes to pay off Lloyd's debts were called in on a moment's notice. As one former millionaire put it, the only thing he could call his own after the fax arrived was the shirt on his back and his gold cufflinks. And while the American investors are now seeking relief in the courts, don't think for a minute that some of the richest families in this country, who never gave the lack of money much thought before, can't feel hot breath raising the hair on the back of their necks.

For the rest of us, the wolf's arrival is less dramatic but just as traumatic. Our wolf tales never even get mentioned in the newspapers: a sudden loss of job that puts a mortgage in jeopardy; a family business that goes under; an elderly parent forced to turn over his house to Medicaid to pay for long-term care; the unexpected expense of infertility and adoption; the bill—payable when services are rendered—that proves veterinary medicine is now state of the art; the roof that needs to be repaired; the termites in the basement; the eight-year-old car that finally can't be resuscitated.

When the wolf arrives, "Our texture of belief has great holes in it," M. F. K. Fisher recalls. "Our pattern lacks pieces." Mary Frances Kennedy Fisher, who was probably this country's greatest food writer, knew all about lean times. In fact, one of her early books was *How to Cook a Wolf*, which she published in 1942 during the worst of the wartime food shortages.

She wrote from personal experience. During much of her life, M. F. K. Fisher had to keep the wolves at bay. Although she was well known—writing for *The New Yorker* as well as many other publications over many years, she was never really well paid and continually had to scratch out a freelancer's hand-to-mouth lifestyle to help support herself, two daughters, and, at various times, three husbands. I say "lifestyle," rather than "existence," because M. F. K. Fisher knew how to live well despite her bank account. She never reduced herself to mere existing, whatever her circumstances. Poverty is always experienced in the soul before it is felt in the pocketbook.

It seems incredible to think of M. F. K. Fisher as lacking for money because she never lacked a simply abundant life. Perhaps she enjoyed the good life because she received it with a grateful heart. She traveled, lived in France and Italy, wrote many magnificent books, knew passionate love, enjoyed a wide circle of friends and admirers, and always savored the everyday epiphanies of eating and drinking well. M. F. K. Fisher's authentic self found outward expression in exuberance.

For those of us who would like to follow in her footsteps, she recommends weeding out desires, leaving only the holy hungers, "so that you can live most agreeably in a world full of an increasing number of disagreeable surprises."

How did she do it? By not running scared when the wolf arrived, by not giving in to her fears that he would blow her house down. She knew that the twists and turns of fate are usually just hot air. Instead, she learned to outsmart, catch, and cook the wolf. By concentrating on the good at hand—a good glass of wine, a good tomato, a good loaf of bread. A beautiful sunset, a lively conversation, a loving relationship. She knew that the good life does not depend on extravagant indulgences. The good life does not deprive. It exults. "You can still live with grace and wisdom," she encourages us—if you rely on "your own innate sense of what you must do with the resources you have to keep the wolf from sniffing too hungrily through the keyhole."

JULY 13

Stocking the Larder

Cooking—yes, and living become simpler rites this month. I have made a list of satisfactory meals planned around only one cooked dish. This list is hung on the door of my kitchen cabinet for reference. When I am lacking in ambition I do not wonder what to have for dinner.

—NELL B. NICHOLS,
WOMAN'S HOME COMPANION, *July 1925*

One of my favorite literary domestics is Nell B. Nichols, a columnist for *Woman's Home Companion* during the 1920s, 1930s, and 1940s. Before Martha Stewart, America had Nell Nichols. There was nothing she couldn't do. But Nell's great gift was that she never made you feel inept; you knew if you followed her blithe instructions carefully, you could also experience domestic bliss.

Nell cooked, canned, cleaned, organized from broom closet to basement with cheerful élan; she tried out new gadgets like the vacuum cleaner and deemed it a "valuable friend," but she also cherished old traditions like bleaching white linens by drying them in the summer sunlight. Reading her columns is like being spoon-fed black-cherry pudding: soothing, comforting, completely satisfying, yet a bit piquant. After an hour with Nell I always want to bob my hair, slip into a simple drop-waist cotton chemise, tie on a checked apron with a bow, and listen to Scott Joplin on the wireless as I dye unbleached muslin curtains "to pretty up the attic windows."

During the decades that Nell Nichols reigned as queen of the home front, "efficiency" was the buzzword in women's magazines. Women were exhorted to consider homemaking not only an art the way their Victorian mothers had, but as a science—home economics. One bit of wisdom for which I'll be eternally grateful to Nell is her plea that women "plan more to work less in the kitchen."

Two homecaring tasks that consume a great deal of creative energy each week are grocery shopping and meal preparation. I've created Simple Abundance strategies for stocking the larder that can help you reclaim a sense of control when cooking. The first is to create a master grocery list. This task will take you only about an hour and will return an abundance of time in the future.

Divide your grocery list into different categories, such as Fresh Produce, Dairy, Meat, Fish, Staples, Paper and Personal Care Products. These will serve as automatic reminders. I have my master list on my computer, and every Friday I print it out and check off what I need. If you prepare yours on a typewriter, get a year's supply of photocopies. Keep a copy of the master list on the refrigerator and instruct family members to add items to the list as they use them up.

We try to grocery shop only once a week, dividing up the task. My husband shops at a food warehouse. I pick up fresh produce—at the farmers' market in the summer and early fall and at an organic grocery the rest of the year. I don't know if it's true for you too, but it seems that every time I go to the supermarket, even if it's just for a gallon of milk and a loaf of bread, $35 disappears. Keep your grocery bills down by making a minimum of visits. (You'll save time, too.)

Before I can make out an efficient grocery list, I need to devise menus, including school or summer camp lunches, so I'll know what we'll be eating that week and what I'll be cooking. By writing out your meals, including side dishes, you'll avoid forgetting any necessary ingredient at the market. I have approximately fifteen different meals that we enjoy seasonally and I rotate them. This gives me an opportunity to control, not just grocery costs, but what we're eating.

A Simple Abundance strategy is to sit down and write out your family's favorite meals; you might even ask for suggestions. Be sure to include side dishes, vegetables, and desserts. Then create a master menu file. Again, I've stored mine on my computer, but you might like to write out your repertoire of menus on index cards. A core of at least a dozen meals enables you to create a sense of variety at dinnertime. Nothing is drearier than eating the same thing over and over again. But it's so easy to get into a rut! Many of us simply don't have time during the week to experiment in the kitchen. To keep your beloved "customers" coming back to your restaurant, try to include two new recipes a month. Save them for weekends, when you have more time and can enjoy the simple pleasure of cooking something new and different.

"Just one word more—please *steal* time every day, if you cannot find it in any other way, to lie on the grass, or in a hammock, under a huge tree this lovely month . . . and relax. What a tonic this is for the soul! What a rest for weary nerves! Our husbands, children, friends—yes, and the nation—will profit by our relaxation. The greatest need today is for calmer homes, and no fireside can be calm unless its guardian is at peace with the world," Nell B. Nichols reassured our grandmothers in the summer of 1924.

"Won't you agree with me, as you lie looking up at the leafy canopy above you, that a home now and in every other month must be a haven to the spirit as well as a place in which the physical needs are supplied?"

Yes, Nell. Yes. Thanks for reminding us.

JULY 14

The Celebrating Table

The table is a meeting place, a gathering ground, the source of sustenance and nourishment, festivity, safety, and satisfaction.
—LAURIE COLWIN

Whether we're single, married, with or without children, we all have to eat dinner. The evening meal should be the highlight of the day. If the day has been peaceful, pleasurable, and profitable, it's time to celebrate. If the day has been difficult and discouraging, it's time for comfort and consolation—blessings by themselves and reason to celebrate. Either way, the celebrating table bids.

Just as there are different food categories, there are different types of dining in: make-do, carryout, home-style, and feasts. All of us make do sometimes, but as a lifestyle choice, a crust of French bread and a heel of salami can quickly lead to psychic starvation and dietary deprivation. Carryout meals can cut corners miraculously, but are extremely expensive, and a steady diet of restaurant food will make you feel as if you've been on the road too long. Home-style is what I call Monday-to-Friday suppers, which, with planning, can be easy, fast, and delicious. Weekends call for your favorite meal one night and a culinary feast the next.

There was a time when I wouldn't begin to think about what to have for dinner each day until four o'clock that afternoon. Today this thought makes me shudder. Planning, shopping, and cooking in the space of an hour is self-abuse, pure and simple. Fear not, there's a great resource for planning your meals and weekly grocery shopping. It's the *Monday to Friday Cookbook* by Michele Urvater. Michele's a professional chef who created this cookbook because, at the end of a long day cooking for other people, she wanted simple but savory, no-fuss suppers for her family. She'll teach you how to stock the pantry with staples, what to fix when schedules clash, and how to avoid the Mother Hubbard's empty cupbord syndrome with style.

"We need time to defuse, to contemplate. Just as in sleep our brains relax and give us dreams, so at some time in the day we need to disconnect, reconnect, and look around us," Laurie Colwin reminds us. "We must turn off the television and the telephone, hunker down in front of our hearths, and leave our briefcases at the office, if for only one night. We must march into the kitchen, en famille or with a friend, and find some easy, heartwarming things to make from scratch, and even if it is but once a week, we must gather at the table, alone or with friends or with lots of friends or with one friend, and eat a meal together. We know that without food we would die. Without fellowship life is not worth living."

Come, the celebrating table bids.

JULY 15

Guess Who's Coming to Dinner?

I learned early on that setting a table is so much more than just laying down knives and forks. It is creating a setting for food and conversation, setting a mood and an aura that lingers long after what was served and who said what was forgotten.

—PERI WOLFMAN

When preparing a meal, the last thing many of us think about, except when we're expecting company, is our table setting. For guests we'll bring out the good china, stemware, and linens, but for ourselves, the everyday, no matter what shape it's in, will have to do. Yes, it will be fine, if it's all you have. But if you continually choose the chipped over the beautiful china behind the glass doors when you don't have to, then making do is not enough.

The rituals of nourishment cry out for the communion cups, the special plates on which to break bread, the candle flame, the circle drawn in the dirt. Ritual protects and heals, ritual symbolizes to all who come to your table seeking rest and renewal that they are enclosed within a sacred space. You may think you're only laying a place at the supper table, but when you trust and follow your creative impulses to bring forth something beautiful, you experience the Sacred in the ordinary. Moses looked for God in the burning bush. We need look no further than our tables, the tables that the Hebrew Psalmist tells us have already been prepared for us so that our cups might runneth over.

"When I think back to our family meals, it isn't the taste or smell of the food that I recall as much as the way the scene looked," reminisces Peri Wolfman, coauthor with her husband, Charles Gold, of *The Perfect Setting* and owner of the New York tableware store Wolfman Gold & Good. "The ambiance of the table, the patina of the wood, the candlelight, the colors, the sense of harmony and order."

Today our style of entertaining has become more casual than the starched linen and polished silver of our grandmothers, yet the sense of harmony that can be conjured up with an inviting table setting has not changed. Nor has the need. If anything, we hunger for harmony more than we do for sustenance. But we don't need to feast from damask everyday: a beautiful pine table set with lovely French linen tea towels as placemats and with lap-sized napkins, pottery plates, oversized water goblets, votive candles, and a small bouquet of summer fruits and flowers is a simply abundant setting that elevates eating into the exquisite pleasure of dining.

When you take extra moments to prepare an attractive table, you're really performing an invocation, welcoming Spirit to be present in recreation and remembrance. Choosing to dine rather than just eat is a small but significant step toward self-nurturance, and one to savor as long as we live. Creating an inviting table is possible more nights than you think, especially if you approach it as another venue of artistic expression in your daily round and confine your efforts, as Peri suggests, to "the simple, the doable, and the affordable."

Today, start using and enjoying the beautiful things that already surround you in your home. Don't save their loveliness only for other people to recognize and appreciate. Using them, you will become aware that authentic aspirations—from setting a pretty table to finding your life's calling—are legitimate longings.

Company *is* coming for dinner tonight. Guess who? It would be a quantum leap in abundance consciousness, if, when your authentic self graces your table, she finds generous portions of the love, respect, and welcome she so richly deserves served up on the most beautiful plate you own.

JULY 16

A Seasonal Feast: The Joy of Anticipation

Why is any day better than another, when all the daylight in the year is from the sun?
By the Lord's decision they were distinguished, and
he appointed the different seasons and feasts;
some of them he exalted and hallowed, and some of
them he made ordinary days.
—ECCLESIASTICUS (ALSO CALLED SIRACH) 33:7–9

The joy of seasonal cooking is the simplest of pleasures, but one of the most overlooked. It brings harmony and rhythm to our days, demonstrating with gentle wisdom that simplicity and abundance are soul mates. The joy of seasonal foods transforms even the ordinary days at the table into hallowed moments, calling to mind the Book of Proverbs' wisdom that "the cheerful heart has a continual feast."

Cooking with the seasons is also thrifty. We often think that using the freshest foods possible, at the peak of their flavor, is a luxury, but seasonal cooking is the best way to eat *well* on a budget. What's more, if your frugality is so subtle and sophisticated, your material girl can't begin to feel deprived—not when she's enjoying a dinner of grilled vegetables with marinated goat cheese, *bruschetta* (toasted Italian bread) topped with tomato, mozzarella, and basil, and peach shortcake with blackberry sauce for dessert.

Summer is when Mother Nature shows off, proving that the Universe is not stingy. Gardens and farmers' markets now overflow with the goodness of the earth. Now, while the summer is offering bountiful home economic lessons, is the perfect time to reconsider how you cook throughout the year.

One of the most wonderful cookbook for seasonal feasts I have ever discovered is *Judith Huxley's Table for Eight*. Judith Huxley was a superb writer, cook, and a gardener, and her love of all three authentic arts is evident on every page of this marvelous book. There are fifty-two sensational menus—a week-by-week walk through the year celebrating the pleasures of the table. I return to this beloved cookbook again and again, usually on Sundays, when I prepare our family feasts.

"There is no season such delight can bring," the English poet William Browne believed, "as summer, autumn, winter and the spring." The simply abundant joy of seasonal foods will convince you that life can be a continual feast at Mother Nature's table.

JULY 17

Loaves and Fishes, Part I

We have here but five loaves, and two fishes.

—MATTHEW 14:17

Do you know the story of Jesus feeding the crowd of five thousand believers, seekers, skeptics, and the simply curious who had come to hear him teach? At the end of the long day, when the disciples wanted to send everybody home, Jesus told them not to be ridiculous, that the people were tired and hungry. "But we only have five loaves of bread and two fishes, barely enough for ourselves," the disciples argued. "How can we feed that many?" "Give me what you have," Jesus told them. Then Jesus looked up to Heaven, offered thanks, blessed the food, and gave it back to the disciples to distribute. Miraculously, after everyone had finished eating as much as they wanted, twelve baskets of leftovers remained.

I love this story because it's such a powerful illustration of abundance consciousness, providing us the model for simply abundant living. The gospels of Matthew and Mark report that Jesus performed this simply abundant miracle *twice*. On the second occasion, four thousand people were fed with seven loaves and a few fishes. By this time the increasingly threatened high priests had started stirring things up. They demanded that Jesus demonstrate more signs and wonders to prove his divinity. He dismissed their taunts and walked away, cautioning the disciples to "beware of the yeast of the Pharisees and Sadducees" (referring, I imagine, to traditional religious hot air). But the apostles took Jesus' warning *literally* and assumed that the bread in that town was spoiled. So they decided not to buy any local bread and planned to eat when they got to the next town.

Hours later they found themselves crossing a lake in a boat, with the journey taking much longer than anyone had expected. The disciples began complaining about not having any bread because of the yeast being tainted. Ravenously hungry, they asked, "What will we do? How will we eat?" Jesus, clearly frustrated at their failure to fully grasp His message, berated them with these words: "You of little faith—why are you talking among yourselves about having no bread? Do you *still not understand*? Don't you remember the five loaves for the five thousand, or the seven loaves for the four thousand? And how many basketfuls you gathered? How is it you don't understand that I was not talking to you about bread? . . . Do you have eyes but fail to see, and ears but fail to hear?"

This is great stuff, because the delicious morsel hidden beneath the story of abundance and lack is that the apostles just *didn't get it*. Miracle after miracle kept occurring before their eyes, but they didn't see what was really going on. That's because they were ordinary human beings, even if their spiritual tutorial was being given by a Master. It still wasn't enough, because they had not personally experienced an inner shift in reality.

The same thing happens with us. How often in our lives, do we still *not get it*? The "it" could be a power struggle going on in an important relationship; an inability to control our credit-card spending; a career problem undermining our self-esteem; the beginnings of addictive behavior in ourselves or our loved ones; or an unconscious form of self-sabotage that has us bouncing from one self-inflicted crisis to another. The "it" doesn't matter. Some such scenario is occurring in most of our lives and will continue, *again and again and again* until the moment we begin to see the pattern. Perhaps we should start paying attention. It doesn't always have to be "déjà vu happening all over again."

When we don't get it, it's usually because we can't interpret the outward experience as it is relayed over the interior intercom. We can't process it in our souls. What's really happening in our outward lives is somehow taking place in a foreign language that we don't understand. So we either assume that the outward manifestation is reality (which it isn't necessarily), or we keep having to repeat the experience until it starts to make sense—rather like learning a foreign language by total immersion. The poet Edna St. Vincent Millay put it this way: "It's not true that life is one damn thing after another—it's one damn thing over and over."

But speaking in tongues is a gift of Spirit. The language of the heart is longing; the language of the mind is rationalizing; the language of emotions is feeling. Spirit speaks them all. Today I would love for all of us to get it at last: not to focus on what we don't have, but to be grateful for what we do. For us to accept, give thanks, bless, and share. For us not to hoard or hold back for fear that there won't be enough. Because Spirit lacks for nothing.

As long as you have a few loaves and fishes, and know what to do with them, all you have is all you need.

JULY 18

Loaves and Fishes, Part II

Hospitality is one form of worship.

—THE TALMUD

Like other simple pleasures in our lives—decorating, gardening, cooking—many of us put off entertaining because we make it such a big deal. We fix more elaborate and expensive meals for guests than we do for ourselves, taking both extra money and extra time to plan, shop, and cook. We make a special effort to create the perfect atmosphere, beginning with a blitzkrieg of housecleaning and ending with a table setting worthy of a photo shoot. The family rhythm is often disrupted for days and includes everything from moving furniture to abandoning regular routines. I have known women who get so rattled that they're swearing "Never again" as they open the front door. It's no wonder that the thought of entertaining overwhelms us. And so it often remains just that—a thought—until a special event is thrust upon us and we must rise to the occasion.

I was heartened to discover that during the Depression the good times didn't completely disappear. Instead, domestic pleasures were scaled to a comfortable dimension. Parties were pared down. Instead of multicourse meals, there was one course which became the theme, such as drinks and finger foods, soup and sandwiches, pancakes or spaghetti, dessert and coffee. Parties moved from the dining room into the kitchen; at kitchen parties a new recipe would be chosen and its preparation was part of the fun. Savory potluck dinners became fashionable, with each couple or guest providing a course until the meal was elevated into a feast.

Potlucks are a marvelous simple pleasure worthy of revival. When invited to a party, most people will ask if there is something they can bring. When everybody brings a special dish, time and cost are kept manageable and the menu can go gourmet even if the party is down-home.

In France, the weekly feast for family and friends is based on *cuisine de femme,* "the food of women," which has "taste and soul and meaning." Mireille Johnston, who was born in Nice, celebrates this simply abundant style of entertaining in her cookbook, *The French Family Feast,* a delightful resource of delicious but not daunting menus that would adapt beautifully to a potluck feast.

One of the most important lessons of the miracle of the loaves and fishes is that the bounty was shared. We need to remind ourselves that good times need to be shared as well, especially if we want more of them in our lives. Mireille Johnston tells us that "Medieval banquets often ended with the guests swearing on a golden pheasant their willingness to depart for the Crusades. Your family and friends will sit at your table exalted and firmly convinced that while the cloudy future may be in the laps of the gods, the glorious present is happily on their plates. And they will leave reassured by the knowledge that the energy and grace, the carefree laughter, and stimulating smells, the power of these great simple dishes—all of these miracles and more can be summoned up again at will."

JULY 19

Carving Out Time for Personal Pursuits That Bring Contentment

It is the soul's duty to be loyal to its own desires. It must abandon itself to its master passion.

—REBECCA WEST

After putting down her pen, novelist Marjorie Kinnan Rawlings cooked up plots as she baked pies. Isak Dinesen arranged flowers. Katharine Hepburn whiled away the long stretches on movie sets by knitting. Queen Victoria filled dozens of sketchbooks with charming watercolors of her children that reveal a glimpse of the real woman who delighted in holding a brush when not ruling an empire.

"We are traditionally rather proud of ourselves for having slipped creative work in there between the domestic chores and obligations," writer Toni Morrison has observed. "I'm not sure we deserve such big A-pluses for that."

But the house calls to us. The children call to us. The work calls to us. When, then, does the painting or the poem call to us?

Probably every day. But we're too busy listening to everybody else instead of to our authentic selves. Maybe it's because we've convinced ourselves that we really don't have the time for personal pursuits that bring us contentment if they take longer than fifteen minutes. Perhaps we don't hear the whispers of authentic longing because we don't *want* to hear. If we hear, we might have to acknowledge, even respond. We're afraid to hear the promptings of the woman who wants to learn how to draw, dance, raise orchids, re-upholster a chair, cook Szechuan. We might have to take a class or buy a book, a pad and pencils, a leotard, a plant, a fabric, or hoisin sauce. No time to be passionate, we have to be practical. Essential, uncompromised longings will have to wait until there's more time: when the children are back in school, when Mom's feeling better, when things let up at the office.

How about an answer we haven't heard before? How about, "My authentic passions will have to wait until I'm ready to admit that pursuing them is essential for my happiness?" How about, "I haven't learned yet how to put myself on the list of priorities?" Notice I didn't suggest putting yourself first; I just want to get you on the list.

The Victorian writer Mary Ann Evans knew how to be practical about her passion for writing. She assumed a man's pen name, George Eliot, so that her novels *Middlemarch*, *Silas Marner*, and *The Mill on the Floss* would be published in an age that discounted the authentic longings of women. This is what she says about master passions: "It seems to me we can never give up longing and wishing while we are thoroughly alive. There are certain things we feel to be beautiful and good and we *must* hunger after them."

Space and time to nurture our creativity may be one of our authentic hungers. Perhaps we think that only food, drink, work, sex, shopping, or pills can reduce the gnawing to a dull throb. But maybe if we took an hour a day to paint, to plot, or to throw pots we wouldn't be in pain—physical or psychic.

Just maybe.

JULY 20

True North

It is good to have an end to journey towards; but it is the journey that matters in the end.

—URSULA K. LeGUIN

I used to believe that happiness could only be found after arriving at my heart's destination. Explorers call it true north. For me true north was enough success to ensure that there was plenty of money to control my own creative destiny, to allow me the luxury to pursue my passions. Now that I have spent far longer on the road from Here to There than I could have ever imagined twenty-five years ago when the adventure began, I have come to an awakening. I've always controlled my own creative destiny, though not always its course. I simply didn't have the common sense to realize it until now.

But more to the point, I've learned that the spirit of our journey is as important, perhaps even more important, than the arrival at our destination. In order for us to realize genuine happiness, we must be willing to court contentment every step of the way. For after all, the journey is really all that most of us will ever know. Day in, day out. The journey is real life.

One day in 1923, the artist Georgia O'Keeffe came to the same conclusion. "I found myself saying to myself . . . I can't live where I want to . . . I can't go where I want to . . . I can't do what I want to. I can't even say what I want to. I decided I was a very stupid fool not to at least paint as I wanted to . . . that seemed to be the only thing I could do that didn't concern anybody but myself."

We may not all be able to paint like Georgia O'Keeffe, who found splendor in bare bones and desert sands as well as flowers, but we can certainly learn slowly to follow her example, to carve out time for rewarding reveries that acquaint us with our authentic selves and give us glimpses of true north.

For it's during our expectant hours—those hours that might once have been called "idle"—that we are most pregnant with our own potential. The English poet Rupert Brooke, who celebrated quiet joys so eloquently, spoke of those few lucky souls who could "store up reservoirs of calm and content . . . and draw on them at later moments when the source isn't there but the need is very great."

This skill—the soulcraft of devoutly caring for our authentic selves—rarely comes naturally or easily. But with practice, with patience, with perseverance, it does come.

JULY 21

The Importance of Solitude

If women were convinced that a day off or an hour of solitude was a reasonable ambition, they would find a way of attaining it. As it is, they feel so unjustified in their demand that they rarely make the attempt.

—ANNE MORROW LINDBERGH

I am convinced that when the end of the world comes it will arrive not as two clashing armies on the brink but as a "last straw": the fax that unravels six months' work in a single sentence, the telephone call that sends us reeling across the room, the seemingly innocent request to perform yet another task. Can we attend one more meeting? Write an additional memo before we leave the office? Bake another batch of cookies? Drive an extra car pool trip this week? Suddenly, without warning, women will rush screaming into the night, leaving men and children shaking their heads in amazement wondering if it was something they said. Always remember, Greta Garbo never declared she wanted to be alone. She said: "I want to be *left* alone." There is a significant difference.

I believe that it's essential for busy women, by which I mean all of us, to pause a moment—this moment—to reconsider the entire subject of solitude. Too many of us approach time alone as if it were a frivolous, expendable luxury rather than a creative necessity. Why should this be so?

Could it be that by shortchanging ourselves, the only thing impoverished is our inner life? And after all, if the lack doesn't show on the surface, if we can pull it off one more time with smoke and mirrors, why, then, of course it doesn't count. Or does it?

"Certain springs are tapped only when we are alone. The artist knows he must be alone to create; the writer, to work out his thoughts; the musician to compose; the saint, to pray. But women need solitude in order to find again the true essence of themselves," Anne Morrow Lindbergh urges us to remember. "The problem is not entirely in finding the room of one's own, the time alone, difficult and necessary as this is. The problem is more how to still the soul in the midst of its activities. In fact the problem is how to feed the soul."

Neglect Not the Gifts Within You

She endured. And survived. Marginally, perhaps, but it is not required of us that we live well.

—ANNE CAMERON

Oh, yes it is! We may come back to enjoy another life—and I'm open to that possibility—but until I know for sure, I don't want to waste the one I'm living right now. I've endured. And survived. And I've lived marginally, but living well *is* all it's cracked up to be.

Over the years, particularly as I have *gradually* tried to honor Spirit's unfolding in my life by not neglecting the gifts within me, I have meditated long and hard about this inner directive, this craving for solitude. For I love the company of my husband and child; I'm excited by brainstorming and creating fabulous projects with a professional team; I adore spending time with close friends. But what I have discovered while composing my authentic concerto is that some of the notes require pauses. I yearn for what May Sarton called "open time, with no obligations except toward the inner world and what is going on there." To maintain inner harmony it is essential for me to ransom at least an hour's worth of solitude out of every twenty-four and to defend this soul-sustaining respite against all intruders and distractions.

Deliberately seeking solitude—quality time spent away from family and friends—may seem selfish. It is not. Solitude is as necessary for our creative spirits to develop and flourish as are sleep and food for our bodies to survive. "It is a difficult lesson to learn today—to leave one's friends and family and deliberately practice the art of solitude for an hour or a day or a week," Anne Morrow Lindbergh admits. "And yet, once it is done, I find there is a quality to being alone that is incredibly precious. Life rushes back into the void, richer, more vivid, fuller than before."

I believe that Anne Morrow Lindbergh, who endured more than any of us could even bear to think about, demonstrated with her courageous and creative life that it is not enough for us simply to endure or survive. We must surmount, learn to excel at playing our notes. We must move to a higher octave or a lower one, whichever is necessary to finding the delicate balance between our deepest personal passions and our commitment to family, friends, lovers, and work. As for me, I have discovered that the surest way to hear the soft strains of harmony is in the Silence.

Snatch Stolen Moments of Solitude

She was not accustomed to taste the joys of solitude except in company.

—EDITH WHARTON

What is needed, then, is a plan.

Through trial and error over the last decade I have tried spending quality time alone in the early morning and late at night when the rest of the house is asleep. Both solutions have proved impractical because I'm too tired to function at those hours, never mind be reflective or creative. I suspect I'm not alone in my need for sleep.

During the school year I seize my solitary hour immediately after my husband leaves for his office and Katie heads off to school. I realize, of course, that I'm very fortunate because I do my work at home and can use the hour I would otherwise spend commuting to the office for my solitary sojourns. In the summer and on school vacations, I grab an hour whenever I can find it, usually in the evening, or when no one else is looking. (It's called being creative and determined.)

If you work in an office, perhaps you can use your lunch hour for solo excursions a few times a week. No one need be privy to this information except you. Is there a beautiful old library, museum, cathedral, or public garden that you can visit for time alone during the middle of the day? Why not investigate the possibilities?

Perhaps, however, your work requires you to conduct business at lunchtime; this is the situation for several of my close friends. Pencil in a half hour in your appointment book for yourself before and after official working hours to close your door and collect your thoughts. One friend thought this was impossible until she began doing it; now her snatched hour is inviolate.

If this seems impossible, then it's vitally important for you to have some quality time alone at home, at least two nights during the week, no matter how busy you are. Schedule "home" on your calendar and commit to it.

Now what if you're home and you're not alone? Claim an hour in the evening, after supper, after the kids are put to bed or while they do their homework, even if you spend half the time soaking in the privacy of the bathtub. Be inventive, even sneaky, if you must. Why not retire an hour earlier than your partner during the week to read and relax in bed by yourself? One of my friends has a high-powered and exciting, but extremely stressful, career as a network television executive and must burn the midnight oil every night during the week. Her solitude solution comes on the weekend when she stays in bed all day on Saturday to recharge, joining her husband for dinner in the evening. If you're juggling family, home responsibilities, and an outside job, claim two hours on Sunday afternoon as your own. Give yourself permission to embrace the sacredness of seclusion.

Or perhaps you're home with young children who aren't yet in school. Plan your solitary pleasures when they take their naps. This is not the time for housecleaning. Use it for your own renewal. And don't be discouraged if your children have outgrown the need for naps (although I don't believe any of us ever do). Change your strategy. Call the hour immediately following lunch "Quiet Time." Take your children to their rooms gently but firmly, offering them a few special toys that they only get to play with at this time. Tell them you will see them in an hour and then retreat to your own special place.

If you spend half your life carpooling, devise personal strategies to help you cope. After the morning run, find yourself a quiet café where you can enjoy a solitary cup of cappuccino. In the afternoon, plan on arriving at school at least a half hour early, with an inviting book to keep you company. Always keep a pad and pen handy to jot down random glimmers of inspiration, which will come once you commit to carving out soulcaring times, even if you have to find them sitting in a parked car. Some of my best work has come while waiting for small people. Be open to the unexpected.

JULY 24

Paying a High Price

[Certain] high-achieving women are imploded with demands, both external and internal, and lack the skills to filter them. These women complain that the first thing they sacrifice is their private time or private pleasures.

—HARRIET B. BRAIKER, PH.D.

Those of us who don't spend regular time alone to rest and recoup are likely to suffer from what psychologists call "privacy deprivation syndrome." Symptoms include increasing resentment, mood swings, chronic fatigue, and depression. Sound familiar? Sound grim? It is! Sufferers struggle through their days in a vacuum of unfulfilled exasperation, only to drop into bed too emotionally depleted to sleep well at night. The littlest thing can set them off, bringing tears and tantrums—and not only from the children in the family. Soon work and personal relationships begin to suffer. Why? Because the never-refreshed are really not that much fun to be around. The cycle may continue unabated until physical illness sets in. Remember the flu you had last year for five weeks? The two weeks you were laid up with lower-back pain last summer? The sinus infection you couldn't shake last month?

We don't have to make ourselves sick before we can call a psychic time out. Unfortunately for many women, it is only when we do get sick that we allow ourselves a dispensation for time and space alone. This may be how real life is for you right now, but it doesn't have to stay that way. If you find yourself secretly looking forward to regular rendezvous with a hot water bottle and NyQuil, then privacy deprivation syndrome is exacting a high price. Let me reassure you there is a better path.

JULY 25

Opening a Door That Separates Two Worlds

There are voices which we hear in solitude, but they grow faint and inaudible as we enter into the world.
—RALPH WALDO EMERSON

It's impossible to experience solitude regularly for any extended length of time without personal passions and authentic longings surging to the surface of your awareness. Once you have embarked on the search for your own authentic style, followed the wisdom of your own heart and have seen the results begin to blossom in your life, you realize that solitude cracks open the door that separates two worlds: the life we lead today and the life we yearn for so deeply.

We can all find ways to regenerate once we realize how essential solitude is to our experience of inner harmony. Tillie Olsen wrote in her story, "Tell Me a Riddle," of a woman who "would not exchange her solitude for anything. *Never again be forced to move to the rhythm of others.*" While most of us probably find ourselves moving to the rhythm of others more than we would like, once we learn to respect and cherish our need for solitude, opportunities will arrive in which we can learn to nourish our imaginations and nurture our souls.

Begin slowly but resolutely. Take comfort in knowing that even stolen moments of solitude—quarter-hour increments—eventually can add up to a lifetime of serenity. Be patient. Don't expect too much too soon, especially when rearranging your schedule means dealing with your family's expectations of what you're supposed to do and when you're supposed to do it. Be patient.

And for those days—maybe even today—when you don't have a moment to yourself, take to heart the advice of photographer Minor White who discovered that "No matter how slow the film, Spirit always stands still long enough for the photographer It has chosen."

JULY 26

Discovering What You'd Like to Do, If You Ever Had the Time

Develop interest in life as you see it; in people, things, literature, music—the world is so rich, simply throbbing with rich treasures, beautiful souls and interesting people. Forget yourself.
—HENRY MILLER

In the beginning spending regular time alone just to collect your thoughts will seem like indulgence enough. Spending time alone to nurture your authentic vision, to express yourself creatively, to enjoy a personal pursuit that brings you contentment and pleasure will seem—well, impossible. Incredulous. Impractical. Inconceivable. Out of the question.

"Right. In another life," is the usual response, along with audible sighs and the rolling of eyes when I broach the subject in my workshops. Then wistful looks appear. "You mean to have fun?" the women want to know.

"Yes. Have fun."

"You mean, by myself?"

"Yes, by yourself. Fun. What would you like to do if you ever had the time?"

"Fun?"

You can see where this leads. Most women I meet have a hard time holding up their end of the conversation when fun is the topic. Let the discourse be on diaper rash or Einstein's Theory of Relativity and we can hold our own. But fun for its own sake? The plain truth is that somewhere between family and careers during the last twenty years, most of us have misplaced an essential part of ourselves. Once we begin embarking on solitary sojourns to get reacquainted with our authentic selves, we usually discover that something is missing.

It's called zest. Exuberance. *Joi de vivre*, as the French would say, or "the love of life." The great delight that comes when the pieces of our particular puzzle finally fit. The heartfelt happiness we derive when something brings us keen pleasure. Something uniquely our own. They used to call this magical something a hobby.

But what to do? The writer Brenda Ueland tells us that our imaginations need "moodling—long, inefficient, happy idling, dawdling and puttering" to flourish. Perhaps we also need a little personal sleuthing to uncover what solitary pleasures might be fun. It's been so long since we've consciously set aside time solely for rewarding reveries that many of us can't fathom what to do (except, of course, take a nap) when we have a couple of golden hours in which to answer to no one but ourselves. We lose what little leisure time we have available through attrition.

Today, give in to your need for "moodling." And while you're dawdling and puttering, consider what rewarding reveries you've put aside that brought you pleasure in the past. "How I think about my work is indistinguishable from the way I think about my needlepoint or cooking: here is the project I'm involved in. It is play. In this sense all my life is spent in play— sewing or needlepoint, or picking flowers or writing, or buying groceries," says writer Diane Johnson. Once you commit to bringing more of a sense of play into your daily round with authentic personal pursuits, life will begin to take on a harmonious lilt.

JULY 27

Solitary Pleasures

Alone, alone, Oh! We have been warned about solitary vices. Have solitary pleasures ever been adequately praised? Do many people know they exist?

—JESSAMYN WEST

Remember, once upon a time, when we all knew how to play? We're going to have to travel back to when we were younger to look for clues. Did you love to play alone when you were ten? What were your favorite extracurricular activities in high school and during college? Nothing in our past lives is wasted. Nothing that once made us feel happy and fulfilled is ever lost. There's a golden thread that runs through each of our lives. We just need to rediscover this thread before the joy of living completely unravels.

Why not have a brainstorming session on paper to excavate your buried bliss? Write out a quick list of ten solitary pleasures. Don't give this a lot of thought, but don't be dismayed if it takes you a few minutes to come up with something.

Need some help? Well, what was your favorite childhood game? Your favorite sport? Your favorite movie as a kid? Your favorite book? Comic strip? Your favorite singer or musical group? What was the best time you ever had as a youngster? As a teenager? As an adult? Can you remember? Can you re-create the memory?

If you could instantly acquire three additional skills, what would they be—playing the piano? figure skating? taking really great photographs? What three outrageous things would you try if no one knew about it— belly dancing? clowning? hot-air ballooning? What three daring things sound intriguing, even if you'd probably never attempt them—stand-up comedy? mountain climbing? scuba diving? What three all-expenses-paid vacations appeal to you—an archeological dig in Egypt? a ride on the Orient Express? a visit to the Paris haute couture collections? Do you like to work with your hands—needlecraft? bookbinding? gardening? Or does the visual appeal to you—framing pictures? working in stained glass? creating shadow boxes?

Get the idea? There's a fabulous world out there just waiting to be explored. We simply have to be willing to experiment. A hobby affords us a marvelous opportunity to awaken our natural talents. It does require a little bit of effort. First of all we have to figure out what we'd like to do to shake the doldrums. Then we have to carve out time to do it. Alice James, the sister of Henry and William James, believed that in life, "Truly nothing is to be expected but the unexpected." By seeking and finding a solitary pleasure that would make you jump out of the bed each morning to pursue it, you'll discover just how right she was.

JULY 28

The Plié of Pleasure

What is your hobby? Every woman ought to have some pet interest in life, outside of the everyday routine which composes her regular occupations. What is yours?
—THE MOTHER'S MAGAZINE, *January 1915*

T here is a vitality, a life force, an energy, a quickening, that is translated through you into action and because there is only one of you in all time this expression is unique," modern dancer Martha Graham advises us. "And if you block it, it will never exist through any other medium and will be lost."

Where are you blocked? A hobby is a wonderful way to start freeing our-selves creatively. That's because no one expects us to be perfect at a hobby. Hobbies allow us to experiment, to dabble with the paint, the poem, the pot, the plié. When ballet dancers speak of doing pliés, they mean bending their knees. Doing pliés at the beginning of rehearsal warms up the leg muscles before the dance begins. Pursuing a hobby warms up our talents and illuminates our natural inclinations. We get to try on imaginary lives and see how they fit.

Now that you've done some moodling and have discovered some per-sonal pastimes that bring you pleasure, today choose one to pursue. If you need materials such as yarn or paint, make a list of the necessary supplies. Give yourself a week to assemble what you need to get going, and one week from today plan an hour to begin. By doing this, you commit to bringing more fun into your life, and what was once inconceivable will soon become impossible to live without.

JULY 29

The Home as a Hobby

Only a very exceptionally gifted mind could cope singly with all the problems which present themselves in the perfecting of a home.
—ARNOLD BENNETT

One of my new hobbies is our home. I began to think of our home as a hobby after discovering a delightful series of magazine essays writ-ten in 1924 by English novelist, essayist, and playwright Arnold Bennett. Although he is largely forgotten now, Arnold Bennett was once as famous as H. G. Wells and George Bernard Shaw. Bennett's niche was as "everyman," a middle-class neurotic who elevated his neurosis to near-genius by brooding, with wit and wisdom, on the meaning of life, its conundrums, and simple pleasures. One of his best-loved books was *How to Live on Twenty-Four Hours a Day*, an art we all should aspire to mas-ter.

In "The Home as a Hobby," Mr. Bennett writes, "The home exists. The home is accepted. Life can be, and is, lived in it. That vase does not suit that mantelpiece. That carpet will not go with that wallpaper . . . The foot of the bed interferes with the swinging of the bedroom door. The whole of the dining-room furniture is seen to have been a mistake. The hall has a poverty-stricken aspect. The two principal pictures in the drawing-room are too high on the wall. A hundred things are just a little wrong and a few things dreadfully wrong! But no matter. The apparatus somehow works. The desire after perfection has failed. The home has become immutable. There the home is! It will do. It must do."

But for the true artist with Real Life as his or her canvas, a golden opportunity awaits, says Bennett. "Nobody has the right to be bored in a half-made home. A home which is not a fair expression of us at our best, a home which lacks what it might have, a home which is in any part more ugly or in any part more uncomfortable than it absolutely need be . . . a home which cannot be run without waste, a home which by any detail gets on the nerves of its inhabitants and so impairs the harmony of their existence—something ought to be done about such a home . . . Why not make the perfecting of the home a hobby?"

An interesting proposition. Most of us don't think of fixing up our homes as a pleasurable pursuit because we usually approach it as a feat requiring more physical, psychic, creative, and financial resources than would be necessary to scale the most formidable mountain in the world. This morning, for instance, I would rather go over Niagara Falls in a barrel than tackle our basement. But I would also love to carve out a little space for an art studio where I would have the space to dabble in my textile designs. To accomplish this, I have to redeem some space from chaos. If I approach our house as a hobby instead of a chore, maybe I'll find the time to stain the front door, refinish a dresser, varnish the hardwood floor, create a nook of my own.

"Your home may be a small one—most people's homes are—but you will never have finished perfecting it," Arnold Bennett tells us. "The subject is vast and knows no bounds." You know, he just may be right.

JULY 30

Habits That Steal Precious Moments

Lost, yesterday, somewhere between sunrise and sunset, two golden hours, each set with sixty diamond minutes. No reward is offered, for they are gone forever.

—HORACE MANN

Nothing dies harder than a bad habit. Usually we know whenever we're doing something that's not good for us because the small voice that resides in the center of our heads can be a pretty vigilant nag. "Please don't," it will whisper when we light up that cigarette, pour an extra glass of wine, or stand in front of the refrigerator inhaling cold spaghetti because we're nervous. The trouble is, of course, that until now, we haven't been willing to listen.

Before changing any behavior, it's helpful to know why you want to get rid of habits that don't nurture or contribute to your sense of well-being. If you change, what will be your positive payback? A healthier lifestyle, more energy and vitality, the joy and serenity of emotional sobriety, a slimmer body? Going within opens up the eyes of your awareness in gentle ways. You start to treat yourself more kindly. As you become more intimate with your authentic self and see glimmers of the woman you truly are inside, you shore up the courage to take the first tentative steps necessary to help her evolve and emerge outwardly.

Soon we'll begin hearing whispers that encourage and comfort, not berate us. Then one thirsty evening, instead of automatically reaching for wine while we fix dinner, we'll enjoy a refreshing glass of sparkling mineral water, especially if it's served with lemon in a pretty cut-glass goblet. Instead of the unconscious snacking every time we enter the kitchen, we'll start eating only when we're sitting down and only what's on our plates, especially if we take the time to prepare delicious meals that satisfy the eye as well as our appetites. Instead of impulsively reaching for a cigarette to bring solace when we're nervous, we'll pick up needlecraft, or even the crossword puzzle.

Too often we're unaware of the ways in which we rob ourselves of precious moments that could be spent nurturing our creativity. These are unconscious habits that the Surgeon General doesn't warn us about but that our authentic selves will. For as long as we continue to cling to bad habits that may not be life-threatening but certainly aren't life-enhancing, we only steal from our potential.

JULY 31

Desire, Ask, Believe, Receive

Difficult times have helped me to understand better than before how infinitely rich and beautiful life is in every way and that so many things that one goes worrying about are of no importance whatsoever.

—ISAK DINESEN

Are you a worrier? We all are to a certain extent, but some of us are more pessimistic than others, and when *we* worry, it's always the worst possible thing that comes first to mind. Worrying is a great thief of time. I have a good friend who can soar from distress to disaster in five seconds, and it has caused her no end of sorrow. Now that she recognizes the pattern and can stop herself in midflight with a gentle reminder, she experiences much more inner harmony even under difficult circumstances. Often when we stew, we think that we're doing something positive about the problem; at least we're thinking about it. Instead, we've set off an escalating spiral that can ruin an entire day—for ourselves and those in our vicinity.

If you find yourself fretting over an issue, instead of working yourself into a frenzy, stop. Now think about everything that's humming along nicely. Can you have a conversation with Spirit? If you don't feel comfortable calling your communion with a Higher Power "prayer," call it a "communication with a good friend." "I learned that simply to ask a blessing upon one's circumstances, whatever they are, is somehow to improve them, and to tap some mysterious source of energy and joy," writer Marjorie Holmes confides. "I came upon one of the most ancient and universal truths—that to affirm and to claim God's help even before it is given, is to receive it." Lift up your worries and ask for grace to get through the rest of the day. There is an abundance of amazing grace available to all of us if we simply learn to ask for it. "Desire, Ask, Believe, Receive," the mystic Stella Terrill Mann advises. Begin praying or conversing in that order and you'll understand why she does.

After praying about your worries, is there a friend you can share your problem with? If not, sit down quietly and write out what's troubling you. Now write out the worst case scenario. What are your greatest fears? If that happened, what would you do? How would you cope? Once you have a solution beyond an "I don't know" response, write it down. One of the reasons we worry is because we feel powerless to control our futures. When we figure out what we'd do if the worst did happen, the sense of hopelessness diminishes. "I have spent most of my life worrying about things that have never happened," Mark Twain admitted at the end of his life. We all do this.

Worrying about the future robs you of the present moment. Try to observe how much worrying you do. And if the nagging worry follows you relentlessly throughout the day, follow Scarlett O'Hara's example. Tell yourself, "I'm not going to think about this right now, I'll think about this tomorrow. After all, tomorrow is another day."

Joyful Simplicities for July

❧ Make the pursuit of happiness real and personal: hang and wave the flag; find a local parade and then share loaves and fishes with family and friends at an old-fashioned potluck picnic. Watch the fireworks in the evening or set off your own authentic sparks. Declare your personal independence: choose to live authentically as a dreamer, not an "expector."

❧ If you have a beach sojourn this month, try to enjoy it at different times: an early morning browse to collect shells before the crowds come, a late afternoon visit to fly kites after they've left. Save one evening for a moonlight walk. If you're not alone, hold hands.

❧ Stand at the water's edge or sit on a towel to gaze out across the water. Just let the rhythm of the waves wash over you. Experience and savor the suspension of time. If you've not yet read Anne Morrow Lindbergh's *Gift from the Sea*, this is the perfect month to do so. Read with a yellow highlighter and mark the passages that speak to your soul. Date them in the margin.

❧ While at the shore, get a yard of fisherman's netting in a shell shop or five-and-dime. Hang it in a window or drape it over a tabletop and create a seashore vignette. Bring home a bottle of sand; place the sand on a tray and arrange different seashells around it for a lovely summer centerpiece. (If you're in a meditative mood, do your shell searching on the shore. The most exotically decorative seashells are usually to be found at shell shops—unless you do your beachcombing at Fiji.)

❧ When was the last time you stargazed? One clear summer's evening lie on a big blanket in your backyard with a good bottle of wine or sparkling cider, cheese, biscuits, and fresh fruit. Look up into the night sky. Realize that you've got a Friend up there. Stargazing is one of the oldest human pastimes and there's good reason for it. Gazing at the stars reminds us that there's more than we'll ever realize and that every day is another chance to follow the clues. Find a star to wish upon.

❧ During a summer thunderstorm, sit in the middle of your bed in the dark and watch out the window or from a screened-in porch. Experience the beauty and power of Nature unleashed. Now think about harnessing that Power in your life by asking for the Light to be switched on.

❧ Whether you know the Bible or not, a marvelous way to rediscover it is through the eyes of other women. A wonderful collection of essays by women writers exploring their favorite Bible stories is *Out of the Garden: Women Writers on the Bible*, edited by Christina Buchmann and Celina Spiegel. Twenty-eight great women writers—including Cynthia Ozick, Ursula K. LeGuin, Patricia Hampl, Fay Weldon, and Louise Erdrich—reflect thoughtfully, playfully, and provocatively on Old Testament stories, characters, and poetry that mean the most to them. To savor the experience even more, munch on the biggest, reddest, and juiciest apple you can find while you read. As the editors observe: "Unlike the Garden of Eden, the Bible is a source women can return to, and as with all great works of literature, it is a book that changes as we change. For curiosity we were thrown out of the Garden, and with curiosity we return."

❧ While waiting for the potatoes to boil, or lying in a hammock, dip into books with culinary themes, such as the romantic and bittersweet novel, *Like Water for Chocolate* by Laura Esquivel or Jacqueline Deval's *Reckless Appetite: A Culinary Romance*. There's a continual feast of cooking mysteries simmering on library and bookstore shelves. Especially fulfilling: Diane Mott Davidson's delicious series featuring a caterer turned sleuth in *Catering to Nobody*, *Dying for Chocolate*, and *Cereal Murders*.

◆§ Arranging a dinner around a film might seem old hat, but not if you pair the cuisine with the film. Enjoy Mexican enchiladas with chocolate *molé* sauce while watching the sensuous *Like Water for Chocolate*; order Chinese carryout to accompany the delectable *Eat, Drink, Man, Woman*; make French *cuisine de femme* to counterpoint the sumptuous *Babette's Feast*. (Since *all* the passionate hungers are explored in these foreign films, they're definitely for viewing *after* the children are in bed.)

◆§ To make your cake-baking meditation as inspirational as possible, you might want to take a look at *The Cake Bible* by Rose Levy Beranbaum with its over-two-hundred suggestions for meditations you'll never forget. Remember, no matter what life throws at us, we can *always* bake a cake.

AUGUST

Summer's lease hath all too short a date.
—WILLIAM SHAKESPEARE

Aficionados of August revel in relinquishment. When it's one hundred degrees in the shade, it's too hot to be anything but receptive and reflective. Let a seasonally sanctioned sojourn of slow joys refill the authentic reservoir of creative energy. This month on the Simple Abundance path we commit to discovering, acknowledging, appreciating, owning, and honoring our authentic gifts, transforming not only our own lives, but the lives of those we love.

AUGUST 1

The Harmonic Convergence
of an Authentic Life

But if you have nothing at all to create, then perhaps you create yourself.

—CARL JUNG

Do you remember what you were doing the weekend of August 16–17, 1987? I don't. If you do, perhaps you were among the more than 144,000 people who journeyed to "power points" around the world, such as Egypt's Great Pyramids; Peru's Machu Picchu; Japan's Mount Fuji; the Temples of Delphi in Greece; Mount Shasta, California; Sedona, Arizona; the Black Hills of South Dakota; and New York's Central Park to hold hands, hum, and "resonate in harmony" in the New Age global event known as the Harmonic Convergence.

What made this weekend so significant was a rare astronomical occurrence known as "a grand trine" (when all nine planets were in their astrological fire signs and positioned exactly one hundred twenty-three degrees apart from each other). It had been 23,412 years since the last one. Now add an esoteric interpretation of ancient Mayan and Aztec calendars and a Hopi legend about a gathering of enlightened teachers meant to awaken humanity, and it's not surprising that thousands of New Agers decided that circumstances were as perfect as they'd ever be to direct the earth, through meditation, toward a peaceful spiritual awakening instead of a cataclysmic one in the next millennium.

It seems to have worked. Each week another visionary book is published encouraging spiritual evolution as "the road less traveled" becomes the inspirational superhighway. But there are so many voices offering clues, glimmers, and insights on how to achieve harmony through the Divine grand trine of mind, body, and Spirit. How do you discern your own truth? And there are so many spiritual paths. Which one should you follow? "In undertaking a spiritual life, what matters is simple," American Buddhist master and teacher Jack Kornfield reassures us in his wonderful book *A Path with Heart: A Guide Through the Perils and Promises of Spiritual Life*. "*We must make certain that our path is connected with our heart. . . .* When we ask, 'Am I following a path with heart?' we discover that no one can define for us exactly what our path should be. Instead, we must allow the mystery and beauty of this question to resonate within our being. Then somewhere within us an answer will come and understanding will arise. If we are still and listen deeply, even for a moment, we will know if we are following a path with heart."

For me, bearing witness to my authentic self is the most joyous and fulfilling spiritual path I have ever followed. It is truly "a path with heart." It began when I acknowledged that creativity is holy. Perhaps this August you might like to convene a personal harmonic convergence through rediscovering, recovering, and celebrating your creativity, the sacred conduit to access your authentic self. It's never too late to reclaim your individual gifts, resuscitate a dream, create an authentic life. Consider this: what if "original sin" is *denying* instead of *celebrating* your originality?

Each of us possesses an exquisite, extraordinary gift: the opportunity to give expression to Divinity on earth through our everyday lives. When we choose to honor this priceless gift, we participate in the re-creation of the world. When we follow our authentic path with love, embracing our creative impulses, we live truth even if what we think we're doing is just planting a flower bed, cooking a meal, nurturing a child, editing a book, producing a television show, sewing a curtain, writing a brief, painting a picture, teaching a craft, composing a song, or closing a deal. As the Vietnamese Buddhist monk, poet, and writer Thich Nhat Hanh reminds us, "Our own life is the instrument with which we experiment with truth."

AUGUST 2

The Gentlest Lessons Teach Us the Most

What a wonderful life I've had! I only wish I'd realized it sooner.
—COLETTE

All of us know about learning life's lessons through pain, struggle, and loss. But few of us realize that it is often the gentlest lessons that teach us most.

Seven years ago our family went to a political convention held at a beach resort. While my husband attended workshops, Katie and I played on the beach. One afternoon there was a surprise activity for the children: a ride on an elephant around the hotel parking lot. Katie was delirious with excitement. That night, as my husband and I tucked her into bed, I said, "Life is always full of wonderful surprises if we're open to them. Some mornings you wake up not knowing what will happen during the day and you get to ride an elephant!"

A couple of days later we returned home and awaiting me was an invitation to join a group of American journalists on an all-expenses-paid, weeklong junket to Ireland to cover Dublin's celebration of its millennium.

The group was departing in ten days. Now there are many things that I am, but spontaneous is not one of them. After I had come up with every conceivable reason to turn down a free trip to my favorite country in the world—my passport was out of date, who would look after Katie, I'd have to juggle my work schedule, I'd just *returned* from a vacation—my husband said quietly, "So you're not going to ride the elephant?" I smiled at him, gently learned the important lesson about being open to receive, and enjoyed one of the most delightful weeks of my life.

If we are willing to learn our lessons gently, they patiently await us in countless ways. Today, try listening to the wisdom of children; accepting the loving kindness of a friend; reaching out to those in need; asking a colleague for advice; acting on your intuition; laughing at your foibles and frailties and accepting them with love; observing how your pets live so contentedly in the present moment; rediscovering the surprising healing power of spontaneity; focusing on the good in any situation you are now encountering; expecting the best of every day; and realizing what a wonderful life you're living—sooner rather than later.

Of course, the unexpected often catches us by surprise. But if we are open to and grateful for gentle lessons, new teachers will appear in our path. Serendipity can instruct us as much as sorrow.

AUGUST 3

A Net for Catching Days

A schedule defends from chaos and whim. It is a net for catching days. . . . A schedule is a mock-up of reason and order—willed, faked, and so brought into being.

—ANNIE DILLARD

A friend of mine has a theory that it's not so much all we *actually* have to do in any one week that kills us, it's *thinking* about all we have to do.

Alice came to this awareness the week she forgot to attend the annual mothers' volunteering session for her daughter's Girl Scout troop. Being an extremely organized person, she assumed she'd remember it. *No need to write it down.* But she forgot because on that crucial day she experienced scheduling system failure, when all available RAMs of memory in the brain's circuitry become overloaded. The next morning, when a sinking feeling in the pit of her stomach awakened her, it was too late. All the easy jobs were gone, only one job remained. Which is how Alice became this year's Girl Scout cookie sales manager.

Here's a Simple Abundance strategy—even for the organizationally challenged—to bring more harmony into your life. It will free up those vital memory RAMs so you don't end up tracking the sale of samoas versus chocolate thin mints. Unless, of course, you want to, in which case perhaps you'd like to get in touch with Alice. Take twenty minutes each Sunday and sit down with your calendar, a pad, pen, and yellow highlighter to map out the next six days with a thorough "To Do" list, then take a preliminary look at the following three weeks.

In order to cast a net that really catches days, you need to consider all the tasks you do in one week, both professional and private. This is not for the fainthearted, but it's crucial. Be of good courage. Here's what we really do each week.

THE UNIVERSAL "TO DO" LIST

Work:
(Meetings, prospecting, marketing/publicity, desk tasks, planning, billing, reading, researching, writing, traveling)

Errands:
(Banking, cleaners, library, gas station, video store, post office)

Children:
(School, health, lessons, sports, scouts, car pool, clubs, play dates, parties)

Appointments:
(Health, fitness, beauty, automotive, animals)

Shopping:
(Food, clothing, drugstore items, home, gifts)

Correspondence:
(Bills, letters, cards, and packages)

Telephone/Fax:

Home:
(Cleaning, laundry, decorating, improvements, cooking, repairs, entertaining, gardening)

Family:

Friends:

Church/Community:

Personal:
(Inspiration, introspection, rest, recuperation, relaxation, grooming, creative excursions, educational, pleasurable pursuits)

After doing most of the above, it would seem there'd be no time left for the last and most important category: personal. The way to solve this real-life dilemma is to move Personal from last to first, making it a top priority as you plan. Start by taking your yellow marker and blocking out an hour each day on the calendar; on your list write out your initials six times as a subliminal code for self-nurturance. The subversive beauty of this method is that once a task is committed to a list, whether it be errands or personal, you don't have to give it another conscious thought because the left side of your brain—the location of logic—*loves lists*. It goes on automatic pilot when making lists, sorting and shifting until a schedule appears that can accommodate everything. Sometimes it's even manageable. If you ever hope to get it done, write it down.

Scan your list morning and night. When you've completed a task, ceremoniously cross it off with a red marker—I prefer a red calligraphy pen. It imparts a great sense of satisfaction to see the list fill up in red during the week. If you feel you spend too many days accomplishing little or nothing, keep a "What I've Done" list for a week. You may discover that you do a lot more than you realize—or give yourself credit for. You'll probably also discover that golden moments were unconsciously squandered because there was no net to catch them. Moments to grow, to dream, to nurture your authentic vision. Writer Annie Dillard believes, "How we spend our days is, of course, how we spend our lives." And we all know truth when we hear it.

AUGUST 4

Preserving Prime Time

There are days when any electrical appliance in the house, including the vacuum cleaner, seems to offer more entertainment possibilities than the TV set.

—HARRIET VAN HORNE

Do you watch too much television? It is, on the surface, an innocent addiction, because there are no obvious side effects.

We know what happens when our children watch too much television. They become passive, disinterested in other activities, and easily bored. Their attention span is drastically shortened and their dissatisfaction with life is frequently expressed to anyone who will listen. Their mothers exhibit similar symptoms when they watch too much television. If you are staying at home with your children, ask yourself if you really need the television on during the day. If you work outside the home and find yourself regularly sitting down in front of the television in the evening without even considering what else you might be doing, isn't it about time you did? Alice Walker is always "amazed that people will actually choose to sit in front of the television and just be savaged by stuff that belittles their intelligence." Anyone who watches television more than five hours a week should agree with her. I was a television critic for several years and I could not believe the stuff I had to watch. At least I was paid!

But there is much on television that is entertaining and informative. In that case, if there's a program you'd really like to see, why not tape it and watch it another time? It's really a matter of making conscious choices. Over the last few years, I have practically weaned myself from television and was simply amazed at the time I've found for more pleasurable and rewarding pursuits.

This week, become aware of how much television you watch so that you can start preserving prime time. Writer Barbara Ehrenreich believes television's lure is that it reveals what we crave the most in the deepest recesses of our hearts: "a rich, new, participatory life." Perhaps you might begin living the authentic life you crave once you stop letting the one you have go down the tube.

AUGUST 5

The Gift of Sacred Idleness

Work is not always required . . . there is such a thing as sacred idleness, the cultivation of which is now fearfully neglected.
—GEORGE MACDONALD

It was a gorgeous summer's morning—sunny, but not too hot or humid. The kind of day that should make you feel grateful to be alive. But I was too exhausted to acknowledge the gift. All night I'd tossed and turned, drifting in and out of consciousness but not really sleep. With a work deadline looming, the end of summer camp but another month to go before school resumed, and the need to visit my sick mother, I had new appreciation for what the English poet Stevie Smith meant when she confessed that she was "not waving but drowning."

Letting the cats into the backyard, I stepped outside for a brief moment. A refreshing breeze rustled the green branches. Sun-dappled patterns of light and shadow created a lovely mosaic on the grass that I'd never noticed before. A natural concerto—birds singing, cicadas chirping, bees buzzing—resonated in the early morning stillness. The hush of harmony hovered around me. I didn't want to leave. Reluctantly I went inside to get a start before Katie woke up.

But the sight of my books and papers sprawled on the floor near my bed where I'd wearily flung them late the night before, gave outward expression to my inner chaos and overwhelmed me. I burst into tears.

After I'd had a good cry, the gentle, reassuring voice I have come to know as Spirit suggested that I return to the backyard. Oddly enough, instead of protesting, I did. I spread an old cotton bedspread on the ground, borrowed pillows from the living room love seat and propped them up against a tall oak tree to create a chaise lounge on the earth. Then I carried out a tea tray and my work basket, assuming I was settling outside to write. But when I sat down, all I could bring myself to do was sit quietly and breathe slowly. I didn't want to meditate, have an authentic conversation with anyone, think, create, be clever, or be a conduit. So I just sat there, sipped tea, looked up at the blue sky through the leafy canopy overhead and observed a butterfly's graceful path through the garden. My surroundings were ordinary, but this morning, so beautiful—so familiar, yet so different.

Within a few minutes my dark mood began to lift. Soon the cats joined me, curious at this unusual detour in the day's rhythm. A little while later, Katie wandered out, still drowsy with sleep, carrying a blanket and pillow to nest and read with us. She asked what I was doing. I told her, for want of a better explanation, that I was conducting research: letting Mother Nature nurture so that I could write a meditation. I invited her to join me. Because Mom seemed so calm and receptive, she decided to seize the day and asked me to sort through the boxes of her baby memorabilia. Who knew how long this unusual opportunity would last? Well, it lasted for eight lovely, languid, summer hours and included an alfresco lunch as well as a nap. In between laughter, family stories, confidence sharing, animal watching, and dreaming aloud, I did absolutely nothing at all except live and love.

At the end of this simply abundant day of bliss, I realized that I'd been given a restorative gift: sacred idleness. An unexpected, melodic day of undoing to balance the discordant days of doing too much. Like grace, this blessing had come out of the blue; it was completely impractical but absolutely necessary, and it was savored with thanksgiving.

AUGUST 6

Letting Mother Nature Nurture

Meaning, moods, the whole scale of our inner experience, finds in nature "the correspondences" through which we may know our boundless selves.

—KATHLEEN RAINE

A friend of mine is a naturalist writer who, ironically enough, lives in the inner city. Behind Pat's Victorian brownstone is an alley that abuts a rough neighborhood where prostitutes, drug dealers, the homeless, and the mentally abandoned painfully coexist with determined urban pioneers. As would most of us in her circumstances, Pat admits that it's hard to relate compassionately to people who urinate on her steps, throw liquor bottles at pets, mug, and murder. Repeated efforts to clean up her alley have been unsuccessful and discouraging. But this year, Pat—who possesses an intuitive ability to turn a wasteland into an oasis—created a beautiful English butterfly garden next to her steps leading to the alley. Her tiny garden—a four-foot triangle—is abundant with gorgeous flowers and plants that attract hundreds of exquisite butterflies. The garden has also attracted her street neighbors, who will often come to spend a few quiet moments glimpsing the only nature available to them. Now the alley is kept spotless as a pathway to the garden by those who used to trash it; not even a gum wrapper can be found. When Pat looks out her window and watches the people she felt so estranged from before, she feels good about bringing some beauty into their lives. It's a gentle but powerful reminder of "biophilia"—Spirit's silent wake-up call that all of life is a sacred continuum.

Biophilia is the exciting new psychological theory championed by Pulitzer Prize-winning conservation biologist Edward O. Wilson, who believes our biophilial urges—the "love of living things"—plants, wildlife and the great outdoors is genetic, encoded in human beings to ensure balance, harmony, and preservation. "Attraction to natural environments is not simply a cultural phenomenon," Dr. Wilson explains. "There is evidence it is a deeper, biological urge."

Some of this evidence is rooted in our ancient ancestors' lifestyle. As early humans evolved over two million years, they existed in bands of hunters and food gatherers; only those who became one with the natural world survived. Dr. Wilson points out, "The glimpse of one small animal hidden in the grass could make the difference between eating and going hungry."

If we are to thrive today, becoming one with nature is just as essential as it was millions of years ago. In fact, many therapists who specialize in "ecopsychology" believe that deepening our emotional ties to nature is as vital to our well-being as the close personal bonds we pursue with family and friends. When we follow our instincts to leave the city for a weekend in the country, garden in the early morning, opt for a picnic in the park instead of a restaurant lunch, hang up a bird feeder, visit the zoo, or adopt a stray animal, we are responding positively to physiological and psychological urges to connect for survival. We might not consciously understand it, but we need to reinforce our strand in the web of life. When we honor this holy hunger by getting in tune with nature, we experience personal harmony.

Today you may not be able to spend a day completely outdoors, but you can soothe away stress by letting Mother Nature nurture. Take off your shoes. Feel the earth beneath your feet. Bend over a blossom and breathe in the fragrance. Lie under a tree and look up at the sky through the branches. Give it a few moments. Now how do you feel?

Mother does know best.

AUGUST 7

Creature Comforts

Our perfect companions never have fewer than four feet.

—COLETTE

The most important life lesson I have ever learned—the transformative power of unconditional love—was taught to me by a four-legged mystical master. Jack was a feral cat who showed up in our backyard nine summers ago. Even though he was obviously starving, for the first week he simply watched, sizing me up as he cased the joint. I set food for him outside the kitchen door, but it was at least a month before he would eat in my presence. Gradually, I was permitted to pet him and he would reward me with a deep, resonant purr of contentment. One chilly morning, as autumn turned to winter, he decided to finalize my adoption and came indoors to live with me and be my love.

Soon after our passionate affair began, Jack developed an eye infection; I took him to our vet and discovered that he had feline leukemia. The diagnosis was devastating. But my veterinarian practiced holistic as well as conventional medicine and suggested along with antibiotics, a course of homeopathic remedies, massage and meditation (rhythmically stroking him for ten minutes to induce deep relaxation) which bolstered both our immune systems.

Eight comforting years of constant companionship passed. Jack became known as the "miracle" cat because he lived longer after having been diagnosed with feline leukemia than any other cat the clinic treated. In fact, Jack appeared so healthy that occasionally his doctor would test him to see if he'd not had a spontaneous remission.

But last summer our time together became finite and Jack began to fail rapidly. Every cutting-edge veterinary procedure was attempted in order to buy us just a little more time. Finally, the moment of profound loss that no prayer could put off arrived. "Only his love for you is keeping him alive," my vet said softly. "Your love for him must now let him go." Gently I wrapped my soul mate in my old bathrobe and cradled him in my arms. As I kissed Jack farewell, he licked away my tears and purred until his last heartbeat. It was one of the holiest moments I have ever known.

Jack's buried in our backyard, where he once played. A little brass marker offers the Scottish poet Robert Burns's remembrance to the "harried orphan who found tender refuge in our hungry hearts." It's a sentiment that applies not only to the cats we have loved, lost, and mourned, but to those who share our lives today: Pussy, Mikey, Morris, and Griffin, a feral cat who now permits me to pet him while he eats outside my kitchen door.

Physicians and psychologists say that loving, caring for, and spending time with animals enhances our well-being. Anyone who has ever been adored by a dog or adopted by a cat probably can't convey in words the emotional bond that grows between them. That's because dogs love us unconditionally and cats are big on redemption. Our sins and shortcomings don't bother them as long as we delight in their presence.

If you don't have animals living with you, this doesn't mean you can't make a connection: visit the zoo at different seasons, offer to pet-sit for a friend, walk a neighbor's dog, put out dried corn and nuts for the squirrels in your backyard, or toss bread to the ducks on a pond, the pigeons in the park, the seagulls at the beach.

If you do have pets, don't just feed, walk, and ignore them. You invited them into your life, so open your heart. Pets need to be stroked, cuddled, caressed, indulged, pampered, and played with; dote on them and they'll return the kind of devotion most of us can only dream about receiving from human beings. Talk to them and you'll discover a trusted confidante who'll never betray your secrets. Laugh at their silly antics—a sure stressbuster—and learn how to live by observing them. Dogs make friends easily, are loyal, and aren't moody. Cats are spontaneous, content to live in the present moment. They're small, shedding, scratching, inscrutable Zen masters sent to teach us the paradox of undoing in a hectic world where things always have to be done. As the ball of fur presently curled up on my desk clearly demonstrates, the more naps you take, the more awakenings you experience.

Today, be grateful for the gift of sharing your earthly span with creatures who comfort. Animals are our spiritual companions, living proof of a simply abundant source of Love. None of us need feel alone. And if there is a gift, then surely, there must be a Giver.

AUGUST 8

The Pleasurable Pull of the Past: Antiquing

It is not that I belong to the past, but the past that belongs to me.
—MARY ANTIN

Like many women, I adore antiquing. Perhaps it is because I have learned more about life—how to live it, how to change it for the better, and how to cherish it—in antique shops than anywhere else. Above all, the powerful and pleasurable pull of the past has awakened my passion for social history. Among the artifacts of days gone by, I have discovered that history is really your story and my story. Stories that heal our souls.

Historian Harvey Green makes a fascinating point in his illuminating book *The Light of the Home: An Intimate View of the Lives of Women in Victorian America*. "What was once used to feed a family, nurse a child, clean and polish a teapot, or carry on the social graces and customs of another era has a different function in the present. These objects from the past suggest some sort of life that seems like ours but is foreign."

Certainly I felt a foreigner in another woman's world twelve summers ago when, in a Maine antique shop, I purchased a trunk full of pristine Victorian women's and children's magazines. Serendipity is the fairy-tale faculty of finding valuable things not consciously sought. These magazines, full of the pleasures of "rainy-day occupations" and family pastimes for "cozy home-circle evenings," became my passports to the past. Little did I realize at the time that my personal time machine would take me back to the future, altering the trajectory of my career and life in wondrous ways. I became fascinated with the Victorian era, researching nineteenth-century domestic life in depth, which led to a newspaper column, workshops, and the writing of two books.

The best adventures I have had antiquing occur when my plan is just to browse. I rarely go intending to buy but rather to be surprised. This openness to receiving riches from the past often results in delightful lessons about trusting your instincts, experimenting with different styles, listening to your heart, honoring your creative impulses, stepping out in faith, and above all, realizing there is no lack. How can there be lack in our lives when even the commonplace, through the passage of time, becomes precious? If you ever need to jump-start your own abundant consciousness, spend an entire day at an antique flea market. Even if money were no object, you couldn't bring home everything you see. There's only so much we need or really want. We just keep forgetting this.

Isabelle Eberhardt wrote in 1900 that to think about "what was good and beautiful" in the past amounts to a "*seasoning* of the present." Remember this the next time you feel the need for an official excuse to time-travel pleasantly on a summer's afternoon.

Eighth Day of Creation:
Honoring Our Personal Gifts

Explore daily the will of God.

—CARL JUNG

Martin Buber, the great Jewish philosopher, told a story about a Hasidic *tzaddick*, or enlightened master, named Rabbi Zusya, who often pondered whether he was living an authentic life: "If they ask me in the next world, 'Why were you not Moses?' I will know the answer. But if they ask me, 'Why were you not Zusya?' I will have nothing to say."

How well we'll hold up our end of this revealing conversation is what begins to interest us now, as the fourth Simple Abundance principle—harmony—starts to stir within our souls. Discerning our personal gifts is essential if we are to experience harmony in our lives. "Because our gifts carry us out into the world and make us participants in life, the uncovering of them is one of the most important tasks confronting any one of us," Elizabeth O'Connor writes in the *Eighth Day of Creation: Gifts and Creativity*. "When we talk about being true to ourselves—being the persons we are intended to be—we are talking about gifts. We cannot be ourselves unless we are true to our gifts."

However, it's difficult to be true to our gifts if we don't know what they are. And while masters, mystics, saints, sages, poets, and philosophers have borne witness to the authentic path down through the ages, many of us have tuned out. Why? I believe it's because the lesson of authenticity is often prefaced with the four most terrifying words known to the human race: *the will of God*. Divine Will is frequently associated with suffering, so it's no wonder many of us choose—consciously or not—to slip into a spiritual abyss of unknowing. Trust God? Been there, done that. Thanks, but no. Prefer to go it alone.

But even in the black hole of doubt, we want to believe that a Force greater than our own power or understanding is with us. And it is. The Force is with your authentic self. As Obi Wan Kenobi tells Luke Skywalker in *Star Wars*, "The Force is an energy field created by all living things. It surrounds us, it penetrates us, it binds galaxies together." The Force binds your dreams and desires with your personal gifts so they can find outward expression. "Follow your feelings, trust your feelings," the Jedi knight urges us all, because it is within the Force that we live and move and have our being.

The Force is Love.

Love wants, wishes, and wills nothing less than your *unconditional* happiness, harmony, Wholeness.

Commit to discovering, acknowledging, appreciating, owning, and honoring your personal gifts.

And may the Force be with you.

AUGUST 10

Calling Forth Our Gifts

Do not weep; do not wax indignant. Understand.

—BARUCH SPINOZA

You long to call forth your gifts. To explore your talents. To discover and recover your creativity. But where do you begin? You begin by offering an open heart and a willingness to serve.

"The artist is a servant who is willing to be a birthgiver," writer Madeleine L'Engle tells us in *Walking on Water: Reflections on Faith and Art*. "I believe that each work of art, whether it is a work of great genius, or something very small, comes to the artist and says, 'Here I am. Enflesh me. Give birth to me.' And the artist either says, 'My soul doth magnify the Lord,' and willingly becomes the bearer of the work, or refuses."

Whether or not we serve is entirely our choice. God's first gift to us is free will, which distinguishes mortals from the angels, who—after having seen the glory—joyfully exchanged free will for the passion of serving. Being higher than the angels, we can have the best of both worlds: free will *and* the passion of serving. Perhaps one day we'll realize it's *not* the will of God we need fear as much as being left to our own deceits and devices. We can always choose to say "No" to the next *Wuthering Heights*, *The Piano*, or Barney.

"Sorry, find someone else."

And Spirit will.

To be fair, sometimes we don't literally use those words. Sometimes we say, "Sorry, I just can't get my act together right now. Come back later."

So the Great Creator moves on until a willing artist with an open heart offers to become the creative conduit.

This scenario goes a long way toward explaining why you are heartbroken, bewildered, and furious when, after diddling around for years, someone else takes out a patent on an infant carrier that resembles the one you designed for your first baby; distributes her greeting card line for single parents while yours is half-finished on the drawing board; trademarks the name of your fantasy store; nationally syndicates the same column topic you've been writing in your head the last five years but never got around to marketing; or wins the Pillsbury Bake-Off with a chocolate decadence cookie recipe just like the one you've been perfecting through years of family taste trials.

Now I don't mean that someone else has literally ripped off your exact book, design, name, or recipe. What I'm talking about occurs when someone else introduces into the world a creative idea so similar to yours it makes you swoon. You feel crushed, but you're also freaked. How on earth could this be possible unless somebody read your mind?

Well, it wasn't *your* mind that was tapped. It was Divine Mind. Remember, before anything exists on earth, it exists fully formed in Spirit. The Great Creator does not play favorites; each of us came into being to carry on the re-creation of the world through our gifts.

And while you are offered many dizzying opportunities in a lifetime, Spirit only comes once for each Work seeking creative expression through you, then moves on. The bottom line is that the Work must be brought forth. If you don't do it, someone else will. So when that great idea flashes across your mind surrounded by Light, pay attention! Once it exists in your mind, realize that other brainwaves soon will be able to pick up the creative energy pattern if they are receptive. Think of your mind as a satellite dish. Creative celestial messages are continuously being transmitted. The frequency is jammed—privy to your soul only—for an infinitesimal, proprietary moment. Just long enough for you to lift up your heart, accept the assignment, and give thanks.

Is the idea absolutely fabulous? Can you see it completely finished in your mind's eye? Does it take your breath away? Novelist Gail Godwin tells us that "Some things . . . arrive in their own mysterious hour, on their own terms and not yours, to be seized or relinquished forever."

So for God's sake—and your own—just say "Yes."

AUGUST 11

Second Thoughts

Whatever you can do or dream you can, begin it;
Boldness has genius, power and magic in it.
—JOHANN WOLFGANG VON GOETHE

Today you realize how blessed you are. In secret you nurture the nascent dream—the Work entrusted to you for safekeeping—in the sanctuary of your soul. In quiet moments you overflow with excitement at the golden possibilities that stretch endlessly before you. Because happiness is the most difficult emotion to bear alone, you confide your dream to your partner, best friend, lover, sister, mother, children.

Their lack of enthusiasm hits you at point-blank range. The "for your own good" litany pours forth: you're too old, too overextended to try something new right now, too broke, too inexperienced. You don't have the resources, the talent, the contacts, or one chance in a million to bring this dream to fruition. Oh, really? Consider the track record of your naysayers. How many dreams have *they* successfully brought into the world?

I thought so. *Please* be careful about confiding your sacred dreams, especially in the first trimester after creative conception—the period that Sören Kierkegaard called the "dreaming consciousness" prior to creation. A disgruntled dreamer is a risky mentor. Never seek somebody's advice if you even *suspect* you know what they'll say. You cannot afford to hear the negative tape again. Second thoughts have aborted more dreams than all the difficult circumstances, overwhelming obstacles, and dangerous detours fate ever could throw at you. Undermining your authenticity by succumbing to someone else's second thoughts is a sinister, subtle, and seductive form of self-abuse. Few of us are immune to the opinions of others. We need to learn how to dispassionately assess advice, ponder the source, weigh the opinion. If the information is insightful and is something you hadn't considered, retain it. If it's discouraging, let it go. End your conversation politely but firmly. Better yet, in the future, don't even start it.

William Hutchinson Murray, the leader of the Scottish Himalayan Expedition team that scaled Mount Everest in 1951, urges the dreamer in you to take a leap of faith: "Concerning all acts of initiative (and creation), there is one elementary truth, the ignorance of which kills countless ideas and splendid plans; that the moment one definitely commits oneself, then Providence moves too. All sorts of things occur to help one that would never otherwise have occurred. A whole stream of events issue from the decision, raising in one's favor all manner of unforeseen incidents and meetings and material assistance which no man could have dreamed would have come his way."

AUGUST 12

The Great Collaboration

We can't take any credit for our talents. It's how we use them that counts.

—MADELEINE L'ENGLE

Don't worry that your talent won't be adequate to the task. Spirit always chooses us as servants of work *perfectly* suited to our personal gifts, even if we beg to differ. A low opinion of our abilities is a handy cop-out when facing creative challenges, but the Great Creator is on to us by now. Actually, feeling inadequate to the task we're asked to do seems to be a spiritual prerequisite.

Anyway, our degree of talent is a moot point, because the Work *always* knows more than we do—a fact for which we can all be eternally grateful. Agreeing to serve really means just showing up to make the calls, mix the paint, pick up the pen, pluck the strings, shape the pot, and get out of the way.

We do not create in a vacuum. Art is a Divine Collaboration, a sacred covenant between the artist and the Great Creator. Inspired artists, the ones who write the books you can't put down, pen the poems you must memorize, paint the pictures you can't walk away from, and compose the music you must listen to over and over again, are the first ones to admit it. The great Italian composer, Giacomo Puccini, confessed that his opera, *Madame Butterfly,* "was dictated to me by God; I was merely instrumental in putting it on paper and communicating it to the public." Harriet Beecher Stowe swore that it was "Another Hand" writing through her at the kitchen table—in between caring for six children, cooking, and sewing—because she never knew what was going to come next in *Uncle Tom's Cabin.* George Frederick Handel believed he was hallucinating for twenty frenzied days as he composed *The Messiah:* "I did think I did see all Heaven before me, and the great God Himself." Painters from Piet Mondrian to Robert Motherwell have viewed their role as channels. Motherwell knew that to let the brush take over was the surest way to render the vision on canvas: "It will stumble on what one couldn't do by oneself."

And once you begin to nurture Divinity's dream—with your creativity, craft, courage, discipline, devotion, discernment, energy, enthusiasm, emotion, intelligence, imagination, inventiveness, passion, perseverance, patience, skill, sweat, savvy, tenacity, tears, and tantrums—you will *grow* into your talent. What's more, you'll be astonished at what the Great Artistic Alliance accomplishes.

The world needs your gift as much as you need to bestow it. May Sarton warns us that "The gift turned inward, unable to be given, becomes a heavy burden, even sometimes a kind of poison. It is as though the flow of life were backed up."

As long as you remember that you're not creating alone, the Flow cannot be stopped.

The Artist's Way: Tuning to the Higher Harmonic

Become willing to see the hand of God and accept it as a friend's offer to help you with what you are doing.

—JULIA CAMERON

Many of us wish we were more creative. Many of us sense we *are* creative, but unable to effectively tap that creativity. Our dreams elude us. Our lives feel somehow flat. Often, we have great ideas, wonderful dreams, but are unable to actualize them for ourselves," Julia Cameron concedes in her peerless *The Artist's Way: A Spiritual Path to Higher Creativity*. "Sometimes we have specific creative longings we would love to be able to fulfill—learning to play the piano, painting, taking an acting class, or writing. Sometimes our goal is more diffuse. We hunger for what might be called creative living—an expanded sense of creativity in our business lives, in sharing with our children, our spouse, our friends."

Many of us have unconsciously erected seemingly insurmountable barriers to protect ourselves from failing or succeeding. We may think we're protecting ourselves by ignoring or denying our creative impulses, but really all we're doing is burying our authentic selves alive. As you slowly learn to remove the rubble of the opinions and judgments of others (including your own internal censor) and exchange a limiting, toxic interpretation of a miserly, mean-spirited God for what Julia calls the *"good, orderly direction"* of a loving and supportive Great Creator, not only will you encounter the inner artist, but you'll come to respect your art as a personal form of worship.

"Once you accept that it is natural to create, you can begin to accept a second idea—that the Creator will hand you whatever you need for the project," Julia reassures us. "The minute you are willing to accept the help of this collaborator, you will see useful bits of help everywhere in your life. Be alert: there is a higher harmonic, adding to and augmenting your inner creative voice."

Spirit speaks to you constantly throughout the day. You may experience a hunch, perk up at the suggestion of a friend, or follow an urge to try something new on a whim. Train your heart to listen. Today, adjust your spiritual satellite. Tune in to the higher harmonic frequency for help as you continue your authentic, artistic pilgrimage to Wholeness.

The Courage to Create

No tears in the writer, no tears in the reader.
No surprise for the writer, no surprise for the reader.
—ROBERT FROST

Perhaps one of the reasons we fear excavating our authentic selves or encountering the inner artist is because creativity seems too risky. We hear the word "artist" and we associate the calling with dramatic, self-inflicted doom: Edna St. Vincent Millay's solitary sips, Dorothy Parker's binges, Judy Garland's sleeping pills, Billie Holiday's heroin, Anne Sexton's final nap in a car filled with carbon monoxide. The number of suffering souls sacrificed on the altar of art by self-abasement goes a long way toward explaining why many women, especially with children, hesitate to call themselves artists. It's safer to dabble. No one really expects a dilettante to deliver the goods. Creating costs too much, especially if you believe creating only comes by the crucifixion technique.

Why should this be so? Rollo May, who wrote *The Courage to Create*, explains that "Down through the ages, authentically creative figures have consistently found themselves in . . . a struggle." But is it the struggle to create or to stay blocked because we fear where the creative life will lead? "Write the truest sentence you know," Ernest Hemingway encourages the writer in you. Paint the truest image you can render. Wait all day with camera poised to capture the five-second sliver of light. Express the rage and range of raw emotion through your dialogue. Convey passion's power with the curve of your dancer's body honed through discipline and denial. Set the angel free when you carve. Make the heavens weep when you compose.

But in order to be true to a creative work, the artist must journey to the center of the self. Past the conscious sentries in the brain, beyond the barbed wire barricades of the heart, into the trenches of "truth or dare." You can't write a true sentence or live authentically if you don't trust yourself. You can't trust yourself without courage.

Perhaps this is why Annie Dillard compares the altered state of consciousness needed to create to a Zulu warrior's frenzied rite of banging drums or an Aztec maiden's purification ritual before she is sacrificed to the gods. "But how, if you are neither Zulu warrior nor Aztec maiden, do you prepare yourself, all alone, to enter an extraordinary state on an ordinary morning," she wonders for herself and all of us.

By showing up. Day in, day out. By not judging how it's going. If it's going at all, that's enough. You can't afford to think about how the work will be received when you're finished. That's not your job. Remember, we're learning to surrender the delivery details of our dreams. Our job, then, is just to do it. It can't be published, produced, performed, or purchased if it doesn't exist.

Consider this: what if the woman who wrestles with God but doesn't live to tell the tale is the one who refuses to create—a work of art, an authentic life? What if the fatal wound, the one from which we never recover, is regret?

Today it's time for authentic "truth or dare." Dare yourself to believe in your creativity, wherever it may lead you. Trust that where it leads is exactly where you're supposed to be. The word *courage* comes from the French word for the heart, *coeur*. Your authentic self knows where you're headed. Don't wrestle with Spirit. Collaborate with It.

AUGUST 15

Sometimes Ignorance Is Bliss

Ignorance gives one a large range of probabilities.
—GEORGE ELIOT

Trust me, you don't want to know. Ignorance is a protective blessing. Do you really want to know that your play about a woman determined to chart her own destiny (considered so promising at the new playwrights' reading) will be savaged when it receives a full-scale production because the theater critic's wife just left him? Do you want to know that eight months after your newspaper column is picked up for national syndication, the syndicate will be sold and your column will be dropped? Do you want to know that you won't get the grant, that it will be your third novel that gets published first, that your television acting debut will end up on the cutting-room floor, or that none of your pots will sell at next week's crafts fair?

I don't think so. "Ever tried? Ever failed? No matter," Samuel Beckett insists. "Try again. Fail again. Fail better." Would you revise the play, market the column, apply for the grant, attend the audition, rent the kiln, if you knew that failure always precedes success? Failure is a crucial part of the creative process. Authentic success arrives only after we have mastered failing better.

Other things we don't need to know: just how much we've taken on when we accepted the artistic assignment. "I must frankly own, that if I had known, beforehand, that this book would have cost me the labour which it has, I should never have been courageous enough to commence it," Isabella Beeton confessed about her *Book of Household Management*, written in 1861—a book that has yet to go out of print.

There's a reason Isabella Beeton was kept in the dark, as we all are when creating. If we ever had an inkling of the intense labor required to bring the Work into the world, we'd be out of here. When the visitation comes, it's the razzle-dazzle of golden possibilities that seduces us. Ignorance is part of Infinite Intelligence's inviting come-hither. Why else are heavenly encounters accompanied by brilliant, blinding Light? Because we're not supposed to see too far ahead. We're not supposed to know. Don't forget that the forbidden fruit in the Garden of Eden was from the Tree of Knowledge.

In the military and high-tech industries, there is a qualifying code assigned to information: "Need to know." If you can do your job effectively without knowing the big picture, you're kept in the dark. All we need to know is that the Spirit knows what we don't. If we get out of the way, we'll be shown the next step, including how not to sell ourselves short as we gracefully grow into our gifts.

AUGUST 16

You Can't Be Original—You Can Be Authentic

To believe your own thought, to believe that what is true for you in your private heart is true for all men—that is genius.
—RALPH WALDO EMERSON

One of the reasons many of us have trouble getting our Work out into the world is that unconsciously we're competing instead of creating, which always short-circuits the flow of inspiration. A friend of mine is a gifted playwright. She denies herself the pleasure of seeing anything on the stage other than revivals of classics, preferably Greek. It's too painful for her to watch contemporary work because she is addicted to comparisons.

Why do we make ourselves sick competing against strangers? I believe it's just another sophisticated, seditious form of self-sabotage. If we don't measure up, why even try? The fault line of comparison runs so deep in the lives of many of us it's heartbreaking. I know women who quake at the thought of school bake sales because their brownies don't sell as fast as those of another mother, and the psychic phobia over Halloween costumes is the last frontier in feminine psychology.

Five years ago when I published my first book, which updated Victorian family traditions, there were few popular books on the Victorian era available. But the late nineteenth century was just about to be rediscovered, and within two years there were so many books in the stores the market was completely saturated. Today it would be extremely difficult to find a commercial publisher for a Victorian book even if you channeled Queen Victoria as a spirit guide. This doesn't mean if you are writing one that you should stop. The cycle of creation is cyclical. There's a reason the past is prologue.

Sometimes you're ahead of your time. Mozart was known to qualify his genius by declaring he was composing for future generations. There are literally millions of aspiring and working artists writing books, publishing poems, selling scripts, directing movies, auditioning for roles, designing clothes, entering juried craft exhibitions, starting home-based businesses, looking for an agent, praying for a lucky break. *Don't panic*. It is impossible for you to be an original. But you *can* be authentic.

"God has lots of movie ideas, novel ideas, poems, songs, paintings, acting jobs," Julia Cameron reassures us. "By listening to the creator within, we are led to our right path." You aren't the only one starting a mail-order catalog this year, but that doesn't mean that you don't know exactly what niche yours will fill perfectly. Why do you think *you* were offered the spiritual and creative opportunity?

Once you accept an artistic assignment from the Great Creator, it's yours. Nobody can take it away from you, unless, of course, you relinquish it. Nobody can duplicate your work because there's no one in the world like you. They can imitate, but they can't duplicate. Your work is born of your sensibilities, temperament, experience, emotion, passion, perseverance, attention to detail, idiosyncrasies, and eccentricities.

When you're authentic, so is your art.

AUGUST 17

Taking On Quite a Task

To live fully, outwardly and inwardly, not to ignore external reality for the sake of the inner life, or the reverse—that's quite a task.
—ETTY HILLESUM

I had a difficult time after my first book was published because it was impossible for me to believe that I had actually written a successful book, especially since I had created a character who had a life of her own. Fictional though she was, my character, Mrs. Sharp, was the storybook mother we all longed to have, and if we have children of our own, the mother we all try to be. It was frequently pointed out to me that this "perfect" Victorian mother was my alter ego, but I passionately denied it.

To my way of thinking, Mrs. Sharp was everything I clearly was not: serene, incurably optimistic, and deeply spiritual. Her life was harmonious because she successfully managed the delicate balance of living in the world yet remaining apart from it. She lived each day to the fullest with a deep appreciation of the past, an enriched sense of the present, and a joyous anticipation of the future. Her home was a haven of hospitality, reflecting in its beauty, order, comfort, and good taste her authentic style. She was a compassionate confidante and true friend, who empathized, encouraged, and inspired. I absolutely adored Mrs. Sharp and so did many other women.

How could I claim to be this extraordinary woman's alter ego? The closest thing I could claim was that I was her amanuensis, someone who takes down dictation. Good or bad, the book was Mrs. Sharp's. But by distancing myself from the creation of the book, I became unable to bask in the accomplishment of bringing it into the world, although it represented five years of work and struggle. I accepted compliments, praise, even gratitude for having written it, as graciously as a bewildered go-between could muster. Having achieved a long-sought goal, I wondered why I felt so empty, unfulfilled, and confused.

A couple of years later I was having a heart-to-heart with my sister. Throughout our conversation, unconsciously I kept referring to Mrs. Sharp. "Stop this," Maureen said gently but firmly. "Stop referring to Mrs. Sharp as if she's a separate person. You're Mrs. Sharp, even if you don't believe it. She is who you are deep within. You have got to start owning your talent or you'll lose it."

Maureen believed the source of my discontent was that I was refusing to accept responsibility for my talent. I wouldn't "own" my talent, as in "claim it." Nor would I "own up," as in "admit to," the truth that I was an artist even if I lived in a suburban home and not a New York loft. The most credit I would give myself was that I was a diligent wordsmith who worked very hard at putting one word after another until she had sentences, paragraphs, pages, columns, features, finished books. I had bludgeoned my true identity as an artist with the blunt instrument of disbelief, then buried my authentic self with denial.

But *why* didn't I own my talent? This is a question I have been asking myself for years. Perhaps it was because if I failed, I would have to own any failure as much as any success, and I didn't want to "fail better" anymore. I wanted to live a creative life and I thought my creativity could only be owned if the world acknowledged that I possessed it. I had many lessons to learn before acknowledging that Spirit had used my personal gifts to give outward expression to something that would not have existed if I had refused to take up my pen. And, having accepted the Great Creator's assignment and run with it, I had both the right and obligation to own—and to share—the work that resulted.

AUGUST 18

Owning Your Talent

Each time I write a book, every time I face that yellow pad, the challenge is so great. I have written eleven books, but each time I think, "Uh, oh, they're going to find out now. I've run a game on everybody and they're going to find me out."

—MAYA ANGELOU

I ran into an old friend, a radio producer, at a party. "I hear you're on your third book," he baited me. "How long do you think you can keep this sting going?"

"It's a great scam." I laughed. "As long as I can."

Perhaps because I so often feel like a fraud, authenticity decided I'd be the perfect host. "Explore me," she whispered. "Peer behind the curtain. Look under the rock. See who's really there." Believe me, I had no inkling when I started Simple Abundance that I was embarking on a safari to discover my authentic self. To give you an idea of how little I knew in the beginning, I thought I was conceiving a lifestyle book on downshifting.

Many artists feel they'll be "found out," sooner or later—and probably sooner. For when we create, although we know that a Higher Power works with us and through us, the Work comes into the world with our name on it. This is the artist's struggle. If we don't create, we snuff out the Divine Spark. If we do create, we feel we're showing a false face to the world because we know we didn't do it alone, even if nobody else does.

But the struggle and the scam stop once we cease denying our talent and become willing to own it—humbly, gratefully, and respectfully—and then *share* it with the world. As long as we're not exploiting our gifts only for our own good, we're covered. In a New Testament parable, a rich man is about to go on a journey, so he entrusts to three of his servants "talents" of money. The first servant is given five talents, the second, two, and the last, one. The first servant immediately puts his talents to work and doubles his owner's investment, as does the servant with two talents. The servant with one talent, however, is afraid of the responsibility, so he buries his talent in the ground.

When the rich man returns, his servants are called for an accounting of their work. Both servants who have increased their talents receive praise for their efforts. They have done wonderfully, so they're invited to share in their master's happiness.

Now the third servant arrives to explain that because the rich man is such a hard taskmaster, he thought it better to play it safe by burying his talent so that nothing would happen to it. The master is so enraged that the fool didn't possess the common sense to deposit the money in the bank, where at least it could have collected interest, that he angrily seizes it back and gives it to the most successful servant. The master then says, "For everyone who has will be given more and he shall have an abundance." The cautious servant is thrown out into the darkness where he begins weeping, wailing, and gnashing his teeth—and with good reason. It hurts like hell when the world won't invest in you. But it's excruciating, almost more than you can bear, when you don't believe and invest in yourself.

This is a parable about creative risk. We feel sorry for the servant who buried his talent because, as Elizabeth O' Connor points out, "his cautious, protective measures seem very reasonable." The master comes off as a thug, throwing the poor soul into darkness without comfort or pity just because he's played it safe. Since most of us do play it safe in life, this story makes us very nervous.

It's meant to.

Many of us squander precious natural resources—time, creative energy, emotion—comparing the size of our talents to those of others. Today, ask Spirit to call forth your authentic gifts, so that you might know them, acknowledge them, and own them. Do you want to live more abundantly? Have you buried your talents? How can we live richer, deeper, and more passionately if we aren't willing to invest in ourselves? Many of us have played it safe for too long and wonder why we are miserable.

Playing it safe is the riskiest choice we can ever make.

AUGUST 19

Spinning Straw into Gold

Stories are medicine. . . . They have such power; they do not require that we do, be, act anything—we need only listen. The remedies for repair or reclamation of any lost psychic drive are contained in stories.

—CLARISSA PINKOLA ESTES, PH.D.

Next to knowing what to do with a few loaves and fishes, knowing how to spin straw into gold is probably the most important talent a woman can possess. It can make the difference between living a life of lack and living one of Simple Abundance. Gratefully, this gift was bestowed on all of us. But, like any other talent, the gift of alchemy must be called forth, treasured, owned, respected, and nurtured.

As the story goes, a poor miller who is given to bragging meets a king who is known for his interest in accumulating riches. Wanting to impress him, the miller tells the king that his daughter possesses a rare talent—the ability to spin straw into gold. Skeptical but intrigued, the king orders the maiden to his castle, where he shows her a large room filled with straw. He then commands her to transform the straw into gold by the morning or lose her life.

Because this is an impossible task, the young woman succumbs to anguished weeping. What can save her? Suddenly, a strange little man appears in the room. "*I* can spin straw into gold. What will you give me in return?" he says. Stunned, the miller's daughter takes off a necklace that had been her mother's and gives it to him. At once the little man sets to work. The last thing the maiden remembers before she falls into a deep slumber is the soft droning of the spinning wheel. At dawn the king finds the miller's daughter still asleep, surrounded by hundreds of spools of golden thread and not one wisp of straw.

The king is delirious with joy at what she's accomplished. And though she wants to explain that it isn't she who's performed this incredible feat, she cannot bring herself to admit her incompetence. If she did, what would become of her? But her silence only increases her dilemma, for the greedy king leads her to an even larger room filled with straw, and again, she hears the royal command to spin it into gold if she values her life.

The second night passes like the first. This time the maiden offers the strange little man her ring in exchange for his magic. The following morning the king is again ecstatic to find the room overflowing with golden spools. But the miller's daughter still conceals the real story. By the time the king leads her to a third straw-filled room, this one the size of a great hall, she realizes she has made a terrible mistake. Why has she not confessed her secret collaboration? But it's already too late, for the king has promised to make her his bride if she will spin the straw into gold once more.

This time, when the mysterious little man arrives during the night, he finds the miller's daughter nearly beside herself because she has nothing left to offer him. "Never mind," he says. "I will help you one more time in exchange for your firstborn child."

"How can I possibly make so terrible a promise?" she asks herself. Then she reasons that, since no one will ever know about her secret accomplice, she won't have to keep her end of the bargain. And so, with her consent, the little man spins the straw into gold for the third time. The next day, the king makes the miller's daughter his queen, and, in her happiness, she soon forgets her promise.

A year passes and the queen gives birth to a handsome baby boy. However, soon afterward, the little magician suddenly reappears in her bedchamber and demands the baby. The queen pleads for her child, offering the little man all the wealth of the royal kingdom, but he refuses. Overcome with grief, she falls to the floor weeping. Her clandestine collaborator, moved to pity, grants the queen three days to discover his name, which he has always kept a secret. "If, by the end of that time, you can name my name, you may keep your child." Eventually, with the help of a clever, faithful servant, the queen discovers that the little magician is called Rumpelstiltskin. She is able to keep her child, her crown, and her contentment.

"Stories are embedded with instructions which guide us about the complexities of life," Jungian analyst and *cantadora* storyteller, Clarissa Pinkola Estes, reminds us in her powerful evocation of the female psyche, *Women Who Run with the Wolves*. Today, contemplate the psychic path taken in this story. When reflecting on dreams or fairy stories, it's important to remember that all the characters are inner aspects of ourselves. You are not only the miller's daughter, but the miller, the king, the faithful servant, the baby, and Rumpelstiltskin. Even more important, you are the straw and the gold.

AUGUST 20

The Golden Storehouse of the Subconscious Mind

Infinite riches are all around you if you will open your mental eyes and behold the treasure house of infinity within you. There is a gold mine within you from which you can extract everything you need to live life gloriously, joyously, and abundantly.

—JOSEPH MURPHY

Did you figure out who Rumpelstiltskin really was? He was the miller's daughter's subconscious mind. "You can bring into your life more power, more wealth, more health, more happiness and more joy by learning to contact and release the hidden power of your subconscious mind," than any wizard could ever conjure, Joseph Murphy tells us in his classic work on metaphysical principles, *The Power of Your Subconscious Mind*. Just as there are two sides of the brain, there are two spheres to our minds. The conscious mind is where reason resides and the subconscious, or deeper mind, is where our emotions and creativity dwell.

"The main point to remember is once the subconscious mind accepts an idea, it begins to execute it," Dr. Murphy explains. "It works by association of ideas and uses every bit of knowledge that you have gathered in your lifetime to bring about its purpose. It draws on the infinite power, energy, and wisdom within you. It lines up all the laws of nature to get its way. Sometimes it seems to bring about an immediate solution to your difficulties, but at other times it may take days, weeks or longer. . . . *Its ways are past finding out."*

In the fable Rumpelstiltskin, the cycle of creation begins with the command given to the subconscious mind. For dreams to be called forth to the physical plane, a declaration must be made: "My daughter can spin straw into gold."

Sometimes the task we agree to take on seems virtually impossible. We think we don't have the time, talent, resources, or support to achieve it. But we are intrigued by the possibilities, just as the king is captivated by the thought of more wealth. Our authentic longings embolden us to obey the command: spin the straw into gold or suffer the consequences. Let the dream die and with it will die the authentic life for which we long.

So we try to spin our straw, using all the skills of our rational mind—our reasoning, our experience, our craft. But when we rely solely on reason to manifest dreams, all we end up with is straw. However, we have a strange creative collaborator who knows how to spin straw into gold. It is Rumpelstiltskin, our subconscious mind. Instead of a necklace or a ring, we surrender pride and control of the dream. Instead of our firstborn child, we surrender our ego; we admit we cannot do it alone. We must give the order to our subconscious to work it out, then slip into a creative slumber in order that the subconscious mind can go to work on our behalf.

When you are creating and you find yourself stuck, let go and turn it over to the Deeper Wisdom dwelling beyond your reasoning. When you are perplexed, you need to ask the subconscious to take over, preferably at night. In the morning, the answer should be forthcoming. But if it's not, continue asking questions before you go to sleep. How do I proceed? How do I spin my straw into gold? Tell your subconscious mind to awaken you with the answer. By the third morning—three is a very mystical number—the answers should start to be revealed.

Amazingly, when we harness the incredible power of the subconscious in our lives, we can accomplish whatever we set out to do, no matter what obstacles we have to overcome. Hold the vision of the completed dream in your mind. See your heart's desire. Feel the thrill of accomplishment. Offer grateful thanks in advance. Don't ask how it will come to pass, just know that it will. Now go to work.

Today, prepare to evolve from a poor miller's daughter into a queen. In your heart, mind, and soul, be willing to turn it over to Infinite Intelligence. Get out of the way, name the source of your Power, and begin to spin straw into gold.

The Comfort Found in Good Old Books

We read books to find out who we are. What other people, real or imaginary, do and think and feel is an essential guide to our understanding of what we ourselves are and may become.
—URSULA K. LEGUIN

Have you read a good book lately? I certainly hope so. But there are many additional ways to enjoy books as a personal pursuit besides reading them: belonging to a book club, rediscovering the old favorites you loved as a child, and searching for that next irresistible volume in which to lose yourself. Unfortunately, the good books that provide comfort, consolation, chuckles, and the companionship we all crave cannot be conjured up instantly. Since the choice of what we curl up with is often crucial for our solace and sanity, we need to learn how to nurture the talent of selection.

Book browsing is a meditative art. Every woman should have three well-paved avenues for page-turning adventures: a proper bookstore stocked by bibliophiles, a choice secondhand haunt, and a civilized lending library. Books are as essential as breathing. In my experience, when going down for the third time, it was often word-to-word resuscitation that saved the day.

We have much to be grateful for: proper bookstores are not as rare as they once were because the art form is enjoying a revival, and libraries abound. But probably you'll have to do a bit of sleuthing to uncover a really good secondhand haunt. Visiting a special secondhand-book store can trigger a religious experience for me. Here I glimpse Eternity as time stands still: hours become minutes and I am suspended in the Hereafter. The dog-eared, gilded-paged, embossed, and foxed with age receive me with the knowing of an old flame. But instead of arms, I am enveloped by the fragrance of leather mingled with a slight, sweet, musty scent. Occasionally, stumbling down a dusky corridor, I will be embraced by the Light, as a sunbeam sliver or an angel's wing leads me to exactly the book I need but wasn't consciously aware of. Frankly, this has happened so many times it's no longer paranormal but standard operating procedure. If you'd like to become more aware of hidden helpers as you begin to call forth your talents, a visit to a great secondhand-book shop is a fabulous way to begin. My favorite book exploration invocation is: "Divine Guidance is my only reality and Divine Guidance richly manifests for me in the perfect book at the perfect price. As I seek, I shall find and I give thanks."

Some secondhand stores are ramshackle affairs with vague subject categories stacked helter skelter. Certainly they are worth wandering into, because you never know what you will find, and we must always be open to receiving abundantly. But the choice secondhand stores have entire rooms devoted to subject categories like cooking, crafts, gardening, arts, women's fiction, classics, social history, mysteries, and inspirational books. You'll find them alphabetized according to author and book series, and occasionally still in their original jackets. Here's where I find my treasures, the lost domestic tomes from the turn of the century to the 1950s, the ghosts of all things once bright and beautiful. Here's where I also find old magazines and booklets that were given away as free bonuses from manufacturers which are a wealth of inspiration and information.

Virginia Woolf believed that "a perfect treat must include a visit to the second-hand bookshop." Put finding a fabulous one on your list of personal priorities.

AUGUST 22

The Poetry Prescription

Poetry affords us a respite in which we may gather renewed strength for the old struggle to adapt ourselves to reality.
—ROBERT HAVEN SCHAUFFLER

One of the gems I unearthed in a choice secondhand-book haunt was the October 1925 issue of *Good Housekeeping*. In it was a novel remedy for weariness called "The Poetry Cure." It suggested that when we are frazzled, ruminating on a line or a stanza of poetry can induce a sense of serenity. This suggestion led me to a marvelous form of meditation, especially if I think I don't have twenty minutes to sit down or take a walk—a situation which happens more often than I care to admit.

Many of us resist the power of poetry to illuminate our path because we have such bad memories of dissecting stanzas in high school English. Some of us also have an inferiority complex about poetry, viewing it as a mantric art that only the well-educated, literate, and erudite can appreciate. But poets are the first to disagree; they know poetry is real and personal.

Rita Dove, America's youngest and first African American poet laureate, says that "Poetry connects you to yourself, to the self that doesn't know how to talk or negotiate." When we allow poetry to slip slowly beneath the sinews of our conscious mind, connection to our authentic selves becomes simpler; an emotion or an experience is captured in evocative word melodies that bestow harmony on everyday encounters. Rita Dove believes that poetry has the ability to restore "a sense of mystery, a sense of wonder" to our daily round. Once I heard her read on the radio a poem she had written about waiting to board an airplane flight to go home. I was cooking, but in that instant I was waiting to board my own flight. It was an exquisite reminder that our specific lives can mirror the universal experience. Nowhere is this more passionately expressed than in poetry.

To begin exploring this simply abundant art, bring home a book of poetry from the library this week. Listening to the varied voices of women poets—Rita Dove, Anne Sexton, Louise Bogan, Diane Wakoski, Emily Dickinson, Maya Angelou, Adrienne Rich, Audre Lorde, Muriel Rukeyser, Judith Viorst, Elizabeth Barrett Browning, Maxine Kumin, Diane Ackerman, Shirley Kaufman, May Sarton, Cherríe Moraga, Marianne Moore—can help you find your own. Read one poem a day. Write a favorite verse from it on a card and commit it to memory. Poetry possesses many secrets just waiting to be revealed to patient seekers of truth. I love to meditate on a line just before drifting off to sleep.

Explore writing your own poems. Don't tell me you're too old or that none of us is interested in what you have to say. Few literary debuts were as stunning as the publication of Amy Clampitt's first full-length book of poetry, *The Kingfisher*, in 1983, when she was 63. Although she had been a poet all her life, she didn't find her authentic voice until she was in her fifties. If you have lived all your life hearing another voice in your heart, maybe it's time to channel her.

Make a poem of one day's dialogue with your authentic self. Attend poetry readings at bookstores, cafés, libraries, college campuses. Trust that you will discover, as did the Russian-born writer Anzia Yezierska, that "The real thing creates its own poetry."

AUGUST 23

Music as Therapy

I think I should have no other mortal wants, if I could always have plenty of music. It seems to infuse strength into my limbs and ideas into my brain. Life seems to go on without effort, when I am filled with music.

—GEORGE ELIOT

You already know that music can be an exquisite source of pleasure and entertainment. But did you also know that it can be a powerful form of prayer, meditation, and healing? Actually, musical therapy is an ancient tradition. Since the dawn of humanity, spiritual healers known as shamans have used drums, bells, and rattles to drive disease from the body, depression from the mind, despair from the soul.

Because music can reach beyond the barriers of our conscious mind, neurolgist Oliver Sacks, author of *Awakenings*, believes it can become a key to unlocking a sense of self. Even Alzheimer patients who have lost their inner bearings often respond to music when all else has failed.

Finding the personal music that calls to us authentically can be empowering as you learn to nurture your creativity. Music loosens the grip of our conscious mind during the process of creation. I listen to classical music when I'm researching and to soaring movie themes while I'm writing. Anaïs Nin believed that music was "a stimulant of the highest order, far more potent than wine" when creating. Novelist Amy Tan listens to the same music each day as she writes, because it helps her pick up her narrative thread where she left off. This technique also works with other creative projects—painting, sculpting, pottery, handicrafts—which are started and stopped over a space of time. If you need to focus your concentration, listening to Mozart can increase your clarity—which is why it's the recommended accompaniment for exam cramming as well as creative brainstorming. Given the fact that Mozart was a genius, it's not surprising that his arrangement of musical notes affects our brain patterns positively.

Piano nocturnes—romantic, resonant, ruminative compositions for solo piano—are a virtual musical pharmacy. No woman should be without a soothing tape or compact disc to play when stressed. I have even used piano noctures to calm our cats when they're confined indoors because of injury, illness, or inclement weather. Instead of smoking or sipping the next time you're extremely nervous, try Camille Saint-Saëns, Robert Schumann, Erik Satie, or Stephen Sondheim's contemporary nocturnes in the musical *A Little Night Music*. When your hormones are playing havoc with your humor, try Haydn. Bach's preludes and fugues are an exquisite balm for the blues. Gabriel Fauré is a personal favorite when I'm frazzled, and Frederic Chopin's exquisite nocturnes can restore a ravished soul even if a broken heart can't be mended.

On another note, ten minutes of boogie-woogie can shake the deepest doldrums because rhythm reduces anxiety. If I have to work at night I find light jazz energizing, but for cooking I adore listening to songs of passionate hunger—traditional Irish music or opera. Soft rock or show tunes keep me moving while I clean, and I love to listen to country music when I carpool. When you crave more than the sounds of silence, there is music for every mood. Acknowledging your mood swings and honoring their reality with music to accompany the experience is soulcraft.

Gradually build a personal collection of musical selections to help you calm down, collect your thoughts, channel your creative energy and call forth your gifts.

Eye of the Beholder

The work of art which I do not make, none other will ever make.
—SIMONE WEIL

When we think of famous women artists, three painters usually come to mind: Mary Cassatt, Georgia O'Keeffe, and Grandma Moses. But there are many, many more women artists who deserve to be just as famous and whose paintings, sculptures, photographs, designs, and illustrations are waiting to be explored and savored.

The American impressionist painter Lilla Cabot Perry is a favorite of mine. She was also the artist friend of the great French impressionist Claude Monet and introduced his work to America. Monet so loved Lilla's work that he hung one of her paintings in his bedroom at Giverny so that he might see it first thing every morning.

Like Mary Cassatt, whose days consisted of "housekeeping, painting and oyster frying," Lilla Cabot Perry was a Victorian "working mother," a century before that ridiculously redundant phrase entered American conversation. In an age when women were expected to choose home and family over career, many women found an authentic way to turn their everyday experience into art. Their determination is a wellspring of inspiration.

Lilla was thirty when she painted her first picture—a portrait of her baby, Margaret. She thought painting might offer her the creative expression she craved after it became necessary to abandon poetry because "it was too absorbing an occupation for a mother of three small children." But painting allowed her to merge motherhood and art, for her work celebrated what she knew and loved best: her children. Eventually her painting became as much a part of the family's daily round as eating and sleeping, as she cleverly enticed her little models to stand still by paying them each a nickel an hour. Later Lilla admitted her passion for self-expression reminded her of "a cooking stove which has too much coal in it and it has to have one of the holes open to keep it from becoming red-hot. It did not matter whether it was the poetry hole or the painting hole, but the lid had to come off."

What artist's lid have you taken off to keep from exploding in fiery frustration? As Lilla says, it doesn't matter whether it's painting or poetry. All that matters is that your creative passion does not get driven inward to become self-immolation. Today, consider all the different and rewarding paths of personal expression open to you by way of your eyes.

Have you ever taken a watercolor, oil, or still-life drawing course just for fun? If an easel doesn't entice, what about the lure of a slanted artist's table: textile, product, fashion, graphic, greeting-card, or book illustration and design. Don't overlook printmaking, collage, sculpture, and photography.

Imogen Cunningham, another artist/mother, was also one of the most celebrated photographers of the twentieth century, capturing 50,000 images over seven decades by keeping "one hand in the dishpan, the other in the darkroom" and never going anywhere without her camera. Pursuing authenticity and raising a family needn't be mutually exclusive unless we insist on making them so.

Even if you think that a "shutter" only hangs on a window or are convinced that you can't even draw a straight line, don't dismiss the visual arts until you've explored the possibility of letting your eyes and hands collaborate with your heart.

The painter Gwendolen John confessed, "My religion is my art; for me, it's everything in life." The visual arts may not be your religion, but they can surely deepen your awareness of Divinity.

AUGUST 25

The Smell of the Greasepaint, the Roar of the Crowd

I seem to wish to have some importance in the play of time. . . . What is deep, as love is deep, I'll have Deeply. What is good, as love is good, I'll have well. Then if time and space have any purpose, I shall belong to it.

—JENNET JOURDEMAYNE
(CHRISTOPHER FRY)

Obviously, I was not destined to become a famous actress. It was the first road taken but it wasn't my authentic path. Although I adored acting—the art, the craft, the lifestyle—I reached the point where I could no longer handle the pain of rejection when I didn't get a part—which happened most of the time. Casting has absolutely nothing to do with how talented an actress you are and everything to do with how you look. If your physical appearance doesn't match the director's interior preconception of what the character looks like, you may not even be able to read for the part.

Holly Hunter stalked Australian film director Jane Campion for over a year while Jane was searching the world for an actress to play Ada, her mute, mid-nineteenth-century Scottish heroine in *The Piano*. Campion didn't initially believe that Holly was right for the part, probably because she couldn't get the indelible image of Holly's previous incarnations as a southern floozy out of her mind. But Holly possessed soul knowledge; she knew this part had been the reason for all those piano lessons as a child and she knew this part was the role she was born to bring to life. The tremendous obstacles she had to overcome in order to get the role must have made winning an Oscar for her soul-stirring performance all the more sweet. I know it did for me, as I watched her accept it.

Rejection, self-doubt, financial insecurity, and public criticism are all part of an actress's daily round. We forget this when we watch those glorious women all dressed up for the Academy Awards. Another actress in *The Piano*, eleven-year-old Anna Paquin, won an Oscar for her role as Ada's obstinate daughter. Anna's only previous acting experience had been as skunk in a school ballet, but she beat out five thousand other little girls in an open audition. Now this is the stuff that dreams are made of: sagas on which entire lives can turn. Why then, was I surprised when Katie—who's a very gifted visual artist—informed me she would not be returning to the art school she had attended for the past three summers, but would be signing up for a young actors' workshop run by a professional theater company? Oh God, the twig is bent early.

The moment we walked into the darkened theater and I saw the bare stage and spotlights, it all rushed back: the smell of the greasepaint, the roar of the crowd, the chills, thrills, magic, mystery, and wonder. An empty theater pulsates with palpable creative energy. Katie's face was flushed with excitement, her eyes were ablaze, and she radiated joy. I wondered if I had ever seen her like that before; surely I would have remembered, wouldn't I? Wistfully, I exited the stage door that had just opened for her.

Over the summer we worked together on her monologue, as character motivation, line reads, rehearsals, and costumes became part of my everyday life again in a recycled sort of way. I shared memorization and makeup tricks, the power of pacing and pausing, and stories from my illustrious stage past. When she got anxious, nervous, and hysterical, I reassured her that tension is an important part of the creative process and tried to show her how to work with it instead of fighting it. Being a traditionalist, I wanted her first opening night to be unforgettable, rich in stage lore and luck. Aunt Dona sent her a telegram from Hollywood (which certainly created a buzz backstage), her dad bought her a beautiful bouquet of flowers, and I told her to "break a leg," the stage invocation for success.

Katie's theatrical debut was terrific—her intensity, energy, and passion caught me completely off guard. I was very surprised and so proud I thought I'd burst. The next day, when I excitedly shared all the details with Dona, she laughed, "Well, what were you expecting? She's *your* daughter." Then my old friend gave me a memory gift. She vividly recalled another passionate young actress wearing a red wool vest, matching gauchos, and black riding boots who confidently walked into an open audition for Christopher Fry's play *The Lady's Not for Burning* as if she knew something the director did not. "She had fire in her eyes and possessed more theatricality just walking to the stage than most people have on it. At that moment I knew I'd found my Jennet Jourdemayne." Jennet, Fry's high-spirited heroine, was my first leading role.

No matter how brilliant we are, a life in the performing arts is not always possible. But a life enhanced by the performing arts is. We don't have to join Actors' Equity to explore the world of theater, dance, or opera as a passionate, personal pursuit. Either side of the footlights can illuminate your path toward authenticity. As the English poet Francis Bacon reminds us, in life's theater only God and the angels are permitted to be onlookers.

AUGUST 26

Reel Life Lessons

Good movies make you care, make you believe in possibilities again.

—PAULINE KAEL

Instead of meditating today, let's just watch a movie. Sneak away in the middle of the day, hunker down in the dark with a box or bowl of popcorn to ponder the meaning of life. It doesn't matter whether we choose a home video or a bargain matinee at the mall, truth can pleasurably be discerned one frame at a time. "Studying movies for their mystical message empowers us. We gain insight and greater self-awareness," Marsha Sinetar suggests in her fascinating book *Reel Power: Spiritual Growth Through Film.* "So much of life today is centered on problems, recovery, and the painful struggles of *trying* to meet the unrelenting demands of twenty-first century living. Unfortunately, by dwelling only on problems, and thus failing to see ourselves and our dilemmas in a heroic, promising light, we limit ourselves. Movies elevate our sights, enlarge imagination. Film, like poetry, is one of our heart's most subtle agents. It reminds us of what we know, helps us stretch and change, provides us with a sensory catalyst for creative, cutting-edge change." Reel power is "the ability to dig out, and use, whatever is spiritually valuable in a movie."

Films are celluloid fairy tales for a culture that no longer sits around the campfire listening to the wisdom of its elders. I use movies to replenish my creative well—usually videos, which we watch on the weekend. I crave period films with lush sets and costumes for my visual fix, rely on comedies for relief from stress, and seek out black-and-white mysteries and romantic classics from the 1930s and 1940s for sheer escape. I collect movies about angels, reincarnation, the afterlife, and everlasting love. I won't watch scary movies or films with senseless violence—nor should you, because once an image is imprinted on your consciousness it's there forever. I think we all need the uplift provided by films that inspire, encourage, affirm, and celebrate the human spirit.

Meditatively matching your mood to a movie is very restorative and rewarding. This week go to a large video store and browse. Take your time. Scan all the different categories and write down the names of movies that appeal to you. Then, on those occasions when you can't get a new video release, refer back to your list so that you always have something worth watching at least once a week. But occasionally it's great fun—an affordable luxury—to experience the first-run magic of the big screen.

"Movies mirror us and invite us to go beyond the obvious. Their themes and images can powerfully equip us to see ourselves as we are at our worst, and at our best, or to help us invent new scripts about who we hope to be," Marsha Sinetar believes. "Everything placed in our path can help us. . . . Certain films—like certain lovely people, glorious works of art or music, and special instances of prayer—seem a grace expressly given for our edification."

AUGUST 27

Meditative Handwork

Hands to work, hearts to God.

—SHAKER AXIOM

Many women, especially if they have children, simply can't find twenty uninterrupted minutes every day to meditate. But those of us who *can* carve out those precious minutes to sit down and be still often find our minds racing on without us. The truth is that traditional meditation methods take time, practice, and discipline before they yield restorative rewards; after a few attempts in which nothing happens, many of us get discouraged and give up. Because this is real life, I've tried to find other ways to induce a meditative state, even in the midst of chaos. One of the best methods is through meditative handwork. When other people see that our hands are busy, they often give us a few moments' peace before making their next request. What they don't know (and we shall never reveal) is that when our hands are busy, our minds can rest.

The creative artistry of handicrafts has been a part of women's domestic daily round for centuries. Handwork in all its many varieties was high art for Victorian women. This intimate and intricate soulcraft gave exquisite outward expression to countless authentic artists who were often strait-jacketed by the expectations of a rigid society. It's only in the last thirty years that what was once esteemed has been demeaned, as handicrafts have been demoted from being every woman's accomplishment to the personal pursuits of a chosen few.

I know the argument well: women today don't have the time for crafts the way our foremothers did. Victorian women had more time on their hands because they didn't work outside the home. As far as I'm aware, Victorian women had twenty-four hours each day to spend, savor, save, or squander. And while they weren't commuting to a job outside their homes, they were beating rugs, washing dirty *cotton* diapers by hand, hanging the laundry to dry on a line, cooking without electricity and refrigeration, baking from scratch, tending the sick without modern medicines, and nurturing families larger than most of us do today. The sense of time certainly has speeded up in the last century, but not the amount of it available. In fact, Victorian women probably had less time than we do; they didn't live as long as women today, and without electricity they weren't able to blur the distinction between day and night the way we do. Frankly, women have *always* had too much to do. It's just that Victorian women often coped better than we do; they realized the restorative power of rhythm, routine, rest, recreation, and ritual. They preserved their energy by alternating household and childcare tasks with centering pastimes that provided creative fulfillment and relief from tension.

No matter what your personal inclinations, there are so many different kinds of handicrafts available that every woman can find one that appeals if she's willing to explore. Consider weaving, basketry, bead craft, needle craft (embroidery, needlepoint, tatting, cross-stitching, lace making, smocking), sewing, knitting, crocheting, quilting, leather craft, rug hooking, pottery, stained glass, ribbon craft, paper craft (decoupage, collage, marbling, papercutting), bookbinding, framing, and carpentry. A friend of mine took up carpentry several years ago because she wanted to make some hanging bookshelves. She started with Shaker reproduction kits available from a catalog. Now she wields a lathe as if it were a sewing needle and sells beautiful pieces of art.

Start small. You don't even have to sign up for a class if you don't think you have the time. Many marvelous and reasonably priced kits are available at craft shops and through mail order. The important thing is to keep trying one thing new each season until you find something you love.

Whatever handicraft you choose to pursue, be sure to keep your favorite project in clear view. If you store your unfinished needlepoint canvas in the closet, that's where it'll remain. Find an attractive basket to hold everything in one place, so the next time you find a few minutes you don't waste them by looking for your supplies.

The Austrian novelist Marie von Ebner-Eschenback wrote in 1905 that "Nothing is so often irretrievably missed as a daily opportunity." For many of us the daily opportunity missed is the pursuit of pleasure. The next time the fabric of real life seems to unravel before your eyes, get busy with your hands, so that your mind can serenely sort out where to pick up the next stitch.

AUGUST 28

Home Art

Home is the heart of life. . . . Home is where we feel at ease, where we belong, where we can create surroundings that reflect our tastes and pleasures. . . . Making a home is a form of creativity open to everyone.

—TERENCE CONRAN

Even if you feel you haven't the eyes to excel in the visual arts, the personality for the performing arts, or the patience for hand arts, you can still explore the delights and pleasures of making your home an authentic art.

There are many decorating and artistic skills involved when the home becomes a hobby. Craft can become art when we refinish furniture, paint a wall a personalized hue, apply faux finishes to flea market finds, rewire an old lamp, upholster a chair, sew a slipcover, lay tile, stencil a favorite line of poetry on a kitchen wall, trim a pillow, lay a flower bed.

Artist Judyth van Amringe lives with daring, one-of-a-kind conversation pieces—lamps, chairs, pillows, tables—which she calls "home art." Learning to create your own authentic home furnishings can also wake up your identity as an artist. "Put your preconceptions of what should and shouldn't go together away—do exactly the opposite of what your old sense would tell you and you will find yourself in a whole new creative landscape," she urges us in *Home Art: Creating Romance and Magic with Everyday Objects*. Home art begins with recycling. "We all know how much appalling waste goes on all around us every day. My credo is to re-use as much stuff as possible always—whether it's mine, my neighbor's, something from a tag sale, a flea market, the street—because if you make something wonderful out of a castoff you are saving its energy and making a little less clutter. Here is the challenge: to turn a piece around, rework it, make it totally your own, your style, your signature."

Judyth's signature and style is bolder than most—a flamenco television cozy isn't a look we might feel comfortable with in our living rooms. But her belief that we should live surrounded by the very personal as well as quirky things we adore is authentic wisdom and definitely worth meditating upon. With a little elbow grease, ingenuity and the sweat equity of time, the marvelous can materialize right before our eyes.

Today, be willing to be adventurous with just one small project: create a new lampshade, hang a whimsical curtain treatment, decoupage a tea tray, gild that tag sale picture frame and turn it into a mirror. I *know* there's some home art project you've been thinking about tackling for a long time. I know because I have several. Throw out your preconceptions, follow your heart, honor your creative impulses, trust your eye. Feathering your own nest is a perfect way for you to spread your wings as an artist.

AUGUST 29

Artists of the Everyday:
Loving, Knowing, Doing

Love is the spirit that motivates the artist's journey. The love may be sublime, raw, obsessive, passionate, awful, or thrilling, but whatever its quality, it's a powerful motive in the artist's life.
—ERIC MAISEL

The other day a friend and I were talking about the difficulty that most of us have in grasping the concept that we are artists—that life is our canvas. She confessed that she herself could barely bake a cake and didn't think of herself as a particularly creative person. I adamantly disagree. I believe with all my heart that the ability to bring forth art from real life is a gift every woman possesses. Whether we choose to nurture this perfectly natural endowment is quite another matter. Admittedly, the concept is almost impossible to register when we're exhausted, overwhelmed, and frazzled. But it's certainly worth meditating on as we savor the last days of summer.

You may not draw, paint, sculpt, knit, sing, dance, or act, but baking a cake *could* be as much a work of art as choreographing a ballet, if you approach it with as much dedication. So is coaxing a tired, hungry toddler (with infinite patience and persuasion) to do whatever it is you need him to do at a given moment. So is graciously entertaining unexpected company with what's on hand and turning it into a memorable feast with candlelight, wine, laughter, and lively conversation. So is helping a friend through a personal crisis, comforting an aging parent, or planning a preteen's birthday party. Whatever you're about to do today *can* be transformed into art, if your heart is open and you're willing to be the Great Creator's conduit. Women are artists of the everyday. The world does not acknowledge or applaud everyday art, so we must. We are the keepers of a sacred truth. We must cherish this wisdom and pass it on to those we love.

As an artist I have come to know that there are three very different layers to creation: the labor, the craft, and the elevation. St. Francis of Assisi explains the creative process this way: the woman who works with her hands only is a laborer; the woman who works with her hands and her head is a craftswoman; the woman who works with her hands, her head, and her heart is an artist.

Labor in creation is showing up to do the Work. Craft is *how* you go about doing it. Are you there in mind, body, and spirit? Are you taking your time or are you rushing? Are you concentrating on whatever it is you are doing or thinking about twenty other things that need to be done? Do you just throw the flour, eggs, butter, sugar, and salt into a bowl all at once, stir the lumpy mess with a flick of your wrist, stick it in the oven, and hope for the best? Or do you sift the flour three times, beat the eggs, cream the butter and sugar together before you combine them? Do you spend fifteen minutes stirring the batter? Do you preheat the oven, grease and flour the pan? Do you hum while you're doing it, enjoying the process of creating, as well as the anticipation of the product? If you do, Love is present. Love is the spiritual energy that induces elevation—the transcendent moment in creation when craft becomes art.

It takes a lifetime to create the work of art for which we were born: an authentic life. But it only takes five minutes to center yourself before you begin each new task today. Five minutes to acknowledge in your soul that you are an artist of the everyday. Five minutes to give thanks for your personal gifts. Five minutes to offer your love, creative energies, and enormous talents to the person, idea, or project awaiting your attention.

Say it aloud: I am a brilliant, gifted artist of the everyday. My art is a blessing for me and mine.

AUGUST 30

If Not Now, Then When?

Procrastination is the thief of time.

—EDWARD YOUNG

I have a friend who's organizing a new women's movement called If Not Now, Then When? We're all invited to become charter members. The movement's mission is to drive a stake into the heart of the procrastination that perpetually robs us of personal pleasure.

Another friend is an antique jewelry dealer who travels to England frequently on business. She's also a politician's wife and the mother of two children. Still, she's signed up for Italian and yoga and is thinking about a watercolor class. We have to make time for ourselves, she insists, and I agree (if not now, then when?). She asks if I would like to join her new nineteenth-century book club. The club will meet one Sunday afternoon a month over tea and sherry. Everyone will bring a savory or a sweet so that there's more than just food for our minds available. I think the club sounds marvelous. I'll get back to her after I finish writing this book on creating an authentic life.

"Life, as it is called, is for most of us one long postponement," Henry Miller wrote wistfully in 1947. What pleasure are you postponing? I just postponed joining a fabulous book club. I'm going to call my busy friend back. It's faint, but I can still feel a pulse.

AUGUST 31

This Too, Is God

One must also accept that one has "uncreative" moments. The more honestly one can accept that, the quicker these moments will pass. One must have the courage to call a halt, to feel empty and discouraged.

—ETTY HILLESUM

Whether you're a poet, parent, or performance artist, one morning you'll wake up, put the coffee on, begin to prime the well to continue in the re-creation of your authentic life, only to discover that the well has run dry. It might seem disconcerting to end this month of meditations on a downbeat, but accepting uncreative days as part of the creative cycle is crucial to your serenity. Uncreative days are real life. Every artist knows them, although few of us care to acknowledge this except in confidential whispers. But as you make authenticity your art you will know them, too. Uncreative days are the part of the yin/yang of artistic yearning.

Once in the middle of a creative drought I sat in a New York coffee shop with my agent and confessed softly, as if I was admitting a great personal failing or the discovery of a terminal illness, that for months I had been unable to dream. I couldn't fantasize, visualize, or even make a wish. Since I'm Irish, the inability to dream is the emotional equivalent of a chemical imbalance in the soul. I needed her advice because Chris has a knack for knowing how to finesse things. We'd just come from a meeting with an advertising agency where she'd made a deal for my creative consulting services that astounded me, especially since at that moment I was convinced there was nothing going on inside worth more than two nickels.

"What do I do?"

"You don't do anything," she told me. Zilch. Nada. Zip. Wait it out. Accept the fallow period as graciously as you can, and get ready for a quantum leap in creativity or consciousness.

It is so difficult to come to a halt, especially when we want to get on with our careers, relationships, health, creativity. But when you're too parched to pray, beyond tears, or too drained to give a damn, it's time to cease and desist. Not all our hours are billable.

No, this does not mean you can quit. You still have to go through the motions, keep showing up for work: on the page, at the drawing board, stove, sewing machine, computer. Continue to prepare the canvas, moisten the clay. Pretend you're a creative temp, here to fill in until your authentic self arrives. In the meantime, defer making any life-altering creative decisions until you receive operating instructions. Your only assignment is to replenish the well. Search for the underground spring through creative excursions. Keep in touch with your authentic self with the daily dialogue. Resurrect any old creative projects that might have fallen into the sinkhole of second thoughts or back of the closet. Give them another glance. When I'm deeply discouraged, I retreat to my illustrated discovery journal searching for visual clues to indicate the next turn in the path.

Often the derailment of too many dreams can bring on a drought, but whenever there's a dry period, there's still plenty of Light. We're just blinded by dark dust storms. Arid despair can often result from nurturance deprivation: not eating well, not sleeping enough, working too hard and too long without anything to look forward to. If you're creatively barren, give yourself a break. Dona Cooper, one of the most creative and productive women I know, frequently reminds me, especially when my plans don't proceed at the speed of light, that "This too, is God."

And it is. Four months after I stopped trying so hard, the creative incarnation of Simple Abundance occurred. The hardest thing we'll ever do as artists of the everyday is learn to call an occasional halt. Today, if you're feeling uncreative, don't despair. Start getting excited and save your strength. You're being prepared for a quantum leap in authenticity.

In the natural world, droughts depart as suddenly and as mysteriously as they arrive. This too, is God.

Joyful Simplicities for August

ﻬ Rediscover the books you loved as a child. Head off to a good library (the older the better) and wander into the children's section (with or without your own little ones). Sit in the childsized chairs and recall moments of contentment curled up with a good book. What was it? *Little Women? Black Beauty? Anne of Green Gables?* The Bobbsey Twins? The Little House books of Laura Ingalls Wilder? The vintage adventures of the ace girl detective Nancy Drew? (Remember Nancy's little red roadster, twinsets, Bess, George, and Ned, and such baffling cases as *Secret in the Old Attic* and *The Mystery at the Moss-Covered Mansion?* Solve them once more with feeling.)

Gloria Steinem tells us it's never too late to have a happy childhood and I believe her. The childhood I would have chosen is captured in Maud Hart Lovelace's wonderful "Betsy-Tacy" series. If you want pure and simple escapism run away to Deep Valley, Minnesota, at the turn of the century to enjoy escapades with Betsy Ray and her friends, Tacy Kelly and Tib Muller. There are ten books in the series, beginning when Betsy and Tacy are five in 1892, and ending with Betsy's wedding after World War I. What I like most about reading children's books from the past (now that I'm old enough to appreciate the subtle nuances) are the charming domestic details of these cozy worlds—the kinds of cooking, decorating, entertainments, and pastimes that filled their lives.

ﻬ Consider joining or starting a book club. Sharing a good book is as rewarding as reading one. Explore plot twists and character development over food and drink with a congenial group of people once a month. Pick a theme: women's fiction, Victoriana, mysteries, or the classics. A resource called *500 Great Books by Women* by Erica Bauermeister, Jesse Larsen, and Holly Smith will dazzle you with possible selections. Most of us don't have enough intellectually stimulating conversations devoted to the exchange of ideas, although I can't imagine why not. But in order to nourish our souls, we need to feed our minds. A book club is a great antidote if you're spending too much time in Mister Roger's neighborhood. Your local bookstore might also be able to steer you toward an existing club.

ﻬ Start your search for a choice secondhand-book shop in the Yellow Pages to see what's in your area. Send for a copy of the *A B Bookman's Weekly,* the specialty publication for used-book dealers (P. O. AB, Clifton, New Jersey 07015, 201-772-0020). You'll find advertisements from dealers searching for books, which will help you search for their shops. To assist you in your quest, Book Hunter Press (419 Granite Springs Road, Yorktown Heights, New York 10598, 914-245-6608) publishes *The Used Book Lover's Guides,* geographical listings of over three thousand shops in forty-six states.

ﻬ "There is the Music of Heaven in all things," the twelfth-century mystic Hildegard of Bingen reminds us. Experience Heaven on earth with an assortment of sacred sounds that soothe. My serenity invocation ritual includes *Chant* by the Benedictine Monks of Santo Domingo De Silos (Angel Records); *Rosa Mystica* by Therese Schroeder-Sheker; *Vox De Nube* by Gaelic singer Nóirín Ní Riain and the Irish Monks of Glenstal Abbey (Sounds True Catalog, 735 Walnut Street, Boulder, Colorado 80302, 1-800-333-9185); *A Feather on the Breath of God: Gothic Voices with Emma Kirkby* (Harmonia Mundi, 2037 Grandville Avenue, Los Angeles, California, 310-559-0802); and *Vision: The Music of Hildegard von Bingen* (Angel Records). Experience the profound healing power of piano nocturnes on *Piano Reflections* by Kelly Yost (available through Channel Productions, P. O. Box 454, Twin Falls, Idaho 83303, 208-734-8668).

✎ Artists need to support one another in their sacred endeavors. I cannot praise Julia Cameron's compassionate and compelling *The Artist's Way* highly enough. It's the first book I recommend to my workshop participants. Her twelve-week course in discovering and recovering your creative self is an intimate tutorial with a gifted and generous mentor. Julia also has a marvelous audio seminar available from the Sounds True Catalog.

✎ I dare you to glance through the Flax Art & Design catalog (P. O. Box 7216, San Francisco, California 94120, 1-800-547-7778) and not find a visual arts or intriguing handicraft project. What have you got to lose but your false assumption that you're not creative?

✎ Reading specialty publications is a fascinating way to explore a new pursuit. Glance through *American Artist*, *Dance*, *Theatre Crafts*, *Opera News*, or *American Craft* for a glimmer of exciting parallel realities.

✎ Treat yourself to a deluxe box of Crayola crayons with *all* the colors, or a wonderful set of colored pencils. Create a poster that reads "If Not Now, Then When?" and hang it where you'll see it every day.

SEPTEMBER

September, the harvest month . . . Summer is over and autumn has arrived.

—CYNTHIA WICKHAM

September's song is a two-part harmony, as summer's lighthearted sere-nade ends and a deeper melody begins. For eight months we've plowed and sowed the soulful seeds of gratitude, simplicity, order, and harmony into our lives. Now an authentic harvest of contentment waits to be gathered in, as the fifth Simple Abundance principle—Beauty—beckons us to partake in her bounty. Begin to reap the rich harvest that Love hath sown.

SEPTEMBER 1

Turning Over a New Leaf

Autumn to winter, winter to spring,
Spring into summer, summer into fall—
So rolls the changing year, and so we change;
Motion so swift, we know not that we move.

—DINAH MULOCK CRAIK

Since ancient times, September has been viewed as the beginning of the new year, a time for reflection and resolution. Jews observe the High Holiday of Yom Kippur, the day of public and private atonement, a sacred withdrawal from the world for twenty-four hours in order to become right with God and others, so that real life might be renewed with passion and purpose.

Change in the natural world is subtle but relentless; seasons seem to give way gently to one another, even if the monthly motion is so swift we don't realize we're moving. But when the leaves start turning colors, it's time for turning over a personal new leaf so that our lives might be restored. "What we need in autumn is an emotional or spiritual shot in the arm," Katharine Elizabeth Fite wrote in *Good Housekeeping* in 1949, urging the beginning of a new tradition for women: personal and positive resolutions in September. "Why do you suppose so many of us waste the autumn? Why don't we make the effort that would provide something new in our lives?" January's negative resolutions "are made when we are worn out in spirit, body, and pocketbook, and have no real urge to do anything but rest."

It seems to me that January resolutions are about will; September resolutions are about authentic wants. What do you want more or less of in your life, so that you can love the life you're leading? It could be as simple as seeing friends more often, setting aside time to have adventures with your children while they still want your companionship, rekindling romance in your daily round, calling a solitary hour a day your own, or just taking more walks in the dazzling sunshine.

The beauty of autumnal resolutions is that no one else knows we're making them. Autumnal resolutions don't require horns, confetti, and champagne. September resolutions ask only that we be open to positive change. I can try to do that. So can you.

The Work of Understanding

Somewhere there is an ancient enmity between our daily life and the great work. Help me in saying it, to understand it.
—RAINER MARIA RILKE

Many of us believe that if Adam and Eve hadn't blown it in Paradise, we wouldn't have had to work for a living and we'd be on easy street in Eden. Unfortunately, that biblical interpretation is fanciful. For if you read Adam and Eve's story more carefully, you'll discover that God always intended for human beings to work and for work to be a joy. Consider Adam's soulful occupations: to name all living things after studying them and to tend a beautiful garden. In the beginning, work was meant as a gift.

But then came the Fall and Adam's work became Eve's labor. Consider the daughters of Eve's daily round. There are private works: nurturing children, homecaring, preparing meals, chauffeuring, financial management, horticulture, tending animals, and for some of us, husbandry. Then there are public works: employment, school and church activities, youth groups, community and charitable volunteering. Fifty-eight million American women have the responsibilities of worldly employment; almost half of all employed women have children under the age of eighteen. Seventy percent of mothers with little ones three and under aren't able to care for them during the day, because they're taking care of the business of reality. In real life we must take care of reality, so that we can afford to take care of what's Real.

If you're employed outside of your home, you're paid money for your efforts. But the greatest portion of a woman's work is gratis and largely unsung. Because we spend so much of our earthly span working, one way or another, this deserves profound contemplation and I'm not just referring to coping with the hassles of commutes, day care, sick children, snow days, teacher conferences, and deadlines. Juggling swords, flaming torches, and conflicting commitments deserves its own meditation. But so does the numinous nature of work. Each of us was created to give outward expression to Divinity through our personal gifts. Sharing our gifts with the world is our Great Work, no matter what our job description might be or how our resume reads.

I don't think many women today can honestly say that their work life— private and public—is in balance with their personal life, whether or not they have children. Matthew Fox, the radical philosopher and former Catholic priest, believes "to live well is to work well." I wholeheartedly agree. But just how do women in the 1990s accomplish that? I wish I could serve up a quick and easy solution to such a complicated, emotionally charged dilemma. For we can't work well or live well if we don't live authentically. Like Rilke, we need to acknowledge aloud the ancient enmity between Real Life and work. It exists. It tears us to pieces every day. We need to help each other understand it, because we will never understand it on our own. We can start by holding one another's hands, by listening to one another's concerns, by reassuring one another, today, that everything will be all right.

Somehow, together, we will figure it out.

SEPTEMBER 3

Scrambled or Fried?

At work, you think of the children you have left at home. At home, you think of the work you've left unfinished. Such a struggle is unleashed within yourself. Your heart is rent.

—GOLDA MEIR

More women than you realize have a secret fantasy that has absolutely nothing to do with erotica. But in its own way, it focuses on the forbidden. I call this fantasy, "Scrambled or Fried?"

One more perfectly normal day of incessant demands, neglected children, and unfinished work and you feel you can't take it anymore. An overwhelming impulse to disappear without a trace comes over you. Methodically, you withdraw all the cash you can from your bank account (credit cards can be traced), pack a small suitcase, head for the bus terminal and begin life all over again as a waitress in a diner somewhere out West. In this fantasy some women take their children with them, especially if the kids are small; other women don't, but usually their kids are teenagers.

Of course, you're not going to do it, but contemplating a plan of escape is an imaginary mechanism to let off steam from life's pressure cooker. No more overdue bills, arguments over cooking, cleaning, carrying out the garbage, charge accounts, or custody; no more clashes between children and career, no more exhausting caretaking of an elderly parent, no more responsibility than you can handle in any twenty-four-hour period. When you think you can't take it anymore, a life that revolves around asking customers if they want their eggs scrambled or fried holds a certain appeal.

Recently, a thirty-nine-year-old woman, the mother of five children between the ages of eight and sixteen, vanished off the face of the earth not far from where we live. Earlier in the day she had been a chaperone on an elementary school field trip. After the class returned to school, she put her daughter on a bus for a basketball game and told her that she would walk the short distance home since it was such a beautiful day. She never arrived. Around dinnertime, her frantic family called the police and a massive search began, complete with prayer vigils. Of course, everyone feared the worst, because for this particular woman to disappear without a trace was completely out of character. She had everything: a Wellesley education, a beautiful family, a lovely home, an extremely comfortable lifestyle, and a perfect marriage to a diplomat. Three days later the woman who had everything, but obviously not enough of what she really needed, turned up unharmed (thank heavens), confused by her own conduct, and dazed by all the commotion.

Here's what happened. As she started for home, she sought a solitary spot to sort some things out. On the spur of the moment she walked a few miles to her favorite place, Washington's National Cathedral, an exquisite sanctuary. In the silence she could hear herself think. After a few hours she could not bring herself to leave its peace to return to the chaos engulfing her at home, so she slept for two days in a small chapel. As of this writing, she's still not returned home and no one really knows when or if she will. This much we do know: for whatever reason, her heart was rent. Her center could not hold. Her life was not, after all, as perfect as it appeared. Real lives seldom are, even if the surface has a pretty sheen. I only wish I'd been able to say to her, "Disappear if you must, but phone home and let the children know that you're okay."

When I heard on the radio that she hadn't been abducted but had voluntarily vanished, I felt a tremendous sense of relief and said as much to my husband. His response was that this woman was obviously mentally unstable. Unbalanced. There was no other explanation for her bizarre behavior. I agreed that the weight of her life was too heavy to carry alone, but as I had a meditation to write (on coping with stress), I chose not to challenge his interpretation. A long conversational detour would have been necessary to point out that under her particular circumstances, which of course we did not know, her disappearing act might have been extremely sane. Desperate, no doubt. Heartrending, no question. But not necessarily crazy.

When our waitress fantasy surfaces, we're physically, emotionally, psychologically, and spiritually exhausted by the struggle within and without that pulls us in a hundred different directions. We're seriously wounded by the ancient enmity between daily life and the Great Work. Band-Aids don't work anymore.

Actually, the fantasy of running away can be very therapeutic because it waves a psychic red flag that tells us real life has become unmanageable. Changes need to occur, creative choices need to be made, conversations need to be started and *finished*. If the fantasy persists to the point of action, asking for help is much better than buying a one-way bus ticket.

"If you knew how often I say to myself: to hell with everything, to hell with everybody, I've done my share, let the others do theirs now, enough, enough, enough," Golda Meir, the only woman prime minister of Israel, once confessed candidly.

You won't have to run away if you can learn to just say: enough, enough, enough.

And mean it.

SEPTEMBER 4

Answering a Higher Call

Your work is to discover your work and then with all your heart to give yourself to it.

—BUDDHA

When I attended Catholic high school during the early sixties, the word "vocation"—from the Latin *vocare* meaning "to call"—was synomous with entering a religious community. Like most sixteen-year-old girls, I wanted to be swept off my feet by a handsome man, get married, have children, and live happily ever after. Becoming a bride of Christ held little allure, perhaps because a gruesome crucifix watched over the classroom. (I swear the eyes moved.)

However, I must admit I found incredibly romantic the notion of women being called out from the world because they were chosen by God. I also thought the nuns' black-and-white habits rather dashing. But this does not a calling make.

Twenty years later I was happily married, living in the Maryland suburbs and the mother of a beautiful daughter I cherished. But needing some time out, I went on a retreat to an Episcopal convent. The moment I drove into its grounds it seemed as if a spell had come over me; by the time I walked down the hushed stone hallway to enter the chapel, I felt as if I had arrived home. It was very unsettling.

After a silent weekend, spent praying and working beside the cloistered women who had answered God's call so dramatically, I felt compelled to reconcile the irreconcilable. I sought out a confessor, a lovely nun about my age, and admitted in the golden autumn sunlight of the convent garden that I now believed I had been blessed with a calling, but that I had said "no" to God. My sorrow was not because I had chosen not to take a certain path in life, but because I hadn't even had the courage to consider the road less traveled. Now it was too late. She in turn confided that she sometimes wondered if she could have served God better in the world as a wife and mother. "But when our hearts are open, Providence makes straight our path," she reassured me. Then she asked quietly: "Why do you assume that you have not already answered God's call? God needs mothers. God needs writers. There must be some special work that only you can bring into the world for God." She shared St. Teresa of Avila's urging for those seeking their calling: "Christ has no body now on earth but yours; yours are the only hands with which he can do his work, yours are the only feet with which he can go about the world, yours are the only eyes through which his compassion can shine forth upon a troubled world. Christ has no body on earth now but yours." With a hopeful heart, I returned home to my husband, child, and work in the world.

Now, a decade later, it has not escaped my attention that I am living my unsought vocation. Dusk is falling as I write, the house is hushed. Ed and Katie are at a double-feature matinee, allowing me to work in peace. In the background, beautiful medieval hymns of prayer, praise, and thanksgiving are being offered to Heaven through my compact disc player. As I draw closer to finishing this book, my home has become a cloister, my passion my calling, my work personal worship. I'm even wearing black. God is in the subtle nuances.

Today realize that Spirit has no hands, head, or heart like yours. No other woman on earth can do what you alone are called to do, can give to the world what you alone were sent to give through your authentic gifts. The call may be so faint you can barely make out the message, but if you listen, *you will hear it.*

SEPTEMBER 5

Job, Career, or Calling?

The pitcher cries for water to carry
and a person for work that is Real.

—MARGE PIERCY

There is a significant difference between a job, a career, and a calling. Jobs are what we do to keep bodies, souls, and families together. But as Studs Terkel wisely points out in his oral history *Working*, daily meaning is as important as daily bread, and recognition as necessary as cash. For when we work, we are searching "for a sort of life rather than a Monday through Friday sort of dying."

One of the people Studs Terkel interviewed was Nora Watson, who then worked as a staff writer for a health-care magazine: "I think most of us are looking for a calling, not a job. Most of us, like the assembly line worker, have jobs that are too small for our spirit. Jobs are not big enough for people." But jobs are crucial; we need to "earn a living," which becomes more difficult each day in the uncertain economic climate of the 1990s.

A career can be a calling, but not necessarily. Usually a career occurs when we stick to an occupational path—accounting, advertising, nursing, publishing—because we do what we do quite well and get paid for doing it. Sometimes careers resemble long-standing marriages in which passion is exchanged for comfort, security, and predictability in an uncertain world. Of course, there is nothing wrong with this choice; for many women it is absolutely the right one—though some may wonder what psychic price is being exacted for playing it safe. It is certainly true that every day we don't strive to live authentically we do pay a price, with compounded interest.

Many of us eventually move from jobs to careers, but often we hesitate to answer an authentic calling, especially in midlife, because we're torn—between the financial realities of raising children and caring for aging parents, between a proven track record and the unknown, between a regular paycheck and uncertainty, between circumstance and creative choice. But it's a mistake to accept as our reality the illusion that many are called to fulfillment but few are chosen. What Spirit has done for other women, can be done for you—when you're ready. The truth is, we're all chosen; most of us just forget to rsvp.

Novelist Mary Morris tells us that "Pursuing what you want to do and achieving your goal is not like finding the burning bush or discovering a gold mine. There are usually no epiphanies, no sudden reversals of fortune. Fulfillment comes in fits and starts. . . . Fulfillment comes in many guises, and it can come to us in our lives at any time. . . . But only *we* can make sure we will be fulfilled. If we feel empty, no amount of water can fill our well. It has to come from within, from the underground springs and streams."

Working from the Heart

Work is love made visible.

—KAHLIL GIBRAN

Most of us do not consider our work a personal form of worship. Work is worldly. Worship is withdrawing from the world to honor Spirit. But could there be a more beautiful way to honor the Great Creator than by contributing to the re-creation of the world through our gifts? This is what we're called to do each day through our work. Yet it is very difficult to get even a glimmer of the holy when we are harassed, unappreciated, over-whelmed, frazzled, and burned-out.

Marianne Williamson believes that the workplace is "but a front for a temple, a healing place where people [can] be lifted above the insanity of a frightened world." Once, when she was working as a cocktail waitress—years before she answered her calling to become a spiritual guide and writer—she realized that people only thought they were coming to a bar for a drink. Really the bar was a church in disguise and she could minister to people with warmth, conversation, and compassion. "No matter what we do, we can make it our ministry," she writes in her illuminating *A Return to Love: Reflections on the Principles of a Course in Miracles*. "No matter what form our job or activity takes, the content is the same as everyone else's; we are here to minister to human hearts. If we talk to anyone, or see any-one, or even think of anyone, then we have the opportunity to bring more love into the universe. From a waitress to the head of a movie studio, from an elevator operator to the president of a nation, there is no one whose job is unimportant to God."

It's easier to imagine that our work could be our worship if we could perceive the sacred in how we spend at least eight hours of the day. Perhaps the secret to coming to this awareness, no matter what our present cir-cumstances, is to discover the work we would *love* to do. But until we do, we need to learn to love the work we're presently doing.

Today you can begin to transform your workplace and your working style by considering how much you have to be grateful for. If you have a job, even one you dislike, it's a safety net as you take a leap of faith toward your authenticity; if you're out of work, the path already has been cleared for you to answer your authentic calling. Invoke Spirit as your personal career coun-selor. The mystical poet Kahlil Gibran tells us, "When you work, you fulfill a part of earth's fondest dream assigned to you when that dream is born."

Fulfilling your part of the earth's fondest dream occurs when you work from the heart.

Wishcraft: Getting from Here to There

Oh, the secret life of man and woman—dreaming how much bet-
ter we would be than we are if we were somebody else or even our-
selves, and feeling that our estate has been unexploited to its
fullest.

—ZELDA FITZGERALD

I can't be the only grown woman in the world who dissolves into tears
whenever Jiminy Cricket stares out of kindly old Geppetto's window, sees
the first star of the evening, and begins to sing, "When you wish upon a
star . . ." in the movie *Pinocchio*. Perhaps I cry, as might you, because we
wish on stars and hope with all our hearts that our dreams will come true.
But turning a wooden puppet into a real boy or a precious dream into reality requires something more in the 1990s than just waving a magic wand.
How about a wise, compassionate, and savvy fairy godmother who's never
heard a dream she thought was frivolous or one that couldn't be wrestled
from fate with mystical moxie?

Barbara Sher is that fairy godmother, one with an attitude. She knows all
about "life makeovers," as she calls pursuing our authentic dreams. She
went from being a divorced mother on welfare to being a pyschotherapist
and career consultant—as dramatic a life makeover as one could imagine.
As a therapist she began to suspect that many of her depressed patients didn't
really need long-term therapy as much as they needed a reason to get out
of bed every morning. Since Barbara had transformed her own life, she fig-
ured she knew as much as anybody about making dreams come true, so she
began offering life-direction seminars. The success of the workshops led to
her first book *Wishcraft: How to Get What You Really Want* (written with Annie
Gottlieb). Here you can find practical advice to help shape vague yearnings into authentic adventures so that "you have a life you love, so that you
wake up every morning excited about the day ahead and delighted to be
doing what you're doing, even if you're sometimes a little nervous and
scared."

I was a freelance writer who dreamed of writing and publishing books
when I took one of her seminars in the early 1980s. One of the first things
Barbara teaches is that in order "to create the life you want, you don't need
mantras, self-hypnosis, a character-building program, or a new toothpaste.
You do need practical techniques for problem-solving, planning, and getting your hands on materials, skills, information and contacts. . . . You need
commonsense strategies for coping with human feelings and foibles that

aren't going to go away, like fear, depression and laziness. . . . And you need ways of riding out the temporary emotional storms your life changes can cause in your closest relationships—while still getting the extra emotional support you need for risk-taking."

The world needs dreamers and the world needs doers. But above all, the world needs dreamers who do. Don't just entrust your hopes and wishes to the stars. Today, begin learning the craft that will enable you to reach for them.

SEPTEMBER 8

Getting from Here to There: When You Haven't a Clue What to Do

Life is either a daring adventure or nothing. To keep our faces toward change and behave like free spirits in the presence of fate is strength undefeatable.

—HELEN KELLER

Some of us hear our passion calling when we're very young, but most of us do not because we're too busy listening to what other people, especially our parents, are telling us. So we embark on a vocational path, trying on different lives for size until we find one we can wear even if it doesn't necessarily fit.

Perhaps you're conflicted about continuing the journey you started twenty-five years ago but have outgrown. You know you're not heading in the direction you want to go, but at least your daily motions are familiar. And familiar feels safe. In today's uncertain world, feeling safe and secure seems the emotional definition of sanity.

Perhaps you're skilled in one occupation but not thrilled about using those skills anymore. Some other work does secretly thrill you. But the stakes seem too high. Perhaps you're dismayed, even embarrassed, by the thought that you don't know what Great Work waits for you.

Not knowing what you want to do can be very disconcerting. You want to go forward but find yourself standing still, overwhelmed by the options or the risks. This doesn't surprise Barbara Sher. In the ten years since *Wishcraft* was published, she's heard many people claim that they wanted to live passionately, but that they were stymied and unable to use her *Wishcraft* strategy because they didn't have the foggiest idea what excited them. This made her extremely curious, so she started meeting with groups of people who didn't know what they wanted out of life. As they shared their stories, she discovered a common thread of discontent; everyone was unconsciously engaged in an internal battle for control of direction. But however directionless they felt, their lives were filled with authentic clues. They just didn't know how to look for them.

Some of the reasons Barbara heard for not pursuing a passionate life included:

- "I'd have to quit my job to get what I really want and I can't do that—I'd starve."
- "Every time I try to go after what I want, I drop the ball and I don't know why."
- "I want to do so many things, I'll never be able to pick only one."
- "How can I walk away from success? And what will I live on if I do?"
- "I want something I shouldn't want—it's trivial or unworthy."
- "I don't have Idea One what to do now."
- "I've tried so many things and nothing does it for me."
- "It's not my fault I'm not doing what I want—the world won't give me a break."
- "I'm trying to go after something, but my heart's not really in it, and I don't know why."

After helping these people realize that they really did know what they wanted to do, she knew there was another book to write: *I Could Do Anything If I Only Knew What It Was* (written with Barbara Smith). Whether we realize it or not, there's a good reason behind everything we do or don't do, every choice we make or avoid. We can't go forward if we don't know what's holding us back. Knowing the truth does set you free. If you suspect that one of those frustrated, angry, discouraged, or timid voices sounds awfully familiar, you'll find wisdom and reassurance in Barbara Sher's suggestions for discovering your authentic dream.

The price we pay for authenticity may seem high, but who among us can truly afford to continue living as a spendthrift of the self?

The Courage to Answer the Call

You gain strength, courage and confidence by every experience in which you really stop to look fear in the face. . . .You must do the thing you cannot do.

—ELEANOR ROOSEVELT

No coward soul is mine/No trembler in the world's stormtroubled sphere," Emily Brontë wrote just before her death in 1848. She was only thirty. At her end, which is really only the beginning for many of us, came the inner awareness that she had lived courageously. She had lived authentically.

Of course, she had known dark moments, but in the darkness she'd come to trust that a Power greater than her own would never leave nor forsake her. This Love was so transformative she wrote to her sister, Charlotte, that It "Changes, sustains, dissolves, creates and rears" as It leads. This steadfast Love endowed her with courage and confidence as her great novel *Wuthering Heights* was rejected by one publisher after another.

Make no mistake, when you start on the path to authenticity, Love will change you, transforming your life in countless ways. Your family and friends might not notice the changes in the beginning because they're so small. But you will, and you'll know that miracles are taking place. Love will sustain you when passion's path takes unexpected twists and turns. Love will dissolve your fears by creating opportunities you couldn't have imagined before you began the search to discover and recover your authentic self. And when doubt, despair, and denial threaten to dismantle your dreams, Love will rear up in your defense. The next time you feel frightened and fragile, stand very still. If you do, you might feel the tip of an angel's wing brush against your shoulder.

No coward's soul is yours. I know this, even if today you don't. I know this because you wouldn't have come this far on the Simple Abundance journey if you were a coward. Reluctantly (actually kicking and screaming), I come to the realization that feeling afraid is Spirit's signal to ask for grace and Power. So take a deep breath, seek your quiet center, and push on. One of the hardest lessons we ever have to master is accepting that all fear comes from within however major are the real life's circumstances assaulting us. The closer we get to giving our dream to the world, the fiercer the struggle becomes to bring it forth. Why should this be so? Because we will be inexorably changed, and life can never return to the way it once was. Of course we're scared; we wouldn't be sane if we weren't. But how many exquisite, glorious dreams sent to heal the world has Heaven mourned because the dreamer, weary and discouraged, relied only on her own strength and could do no more?

Today if you feel afraid, take comfort in remembering that courage is fear that has said her prayers. "I've dreamt in my life dreams that have stayed with me ever after, and changed my ideas," Emily Brontë confessed. "They've gone through and through me, like wine through water, and altered the color of my mind." Dreams are gifts of Spirit meant to alter us. Trust that the same Power that gifted you with your dream knows how to help you make it come true.

SEPTEMBER 10

Setting Your Own Pace

One sad thing about this world is that the acts that take the most out of you are usually the ones that other people will never know about.
—ANNE TYLER

Novelist Anne Tyler tells a wonderful cautionary tale about pursuing your authentic calling. Arriving to pick up her children at school one afternoon, she was met by another mother who casually asked, "Have you found work yet? Or are you still just writing?" Simply because you do it doesn't mean the rest of the world will think it's wonderful or even worthwhile. The sooner you realize that other people won't necessarily bless or appreciate your efforts to follow your calling, the happier you'll be. A lot of people—including your partner and children—might wonder aloud for years if you're ever going to become sensible again.

No, you're not. So shrug off their skepticism with a smile and go back to mining your acre of diamonds. Eventually they'll come around, either as cheerleaders or as astonished spectators. In the meantime, do your best to pay as little attention as possible to doom, doubt, and derision. You've only got so much psychic energy. If it's squandered on converting the heathens, you won't have any left to do the work waiting for you. Remember, the prophetess is rarely recognized in her own household.

Next, if you're trying to bring forth a dream while caring for a family and holding down a job, you must set your own pace. You know your commitments better than anyone else. We've all got to live with them as well as work around them. Authentic fulfillment through your work is a marathon, not a sprint. Long-distance runners prepare for marathons with a lot of shorter runs, increasing their length and speed as they become stronger. In order to hear your calling and answer it, you must generously give yourself the gift of time. Certainly, no one else in the world will do it. If you have children living with you or are employed full time during the day, you should have a three-year plan to secure that dream job, publish that book, organize a one-woman show, win that grant, send out your mail-order catalog. It took me three years and thirty rejections to launch a nationally syndicated newspaper column. The bottom line is not how fast you make your dream come true, but how steadily you pursue it.

Anne Tyler reveals in a collection of essays, *The Writer on Her Work,* how difficult it is to create around family life. Writing is her frame of reference, as it is mine, but the same principle applies to any passion. One March a character arrived in her consciousness as she was painting the downstairs hall. She knew if she "sat down and organized this character on paper, a novel would grow up around him. But it was March and the children's spring vacation began the next day, so I waited." By July she was finally able to start. Even with the inevitable creative delays that daily life brings, there is tremendous gain in the struggle to answer your calling with children growing up all around you. "It seems to me that since I've had children, I've grown richer and deeper," Anne Tyler confesses. "They may have slowed down my writing for a while, but when I did write, I had more of a self to speak from."

SEPTEMBER 11

A Psalm for Life

Let us, then, be up and doing
With a heart for any fate;
Still achieving, still pursuing,
Learn to labor and to wait.

—HENRY WADSWORTH LONGFELLOW

Here, in four lines, is the essence of mystical moxie: the secret to achieving what you want out of your life. Written more than a hundred years ago, this wisdom is as relevant today as when it was penned. This psalm to life is one of my favorite poetry meditations, especially when I'm discouraged because I'm not seeing results as quickly as I'd like to. I know that if you mull over Longfellow's advice, you'll receive an emotional and spiritual boost today.

"*Let us, then, be up and doing . . .*" Dreams are not enough. They must be backed up with effort. Success is as simple and as profound as that. Always remember that *striving* and *struggle* precede success, even in the dictionary.

We must be doing something about bringing our dreams into the world *every day*, even if we only have fifteen minutes out of every twenty-four hours to concentrate on our calling. Is there a phone call you can make? A letter you can send? One page that you can write? A mailing list you can get yourself on? Five pages of a book you can read? An organization in your dream field that you can volunteer your way into? You'll be amazed at the power of fifteen focused minutes.

"With a heart for any fate . . ." Opening our hearts to the possibility of failing is easier said than done. That's why we have to surrender expectations, delivery details, and the world's reception to Spirit. Become open to Divine fine-tuning or finishing touches. Birthing a dream is a collaborative effort.

"Still achieving, still pursuing . . ." As long as you're actively pursuing your dream with a practical plan, you're still achieving, even if it feels as though you're going nowhere fast. It's been my experience that the very moment I feel like giving up, I'm only one step from a breakthrough. Hang on long enough and circumstances will change, too. Trust in yourself, your dream and Spirit.

"Learn to labor and to wait." This is the most difficult of Longfellow's suggestions. Most of the time we wait much longer for a dream to manifest itself in our lives than we ever imagined we would have to at its conception. That's because *our* concept of time and Spirit's are not the same. Be extra kind to yourself while waiting, making it as pleasurable as possible. Remember, the longer it takes for a dream to make itself manifest, the more comfortable you'll feel owning your talent.

SEPTEMBER 12

Uncommon Women and Others

Our aspirations are our possibilities.

—SAMUEL JOHNSON

When we're twenty-five," Rita declares, "we'll be *pretty* incredible." Rita is one of seven Mount Holyoke seniors featured in Wendy Wasserstein's play *Uncommon Women and Others*. The young women are about to leave their privileged and sheltered college existence to seek fame and fortune in the real world. They will discover that fulfillment is a lifelong process, even for uncommon women. At the end of the play, six years later, their lives have changed in unexpected ways, but Rita still has high hopes: "When we're forty-five, we can be *pretty* amazing."

Uncommon Women and Others' first professional reading was during the summer of 1977 at the Eugene O'Neill Theater Center in Waterford,

Connecticut—an elite, idyllic, three-week summer camp for the country's most promising young playwrights and theater critics. Each year ten new plays are selected from the thousands submitted in hopes of receiving a high-gloss polishing by the professional actors, actresses, directors, and script doctors who are assigned to each young playwright. After two weeks of preparation, showcase evenings are performed in the handsome white wooden barn and attended by representatives of regional theaters around the country and off-Broadway. Everyone who visits the beautiful farm overlooking the Long Island Sound is searching for the next season's hit. Of course they're supposed to be focusing on promise, but it's the next Sure Thing that always has the famous and near-famous buzzing in the O'Neill Center's cafeteria line.

Although it didn't receive the most attention during the session, Wasserstein's play turned out to be the jewel in the O'Neill's crown that summer, launching a major career for her as well as for some of the actresses who appeared in the New York production: Glenn Close, Swoozie Kurtz, and Jill Eikenberry. In 1988, Wasserstein's promise was confirmed when she won both the Tony Award and the Pulitzer Prize for her play *The Heidi Chronicles*.

Like the self-absorbed *Uncommon* characters, most of the playwrights, actors, directors, and critics at the O'Neill Center were very full of themselves—puffed up with their reputations or potential. However, I remember Wendy Wasserstein as a rather shy, funny, and self-deprecating young woman who stood apart from the glitterati. She seemed much more focused on the work at hand—which was getting her play into shape for a professional production—rather than on making contacts. Of course, it was precisely because she concentrated on calling forth her authentic gifts that the play was eventually such a success and the theater world began lining up to contact her.

One of the most wonderful truths you will discover on the path to authenticity is that your aspirations *are* your possibilities. "Each year I resolve to believe there will be possibilities," Wendy Wasserstein confides now. "Every year I resolve to be a little less the me I know and leave a little room for the me I could be. Every year I make a note not to feel left behind by my friends and family who have managed to change far more than I." This passion for authenticity is what makes Wendy Wasserstein not only an uncommon woman but an extraordinary one. And it can for you as well.

Thoughts on Success

*A tragic irony of life is that we so often achieve success or finan-
cial independence after the reason for which we sought it has
passed.*

—ELLEN GLASGOW

Few women *believe* they are successful because they don't *feel* successful.
In the deepest recesses of our hearts, we feel like failures—counterfeits,
frauds. But even if we know we are successful, we rarely admit it. The
world does not like braggarts. And we want the world—every last person
in it—to like us. We suffer from a potent combination of public and private
conditioning over a lifetime.

Webster's Dictionary defines success as "the attaining of a desired end," as
well as "the attainment of wealth, favor or eminence." When we succeed,
we "prosper, thrive, flourish." When we don't, we want to sink to the center of the earth until the shame subsides. Success and failure are a black-
and-white issue. It's good or bad. It's a lucky break or tough luck. Actually
it's none of these things. Failure and success are the yin and yang of achievement, the two forces in the Universe over which we have absolutely no
control. We keep forgetting that all we can control is our *response* to failure
and success.

During the Victorian era, success, power, and wealth were considered
physical manifestations of Providence's divine approval. They still are.
William James considered the pursuit of success "our national disease" and
cautioned that the "exclusive worship of the bitch goddess" could kill you
if you weren't careful. Few Victorians believed him. A century later, even
though we can see the bodies dropping all around us, we still don't believe
him. We must *never* forget that what the world giveth, the world can taketh
away—and frequently does.

Most of us were not taught that there are two kinds of success: worldly
and authentic. But in order to live happy and fulfilled lives, we need to
know the difference between what's Real and what's not, because success
is part of Life University's required curriculum. There is absolutely nothing wrong with the pursuit of worldly success and financial independence;
I'm pursuing it as I write this meditation. But Simple Abundance has taught
me, as I know it will teach you, that authentic success is living by your own
lights, not the glare of popping flashbulbs.

And they can't take *that* away from us.

Giving Yourself Credit

*It was the first operatic mountain I climbed, and the view from it
was astounding, exhilarating, stupefying.*

—Leontyne Price

One of the reasons women often don't feel successful is we never give
ourselves credit. Should we slip for a moment and bask in the glow of
accomplishment, we immediately feel the need to downplay our achievement, especially in front of our family and friends. Before we know it,
we're practically denying we ever attained anything. But many successful
people do revel in their achievements, covering the walls of their offices
and homes with their photographs, and magazine covers, displaying golden
statuettes and awards on their mantels or in specially built cabinets. They've
succeeded, and not only does the world applaud them, they congratulate
themselves.

Do you remember the song we used to sing as children on lengthy family car trips? "The bear went over the mountain, the bear went over the
mountain, the bear went over the mountain, and what do you think he saw?
He saw another mountain, he saw another mountain, he saw another
mountain, and what do you think he did? He climbed that other mountain,
he climbed that other mountain. . . ." And so on, until our parents wanted
to shoot *him*, strangle *us*, or maybe *both*!

Many women suffer from the climbing-bear syndrome. We scale one
mountain after another, overcome every obstacle, smash the glass ceiling.
But is the promotion savored? Do we celebrate graduating from night
school, closing the deal, delivering the goods? No! We shrug off our personal triumphs as if they were flukes, then wonder why we feel so unfulfilled.

If we trace this unnurturing behavior back to its source, many of us will
find ourselves standing quietly, waiting patiently for the parental approval
that never came, no matter what we achieved. Decades later, because we
have been conditioned to believe that *nothing* we do is ever good enough,
we continue this destructive cycle of withholding approval from ourselves.

Once, over a five-year period, I wrote and narrated a twelve-part series
for public radio, launched a nationally syndicated newspaper column,
wrote and published two books, and gave numerous lectures and workshops. On the surface I looked successful. Looking back, I now recognize
this frenzy to "succeed" was the climbing-bear syndrome. But I had also
succumbed to the self-destructive illusion of believing that the next cre-

ative project would be *the one* that would bring me the recognition I'd been hungering for all my life. The big break would finally arrive, the brass ring would at last be within my reach, or my ship would come in. Since I hadn't received recognition or approval from my parents and certainly didn't give it to myself, the only possible source was the outside world. Surely the world would notice, in a meaningful way, my next project.

I experienced this awakening one day when I was rewriting my résumé for a new venture. As I listed my accomplishments, I wondered "Who is this woman? Do I know her? Do I have multiple personalities?" For if detectives arrived at my door to search for her, they wouldn't have found a shred of physical evidence. So I started searching for clues, rescuing proof that mountains had been climbed from cardboard boxes buried in the basement. I took some of my favorite memorabilia—my book covers, the announcement of my column—to the framers. When I hung them up in our living room, I stood back and looked at them the way a stranger might. Wow! It was astounding, exhilarating, stupefying. Then I began to congratulate myself out loud for jobs well done. Now I seize moments of achievement by making them concrete. Having the physical evidence of accomplishment has gone a long way toward making me feel successful. I've also had mementos of my husband's political career framed, and I honor Katie's accomplishments with her own gallery in the family's public spaces.

Although it may crown you Queen for a Day, the world cannot confer the recognition that will make you feel fulfilled. Only *you* can. So chill a bottle of champagne and toast yourself upon the *completion* of a creative project, personal accomplishment, professional achievement. Can we really afford to wait for the world's approval? "I am doomed to an eternity of compulsive work," Bette Davis confessed in her memoir, *The Lonely Life*. "No set goal achieved satisfies. Success only breeds a new goal. The golden apple devoured has seeds. It is endless."

SEPTEMBER 15

Authentic Success

We must all pay with the current coin of life
For the honey that we taste.

—RACHEL BLUMSTEIN

Authentic success is different for each of us. No single definition fits all because we come in all sizes. One autumn afternoon years ago, while wandering through an abandoned cemetery, I discovered a wonderful definition of authentic success inscribed on the headstone of a woman who died in 1820: "The only pain she ever caused was when she left us."

Authentic success is having time enough to pursue personal pursuits that bring you pleasure, time enough to make the loving gestures for your family you long to do, time enough to care for your home, tend your garden, nurture your soul. Authentic success is never having to tell yourself or those you love, "maybe next year." Authentic success is knowing that if today were your last day on earth, you could leave without regret. Authentic success is feeling focused and serene when you work, not fragmented. It's knowing that you've done the best that you possibly can, no matter what circumstances you faced; it's knowing in your soul that the best you can do is *all* you can do, and that the best you can do is always enough.

Authentic success is accepting your limitations, making peace with your past, and reveling in your passions so that your future may unfold according to a Divine Plan. It's discovering and calling forth your gifts and offering them to the world to help heal its ravaged heart. It's making a difference in other lives and believing that if you can do that for just one person each day, through a smile, a shared laugh, a caress, a kind word, or a helping hand, blessed are you among women.

Authentic success is not just money in the bank but a contented heart and peace of mind. It's earning what you feel you deserve for the work you do and knowing that you're worth it. Authentic success is paying your bills with ease, taking care of all your needs and the needs of those you love, indulging some wants, and having enough left over to save and share. Authentic success is not about accumulating but letting go, because all you have is all you truly need. Authentic success is feeling good about who you are, appreciating where you've been, celebrating your achievements, and honoring the distance you've already come. Authentic success is reaching the point where *being* is as important as *doing*. It's the steady pursuit of a dream. It's realizing that no matter how much time it takes for a dream to come true in the physical world, no day is ever wasted. It's valuing inner, as well as outer, labor—both your own and others'. It's elevating labor to a craft and craft to an art by bestowing Love on every task you undertake.

Authentic success is knowing how simply abundant your life is *exactly as it is today*. Authentic success is being so grateful for the many blessings bestowed on you and yours that you can share your portion with others.

Authentic success is living each day with a heart overflowing.

The Fear of Success

The conflict between what one is and who one is expected to be touches all of us. And sometimes, rather than reach for what one could be, we choose the comfort of the failed role, preferring to be the victim of circumstance, the person who didn't have a chance.
—MERLE SHAIN

Many women fear success much more than failure. Failure we can handle, failure feels familiar. But success means we must leave our comfort zone, the well-padded perimeter of predictability. Whether or not we like or admit it, a woman's success is secondary to her relationships. We fear success because we fear the impact it will have (and it most assuredly will), not only on our own lives, but on the lives of those we love.

Even the financial rewards of success don't entirely belong to us, unless we're single and without children or elderly parents to care for. If we're not, the checks may have our name on them, but they go to pay grocery bills, tuition, winter coats, car repairs, braces, summer camp, vacations, home improvements, social security supplements. Millions of women are also responsible for mortgages or rent, utilities, food, health insurance and much, much more. Why should it come as a surprise that personal indulgences become figments of feminine imagination?

As for relationships, if you're single and reach a certain level of success (not to mention a certain age), you worry about meeting a man who won't be intimidated by your achievements or your income. If you're married, you worry about how your success will affect your relationship with your husband. It is one of life's paradoxes that the higher a woman ascends in the world, the more the earth rumbles beneath her on the home front. This is because success questions the validity of the unspoken covenant we make when we say "I do." (Unfortunately, many of the emotional and economic assumptions we have when we utter these words are based on where we are at the time, not on where we're headed.)

If she has children, a woman's ascent is thwarted by an even stronger gravitational pull than the discomfort of her partner. Nothing weighs more than maternal guilt. Men (with some exceptions) rarely work around the needs of their children; women rarely work any other way. The novelist Fay Weldon was once asked why she wrote longer sentences in her later novels. She answered that it was because as her children grew older, she had fewer interruptions.

So we fear success with good reason. We've got a lot at stake. Success brings change, and change is uncomfortable. But by attempting to achieve one challenge at a time, we redefine success for ourselves and those we love. As we become more comfortable with our accomplishments, we learn that success doesn't have to pull, tug, or chafe if we wear our real size.

SEPTEMBER 17

Having Your Cake and Eating It, Too

Life itself is the proper binge.

—Julia Child

Authentic success and worldly success are not mutually exclusive. Granted, it is easier to achieve them one at a time, but pursuing both is not the impossible dream once you realize the important distinctions between the two. We need not choose between them. We must only discern which of the two helps us care for our soul and the souls of those we love, and pursue that one first.

The Bible tells us we cannot serve two masters—God and money. But what about having your cake and eating it, too? On this, the scripture is silent. Actually, it's quite possible to eat and have, provided you bake two cakes at the same time. Any cook knows that doubling the amount of your batter is no big deal. But going into the kitchen to make a second cake after you've baked and iced your first and washed the dirty dishes requires a tremendous amount of psychic and physical energy. That's why you need to double your dreams when you conceive them; doubling the size of your dream creates space for a lifestyle based on authentic success, but it can be iced with as much worldly success as you are willing to pay for with the coin of life. Some of us like sweets more than others.

"Success is important only to the extent that it puts one in a position to do more things one likes to do," Sarah Caldwell tells us. I love baking cakes. How about you?

The Gift of Failure

Flops are part of life's menu and I'm never a girl to miss out on a course.

—ROSALIND RUSSELL

In the eyes of the world, Clare Booth Luce was one of the most successful women in the twentieth century. She was a playwright and author, a two-term Congresswoman, and Ambassador to Italy. She was also a mother and the wife of publishing magnate Henry Luce, cofounder of *Life* and *Time* magazines. But this extraordinary woman confessed that she often thought "if I were to write my autobiography, my title would be *The Autobiography of a Failure.*"

Now I ask you, if Clare Booth Luce felt this way about herself and her brilliant career, what hope is there for the rest of us?

Gratefully, there is a great deal of hope as long as we stay on the path to authenticity. Clare Booth Luce felt like a failure because she believed she had lived inauthentically, having not followed her true calling. "I would say my worst failure, paradoxically, was a rather long-drawn-out series of relative successes, none of which were in theater. In other words, my failure was not to return to the real vocation I had, which was writing. I don't remember from childhood ever wanting to do or be anything except a writer."

To begin with, she *never* wanted to run for Congress, it was entirely her husband's idea; Henry Luce was a powerful man because he knew how to wield power for his own benefit. Clare Booth's theatrical career was thriving (she had written five plays) when she married Luce in 1935, and her play *The Women* became a smash hit on Broadway the following year. But her husband believed that theater was an avocation, nothing more than "night work." So, when Clare Booth added Luce to her name, she reluctantly sublimated her passion. After two terms in Congress, she tried to resign from political life to resume her writing. Then, in rapid succession, came a series of staggering losses: the deaths of her mother, brother, and of her only child, a daughter, in an accident. For Clare Booth Luce, life came to an abrupt halt, and it was a long time before she felt able to continue as an active participant. After a while, she began to tell herself, "Maybe you're not a writer. Maybe you'll never be a writer again." And although she did eventually write articles and books, she never went back to her first love, the theater. She mourned the path she had abandoned for the rest of her life.

Clare Booth Luce's loss was a hidden one, Carole Hyatt and Linda Gottlieb tell us in their inspirational and practical primer on surmounting failure, *When Smart People Fail: Rebuilding Yourself for Success*. "Hidden failures suffer less from a sharp sense of loss than a chronic sense of disappointment. But they suffer nonetheless, longing somehow to change, often as scared and ashamed as those who have been fired. How many people, laid off jobs through no fault of their own, nevertheless feel they have somehow failed? How many of us feel stuck in jobs we hate, are terrified to risk change, and despise ourselves for doing less than our best? Often at the very moment the world is praising us, we know in some corner of our minds that we have failed our own best hopes."

Each one of us is terrified of failing. But whether we risk it all or play it safe, we cannot avoid failure—public or hidden—all our lives. "Real strength comes from knowing we can survive," Carole Hyatt and Linda Gottlieb reassure us. Failure stretches us beyond our conscious capacity so that we can grow into our authentic selves. This is failure's generous gift. In life the worst thing that can happen isn't failing. It's never having tried. "Seen in that light, smart people can never fail."

SEPTEMBER 19

Affinities

Oh, it's delightful to have ambitions. . . . And there never seems to be any end to them—that's the best of it. Just as soon as you attain to one ambition you see another one glittering higher up still. It does make life so interesting.

—ANNE SHIRLEY (L. M. MONTGOMERY)

Ambition is achievement's soul mate. Action is the matchmaker that brings these affinities together so that sparks can begin to fly and we can set the world on fire.

We think highly of achievement. He's a fine fellow—honorable, desirable, the perfect gentleman. But ambition is considered more of a tramp than a lady, a vixen rather than a virtue. If her passion and power aren't creatively and constructively channeled, she could turn on the one who invoked her presence. Just as electricity can be life enhancing or destructive, so can ambition. What ambition really needs is a new press agent. The only time we ever hear about her is when she's blamed for somebody's downfall.

But ambition only becomes dangerous when, blinded by her charms, we become easy marks for greed. When the soul is impoverished, the ego is easily seduced. Greed is a very effective pimp for the dark side.

It's no wonder that many women flee from authenticity. It's too dangerous to admit, even to ourselves, that we possess not only aspirations but ambitions.

But what if ambition is a gift of Spirit? What if ambition is part of the authentic package, generously bestowed on us all when we were given our personal gifts? If sex can be both sacred and profane, if power blesses as well as destroys, why should the nature of ambition be any different? What if we are *supposed* to be ambitious? What if our refusal to channel our ambitions for our highest good, the highest good of those we love and the rest of the world, is the real corruption of Power? Think of all that could be accomplished if women cherished their ambitions and brought them into the Light where they belong. Think of how our lives could be transformed if we respected ambition and gave grateful thanks for being entrusted with such a miraculous gift.

One thing is certain. We cannot achieve without ambition. Action—ambition in motion—is what produces achievement. "All serious daring starts from within," Eudora Welty reminds us. Today the most serious daring you might engage in is an unusual creative brainstorming session. Invite ambition to sit down with your authentic self. Tell her what you'd like to achieve. Listen to her suggestions. Then take a closer look. Those horns you think you see might actually be a slightly off-center halo.

SEPTEMBER 20

The Enemy Within

We have met the enemy and he is us.

—POGO (WALT KELLY)

It's hard to accept that you can be your own worst enemy. In fact, this realization is so painful that we go to great lengths to prove otherwise. It's always fate, circumstances, or lousy luck that messes up our best-laid plans.

When all you encounter is disappointment after disappointment as you pursue your dreams, it's natural to start feeling sorry for yourself. But if you constantly think the chips are stacked against you or that the cards are marked, pray today for the courage to check out the dealer at your game of chance. Does she seem a bit familiar? She should, because she's your authentic self's evil twin: the ego.

The ego has everything to lose once your authentic self grows strong enough to act consciously on your behalf, guiding your creative choices, decisions, ambitions, and actions for your Highest Good. What was standard operating procedure before—denial, sublimation, repression—is recognized for what it is: subtle self-abuse. When you become authentic, you become greater than you ever thought you could be, and this greatness allows you to heal yourself, your family, and your world. Your authentic self is your ego's worst nightmare, and the ego will do everything in its power to eliminate her rival's influence from your daily round. The way the ego goes about this is to bring out the heavy guns: fear and intimidation.

Fear has derailed more dreams than we can ever know. Physical distress—a racing heart, pounding head, nervous stomach—is the first assault when we edge to the perimeter of our comfort zone. It's a natural, primordial instinct, a remnant of the fight-or-flight syndrome. But although it may feel excruciating, making a telephone call, speaking up during a business meeting, or dropping off your portfolio with a prospective employer is not the same as fighting off the charge of a woolly mammoth. We don't have to run scared. We *do* have to learn to recognize the physical manifestations of fear and acknowledge them. The next time you're physically sick at the thought of leaving your comfort zone, calmly reassure your conscious self that the feeling of fear is passing *through* you and will dissipate as long as you keep on moving forward. Many actresses are so scared that they feel nauseous just before walking on stage, but they've learned how to transform fear into the creative energy of forward motion. They burst through to the other side of stage fright to applause.

Intimidation works differently from naked fear. She's a shapechanger, capable of adopting different guises to control you. The moment you step bravely out from the bounds of your comfort zone, she's likely to rise up inside you like a lion tamer, complete with whip and chair. "Get back!" she'll scream. "Who do you think you are? You'll make a fool of yourself! You're risking your marriage! You're neglecting your children! Get back to your cage immediately!"

When these scare tactics are no longer effective, intimidation often takes another shape, as the voice of reason: "Look, I don't want to alarm you but . . . You know you've taken on quite a lot, I wouldn't if I were you . . ."

The worst thing about intimidation is that she knows all our buttons and just when to push them. But if she doesn't succeed with scare tactics, she'll kill your dreams with kindness. She's your best friend: she'll enable you to dig your own creative grave by handing you the shovel. She's the only one who knows how tired you really are, so she'll encourage you to take a nap instead of writing prospecting letters. She understands that you just don't have much time for relaxation, so what's the harm of a catching a soap opera in the early afternoon instead of working on your résumé before the kids come home from school? Relax, she tells you, "*You've got plenty of time. . . .* If it doesn't get taken care of today, there's always tomorrow . . ."

If none of the above works because now you're older, wiser, and more experienced, she'll begin a whispering campaign, sounding very similar to your intuitive voice. How will you know the difference? If the suggestion you hear doesn't bring you a sense of peace, *it is not the voice of your authentic self.* It's the ego in one of her many guises. Tell her to shut up. Then turn on some beautiful music that uplifts, inspires, and drowns her out.

Today, just begin observing your behavior pattern. Every woman—even the megastars whose lives seem so glamorous—experiences ambivalence about success. One significant quality found in the women we admire is that they have identified their personal patterns of self-sabotage and learned to let their own best friend—their authentic self—outsmart the enemy within. And so can you.

SEPTEMBER 21

The Spiral Path

My joy, my grief, my hope, my love,
Did all within this circle move!

—EDMUND WALLER

I am often asked if I am now living authentically after following the Simple Abundance path for the last four years. Some moments, some hours, some days feel wholly right, completely authentic. And more frequently than not, I can attest that my conversations with family, friends, colleagues, even aquaintances and strangers are authentic encounters. So are my choices, even the difficult ones, and my joys, my griefs, my hopes, my loves. But every minute of every day is not yet authentic. I think it takes an entire life-time to live authentically. It is the *striving* to be authentic that makes you so, not the end result. When you think you've arrived, you realize you've come all this way just to prepare yourself to begin again.

The biggest surprise on the soulful journey to authenticity, whether as a philosophy or a spiritual path, is that the path is a spiral. We go up, but we go in circles. Each time around, the view gets a little bit wider. The psychologist Carl Jung believed that our spiritual experience of "the Self," which I call the authentic self, could only be truly realized by *"circumambulating."*

The ancients revered the power of the circle. In the African tradition, as well as in Disney movies, our earthly span is called "the circle of life." Black Elk, the leader of the Oglala Sioux, taught that "The power of the world always works in circles." Buddhist and Hindu pilgrims circle the base of Tibet's Mount Kailas as an act of worship. Muslims circle the Kabah in Mecca. For thousands of years the creation of mandalas—circular, geometric designs—has been part of both Eastern and Western spiritual traditions. Seekers create personal mandalas in order to invoke the sacred through the visual. Circles are found at sacred sites throughout the world. There is a circular maze at the base of Chartres Cathedral in France. The gigantic prehistoric sculptures at Stonehenge, England, form a circle. The communion host offered at Catholic mass is a round wafer. If we search for circles, we will find them everywhere. Plato believed the soul was a circle. If it is, and the authentic self is the Soul made visible, how could our awakening to authenticity be straight and not circular?

I am reminded of just how much of a spiral the authentic journey is when I get stuck in a set of circumstances from which escape seems impossible. When this occurs, I ask myself, "What's the lesson here, so that I can move on?" I usually discover that I've stopped using the principles of Simple Abundance as my stepping-stones to Wholeness. I've been too busy to write in my gratitude journal; I've begun dropping in my tracks because I've been unable to say "no"; I'm cranky because my house is cluttered and I can't find anything; I'm frazzled because I've let myself forget that moments of solitude and meditation are necessary to center myself. I've been this route many times. I *know* that if I'm not experiencing harmony in my daily round, I'm not participating in the process.

So I start again. Begin at the beginning. Make gratitude an active rather than a passive prayer, consciously bring simplicity and order to my daily round, honor moments of *being* rather than of doing. It's not enough to know or write about Simple Abundance; it must be *lived* to realize its beauty and joy. When I do resume living by my own lights, I usually discover that I'm able to move on. But even if I can't change my outside circumstances, Simple Abundance enables me to change how I react to them.

"The life we want is not merely the one we have chosen and made," poet Wendell Berry tells us. "It is the one we must be choosing and making."

SEPTEMBER 22

Real Life Has a Steep Learning Curve

I would like to learn, or remember, how to live.
—ANNIE DILLARD

Now the revelations come very quickly and from all quarters because you're ready to start making connections. In the Old Testament, God uses donkeys, rocks, and burning bushes to deliver Divine messages, so don't question the validity of what you hear or how you hear it *if the truth resonates within.* You might be reading a story, watching a video, or chatting casually with a friendly grocery clerk. Don't cut yourself off from sources of inspiration.

One of the quantum leaps that comes about on the Simple Abundance path is the sudden awareness that you've spent your entire life going backward instead of forward. You may have believed that seeking a spiritual path was all about submission, sacrifice, and suffering and that only the worldly path could provide freedom, fulfillment, and good fortune. Then, one morning—maybe even this morning—you make a connection. And when you do, you realize that you have to unlearn practically everything you've taken for granted—chapter and verse.

Don't panic. This really isn't as hard as it sounds. Has the other path worked? Have any of the world's gifts given you authentic happiness? Has the perfect job, relationship, house, money, or anything else you thought would do it for you, fulfilled you for longer than a week? So trust your experiences and impulses; you've had them for a reason. Real Life has a steep learning curve, but once you respond from personal knowledge instead of by rote, it's easier than you might have thought. What's more, Real Life actually becomes fun.

Here's what I think happens. Just before we come to earth to begin this life, we are given a photograph of our futures—the Divine Plan—to get us excited about the great adventure ahead. As the photo pops out of the celestial camera, we're in such a hurry to get on with it, we grab the negative instead of the photograph. Now we've got the pattern of a fabulous life, but the perspective is reversed. What's white looks black. What's black appears white. We've got the big picture, but it's backward. So we cry when we should be laughing, are envious when we should feel inspired, experience deprivation instead of abundance, do it the hard way instead of the easy way, pull back instead of reaching out. And worst of all, we close our hearts so we won't get hurt, when opening them is the only way we'll ever know joy.

How many times have we waited for Spirit to move for us, when in fact, Spirit is waiting to work *with* us? Today, take the negative of your Divine Plan and let Love develop it so that you can begin living the life for which you were created.

It's time to move forward.

For Thine Is the Kingdom, and the Power, and the Glory

When I look into the future, it's so bright it burns my eyes.
—OPRAH WINFREY

Several years ago I read a profile of Oprah Winfrey in *The New York Times* magazine. In it she expressed her belief that the concept of God never giving us more than we can handle refers to much more than just the stoic bearing of pain and suffering. God's giving also includes the goodies—wealth, worldly success, power. If you think you're not strong enough to bear the Glory, rest assured, it *will* be withheld until you believe you can and ask for it.

Today, meditate on this possibility. I know I've been thinking about it for years and it's just beginning to register.

We know that Power is available to each of us, every moment of every day, but we have to ask that the spiritual switch be turned on. Next, we've got to be ready to bear the Glory. We prepare ourselves by gradually growing into our talents, one creative challenge at a time. With each accomplishment that is personally acknowledged and celebrated, our self-confidence increases, and we begin to trust our abilities. Furthermore, we realize we weren't intended to do this alone. That takes care of the Power and the Glory. Now what about the Kingdom?

Spiritual seekers are told to search for the Kingdom of Heaven before anything else. Could the Kingdom of Heaven be an authentic life? I believe so. Because once you find your authentic path and follow it, all the other puzzle pieces start to fall into place: the money, the job, the relationship.

Joseph Campbell tells us to "follow our bliss" if we want life to be rich, deep, and meaningful. Follow your bliss and doors will open. Follow your bliss, and you'll get on the track created especially for you at the beginning of time.

Could your bliss and an authentic life be one and the same? What if, whatever it is that makes you ecstatic, brings you joy, sends you soaring, satisfies your hunger, fulfills your yearning, ignites your passion, makes you reach out to others, and gives you peace—in other words, your bliss—*is* also the Kingdom of Heaven?

"Thy kingdom come, thy will be done, on earth as it is in heaven . . ."

"Only connect!" E. M. Forster urges us. "Only connect the prose and the passion, and both will be exalted, and human love will be seen at its height. Live in fragments no longer. Only connect, and the . . . isolation that is life . . . will die."

"Only connect." Then and only then can the Kingdom and the Power and the Glory be yours. Forever and ever.

Amen.

Do What You Love and the Money Will Follow—or So They Say

Do what you love, and the money will follow.

—MARSHA SINETAR

I love the optimism of this quotation, and I believe it's true. If you've not read her, Marsha Sinetar can make a believer out of you as well. I think you'll find her book (by the same title) a practical and inspirational primer on getting your passion to pay off.

Sinetar is actually not the first to advise us along these lines. Countless sages, poets, and philosophers have done so, though each has put it differently. One of Buddha's main steps for achieving enlightenment, for example, is discovering your right livelihood. And at the other end of the spectrum, John D. Rockefeller believed that the power to make money was a gift from God, which is simply another way of saying, "Do what you love and the money will follow."

But still we ask: Does it *really*?

Yes. But not the way you're used to getting it.

In the first place, the money usually doesn't come all at once, especially in the beginning.

In the second place, the money will come from unexpected sources. But it will come, and here's why. When you start following your authentic path, you're finally using the gifts Spirit expects you to use. You're actively searching for the Kingdom of Heaven here on earth. You're holding up your end of the bargain. Spirit's part of the pact is to make sure you have everything you need to make you truly happy. This includes money. Spirit knows that the rate of exchange used here on earth is cash, not clamshells or sheep. But the rate of exchange in Heaven is wonder. Doing what you love is not about money, it's about wonder. As soon as you understand you're supposed to be asking for wonder instead of money, you'll start experiencing abundance. Trust me, doing what you love does eventually lead to the ATM. But you might have a few detours before you get there.

Which brings us to the third and final caveat: *We must not tell Spirit how* the money should be delivered, when it should arrive, or in what denomination. This is not a ransom. Spirit's been delivering the goods for a long time now. Spirit doesn't need our input, although it's been my experience that friendly suggestions and reminders every now and then about exactly what bills need to be paid doesn't seem out of line.

Essentially what happens when you begin to do what you love is that you get a new employer: Spirit. Spirit always pays us in proportion to how hard we work. It's probably the first time that many of us will find ourselves being compensated fairly. But the paycheck doesn't arrive every Friday or even once a month. I don't want to scare you, but sometimes it can even take years. Still, it does arrive. And the first time you get paid for doing what you love to do will be one of the most thrilling moments of your life.

It's worth the wait. It's glorious. It's bliss. It's nothing less than experiencing Heaven on earth. As the English novelist Enid Bagnold reminds us, "There may be wonder in money, but, dear God, there is money in wonder."

SEPTEMBER 25

If One Woman Has Done It, So Can You— And If Not, Why Not You?

I've always believed that one woman's success can only help another woman's success.

—GLORIA VANDERBILT

If there's something you want to do with your life and another woman has done it before you, there's no reason you can't achieve it too. And if no woman has ever done what you dream of doing, there's no reason you can't be the first. Someone has to be. Who are the women you most admire? Why? Find out everything you can about their lives because they have secrets to share with you.

In 1908, Napoleon Hill was a college student and a fledgling freelance writer. He obtained an interview with Andrew Carnegie, who was then the world's richest man. Hill wanted to write a profile that would reveal Carnegie's secrets for accumulating his vast fortune. Carnegie was so impressed with the young man that the initial three-hour interview stretched into three days.

During this time Carnegie asked Hill if he would be willing to devote the next twenty years to one of the millionaire's pet projects: interviewing other successful entrepreneurs and distilling their success secrets into a formula that average men and women could use to achieve their dreams. Carnegie offered Hill no financial incentive but he did promise him introductions to such famous men as Thomas Edison, Henry Ford, Harvey Firestone, and Luther Burbank. Hill jumped at the chance.

The result was an immensely successful writing career that eventually led in 1937 to the publication of Hill's philosophy of personal achievement, *Think and Grow Rich*. Coming as it did in the midst of the Great Depression, the book's uplifting message, "Whatever the mind can conceive and believe . . . it can achieve," captured the country's imagination. Hill's book eventually became one of the most influential ever published, selling over ten million copies. It spawned the self-actualization publishing genre.

One of the secrets that Hill discovered was that many successful dreamers enjoy personal reveries with their role models. Hill suggests creating an imaginary council with a group of "Invisible Counselors," composed of the people you most admire. At night before you go to sleep, close your eyes and conduct success strategy sessions in which you seek the advice of your heroines. While the meetings are "purely imaginary," Hill believes they make us more "receptive to ideas, thoughts, and knowledge" which reaches us through our sixth sense, intuition.

If your role models are alive and achieving, think of them as clearing the brush for you. Follow their tracks. Research everything you can about their personal journeys. Do they make personal appearances, give lectures or workshops you can attend? Join women's business associations, network at conferences, ask for advice and occasionally look down at the floor. Someone has laid down a path for you to follow.

SEPTEMBER 26

The Tao of Success

Nothing in the world can take the place of Persistence.
Talent will not; nothing is more commonplace than unsuccessful
*   men with talent.*
Genius will not; unrewarded genius is almost a proverb.
Education alone will not; the world is full of educated derelicts.
Persistence and Determination alone are omnipotent.
—CALVIN COOLIDGE

This is the Tao of success—the Way—and like every other truth, it's at once very simple and very difficult. Not the understanding as much as the doing, because the Tao of success is Patience and Persistence.

Patience is the art of waiting. Like all high arts, it takes time to master, which shouldn't be surprising, since patience is the knowledge of time. How to use time to your advantage, how to be at the right place at the right time, how to pick your moments, how to bite your tongue. Patience is discovering the mysterious pattern of cycles that cradle the Universe and ensure that everything that has happened once will recur.

Perseverance in life is being steadfast; persistence is being stubborn. Persistence is grittier than perseverance. Perseverance is achievement's perspiration; persistence is its sweat. Persistence is knocking on Heaven's doors so often and so loudly on behalf of your dreams that eventually you'll be given what you want, just to shut you up. For example, think of an eleven-year-old child who wants to get her ears pierced sooner than her sixteenth birthday, the age her old-fashioned mother thinks is appropriate. The first request, even if it comes in a burst of emotion, doesn't succeed. Nor does the second, the third, or even the fourth. But the child who goes at you, morning, afternoon, and night, week after week, month after month; this child's voice is water to the rock of your reason. This stubborn but patient child wears you down, which is why you end up at the mall on her twelfth birthday, shaking your head as you pay to adorn her earlobes with tiny gold balls.

The potent alchemy of patience and persistence, which together become endurance, must have been what the Lebanese poet Hoda al-Namai was meditating on when she wrote:

I have not withdrawn into despair,
I did not go mad in gathering honey,
I did not go mad,
I did not go mad,
I did not go mad.

If you are determined to gather life's honey, to stick your hand into the hive again and again and again, to be stung so many times that you become numb to the pain, to persevere and persist till those who know and love you become unable to think of you as *a fairly normal woman*, you will not be called mad.

You will be called authentic.

Only the Heart Knows

Only the heart knows how to find what is precious.
—Fyodor Dostoyevsky

When Anna Quindlen, the Pulitizer Prize-winning columnist for *The New York Times,* stepped off journalism's fast track to devote her time, emotion, and creative energy to writing novels and raising her three children full time, her peers were aghast, and her woman readers were astonished. Half her readers—women who had decided to put family before career—applauded her choice. The other half—women who were trying desperately to raise happy kids and work full time—felt betrayed. Anna Quindlen was not just Supermom, but the archetype for women who wanted to have it all. Her personal decision resurrected the old debate between mothers with careers versus mothers who work at home. If she couldn't take the juggling any longer, what hope was there for the rest of us?

But Anna Quindlen's creative choice wasn't about career versus family. It was about worldly success versus authentic success. She dreamed of writing novels instead of newspaper columns. She wanted to be there when her children came home from school. She wanted to live by her own lights. She wanted to listen to her heart. And she had the financial means to do so.

Only the heart knows what's working in our lives. The heart is our authentic compass. If we consult her, the heart can tell us if we're headed in the right direction. But the heart also tells us when we've made a wrong turn or when it's time for a U-turn. For a lot of us, this is information we don't want to know. Knowing might mean choice, and choice often means change.

I don't doubt that there are ten million women who would love to make the choice that Anna Quindlen did, but they're not in the financial position to do so. But just because you can't do it today or tomorrow doesn't mean you can't ever do it. Dreams deferred come true every day. Delay doesn't mean denial.

The heart does not charge for consultations, conversations, creative brainstorming sessions, or carrying a dream from conception to delivery, no matter how long it takes. "Dreams pass into the reality of action," Anaïs Nin reassures us. "From the action stems the dream again; and this interdependence produces the highest form of living."

A Time for Everything

There is a time for everything,
And a season for every activity under heaven.

—ECCLESIASTES 3:1

Yes, but they are not the same time.

You cannot raise happy, secure, emotionally well-adjusted children, revel in a fabulous marriage, and work a sixty-hour week.

You want to, I know. So do I. But we can't. It is physically, emotionally, psychologically, and spiritually impossible. We have tried. We have failed.

We cannot circumvent the laws of Heaven and Earth just because it would be convenient. Just because it would fit nicely into our plans. We have tried. We have failed.

When we cannot do it all at the same time, we are meant to do only some of it. In order to find out what that "some" is to be, we need to ask: What is it I truly want right now? What is it I truly need? How do I get it? How much does it cost in life's currency?

This might be the season for you to wipe a runny nose. That doesn't mean the season of running your own business won't occur. This might be the season of living out of a suitcase. That doesn't mean the season of restoring a colonial farmhouse will never come. Making deals doesn't mean that someday you won't be making school lunches. The seasons of life are not meant to be frenetic, just full.

"You probably can have it all," Anna Quindlen muses. "Just not all at the same time. And . . . you might have to make certain compromises when your children are small. But your children are going to be small for a very short period of time . . . it will go by in a blink of an eye, and you will only be 40, 50, or 60 with another 15 or 25 years ahead of you." A quarter of a century to do what you want to do, the way you want to do it.

Blessed is the woman who knows her own limits.

SEPTEMBER 29

Self-Nurturing on the Job

When we truly care for ourselves, it becomes possible to care far more profoundly about other people. The more alert and sensitive we are to our own needs, the more loving and generous we can be toward others.

—EDA LeSHAN

Rituals of self-nurturance are the mortar that holds the day together, especially when you're spending eight to ten hours away from home. Think of a favorite cup and indulgent brews that can be warmed in the microwave (an assortment of coffees, teas, hot cocoa, and cider). Set aside ten minutes at your desk with your cup and a closed door before the day officially begins; it can center you as you thoughtfully review what needs to be done. Ten minutes of quiet at the end of the day, straightening the piles on your desk, looking over tomorrow's agenda, can help bring an orderly closure to your day before you shift gears. Ten minutes in the morning, ten minutes at night. No matter how busy we are, we all can invest twenty minutes to preserve the precious resources of time, creative energy, and emotion.

Create a pleasing and pretty workspace. Aim for creating a comfortable nest instead of a sterile environment. Bring in a wonderful desk lamp, baskets and wooden boxes to hold paper and projects, a flowering plant in the winter, and a small bouquet of seasonal flowers in spring, summer, and fall. Find yourself a personal talisman—an object with special meaning—that reminds you that you're headed in the right direction. Keep an ample supply of your favorite pens and pencils in cups on your desk; be on the lookout for notepads or cards that suit your idiosyncrasies and delight your senses. My trademark is using note cards three by five inches in size that are a cross between a business and a note card. Little civilizing details can make a tremendous difference. Search for a handsome pillow for your chair. Add dashes of color wherever you can—your paperclips and folders, for example. Hang a bulletin board near your desk for clippings, cards, cartoons, inspiration, and reminders. If you have a private office and can hang pictures, keep the walls blank until you find something you'll never tire of looking at.

Now create a comfort drawer. Fill it with everything you ever wanted at work and didn't have: a small sewing kit; safety pins; tampons; an extra pair of hose and reading glasses; pain relief; Band-Aids and a small tube of antiseptic ointment; small packets of tissues. Tuck in breath mints, a chocolate bar, and a couple of blank greeting cards for quick notes to distant friends.

Remember your toy box at home? Create a small one at work for those moments when you don't want to be or simply can't be a grown-up anymore, usually in the late afternoon: three-dimensional puzzles, tarot cards, a yo-yo, paddleball, pick-up sticks, Chinese health balls, Silly Putty, a miniature kaleidoscope, or a gravity-defying bouncing ball that is the replica of the planet Jupiter. You get the idea.

Outfit a pretty cosmetic bag to keep in your desk with dental items, deodorant, scented hand cream, emery boards, eyedrops, comb, brush, a small spray of your favorite cologne, in order to freshen up midday or if you can't go home before going out in the evening.

If you work in an enlightened office or have a private one, music, especially classical selections, can be a powerful tool for productivity. Aromatherapy can work wonders in an office setting; get a sculptural scent diffuser (the size of a small vase). The top of the diffuser holds a half cup of water and about five drops of essential oils, which are heated by a votive candle. The warm fragrant water will discreetly put moisture back into the air around your desk (very important in heated offices), and the scent is very soothing or invigorating depending upon your needs. The only drawback to using aromatherapy in the workplace is that more people might be drawn to your desk because the environment is so pleasant.

Stretch twice a day, especially if you work at a computer for long periods of time. Read Dr. Seuss aloud, especially *Oh the Places You'll Go.*

Remember feng-shui—the art of placement? Don't scoff. Does it hurt to position your desk advantageously so that your *chi,* or energy, is flowing and not blocked? No. Can it help? Yes! There must be a reason it's been practiced for the last three thousand years.

Every week or so, bring in something good to eat (it doesn't have to be fattening) in a pretty tin or basket to share.

Treating yourself well on the job is not impossible. It can serve as a source of inspiration to bring out your best. When starting a new project, ask yourself, is there anything I can do to make this task more pleasurable? If there is, do it.

The therapeutic value of treats in the workplace is probably the last thing employers think about as a benefit, but it shouldn't be. Working happier accomplishes much more than working harder.

Traveling on Business

Is there anything *as horrible as* starting *on a trip? Once you're off that's all right, but the last moments are earthquake and convulsion, and the feeling that you are a snail being pulled off your rock.*

—ANNE MORROW LINDBERGH

About this time every year, the earth starts to quake beneath the feet of two good friends of mine who work in publishing and are compelled to attend the international booksellers' convention held in Germany each autumn. Some women race dogsled teams in the Iditarod, a 1,150-mile marathon across frozen Alaskan tundra; some sell books in Frankfurt. The grueling tactics of the two competitive events seem about even in terms of the psychic and physical endurance required to live to tell the tale.

Fear and loathing is not too strong a description of the visceral reaction many of us experience when a business trip looms. Actually, the anticipation of the trip is often more horrendous than the reality, even if it consists of seven days of smiling while attempting to strike deals in forty different languages. But no matter what faces you on a business trip, if you intuitively plan for yourself the way you would for a child about to go away on her first weeklong camping trip—preparing both for the unexpected and for maximum comfort—you'll not only cope, but have a very good chance of enjoying the change of scene.

Here are some soothing strategies for easing hectic moments so that your trip might be pleasant and productive.

You've heard it before, but pack as lightly as possible, leaving room in your suitcase for your favorite sleeping pillow. This can make the difference between a good night's sleep and tossing fitfully in a strange bed. It doesn't help to look haggard and feel exhausted at the beginning of the trip.

Your airplane carry-on bag should be large enough to hold a complete outfit appropriate for business, as well as your cosmetics, toiletries, and vital business papers in a portfolio if you're not carrying a briefcase. Should your luggage be lost or delayed, you can manage, at least for a day.

No matter what the season or where you're traveling, pack at least a few warm items that can be layered: seasonless knits in coordinating colors, a dressy sweater, and socks. The coldest I've ever been was during a numbing week of Irish downpours in August; it *snowed* on a trip to Paris during May; and San Francisco in June can make your teeth chatter. Pack a portable umbrella, gloves, scarf, and hat. Wear a raincoat with a warm removable lining.

Create a comfort bag for traveling. Mine includes a small tape recorder and earphones with favorite tapes; small packets of nuts, crackers, and cheese; my favorite tea in bags; a couple of small plastic bottles of mineral water and individual-serving-size bottles of wine; sachets or a small scented candle (hotel rooms can be very stuffy and often you can't open the windows); and a special bath indulgence.

Many hotels have gyms and swimming pools; don't forget your aerobic shoes, workout clothes, and swim suit, so that you can unwind in the evening.

If you're attending an all-day conference or convention and won't be back at your hotel until night, tuck the following lifesavers into your briefcase or backpack: headache relief, a small bottle of water or juice and nibbles in case you miss lunch; and a travel-size toothbrush, toothpaste, mouth wash, and a string of dental floss.

Remember to pace yourself as much as possible. If your day is spent in back-to-back meetings, try to squeeze in mini-breaks; you need fresh air as much as you do a cup of coffee and trips to the ladies' room. When your days are crammed with appointments, one quiet night on your own is essential.

Build breathing space into your schedule, *especially* if you think you can't possibly do it. Get up an hour earlier than you really have to. Lie in bed quietly to collect your thoughts, and then luxuriate with breakfast in bed. It may be the only peaceful hour of your day. If you have a breakfast meeting scheduled, at least have your first wake-up cup in private. If you have evening engagements, try to return to your hotel beforehand to revive. Lie down for twenty minutes, take a quick shower, put on fresh makeup, and change for dinner. You'll feel a surge of new energy and enthusiasm. Try to arrive at your hotel the day before meetings begin so that you can settle in; pack up your room the night before you go home so that you don't have a mad-dash departure.

If something has started to annoy you but isn't quite a nag—a sensitive tooth or a twinge when you go to the bathroom—check it out before you leave. There is absolutely nothing worse than needing an emergency root canal or having a urinary infection flare up while traveling.

Always travel with different absorbing kinds of reading: serious, light, trash, and inspirational. You can't predict what your mood will be on the way there, coming back, or in-between. I collect novels throughout the year and save them for trips; treat yourself to magazines you don't normally read at home.

Pack at least one collapsible bag to fill up with anything you might want to bring back. I'm always on the lookout for unusual small gifts when on trips.

Whether you're in a new city or returning to an old favorite, carve out a couple of hours for a solo creative excursion: shopping, visiting a museum, taking a walk in a beautiful park or public garden, savoring a drink in an inviting café. Above all, enjoy your trip as much as possible—the solitude of your hotel room, the luxury of room service, not having to worry about cooking or carpooling, the novelty of different newspapers and scenery. Be grateful for the opportunities to meet new people, see new places, enlarge your horizons. Realize that your work is important and makes such a contribution to the simply abundant lives of others, as well as to your own, that the world is waiting to hear from you. "Through travel I first became aware of the outside world," Eudora Welty confides. "It was through travel that I found my own introspective way into becoming a part of it."

Joyful Simplicities for September

⋙ *L' été c'est fini*, as the French say, so end summer on a high note. Make a really big deal out of the last cookout of the summer. Serve your favorite summer recipes with a final flourish. Linger in the twilight, watch the sun go down, and bid summer a fond adieu.

⋙ On Labor Day weekend take fifteen minutes to write down all the things you wanted to do over the summer but never got around to. Put your list in an envelope. When you get your next year's calendar, paperclip the envelope to the first day of June and open it then. Try to block in some time on your calendar to make postponed pleasures a priority when summer returns.

⋙ Stock up on your own school supplies. They're on sale this month. Get your own pads, notebooks, scissors, tape, and crayons. Send away (to Lillian Vernon or Miles Kimball) and get pencils imprinted with your name on them. It's inexpensive and fun. Take a creative excursion to find exactly the kind of pen you prefer writing with. Go to an artists' supply store. Experiment with every type of pen you can find until you discover one that writes wonderfully. Once you've identified your brand, stock up on them at discount office supply stores.

⋙ Make taffy apples.

⋙ Enjoy fresh apple cider and pear nectar.

⋙ Experiment with different types of popcorn.

⋙ Pack away your swimsuit. Bring out your woolens. Do you have a favorite sweater that you absolutely adore? If not, why not?

⋙ Celebrate the autumn equinox with a festive dinner of homestyle cooking. Do this especially if you live alone and rarely cook a decent meal for yourself. Bring home a small pot of mums for your dining table. Draw hearthside and light the candles, pour the wine or cider, and enjoy the simple pleasures of comfort food. Have you ever tried an English "fidget pie," a traditional harvest meal? It's composed of potatoes, onions, apples, and ham pieces in a vegetable stock seasoned with a little brown sugar, salt, and pepper. Pour into a pastry shell, cover with a top crust and bake as you would any filled pie.

❧ Gradually assemble your treats for the office.

❧ Observe the autumnal festival of Michaelmas on September 29, which is the feast day of St. Michael the Archangel. This ancient English harvest festival dates back to the sixth century. Legend has it that on this day the devil was driven out of Heaven by St. Michael and landed in a patch of blackberry brambles. It's traditional to have blackberry treats—pies, tarts, or jam on scones for tea on this day.

❧ Start making your Christmas list this month so that you won't be frantic in December.

❧ If you have children, this is the time to have them decide on their Halloween costumes. Don't despair. They don't divide the children into two groups at school: those wearing store-bought costumes and those wearing homemade ones! Order the costume from a catalog this month or assemble all your supplies. Soon everything will be picked over, and there's nothing so disappointing for children (or so frustrating for you) as discovering you can't find exactly what you need. If you do construct homemade costumes, always keep in mind exactly whose costume it is you're making. Some of us get carried away and end up creating costumes designed more to impress each other than to please our children.

❧ Take a walk under the huntress moon.

❧ Look at farmers' markets for dried flowers to create your own bouquet. Prepared bouquets can be wonderful, but they're expensive. Creating your own bouquet on a September Sunday afternoon is a relaxing restorative that reminds you all winter long that beauty is simply abundant if you look for it.

OCTOBER

The fields are harvested and bare,
And Winter whistles through the square.
October dresses in flame and gold
Like a woman afraid of growing old.
—ANNE MARY LAWLER

Now Indian summer arrives, a change of season that's more a sense memory than a date on the calendar. Finally, the heat is passing. Gradually familiar surroundings don a rustic palate of jewel tones that dazzle with their beauty. Let October seduce you with her charms. "Beguile us in the way you know," poet Robert Frost entreated this season of abundance. "Release one leaf at the break of day."

Recognizing Burnout Before You're Charred

My candle burns at both ends;
It will not last the night.

—EDNA ST. VINCENT MILLAY

Burnt offerings.
Burned to a crisp.
Burned beyond recognition.
Burned alive.
Burned out.

Setting the world on fire comes with risks. Unfortunately we usually don't realize this until smoke gets in our eyes.

Burnout is a condition caused by unbalance: too much work or responsibility, too little time to do it, over too long a period. We've been cruising in the fast lane but we've been running on fumes rather than on fuel. Often we think that burnout is something that just happens to other women—to workaholics and perfectionists. But careaholics are also at risk—women who care deeply about their children, work, relationships, parents, siblings, friends, communities, issues. This sounds like every woman I know. Perhaps we would pay more attention to burnout if it were as dramatic as a heart attack. But a smoldering flame can be just as deadly as a flash fire.

Sometimes burnout manifests itself as a sense of complete exhaustion at the end of a project that has taken months of challenging and intense work. Taking a week off to rest, then resuming work at a slower pace is usually enough to bring about a speedy recovery. But first-degree burnout—the soul snuffer—comes from living unbalanced for years; when what was supposed to be a temporary situation becomes a lifestyle.

Burnout often begins with illness—anything from a bout of flu you can't shake to chronic fatigue syndrome—and is usually accompanied by depression. Sometimes burnout is hard to distinguish from a creative dry spell, especially if you're good at denial, which most women are.

It's burnout when you go to bed exhausted every night and wake up tired every morning—when no amount of sleep refreshes you, month after weary month. It's burnout when everything becomes too much effort: combing your hair, going out to dinner, visiting friends for the weekend, even going on vacation. It's burnout when you can't believe, under any circumstances, that you'll ever want to make love again. It's burnout when you find yourself cranky all the time, bursting into tears or going into fits of rage at the slightest provocation. It's burnout when you dread the next phone call. It's burnout when you feel trapped and hopeless, unable to dream, experience pleasure, or find contentment. It's burnout when neither big thrills nor little moments have the power to move you—when nothing satisfies you because you haven't a clue what's wrong or how to fix it. Because everything's wrong. Because something is terribly out of whack: you. It's burnout when you feel there is not one other person on the face of the earth who can help you.

And you're right.

When you're suffering from burnout, you *are* the only person on earth who can help because you're the only one who can make the lifestyle changes that need to be made: to call a halt, to take a slower path, to make a detour. When you have no strength left, you have no choice but to rely on the strength of a saner Power to restore you to Wholeness. In the pursuit of our souls, Spirit takes no prisoners.

OCTOBER 2

The Ultimate Seduction

It is your work in life that is the ultimate seduction.
—PABLO PICASSO

Like a phantom lover, work charms, cajoles, comforts, and caresses. Our work—especially if it's our grand passion—can be so seductive that we can find ourselves completely caught up in its rapture, unable to resist. However, work doesn't have to be a grand passion for us to be swept away; an infatuation can just as conveniently distract us from whatever is disappointing, disagreeable, or disturbing elsewhere in our lives. When you simply can't deal with real life, a fax that needs to be answered immediately can be a fine friend.

The ultimate seduction is often accompanied by the ultimate addictions: workaholism and perfectionism. What makes these two reckless behavior patterns so dangerous is that they're sanctioned, supported, and sustained by a society still shackled to the Puritan work ethic. The Puritans frowned on anything enjoyable, believing that God's favor could be achieved only by grueling struggle, stringent self-discipline, and backbreaking work. But Spirit can't use us to heal the world if we can't heal ourselves.

I and many of my friends are workaholics. Even kryptonite can't stop us. For years, we've all vehemently denied it. Now, in conversations, we're able to admit "tendencies toward," much the way an alcoholic admits to being a social drinker. These tendencies include working long hours during the week; bringing work home with you on weekends and vacations; turning on the computer after the kids are in bed; sneaking in work, one way or another, seven days a week; referring to the perusal of contracts as "reading"; canceling dates with friends and family to finish up "one more thing"; postponing pleasure until a deadline is met; carrying a cellular phone; installing a fax at the beach condo; starting one project before finishing another; letting work interrupt precious private or family time; taking eighteen-hour round trips to Los Angeles; and squeezing the only "vacations" into business trips.

Tendencies?

If you hear yourself frequently muttering under your breath, "This is insane," the time has come to quietly scrutinize your working style. Authentic success doesn't come wrapped in a shroud.

Start small. Be sneaky. Think baby steps. The same savvy that got you into this mess can help you escape. Take the work home but don't open the briefcase. Turn on the answering machine during dinner and in the evening. Take a day off every two weeks. A woman I know has reached the point of taking one Sunday off a month, whether she needs it or not. Secretly she believes it's her most astonishing accomplishment.

When we succumb to workaholism, what's really happening is that we've lost faith in Spirit's willingness to help us achieve success. We've separated the secular from the spiritual. Asking for grace doesn't seem as practical as working round the clock.

When was the last time Spirit accompanied you to work?

When was the last time you asked It to?

OCTOBER 3

Little Miss Perfect

Perfectionism is the voice of the oppressor, the enemy of the people. It will keep you cramped and insane your whole life.
—ANNE LAMOTT

The road to hell is paved by perfectionists working with grains of sand. Uh-oh . . . missed a spot . . .

Like workaholism, aspiring to be Little Miss Perfect is an addiction of low self-worth. When we were young, nothing we did was ever good enough, so we just kept on doing until doing was all we could do. When doing more and more didn't make a difference, we thought if we did our work perfectly, we'd hit the mark. When we did, suddenly voices other than our own sang our praises. It sounded like the Heavenly hosts. Champagne or chocolate couldn't begin to compare with the ecstasy of genuine compliments. We're creatures who live by our senses, and since the response we got for perfection felt wonderful—even if for only ten seconds—we wanted to repeat the experience. So we committed to doing everything perfectly, setting in motion a cycle of self-destruction that frequently felt as comfortable as a straitjacket. Still, the pursuit of perfection is the opiate of choice for millions of women.

I could tell you to stop reading the magazines, watching the videos, and going to the movies that continuously reinforce our belief that perfection is possible, but you're not going to listen to me. Instead, next time you see a gorgeous woman on the cover of a magazine, a room to die for, or a meal that would take a professional chef a week to prepare, begin to chant, "You're not real. You're not real. *You're not real.* I refuse to grant you the power to make me miserable." (This spell breaker is even more effective if chanted aloud in a grocery checkout line.) The woman, the room, and the meal that are depicted to inspire (but that really diminish us) are illusions conjured up by professionals paid handsomely to manipulate reality.

Once a close friend gave me a priceless gift. She convinced me that my sanity is much more important than the subtle nuances that I adore. The subtle nuances are the essence of perfection. The subtle nuances trigger the "Ah" response. But a life spent seeking the subtle nuances leaves little time to enjoy the big picture. Now, as a recovering perfectionist, I try to leave the subtle nuances to Spirit, who shows off better than I do.

Today, I would like to give you that gift: *Your sanity is much more important than the subtle nuances.*

Get yourself a small hourglass filled with sand. Place it prominently where you can see it—in the kitchen or on your desk. Turn it over once a day. Watch how fast the grains of sand flow. Those are the minutes of your life. Live them. Pave with them. Everyday it's your call.

A point worth pondering: Upon completing the Universe, the Great Creator pronounced it "very good." Not *"perfect."*

Homework

There are some things you learn best in calm, and some in storm.
—WILLA CATHER

And some things you learn best at home, such as your authentic working style. Working from home is becoming an attractive economic alternative as women try to bring more harmony into their daily round. Many
women are leaving the downsized corporate world to start home-based
businesses; three out of every four sole proprietorships are now owned by
women. Other women are negotiating computer commuting as a benefit,
so that they might be more available to their families during the week, especially on those occasions sent to try mothers' souls: sick days, snow days,
and school breaks. Still more women are discovering that working from
home, at least part of the week, is more productive than working at the
office because, with fewer interruptions, it provides a more serene environment in which to concentrate.

Working from home is great, but it's not exactly as you might imagine
it to be, especially if your current workplace is still at another location. Yes,
it's fabulous to be able to work in pajamas or sweats, handy to throw a load
of laundry into the washing machine while sending a fax, convenient to
start spaghetti sauce simmering in the early afternoon while conducting
telephone conferences. But if you're not careful, it's *very easy* to blur the
distinction between the two spheres—home and work—until you have
only "homework," which is horrendous. Homework is rolling out of bed
and waking up on-line, only to fall asleep at the computer sixteen hours
later. Homework is a soulless, repetitive cycle of brutality brought on by
the ease and convenience of technology.

Does the Bataan Death March mean anything to you?

I've been working from home for nearly twenty years, and now I can't
imagine another working style. But like any life choice, you have to be suited to it. A dear friend fantasized about working from home for years; after
a couple of months she resumed working at her office most of the time
because the isolation was numbing.

You also have to be extremely focused to work from home, because *you
must work.* When the family heads out the door in the mornings, you must
head into your office and not give homecaring another thought until your
business for the day is complete. This response is not automatic; it requires
rigorous discipline not to "pick up" the house before settling down to work.
I recommend a blindfold when walking through the house during the day.

Once you realize how comfortable, even pleasurable, it can be to work at home, it's easy to become reckless, taking on more than you can handle reasonably. That's because your work week is no longer structured around five days and eight to ten hours; the office is always open. Since you don't have a commute, you start working an hour earlier and continue an hour later than if you were working in an office. Since the office is right down the hall, it's easy to just pop in there after the kids are settled for the night to "finish up." Weekends are all too perfect for "catching up" on last week's leftovers or for "getting a head start" on next week's load. Eventually the days have no distinction and your working style is a sinkhole. Gradually your homework begins to resemble the slave labor of immigrants who were paid pennies for the piecework they produced in their tenement homes. But even if you're earning more money than before, if you no longer have a life at home you must learn to set limits.

Working from home can be a genuine step toward self-determination, once we honor the sense of balance we originally sought away from the office. "If people are highly successful in their profession they lose their senses," Virginia Woolf, who worked at home, cautions us. "Sight goes. They have no time to look at pictures. Sound goes. They have no time to listen to music. Speech goes. They have no time for conversation. They lose their sense of proportion—the relations between one thing and another. Humanity goes."

Heed her words.

OCTOBER 5

Mediation as Meditation

Most important for us is a good spiritual relationship between employees and management.

—Tatsuhiko Andoh

One morning your predictable conscious self surprises you. The alarm rings. She shuts it off and rolls over. Doesn't get out of bed. Shows no intention of getting dressed. She's on strike. Grievances have been ignored for years, maybe a lifetime. Working conditions are intolerable.

Annie Dillard tells us what happens next: "[Y]our worker—your one and only, your prized, coddled, and driven worker—is not going out on that job. Will not budge, not even for you, boss. Has been at it long enough to know when the air smells wrong; can sense a tremor through boot soles. Nonsense, you say; it is perfectly safe. But the worker will not go. Will not even look at the site. Just developed heart trouble. Would rather starve."

Maybe you haven't burned or bummed out, run away, landed in the hospital, or had a complete nervous breakdown. Yet. Maybe your family is still intact. At least they were still all accounted for at dinner last night. Maybe your friends are still speaking to you. Who knows? It's been six months since any of them saw you.

Today you're a very lucky woman. Don't push it. Life with you has been as much fun as serving time in a Siberian labor camp. You were a walkout waiting to happen. Management—the ego—can fend for herself until a new contract is agreed on. There are labor laws but none to protect against self-exploitation. The picket line will not be crossed until there are.

The time has come for mediation as meditation. Get a soothing cup of comfort and think about your ideal working day. If you could work in any style or setting, what would it be? What are your ideal working hours? Imagine your ideal workplace surroundings. What do you see? Now compare the ideal with the real. Is there any common ground? Can you introduce one ideal element into your present working environment? Few women can wave their hands and start an authentic life over from scratch. But all of us can begin working with what we've got. Working with our real life circumstances is *how* we render reality perfected. Perfection is unattainable. "Perfected" is possible.

Today, begin a little creative collective bargaining between choice and circumstances. "A work force is willing to go through many painful things if it believes in the long-term goals," labor economist Richard Belous reminds us. Creating an authentic working style is a long-term goal worth the wait.

OCTOBER 6

Downshifting: Living in Lower Gear

Things do not change; we change.

—HENRY DAVID THOREAU

Henry David Thoreau didn't set out to become the patron saint of simplicity. Actually, he sought a job as highway surveyor with the city of Concord, Massachusetts, in order to support his meager earnings as a writer. For years he had been the de facto keeper of passable paths around the town and the public had testified to the quality of his work. Nonetheless, the town officers declined to pay him a salary for his efforts. Packing his pens, bottles of ink, and paper, the would-be municipal employee borrowed an axe and headed for Walden Pond to conduct an experiment with life.

A century and a half later, Thoreau's experiment, reinterpreted for the

1990s, is called "downshifting," a word coined by business writer Amy Saltzman. It describes the emergence of a new breed of workplace trend-setters who are no longer willing to allow their work to ride roughshod over their lives. Like Thoreau, these career professionals are choosing not to keep pace with their fast-track peers. By setting career limits, they're slowing down in order to devote more time and creative energy to their families, communities, and personal needs. Saltzman documented the different ways in which these enlightened pathfinders have found authentic success in her thought provoking book *Downshifting: Reinventing Success on a Slower Track.*

Saltzman began tracking the downshifting trend in the late 1980s while working in New York as a senior editor at *Success* magazine. At the same time she was wrestling with maintaining some control over her own life while meeting the "intellectual and creative challenges of helping a young publication take hold in a competitive field." But she explains in her book: "I found myself feeling increasingly ill at ease with the message of a magazine that typically defined success in narrow, self-interested terms."

Then a chance encounter with a friend who was working as an editor for another magazine solidified Saltzman's misgivings about the fast track. As her friend assumed a "Gotta run, I'll call you, we'll do lunch" pose before dashing off down Madison Avenue, she inquired how Saltzman was doing. Saltzman told her friend that "things were fine, work was interesting, although I wasn't allowing it to take over my life; I was doing volunteer work a few evenings a week, reading a lot and working on a short story that I didn't think would ever get published but was enjoying it anyway."

This laissez-faire attitude baffled her friend, Saltzman recalls, because she was "unable to grasp the idea that I wasn't particularly busy at work and enjoying it." But Saltzman had made "a conscious decision to take life a lit-tle slower." In fact, she'd deliberately not gone after a promotion because she knew the job would eat up too many evenings and weekends. "Besides, while it might have looked impressive, I wasn't sure the position suited me at that point in my life. The decision, however, had not been made lightly and had continued to nag at me. When I saw my friend, I realized why. If we weren't always moving ahead and aiming for something higher and more impressive, if we didn't have that look of constantly being busy and in motion, we were somehow boring or even losers."

But no matter what her life might have looked like to an outsider, the reality of Saltzman's decision to take things more slowly was that her "life felt fuller, more interesting and more worthwhile than I could ever remember." By slowing down, Amy Saltzman discovered that "the fast track shackles us to a set of standards and rules that prohibit us from leading truly successful, happy lives."

When we begin to search for our authentic working style, we can make that discovery our own.

Learning to Create Boundaries

Before I built a wall I'd ask to know
What I was walling in or walling out.

—ROBERT FROST

Limits are the barbed wire of real life. Boundaries are split-rail fences. When you push past limits, personal or professional, there's a good chance of being pricked as you hurtle up and over. But boundaries set apart the Sacred with simple grace. There's always enough room to maneuver between the rails if you're willing to bend.

We want our lives to feel limitless, so we must learn the art of creating boundaries that protect, nurture, and sustain all we cherish. For most women, creating boundaries is excruciating, so we don't do it until we're pushed to the outer edge of tolerance. To create boundaries we must learn to say, *thus far and no further.* This means speaking up. Expressing our needs. Indicating our preferences. These moments are tense and can easily escalate into confrontations complete with tears, misunderstandings, and hurt feelings. This is why many women stay quiet, rendered virtually mute by unexpressed rage and unable to articulate any needs at all.

But even if we are mute, we're not powerless to draw a line in the sand. A talented friend of mine who has several books to her credit has long been married to an intelligent, charming, but critical man. Because her husband is more educated than she, she's always asked him to read her work and make suggestions about it. Unfortunately, he's often been rather harsh in his efforts to help and didn't realize how much of a sting his words inflicted. Sometimes he would even leave her work lying around before looking at it—long enough to convey, if not disdain, then certainly disrespect. After each such episode, it would take his wife days to pick up her pen again. Finally, she stopped showing her work to him, creating an unspoken boundary to protect her dreams. When she finally published her break-through novel, her husband was astonished at all the praise she was receiving and seemed embarrassed that he didn't understand what people were raving about. One night, she told me, she discovered him reading her best-seller. "This is good. This is very good," he told her in a surprised voice. "But why didn't you ask me to read it first?"

"Because you had no idea I was capable of this," she replied, with relish, finding her authentic voice at last.

Speaking the language of "no" is a good place to start creating boundaries. "'No' can be a beautiful word, every bit as beautiful as 'yes,'" writers

John Robbins and Ann Mortifee declare. "Whenever we deny our need to say 'no,' our self-respect diminishes," they tell us in *In Search of Balance: Discovering Harmony in a Changing World*. "It is not only our right at certain times to say 'no'; it is our deepest responsibility. For it is a gift to ourselves when we say 'no' to those old habits that dissipate our energy, 'no' to what robs us of our inner joy, 'no' to what distracts us from our purpose. And it is a gift to others to say 'no' when their expectations do not ring true for us, for in so doing we free them to discover more fully the truth of their own path. Saying 'no' can be liberating when it expresses our commitment to take a stand for what we believe we truly need."

OCTOBER 8

A Passion for Beauty

Beauty is an ecstasy; it is as simple as hunger.
—W. SOMERSET MAUGHAM

One baby step forward. Three giant steps back. I'd been experimenting with the first four Simple Abundance principles for almost a year and thought I had overcome the "buy me" syndrome. I enjoyed window shopping and did not feel diminished because I couldn't purchase something that captured my eye. Then I discovered a $45 lifestyle book crammed with pictures of things I love. Lush arrangements of flowers. Groupings of silver picture frames. Rose chintz. I flipped through visions I wanted to live in. Angrily I returned it to the bookstore shelf, furious that I couldn't afford the book and fed up that I was not living the lifestyle I thought I wanted. All I had may very well have been all I needed, but it certainly wasn't all I wanted.

After several hours of churning, I stopped. Something was going on within; this emotional response was occurring for a reason. I meditated on what had pushed my buttons. Was it that I had been living too stringently on a budget? Was I depressed about my lack of money for decorating trifles that I could once have purchased without a thought? Or was something deeper happening? The more I thought about it, the more I realized that I hadn't been paying enough attention to my passion for beauty. My deprivation was caused by not appreciating, savoring, or celebrating the beauty that already existed in my life—so much so that my soul had erupted into a volcano of protest. When something calls to us on a deep enough level to engage our emotions, our conscious attention is sought. Beauty was calling to me, not objects. After I realized this, I headed for a farmers' market for flowers. But instead of one bouquet, I treated myself to two. When I set my lush arrangement of flowers in the living room, my authentic craving for beauty was satisfied very inexpensively and the wants immediately quieted down.

Don't feel you have to deny or ignore your feelings when you want something beautiful but can't afford it. The desire offers clues to satisfy this holy hunger. Explore why you behold something as beautiful; use your impressions to jump-start your imagination. Beauty surrounds us. It is everywhere if we search for it, if we're open to having more of it in our lives. "Here we are, sitting in a shower of gold," the Australian novelist Christia Stead wrote in 1938, with "nothing to hold up but a pitchfork."

OCTOBER 9

Coping with Stress

In this world without quiet corners, there can be no easy escapes … from hullabaloo, from terrible, unquiet fuss.
—SALMAN RUSHDIE

Is there a woman alive who doesn't suffer from stress? If there is, seek her out, ask her to share her wisdom. When you find her, I'd be willing to bet she'll offer the following suggestions:

Cultivate gratitude.
Carve out an hour a day for solitude.
Begin and end the day with prayer, meditation, reflection.
Keep it simple.
Keep your house picked up.
Don't overschedule.
Strive for realistic deadlines.
Never make a promise you can't keep.
Allow an extra half hour for everything you do.
Create quiet surroundings at home and at work.
Go to bed at nine o'clock twice a week.
Always carry something interesting to read.
Breathe—deeply and often.
Move—walk, dance, run, find a sport you enjoy.
Drink pure spring water. Lots of it.
Eat only when hungry.
If it's not delicious, don't eat it.
Be instead of *do*.

Set aside one day a week for rest and renewal.
Laugh more often.
Luxuriate in your senses.
Always opt for comfort.
If you don't love it, live without it.
Let Mother Nature nurture.
Don't answer the telephone during dinner.
Stop trying to please everybody.
Start pleasing yourself.
Stay away from negative people.
Don't squander precious resources: time, creative energy, emotion.
Nurture friendships.
Don't be afraid of your passion.
Approach problems as challenges.
Honor your aspirations.
Set achievable goals.
Surrender expectations.
Savor beauty.
Create boundaries.
For every "yes," let there be a "no."
Don't worry; be happy.
Remember, happiness is a *living* emotion.
Exchange security for serenity.
Care for your soul.
Cherish your dreams.
Express love every day.
Search for your authentic self until you find her.

OCTOBER 10

Poise Wreckers

No quality is more attractive than poise—that deep sense of being at ease with yourself and the world.
—GOOD HOUSEKEEPING, *September 1947*

One of the most miserable days in my life graciously bestowed on me a priceless gift: the awareness that everyday poise is acquired or lost before we leave our homes.

Early in my writing career I was summoned to New York for an important meeting with a woman who, it was whispered, made Medea seem beatific. I decided I should prepare for this encounter by appearing just as formidable. Since deep within I was paralyzed with fear, I attempted to overcompensate for it with outward trappings. In a frenzy, I bought an expensive outfit that screamed "woman of substance," although it most assuredly didn't look like me. I also dramatically changed my hairstyle and makeup.

Because I felt so strange with my sophisticated new getup, I stayed up far too late the night before my trip fussing with everything instead of relaxing, packing leisurely, and getting some much-needed sleep. I was exhausted when I finally dropped into bed, so I just left my makeup, personal care necessities, and accessories strewn on top of the dresser.

In order to arrive in New York in time for the meeting, I had to get up at 4:30 A.M. It had never occurred to me that I would be virtually dressing in the dark, so as not to wake up Ed and Katie. It was difficult and frustrating feeling my way to find what I needed. I ended up rushing out in a state of utter panic to catch my train.

The meeting had not even begun before I became hot and sweaty. This was right after I felt the left sleeve of my blouse rip beneath my suit jacket. Since I'd never worn this outfit before, I didn't realize how tight the arms were or how much the skirt rode up on my hips when I sat down. The deep red nail polish that had looked so elegant in the salon the day before had chipped en route; naturally, I had no way of touching up my nails, so I tried to hide my hands. Several cups of coffee on the train, combined with raw nerves, had made my mouth dry, but I hadn't thought to carry breath freshener in my purse or ask for a glass of water before the meeting started.

I was so self-conscious during the meeting that I had difficulty focusing and certainly didn't have the confidence to offer my opinion, even though I felt very strongly about some of the decisions being made on my publishing project. Two excruciating hours later, the conference-from-hell was over. As the elevator doors closed, I swore I would never again leave another business meeting hot and sweaty, much the way Scarlett O'Hara swore with raised fist that she'd never again go hungry.

Of course, I realize I'm probably the only woman in the world to endure such humiliation at her own hands. But into each of our lives come important meetings, public appearances, and special occasions. Here are some practical antidotes for public awkwardness:

Never dress to impress others: dress to express your authentic sense of style. The only way we become truly at ease with ourselves is by knowing who we are. Never wear an outfit that you've never worn before to an important event; if your clothes need constant adjustment—pulling down a too-short skirt, hitching up a shoulder strap—you'll be unable to relax, focus, and function. If you buy something new, give it a trial run. *Never* drastically change your hair and makeup just before meeting new people for the first time. If you want a new look, put it together thoughtfully and gradually, so that you'll be at ease with the final effect.

If your dressing table is cluttered and your closet jumbled, you're bound to feel less than confident and serene when you're trying to put together a look that presents you at your best. To achieve order within, begin with outward order.

If your hair needs washing, your breath isn't fresh, or your makeup is stale, if your nails are rough or chipped or your antiperspirant is fading, you'll self-consciously avoid close encounters, giving others the wrong impression. Poise and personal grooming are soul mates. Women known for their sense of style and poise are impeccably groomed.

Poise is often overlooked when we think of putting together our authentic look. And why is developing poise so important? Because when we're not obsessively focusing on ourselves or our shortcomings, our smiles become warmer, our laughter more spontaneous, and our thoughtfulness blossoms. Outer poise mirrors inner poise. Moments spent in quiet contemplation to nurture our inner poise should be an essential part of every woman's daily beauty ritual. Self-possession costs us only time and self-nurturance. When we feel at ease with ourselves, we feel at ease in the world.

OCTOBER 11

It's Always Something

It's always something.
—ROSEANNE ROSEANNADANNA (GILDA RADNER)

And, of course, it is. Sometimes it's a damn nuisance. Sometimes it's soul shattering. But it's always something. It's real life.

After Gilda Radner left *Saturday Night Live* where she created some unforgettable, funny women characters—Roseanne Roseannadanna, Emily Litella—she set out to create a life for herself. For a decade she had been a successful workaholic as life whizzed by. Falling in love with Gene Wilder helped her realize the pleasure of lowering gears. By the time they married in 1984, she wanted to pursue her dream of becoming a writer. Always observant and knowing rich material when she found it, she began a book called *Portrait of the Artist as a Housewife*, a collection of stories, poems, and vignettes celebrating domesticity and the humor inherent in toaster ovens and plumbers. It would have been hilarious.

But real life grabbed her attention with a diagnosis of ovarian cancer, and a grittier book emerged, *It's Always Something*, a defiantly irreverent, moving memoir. Like other women who struggle with life-threatening illness, Gilda mourned "my lost joy, my happiness, my exhilaration with life." The day before her diagnosis, life stretched before her, luminous in its limitless possibilities. The moment after being told she had cancer, life's dimensions shrank to twenty-four-hour stretches.

In a moving essay contained in *Minding the Body*: *Women Writers on Body and Soul*, Judith Hooper rightly admonishes us: "We go around thinking that real life is about adding a rec room to the basement, but this is not about real life. Cancer is real life. When you accept cancer, it is as if new systems within the organism automatically open—like the oxygen masks and flotation systems that automatically drop in your lap on a 747 in an emergency. When you walk this earth on borrowed time, each day on the calendar is a beloved friend you know for only a short time."

You begin to *live*.

Why must we find a lump in our breast before this occurs? Do you know? Because I certainly don't. But I do know a wonderful woman who was very active at her children's school for many years, largely because after she had volunteered a generous amount of personal time, no one else came forward to take her place. The hours she put into her PTA related work were the equivalent of a full-time but unpaid second job. When she made the terrible discovery that she had breast cancer, she admitted to close friends that in a strange way, she was relieved. Cancer meant she could start saying "No," create boundaries, and finally put down the school committee burden without guilt. Now she could ransom back her life. After all, no one expects a woman fighting breast cancer to do anything but take care of herself. Of course, she was right.

When I heard this story I wanted to scream and cry: it was almost too much to take in. Yes, it's always something. *But it doesn't always have to have your name on it.* I pray we never find a lump, but I pray just as fervently that we never squander or surrender another precious day for whatever reason.

And if you've already found a lump, I pray that you'll grow Whole and old in joy, peace, and grace, gifting us for many years with your wisdom.

Heaven knows, we need it.

OCTOBER 12

A Tale of Two Times

It was the best of times, it was the worst of times.

—CHARLES DICKENS

Once upon a time.
Up until this time.
For the time being.

Time and time again.

All in good time.

Time's up!

Since the dawn of Time, we've tried to understand her nature. Why? In order to control her. But time is a holy mystery, an extravagant gift meant to be experienced, not understood. Certainly not controlled. Why do you think we're crazed half the time?

Time's mystery is difficult for most women to appreciate because we've so little of it. Although we've all been allotted twenty-four hours each day, it doesn't seem to go very far. So if we experience anything at all, it's dread, because we keep running out of time. Again and again. And it doesn't matter what *kind* of time it is—Greenwich, daylight saving, standard, eastern, mountain, central, or pacific. All that matters is we never seem to have enough of it. Which is why all the women I know constantly feel time-worn.

For centuries those with time on their hands—saints, poets, mystics, masters, sages, and philosophers—have pondered time's enigma. They've discovered her duality. As the sculptor and poet Henry Van Dyke explains: "Time is/ Too slow for those who Wait/ Too swift for those who Fear/ Too long for those who grieve/ Too short for those who Rejoice . . ." Slow and swift are time's parallel realities, the yin and yang of existence.

In order to know a semblance of serenity during the days of our lives, we also need to discover Time's twin nature, which the ancient Greeks called *chronos* and *kairos*.

Chronos is clocks, deadlines, watches, calendars, agendas, planners, schedules, beepers. Chronos is time at her worst. Chronos keeps track. Chronos is a delusion of grandeur. Chronos is running the Marine Corps marathon in heels. In chronos we think only of ourselves. Chronos is the world's time.

Kairos is transcendence, infinity, reverence, joy, passion, love, the Sacred. Kairos is intimacy with the Real. Kairos is time at her best. Kairos lets go. In kairos we escape the dungeon of self. Kairos is a Schubert waltz in nineteenth-century Vienna with your soul mate. Kairos is Spirit's time.

We exist in chronos. We long for kairos. That's *our* duality. Chronos requires speed so that it won't be wasted. Kairos requires space so that it might be savored. We *do* in chronos. In kairos we're allowed *to be*.

We think we've never known kairos, but we have: when making love, when meditating or praying, when lost in music's rapture or literature's reverie, when planting bulbs or pulling weeds, when watching over a sleeping child, when reading the Sunday comics together in bed, when delighting in a sunset, when exulting in our passions. We know joy in kairos, glimpse beauty in kairos, remember what it means to be alive in kairos, reconnect with our Divinity in kairos.

So how do we exchange chronos for kairos?

By slowing down.

By concentrating on one thing at a time.

By going about whatever we are doing as if it were the only thing worth doing at that moment.

By pretending we have all the time in the world, so that our subconscious will kick in and make it so.

By making time.

By taking time.

It only takes a moment to cross over from chronos into kairos, but it does take *a moment*. All that kairos asks is our willingness to stop running long enough to hear the music of the spheres.

Today, be willing to join in the dance.

Now you're in kairos.

OCTOBER 13

Absolutely Fabulous

I have a little shadow that goes in and out with me,
And what can be the use of [her] is more than I can see.
                                                    —ROBERT LOUIS STEVENSON

For many years I've had difficulty identifying, imagining, and personalizing my "shadow," Carl Jung's name for the darker self lurking deep within. Jung believed that our shadows are the composite of all the shameful emotions, nasty impulses, and negative aspects of our personalities that we attempt to bury in order to show an acceptable face to the world. Think of the raving lunatic the family keeps locked in a tower in gothic novels, or Robert Louis Stevenson's Dr. Jekyll and Mr. Hyde, and you get the idea.

Unfortunately, not knowing *is* what hurts us, especially when sublimating our shadow. In *Guilt Is the Teacher, Love Is the Lesson*, Joan Borysenko describes the fermentation of our "ghostly double" as "getting up a head of steam, getting wilder and wilder inside us, informing our behaviors without our consciously knowing they are there" until they express themselves "quite suddenly and explosively in accidents, impulsive behavior, illness, lapses of judgment. . . . In other words, an unexplored shadow leaves us stuck without understanding why, assaulted by strange impulses, and powerless to change."

To be honest, even though I understood Jung's concept of the shadow, I had no real desire to get to know her better. Then another of life's lessons opened up my eyes. What I discovered shocked me, but didn't send me shrieking in terror. It made me laugh.

Have you ever seen the wicked British sitcom *Absolutely Fabulous*? It's the

Fawlty Towers of the fashion world and revolves around two fortysomething debauchees—Edina and Patsy—whose only redeeming social value is their loyalty to each other. Edina—known as "Edie" by her intimates—is a dizzy, pudgy fashion publicist, whose greatest ambition is to "look completely happening." She has two ex-husbands, one long-suffering, sensible, and disapproving teenage daughter, and a mother who can't figure out where she went wrong. There isn't a New Age fad Edie hasn't embraced in a futile effort to find enlightenment, including chanting, colonic irrigation, and isolation chambers. Patsy is an anorexic, alcoholic, nymphomaniac fashion editor with a blond beehive the size of Trump Tower—an homage to her icon, Ivana. Edie's never seen in anything but designer hallucinations; Patsy's never seen without a cigarette dangling from her red lips or a glass of champagne in her hand. To Edie and Patsy, everyone is either "sweetie," "darling," or "sweetie darling"; anything pleasurable is "absolutely fabulous," including their opinions of each other.

They're vile, vain, vapid, vacuous. Shallow, selfish. Dumb and dumber. Hilarious. They're certainly not role models, but most assuredly, they're the stuff of our shadows.

The first time I watched Edie and Patsy cavorting around London, I fell off the couch in tears, hooting, howling, and holding my sides. Edie was my evil twin, my shadow. I recognized her instantly. Edie gives new meaning to the awareness of "there but for the grace of God." But I love her despite all her flaws, or maybe because of them.

I suspect there are many women who identify with some part of Edie and Patsy. Or Thelma and Louise. All these women are out of control, so watch out. But we can't afford to be; there are people who need care and there are jobs waiting to be done. But if we could shed every responsibility and inhibition for a half a day, perhaps we'd resemble one of these dolls. And while that's amusing, it's not pretty. Still, whenever I am stressed to the max, I'll relax with a glass of wine and watch my Ab Fab videos. I always come back to real life chuckling and, in a strange way, renewed. Edie happily goes back into the dark, having basked in my undivided attention, and I contentedly return to writing, carpooling, and making meat loaf and mashed potatoes for supper.

Our shadows are only to be feared if we repress them, if we refuse to give them the recognition they need. In her book *Women Who Run with the Wolves*, Clarissa Pinkola Estes suggests "opening the door to the shadow realm a little and letting out various elements a few at a time, relating to them, finding use for them, . . ." so that we can "reduce [the risk of] being surprised by shadow sneak attacks and unexpected explosions" like a "Roman candle gone berserk."

Edie, self-medicating with booze, cigarettes, drugs, shopping, and sex to mask her pain, blindly embraces self-awareness trends because she's afraid to follow the wisdom of her heart. She's consumed with her appearance to avoid recognizing deeper concerns; she's a slave to fashion because she doesn't trust her instincts. But as Dr. Estes reassures us, the shadow "can contain the divine, the luscious, beautiful and powerful aspects of personhood" such as "the woman who can speak well of herself without denigration, who can face herself without cringing, who works to perfect her craft."

Edie's craft, like our own, is discovering her authenticity. But in our search, sweetie darling, we must not ignore what Dr. Estes calls "these discarded, devalued, and unacceptable aspects of soul and self," even if they make us feel uncomfortable. Especially—sweetie darling—if we long for our lives to be rich, deep, and absolutely fabulous.

Kiss, kiss.

OCTOBER 14

The Ultimate Result of All Ambition

To be happy at home is the ultimate result of all ambition.
—SAMUEL JOHNSON

The wisdom contained in this one sentence is worth meditating on for the rest of our lives; it's probably the reason Dr. Johnson earned his final resting place with the "Immortals" in Westminster Abbey.

Why are you working so hard? To be happy at home. But you're never *at home*—in mind, body, or spirit—because you're always working. So why are you working so hard? To be happy at home.

This is not a Zen koan. Life *is* a paradox, but we don't have to make it any harder than it is already. We've been on this path for ten months, but if you're on the cusp of grasping this insight, you're miles ahead of most of us.

Hold this thought: *the ultimate result of all ambition is to be happy at home.* Engrave this truth on your consciousness. Lay the track deeply, so that even when you're on your own version of automatic pilot, you'll be homeward bound. Write it on the palm of your hand; sneak a peek at it three times a day. Mutter it under your breath before attending a budget review that starts a half hour before the children need to be picked up; before agreeing to entertain out-of-town clients on your anniversary; before answering faxes on Sunday or leaving voice mail messages at midnight.

What is the ultimate result of all ambition?

You know.

Inscribe it on your heart. Needlepoint it on a pillow. Say it out loud when you get up and just before retiring. Make it your *mantra*—that personal phrase that brings all things into focus. Doing so will help remind you that the greatest adventure of our lives is finding our way back home.

OCTOBER 15

The Quality of the Day

To affect the quality of the day, that is the highest of arts.
—Henry David Thoreau

We know now that there are many aspects to real life in which our opinion is neither sought nor required. Sometimes, despite our best efforts and positive thinking, health, fortune, and/or peace elude us. But the one thing we do have absolute control over is the quality of our days. Even when we're grief stricken, racked with pain, sick from worry, deeply depressed, squeezed by circumstances—how we greet, meet, and complete each day is our choosing.

We hate to hear this.

Of course, when we're sick, worried, grieving, depressed, or frantic, we're not very interested in the day's quality; we just want the misery to end. But wishing the day away is also a creative choice, even if it's not a deliberate one.

Artists of the everyday excel in elevating the simple to the level of the Sacred. You can use whatever you have on hand—a meal, a conversation, humor, affection—to create comfort and contentment—to put a positive spin, if not on the overall quality of the day, then on critical moments of it. For some time now I have been conducting a top-secret experiment with life, as Thoreau suggests we do. I wanted to see just how much influence I really had on the day's character. So the first words I speak in the morning are: "Thank you for the gift of this wonderful day."

Here are the initial findings, but you will not like them. Nor did I.

- All days are wonderful in direct proportion to the creative energy invested in them. No investment, no return.
- Even lousy days possess hidden wonder. Sometimes all you need is a moment of attitude adjustment to shift your perception of an entire afternoon and move forward into a pleasant evening.
- Weather does not seem to affect the experiment. Gray, cold, and rainy days spent in an office are just as susceptible to the warming influence of enthusiasm as are sunny days spent lying in a hammock sipping sangria.
- Days that are expected to be wonderful before they begin turn out to be so much more frequently than days greeted with grumbling.
- The results of this experiment suggest that it doesn't matter whether a day is good or bad. What matters is what we do with it.

We knew that.

Ceremonials for Common Days

How, but in custom and ceremony,
Are innocence and beauty born?

—W. B. YEATS

Ceremony and custom give birth to beauty, restoring a sense of wonder to our daily round. Most of us are far too jaded for our own good. We've seen it all. Nothing surprises us anymore.

Which is precisely our problem. We only *think* we've seen it all. What we haven't begun to see is the abundance that surrounds us, the beauty that gift wraps the extravagance of each day.

The best way to renew our sense of the Sacred is through personal rituals. I treasure a little book called *Ceremonials of Common Days* written in 1923 by Abbie Graham. I found it languishing on a dark, dusty secondhand bookshelf and ransomed it for a dollar. Now my hand-printed oracle, with its blackboard cover of yellow and green woodcut flowers, sits on my desk. The gold lettering on its spine reminds me that perception comes only when we pace ourselves. Nothing is too insignificant in the eyes of the authentic self. Nothing is beneath notice.

There are numerous holidays (from the Old English "holy day") throughout the year, falling just when we need cheering up. We respond to them as if company's come to call, bringing out our special dishes, linens, crystal, flowers, and candles.

We actually do most of our living among the common days, taking them for granted just the way we do the people we love. Yet myriad occasions during the course of each day cry out for consecration.

A liturgy of commonplace moments ripe for personal ritual might include sipping the first cup of coffee; putting on one's public face; eating at one's desk; window shopping; making a long-desired purchase; crossing the threshold at night; changing into comfortable clothes; hearing the sound of a loved one's homecoming footsteps; sitting down to a simple meal; being paid; traveling on business; sharing a laugh, or a confidence, or both; indulging in rainy day reveries; curling up to watch videos at home; sleeping late and having breakfast in bed; starting a good book; losing five pounds; having a good cry; and so to bed. There is no shortage of common day ceremonies waiting to be enjoyed, only weary imaginations in need of inspirational transfusions.

"To make a day, it took an Evening and a Morning—at least to make the first day. But that was when the world was new and there was in it only light and darkness, day and night, and God," Abbie Graham calls to our remembrance. "The world has grown more complicated since that creative era. To make a day now it takes bells and whistles and clocks and desks and committees and meetings and money and a serial of daily newspaper editions, and hungry people, and people who are too tired, and luncheon engagements and telephones, and noise and shouting and much hurrying. All these things and many others it takes now, in addition to an evening and a morning.

"Perhaps these ingredients are necessary for the concoction of a day; but when I come to observe the Ceremonial of Evenings and Mornings, they do not seem to be the reason why light and darkness were separated and day and night created. Whatever be my philosophy, I, too, must work to make enough money to pay my share toward the bells and whistles and the trains and the luncheon engagements and the privilege of hurrying.

"But as I watch the stars of evening, and in the morning open my window toward the east, I shall observe the Ceremonial of quietness of heart, of simplicity, and poise of spirit, that I may keep my soul and the souls of others free from entanglements in the machinery of a day."

OCTOBER 17

The Habit of Being

So many worlds, so much to do
So little done, such things to be.

—ALFRED, LORD TENNYSON

During her lifetime (1925–1964), neither the camera nor the critics were very kind to Flannery O'Connor. She was as unphotogenic as she was unapologetic. The camera's harsh lens couldn't capture the intelligence, passion, imagination, exuberance, wit, and grace her family and friends knew and loved. For much of her adult life, the camera only recorded a body and face ravaged by illness. Her critics didn't appreciate her finely honed sense of the grotesque—that Southern specialty—with all its satire, black humor, and pathos, nor her obsession with religion. She was a cartographer of the human soul, and her searing words gave expression to the yearning of misfits. The characters in her novels and short stories were forlorn and flawed, searching for redemption whether they knew it or not.

Redemption was a major theme in Flannery's work as well as the thread that held her life together. "There are some of us who have to pay for our faith every step of the way and who have to work out dramatically what it would be like without it," she wrote, "and if being without it would ultimately be possible or not." Her rural Georgia surroundings, coupled with her affliction with lupus at twenty-five (the disease that killed her father when she was a child), contributed to a deep sense of isolation, for she was unable to care for herself and lived, until her death at thirty-nine, with her mother.

What her close friends remember best about Flannery was her determination to revere and savor the gift of every day. Her close friend (and editor of her letters), Sally Fitzgerald, calls it "the habit of being," a deep joie de vivre that animated her daily round. Flannery's passion for life, Sally Fitzgerald tells us, was "rooted in her talent and the possibilities of her work, which she correctly saw as compensating her fully for any deprivations she had to accept, and as offering a scope for living that most of us never dream of encompassing." Her mornings were sacred, reserved for her writing, but the rest of the day was devoted to being Flannery.

The habit of being—the exultation in the present moment—is an exquisite concept, one that could enrich our lives beyond measure. We're all habitual creatures, but usually we practice the *habits of doing*: getting up, making breakfast, getting children off to school and getting ourselves to work. Then there are our *habits of brooding*: projecting into the future, dwelling on the past, nursing old wounds, holding imaginary conversations, indulging in comparisons, conducting endless mental calculations about money, gnawing on regrets, second-guessing inspiration, ruminating on problems at work, anticipating the worst. The habits of brooding are rooted in the past or the future, and they can rob the present moment of all harmony, beauty, and joy.

But what if, as curators of our own contentment, we deliberately cultivated the *habit of being*: a heightened awareness of Real Life's abundance? The habit of being is a grateful appreciation for the good surrounding us, no matter what our circumstances might be today. What if you knew there was always going to be a simple pleasure to look forward to every few hours? What if you made sure there was? How do you think you would greet the day?

Flannery O'Connor generously offered struggling writers advice. To one she wrote: "Wouldn't it be better for you to discover a meaning in what you write than to impose one? Nothing you write will lack meaning because the meaning is in you." I believe this passion for discovering meaning extends to the art of the everyday as well. Once you commit to cultivating the habit of being, nothing in your daily round will lack meaning because you'll discover that the meaning is within you.

OCTOBER 18

A Lesson from Loss

Loss as muse. Loss as character. Loss as life.

—ANNA QUINDLEN

It was just another manic Monday for Nancy, Cheryl, Valerie, Kathleen, Gilda, Elizabeth, and Patricia. Just another business trip, another swing on the flying trapeze. Children were kissed and sent off to school; babies were left with sitters; spouses were reminded about soccer practice, the casserole in the freezer, the laundry that needed to be picked up. Their day was frazzled or pleasant, successful or disappointing. Does it really matter? At the end of it, perhaps there was an opportunity to grab some small treat in the gift shop before boarding American Eagle commuter Flight 4148 to Chicago's O'Hare Airport. Waiting for them were loved ones eager to report on the day's happenings, cabs to catch, connections to make.

Instead, there were news bulletins, phone calls, disbelief, devastation, shock, pain, grief, hearts broken, dreams dashed. Nancy (forty-eight), Cheryl (forty-four), Valerie (forty-four), Kathleen (forty-seven), Gilda (forty-three), Elizabeth (thirty-seven), and Patricia (forty-two) never made it home. For, as the plane was descending, the inconceivable occurred. All the women perished in a fiery crash, along with sixty-one other souls. In their final moments, did they realize they weren't going to make it? What were their last thoughts?

It certainly wasn't the deal made or lost or how hassled their day had been. Surely their last thoughts were Real. Maybe the faces of those they loved pushed away the fear. Maybe there was no time for regrets. I hope so. I pray so.

If we are alive, we cannot escape loss. Loss is a part of real life. "Have you ever thought, when something dreadful happens, a moment ago things were not like this; let it be *then* not *now*, anything but *now*?" the English novelist Mary Stewart asks. "And you try and try to remake *then*, but you know you can't. So you try to hold the moment quite still and not let it move on and show itself."

Today might be tough for you. You might not want the next moment to show itself, to reveal the twists and turns of life's mystery. But at least you have it. You still have life. A choice as to how you will live this precious day.

Don't wish it away. Don't waste it. For the love of all that's holy, redeem one hour. Hold it close. Cherish it. Above all, be grateful for it. Let your thanksgiving rise above the din of disappointment—opportunities lost, mistakes made, the clamor of all that has not yet come.

And if today is so horrendous that the gift doesn't seem worth acknowledging; if you can't find one moment to enjoy, one simple pleasure to savor, one friend to call, one person to love, one thing to share, one smile to offer; if life is so difficult you don't want to bother living it to the fullest, then don't live today for yourself.

Live it for Nancy, Cheryl, Valerie, Kathleen, Gilda, Elizabeth, and Patricia.

OCTOBER 19

Compliments

Nowadays we are all of us so hard up that the only pleasant things to pay are compliments.

—OSCAR WILDE

All women need more compliments in their lives. We need to give more of them to our families, friends, and strangers. We need to hear more of them, even if we have to give them to ourselves. But most of all, we need to bask in them.

In our heart of hearts, most of us feel that we deserve more compliments than we receive. But maybe one of the reasons we don't hear as many compliments as we'd like is because whenever one has our name on it, we return it to the sender.

"Oh, this old thing?"
"I got it on sale."
"It's from a flea market."
"Do you really think so?"
"It was nothing."

Remember, if we send good things away or aren't open to receiving them, at some point the Universe may no longer bother with us. And who would blame it? No one enjoys hanging around an ingrate, and that's exactly what we are when we discount the marvelous about ourselves.

It's interesting that the first dictionary definition of a compliment is "an expression of esteem." Perhaps we have a difficult time accepting compliments because deep down we don't believe we deserve them. When we aren't willing to receive praise, it's because our self-esteem is flagging.

Today, be receptive. Start with the assumption that you're beautiful, dazzling, absolutely fabulous. Ask Spirit to reveal how gorgeous and brilliant you really are. Every time someone pays you a compliment, accept it as if an angel had just whispered Spirit's appreciation. Smile and say, "Thank you. How nice of you to notice." Become abundant with your compliments to others. We're all so fragile, especially when we put on a brave face. A sincere compliment can penetrate beneath even the most sophisticated masks to soothe troubled souls. The woman you think needs compliments the least is probably the one who needs them most.

Cultivate the habit of giving at least one compliment a day to another human being, as well as to yourself. You'll feel good when you do, and soon it will become one of your habits of being. Just as words can hurt, words can heal.

OCTOBER 20

Complaints

If you have not slept, or if you have slept, or if you have headache, or sciatica, or leprosy, or thunder-stroke, I beseech you, by all angels, to hold your peace, and not pollute the morning.
—RALPH WALDO EMERSON

Complaints we know. Complaints we're good at. Most of us have already mastered the art of the complaint in all its many variations: gripe, groan, moan, kvetch, bitch, whine. Probably the only woman on the face of the earth who doesn't carry on the way we do is Mother Teresa.

One of the reasons we love our close friends so dearly is that they allow us to complain knowing that we'll return the favor. But if we really love them, don't you think it's about time we started sparing them? Some of us spend half our lives griping. It's time to get a grip. When we bitch and moan we're not much fun to listen to; just because you can't see the eyes at the other end of the receiver doesn't mean they're not rolling or shut. Try new outlets to channel hostility: moan on your dialogue pages, shout in the shower, blow off steam as you walk, or scream in your car as you wait in traffic. Spirit's big enough to take it. Besides, it's all been heard before. There's nothing new under the sun.

I'm not suggesting that we suppress our negative feelings. But the petty stuff we're often foaming at the mouth about isn't worth the breath it steals. Our words are powerful, so powerful that they can change our reality—the quality of our days and nights. Moaning rarely makes either us or those around us feel better. In fact, it often makes everyone feel worse. Learning to shrug is the beginning of wisdom.

Alternatively, learn to be creative about your complaining. Barbara Sher believes "in the efficacy of complaining the way some people believe in the efficacy of prayer." In fact, she encourages "hard time sessions." In her book *Wishcraft*, Sher suggests that the next time you feel as though you'll explode, announce beforehand that you need a hard time session. Tell anyone in close range that you're mad, nervous, fed up, and not going to take it anymore. Tell them for the next five minutes you're going to lose it. Tell them not to pay any attention and not to take it personally. Then run amok. You'll probably end up feeling much better without having to offer apologies or wipe away tears. You may even end up laughing.

Today, if you must complain, at least be creative about it.

OCTOBER 21

Comparisons

Let me remember that each life must follow its own course, and that what happens to other people has absolutely nothing to do with what happens to me.

—MARJORIE HOLMES

Comparisons are irresistible but insidious, odious, and very often our self-torture of choice.

Today, let's meditate on not coveting our neighbor's husband, figure, home, clothes, income, or career. Not to mention her accomplishments, achievements, awards, recognition, and fame. Usually it's only one woman whose bounteous blessings push our buttons of raging insecurity; we really don't care if most of the world has more than we have, we only care that "she" has and we have not. Often the subject of our hostility is not personally known to us, though the life she leads in print is. Secretly we stalk the newspapers and magazines accumulating evidence of *her* good fortune. Or she could be one of your friends (deepest sympathy) which is horrendous, because you must hear firsthand accounts of all you're missing at the moment. Whoever she is, she's the devil in disguise, because you insist on measuring your life, success, bank account, and self-worth against hers.

Obviously, I couldn't ruminate on coveting, jealousy, envy, and making oneself utterly miserable with comparisons unless I was vaguely familiar with this sin against authenticity. (All right, intimately familiar.) Would you believe my favorite poem (and probably that of every other writer in the world) is Clive James's funny, spiteful ode, "The Book of My Enemy Has Been Remaindered"?

This is not good. This is not enlightenment. We're grown women. We're bigger than this. Aren't we?

Well, even if we aren't, comparisons hurt us in profound ways. They undermine our confidence. Shut down our flow of creative energy. Short-circuit our access to Power. Deplete our self-esteem. Suck the life force from our marrow. Coveting destroys what is Sacred within. Instead of comparing yourself to another woman, why not just take a wet leather lash and beat yourself senseless? It's easier to recover from physical abuse than self-inflicted psychic brutality.

The next time you're tempted to compare your life to another's, pause for a moment. Remind yourself, over and over, that *there is no competition on the spiritual plane.* The blessings your nemesis has received also can be yours as soon as you are *really* ready to receive with an open heart all the good fortune created just for you.

And when will that be? As soon as you can bless the woman you secretly curse; as soon as you can give thanks for her happiness and success as much as your own because it demonstrates the abundance of Real Life.

OCTOBER 22

Compromises

Compromise, if not the spice of life, is its solidity.
—Phyllis McGinley

Whether you're single, married, with children or without, it's not possible to get through the day without agreeing to at least one compromise. There are little compromises, like car pool schedules and homecaring jobs, and there are bigger ones like working conditions and coexisting with teenagers. Tolerable compromises are those we enter into fully—with complete knowledge in advance of exactly what we're surrendering. The other kind of compromises—the ones many of us make day in day out—are the strong, silent type. They're strong because we're stuck with them and silent because they're unconscious or unspoken.

Compromises are the art of the bottom line. We can bend only so far and then we break. Knowing just how far you can bend is the first step in making sane agreements, but this isn't as easy as it sounds.

The more complicated life becomes, the simpler your bottom line must be. How about this. What *must* you have from this situation? What do you absolutely *need*? If you need it, you must have it. It's non-negotiable. If you didn't *need* it to survive, it—whatever "it" is—wouldn't be a need. Then it would be a want. Unfortunately "wants" are the currency of compromise. I want, you want, we all want, which is why we bargain. Keep in mind that your want might be another's legitimate need. The best compromises, like a workable lifestyle, cover all your needs while satisfying a few of your wants.

If you dread it, don't agree to it. If you do end up doing it despite your dread, you'll depise the whole deal, including the woman who agreed to it: you.

Be affable. Try to see the other person's point of view. Be flexible. Be as generous as you can without gagging. Ask that the highest good for all parties be achieved. Trust your instincts. Pay attention to physical clues, especially your gut; it's there not only to aid in digestion, but to serve as a reliable aid in discerning what's best for you.

Above all, follow Janis Joplin's advice: "Don't compromise yourself. You are all you've got."

OCTOBER 23

Money and the Meaning of Life

The problem of money dogs our steps throughout the whole of our lives, exerting a pressure that, in its way, is as powerful and insistent as any other problem of human existence. And it haunts the spiritual search as well.

—JACOB NEEDLEMAN

Take a deep breath. Relax. Be open. For the next week, we're going to think about money. The love of it. The lack of it. How we accumulate, spend, save, and squander it, lust for it, worship it, worry about it, work for it. Like success, money is an emotionally volatile issue for most women. It's probably the most complicated relationship we have—and the one that most controls our lives because we let it.

"Our lives are hell not because money is so important to us, but because it is not important enough," insists Jacob Needleman, author of the illuminating meditation *Money and the Meaning of Life*. If money were more important to us, we would seek to understand its impact and how it influences every aspect of our lives.

In October 1967 Jacob Needleman, a mild-mannered college professor of philosophy and comparative religion, wandered into a San Francisco boutique that sold spiritual memorabilia. A beautiful Jewish prayer shawl caught his eye, and he decided to buy it. But the shop manager refused to let him pay for it with a personal check. Totally out of character, the professor threw a tantrum. It didn't work, but it did start him thinking about the role that money plays in our lives.

"Think of our relationship to nature, to ideas, to pleasure," he challenges us. "Think of our sense of self-identity and self-respect; think of where we live and with what things we surround ourselves; think of all our impulses to help others or serve a larger cause; where we go, how we travel, with whom we associate—or just think of what you were doing yesterday, or what you will be doing tomorrow, or in an hour. The money factor is there, wrapped around or lodged inside everything. Think of what you want or what you dream of, for now, or next year, or for the rest of your life. It will take money, a certain, definite amount."

It would have taken only $35 for Professor Needleman to obtain the coveted prayer shawl if he'd had the cash in his pocket. Because he did not, that object of desire, over a quarter of a century later, remains a vivid memory. "It [was] a beauty—fine, delicately knotted fringes; rich deep pure white silk." It was not to be his. But "in such personal, apparently trivial events, the likes of which are experienced daily by all of us, we may see what really lies behind our attitudes toward money."

One of the things we probably don't realize is how hypocritical we are about money. We want it but we don't want to appear as if we do; we fear and desire it in the same heartbeat. Professor Needleman believes that money is a force we must face in the late twentieth century in much the same way that sex was an issue for previous generations. What is undeniable is that money is the raw material from which we build our lives, whether we like it or not.

One of our difficulties is that too often we confuse spiritual yearnings with material wants. For instance, you long for serenity. You assume that serenity is a resident comma in your checking account balance. And while being able to pay your bills easily—a practical definition of serenity—often comes with a fatter paycheck, the comma requires an expenditure of more time, creative energy, and emotion. The redistribution of your life force means subtracting it from the seemingly "disposable" segments of your life—family time, personal pursuits, spiritual growth, rest, and recreation—and moving it to your work allotment. More work, more pay, more stress. More stress, less serenity, no matter how much money you're earning. In becoming experts at quantity instead of quality, we rob our souls of Real Life's richness.

In order to find balance between the two spheres that pull us in opposite directions—material and spiritual—Jacob Needleman suggests we consider the practical advice in the ancient admonishment "Render unto Caesar that which is Caesar's and unto God that which is God's."

"The entire problem of life in contemporary culture can be defined as the challenge to understand that saying of Jesus," Needleman writes. "It is not so simple; in fact, it is immensely difficult. It requires that we begin to understand what in ourselves belongs to the transcendent realm and what to the material realm. And then to give to each what is due to each—no more and no less. This is what it means to be human. Meaning can come from no other source than this."

OCTOBER 24

Worrying about Money

Concern should drive us into action and not into a depression.
—KAREN HORNEY

Worrying about money never paid a bill. If it did, at least there'd be a legitimate reason for indulging in worry. Actually, worrying about money repels, rather than attracts, prosperity—not exactly what we had in mind. Worrying about money sends toxic signals: fear, lack, deprivation. When your subconscious mind continually receives negative impulses, it duplicates in your daily round whatever it was instructed to manifest, such as fear, lack, deprivation.

Don't panic. Every little thought you've ever had doesn't instantly materialize. Thank God. The results of our thinking can take years to appear in our lives, but as a woman thinketh, so doth she experience.

Here's a perfect example. Many people assume that the reason that Amy Dacyczyn, the best-selling author of *The Tightwad Gazette* (and a newsletter of the same name), raked in her first $1 million, paid off her mortgage, and hired financial planners, is because her parsimonious philosophy was timely.

Well, that's one explanation. A metaphysical one could be that Amy loves money. For over a decade before she started her newsletter, which led to her book, she reveled in her passion every day. This love of money was characterized by a zealous frugality and fanatical economizing. It still is. Here is a woman who does not spend a penny unless it's pried loose from her hand. Now Love is the most powerful positive emotion in existence. Love attracts. Amy's positive cash fixation was expressed in continuous thought. As she sowed, so she reaped. Eventually money began arriving at her doorstep in royalty and subscription checks.

Now thinking about money every minute of every day until the millennium isn't how I choose to live. But what are the alternatives to worry?

First, calculate whether you have enough money for all your needs *today*. If you do, stop focusing on lack this minute. You probably have all the money you need to take care of today's needs and more. It doesn't matter how much more. Anytime you have more than you need, you have abundance. Catch yourself the next time you start dwelling on what you don't have; switch tracks by noticing and appreciating all you do have. As this becomes a personal habit, you'll find yourself coping well with any amount of money you have, rather than worrying about it.

Worry is a future-tense emotion. Worry is a projection of a possible— not necessarily probable—scenario. *Will* there be enough? Where *will* it come from? How long *will* it last?

My favorite anti-worrying-about-money suggestion comes from Sanaya Roman and Duane Packer, the authors of *Creating Money: Keys to Abundance*. Instead of worrying, consider what actions you could take to create money. "Ask yourself, 'How can I *create* money today?' There is an enormous difference in the energy you send out to the universe when you focus on creating money rather than needing money; the first is magnetic to money and the latter is not."

Transforming every "What will I do?" into "What can I do?" fuels your fiscal creativity, restoring a sense of peace as you pursue prosperity.

"'Constant worry about money blocks your creativity and clear thinking," Roman and Packer remind us. "When you have very little money, you are learning many lessons that will make it easier to handle money when it comes. To break through this level, you may need to keep your life simple and uncomplicated in terms of money, expenses, demands and needs. Think of yourself as the rose bush that is cut back in the winter so that it may grow strong in the spring."

OCTOBER 25

On Paying Bills

Here are the bills again.
I always dread them a little.
They are familiar presences:
first in the mail box, then in the bill drawer,
now on the desk. Services Rendered.
My life is dependent on services rendered.

—GUNILLA NORRIS

I've paid bills when I could comfortably write the checks, and I've paid bills when it gave me palpitations to do so. Believe me, solvency feels better.

Which is one reason why many of us put off paying bills until the next paycheck, or next month, setting in motion a cycle of misery. Bill paying becomes a painful issue, releasing toxic emotions that keep us locked in lack.

Of course we're not trying to stiff anybody. All we're trying to do is make ends meet, which seems to get harder each week. And then, when the ends don't meet, we panic. A few bucks in our hands makes more sense than in an envelope on its way to a faceless institution. But thinking this way only worsens our financial situation.

If money doesn't make the world go round, "services rendered" certainly does. We can pay for those services more serenely, even when we're strapped, by remembering that all financial transactions really boil down to an exchange of energy. Someone provides us with energy in the form of heat, light, food, gas, clothing, shelter, the ability to speak to others over airwaves, or watch movies from the comfort of our couches. We reciprocate by paying for those services through energy in the form of money. If we pay with a check or a computer transaction, no cash is even exchanged. Only energy has been shuffled. If there's unlimited energy in the Universe, we can tap into the supply if we make sure we don't block the Universe's stream of good with our own negative attitudes. We can keep a constant flow of money in our daily round through giving with love and paying what we owe with gratitude.

Once, in a flush season when I had no reason to worry about money, I created a ritual for paying bills. At the beginning and the middle of each month, I would set aside a half hour to quietly, consciously settle my accounts. I'd clear my desktop, leaving only my bills, checkbook, calculator, envelopes, and stamps in view. As I worked, I'd play soft, soothing music, and sip a lovely cup of tea, and pay loving attention to what I was doing. As a result, I actually began to enjoy the experience.

When leaner times arrived, I still relied on the power of ritual to keep me positive. If I was feeling frightened, I would retrieve the memories of when I paid bills with ease, recalling the positive feelings of plenty: well-being, peace, security, freedom. Since our subconscious minds cannot distinguish between reality and fantasy, I would begin to relax. Even if my reality was not set during a season of plenty, I gradually came to know contentment in the season of enough.

This does not mean I don't still have moments of panic when a big bill arrives. But I have taught myself how to achieve virtual reality when paying bills and so can anyone.

Right now go to your wallet and take out a dollar bill. Turn it over. What do you see?

In God We Trust.

Place that bill, with the trusting side facing you, where you can see it the next time you settle your accounts.

"Guard me against the arrogance of privilege, against the indulgence of feeling that I don't have enough, and the poverty of spirit that refuses to acknowledge what is daily given me," Gunilla Norris writes in her beautiful book of meditations, *Being Home*. "Keep me truthful in knowing where I spend, where my values actually are.

"Let me not skip this monthly knowing," Gunilla asks of Spirit, as we all should. "Instruct me in judicious spending and in gratitude with no holds barred."

OCTOBER 26

Spending Habits

I don't know much about being a millionaire, but I'll bet I'd be darling at it.

—DOROTHY PARKER

Without a doubt, we'd all be darling millionaires. We know that money can't buy happiness, but we also know where to shop. The problem for many of us is that too often we act as if we're already millionaires. "Acting as if" is a very powerful psychological tool to help us make positive life changes. We act as if we're confident and we become so. We act as if we're clean and sober and we stay so. We act as if we're serene and we experience more moments of calm in our daily round. "Acting as if" can improve the quality of our lives enormously, with one exception: spending money. You can't act as if you have all the money in the world if you don't. You can't spend money as if there were no tomorrow if you can't cover the check, pay off the charge card bill monthly or barely make your minimum. As far as paying for your pleasure is concerned, tomorrow *always* arrives in a white envelope at the end of the month.

I grew up in a family of spenders. My husband grew up in a family of savers. When we got married we were the yin and yang of money handlers. Now, after sixteen years, one of us has evolved into that space of harmony that Aristotle called "the Golden Mean" and Buddha called "the Middle Way." The other still saves.

Taking the middle path of money—Simple Abundance—is really taking the best from both approaches; extravagance and asceticism. Extravagance offers gratification and a feeling of abundance. Asceticism endows simplicity and a sense of security. Simple Abundance offers it all.

One of the greatest gifts my husband has ever given me is the ability to think before I spend. This is how savers behave. Savers don't get a high from recreational shopping. Savers don't shop in order to make themselves feel better. Savers have seen many sales they can walk away from. Should they have to spend money, savers will ask, "Do I really want this? Do I really need this? Can I do without this? Where can I find this 50 percent off?" Like naturally thin people who don't eat when they're not hungry, savers don't spend if they don't have to. And they certainly never squander money. Savers put aside for rainy days, which is why they don't panic when the roof starts leaking.

An interesting eye-opener is to discover how much money you've earned in your lifetime. Think back to every job and guestimate your earnings. If you've stayed at home and your husband is the chief wage earner, calculate his salary. You will be astounded at how much money has passed through your hands. It's even possible that you've seen several million dollars come and go.

This comes as no surprise to Joe Dominguez and Vicki Robin, authors of *Your Money or Your Life*, a guide to achieving financial independence by transforming your relationship to money. "Money is something we choose to trade our life energy for. Our life energy is our allotment of time here on earth, the hours of precious life available to us. . . . it is limited and irretrievable. . . . our choices about how we use it express the meaning and purpose of our time here on earth."

It's amazing how this enlightened definition of money can alter the shopping experience. Is that $90 blouse really worth six hours of your life?

This week, keep track of your *every expenditure*, be it large or small, routine or one-time-only, for services rendered or for actual purchases, and whether made with cash, check, or credit card. Carry a small notebook or index cards—one card for each day—to track your spending and see where the money goes. At the end of the week, take a sheet of paper and list your expenditures under these headings: Necessities, Comforts, Wants, Indulgences, Extravagances, Insanity. How much life energy did you spend? What was worth it? What expenditures make you sigh? With happy recollection or with regret?

Now look at the choices that make you feel uncomfortable. What could you have passed up without a sense of deprivation kicking in? Now take that amount and multiply it by fifty-two. I'd be willing to bet that the total amounts to a nice chunk of change that could have been saved either for an authentic want that would thrill you or for a peace-of-mind savings investment. And you probably wouldn't even have missed it.

Other suggestions for moving your spending habits into the golden mean include leaving your credit cards and checkbook at home and buying only with cash; enlisting the help of a friend who also wants to bring her spending under control and acting as each other's conscience; and not hiding your purchases. When you can walk into the house with your shopping bags in the light of day instead of hiding them in the trunk until dark, you'll know you've entered the moderate zone.

Today, be willing to gently explore your life-energy expenditures. Don't blame yourself for bad choices. Do attempt to make better ones. Most of our problems in handling money stem from unexamined patterns rather than from uncontrollable urges.

OCTOBER 27

Quieting the Wants

There must be more to life than having everything.
—MAURICE SENDAK

Yes, there is, but your material girl doesn't know it. About this time of the year the shopper from hell reappears, and she's hungry. Be careful, she can undermine every bit of progress you've made on this path if you're not careful. Each day's mail brings luscious mail-order catalogs, the preholiday sales have begun, and you've started thinking about your gift list. Your material girl wants her share. Even if you're experiencing "less is more" contentment, the world is putting on the Ritz and it's hard not to be dazzled by all that's displayed. So many choices, so many wants, so many beautiful things beckoning you to buy.

Attempts at deprivation or reason in these year-end weeks of temptation are fruitless. But there is a savvy way to quiet the wants. Don't deny them. Indulge them. Revel in your wants. Exult in extravagance. Surrender to them. Let yourself go.

Don't worry. I've not lost my senses, but found them. You can as well, and you won't have to spend a cent. Here's how: collect those mail-order catalogs each day, but don't quickly flip through them. Wait until you can enjoy shopping slowly. Circle in red *everything* that captures your material girl's fancy. Don't let price influence you. Spiritually you have all the money you need. Go on a shopping spree on paper. Visualize wearing that elegant cashmere blazer, sitting down in that gorgeous chair, putting on that gold necklace, entertaining with those beautiful dishes. Mentally claim them as your own. Tell yourself "I can have that." Write down all the particulars on a piece of paper, insert it in the catalog, and put all your catalogs into a basket of their own. Now forget about things for you and focus only on the gifts you need to get for other people. If your material girl starts to whine, reassure her that you've already taken care of her wants. Then, after the holidays are over, peruse your catalogs again. See if the wants are still there. Maybe you were given a gift that satisfied the yearning. Maybe your original favorite has gone on sale. But don't be surprised if you're no longer interested. Why? Because you satisfied the material girl. You fed her wants with attention. You didn't ignore, dismiss, or deprive her. You told her she could have anything she wanted. But all she really wants is to hear you give her permission.

What you're actually doing with this exercise is expanding your abundance consciousness by releasing mental limitations, the ones that really hold you back. "When you repeatedly say, 'I can't afford it,' your subconscious mind takes you at your word and sees to it that you will not be in a position to purchase what you want," Joseph Murphy explains in *The Power of Your Subconscious Mind*. "As long as you persist in saying, 'I can't afford that car, that trip to Europe, that home' . . . you can rest assured that your subconscious mind will follow your orders, and you will go through life experiencing the lack of all these things."

We quiet our wants when we acknowledge them. We can do that on the material or a metaphysical plane. The best things in life might not all come free, but the best bargains are discovered by your own personal shopper: your subconscious mind. Honor your desires by winnowing them out, so that all that remain are authentic.

OCTOBER 28

Financial Serenity

A little bit added to what you've already got gives you a little bit more.

—P. G. WODEHOUSE

We're zealots at pursuing financial security when what we really hunger for is financial serenity. Financial security is never having to worry about money again because you've accumulated all you'll ever need. In today's uncertain economic climate—when the only thing we can expect is the unexpected—how long do you think it will take for us to accomplish this?

Financial serenity is never having to worry about money again because you've discovered the true Source. You have access to an inexhaustible, invisible storehouse of good. We don't have to wait another moment for financial serenity. We can begin to experience it today regardless of our economic condition.

Financial serenity starts when we accept as our truth that money is a state of mind and that abundance is a state of belief. When we choose abundance, we become rich in the Real. We attain true wealth. Of course, money is part of personal wealth, but so is love, inner peace, harmony, beauty, joy, perfect health, authentic expression, discovering your bliss, pursuing your passions, fulfilling your Divine destiny.

However, there are certain actions we can take to increase our wealth. The first is choosing to live on less than we earn, so that we can save and share more. Many of us want savings accounts in theory, but psychologically resist them. That's because we associate savings with deprivation instead of gratification. For in order to save we must do without something else. What we don't consider is that having a savings account enables us eventually to experience authentic satisfaction instead of the cheap imitation of instant gratification.

The way to start saving money on a regular basis is to think of it as a positive choice, one that affirms your abundance. I call mine my serenity account. As you save money, you begin to let go of limiting thought patterns. How much should you save? Start with whatever you can, but aim for ten percent of whatever money comes your way, depositing it in your account before it goes somewhere else.

Your savings is a "positive affirmation that you have more than you need at the moment," Sanaya Roman and Duane Packer remind us in *Creating Money*. "As you feel abundant, you become magnetic to even more money. . . . Think of how much you would like in your savings account; imagine it as vividly as you can. Imagine the balance you would like in your passbook. Envision yourself putting money into your account. Feel the joy you will have when you look at the balance. Picture your savings as your wealth account. View it as money that is teaching you how to handle a larger and larger flow of prosperity."

OCTOBER 29

Affirming Abundance

Whoever thinks that [she] is helping to keep God's work going on the earth cannot help but believe that God will help [her].
— CHARLES FILLMORE

Another step toward financial serenity is taking on a "Silent Partner" with a vested interest in your prosperity. This is done through tithing: returning a portion of your wealth to the work of Spirit. When you tithe, you acknowledge and honor the true Source of your supply. Tithing is an ancient spiritual tradition and a universal prosperity law used by the great wealthy civilizations—Egyptians, Babylonians, Chinese, Greeks, and Romans—to ensure abundance.

Unless you were raised in a spiritual tradition that honors tithing, such as Judaism and Mormonism, you may be unfamiliar with the practice and uncertain about what it involves.

Understanding how tithing works metaphysically helps skeptics become more open to the ways in which its practice can enrich our lives. Spiritual law, no matter which path, tells us as we give, so shall we receive. We realize that money is a form of energy. Energy does not increase if it's hoarded. Energy must circulate freely for power to be released. When we receive an increase of money in our lives, giving away a portion of that money keeps the channels of abundance circulating freely, as Spirit intended.

On a practical level, tithing allows us to express our thanksgiving with action. Returning some of the material good we receive is a tangible demonstration of trust. But also, tithing changes our attitudes about money. We become èxpectant, anticipating the best. We've kept our part of the bargain. Now that we are givers, we can ready ourselves to receive.

Tithing *will* make you more magnetic to money, whether you believe it or not. The mechanics of tithing involve taking one-tenth of all money you receive—from earnings, gifts, or interest on savings and investments—and regularly donating it to the church, temple, mosque, or other spiritual organization that inspires, uplifts, and encourages your personal growth. If there isn't one, your tithe can be given to a nonprofit organization that carries on Spirit's work in the world, caring for those unable to care for themselves—the sick, the hungry, and the homeless. This is how I tithe. But each woman should consult her own heart.

My experience with tithing on the Simple Abundance path has been erratic but amazing. When I tithe, I experience more financial serenity than when I don't. The money seems to stretch further or my expenses diminish. When I tithe I'm able to save more with ease, and new moneymaking opportunities arrive, often unsolicited. The floodgates of heaven do shower me with blessings, although I've not yet reached the point at which I can't find room for more.

When I don't tithe, I'm not struck down, but I do start to worry about money. There seem to be longer stretches between bank deposits and more unexpected expenses, which *always* end up costing me more than the amount my tithe would have been. So I know it's time to write a check. Wait and watch what happens. Very quickly, the ebb recedes and the flow begins again. Coincidence?

Some people say if you don't have much money to spare, it's just as good to tithe your time or goods. It's been my discovery that when I tithe time, I receive more time. When I tithe goods, I receive gifts. If I want more money in my life, I tithe money.

When we're in great financial straits, we think we can't afford to tithe.

But when our financial needs are great, can we afford *not* to try tithing? Or we tell ourselves that if we ever get to a point in our life at which money is not an issue, we'll be generous givers. I have no doubt. But money will cease to be an issue only when we relax about it. Affirming our abundance now, by becoming generous givers, dramatically demonstrates our prosperity to the doubter within. Let your authentic self convince her and watch what happens.

OCTOBER 30

Becoming More Magnetic to Money

A lean purse is easier to cure than endure.
—GEORGE S. CLASON

The wealthiest civilization in the ancient world was Babylon. Babylon was famous for its fortune because its people as well as its king were rich, enjoying a level of personal wealth beyond our contemporary comprehension. The poor Babylonian was the exception, because knowledge of the laws of prosperity was available to everyone.

The man-made laws of money created by the Babylonians were very simple, even for the financially impaired. And they're just as true today as they were eight thousand years ago. The path to personal wealth is regular saving and sharing, controlling expenditures, living debt-free, increasing prosperity through prudent investment, protecting the bulk of your wealth from loss, owning property, establishing a future income for old age, and increasing the ability to earn money through perseverance.

During the late 1920s and the Depression years of the 1930s, many banks and large insurance companies distributed free pamphlets explaining these ancient laws of thrift and personal wealth through parables written by George S. Clason. In 1955 a collection of them was published as *The Richest Man in Babylon*, becoming an inspirational classic.

The first of the Babylonian secrets for achieving personal wealth was to "Start thy purse to fattening." This was accomplished by taking a part of all one earned—not less than ten percent—and claiming it as one's own. This money was kept in a purse usually worn at the waist. The purpose of the purse wasn't simply to save money but to act as a money magnet, endowing its owner with a sense of financial serenity as it grew fatter. When the purse became too heavy to wear, some of the money could be transferred to a larger savings chest and used for lending, trading, acquiring property, and making investments. But a portion of the money remained in the purse to attract more. Babylon's richest always kept a fat purse close by as physical proof of their prosperity.

Creating a money magnet is a fabulous psychological ploy to jump-start a sense of financial serenity if you're worried about money. A money magnet is not a savings account; it's in addition to the money you deposit in your savings account. You keep your money magnet close at hand so that you can *see* your prosperity—touch it or count it as often as you like. You need some money that is completely yours, which is why the existence of your money magnet is to be kept secret. It's not intended to pay the pizza delivery boy.

A symbolic money magnet that's a personal favorite is to carry a hidden $100 bill in addition to whatever money I think I need when I go out. The reason for this is that, no matter what happens, I'll always have $100 to spend as I wish or for emergencies. But it must be *a $100 bill*, not merely $100. You'll spend $100, but you'll rarely break a $100 bill. (At least I won't.) This way you always feel abundant without spending money. It's a terrific reconditioning tool to teach us that abundance must occur in our minds before it can manifest itself in our lives.

OCTOBER 31

Make Room for Mystery, Awaken to the Magic

To work magic is to weave the unseen forces into form; to soar beyond sight; to explore the uncharted dream realm of the hidden reality.

—STARHAWK

At last the bewitching hour has arrived: All Hallow's Eve. Some of us will be accompanying little goblins on their appointed rounds; our love, care, and concern providing their protection during the dark of night. Many other women will be greeting high spirits at the front door with sweet bribes, choosing to treat rather than be tricked. Wise choice.

Halloween comes down to us from the pre-Christian Celtic festival of Samhaim, held October 31, the last autumn night before the cold and bleakness of winter. On this night—considered the Celtic New Year—the Druids believed that the supernatural world drew closer to the physical world, so human beings were more susceptible to the power and influence of the unseen. Magic spells could be cast more easily, divination (predicting fortunes) was more revealing, and dreams held special significance.

Being Celtic, I still believe this. Being human, I believe Halloween is the perfect reminder that Magic flows through us, mystery infuses every encounter of every day. We conjure up the shoe that cannot be found anywhere in the house, transform leftovers into a feast, coax bounty from barren earth, banish fear, heal hurts, make money stretch till the end of the month. We carry, cradle, nurture, and sustain life. We do all this and much more. But most women are not aware of their tremendous power for good. We are asleep to our Divinity. We've not consciously awakened to the realization that we are descendants of an ancient, sacred lineage: the She.

Isn't magic what you're performing when you create an authentic lifestyle for yourself and those you love? Aren't you shaping unseen forces with your creativity and soulcrafts, bringing into the physical world through passion what has only existed in the spiritual realm? If you can do this unconsciously, how much more could you accomplish if you were fully aware of your powers?

O daughter of the She, much power has been gifted you. It is the power of Love. Tonight by candlelight or by the light of the full moon in your backyard, commit to use your power wisely for the Highest Good of all. *You have no idea of the countless lives you touch in the course of your lifetime.* Souls searching for Wholeness that could be healed with the magic at your command. Go directly to the Source. Acknowledge your lineage and your authentic gifts with a grateful heart. "I am sure there is Magic in everything," Frances Hodgson Burnett observed, "only we have not sense enough to get hold of it and make it do things for us."

Now we do.

Joyful Simplicities for October

✒ Plan an outing to a pumpkin patch or farmers' market. Select the perfect jack-o'-lantern, but get an assortment of smaller pumpkins on which to carve different designs, like checkerboards, hearts, or the moon and stars. Pie pumpkins are the perfect size for creating luminaries for steps or driveways, and the midget pumpkins make charming votive candle holders for dinner tables.

✒ Create a seasonal table. Set aside one small space on which to arrange an autumnal still life: wheat sheaves, pumpkins, gourds, Indian corn, or bittersweet, with bouquets of dried flowers and preserved autumn leaves.

✒ Preserving autumn leaves was a favorite pastime for Victorian women. Select large branches, when the leaves have first turned their beautiful crimson, orange, and gold, and before they start to fall, just as you would flowers. Split the stems of your branches about three inches from the bottom; stand them in a bucket of warm water for several hours. If any leaves begin to curl, remove them. Prepare a solution of glycerine (available at pharmacies) and water by combining one part glycerine with two parts water. Bring the solution to a boil, simmer gently for ten minutes, and let it sit until completely cool. Cut the bottom of your stems at a very sharp angle and lightly hammer the ends; stand your branches in the mixture, storing your container in a cool, dark place until all the glycerine mixture has been absorbed (about a week to ten days). When you first notice tiny beads of glycerine forming on the leaves, remove the stems, wipe down the leaves with a damp paper towel, and dry thoroughly. Your leaves will stay beautiful and bright for several seasons.

⤐ Pumpkins make very attractive natural vases for autumn bouquets. Scoop out the center as you would for a lantern and fill with a damp oasis (the floral sponge) cut to size. Arrange jewel-tone flowers, preserved leaves, and vines in the oasis for a long-lasting arrangement. Occasionally test the oasis to see if you need to add more water.

⤐ Halloween is traditionally the night for fortune-telling. A delicious way to do this is with a Victorian fate cake. Make a spice cake and insert specially made silver charms into the batter after it is poured into the pan. When the cake is cut, the charms will reveal the future: the bell is a wedding; the thimble blesses the owner; the wishbone grants one wish; the coin promises prosperity; the horseshoe ensures good luck; and the button, domestic bliss. A set of English silver fate charms (which can be used again for Christmas pudding) is available from the Seasons mail-order catalog. (1-800-776-9677).

⤐ Dress up for Halloween, or at least find yourself a wonderful mask to wear when opening the front door.

⤐ This is the month to plant crocus, daffodils, and tulips outdoors for next spring's season of showing off.

⤐ If you live in a four-season climate, take a Sunday drive in the country to revel in Mother Nature's flamboyant fancy dress. Pack a picnic. Linger as long as you can.

⤐ Mull cider and/or wine on the weekends for an autumn cup of cheer, especially delightful after raking leaves! The best mulling spices I've ever found are the William-Sonoma brand, available from their shops and catalog (1-800-541-2233).

NOVEMBER

*All freezes again—
among the pines, winds
whispering a prayer.*
—Riei, Eighteenth-Century Japanese Poet

November silently sneaks up on us, catching our senses by surprise. Suddenly, as the English poet Thomas Hood sullenly observed two centuries ago, there's "no shade, no shine, no butterflies, no bees, no fruits, no flowers, no leaves, no birds." Outside, silvery gray shafts reveal a familiar landscape stripped of pretense. Behind closed doors, glowing amber fires shed light upon the Real. Like a woman who has found her authenticity, November's beauty radiates from within.

Embracing the Ebb

The season when to come, and when to go,
To sing, or cease to sing, we never know.

—ALEXANDER POPE

There once was a mighty queen with a short fuse. One autumn, as the year was beginning to ebb, the queen fell into a deep melancholy. She could neither eat nor slumber, and tears of an unknown origin fell frequently, which infuriated her, triggering angry fits that made those around her quake in fear.

Each day the queen summoned a new adviser from her esteemed circle of sages to explain the cause of her baffling condition. In they came and out they went: the court physician, the stargazer, the psychic, the alchemist, the herbalist, the philosopher. All were dismissed as charlatans for their inability to unravel the mystery of the royal black spell. They counted themselves lucky to have only their illustrious careers shortened.

"Surely there must be one among you who knows the source of my suffering," the queen cried in despair. But her pathetic wail was greeted only with awkward silence, for all were wary of her wrath. Finally, the royal gardener was moved by compassion for the poor woman and slowly approached her throne.

"Come into the garden, Majesty, beyond the walls of your self-imprisonment, and I will disclose your dilemma." The queen was so desperate, she did as she was bid. When she went out to the garden for the first time in many weeks, she noticed that the bright, vivid colors of summer had faded and the garden seemed bare. But it was not, she saw, wholly bereft of beauty, for it was regal in autumn's brilliant hues of crimson and gold. The air was refreshingly cool and crisp, and the sky, pure blue. "Speak, gardener," the queen ordered, "but choose your words carefully, for I seek the truth."

"Majesty, it is not your body or your mind that is ailing. It is your soul that is in need of healing. For while you are a mighty and powerful queen, you are not Divine. You are suffering from a human condition that afflicts us all. Earthly souls ebb and flow in sorrow and joy according to the seasons of emotion, just as the seasons of the natural world move through the cycle of life, death, and rebirth. These are the days to be grateful for the harvest of the heart, however humble it might be, and to prepare for the coming of the year's closure. Even now, the season of daylight diminishes and the time of darkness increases. But the true Light is never extinguished in the natural world, and it is the same in your soul. Embrace the ebb, my beloved queen, and do not fear the darkness. For as night follows day, the

Light will return and you will know contented hours once again. Of this I am sure."

The unhappy queen considered this wisdom thoughtfully and asked the gardener how she possessed the secret knowledge of inner peace during the seasons of emotion. The gardener led her to a brass sundial. It read:

This too, shall pass.

NOVEMBER 2

Caring for Your Soul

Let us imagine care of the soul, then, as an application of poetics to everyday life.

—THOMAS MOORE

Soul. Created on the sixth day. After the cherubim and seraphim. After the dominions, virtues, powers, principalities, archangels, and angels. After Light was called forth from the void of darkness. After morning and evening were delineated. After space and time. After air, fire, water, earth. After the sun, moon, and stars were hung in the heavens. After the Universe began spinning. After its Power was switched on and its Energy was charged. After the music of the spheres began the celestial concerto. After the beasts ran upon the fields and birds soared. After the garden was in full bloom.

Only after *all* was made ready—and the Great Creator pronounced it very good—only then, was it the Beloved's moment. For the Beloved—to be known through all eternity as Soul—was sent into the world on Divine breath as Spirit laughed and cried. Soul was born in both joy and pain. Blown into a handful of dust. Divinity was to live and move and have its being in a creature made of mud.

There you have it. Go figure. Which is precisely what men and women have tried to do down through the ages. But even reason, intellect, imagination, passion, poetry, prayer, art, sex, song, and saxophone cannot unravel or fully reveal the mystical nature of our souls. Let alone understand it.

Obviously, after twenty-five thousand years of trying, we're not meant to understand the essence of Soul. But we can come to know her. For we were created *for no other reason* than to love, nurture, nourish, sustain, protect, uplift, inspire, delight, charm, and comfort the beloved presence within each of us. Psychotherapist and writer Thomas Moore calls this profound attention to the authentic needs that stir deep within "caring for our souls."

Today is All Souls' Day, a solemn day set aside since the Middle Ages for remembrance of the beloveds who no longer laugh and cry with us on earth. But All Souls' Day is a beautiful occasion for contemplating how we care for our own souls, the degree of hospitality we extend to these guests in our daily round, and the quality of their visit so far. In order to approach "the depth that is the domain of the soul," Moore urges us to become "artists and theologians of our own lives."

It is through "the small details of everyday life" that we make our souls feel welcome. "Tending the things around us and becoming sensitive to the importance of home, daily schedule, and maybe even the clothes we wear are ways of caring for the soul," Moore tells us in his deeply moving meditation, *Care of the Soul: A Guide for Cultivating Depth and Sacredness in Everyday Life*.

Today, be willing to ask your Guest what she requires to make her stay more pleasurable. Ask often: "What do you need at this moment? What would bring you peace, contentment, joy? It may be to slow down, take a walk, hug a child, caress a cat. Flip through a magazine. Call your sister. Send a funny card to a friend. Take a nap. Order Chinese carryout. Watch a favorite movie. Have a good cry. Find a drugstore with an old-fashioned soda fountain that serves cherry phosphates. Solve an English mystery. Turn in early. Dream. Fantasize. Pray. Whatever it might be, she will tell you. Ask.

"'Stay' is a charming word in a friend's vocabulary," Louisa May Alcott reminds us. Stay, my Beloved. Stay. Say it now. Say it often. Come live with me and be my love.

Stay.

NOVEMBER 3

Becoming Real

Once you are Real you can't become unreal again. It lasts for always.

—MARGERY WILLIAMS

On Christmas morning the bunny sitting in the top of the Boy's stocking with a sprig of holly between his paws looked quite splendid. He was fat and bunchy in all the right places, with a soft, spotted white-and-brown coat, thread whiskers, and ears lined in pink sateen. The Boy was enchanted and played with the rabbit for two whole hours until the family directed his attention to all the other wonderful parcels lying under the tree "and in the excitement of looking at all the new presents the Velveteen Rabbit [was] forgotten."

For a long time, the bunny remained just another plaything in the nursery. But he didn't mind because he was able to carry on long, philosophical discussions with the old Skin Horse who was very old, wise, and experienced in the strange ways of nursery magic. One of the rabbit's favorite topics of conversation was on becoming "Real." Here is the heart of Margery Williams's mystical tale of the transformative power of love, *The Velveteen Rabbit*, written in 1927.

The Skin Horse patiently explained to the bunny that "Real isn't how you are made. It's a thing that happens to you. When a child loves you for a long, long time, not just to play with, but REALLY loves you, then you become Real."

Becoming Real doesn't happen overnight to toys or people. "Generally, by the time you are Real, most of your hair has been loved off, and your eyes drop out and you get loose in the joints and very shabby. But these things don't matter at all, because once you are Real, you can't be ugly, except to people who don't understand."

In order for toys to become Real, they must be loved by a child. In order for us to become Real, we must become lovers of real life in all its complexity and uncertainty. Like the Velveteen Rabbit, we long to become Real, to know what authenticity feels like. Sometimes this hurts. The thought of losing our whiskers and having our tail come unsewn is frightening. In a world that judges by appearances, it's embarrassing having all the pink rubbed off your nose. The Velveteen Rabbit isn't alone in wishing to become Real without any uncomfortable or unpleasant things happening.

One of the ways that we become Real without too much discomfort is by growing gradually into our authenticity. As you learn to acknowledge, accept, and appreciate what it is that makes you different from all the other toys in the cupboard, the process begins. As you learn to trust the wisdom of your heart and make creative choices based on what you know is right for you, process becomes progress. As you learn to endow even the smallest moment of each day with Love, progress becomes reality perfected. Your black-button eyes might have lost their polish, but now these windows to the soul see only beauty. You become not only Real to those who know and love you, but Real to everyone. You become authentic.

NOVEMBER 4

Return of the Goddess

And write about it, Goddess, and about it.
—ALEXANDER POPE

She's ba-aa-aak! The goddess has returned with another book to lead us from desire to fulfillment. Which one? Doesn't really matter! The goddesses of gracious living, entertaining, decorating, fitness, fashion, beauty, and relationships regularly appear this time of year, keeping in motion the cycle of worship and words. It used to be that goddesses performed miracles. Now they write books telling us how to perform our own.

Four o'clock on a cold November afternoon, and it's already dark. Disciples from all over the Washington area have left their jobs, homes, and families to await the Appearance, Signing, and Rapture at the ceremony of the book-signing. The goddess will not arrive for another hour, but already the faithful number two hundred. We're everywoman: suburban mothers with small children in tow, executive women in power suits with briefcases and cellular phones. The first in line have camped out here all day. My daughter and I have only been here for half an hour conducting field research on the contemporary goddess scene, but already there are two dozen well-dressed women behind me.

Every now and then a bookstore employee comes out to remind the flock that the goddess is signing *only* her latest offering and *only* two books per customer. This particularly irks one woman who just minutes ago bought ten copies of the latest tome to give to family and friends as Christmas presents; no one ringing up the $250 sale told her she couldn't get eight of them signed. Now there is much grumbling about nerve, fame, wealth, business empires, and goddesses who forget who elevated them from divas to divinities. But we are resourceful. Not all of us have more than one book for signing; up and down the line the books are distributed and the problem is solved.

Instead of loaves and fishes there will be canapés. Every once in a while, Katie comes back to give my aisle the latest reconnaissance on the goddess's estimated time of arrival. Katie is starved; it never occurred to me to pack provisions. I snatch two cranberry tartlets the size of postage stamps from a passing tray, wrapping them in a tissue for safekeeping in my pocket until her next report.

After another hour, fearing that I won't get to the front before the great one must leave, I sneak behind the barricades up to the front. I haven't waited this long not to get at least a glimpse of the goddess in the flesh.

But I get much more than I imagined. For behind her is an altar: a gorgeous French country table of washed pine covered in checked homespun. Upon it are mountains of fruits, vegetables, loaves of bread, copper cooking utensils, and candles. In front of the altar, she sits in a tapestry chair behind a cherry Queen Anne desk bearing an arrangement of exquisite flowers that are only in season in designer floral shops. Nearby, tokens of devotion from the disciples have created a shrine; individual bouquets of flowers and a large pile of presents, many of them wrapped in homemade wrapping paper, variations on a theme of potato stencils.

Frankly, I've seen more than enough. The goddess is as lovely as her images; the altar is beyond belief, except that I saw it with my own eyes. It gives me the shivers. I want to leave, but Katie is horrified at the thought of going without getting our book signed. We stay.

By now, it's much too late to cook dinner, so we stop off for burgers and fries. A few minutes later, I'm fishing for my house keys and pull out the crushed tissue containing the cranberry tartlets. The house is dark, cold, and forlorn. No fire, no candlelight, no animation, no inviting aromas to welcome us. "A house is no home unless it contains food and fire for the mind as well as for the body," Margaret Fuller wrote in *Woman in the Nineteenth Century* in 1845. The crust is delicious, but the cranberry tartlet is not as filling as I imagined it would be.

NOVEMBER 5

The Goddess Within

Come, Vesta, to live in this Beautiful Home.
Come with warm feelings of friendship.
Bring your intelligence,
Your energy and your Passion
To join with your Good Work.
Burn always in my Soul.
You are welcome here.
I remember you.
—HOMERIC HYMN (TRANSLATION BY FRANCES BERNSTEIN)

Ever since civilization began, women have turned to goddesses for intercession and inspiration. For Roman women, the most beloved goddess was Vesta. She, like her Greek counterpart, Hestia, was the goddess of the hearth. Vesta is the one who urges women to be quiet, to sit, to gaze, to listen, to prepare delicious meals, to bring beauty into our daily round, to live through our six senses, to create a sacred haven of security and serenity set apart from the world in order to protect all we cherish. Vesta is the ancient goddess who calls on us to focus our creative energies on the Real.

In an unpublished book on ancient women's spirituality, Frances Bernstein notes that the Latin word for hearth is *focus*. Focusing is the sacred art of Vesta. Focusing is also a crucial need today for women who spend much of their time rushing to fulfill the inexhaustible demands of family and work. The faster we run, the more conflicted we become. As we get nowhere fast, we lose focus and clarity, existing in a perpetual state of confusion. Many times during the day we'll speak of feeling "out of kilter," "spaced out," or "off the wall." These expressions are quite apt because they accurately describe a lack of centering within. When the center isn't holding, it's because we've lost touch with the tremendous healing power of our Vesta aspect. We have wandered far away from the sacred hearth and don't know how to find our way back to heat, light, and warmth.

In order to regain focus, women need to restore a sense of "at homeness" to their lives, which is what we are really attempting to do when we create domestic goddesses. We glorify women whose public careers exploit our private yearnings. It's far easier to live vicariously through their books, videos, magazines, newsletters, television shows, or infomercials than it is to nurture our own gifts. It is much more comfortable to create goddesses than honor our own Divinity.

Don't misunderstand me. I love the goddesses. They are clever, savvy, and possess marvelous creative talents. They have much good to offer us; certainly I've done my share to make them all wealthy women. I need a new low-fat risotto recipe just as much as you do. But there is a significant difference between being an avid fan and a rabid follower. You don't have to belong to a cult to become brainwashed.

When admiration leads to adoration, we unconsciously create graven images that diminish rather than enrich our lives. We deny our own authenticity. Disown our passion. Siphon off our own power by endowing women who clearly have enough our portion. Is this what "the rich get richer and the poor get poorer" really means? Being poor in self-confidence and creative energy keeps us in lack much more than a lean purse.

By worshipping false goddesses, we make another woman the Creatrix, instead of honoring the Creatrix within. If you're really seeking an authentic goddess, you know where to find her.

Rising to the Occasion

To be really great in little things, to be truly noble and heroic in the insipid details of everyday life, is a virtue so rare as to be worthy of canonization.

—HARRIET BEECHER STOWE

In real life, serenity depends on coping and coping well. Rising to the occasion.

Consider the following scenarios. You have a flat tire on the way to an important business meeting. You find yourself locked out of the house. You discover that your husband's college roommate is coming for dinner in two hours. The pipes freeze. The puppy swallows an earring. Someone's sick or snowed in. You're asked to send money, switch car pool trips, show up for jury duty. One minute you're called out of town, the next you're asked to step in on a moment's notice to save the school bazaar.

Real life is the collison—day in, day out—of the improbable with the impossible. Longfellow believed that situations that call forth our coping abilities are "celestial benedictions" in dark disguises, sent not to try our souls, but to enlarge them. Just as dough rises in a bowl, expanding before it becomes bread, we become larger than we ever thought possible when we rise to occasions, performing miracles with good humor and grace. Coping well enables you to see beyond the circumference of circumstance, so that the Real in the center of your daily round is not hidden by happenstance.

Most women are geniuses at rising to the occasion. But we've never realized how extraordinary this talent really is, because it's second nature by now. We've never given credit where credit is due, because we've never given coping much thought. But if women who cope well ran everything, Nirvana wouldn't only be the name of a grunge band.

We become more adept at rising to the occasion each time we see ourselves doing it. Every time we cope well with whatever real life throws our way, it's another deposit of confidence, creativity, and courage in our self-esteem account. So congratulate yourself each night for handling the unexpected with finesse. Well done.

Today, when you need to rise to the occasion, do it with style. Do it with a knowing smile. Confound them. Astound yourself. Make it look easy, and it will become so.

NOVEMBER 7

Shepheard's Hotel

She had been forced into prudence in her youth. She learned romance as she grew older—the natural sequence of an unnatural beginning.

—JANE AUSTEN

Christmas. Dublin. 1878. I'm hiding a handsome Irish patriot on the run from the British police in a room beneath Neary's pub. No thought of the risk.

But that's just one of my many lives. Other nights it's 1915 and I'm on the veranda of the Muthaiga Club, the "Moulin Rouge of Africa." Or I may be watching for the guanacos in the mist of the Andes, running bulls with Hemingway in Pamplona, sailing down the Nile, trekking through Karakoram, whizzing across the frozen Neva River in a sleigh driven by my devoted Cossack manservant, descending the steps at the Paris Opera House with a suave Guy de Maupassant (or is it the fiery young Toscanini?).

Neither. It's J. Peterman, the last romantic man on the earth. Peterman believes I'm mysterious, powerful, irresistible, smart, sharp, sassy, funny, sexy. And beautiful, it goes without saying. The kind of woman for whom a man would commit perjury or embezzle. (Doesn't really have to do it, mind you, it's the offer that counts.) The kind of woman others spend their entire lives remembering and envying. Not too surprisingly, when I'm with him, I become that woman. My authentic self. Sentimental. Incurably romantic. Emotional. Impulsive. Passionate.

Like Peterman, I lament the passing of a lost way of life, especially since most of it was lost before we were born, when romance was a part of the daily round. With Peterman's help, the days of ocean liners, crepe de chine, train cases with secret compartments, and Morris Minor roadsters can be summoned back at will. He travels the world in search of the last vestiges of real romance. When he finds a little piece of it, he has it reproduced and tells me about it in his mail-order catalogs known as "Owner's Manuals." No glossy pictures, no hard sell. Just personal vignettes of what we were doing the last time I wore or used it, accompanied by evocative watercolor sketches to jog my memory. I wait for J. Peterman in the post the way some women wait for Fabio's appearance at the mall.

My trysts with Peterman are nocturnal, and always take place in bed. There my soul mate and I reminisce, retrace roads not taken, and recall risks not ventured, until there is no longer a trace of regret, only fond remembrance. I knew J. Peterman was my soul mate when he poured out his regrets for not spending a night in Shepheard's Hotel in Cairo. It burned to the ground in 1952 before he could afford to check in. "That night, it became my code word for everything unobtained, undone." I'd thought there wasn't another soul on the face of the earth who mourned missing out on one-impossibly-perfect-night-at-Shepheard's-Hotel-in-Cairo.

Peterman knows the woman I truly am, even if I forget. He knows that I was created in a burst of passion, for romance. So were you. Plumb the female psyche and you will find an elegy of romantic remorse—the unobtained, the undone. Melancholy fragments of unrequited loves that stretch from our cradles to our graves. Regrets not necessarily caused by lovers who chose to live without us, so much as by recollections of the things we loved once but learned to live without. It could be the novel you abandoned writing, the art fellowship in Paris you never pursued, the black velvet cape that finally found you at an antique stall but you passed up because, where would you wear it? (Everywhere.) The love you couldn't return, the love that frightened you, the love that you were afraid to express. The loving gesture that died in hesitation. The romance of living that we let slip away every day because real life forces us into prudence.

When you acknowledge your romantic impulses, no matter how implausible or impractical, you strengthen the intimate connection with your authentic self. Connection with those who cherish and love you unconditionally. Connection with those things that fuel your passions, feed your soul, keep you alive.

Today, check into Shepheard's Hotel. What must you do before you die? Where must you go? What worlds must you conquer? Begin exploring, today, small ways in which to honor your sacred yearning for romance, even if it's just by telephoning for a mail-order catalog.

Bogart and Bergman will always have Paris. Peterman and I will always have Cairo. I have the bathrobe to prove it.

NOVEMBER 8

Everyday Life Is the Prayer

More things are wrought by prayer than
this world dreams of.

—ALFRED, LORD TENNYSON

In the beginning was the Word.
And the Word was with God.
And the Word was God.
Might I have a word?

Some women know they pray. Other women think they don't because they aren't down on their knees morning and night. But they're up in the dark with sick children, visiting an elderly parent on their lunch hour, supporting the dreams of those they love with their work, helping a friend bear grief or rejoice, nourishing bodies and souls. This, too, is prayer.

For whether we realize it or not, with every breath, with every heartbeat, women pray. We pray with desire, longing, hunger, thirst, sighs, remorse, regret. We pray with disappointment, discouragement, despair, disbelief. We pray with anger, rage, jealousy, envy. We pray with pleasure, contentment, happiness, exultation, joy. We pray with gratefulness, acknowledgment, appreciation, acceptance, relief. We pray when we comfort, cheer, console. We pray when we laugh. We pray when we cry. We pray when we work and play. We pray when we make love or make a meal. We pray when we create and admire creation. One way or another, we pray. Everyday life *is* the prayer. How we conduct it, celebrate it, consecrate it. It's just that some prayers are better than others. Conscious prayers are the best.

In its purest form, prayer is conversation. Communion. Connection. Intimacy. Prayer is the dialect of Divinity. Prayer is actually the authentic conversation because you don't have to hold back; you can say whatever needs to be said, exactly the way you want to express it, when you want to express it. You won't be judged. You won't risk losing love; instead, by praying you will increase your awareness of it. You won't have to phrase your words carefully lest there be misunderstandings, because you can't be misunderstood. Even if you don't know what you want or need, Spirit knows what you're about to say, ask, beg, scream, or praise before you utter a syllable.

Then why do we need to lift up our voice in prayer?

Because it's not good for women to be silent. We need to get real life off our chests. Get whatever's bedeviling us out into the open, so that we can get on with it. We can't do that when we're stuck, and women do get stuck, in a kind of self-destructive holding pattern, when they're silent. "Every person's life is lived as a series of conversations," Deborah Tannen tells us. Women pray because we need to talk to Someone who's really listening.

NOVEMBER 9

The Sacrament of the Present Moment

There is nothing so secular that it cannot be sacred, and that is one of the deepest messages of the Incarnation.
—MADELEINE L'ENGLE

If everyday life is our prayer, the moments we offer up to create an authentic life are our sacraments. *The Book of Common Prayer* defines a sacrament as "an outward and visible sign of an inward and spiritual grace." The outward and visible way in which we move through our daily round—the time, creative energy, emotion, attitude, and attention with which we endow our tasks—is how we elevate the mundane to the transcendent. Moments of illumination aren't just experienced by saints, mystics, and poets.

There are seven traditional Christian sacraments: baptism, penance, eucharist, confirmation, marriage, ordination, and healing the sick. But we don't have to think of the sacraments only in religious terms, as Matthew Fox notes, for "the Sacred is everywhere."

When we welcome the new day, we baptize it with our gratitude and enthusiasm; when we reconcile with another or ourselves and make amends, we experience penance. Confirmation bestows wisdom. Marriage is the sacrament of relationships. Eucharist is the sacrament of nourishment. Holy orders or ordination is the sacrament of authority, and healing the sick is the sacrament of Wholeness. It *does* matter how we braid her hair, pack his lunch, send them on their way, greet their return, make suggestions, change the contract, return the telephone call, pass the pasta, pour the wine, listen to a friend, lift a burden, share a secret, visit him in a nursing home, check for monsters under the bed.

"For the wonderful thing about saints is that they were *human*," Phyllis McGinley reassures us in *Saint-Watching*. "They lost their tempers, got hungry, scolded God, were egotistical, or testy or impatient in their turns, made mistakes and regretted them. Still they went on doggedly blundering toward heaven."

NOVEMBER 10

The Gaps

Where so many hours have been spent in convincing myself that I am right, is there not some reason to fear I may be wrong?
—JANE AUSTEN

It's difficult for me to write about faith without also writing about doubt. I'd love to write a meditation on the comfort of absolute faith, the faith of Abraham walking in the desert with his beautiful little boy, Isaac, on their way to make a burnt offering to God. They have the fire, they have the wood. But where is the lamb? Isaac asks his father. God will provide the lamb for the burnt offering, Abraham tells the son he prayed seven decades for. Of course, this being a story about absolute faith, God does provide. After an altar is built, the wood is arranged, the child is bound, and the knife is unsheathed, an angel intervenes. God provides. Faith breaks a heart in order to make it Whole. But I can't write about the comfort of an absolute faith like Abraham's because you'd never have found me walking in the desert with fire, wood, my child, and no lamb.

For Abraham, there were no gaping black holes of doubt. Or were there? Not even as he held the knife aloft? Once a friend told me of a conversation she'd had with another mutual friend on God, faith, and doubt. In passing, she mentioned that they both wished that they possessed my faith. I have no recollection of the rest of the conversation. I do recall, however, my need to hang up the phone, shocked that anyone should believe my fragile faith worth emulating.

Annie Dillard tells that the Old Testament prophet Ezekiel was wary of those who hadn't floundered in the gaps before finding their way back across deserts of the heart. "The gaps are the thing," she points out. "The gaps are the spirit's one home, the altitudes and latitudes so dazzlingly spare and clean that the spirit can discover itself for the first time like a once-blind man unbound." I hope to God she's right.

For perhaps the gaps are what make faith possible, especially when the pain is unbearable. If there were no doubt, why would we need faith? Perhaps the doubts must be acknowledged, accepted, embraced, and pushed past before our faith is strong enough, not just to talk about, but to sustain.

It's okay if you hold your breath when you leap. Just don't look down.

"Faith is not *being sure*. It is *not being sure*, but betting with your last cent," Mary Jean Irion reassures us in *Yes, World*. "Faith is not making religious-sounding noises in the daytime. It is asking your inmost self questions at night—and then getting up and going to work."

NOVEMBER 11

Amazing Grace

Grace fills empty spaces, but it can only enter where there is a void
to receive it, and it is grace itself which makes this void.
—SIMONE WEIL

Grace is direct Divine intervention on our behalf that circumvents the laws of nature—time, space, cause and effect, the availability of parking—for our Highest Good. Theologians tell us that grace is an unmerited demonstration of God's love, proof that we're not in this alone. Considering that most of us operate under the assumption that daily life is a one-woman battleground, it's no wonder we're amazed when out of the blue, the Force suddenly seems to be with us. Grace is the Force—a spiritual energy field that protects and assists. Grace is Spirit's test flight; we seem to glide through the moment, the encounter, the day, without friction. We experience Real Life.

We access grace like every other spiritual tool, by asking for it specifically and regularly. In the morning you brush your teeth, put on the kettle or the coffee maker. Now that you're awake, gratefully and expectantly ask for one day's portion of grace. The kids eat their breakfast, get dressed without fuss, and are out the door on time. The bus driver waits for you. The day unfolds in blissful uneventfulness. Someone asks if you've lost weight. You realize you're smiling at four o'clock in the afternoon. You think, maybe there's something to this. The next day you ask for grace. Eventually you get to the point where asking for grace is as natural and as necessary as breathing.

Celestine Moments

These are only hints and guesses,
Hints followed by guesses, and the rest
Is prayer, observance, discipline, thought and action.

—T. S. ELIOT

Carl Jung called it "synchronicity": two seemingly unrelated events that cannot be explained by cause and effect but are uniquely linked by personal meaning.

We call it coincidence. Serendipity. Luck. Chance. Fate. We call it everything, but what it really is: Grace. God. When chance events occur "at just the right moment, and bring forth just the right individuals to suddenly send our lives in a new and important direction," James Redfield tells us in *The Celestine Prophecy*, we're meant to "intuit higher meanings in these mysterious happenings."

But most of the time we're too busy to pay attention. Too busy with real life to give Real Life more than a passing nod. So the celestine moment is written off with an "Isn't that interesting?" shrug instead of a "What do you suppose this means?" inquiry. And instead of waiting for Spirit's reply, we're off again in a thousand directions.

Artists depend on the higher harmonic of synchronicity. And because they expect it, they receive it. Today, begin an experiment in enlightenment. For one week operate on the assumption that *nothing* that happens in your daily round is accidental. Cast a wider net. Pay close attention to your dreams. Follow your urges. Honor your hunches. Use intuition as the spiritual tool it is. Consider what movies you're interested in seeing. Really listen to the lyrics of songs. If someone suggests something new for you to do, try it. If a lecture or workshop sounds interesting, go to it. Notice what books you're drawn to. Strike up conversations with strangers who sit next to you or someone interesting-looking who makes eye contact. Be receptive and alert. See how many celestine moments you can accumulate in the course of a day. The more open you are to synchronicity's role in your life, the more magnetic you become to Divine assistance.

NOVEMBER 13

Answered Prayers

God answers sharp and sudden on some prayers,
And thrusts the thing we have prayed for in our face,
A gauntlet with a gift in "it."
—ELIZABETH BARRETT BROWNING

O scar Wilde believed that there were only two tragedies in life: not getting what you pray for and getting it.

"Answered prayers are scary," Julia Cameron admits in *The Artist's Way*. "They imply responsibility. You asked for it. Now that you've got it, what are you going to do? Why else the cautionary phrase 'Watch out for what you pray for; you just might get it'? Answered prayers deliver us back to our own hand. This is not comfortable."

Very often the reason we're uncomfortable is because we've not been praying for the right thing, and on some deep level we know it. We pray to meet our soul mate, instead of praying for the grace to become the woman our soul mate would be attracted to; we pray for worldly success when what we really long for is a sense of authentic accomplishment; we pray for more money, when what we need is a change in our relationship to money. We pray for a certain outcome in any given situation, when what we should be praying for is peace of mind, no matter which outcome occurs.

Actually, our prayers are always being answered. We just don't like to think that "no" is a reasonable response to our very reasonable requests. Writer Madeleine L'Engle admits, in *The Irrational Season*—surely speaking for us all—"We don't like Noes; and sometimes we like the Noes of God less than any other No."

The "noes" of Spirit are more of a Holy Mystery than the "yeses"; more meaningful to meditate upon, after the tears, the fury, and the cursing subside. The "Noes" of God don't make sense to our conscious, rational mind, especially since we're convinced we know what's best. But do we? Really?

We want the "yes," but sometimes we need the "no." Consider the disaster that would ensue if we answered a child's every request with a "yes." That's too frightening even to contemplate. But we're children of Divinity. We can't begin to envision the big picture; nor do we weigh our requests against the prayers of others. Spirit hears both the hopeful entreaties for a sunny family reunion picnic and the farmer's plea for rain.

You would be astounded at the relief that comes once you stop assuming you have *all* the answers.

When your prayers seem delayed or denied, you need to ask Spirit if you're praying for the right thing. If you're not, ask that the right prayer might be revealed to you. Very often when we're told "No," it's to allow us more time, space, wisdom, and experience to prepare for the glorious moment when, because you're finally ready, willing, and able, Spirit answers you with a sharp, sudden, and resounding "Yes!"

NOVEMBER 14

Miracles

There are only two ways to live your life. One is as though nothing is a miracle. The other is as though everything is a miracle.
—ALBERT EINSTEIN

We think of a miracle, such as a sudden physical healing, as an event. Actually, the real miracle is not the event, but how we perceive the event in our lives. Ask yourself which is the *real* miracle: when the check finally arrives, the deadline is extended, the lawsuit is settled, the exception is made? Or when you cope, serene and smiling in the face of unbearable circumstances, triumphantly blowing everybody's mind—including your own—with your poise and courage?

Marianne Williamson describes a miracle as "a parting of the mists, a shift in perception, a return to love." The sacred continuum of Love is what makes miracles possible: Spirit's love for us, our love for each other, our love for Spirit. In her book *A Return to Love: Reflections on the Principles of a Course in Miracles*, she tells us that once miracles were all we knew, because we existed in Love. Then we woke up on earth and "were taught thoughts like competition, struggle, sickness, finite resources, limitation, guilt, bad, death, scarcity, and loss. We began to think these things, and so we began to know them." Love was replaced by fear.

When we exist in fear—which for many of us is real life—miracles become the exception, not the daily round. But it doesn't have to stay that way. What we need to do is find our way back home, back to our authentic self.

There are many paths to Wholeness. The one Marianne Williamson began taking in 1977 was *A Course in Miracles*, which she explains is a "self study program of spiritual psychotherapy" based on universal spiritual truths transcribed by a Jewish psychologist in mystical dictation sessions during the mid-1960s. Through a daily meditation and workbook exercise, seekers learn to surrender all the ego's preconceptions—what we want, need, and think will make us happy—exchanging it only for the practical daily application of Love in our lives. "Whether our psychic pain is in the area of relationships, health, career, or elsewhere, love is a potent force, the cure, the Answer," she reassures us.

The introduction to *A Course in Miracles* states that the crux of the three-volume, 1,188-page course is very simple:

Nothing real can be threatened.
Nothing unreal exists.
Herein lives the peace of God.

In becoming aware of this, we experience the miracle of Real Life. "In asking for miracles, we are seeking a practical goal," Marianne Williamson reminds us, "a return to inner peace. We're not asking for something outside us to change, but for something inside us to change."

NOVEMBER 15

Heaven Watching Over You

We all have angels guiding us. . . . They look after us. They heal us, touch us, comfort us with invisible warm hands. . . . What will bring their help? Asking. Giving thanks.

—SOPHY BURNHAM

Do you remember the comfort and joy of an imaginary playmate when you were a child? Just because the rest of the world couldn't see your constant companion, didn't mean he or she wasn't Real. What's more, your reassuring companion spirit is still an immediate presence in your daily round—guarding, protecting, guiding, inspiring, and loving you—even if it's been a long time since you made mud pies together in the backyard.

Angels are our proof of God's love for us, continuous reminders that we're not alone. Almost everyone has had an experience of being pulled back from danger by an invisible force. At that moment we felt that Heaven was truly watching over us. And we were right. While over two-thirds of us believe in the existence of angels, not everyone is ready for an intimate earthly relationship with a Heavenly superior being.

For the last three years I've enjoyed an intimate relationship with my guardian angel, whom I call Annie. As I committed to my spiritual growth, I consciously sought a mystical friendship, and it has brought me great joy, comfort, security, and peace. Annie's greatest gift has been helping me relax. She frequently reminds me that Real Life isn't a one-woman melodrama although I have a tendency to keep rewriting the script. However much I'd like to, I've never seen her. Angels cannot be conjured up on demand; they're not genies in magic lamps. However, we can call on these constant companions to guide, help, and inspire us.

"Our angels know us more intimately than our parents or our spouses. They care passionately about our well-being, and about our physical health, too," Eileen Elias Freeman tells us. "They know what we do, what we pray, what we see and say. They watch over the life and death of every single cell, and they love us, because they are beings who come from God, and God is love."

Although there are more books on angels today than ever danced on the head of a pin, Freeman's books, *Touched By Angels* and *Angelic Healing*, are my favorites. She argues convincingly that deep and abiding angelic encounters are only possible when we become aware that the special relationship we really seek is with Spirit. We may love the message and the messenger, but we should never forget the One who sent it.

As with every spiritual gift, we must ask our angels to help us. We must ask Spirit to deepen our relationship with our Heavenly guardians, offering thanks that the lines of celestial communication are continuously open.

NOVEMBER 16

Riding the Big Kahuna

Ask yourself whether you are happy and you cease to be so.
—J. S. MILL

Go with the flow. Catch the wave. Ride the big Kahuna. Wouldn't I just love to! How about you? But real life these days rarely includes a stop at Surf City unless you live in Malibu.

Whenever we experience the Flow, we experience a luminous liftoff: we're alert, soaring, unselfconscious, authentic, moving at the peak of our abilities. We forget food, drink, sex, sleep. Why? We're fueled by high-octane Love. Calling forth our gifts at the top of our lungs to a celestial "Bravo!" Reveling in our passion. We don't need positive-thinking mantras to motivate us; happiness propels us at Warp 9 toward our aspirations. Obstacles dissolve in the Flow. Toxic emotions, anxieties, and depression disappear. We're in this world, but certainly not of it. Here we experience a profound pleasure not found in the erogenous or erroneous zones, a peace that surpasses our puny understanding. Exhilaration. Joy. Transformative transcendence. What you're really looking for when you ask the doctor for Prozac. What you thought sex was when you were sixteen.

The bad news is that we don't ride the big Kahuna often enough. The good news is that the Flow can be invoked and induced; it's even expected to become one of the most productive specialties of psychological research in the next decade. For the last twenty years Mihaly Csikszentmihalyi has been pioneering the scientific study of joy, scrutinizing altered states of "optimal experience," those moments when we feel deeply connected with Real Life, which he labels "flow." He believes that exhilaration can be part of everyday life, and I'm a believer. Reading his incredible book *Flow: The Psychology of Optimal Experience* might make a believer out of you.

What's more, going with the Flow is most often attained with simple pleasures, even work, when we bring the right attitude and attention to our tasks. Complete consciousness—focusing our psychic energy on what we're doing—induces the Flow. As we learn to shut out chaos, concentrating our creative energies within, our attention fuels our ability to accelerate beyond our normal capacities.

When working, playing, or creating, ritual plays an important role in preparing our minds, bodies, and souls to tap into the mother lode. The particular way you arrange your desk at the beginning of the day, the soft pencil you prefer, the music you listen to when you write in your discovery journal is an invocation to the Flow. Small moments—reading, gardening, cooking, arts, and crafts—take on new meaning when we honor them as waves on which to catch the Flow. Exploring your family's heritage, commemorating special moments or people in your life by collecting and displaying talismans, can invite the Flow by linking the past with the present.

Varying the routines of your daily round can induce the Flow because novelty increases the frequency of the waves; thinking of lovemaking in new ways can fan waves of desire previously doused with familiarity. Memorizing favorite quotes, poetry, songs, and facts and enlivening our conversation with them, evokes the Flow. Mastering a game, sport, or new skill activates the Flow process. But so does solitude and daydreaming. Indulging your imagination brings the big Kahuna within reach, because your imagination is your soul's way of communicating with your conscious mind.

"How we feel about ourselves, the joy we get from living, ultimately depends directly on how the mind filters and interprets everday experiences," Mihaly Csikszentmihalyi reminds us. "Whether we are happy depends on inner harmony, not on the controls we are able to exert over the great forces of the universe."

NOVEMBER 17

Weather Report

It's terribly amusing how many different climates of feeling one can go through in a day.
—ANNE MORROW LINDBERGH

Today, variably cloudy. Moody. Didn't sleep well last night; up twice with children. Much tossing, turning, churning. Could be time of month, bills due. Heavy water retention. Alternating gray punctuated by streaks of light, some levity but not quite sunny. Most likely at lunchtime, if with friends. Foreboding, if lunching at desk. During the afternoon, expect thunderstorms due to deadline approaching, boss's frustrations, revised sales figures. Tonight, turning colder. Didn't resolve argument with husband over upcoming holidays. Possible frost late tonight, which will make for another unsettling day tomorrow.

Many women today are struggling with various addictions to drink, drugs, smoking, food, sex, shopping, or sleeping. Most of these forms of self-abuse are frequently discussed in books, magazine articles, and television specials. But there's another "habit" that affects many of us but gets little airplay, and that's addiction to the highs and lows of emotions.

There was once a period in my life when I could literally cry or rage for hours—and did so frequently. I was an emotional drunk, bingeing on self-abuse with tears and tantrums until I was exhausted, unable to be a loving partner or a productive writer. Emotional binges aren't just a matter of temperament; they can spell termination for relationships, careers, and dreams. The only way I got sober was by acknowledging my dependence on personal drama to a Source stronger than my instinct for self-sabotage and finally surrendering the theatrics. I prayed every day for emotional sobriety. One day at a time. I got therapy. I got better. I became well. But I know that as far as emotions are concerned, I'll always be in recovery.

Sometimes emotional bingeing is precipitated by a physical disorder—PMS, manic-depression, or clinical depression, or by stress, and fatigue. But changes in our emotional climate that disrupt and destroy our daily round are anything but amusing.

Becoming aware of our emotional weather patterns is essential if we want to remain sane, functioning, and well-loved members of the human race. Every woman has a pattern, and everyone's pattern is different. If you don't recognize yours, start paying attention. When an outburst of anger or tears erupts, step back. Breathe deeply. Center yourself. Count to one hundred before issuing an ultimatum. When you're calm, replay the circumstances surrounding your emotional surge. You're frustrated. Why? How much sleep did you have last night? What did you eat for lunch? How many glasses of wine did you drink? When was your last period? Your last physical exercise?

You're enraged. Why? You're grief-stricken. Why? You're resentful. Why? Deal with it. Talk to a friend. Write in your discovery journal. Write a letter you don't send. Update your résumé. Clean a closet or purge files at work. Now that you're calmer, what one practical step could you take to make the situation, if not better, then at least tolerable? Yes, there must be one thing you can do. Do it.

Unfortunately, emotional drunks do not overindulge with the *positive* emotions: gratitude, forgiveness, empathy, admiration, wonder. But we do recover our authenticity and our equilibrium with joy.

Cultivate happiness. Hone your sense of humor; it's the most irresistible asset any of us can possess. Smile, especially if you don't feel like it. The physical workout of the muscles around your mouth increases the positive enzymes in your brain chemistry.

"The truth is that we can overhaul our surroundings, renovate our environment, talk a new game, join a new club, far more easily than we can change the way we behave emotionally," Ellen Goodman observes. "It's easier to change behavior than feelings about that behavior."

But no behavior can be changed before it's acknowledged. And no addiction is beyond the reach of Love.

NOVEMBER 18

The Blessing of Friends

Each friend represents a world in us, a world possibly not born until they arrive, and it is only by this meeting that a new world is born.

—ANAÏS NIN

Angels aren't our only constant reminders of Divinity's devotion to our emotional, physical, and psychological well-being. So are our friends. Angels bestow grace and perform miracles; so do our friends. Angels are Divine messengers; so are friends. God speaks to us through all those intimate chats, conversations, and confessions. Probably because, if we'll listen to anyone, it's to a pal who loves us unconditionally and is committed to our happiness.

Our friends are the jewels in our crown of contentment. We need to treat them as preciously as we truly hold them in our hearts. There are many ways to do this. Rituals of friendship are especially meaningful. Take each other out for festive birthday lunches. Share your favorite books. Read one simultaneously, then get together once a month for afternoon tea or coffee just to discuss it. Be on the lookout for newspaper and magazine articles, recipes, and cartoons you can clip or photocopy and drop them in the mail. Remember friends with cards and thank-you notes. Brief, encouraging notes when tough times hit will be treasured, even more than phone calls. Share resolutions or aspirations with a friend on New Year's Eve. Go on walks together. Make annual outings a tradition: antiquing, flea marketing, or thrifting together in the summer; holiday shopping together in the winter. Once a year, have a swap meet of clothes and accessories. When a friend's sick, deliver a get-well "indulgence basket" filled with bedside comforts: something irresistible to read, cough drops, tissues, assorted fruit teas, homemade soup, a small, flowering plant. Send or give friends flowers: spur-of-the-moment bouquets from a street vendor before you meet for lunch or to bring a smile during dark days. When there's a death in a friend's family, instead of making a contribution in the deceased's name or sending flowers to the funeral (others will do that), wait a couple of days and send her a beautiful plant or bouquet. It will comfort her more than you can imagine. During tough times, put her name on a prayer list. Sometimes our prayers for our friends are the greatest gifts we can give them. Start or continue collections for a friend, adding a new collectible each birthday or at holiday time. When giving a cherished pal a gift, always give her something she'd never give herself, an indulgence. Cook for your friends. During trying times—while a friend is sick or under tremendous stress—double a recipe and deliver a casserole to her home.

Above all, let your friends know how much you love them. Tell them frequently how much you treasure the gift of their friendship. Sadly, significant others come and go. Children grow up. Parents die. Siblings are separated by distance. But our friends are the continuous threads that help hold our lives together. Cherish your friends, not only in thought but in action. "Friends are people who help you be more yourself," Merle Shain reminds us, "more the person you are intended to be."

NOVEMBER 19

The Kindness of Strangers

Whoever you are—I have always depended on the kindness of strangers.

—BLANCHE DUBOIS (TENNESSEE WILLIAMS)

In the Bible, the angels who intervened in the lives of humans were most often strangers who appeared on the scene just once, gave assistance, and then disappeared as mysteriously as they arrived. From all the published firsthand accounts, the standard angelic operating procedure hasn't changed in five thousand years.

From this day forward, start becoming consciously aware of your encounters with strangers. Look for them. Smile. Make eye contact. Strike up a conversation. You never know. Even if it's not an angelic encounter, it might be a celestine moment. Several years ago I was in New York hostessing a week of Victorian lectures at Macy's. One day I was riding in a freight elevator. Not thinking I was doing anything extraordinary, I held the automatic door open for two employees with their arms full, asked what floor they wanted, and made chitchat. "You must not be a New Yorker," one commented. I told them I wasn't, and they broke into laughs. "Knew it. No New Yorker would be this friendly or helpful." Later that day as I was leaving, I was really struggling with two boxes of props and a costume bag when I ran into one of my new acquaintances. Not only did he offer to carry my boxes; he walked out to the street and waited with me until he hailed a cab, sending me on my way with a smile.

Never turn down a stranger's offer of help, unless you're alone in a dark, secluded place, where you shouldn't be in the first place. Life is hard for many women. But gradually, I'm becoming aware that it's really not as hard as we make it. One of the reasons real life is difficult is that we don't ask for assistance—from family, friends, co-workers, strangers. We feel uncomfortable, as if asking for help is confirmation that we're completely inept or spongers.

Stop the rather self-centered assumption that a little help is too much to ask for. Because we become a burden only when we're overwhelmed by our own hubris and have to rely on others to bear our load as well as their own.

Be kind to strangers. Let strangers be kind to you. Think of it as a positive exchange of comfort and compassion in the circle of life. Remember, as St. Paul reminds us, "Some have entertained angels unaware." And some of us have encountered them without knowing, sending them away before receiving their blessing.

Blessed Be the Ties That Bind

Call it a clan, call it a network, call it a tribe, call it a family.
Whatever you call it, whoever you are, you need one.

—JANE HOWARD

Around this time of year we start thinking of family, sometimes lovingly, sometimes with dread. Although the configuration of the family has changed drastically since the Victorian era, what hasn't changed is our need for close ties to those who call us their own.

Real life often frays the ties that bind families. Some families are separated by distance, others by estrangement and obligation. Many women today care not only for their children and spouses but also for their elderly parents. Constant caretaking often creates strain and resentment between us and our parents as we assume more responsibility for their affairs.

But it is possible to draw close to those we love if we plan for it. It seems absurd that we must make time for love, whether it's carving out time for a romantic interlude with a partner, setting up an official lunch date with a sister, or penciling in a long telephone call with a brother or a favorite cousin. But there you have it.

I have a dear friend who is absolutely marvelous about remembering her large extended family and great circle of friends. The way she does it is to buy a stash of cards regularly throughout the year for all occasions. At the beginning of every month, as automatically as she does her bills, she looks at her calendar to see whose birthday is coming up or what holiday. Many times we have the loving impulse to send a get-well, new-baby, or condolence card, but because we have to make a special trip to get one, the loving gesture is lost, not through indifference but inconvenience.

Be creative with your gestures. If you have a favorite meditation book, get one for your sister and mother. Tell them that when you read yours, you'll be thinking of them. Become an inveterate clipper of articles that will interest or amuse family members. I keep scissors handy when I'm reading and place the clips in a special basket. Every couple of weeks, usually when I settle accounts, I'll drop them in the mail. You don't have to write more than "Thought you might like this." The gesture takes a total of five minutes from clipping to putting a stamp on the envelope, but the cheer it brings is amazing.

If you live away from family members, schedule telephone calls on a regular basis. Elderly parents need the reassurance of a weekly check-in that they can count on and look forward to.

We all remember the children in our extended families around the holidays, but it takes a little extra effort to remember the kids' birthdays. There are more hurt and silent feelings smoldering over this one omitted gesture than you can imagine. Try to make the effort. Not having time, or "meaning to," really doesn't cut it. None of us have time, all of us mean to. We *all* can do it, once we make thoughtfulness easy with a system.

Share family stories. Record them on audiotapes so they won't get lost. Especially have your parents and grandparents record their memories. After he's gone, the sound of your father's voice will break your heart but heal your soul. Go through your old family photographs and have copies made for everyone. Start an extended family video record. Try to get together annually.

After a friend's mother died, there was a small amount of insurance money to be divided among the grown children. She and her siblings didn't want to drift apart, but they knew they'd have to make an effort to stay close since everyone lived so far from each other. They created a reunion fund to pay for lodging and food so that everyone could get together each summer. She says it was the first few reunions that were so crucial; after that, a new family tradition had been established. Now my friend feels closer to her brothers and sisters as an adult than she ever did as a child.

Simone Weil believed, "To be rooted is perhaps the most important and least recognized need of the human soul." That's a wonderful thought to meditate upon this Thanksgiving.

NOVEMBER 21

Playing Hooky

You must have been warned against letting the golden hours slip by. Yes, but some of them are golden only because we let them slip.
—J. M. BARRIE

Today let's meditate with our calendars open. How does your week look? Which day could you take off without your world grinding to a halt because you're temporarily unavailable to keep it spinning? Good. Now write in, "mental health day."

Remember the "mental health" days we'd cite in high school in order to drop out for a day? It's time to revive the tradition. Don't feel guilty about calling in sick; this is preventive action. Sometimes I wish I were a physician specializing in women's medicine. I would surprise each one of my patients annually with a written prescription to play hooky for a day. I would convince them that hooky is absolutely necessary for their good health: physical and psychological. Then I would give them an official note excusing them from real life. I think the crucial reason it's so difficult to be a grown-up is that there's no one to write a note for us excusing us from the job, the marriage, caring for Mom, and driving the car pool. Don't worry. I'll write your note. Will you write mine?

Playing hooky is not the same as "sitting one out." When—because you simply can't stand it anymore—you sit one out by taking a sick day or a vacation day, you don't have the creative energy for "hookiness." When we play hooky, the operative word here is "play" and no one's to know it but your authentic self. (Or a good friend who's playing hooky with you.) Send your husband off to work, call in and say you'll see whomever tomorrow, take the kids to day care. If you're at home, call a sitter or arrange with another mother to exchange hooky days.

Now you have approximately eight hours to call your own. Do whatever seems most frivolous, most totally self-indulgent. Get a European body wrap, a pedicure, a cosmetic makeover, or a facial. Treat yourself to an aromatherapy massage. Pretend you're a tourist and take in the local attractions. Go to the movies. Go out to lunch in another part of town. Stay at home watching soap operas, talk shows, classic sitcoms, or cinema on cable. Rent *Ferris Bueller's Day Off*. Read a fabulous novel in one sitting with a small box of Godiva chocolates in your lap. Don't answer the phone. Only do what you want to do, not what needs to be done. Pick up the kids and your favorite carryout food. When your day is over, all you've accomplished is caring for your soul.

Luxuriate in your idleness. "It is impossible to enjoy idling thoroughly unless one has plenty of work to do," the Victorian British writer Jerome K. Jerome confessed. "There's no fun in doing nothing when you have nothing to do. . . . Idleness, like kisses, to be sweet must be stolen."

NOVEMBER 22

Meditation for Bad Girls

It's so easy to be wicked without knowing it, isn't it?
—ANNE SHIRLEY
(L. M. MONTGOMERY)

A friend and I were chatting away on the phone when she blithely confessed doing something totally outrageous but hilarious. "You're so bad," I admonished her with admiration (especially because ninety-nine percent of the time she is too good for her own good). After we stopped laughing long enough to catch our breath, she suggested that bad girls have something to teach the rest of us.

How to spot a bad girl. Bad girls sip only champagne and cocktails—not beer, wine, sherry, mineral water, café látte, or Darjeeling tea. (Think Martinis, Stingers, Black Russians.) Bad girls prefer spandex, halters, high heels, fishnet stockings, silk, suede, leather, or white satin cut on the bias and black satin cut down to here. Bad girls have blond, raven, or flaming tresses, red mouths and nails. Think Mae West, Rita Hayworth, Ava Gardner. (But the baddest girls have mousy brown hair.) Bad girls wear capri pants, mules, cashmere or mohair twinsets, silk scarves covering their pin curls, and black sunglasses to the grocery store, then don black tuxedos and silver fox boas at night.

Bad girls are in touch with their inner bitch because they run with dobermans wearing studded black leather collars. Bad girls travel to Vegas with their ex's gold card while their own name is still on it. Are passionately loyal to their friends. Have been known to torture those who break the hearts of pals. Bad girls call the psychic friends network. Have their own astrologer. Know a cusp is not an intimately transmitted condition. Bad girls listen to Billie Holiday. Know the importance of regular waxing. Bad girls exercise muscles the rest of us don't even know we have. Bad girls smell expensive and never leave the house without wearing fabulous earrings. Read Nietzsche. Buy the *National Enquirer*. Can pronounce Goethe and recite *Fleurs du Mal*. Bad girls use cigarette holders; really bad girls attend cigar dinners.

Bad girls like disguise: they like presenting themselves as perfect moms, ice princesses, and librarians. Bad girls are passionate while the rest of the world is cool. Prefer gold to silver. Bare their midriffs, never their souls. Bad girls make hay on Ralph Lauren sheets. But bad girls never marry for love, which is why they often change their names. Really bad girls have numbered bank accounts. Bad girls know it's not the cards you're dealt but how well you play your hand. Bad girls win at blackjack. Vacation at backgammon tournaments in Monaco. Frequent pool halls but shoot billiards. Have a bookie, accountant, and lawyer on retainer. Bad girls send large checks to good causes and never take a tax deduction. Bad girls don't just *want* to have fun, they make sure they do. Bad girls are committed to the philosophy of personal pleasure.

Most of us are only bad girls in our dreams. But there's a pattern in the bad-girl lifestyle that deserves contemplation. Bad girls buy what they want to buy, eat what they want to eat, wear what they want to wear, sleep when they want to sleep. Bad girls do not have therapists because they don't need them. Instead, bad girls have housekeepers and masseuses.

Bad girls realize this isn't a dress rehearsal. Real life is what you make of it.

You can be bad. You can be good. You just sure as hell better be authentic.

True Thanksgiving

An open home, an open heart,
here grows a bountiful harvest.

—JUDY HAND

The turkey is in the oven, filling the air with the fragrance of anticipation, and my heart is glad. The pies are cooling on the rack, overflowing with the fruits of the earth, and my heart is full. Conversation, companionship, and conviviality transform the rooms of this beloved home, and my heart is at peace.

Soon dear ones—family and cherished friends—will gather at the table to rejoice in our bounty of blessings, and with us lift up their hearts in thanksgiving. As the table is set, my heart gratefully remembers the legacy of love and tradition represented in the talismans of freshly laundered linens, sparkling crystal, and gleaming china. The silver shines, the candles glow, the flowers delight us with their beauty.

This is good. This is very good. Let us hold fast to this authentic moment of Simple Abundance. Let us cherish this feeling of complete contentment. Let us rejoice and praise the Giver of all good. The English novelist Thomas Hardy believed that the days of declining autumn created an inner season in which we could live "in spiritual altitudes more nearly approaching ecstasy" than at any other time of the year. Let us exult in our souls' ecstatic accord.

Come, my thankful sisters, come. Offer grace for the bounty of goodness. Raise the song of harvest home, the glass of good cheer, the heart overflowing with joy. We have so much for which to be thankful. So much about which to smile, so much to share. So much, that in this season of plenty, we can embrace the season of relinquishment. All we have is all we need.

O beloved Spirit, truly you have given us so much, an extravagance of riches. Give us, we pray, one thing more. The gift of grateful hearts. Hearts that will not forget what You have done.

The Blessing of Health

The first wealth is health.

—RALPH WALDO EMERSON

At this time of year our conscious attention often turns to what we don't have rather than what we do—and for a very good reason. The season of non-stop shopping has arrived. With Thanksgiving only just behind us, the race to get ready for the next round of holidays begins. No sooner have we celebrated the season of plenty than, with the advent of the first official days of Christmas shopping, we enter four frenetic weeks of looking, finding, buying, and ordering—but not for ourselves. We feel overwhelmed by a season of lack.

So before we head to the mall, it would do our souls good to have a reality check, in the form, not only of counting our blessings, but of focusing on them. Money is going to have to buy a lot in the next few weeks, but it can't buy the gifts that count most: good health, a loving and supportive marriage, healthy children, the fulfillment of creative expression, and inner peace. We forget this, not because we're ungrateful louts, but because we get distracted with the razzamatazz of real life. Now is the time to remember. What if I gave you a choice. You're guaranteed all the above joys but not a BMW in the driveway. Or you are guaranteed a BMW in the driveway, with the cash to pay comfortably for the luxury home adjacent to it, but you'll have to throw the dice for the Real Life blessings. Which would you choose?

The blessing we'll meditate on today is health. We can't buy good health, no matter how much money we have. We can purchase the best medical treatment available in the world, but good health is not for sale. Health is a priceless gift from Spirit that most of us take for granted until we become sick. "One of the most sublime experiences we can ever have is to wake up feeling healthy after we have been sick," Rabbi Harold Kushner reminds us in *Who Needs God*. "Even if it is only relief from a headache or toothache, the health we take for granted most of the time is suddenly seen to be an incredible blessing." Today, realize if you have nothing else but your health, you are a wealthy woman. If you have a healthy mind, a healthy heart, and reserves of stamina and creative energy to draw on, the world is literally lying at your feet. With your health you have *everything*.

But health is not just the absence of sickness. Good health is vitality, vigor, high energy, emotional equilibrium, mental clarity, and physical endurance. *These* are the gifts to pray for, not just that your credit charge purchases will be approved and you won't have to slink away in disgrace.

Take your vitamins. Thank Spirit for the health you enjoy, and ask for more. If there is only one spiritual lesson I can inscribe on your consciousness, it's to ask. Ask and you shall receive. Ask and if you don't get it, at least you tried. Ask and be *specific*. Today, why not ask for the creative and physical energy you'll need, not just to survive the holiday season, but to enjoy it?

NOVEMBER 25

When You're Sick

Illness is the doctor to whom we pay most heed; to kindness, to knowledge, we make promises only; pain we obey.

—MARCEL PROUST

"You feel like you're dying, you look like you're dying, and you sound like you're dying," my doctor said while studying my lab slips and X ray. "Thankfully, you're not. You've got a relapse of the flu, infected sinuses, and now pleurisy. I want you to take an antibiotic and go back to bed where you belong until you're well enough to be up, which could be another week to ten days." When I feebly protested that I'd already been sick with the flu for three weeks and that I was far behind in my work, my doctor nodded sympathetically. "Well, go home then, take your medicine, put on your pajamas," she advised, "and write a meditation about how important it is to take care of yourself when you're sick. But I will be very angry if the next time we meet it's in the hospital."

I did as I was told. Sort of. I send this dispatch from underneath the covers.

Most women don't go to bed when they're sick because they can't. The children still need to be taken care of, the work still has to get done, the meals still have to be made, life marches on. So you stagger around like Typhoid Mary until you drop. One morning you just can't move and with good reason. You're sick. For a day or two—at the most—you allow yourself a reprieve. Your mate and/or the children of the household solicitously inquire if there's anything you need, then quietly close the bedroom door so you can rest. Frequently, they'll poke their heads in to check on you because the sight of mother prone on the bed for more than two hours registers a 6.5 on their personal Richter scales. "Feeling better yet?" you're asked cheerfully. Eventually, after this question has been posed enough times, you say you do, even if you don't. You get out of bed, get dressed, and get ready once again to swallow swords while juggling flaming torches. The show must go on.

But sometimes we can't get up. Sometimes we're so run-down that we can't shake the flu standing up, or our bad cold becomes bronchitis or we break a bone, slip a disc. Sometimes the unthinkable confronts us: a lump in the breast, a high white-cell blood count, a whack on the head, chest pains that stun us into submission. We're not asked politely if we'd like to pause on the path for a refreshing respite. We're abruptly ordered to a halt.

The deeply spiritual Southern writer Flannery O'Connor came to believe, "In a sense sickness is a place more instructive than a long trip to Europe, and it's always a place where there's no company, where nobody can follow." The next time you're sick, stop feeling guilty about it. And quit operating under the deranged and dangerous delusion that *it's all under your control*. Instead of setting yourself up for a fall, give yourself permission to drop out for as long as you really need to in order to (1) get well and (2) gently explore this strange but temporary detour. Be as open to new insights as an inquisitive tourist would be.

If I'd never sustained a head injury ten years ago, I don't think I would have started my own business, written a syndicated newspaper column, or eventually published three books. My nearly two years' arbitrary sabbatical provided me with the opportunity to strike out on a new path after I recovered. Every illness, from a cold to cancer, has a life-affirming lesson for us if we're willing to be taught. It can be simple or profound. Learning to take better care of ourselves in the future in order to stay healthy. Bringing more harmony into our daily affairs. Balancing our need for rest and recreation with the demands of responsibility. Appreciating the subtle nuances of the dark days as well as the light-filled ones. Seeking Wholeness as well as healing. Searching not just for a possible cure, but for the probable cause.

Flannery O'Connor searched for the positive aspects of her illness until she viewed her tutorial with lupus as "one of God's mercies." We may never become that enlightened. But the next time you're not feeling well, *please* cradle yourself gently with kindness and compassion. You'll be better for it.

NOVEMBER 26

Rx for Harried Hearts and Frazzled Minds

There is hope for all of us. Well, anyway, if you don't die you live through it, day in, day out.

—MARY BECKETT

Some nights waves of weariness beat against our brains, crash against our hearts, wash over our bodies, threatening to erode our best defenses like sand dunes upon the shore. The water is cold, dark, and deep. Diversions that have worked in the past—drink, drugs, food, sex, shopping, work—now obscure a dangerous undertow. Nothing seems to hold back the tide. We need someone to throw us a line, to rescue us from drowning in disappointment.

When these nights come and I find I'm stranded alone on the beach of faltering belief, I have found refuge in a very centering and comforting prayer by Dame Julian of Norwich, a thirteenth-century English mystic:

All shall be well,
And all shall be well,
And all manner of things shall be well.

This simple affirmation of faith is especially comforting because it seems to console the dark submerged sadnesses of the inexplicable, the unexpressed, the unresolved, the unfair and the undeniable that stalk my soul after I close my eyes. I'll say the prayer over and over again softly, under my breath like a mantra, not trying to understand the meaning of the words because I can't. Some mysteries are beyond our comprehension. Some mysteries we will never solve. Never know.

So instead of trying to make sense of it all, I'll simply let the Spirit of the words soothe my frazzled mind and harried heart until sleep comes. Sometimes we can't make sense of it. Sometimes *none of it makes sense.* Sometimes it just is. But if we can hold on long enough for this night to give way to another day, all shall be well, even if it's different from what we had expected. Even if it's different from what we had hoped for and believed with all our hearts would happen.

All shall be well,
And all shall be well,
And all manner of things shall be well.

NOVEMBER 27

What Women Want

The great question . . . which I have not been able to answer, despite my thirty years of research into the feminine soul, is "What does a woman want?"

—SIGMUND FREUD

A nap, Dr. Freud. A nap.

Now. Today. All right, if not today, at least on Sunday afternoon. This is the platform I'll run on: eight hours of work, eight hours of rest, eight hours to do whatever we please. Should one of those pleasant hours be spent napping on your bed under a cozy comforter, door closed, curtains drawn, I would pronounce you a woman of great discernment.

A nap is not to be confused with sleeping. We sleep to recharge our bodies. We nap to care for our souls. When we nap, we are resting our eyes while our imaginations soar. Getting ready for the next round. Sorting, sifting, separating the profound from the profane, the possible from the improbable. Rehearsing our acceptance speech for the Nobel Prize, our surprise on receiving the MacArthur genius award. This requires a prone position. If we're lucky, we might drift off, but we won't drift far. Just far enough to ransom our creativity from chaos.

Where to have a proper nap? Your own bedroom. On the living room couch when you visit your parents because the grandchildren have been told to leave their poor mother alone and go outside to play (just the way you were told when you were little and *your* poor mother wanted to be alone). Or in a hammock. On a chaise lounge. Under an umbrella on the beach. In a wingback chair in front of a fire.

How long do we nap? One hour at the very least.

How do we do this if we have small children at home? We nap when they nap. But they *don't* nap, you say. They do now.

How do you nap at the office? Unfortunately, you don't, unless you shut the door and put your head on the desk for a quickie. Usually this is reserved for when our eyes are sizzling out of their sockets. Which makes the tradition of the Sunday nap all the more essential. If you want to be happy for the rest of your life, napping is not optional.

How do you begin this tradition? Sunday at three o'clock, after the potatoes are peeled and the roast is in the oven, you disappear up the stairs or down the hall. Reassure them you will be back. Tell anyone who might be interested in your whereabouts that you need to sort something out. Alone. If you must look like you're about to do something productive, carry the newspapers with you as if you're going to read. What they don't know can only help you. Now crawl under the covers. Good. You've done it.

"No day is so bad it can't be fixed with a nap," Carrie Snow insists. No day is so good that it can't be made better with a terrific time out.

Daydreams

Reverie is not a mind vacuum. It is rather the gift of an hour which knows the plentitude of the soul.

—GASTON BACHELARD

Were you admonished in no uncertain terms during your wonder years to get your head out of the clouds? Quit daydreaming? Unfortunately, so was I. It's taken me three decades to unlearn the impulse to be practical. Just imagine what you might have accomplished if only you'd been encouraged to honor your creative reveries as spiritual gifts.

Daydreams are the fertile soil in which our imaginations flourish and reach for the Light. Daydreams incubate creativity and make possible reveries, visualization, and maybe even visions. A lot of people think that daydreams are fantasies, but fantasies possess a sense of improbability and often danger. Fantasies are perfectly healthy—we all have them, especially sexual ones—and they're very therapeutic. Fantasies allow our shadows to act out our unacceptable tendencies in the safety of a protective inner hologram. Mrs. Billy Graham was once asked if she ever thought of divorcing her famous evangelist husband to whom she had been married for half a century. No, she confessed, but she'd often thought of murder.

We must enter a daydream—willingly suspend conscious thought of reality with our eyes open—before we can experience the joy of reverie. Poets, artists, writers, musicians, and scientists know that the Muse visits in reverie, even if the subject of the reverie has absolutely nothing to do with the creative project at hand. Reveries seem to be experienced through a scrim, a gauzy curtain, just beyond the other side of consciousness. Reveries are always pleasurable but take time. I need at least fifteen minutes of active daydreaming before I can enter the reverie zone. You'll know you've experienced one if you feel as if you've been pulled back into your body when you're snapped out of it.

Visualizations are daydreaming's virtual reality: a deliberate, positive scene-setting of what you'd like to see happen in your future. When we visualize, we make the interior scene as realistic and detailed as possible, coloring the scene with the senses until what we are viewing is so realistic it triggers an emotional response: happiness, ecstasy, joy, relief, thanksgiving. Since the subconscious mind cannot distinguish between reality and virtual reality, deliberate visualization over a period of time usually results in the desired end. The subconscious mind is the soul's servant; it willingly sets in motion whatever behavior and circumstances are necessary to manifest physically the desired program. The pulse of the subconscious is belief. If you *truly* believe it, you'll eventually see it in your life.

Visions are Divine revelations through supernatural images. Visions are usually the province of saints, mystics, and shamans because these special people are spiritually strong enough to handle them. We can't really induce a vision, although we can invoke one through daydreams. But if you're not successful at visions, think of this as a blessing. Visions utterly, dramatically, vividly, often violently change the course of lives. You don't go back or stay in one place after you've encountered a vision. You're propelled forward in a quantum leap. Those who are able to call forth visions usually prepare themselves for the experience with days of isolation. Native Americans and indigenous people like the Aborigines embark upon "vision quests" as ceremonial rites of passage, and while this is an ancient tradition, it's not one that readily translates into a contemporary woman's real life. There are many marvelous books available offering the wisdom of different spiritual paths, but most of them seem to have been written by people who do not have children; people who are free to travel to ashrams, convents, monasteries, power points and sacred places where Heaven and earth meet. But I believe with all my heart that today's woman can and must find this sacred intersection in her daily round. We've been given the spiritual tools of prayer, meditation, solitude, gratitude, simplicity, order, harmony, beauty, joy, and daydreams. "A dream is a scripture," the Italian novelist Umberto Eco tells us in *The Name of the Rose*. If we seek divine revelation, we'll find it, even if it occurs during a bus ride or while folding laundry.

NOVEMBER 29

Nightscapes

Dreams are illustrations . . . from the book your soul is writing about you.
— MARSHA NORMAN

Last night I dreamed I was at a flea market searching for the Holy Grail, supposedly hidden in a bushel of gold, silver, and copper sugar bowls. I had just spied it when a pink porcelain vase I didn't even know I was holding shattered onto the concrete floor and I had to rush out into a thunderstorm to get the children off a beach. I'm sure there's a message encrypted in there, though I haven't had time today to figure it out. But at least I've written the dream down, so that I can seek divination when an opportunity for reflection presents itself.

While I've been on the path toward authenticity, I've experienced more technicolor nightscapes than I've ever known. We have dreams every night, though we don't always remember them. As you seek your authenticity don't be surprised if you start remembering more dreams. This is not a coincidence. We communicate our willingness for Divine revelation with daydreams, and our authentic self responds with a visual fax in the form of a nightscape.

Our dreams are Divine stories that reveal where we've been and why, where we're headed, and the easiest way to get there. Dreams are our authentic Rosetta stones. Each night new hieroglyphics are inscribed, but not in Egyptian. Our Divine inscriptions are familiar faces, settings, objects, pursuits, dilemmas. We just need to make time to translate them. Dreams are also problem solvers. When we are perplexed about a course of action or need creative direction, we can seek Divine assistance through our dreams. Scientists, inventors, writers, and composers creatively brainstorm with their authentic selves in nightscapes. Beethoven and Brahms would jump out of bed in the middle of the night to write down scores. Thoreau kept a pencil and piece of paper under his pillow. Samuel Taylor Coleridge received the entire text to the poem "Kubla Khan" in a dream, and Robert Louis Stevenson worked out plot developments to *The Strange Case of Dr. Jekyll and Mr. Hyde* while dreaming.

The most informative dreams usually occur when we've gotten a good night's sleep and didn't go to bed exhausted or intoxicated. If you can't pick up a pen the moment you get out of bed because you have children, lie quietly before getting up, and run the dream consciously through your mind several times so that you can remember the gist of it. If you do find time to write it down sometime during the morning, you'll be surprised that your pen will reveal details you didn't even remember. After a few hours of consciousness, however, even vivid nightscapes tend to fade back into the deep.

Jung believed that all the participants in our dreams are aspects of ourselves. If that's the case, then my dream last night was a clear signal from Spirit that Simple Abundance—the search for my authentic self—is the path I need to continue following in order to become the woman I really am. But I don't think the message was meant only for me.

The Holy Grail is our authenticity. It's glimpsed hidden among what is familiar to us—home, family, work, pleasures. But what appears on the surface to be ordinary—sugar bowls—is really a treasure because the sugar bowls are all made of precious metals. The vase that slips to the floor and shatters is who we were before we awakened to our Divinity. Our authenticity begins to emerge in our daily round, but as it does, sudden storms develop as the ego tries to frighten us back into denial. We are the little children huddling on the beach afraid to move forward. We feel alone and helpless. Then, when we look up, we see our authentic self rushing toward us—strong, beautiful, and brave. Gently she scoops us into her arms and reassures us there is nothing to fear. She has come to carry us to safety. To return us to Wholeness. To bring us Home.

The Loss of Control

We are most deeply asleep at the switch when we fancy we control any switches at all.

—ANNIE DILLARD

Life is an illusion," the notorious World War I double agent Mata Hari confessed in 1917, as her eyes met a French firing squad. You know what they say about confessions on the way out: it's the truth whether you believe it or not. Certainly Mata Hari lived the ultimate illusion. She was all things to all men, at least until she gave herself away by assuming she had it all under control. First she seduced French officers into divulging military secrets that she passed along to the Germans. Then she cajoled the Germans into giving her information coveted by the French. But the trouble with illusion, as the famous femme fatale discovered to her regret, is that you can't keep it up forever. Eventually it all goes up in a puff of smoke, and you might not be left standing when the smoke clears.

Illusions are the conscious mind's double agents. The ego doesn't like to think that anybody—especially the authentic self—can do it better than she can. So she seduces the rational mind into believing those things that help us make it through the day—that this time he'll stop drinking, that the kid's just going through a phase, that the argument's over money and not power, that the unworkable will work, *if you just try a little harder*. Now, maybe all of this is true. But if it's not, you're setting yourself up for the double-cross. When that subterfuge succeeds, the master illusion—the mind's Mata Hari—moves in for the kill, convincing you that life can be manipulated.

Life can't. But we can. A few weeks go smoothly, at home and work, and suddenly we secretly succumb to the lure of thinking we can control relationships or the course of events. We line everything up in perfect order so that, through sheer force of will, we'll be at the right place at the right time. But when we become addicted to thinking we can control another person's behavior or a particular outcome, we're as vulnerable as a crack addict who thinks this hit will be her last. High on determination, we assume we can handle the day, the deal, the deadline, the divorce, the disease, if we can just keep everything under control. When we can't, we spin dangerously *out of control* and into a nosedive. As Melanie Beattie reminds us in *The Language of Letting Go*: "Whatever we try to control does have control over us and our life."

And while we might walk away from the wreck, we're often more upset by the loss of the illusion than by the reality of the rubble. The good news is that we can pick up the pieces and salvage the best of a bad situation, but only after we become aware that we have unconsciously betrayed ourselves.

You can never lose something if you never had it to begin with. You were never in control and never will be. Let go of that illusion so that you can cut your losses and move on. Acceptance of the inevitable—as difficult and painful it might be today—is the first step toward an authentic trade-off. "We trade a life that we have tried to control," Melanie Beattie reassures us, "and we receive in return something better—a life that is manageable."

Joyful Simplicities for November

◆§ Call for the J. Peterman Company mail-order catalogs. Trust me, they want to hear from you (tell them SBB sent you). You want both the latest "Owner's Manual" featuring romantic, vintage reproductions of classic and exotic apparel and accessories, and the "Booty, Spoils & Plunder" catalog, which is a collection of furniture, decorative accessories, and anything else that captures Peterman's eye on his travels. If you order these catalogs, you'll have so much fun daydreaming, armchair traveling and remembering, that you'll thank me when we meet. Peterman won't thank me for this tip, however: each January his "Anti-Recession" sale is worth waiting for all year long. (Write the J. Peterman Company, 2444 Palumbo Drive, Lexington, Kentucky 40509; 1-800-231-7341. If you're calling from Sydney, London, or Prague, it's 606-268-2006. Fax: 800-346-3081.)

◆§ If you've been hesistant to strike up a reciprocal relationship with your guardian angel, don't be. You have everything to gain and nothing to lose but your skepticism. I love Terry Lynn Taylor's angel books, *Guardians of Hope*, *Messengers of Light*, and especially, *Creating with the Angels*. Eileen Elias Freeman's *AngelWatch Foundation* gathers information on angels and their work in the world today and features them in the bimonthly *AngelWatch* Magazine. (For information send a stamped self-addressed envelope to P.O. Box 1397, Mountainside, New Jersey 07092.)

◆§ Native American legend reminds us that both good and bad dreams hover over us while we sleep, waiting to capture our minds for the night. In order to ensure a peaceful night's sleep, "dream catchers" were prepared: webs of colored string with a hole in the middle to let happy dreams pass through to the subconscious mind. Bad dreams are caught in the dream catcher's net, where they disappear with the first light of a new day. Dream Catchers made by Native Americans (as well as kits for making them) are available from large craft stores, ethnic gift shops, and catalogs. You can also make one yourself by taking a small embroidery hoop and stringing it with a net made of colored embroidery thread. (Be sure to leave a hole in the middle.) Add festive colored beads (green is the color of abundance; rose or red is the color of love; blue is the color of healing and protection; purple is the color of inner power) and feathers. Hang it over your bed.

🌿 Write your own personal grace and offer it for the first time on Thanksgiving. This is a wonderful restorative, because you must carefully consider those things for which you are truly grateful. To inspire you, peruse *One Hundred Graces* edited by Marcia and Jack Kelly.

🌿 Fill a basket of food and take it to a shelter the day before Thanksgiving. Re-create your family dinner as much as possible, if you can, starting with the turkey. But any contribution you make will be welcome. If you have children, let them help you shop, load the basket, and deliver it with you. This is a very visceral reminder of how much we have for which to give thanks.

🌿 Watch the Macy's Thanksgiving Day parade.

🌿 Don't rush out the day after Thanksgiving to do holiday shopping with the rest of the world. Instead, make a pot of homemade turkey vegetable soup, write out a shopping list for the Christmas pudding ingredients, create an Advent wreath, and start listening to holiday music.

🌿 Have fun choosing your *own* Advent calendar.

DECEMBER

I open the door. The gorgeous guest
from afar sweeps in. In her hands are
her gifts—the gifts of hours and far-seeing
moments, the gift of mornings and evenings,
the gift of spring and summer, the gift
of autumn and winter. She must have searched
the heavens for boons so rare.

—ABBIE GRAHAM

December's gifts—custom, ceremony, celebration, consecration—come to us wrapped up, not in tissue and ribbons, but in cherished memories. This is the month of miracles. The oil that burns for eight days, the royal son born in a stable, the inexplicable return of Light on the longest, darkest night of the year. Where there is Love, there are always miracles. And where there are miracles, there is great joy. Gratefully we weave the golden thread of the sixth principle of Simple Abundance—Joy—into our tapestry of contentment. At last we embrace the miracle of authenticity, changing forever how we view ourselves. Our daily round. Our dreams. Our destinies. Days we once called common, we now call holy.

DECEMBER 1

Charmed Lives

There is entirely too much charm around, and something must be done to stop it.

—Dorothy Parker

Charmed lives. Crammed down our throats in the glossy pages of lifestyle magazines. Paid for with a portion of our life energy. It's sick, I tell you, sick. You know who was celebrated for having a charmed life? Macbeth. Now there's a thought worth meditating on. Did Lady Macbeth share this opinion?

Actually, we all have charmed lives. We just don't have a conscious awareness of it, especially after reading about the airbrushed lives of other women. It takes a 1990s version of Everywoman's story to help us see.

This had been one hell of a year for Everywoman. Just about everything that could go wrong, had gone wrong. Or so it seemed. Money was tight because Everywoman was paid on commission. It didn't seem to matter how hard she worked, the recession kept the paychecks irregular. Because finances were tight, there was tension in her marriage, which increased after their adjustable rate mortgage went through the roof. Her husband worked two jobs. Many of their conversations (when they were speaking) were about her finding a more reliable form of employment. Everywoman enjoyed her work and was good at it; she just needed a little more time to make it pay off. But time seemed to be running out.

That year, her various aches and pains had turned out to be due to a chronic condition. Her doctor told her to make a lifestyle adjustment: eliminate the stress and fatigue that triggered flare-ups. One of her children had required special attention to get him through a rough emotional patch, which only made the other children resentful. Last spring her dad had died suddenly. Soon afterward, her mother had a series of heart attacks and a debilitating stroke. Unable to care for herself, she had to be put into a nursing home. Her widowed mother-in-law fared better. She came to stay "temporarily" during the summer and hadn't left yet. Her teenage daughter frequently complained about having to give up her bedroom for Grandma. Seeing her mother-in-law at the dinner table made Everywoman feel guilty and resentful that she couldn't do the same for her own Mom. Everywoman felt worn to a raveling. Today she begged Anyone Who Might Be Listening to give her a break.

"You're right. It's been tough," the kindly voice of her guardian angel agreed. "Take heart. Every life comes with its hard times. The Boss says there's a holiday special going on right now. Come up and choose another life, or choose the Strength-Wisdom-Grace package. Strength to meet your challenges, Wisdom to embrace real life, and the Grace to be grateful not only for what you have, but what you've escaped."

"I want a charmed life," Everywoman said.

"A charmed life, is it? Well, let's see what's available."

The next thing Everywoman knew she was sitting in front of a celestial computer, as the charmed lives of women all around the world came on-line. The faces were familiar but different in private than in public. Not very glamorous. She was told she could exchange her life for the life of any other woman. A woman's life appeared. "How about her?" an angelic life-exchange counselor asked. "Comfortable—there's a live-in housekeeper—but rather hectic. Had to put aside her career as a famous trial attorney because of her twin daughters' cystic fibrosis."

Everywoman asked to be shown other lives . . .

There was the beautiful woman beaten by her superstar husband . . . The woman whose child was hit by a drunk driver and is now in a coma . . . The infertile woman who finally became pregnant only to discover she had breast cancer . . . The famous woman whose very public husband had a reputation for being a philanderer . . . The woman whose husband is about to go to prison for insider financial manipulation.

Everywoman was shaken. "I asked for women with charmed lives," she moaned. "You've only shown me women with great sorrow, humiliation, pain, and despair in designer clothes."

"Each of these women has been celebrated for her charmed life in those magazines you're so fond of reading. Time's up. What will be it be?"

"Is it too late to choose Strength, Grace, and Wisdom?" Everywoman asked hesitantly.

"Good choice. Has anyone told you lately that you lead a charmed life?"

DECEMBER 2

Passionate Kisses

A kiss can be a comma, a question mark or an exclamation point.
—MISTINGUETT

Every woman knows the subtle nuances of puckering up: fly kisses, bye kisses, real kisses. *Lock-the-door* kisses.

Ah, lock-the-door kisses . . . Vaguely, wistfully recalled. It's been a while since we had some of those. Actually, it's been a while since we've had any kind of kisses around here. For the last month all the kissers in this house have been gripped in a relentless cycle of contagion—strep throat, flu, bronchitis—unvanquished despite megadoses of every antibiotic known to modern medicine. At this moment I don't want to be kissed by anyone on this ward and they certainly don't want to be kissed by me.

The good news is that the same precious natural resources not being pleasurably expended in regular lovemaking can be channeled into your creativity. Waste not, want not. Passion ignites sexual energy or creative energy. Your choice. Every artist, if they're telling the truth, will confess that when they're working at full throttle—writing a book, making a movie, directing a play, preparing for an exhibition, rehearsing for a concert, choreographing a new pas de deux—the sex drive diminishes. Frankly my dear, we don't give a damn. That's because we can make wild, passionate love or make wild, passionate art. Rarely both at the same time.

This natural sublimation process works just as well in reverse. Found yourself in solitary space as far as an intimate relationship is concerned? Don't waste time sulking. Try not to get caught up in what's missing but what's presenting itself to you. Dame Fortune's knocking. Invite her in. This is the perfect time to get serious about that screenplay, sign up and *show up* for the photography class, finish your degree, check in to Shepheard's Hotel, fall in love with your authentic self. *There is nothing sexier than the woman emitting the pheromone of personal fulfillment.* You'll not be alone for long, unless you want to be.

I can think of only one reason on earth why we shouldn't be able to have all the good stuff as well as passionate kisses: real life. Every woman knows times when she's alone: by choice, by chance, by circumstance. Cheer up. Sometimes you haven't found the lips you want to kiss. Sometimes the lips you want to kiss aren't available. Sometimes the one you'd like to kiss is sweaty and chilled, hacking and moaning in the bedroom just down the hall.

DECEMBER 3

No Sex Please, We're Married

Personally I know nothing about sex because I've always been married.

—Zsa Zsa Gabor

Remember when we used to call sex "sleeping together"? How prophetic. There's one that Nostradamus missed.

Having touched on the sublimation of sex for art, let's meditate for a moment on the profound but necessary sublimation of sex for survival. Not survival of the species. Survival of the sleep-starved. The women I know lust after twelve hours of uninterrupted slumber. The only married women having sex as often as the magazines and marriage experts tell us we should be are on the soaps.

Often the real-life demands of family and work mean that married women discover there are many ways to make love besides the missionary position: turning the lights down low, handing him a nightcap, and joining him to watch a weekly news show that presents his political point of view; asking how his favorite teams are doing and listening to the answer; sleeping on the couch so that you can rest when his cough sounds like a foghorn; sending him to the auto show alone; never going to sleep without saying "I love you"; calling once a day just to see how it's going; attending a couples' massage workshop to learn how to do it yourselves; remembering his mother's birthday; wearing socks to bed; telling each other how nice you look; touching; creating a private language; filling up the tank; picking up a magazine he'd like at the newsstand; renewing her books at the library; doing the crossword puzzle together; fixing each other's favorite meals a couple of times a week; reading, talking, laughing, crying together in bed.

"Exhaustion and lack of privacy make intimate moments of raw passion rarer than in our courting days," attorney and writer Linda Aaker reassures the married chaste among us. "Sex is also meeting your partner's eyes over the tousled head of a child. . . . Sex is sometimes just sleeping well beside the person you love, and drinking coffee together."

DECEMBER 4

The Refinement of Everyday Thinking

The whole of science is nothing more than a refinement of every-day thinking.

—ALBERT EINSTEIN

There is a significant difference between thinking you know and actually *knowing*. Just as there's a significant difference between superficial change and change on a cellular level. It's one thing to move the furniture around for a fresh new look; it's quite another to rearrange your "DNA"—your destiny, nature, and aspirations—which is exactly what you're doing when you search for your authenticity. Start to do that and you get a fresh new life.

When I started writing this book, I knew that if I integrated gratitude, simplicity, order, harmony, beauty, and joy into my daily round, a sense of lack diminishes and a sense of abundance increases. That seemed to be quite enough. What I didn't know or even anticipate was the potency of the Simple Abundance process when combined with passionate and persistent reflection over two years. It is virtually impossible to write a book on authenticity as a spiritual and creative path and not be profoundly changed by it.

On paper, Einstein's mathematical equation $E = mc^2$ appears rather benign, doesn't it? But it led to the development of the atomic bomb.

On paper, gratitude/simplicity/order/harmony/beauty/joy = authenticity appears equally benign. But I have discovered that this equation leads to complete personal and spiritual transformation—a mystical metamorphosis of our particular "DNA" that's so deep our egos don't know whether they're coming or going. One minute we're sure of ourselves, the next, we're second-guessing. This can be very disconcerting to our conscious selves.

Of all the definitions of the *ego* I've ever discovered, my favorite is Joseph Campbell's: "What you think you want, what you will to believe, what you think you can afford, what you decide to love, what you regard yourself as bound to." Now, there's one tough babe to reckon with, and she's got a stranglehold on your destiny, nature, and aspirations that's so strong it will take nothing less than a Divine detonation before she lets go.

Don't worry. About this time, you're poised for critical mass—that point when a self-sustaining chain reaction occurs.

In physics, nuclear fusion occurs when two separate elements, like hydrogen and helium, are forced together. Through the exertion of extreme pressure and temperature, a surge of energy as powerful as the sun is suddenly released until the hydrogen and helium are completely transformed, producing an entirely new force in the universe. This is how new stars are created.

In your search for authenticity, a similar process occurs. You fuse the six Simple Abundance principles, or outward lifestyle changes, with your own inner work, or what Einstein called "the refinement of everyday thinking." Now exert real life's pressures and the heat of your own passions on the six principles, and ponder for at least one to two years. The result? One day the transformative process builds to a point at which it can no longer be contained within. A huge surge of creative energy is suddenly released, bringing forth a completely new entity: your authentic self, the visible manifestation of your soul.

When this happens, "what you think you want, what you will to believe, what you think you can afford, what you decide to love, and what you regard yourself as bound to," will seem as if they belonged to another woman. They did.

After passionately and persistently exploring the origins of the universe, Albert Einstein came to know that "Something deeply hidden had to be behind things." When you passionately and persistently search for Wholeness, *you'll* know as well.

DECEMBER 5

Sigh Some More, My Ladies, Sigh Some More

Most of the sighs we hear have been edited.
—STANISLAW JERZY LEC

I have a habit that drives my husband crazy and keeps me sane.

I sigh.

Obviously, I sigh more than I am consciously aware. Yet I've noticed that whenever my sighing is brought to my attention—*"Please don't do that"*—I'm taking deep breaths for a very good reason.

Women sigh so that we won't scream. There are several occasions in the course of any woman's day when, without question, screaming is the appropriate response. However, on this side of an electrified fence, screaming is not considered good form.

So we sigh.

First we breathe in, quickly and sharply, inhaling reality, acknowledging the present situation—the current hassle or disappointment, confrontation or challenge, long wait or lack of cooperation.

We hold our breath for a heartbeat.

Then we breathe out, slowly and deeply, exhaling and letting go of our initial response—our dismay, impatience, frustration, annoyance, disappointment, regret. Letting it out. Letting it go.

The act of sighing is a quiet vote of acceptance—of "getting over it" and moving on.

Women with significant others and/or children sigh more than their solitary sisters because there are more preferences, needs, wants, wills, and demands to be dealt with, if there is to be a state of détente in the daily round. More bending in order not to break.

So should you feel the need to sigh today, by all means breathe slowly and deeply. Breathe expressively. Think of sighing as the hot air that makes rising to the occasion possible. Hot air that's pent up will eventually explode, and steam can burn. But steam that's deliberately allowed to escape through a safety valve can be converted into creative energy. So sigh without hesitation. Sigh without guilt. Sigh without embarrassment. Sigh with pleasure.

Sigh some more, my ladies, sigh some more.

The Festival of Lights

To be a Jew is a destiny.

—VICKI BAUM

In the dark days of December comes the wonderful holiday of Hanukkah, celebrated in Jewish homes. Originally known as the "Festival of Lights," Hanukkah commemorates a miracle that occurred in 165 B.C., after Judas Maccabaeus and his followers reclaimed Jerusalem from a Greek emperor who considered Israel a Greek province.

In an attempt to assimilate conquered nations into a cohesive and controllable society, the Greek empire prohibited any other religion; Jews were forced to abandon their faith and ordered to worship Greek gods. By decree, the Temple of Jerusalem was turned into a Greek shrine, and Jews were forbidden to study the Torah, celebrate their holidays, or practice Jewish customs. Many Jews, disobeying the edict, died for their beliefs. After a three-year guerrilla campaign, the Maccabees were victorious and the temple was restored to Jewish worship. As part of their rededication ceremony (the word "Hanukkah" means dedication) the Maccabees began an eight-day purification rite, only to discover there was barely enough sacred oil to keep the temple *menorah*—a candelabrum with eight branches—lit for one day. Miraculously, the temple lamp burned continuously for eight days. Ever since that time the Jewish people have observed Hanukkah in remembrance of their struggle for religious freedom and the miracle of restoration, symbolized by the abundance of oil.

Many who celebrate Christmas believe that Hanukkah is a festival reserved solely for those who practice Judaism. But as Harold Kushner points out in his enlightening and engaging meditation *To Life: A Celebration of Jewish Being and Thinking*, if it weren't for Hanukkah, we wouldn't be celebrating Christmas. Had the Maccabees not rebelled against the Greeks, the Jewish faith would have faded into Greek culture, never to be heard of again. "There would have been no Jewish community for Jesus to be born into a century and a half later. No one would have remembered the messianic promises he claimed to fulfill. Without Hanukkah, there would have been no Christmas."

When one follows any family tree back far enough, there are bound to be surprises. And those who follow the Christian path will discover, if they truly search for their roots, that by faith, we belong to the House of David. Jesus lived his entire life as an observant Jew. He celebrated Hanukkah as a child; the Last Supper was a Passover seder. All the apostles and most of those who became his early followers were Jewish. The crowds who came to hear Jesus preach called him "Rabbi," the Hebrew word for teacher. Perhaps our similarities and heritage are greater than our differences after all.

Personally, I've come to think of Hanukkah as a celebration of authenticity. The Maccabees refused to surrender what made them authentic—their faith—even if it cost them their lives. Not to be able to live as observant Jews was not to live at all. I also consider the Hanukkah miracle the earliest recorded demonstration of Simple Abundance. Two thousand years ago there was only enough sacred oil for one night. But all that these faithful, courageous, and grateful people had *was all that they needed.*

Sacred oil in a temple. Loaves and fishes on a mountainside. Miracles are of Spirit, not any one faith. Miracles are for anyone who believes. That is the heart of Hanukkah and the soul of Christmas. The more we allow ourselves to recognize the wisdom and truth in other spiritual paths, the closer to Wholeness we become.

DECEMBER 7

Are Women Human?

We are not human beings trying to be spiritual. We are spiritual beings trying to be human.

—JACQUELYN SMALL

Whether women were human fascinated the English writer D. H. Lawrence, who often explored this conundrum in his work. "Man is willing to accept woman as an equal, as a man in skirts, as an angel, a devil, a baby-face, a machine, an instrument, a bosom, a womb, a pair of legs, a servant, an encyclopaedia, an ideal or an obscenity; the one thing he won't accept her as is a human being, a real human being of the feminine sex."

Perhaps the reason men find it so difficult to accept women as human beings is because we're not, and deep down everyone knows it. But often women forget their Divinity as they go about their daily round. How often do we excuse ourselves with the expression, "Well, I'm only human."

No, you're not, and neither am I. We forget we're spiritual beings appearing for a brief span on this planet as humans. I certainly forgot that this morning when my daughter stayed home from school because she's sick. *Again.* In a little while, I'll have to take her to the doctor for a strep test and my entire work day will have been disrupted. I'm frustrated and angry; not at Katie—at real life, at deadlines. But did she realize that, when I rolled my eyes at the thought of another day gone awry? I don't think so.

Spiritual beings do not sweat real life's small stuff. They also know that most of what drives us crazy in real life *is* small stuff. The only thing that isn't small stuff is the reason you're on earth in the first place: to find that portion of the world's lost heart that only you can ransom with your love and authentic gifts and then return it, so that all of us can experience Wholeness.

A spiritual being knows that the work will be waiting for her when she gets back from the doctor's office. A spiritual being knows that there is no such thing as a deadline. Deadlines are *chronos*, the world's time; Divinity knows only *kairos*, Eternity. The deadline will be met if I remember to ask for grace. A spiritual being knows that the only thing that's not small stuff today is caring for and comforting a sick child.

This spiritual being might have also known that this morning if she'd taken five minutes to center herself.

Scripture tells us that men were created a little above the angels. But don't ever forget that women were the climax of the Spirit's creativity cycle. After woman was created, Wisdom realized there was no need to proceed further: this superior being would save the world.

Big things are expected of us.

As for me, there's a lost heart that needs to be ransomed by a spiritual being trying to be human.

DECEMBER 8

Tidings of Comfort and Joy

Gloom we have always with us, a rank and sturdy weed, but joy requires tending.

—BARBARA HOLLAND

This is the week that women's shoulders begin to droop as their list of holiday "should do's" becomes as long and heavy as Jacob Marley's chains. There's card writing, card mailing, gift buying, gift wrapping, gift sending, tree buying, tree trimming, cookie baking, party giving, turkey roasting. By next week, unless a Power greater than ourselves restores us to sanity, women will be dropping in their tracks. Not surprisingly, the Christmas holidays are the height of the flu season. The author of a recent book on simplifying our lives suggests that we "bow out" of the holidays—as if this were an option for real women. Is it for you?

When it begins to look a lot like Christmas, it's because women across the country are wearing red hats and pointed shoes to accessorize their Donna Karan suits, Gap jeans, or Lands' End sweats. In case anyone hasn't noticed, women are the ones who "do" Christmas, performing miracles on demand. Women are Spirit's deus ex machina, making holiday dreams come true from behind the scenes.

The celebration of Christmas as we know it today, with its whirl of festivity, decorations, lavish gifts, parties, and family-centered traditions, was a creation of middle-class Victorians in both England and the United States in the mid-nineteenth century. Victorian women, who were full-time homebodies, began "doing" Christmas in July. However, in the final two decades of the twentieth century, women have been doing lots of other things while we're doing Christmas. Which is why we end up doing ourselves in every December. For many women, this is the season of misery and angst: tears, tantrums, screaming, yelling, hustle, bustle, cash conflicts, royal-pain relations, and holiday humbug.

Wouldn't the real Christmas miracle be if we slowed down long enough to remember the reason for the season, so that our holiday celebrations became authentic and meaningful?

So be of good cheer. Be not frazzled, frustrated, nor frantic, for I bring you tidings of comfort and joy. If *you* do Christmas at your house, you can choose to do it your way. Whatever that way might be. You *can* consciously decide to be happy, loving, fulfilled, generous, peaceful, contented, spiritual, joyous, calm, festive, and emotionally connected to the important people in your life for the holidays this year.

Or you can, unconsciously, choose to be a wreck.

Today, *realize* that you can't do everything. Not all at once. Not in the next sixteen days. Not at all. Period.

Now, *recognize* that one of the reasons Christmas pasts probably didn't live up to your expectations is because you've tried to do too much, too perfectly.

Look at that list.

Choose to let only what you love best about the holidays remain. Cross out two more "musts." Now there's time for gazing out the window at gently falling snow, delighting in the sounds of bells and joyful music, savoring the sweet aromas of hot cider, roast turkey, and gingerbread, sipping hot chocolate and homemade eggnog, reading a holiday story each night at dusk, basking in a fire crackling on the hearth and re-creating cherished customs that care for your soul as well as the souls of those you love. "I do hope your Christmas has . . . a little touch of Eternity in among the rush and pitter patter and all," mystic Evelyn Underhill recommends. "It always seems such a mixing of this world and the next—but that, after all, is the idea!"

DECEMBER 9

The Christmas Letter

This is my letter to the world.

—EMILY DICKINSON

There is a woman still at large—charmed and dangerous. She waves her clever hand over a room and it looks like a page from *House Beautiful*. She waves her creative hand over the fruits of the earth and a feast appears nightly. Her thumb is green, her herb vinegar is curing, her potpourri recipe is sought, her PTA cupcakes are from scratch, her Halloween costumes are legendary, she still wears size 8. Her celebrity lawyer husband adores her, her five *summa cum* children think she's *laude*. She finished her holiday shopping, wrapping, and sending in November. Now she's turning her attention to making her own New Year's Eve confetti out of naturally colored crushed egg shells. I know this because I've just received her annual Christmas letter. Be forewarned. It's speeding its way to your house.

This woman must be stopped. She undermines our domestic tranquillity. She threatens the common good.

Here's the plan. This year, we'll write a letter of our own. We'll write about our exciting safari of the self and Spirit. We'll write about Simple Abundance. We'll write about the tiny changes that have made a great difference in how we approach our daily round. Then we'll write another letter, dated this time next year, in which we'll describe how our dreams came true. In it, we'll outline our glorious ideal lives in detail—exactly what we're doing, how we're doing it, who's doing it with us. But we'll write these two letters in our discovery journals only; they're for our eyes alone. Because this is not merely our letter to the world, this will be our letter to the Universe. What we're really doing is setting down our New Year's aspirations in concrete form. It's the same as writing down our goals but far more creative and fun.

Your Christmas letter to the Universe can be the most powerful of motivational tools because it engages your emotions increasing the pulses of creative energy your subconscious mind needs to transform a reverie into reality perfected.

Many of us react to Christmas letters as if they were fingernails on the blackboard of our brains. But my oldest friend—we lived across the street from each other from birth—writes fabulous annual letters which I look forward to receiving. That's because it's a Real letter; it fills me in on her family's tough times as well as on their achievements and happy times. She may send it to a hundred people, but it's as warm, witty, and authentic as Peg herself, and it reads as if she's written it only to me. So if one of your pleasures is writing seasonal greetings, please don't stop. Just remember that your family and friends don't live edited lives. You needn't either.

As for this year's crop of Christmas letters, I find they make quite absorbent liners for the gerbil cage.

DECEMBER 10

Gifts of the Magi

Christmas won't be Christmas without any presents.
—Jo March
(Louisa May Alcott)

Jo's right. Remember when she grumbled about not having any money for presents in *Little Women*? Christmas *is* about gifts. Always has been. But we feel uncomfortable with this emphasis on gimme, gimme, gimme. Buy, buy, buy. Charge, charge, charge. We admonish our children to remember the reason for the season, even though we have difficulty remembering it ourselves when we're caught up in the chaos and commotion of the holidays.

Today let's ruminate on the Real role of gifts in the Christmas story. Those gifts were wrapped in miracles, which is probably why we can't find them at malls or in mail-order catalogs. The first gift was of Spirit: unconditional Love. The next gift came from a Jewish teenager named Miriam, who was known to her family and friends as Mary. Her Christmas present was selflessness, the complete surrender of ego and will needed to bring Heaven down to earth. The gifts of her fiancé, Joseph, were trust and faith. He trusted that Mary wasn't pregnant with another man's child; he believed there really was a Divine Plan to get them through this mess. The Child brought forgiveness. Wholeness. Second chances. The angels' gifts were tidings of comfort, joy, and peace, the reassurance that there was nothing to fear, so rejoice. The shepherd boy's gift was generosity: his favorite lamb for the baby's birthday present. The innkeeper's wife's gifts were compassion and charity: a warm, dry, safe place for the homeless family to stay, her best coverlet to wrap the new mother and little one, a meal for Joseph, the donkey's fresh hay.

Three kings from the east traveled many hot, dusty miles following a bright star in search of a royal birth. The sages' divination foretold the coming of the "King of Kings"; on their camels' backs were treasures with which to honor his arrival. But when they arrived in Bethlehem, they found the newborn prince in a cow stall instead of a palace. The shocked Wise Men unwrapped gold, frankincense, and myrrh, but their Real gifts were wonder, acceptance, and courage. They offered wonder by surrendering logic, reason, and common sense. Accepting the impossible, they suspended skepticism long enough to double-cross the insane King Herod, frantically searching for the child who would change the world. With courage— at the risk of their own lives—the Wise Men helped the young family escape to a safe haven in Egypt.

Oh, yes. Christmas *is* all about gifts. Nothing but gifts. But such gifts! Gifts tied with heartstrings. Gifts that surprise and delight. Gifts that transform the mundane into the miraculous. Gifts that nurture the souls of both the giver and the given. Perfect gifts. Authentic gifts. The gifts of Spirit, a frightened teenage girl, her bewildered sweetheart, the Child, the angels, the shepherd boy, the inn-keeper's wife. The gifts of the Magi.

Unconditional Love. Selflessness. Trust. Faith. Forgiveness. Wholeness. Second Chances. Comfort. Joy. Peace. Reassurance. Rejoicing. Generosity. Compassion. Charity. Wonder. Acceptance. Courage.

To give such gifts. To truly open our hearts to receive such gifts gratefully. Christmas just won't be Christmas without any presents.

DECEMBER 11

Only Fourteen Shopping Days Till Christmas

Giving presents is a talent; to know what a person wants, to know when and how to get it, to give it lovingly and well.
—PAMELA GLENCONNER

Now that we've accepted that gifts are the center of Christmas, deciding what to give and how to get it comfortably and affordably deserves some reflection, especially considering that there are only fourteen shopping days left until Christmas.

Keep in mind that Christmas will arrive on December 25 whether we're ready for it or not. How're you doing? That frantic? In that case, promise your authentic self that this is *absolutely the last time* you'll shop, wrap, and send all your gifts in the space of four weeks. It took nine months to orchestrate the first Christmas, which is exactly what you're going to aim for in the future.

Next year, you swear, it will be different. But in order for that to happen, you're going to have to get started on it the last week of December. That's just when you're absolutely sick of Christmas, of course, but that's also when you can get next year's wrapping paper, cards, and holiday novelties at bargain prices. In addition, there are regular sales throughout the year. Keeping your eye open for bargains year round, as well as bearing in mind the special interests of your family and friends, will permit you to gather Christmas gifts at a leisurely pace and at the best prices months in advance. You won't find delightful, affordable gifts in department stores at the eleventh hour. Christmas accounts for nearly one-half of annual retail revenues. How many genuine sales do you think are going on in December?

Always work from a list of people you give gifts to, noting their hobbies, personal passions, treasured collections, and sizes. Don't try to carry it all in your head; free up some mental RAMs with written reminders. Try to keep apparel gifts for kids to a minimum; they grow in such spurts, it's virtually impossible to get the size right. Gifts purchased throughout the year, especially on sale or at outlets, aren't always returnable. It's also difficult to keep track of what's in and what's out with kids; presents aren't supposed to make everyone miserable.

Mail order is a spiritual gift, if you really use it to your advantage. When you find a potential gift for someone, stick a note on the front cover. Every month, try to get at least one Christmas gift; spacing out the spending means less stress next December, a personal present of peace of mind that won't go unappreciated.

Making gifts for those we love can be fun and occasionally economical, but only when we've got the time and creative energy to do it properly. This is *not* the day to begin that four-hundred-piece doll quilt for little Minnie May, no matter how darling either of them are. Put the patterns and magazine directions away; find the fabric on a sale table and enjoy beginning a gift of heart and hands one rainy day in March. Celebrating Christmas in July is a fabulous tradition worthy of revival. Resourceful Victorian women made most of their gifts and no one started them later than July. Hold a birthday tea on July 15 in honor of the Reverend Clement Clarke Moore, the author of "The Night Before Christmas" and start planning homemade presents.

If you're buying or making Christmas gifts ahead of time, you need a place to put them. Designate one closet, cabinet, trunk, or drawer as the gift repository. A gift-cache is a sanity saver during the year; gift gathering can become a joyful simplicity. You can't imagine the satisfaction that comes when you open your cache and pull out the perfect gift for an unexpected occasion. But should you choose to delight in your own cleverness by sneaking into your gift closet throughout the year, just remember to restock.

Since you already have your gift wrapping stashed away, you don't have to wait to wrap them in a frantic flurry; you can wrap them creatively and with pleasure. Make your wrappings part of the gift. Forget store-bought bows in big plastic bags; they're hideous and you know it. However, the really great bows can cost more than the gift. Throughout the year you can find gorgeous ribbons, cords, and trimming at fabulous prices, once you're consistently looking for them. *Label* your wrapped gift; who it goes to and what it is. Trying to mentally retrace the origins of mystery packages without opening them is not fun. But plotting a loved one's glee on gazing at your holiday remembrance is a gift of joy you give yourself.

DECEMBER 12

A Partridge in a Pear Tree

There is only one real deprivation . . . and that is not to be able to give one's gifts to those one loves most.

—MAY SARTON

I don't think many of our true loves are waiting with bated breath for a partridge in a pear tree this year. But I do know a one-size-fits-all gift that would be absolutely thrilling for everyone on your list: the gift of yourself. Unfortunately, this most personal gift is very expensive, for it requires large expenditures of our precious, but dwindling, natural resources. Time. Creative Energy. Emotion. It would be far easier to give everyone two turtle doves and be done with it.

This doesn't mean that we don't want to give of ourselves during the holidays. Actually, that's what we're desperately trying to do. Obviously, we're not doing it very well. This is why many of us end up feeling depressed and discouraged as we pack away the ornaments. How did Christmas slip out of our grasp, *again*?

Because we were holding too many things at once: obligations, promises, should-dos, conflicting commitments. "Oh, sure, no problem" is the first indication of the discombobulated mind. First thing: excuse yourself from every evening meeting for the rest of the month. Only accept social events that you *really* want to attend. Your absence might be noticed any other time of the year, but not during the holidays. Everybody's focus is as scattered as yours. You'll not be missed.

Now about those gifts. All those bright, pretty baubles blowing your budget are only symbols of the gifts you really long to give. So this year why don't you try to give them the Right Stuff?

On the first day of Christmas, I gave to my true loves:
The gift of my Undivided Attention
On the second day of Christmas, I gave to my true loves:
The gift of Enthusiasm
On the third day of Christmas, I gave to my true loves:
The gift of Creative Energy

On the fourth day of Christmas, I gave to my true loves:
The gift of Simple Seasonal Pleasures
On the fifth day of Christmas, I gave to my true loves:
The Gift of Tenderness
On the sixth day of Christmas, I gave to my true loves:
The gift of Good Cheer
On the seventh day of Christmas, I gave to my true loves:
The gift of Beauty
On the eighth day of Christmas, I gave to my true loves:
The gift of Communication
On the ninth day of Christmas, I gave to my true loves:
The gift of Surprise
On the tenth day of Christmas, I gave to my true loves:
The gift of Wonder
On the eleventh day of Christmas, I gave to my true loves:
The gift of Peaceful Surroundings
On the twelfth day of Christmas, I gave to my true loves:
The gift of Joy

"Be ready at all times for the gifts of God, and always for new ones," Meister Eckhart urges us in this season of giving. Be ready at all times to give those you love the simply abundant gifts of Spirit. If you do, they'll give you Christmas gifts you'll never forget: happy smiles and contented hearts. And you won't want to exchange them.

DECEMBER 13

Yes, Virginia, There Is a Santa Claus

Nobody can conceive or imagine all the wonders there are unseen and unseeable in the world.

—FRANCIS P. CHURCH

Francis P. Church had no intention of composing a classic essay in inspirational literature that September afternoon in 1897 when he sat down to answer a little girl's query. Virginia O'Hanlon was eight years old, precisely the age when skepticism starts to erode faith. Her friends had told her there was no Santa Claus. When she went to her father for the truth, he was as tongue-tied as many parents are when conversations start to focus on the veracity of North Pole activities. He told her to take her question to the experts on everything: the editors of the newspaper. So Virginia took pen in hand and posed the eternal question of childhood to her local paper: "Papa says, 'If you see it in the *Sun* it's so.' Please tell me the truth, is there a Santa Claus?"

Nearly a hundred Christmases have come and gone since Virginia asked for the truth, but what's Real and what's not hasn't changed. Children *of all ages* have a deep desire to believe in a great, benevolent, and generous gift giver who rewards the good. Christmas allows the child slumbering in each of our souls the chance to be reborn every year, awakening a sense of joy and wonder that even eleven months of doubt, derision, or discouragement can't snuff out. All that's required of us is that we believe.

Believe in what? Believe in whatever means the most to you at this moment. That Love makes it possible to believe in all things, especially miracles. That this is the season of miracles. That there's a miracle with your name on it. That when you wish upon a star, grace steps in to bridge the gaps until your dreams comes true. That there *is* a Santa Claus and you *have* been very, very good this year.

Have you written your letter yet? Yes, I do mean you. If you haven't, do it today with great ceremony. Sit down with a cup of hot cocoa, your best stationery, and your wish list. Pick one worldly gift and tell Santa what you want. Now pick one gift that only Spirit can give. Put your letter in an envelope and send it off. Wait. Watch what happens. Be happy.

For the rest of the season, frequently declare (under your breath is okay) during your daily round: "I believe! I believe! I believe!"

Right now I'm going to believe that Frank Church wrote today's meditation for me, as well as Virginia, a century ago:

> Virginia, your little friends are wrong. They have been affected by the skepticism of a skeptical age. They do not believe except what they see. They think that nothing can be which is not comprehensible by their little minds. All minds, Virginia, whether they be [grown-ups] or children's are little.
>
> Yes, Virginia, there is a Santa Claus. He exists as certainly as love and generosity and devotion exist, and you know that they abound and give to your life its highest beauty and joy. Alas! how dreary would be the world if there were no Santa Claus! It would be as dreary as if there were no Virginias. There would be no childlike faith then, no poetry, no romance to make tolerable this existence. We should have no enjoyment, except in sense and sight. The eternal light with which childhood fills the world would be extinguished.
>
> Not believe in Santa Claus! You might as well not believe in fairies! . . . The most real things in the world are those that neither children nor [grown-ups] can see. Did you ever see fairies dancing on the lawn? Of course not, but that's no proof that they are not there.
>
> You tear apart the baby's rattle and see what makes the noise inside, but there is a veil covering the unseen world which not the

strongest [grown-up] . . . that ever lived, could tear apart. Only faith, fancy, poetry, love, romance, can push aside that curtain and view . . . the beauty and glory beyond. Is it all real? Ah, Virginia, in all this world there is nothing else so real and abiding.

No Santa Claus! Thank God! he lives, and he lives forever. A thousand years from now, Virginia, nay, ten times ten thousand years from now, he will continue to make glad the heart of childhood.

Clap loudly if you believe.

DECEMBER 14

Legacy of Love

All happy families resemble one another, but each unhappy family is unhappy in its own way.
—LEO TOLSTOY

Most people assume that Christmas is hardest for children who've stopped believing in Santa Claus. But I think the holidays are the most difficult for those who have experienced a recent loss, through death or divorce, particularly if this is the first or second holiday after their world has been torn asunder.

Many single mothers often feel uncomfortable at Christmas and unconsciously convey this discomfort to their children. One way this is done is by putting off holiday preparations until the very last moment, then throwing everything together in a halfhearted frenzy. Perhaps one of the reasons single women and single mothers experience difficulty during Christmastime is because, deep in their hearts, they think holiday traditions belong only to perfect Norman Rockwell families. The first time a woman newly on her own opens the ornament box alone (if she even bothers to pull it out), she experiences such a sense of loss she may decide not to continue the holiday rituals she once treasured because the comparison of Christmases Past with Christmas Present is too painful.

"What's the point?" she says.

The point is that we all need the reassuring and healing messages that treasured rituals provide. "One of the most important aspects about family traditions—rituals that families continue to do year after year—is that traditions have symbols and families need symbols," Dr. Steven J. Wolin, a clinical professor of psychiatry at the George Washington University Medical School, explains: "You bring out the old glass, you sing the old songs, you say the same prayer, you wear a certain outfit, you set the table in a certain way." These are the unconscious moments of family ritual that become emotional security blankets to be tugged on in times of stress.

Cherished customs are just as important for grown women as they are for children. When I first began updating Victorian traditions for modern families, I thought the reason I delighted in doing them was so that I could create happy memories for my daughter. But after a few years, I realized that our rituals brought me comfort and joy. I longed for the reassuring rhythm of marking the seasons just as much as Katie did. We *need* to trim the tree, light the menorah, make the Valentines, dye the Easter eggs, attend the Passover seder just as much as our children do. Our souls can never outgrow the yearning for luminous and liminal moments of Wholeness.

So unpack those beloved holiday traditions. Create new ones that express your authenticity, just as you create a new lifestyle. "Traditions are the guideposts driven deep into our subconscious minds," Ellen Goodman tells us. "The most powerful ones are those we can't even describe, aren't even aware of."

DECEMBER 15

Meditation for Women Who Read Too Much

She is too fond of books, and it has turned her brain.
—Louisa May Alcott

Virginia Woolf believed that when we women who read too much arrive at the pearly gates carrying our beloved books with us, the Almighty will tell St. Peter: "Look, these need no reward. We have nothing to give them here. They have loved reading."

In real life there are women who read and women who read too little. There aren't women who read too much because this is an impossible feat. How can one read too much with only twenty-four-hour days? Lifetimes that average only 80 years?

Any time of the day is perfect for reading. Any place. Any excuse. Reading is the last refuge for addictive personalities; there are no bad side effects from reading too much. Louisa May Alcott thinks becoming too fond of books will "turn" our brains. Of course, any woman so fond of books that she felt compelled to write her own can't be all wrong. Books do turn us. Turn us on to our passions and to pursuing our passions. Turn us into authentic women. When a sentence in a book resonates within, it is the voice of your authentic self. Listen to what she's trying to tell you. Spirit is constantly communicating with us. Most of us long to experience Paradise on earth. Women who read do. Whoever said that you can't take it with you obviously never read a good book. For everything you've ever read, loved, and remembered is now a part of your consciousness. What is once cherished can never perish.

"Reading means," Italo Calvino tells us, "[being] ready to catch a voice that makes itself heard when you least expect it, a voice that comes from an unknown source, from somewhere beyond the book, beyond the author, beyond the convention of writing: from the unsaid, from what the world has not yet said of itself and does not yet have the words to say."

DECEMBER 16

Gold-Star Days

Maybe one of these days I'll be able to give myself a gold star for being ordinary, and maybe one of these days I'll give myself a gold star for being extraordinary—for persisting. And maybe one day I won't need to have a star at all.

—SUE BENDER

I haven't yet gotten to the point where I don't need gold stars: gleaming, golden, five-pointed proof that I've accomplished something that was a bit of a stretch, especially if it was remembering to treat myself with the loving kindness that seems so much easier to give to others. Back in the days of blackboards and chalk, gold stars came in a small cardboard box. You'd take the lid off to find five hundred gold, paper-foil stars, stiff with dry glue backs. Running your fingers through the small pile of possibilities, you'd hear the rustling of self-worth. Nowadays gold stars get pulled off self-sticking sheets. You don't even get the taste of success on your tongue, but I love them just the same.

A good friend of mine has a different memory of gold-star days. Her mother maintained star charts for each of her eight children. Every Sunday night after dinner, the past week's reckoning would occur in the dining room as the gridded charts revealed who had excelled at homework, chores, personal hygiene, and behavior—and who hadn't. The striving for gold stars was supposed to be a motivational game. However, accumulating gold stars under duress wasn't fun for Anne, despite the fact that she excelled at everything and was a model "good girl." For her, the pressure of constant evaluation was excruciating. Opening the cardboard box was a psychological and emotional stretching on the rack of self-respect.

But gold-star days are *very* different when we give them to ourselves. When you give yourself a gold star, sticking it to an empty calendar block, the star twinkles, winks, and whispers "Good for you, girl!" I particularly like to give myself gold stars when I'm embarking on a new self-nurturing pastime or reviving one that has fallen by the wayside: walking, creative movement, healthy eating, writing my dialogue pages, meditation, slowing down, balancing work and play. The spirit may be willing, but all too often the flesh gets sidetracked.

The extraordinary days don't need gold stars. But ordinary days sure can be brighter with a shiny, five-pointed pat on the back.

DECEMBER 17

Act Two

For years I wanted to be older, and now I am.
—MARGARET ATWOOD

The other day I switched on the television while I was waiting for the kettle to boil and caught a glimpse of my favorite actress in a cable movie. I was thunderstruck at how much older she seemed since the last time I'd seen her. If this gorgeous, high-maintenance, personal-trainer using, spa-attending woman was visibly maturing, what did a low-maintenace, car-pool schlepping, suburban mother and stressed-out-writer-on-deadline look like?

"How old do I look?" I asked my daughter when I picked her up at school. "Old enough to be my mother," the wag shot back. "Am I showing my age?" I asked a good friend over lunch. "No more than I'm showing mine," she reassured me.

How vividly I remember an evening in my sixteenth year, when a friend of my parents, who I thought was in his dotage (mid-forties) brought his beautiful new fiancée over for dinner to introduce her to the family. Mike had been an eligible bachelor for many years. Susan had been a Miss America runner-up. It was all very romantic, and I wanted all the juicy details. At one point I asked Susan, with that casual, insufferable insouciance of a smart-assed teenager, "How old are you?"

The only sound in the living room was my mother's eyebrows rising. Susan's warm smile broke through the awkward embarrassment. "Thirty-two," she said matter-of-factly.

The gulp of soda I was just about to swallow spurted out into the air. *"Thirty-two? And you're getting married for the first time?"* (It's a miracle I'm alive to recount this tale.) "Young lady," my mortified mother admonished me, "you should be ashamed of yourself. We do not ask women older than ourselves their age. Apologize to Susan immediately."

"No, please," Susan laughed, as the rest of the room broke up. "It's all right. Do you think thirty-two is too old to be a bride?"

Of course I did, unless she was going to be the bride of Methuselah. Except that Susan didn't look "middle-aged," she looked absolutely fabulous. She was the most glamorous "older woman" I had ever seen in person. But waiting until you were that *old* to get married, especially when you were gorgeous, was beyond my conception. Now, of course, I know from personal experience why she was marrying for the first time at such an advanced age. But it was too late. At that moment, Cupid marked me. Two weeks after I married my husband, I celebrated my thirty-second birthday. As I remember, it was a very good year.

Now, like many of my women friends, I'm discovering that Act Two is much more interesting than Act One. Act One just sets the scene—who our heroine is, where she came from, the forces that shaped her. It's in Act Two that the creative tension really begins to build as her story unfolds. Act Two is teeming with twists and turns as the pivotal moment of choice comes into view. Act Two reveals the dramatic center of her authentic plot. What will happen next? How will our heroine cope? How will she change?

We simply can't move into Act Two until we have several decades under our belt. Hopefully we're wiser, more experienced, self-confident, courageous, and canny. Suddenly, there's more depth and breadth to the scripts we create. "In middle age we are apt to reach the horrifying conclusion that all sorrow, all pain, all passionate regret and loss and bitter disillusionment are self-made," the novelist Kathleen Norris confessed in 1931.

But now we know how to change all that.

Don't we?

I'm ready for my close-up, Mr. DeMille.

DECEMBER 18

A Birthday Ritual

The birthday of my life
Is come, my love is come to me.

—CHRISTINA GEORGINA ROSSETTI

Today isn't my birthday, but it might be yours. If it is, I hope you're having a wonderful day—a day of authentic indulgences, joyful simplicities, contemplation, closure, and celebration.

We should all commemorate our birthdays that way. I've reached a point where I'm not really big on major birthday gatherings, but I do need to distinguish the birth day of my life in special ways from the rest of the calendar. So I've created my own birthday ritual to help me commemorate the year just past while invoking illumination for the year to come. First, I take a soothing bath, symbolically washing away the past year's pain, sorrow, regrets, mistakes, and guilt. Then I go alone to my bedroom and light one votive candle for each year. (This is not as daunting as it sounds if you use the tiny "tea lights" that come in their own metal container. Gather them together on a tray or spread them around the room.) My favorite music is playing in the background, fragrant incense fills the air, and beside my bed is a bouquet of my favorite flowers. I put on a brand-new nightgown and get comfortable in my freshly made bed. Then I offer a personal psalm of thanksgiving for my life. As the candles burn I reflect on my personal journey so far. I look at old and recent photographs, then read selections from my journal. So many wonderful moments from the past year have already slipped from my conscious memory; it's comforting to call them back for a brief visit. Next I ask for a birthday gift that only the Giver of Good can bestow: to conceive a wonderful new dream or plan; to realize a dream delayed; to overcome an old fear or be released from an old pain; to experience a new freedom; to discover a new strength; to find a new friend; to achieve a long-sought goal; to reach toward a new aspiration; to overcome a new challenge. I sip a glass of champagne, then slowly open a beautifully wrapped gift from my authentic self. And of course, it's the perfect present.

Many people who love you will try, but no one can celebrate your birthday exactly the way you need for it to be observed. That's because *no one* really knows the year you've just completed; no one else has lived it. What's more, each year is different. Your thirty-second and forty-eighth birthdays won't begin to resemble each other. Your husband, lover, children, friends, and co-workers can be aware of recent events that have unfolded in your life, but only your authentic self knows how deeply these events reverberated. Perhaps a loved one died six months ago. The rest of the world assumes you've moved on, when the reality is that the shock of your loss has only begun to wear off and your grief has just set in. Perhaps the perfect birthday gift is to have a special photograph of your loved one professionally framed or restored. No one else is going to know you need this emotional touchstone, but you do. Maybe you need, not a boisterous family party, but a few private hours to remember, to honor the sacredness of the profound changes that have occurred in your life. Birthdays are new beginnings, but they're also moments of personal closure, which are crucial if we are to grow positively into our authenticity.

Every birthday, not just the ones marking a new decade, is a significant milestone. Every age brings with it three hundred sixty-five Real Life lessons. "We turn, not older with years, but newer every day," Emily Dickinson reassures the birthday girl in all of us. And that's certainly something worth celebrating in grand style.

So: Happy Birthday! Happy birthday to you!

I've got a good feeling that this coming year is going to be your best yet. Heaven *knows* you deserve it.

DECEMBER 19

A Woman of a Certain Age

Men don't make passes at crones with big asses.
—Cybill Shepherd

Grow older, I shall. Grow older gracefully, I shall try. Grow into a crone? Over my dead body.

Crone. What an ugly word to describe such a creative chapter in a woman's story! But no woman need become a crone if she doesn't want to. You can be a Wisewoman without being a hag. Personally, I think invoking the image of a crone as a figure to emulate diminishes a woman's sense of well-being, rather than enhances it. The French call feminine Act-Two players "women of a certain age," and that describes a lot of women very succinctly; we become more certain of ourselves as our authenticity emerges. When it comes to a choice between Lena Horne's sexy chuckle or Madam Mim's gleeful cackle, I'm much more inspired by the lady and her music than by the lady with her magic spells.

I think it's vital for us to change the concept of feminine aging from "invisible" to "vibrant," because a sweeping societal change is waiting in the wings as the millennium approaches. Fasten your seat belts, boys.

Some of you are in for a bumpy ride as the Century of Women begins. By the year 2000, forty-two percent of all adult American women will be fifty or older.

However, we really don't have to wait to start making an attitude adjustment about second acts. We can start today. Contemporary women are already redefining the midlife passage that Gail Sheehy calls "the Flaming Fifties." After five years of research for her book *New Passages: Mapping Your Life Across Time*, she's discovered that the women of the 1990s are in their fifties. And from a look at the company she keeps—Barbra Streisand, Linda Ellerbee, Janet Reno, Judy Collins, Lauren Hutton, Jane Fonda, Martha Stewart, Donna Shalala, Judith Jamison, Barbara Boxer, and Tina Turner—the fiftysomething decade sizzles. "Women at this stage of life find themselves blazing with energy and accomplishment as never before in history. . . . the struggles that sapped so much of their emotional energy have subsided by now. The results [of Sheehy's research] strongly suggest that the dominant influence on a woman's well-being is not income level or marital status; the most decisive factor is age. Older is happier."

Coco Chanel reminds us that "Nature gives you the face you have when you are twenty. Life shapes the face you have at thirty. But it is up to you to earn the face you have at fifty." As long as the face staring back at you is authentic, you can call yourself anything you want to. But you'll find me hanging out backstage with red-hot chanteuses, *not* my "crone-ies."

DECEMBER 20

The Glad Game Reconsidered

Be Glad. Be Good. Be Brave.

—ELEANOR HODGMAN PORTER

Bah! Humbug!

You can't mean that, four days before Christmas!

Oh yes you can, *especially* four days before Christmas! This morning the test-that-tries-women's-souls commences. As with Christmases past, this year the test will be multiple-choice: who sleeps where, who cooks what, who gets custody of Christmas morning, which gifts haven't arrived, which gifts haven't yet been sent, who picks people up at the airport, who checks into Bedlam. Suddenly Ebenezer Scrooge seems like the most maligned and misunderstood figure in literature.

But I know someone whose literary reputation needs rehabilitation even more than Scrooge's. Remember Pollyanna? "The Glad Girl"? Now don't snicker at the thought of her name. Pollyanna's cloying determination to find the good in any situation might seem too saccharine to swallow four days before Christmas, but I think the instructions to her Glad Game should be festively wrapped and put under Everywoman's tree.

Sneer if you must, but the Glad Game is the perfect antidote when a holiday problem flares up suddenly. "Pollyanna did not pretend that everything was good," her creator, Eleanor Hodgman Porter, insists. "Instead she represented a cheery, courageous acceptance of the facts. She understood that unpleasant things are always with us, but she believed in mitigating them by looking for whatever good there is in what is."

When *Pollyanna* was originally published in 1913, no one was more shocked than Mrs. Porter at the sudden and widespread appeal of her eleven-year-old orphan's ability to find the silver lining in any black cloud. Although the book was published without any publicity, word-of-mouth recommendation made it a best-seller, eventually selling over a million copies. *Pollyanna* was translated into a dozen languages and was so popular that the character's name entered the English vernacular to describe irrepressible optimism.

In the novel, Pollyanna Whittier is the daughter of an impoverished missionary who continuously preaches the sermon of gladness to anyone who'll listen. The Reverend Whittier points out that the Bible records *eight hundred* instances of God instructing his children to be glad and rejoice. Obviously, the Reverend concludes, He must have wanted us to live that way, at least some of the time. One Christmas these beliefs are put to a severe test when the annual holiday hamper arrives from the Missionary Ladies Aid Society. Pollyanna has asked for a real china doll for Christmas. But when she opens the hamper on Christmas morning, she finds that the good ladies have mistakenly sent her a pair of children's crutches instead. Naturally, she feels devastated. In an effort to comfort her, the Reverend makes up a game to see if they can find one good thing about receiving a pair of crutches as a Christmas gift. Of course, they do: Pollyanna doesn't need them! Thus, the Glad Game is created.

After Pollyanna's father dies, she's sent to live with her Aunt Polly Harrington, a wealthy but lonely spinster. No one doubts that the reason Miss Polly never married is her very stern and unpleasant personality.

When Pollyanna arrives in the little Vermont town, she soon transforms the community with her spunk and good cheer. The sick become well; the lonely find friends and sweethearts; unhappy marriages are saved. Everyone except Aunt Polly succumbs to looking for life's bright side. But Aunt Polly remains a hard nut to crack. At one point she explodes: "*Will* you stop using that everlasting word 'glad.' It's 'glad'—'glad'—'glad' from morning till night until I think I shall go wild." (A response one could imagine sharing occasionally!) However, even Aunt Polly comes under the Glad spell after Pollyanna has a serious accident and only pulls through because of her own pluck and the goodwill of the community.

Pollyanna may be hopelessly sentimental, old-fashioned, and outdated as a novel, but this business about eight hundred reassurances to *"Cheer up, it's not so bad!"* deserves reconsideration. Perhaps this is exactly the nugget of good news we should meditate on as we deck the halls and roll out the red carpet.

DECEMBER 21

Seasonal Soulcraft

Live in each season as it passes; breathe air, drink the drink, taste the fruit, and resign yourself to the influences of each. Let them be your only diet drink and botanical medicines.
—HENRY DAVID THOREAU

The winter air outside is thin and bracing: sharp, frigid, icy, stinging. We do not saunter; the pace of our steps is quick, mirroring on the outside the accelerated forward motion within as holiday preparations take center stage. Once we close the door, the winter air is warm, heavy, and aromatic: wood burning, fresh evergreens, spicy cinnamon and ginger. Breathe in deeply the fragrance of contentment.

In winter we live in anticipation. Friends come in from the cold to be embraced by the convivial chaos of our family's annual holiday open house. "All year long I dream about your homemade eggnog," a guest confides as soulful gifts are exchanged: heartfelt compliments and a cup of cheer. In the kitchen, frothy hot wassail—spiced cider and dark English ale—is ladled into cups, ransoming hands and hearts from winter's chill. The dining room table groans good-naturedly from the bounty of abundance: roast turkey, baked ham, cheeses, fresh breads. Children of all ages crowd around seasonal sweets and winter's fruits: candy canes and sugarplums, pumpkin, mince, and apple pies.

Souls, sip and savor. Take thine ease. Eat, drink, and be merry in this season of joy.

"The most ancient spiritual wisdom was centered around the predictable shifts in seasonal energies. Rituals revolved around sowing, reaping and the cycles of light and darkness," Joan Borysenko, the respected scientist, gifted therapist, and unabashed mystic, reminds us in her tiny contemplative jewel, *Pocketful of Miracles: Prayers, Meditations, and Affirmations to Nurture Your Spirit Every Day of the Year*. "The seasonal rhythms correlate with our bodily rhythms. . . . Our dream life and inner life grow more insistent in the winter darkness. . . . The old year is put to bed, one's business is finished, and the harvest of spiritual maturity is reaped as wisdom and forgiveness."

For centuries, Eastern healers—particularly practitioners of Chinese medicine—have taken into consideration the impact the seasons have on our bodies, minds, and souls. But the symbiotic relationship between human beings and nature has virtually been ignored by Western medicine until recently. Now physicians acknowledge that some people suffer from a deep depression in the winter because they're extremely sensitive to darkness. Light therapy restores their subtle energies to a healthy balance.

Learning the soulcraft of seasonal healing can bring new depth to our journey toward Wholeness. In the natural world, winter is the season of rest, restoration, and reflection. There's not much of that going on this week, but after the holidays are behind us, consider how you spend whatever time you have at your personal disposal. And if you have as little as I think you do, reflect on how you can change that next year.

The twelfth-century German mystic Hildegard of Bingen suggests a simple way for us to begin exploring the richness of seasonal soulcraft:

Glance at the sun.
See the moon and the stars.
Gaze at the beauty of earth's greenings.
Now,
Think.

DECEMBER 22

Here Comes the Light

There are two ways of spreading light; to be
The candle or the mirror that reflects it.

—EDITH WHARTON

In ancient times, as the days grew shorter and darker, people became increasingly anxious and depressed, fearing that the sun was dying. Without the sun, whom they worshipped as a god, people knew they would perish. In order to coax back the source of their warmth, light, and abundance they created midwinter rituals, culminating in a great festival at Winter Solstice, on or about December 21–22, the longest night of the year. The women would gather greenery to decorate dwellings and prepare elaborate communal feasts. The men would light huge bonfires; in the bright glow of the flames representing the energy of the sun, they would hold revels with music and dance.

Today, celebrating the Winter Solstice is becoming very popular. For people who don't feel comfortable with organized religion or even with exploring an individual spiritual path, honoring the festivals of the natural world fulfills a deep, primordial need to connect with a Power greater than humanity, no matter what the Power is called. Women reviving the ancient feminine traditions celebrate the Solstice as the birthday of the Great Mother. Ecology-minded people, such as many Native Americans, honor the sacredness of their connection with the Earth. Women who have inter-faith marriages and can't make a choice between celebrating Hanukkah and Christmas often view the Winter Solstice as a neutral holiday the whole family can celebrate.

One meaningful way to celebrate the Solstice is to consider it a sacred time of reflection, release, restoration, and renewal. Zsuzsanna Budapest, a leader in the Goddess movement, believes the interval of the winter solstice is the ideal time to reach out to those from whom we feel estranged. In *The Grandmother of Time: A Woman's Book of Celebrations, Spells and Sacred Objects for Every Month of the Year*, she reminds us that "Every so often, we want to make a clean beginning and must therefore atone for the past. I don't mean we have to feel guilty; just the opposite. When you send out your Winter Solstice greeting cards, send some to people with whom you are not on good terms or to those with whom you have quarreled. Just say, 'Hey, let's forget our bad times. Blessings to you.' Each time you share forgiveness, somebody else will forgive." To make sure your forgiveness card is not misunderstood, which might make things worse instead of better, she recommends rubbing the cards with lavender buds or including them in the envelope. The card will offer a heavenly fragrance, surely the sweet scent of reconciliation.

It really doesn't matter whether we reflect the Light through our authentic gifts or whether our authentic calling is to spread it. What matters is that tonight the world is dark, cold, and bleak. Your flame burns so brightly. Share your Love and warmth with others. Watch the Light return.

DECEMBER 23

It's a Wonderful Life

[I]nstead of the usual "Why can't we make movies more like real life?" I think a more pertinent question is "Why can't real life be more like the movies?"

—ERNIE PYLE

Some holiday traditions are sacred. In our house one such tradition is the annual Christmas classic cinema celebration. Over the course of a week, as we hang stockings, wrap packages, and munch more popcorn than we string, we watch *White Christmas*, *Holiday Inn*, *Christmas in Connecticut*, *The Bishop's Wife*, *Miracle on 34th Street*, *A Muppet Christmas Carol*, and of course, *It's a Wonderful Life*, the fabulous three-hanky film fable starring James Stewart and Donna Reed. After nearly fifty holiday seasons, its potent alchemy of idealism and irony still conjures up movie magic.

In 1946, Frank Capra had no idea his sentimental small town fantasy would become a seasonal favorite for the ages. "In its own icky bittersweet way, it's terribly effective," *The New Yorker* begrudingly conceded. It's Christmas Eve, the night of miracles, and George Bailey certainly needs one. After a lifetime of saving the lives of others, he's giving up on his. He's broke, disgraced, facing prison, and in despair over a savings and loan shortage that is truly not his fault. After angrily wishing he'd never been born, he's about to jump off a bridge, when he's rescued by his guardian angel who temporarily grants his wish by showing him what the world would have been like without his authentic contribution.

George believes he's never had a lucky break. But when he steps back to reconsider his choices, he realizes they were the right ones. He's also a rich man: he has a loving and supportive wife, healthy children, work that makes a difference, and more friends than his house can even hold at one time. Quite frankly, it's a wonderful life he was about to throw away.

We can discover just how wonderful our lives are—exactly as they are right at this moment—by doing what George did (without the bridge scene!). We can step back and take another look at our lives and the lives we've touched. One of the unexpected blessings of writing this book is that I've gone back over the ordinary moments of my life, mining them for meaning. Writing a meditation around an encounter, mistake, regret, or conversation is very revealing—even more so than is keeping a journal. Every day in the two years it has taken me to write *Simple Abundance*, I've had a topic to muse upon, usually a title, often a quote, but always a blank page. Most of the time I've found out what I was writing about only after I was well into it. And what I've discovered—as you can—is that I've enjoyed a wonderful life. That knowledge has resonated deep within me and I'm truly grateful. Obviously there are many things I wish I hadn't done or crises I brought upon myself, but now I see that every experience is a loving teacher.

Next year I want you to seriously consider writing your own authentic meditations. Start slowly. Only write one every week or every month. Search for the Sacred in the ordinary and you'll find it. Nothing in your life is too insignificant to be a source of inspiration. As you begin to write your own meditations regularly, you'll be amazed at how much you start remembering or recognizing. The English poet Cecil Day-Lewis confides: "We do not write in order to be understood, we write in order to understand." If you start writing your own authentic meditations, what you'll remember, recognize, and understand is that it's a wonderful life.

Here Is All I've Counted Splendid

Write it down, when I have perished:
Here is everything I've cherished;
That these walls should glow with beauty
Spurred my lagging soul to duty;
That there should be gladness here
Kept me toiling, year by year . . .
Every thought and every act
Were to keep this home intact.

—EDGAR A. GUEST

Tonight is my favorite night of the year. In this quiet moment, Simple Abundance is not a philosophy but reality perfected. My heart is full of *gratitude*; striving for *simplicity* in our holiday obligations has preserved my sanity; *order* has kept all the moving parts moving; a sense of *harmony* has emerged because I finally stopped long enough to balance work and family at least for the holidays; *beauty* surrounds me in the festive decorations throughout the house, now illuminated and intensified with the glow of candles and a cozy fire; and *joy*, the child of laughter and contentment has arrived, the guest of honor at our festive family feast.

After dinner, after we have each opened just one gift and other members of the household are snug in their beds, it's time for my own private Christmas ritual: the preparation of a Nativity tray, an English medieval custom that never fails to bring the true meaning of this special night into sharp focus.

Legend has it that on the night of the Nativity, whosoever ventures out into great snows bearing a succulent bone for a lost and lamenting hound, a wisp of hay for a shivering horse, a warm cloak for a stranded wayfarer, a garland of bright berries for one who has worn chains, a dish of crumbs for all huddled birds who thought their song was dead, and sweetmeats for little children who peer from lonely windows—whosoever prepares this simply abundant tray, "shall be proffered and returned gifts of such an astonishment as will rival the hues of the peacock and the harmonies of heaven."

So I quietly take down from the top of the cupboard a huge willow tray, line it with cloth, and place on it a juicy bone from our standing rib roast dinner; a bowl of cat food; hay from the bale I used for autumn decorations; a warm coat someone has outgrown or grown tired of; a string of cranberries; a dish of fresh bread crumbs and sunflower seeds; and a plate of sugarplums.

Quietly, I sneak out the door and bring it down to the top of the stone wall in front of our house near the street. Sometimes there's snow, sometimes there's not, but it's always cold. I look up to find a bright star; is it *the* Star? It is to my eyes. I'm freezing. Now it's impossible on this holy night not to think of the homeless as I settle the tray into a drift or dirt. Two thousand years ago another homeless family depended on a stranger's charity. They didn't find any until an ordinary, harried, exhausted woman stopped long enough to feel her heart tug. Mine now tugs with guilt; that a basket and presents were dropped off earlier this afternoon to a shelter salves the sting a bit, but I'm disappointed and saddened that I didn't, don't, do more. I will next year, I promise. Sometimes I keep those well-intentioned promises, sometimes real life distracts me from Real Life. I don't do enough, and both Spirit and I know it.

I started preparing the Nativity tray because an almost palpable mysticism seemed to surround the legend. I was also very interested in the promise of astonishing gifts to rival the harmonies of heaven. Every year when I go out on Christmas morning to collect the tray, many of the offerings are gone. One year, even the coat. For all I know, I'm the squirrels' Santa Claus. But it does give me happy pause, wondering whose Christmas dreams came true.

And the astonishing gifts to rival heaven? Everywhere I look. But the best one is that now I can truly see them.

DECEMBER 25

Christmas

If, as Herod, we fill our lives with things, and again with things; if we consider ourselves so unimportant that we must fill every moment of our lives with action, when will we have the time to make the long, slow journey across the desert as did the Magi? Or sit and watch the stars as did the shepherds? Or brood over the coming of the child as did Mary? For each one of us, there is a desert to travel. A star to discover. And a being within ourselves to bring to life.

—Author Unknown

I first discovered this profound expression of Simple Abundance's essence just before I began writing this book. While browsing in a gallery in Vermont, I was drawn across the room to a display of work by the gifted calligraphy and graphic artist Michael Podesta. There it was—an elegant script rendering of exquisite grace. "That's it," my authentic self whispered. "That's Simple Abundance." Of course it was, and I had to have it. But when I spotted the price tag, I knew it wouldn't be at that moment. That's okay, I reassured Herod's daughter, writing the quote down. Just accept the gift of the quote right now; the print will come when it's supposed to. I picked up the artist's mail-order catalog and continued to enjoy a wonderful day with Katie, her cousins, and my sister. Back at my mother's, I mentioned the print and how this quote was the very first one I had for the book. "It's perfect for Christmas," I told her. "It sums up the book in one amazing paragraph."

When I arrived home, Michael Podesta's print was waiting for me, a good luck gift from my mother. After I had cried and laughed and called to thank her, I hung it over my meditation table. Its beauty acts as an anchor to my bedroom, the place where I sit, work, dream, sleep, love, and pray; its timeless message a deep harbor for my restless heart, a soulful safe haven. When I called Michael to ask where the quote came from, he told me that he didn't know; someone had sent it to him anonymously in the mail without attribution. But it spoke to his heart and he knew he needed to make a print using it.

To the unknown poet, giver of wisdom and truth, thank you for this very special gift.

"Oh, would that Christmas lasted the whole year through, as it ought," Charles Dickens lamented. "Would that the spirit of Christmas could live within our hearts every day of the year."

But what is the Christmas spirit? Perhaps the Christmas spirit, like the nature of the Beloved, is meant to be a Holy Mystery. Perhaps the Christmas spirit is our souls' knowledge that things, no matter how beautiful, are only things; that we were created, not always to do, but sometimes simply to be. Perhaps the Christmas spirit is a loving reminder that we must *make* time for the long, slow journey across the desert; we must *take* time to discover our star; we must *honor the time necessary* to brood over the coming of the authentic women we were created by Love to become. It has been said many times that our lives are gifts from God—that what we do with them is our gift in return. Today is the perfect day to remember this.

So this is my Christmas wish for both of us: that behind the toys, tinsel, carols, cards, and convivial chaos, there will come a moment of quiet reflection and peace. That it may be truly said of each of us that we know how to keep Christmas well, if any woman does.

Merry Christmas! and God bless us, God bless us every one!

DECEMBER 26

Two Lives

We must be willing to get rid of the life we've planned, so as to have the life that is waiting for us.

—JOSEPH CAMPBELL

Do you remember the scene in the movie *The Natural*, when Robert Redford is lying in a hospital bed, sick, discouraged, and about to give up? It's the last game in the play-offs and he's not there because he's been poisoned by the woman he thought he loved. Glenn Close, his childhood sweetheart, comes to visit him. Bob's feeling pretty sorry for himself. The doctor's told him that he can't ever play baseball again. But baseball is his life. He's thirty-nine years old and he's just made it to the majors. "I believe we have two lives," Glenn tells him. "The life we learn with and the life we live after that."

Well, she's right, as we've been learning up till now on the Simple Abundance path. And what have we learned? That there are only two classes in the University of Life. Over one door the sign reads: "Heaven on Earth." Over the other door: "Seminar on Understanding the Mechanics of How Heaven Works."

The first course is a hands-on work/study program. We live Real Life. Honest.

The other course is an intellectual seminar. We try to figure out how we can manipulate real life, with a little metaphysical mumbo jumbo. Maybe.

Every morning we're given the opportunity to choose which class it will be for the next twenty-four hours: Real Life or real life? In each class, there will be unexpected pop quizzes. Some of us are not given advance notice of when the final exam is scheduled; some students are more fortunate. There's no way of knowing which group we're in.

"On this narrow planet, we have only the choice between two unknown worlds," Colette instructs us. "One of them tempts us—ah! what a dream, to live in that!—the other stifles us at the first breath."

A Woman of Substance

First we have to believe, *and then we believe.*
— G. C. Lichtenberg

As the season of Believing seems to wind down for the rest of the world, please let me gently make something very clear. Many dreams still wait in the wings. Many aspirations are just within our grasp if we keep stretching. Many hungers need nourishment. Many yearnings must be acknowledged, so that they can be fulfilled. Many authentic sparks must be fanned before Passion performs her perfect work in you. Throw another log on the fire.

This is not the day you quit.

This is not the day you cry.

This is the day you stare down every naysayer in your life who doesn't get it yet. Because *you* do. Finally. And now you *know* that *faith is the substance of things hoped for, the evidence of things not seen.*

This is the day you shout, "I Believe!" Keep on shouting it until you're hoarse. No more muttering under your breath.

Do you know what happens every time a child says, "I don't believe in fairies!" A fairy falls down dead.

Do you know what happens every time a woman says, "I don't believe. It's taking too long!" The woman falls down dead. Inside. Where it counts. But it just might take another forty years before they get around to burying you. And do you know what they'll say as your ashes are scattered? "I don't think I can ever remember a time when she was truly happy." And they'll be right.

This is *not* the time you stop believing. You simply can't afford the luxury of skepticism. And what must you believe with every breath, until you do *believe?* How about the mystical alchemy of style and Spirit. In the past a woman's spirituality has been separated from her lifestyle. But now you know this doesn't make any sense. Never did. Never will.

Now you know that the union of Authentic Style and Spirit creates a woman of Substance.

You.

So keep on believing that you have the passion, intelligence, brilliance, creativity, wisdom, clarity, depth, and savvy to find that quiet center of solace, serenity, and strength necessary to create and sustain an authentic life. Every day is the prayer. An authentic life is the most personal form of worship. When you start believing, you'll discover that all things are really possible.

Clap.

Clap once again.

But let's really hear it this time!
Wow! That's better! Why, it's so loud, it'll wake up the dead.
Good for you.

DECEMBER 28

The Courage to Create the World You Want

You can have anything you want if you want it desperately enough.
You must want it with an exuberance that erupts through the skin
and joins the energy that created the world.

—SHEILA GRAHAM

The first time you think you'd like to do something a little different from the way you've always done it—maybe bring creole shrimp stew to the pot-luck supper instead of your delicious-but-predictable potato-and-peas casserole—you pick up a pebble. The first time you actually do it differently—whether you're delighted or disappointed in the results—you throw the pebble into the pond. The pebble sends out tiny, barely visible ripples of movement toward the center. No one else notices. But the woman who threw the pebble or spent two hours in the kitchen cooking up simple pleasure does if she's paying attention.

It's the same way with courageous acts in your daily round. They may be so small that only you realize something's going on. But one day, all those small but indelible moments of private courage will burst through. And both you and your world will have changed in an authentic moment.

We become authentic the same way we become courageous. By doing it. Not by thinking about it. Rosa Parks didn't think about becoming the symbol of the Civil Rights Movement when she refused to give up her seat and go to the back of the bus. But her authentic and exuberant commitment to equality pushed through her reserve, joining with the Energy that created the world. *Exuberant* means not only "joyously unrestrained" but "displaying something in abundance." Rosa Parks displayed an abundance of authentic courage. And at that defining moment, can we doubt that her soul was "joyously unrestrained" even if her heart was trembling?

This week African-American women begin celebrating a festival honoring faith, unity, heritage, and values. *Kwanzaa*, which means "first fruits of the harvest" in Swahili, was started in 1966 by civil rights activist Maulana Karenga. Over the last three decades the holiday has become widely celebrated by black women who cherish their authenticity. The seven-day celebration, which starts on December 26, is observed by lighting a candle each night to honor a specific value. They are, in order, unity, self-determination, cooperative work and responsibility, cooperative economics, purpose, creativity, and faith. There is no prescribed way to celebrate Kwanzaa except with great festivity.

Not all of us celebrate Kwanzaa, but the courage to embrace authenticity with joyous unrestraint is certainly something to celebrate by lighting a candle, raising a glass, and doing something completely unexpected that lifts our spirits. "We need to feel the cheer and inspiration of meeting each other," Josephine St. Pierre Ruffin believes. "We need to gain the courage and fresh life that comes from the mingling of congenial souls, of those working for the same ends."

DECEMBER 29

A Success Unexpected in Common Hours

I learned this, at least, by my experiment: that if one advances confidently in the direction of [her] dreams, and endeavors to live the life which [she] has imagined, [she] will meet with a success unexpected in common hours.

—HENRY DAVID THOREAU

Some days—and today is one of them—I think of Simple Abundance as the woman's Walden. But Thoreau went off alone to a hut in the woods. We're surrounded by offspring-on-vacation, many of them mopey and miserable because "there's nothing to do." When we point out that there's plenty to do, it's not exactly what they had in mind.

Henry, can we trade?

Today is the day the post-holiday blues usually drop in for their annual visit. After any strenuous exertion, especially one that's lasted several weeks, there's a natural letdown in energy and enthusiasm. "The life in us is like the water in a river," Thoreau tells us. It rises, even floods, but then it recedes until it finds its true level.

The year is drawing to a close; and whether we're aware of it or not, we're balancing our personal books, tallying up the profits and losses. If we're in the red as far as achieving goals, surrendering expectations, reaching for aspirations, coming to terms with situations we can't change, or acknowledging that we could have made changes but chose not to, we're going to end up feeling blue. If we've blown our budget, it's likely our purses will be leaner for a couple of months. Not fun.

To make matters even worse, you're probably not feeling very well. Don't be surprised by nasty colds or lingering chest congestion.

Practitioners of Eastern medicine expect these ailments in the winter; metaphysically the lung is the organ that processes grief. If we've experienced a loss—and all of us have in one way or another this year—we might still be grieving, unable to accept and release it. Old pain is very difficult to give up; by now it's a familiar friend, just not a very nurturing one.

When this happens we need to remember to treat ourselves kindly. This is the time to trust, not make judgments. Soon the children will go back to school. The company will leave. The work will get completed. The bills will be paid. The quiet moment will come. You'll be able to catch your breath, and then you'll notice that it doesn't hurt anymore. Your creative energy and enthusiasm will return. Once again you'll start to advance confidently in the direction of your dreams.

"However mean your life is, meet it and live it; do not shun it and call it hard names. It is not bad. . . . It looks poorest when you are richest. The fault-finder will find faults even in paradise. Love your life, poor as it is. You may perhaps have some pleasant, thrilling, glorious hours, even in a poorhouse," Henry reassures us. "The sun is reflected from the windows of the almshouse as brightly as from the rich man's abode; the snow melts before its door as early in the spring."

DECEMBER 30

Ithaka

As you set out in search of Ithaka
Pray that your journey be long,
full of adventures, full of awakenings.
Do not fear the monsters of old . . .
You will not meet them in your travels
if your thoughts are exalted and remain high,
if authentic passions stir your mind, body and spirit.
You will not encounter fearful monsters
if you do not carry them within your soul,
if your soul does not set them up in front of you.
                    —CONSTANTINE PETER CAVAFY

At the funeral of Jacqueline Kennedy Onassis, many of us heard for the first time the poem "Ithaka," written in 1911 by the Greek poet C. P. Cavafy. This exquisite song of encouragement to travelers setting out on a voyage of self-discovery is often read as an elegy. But I believe "Ithaka" is even more powerful when it becomes a personal affirmation of our Real Life journey.

Ithaka was the beloved island home of the legendary Greek hero, Odysseus. After playing a leading role in the Trojan War, Odysseus roamed the world for ten years, having adventures, meeting challenges, and learning lessons that profoundly changed him. Today an *odyssey* means a long, often exhausting, exhilarating and/or excruciating transformative journey.

The search for authenticity is our personal odyssey. As we move through our daily rounds on the Simple Abundance path as daughters, friends, lovers, wives, mothers, and artists of the everyday—what we are really seeking is the Ultimate Reality. We are seeking Ithaka.

Over the last fifty years, there have been several fine translations of Cavafy's poem, but for me, they've always seemed as if they had been written for men. This is not too surprising, as they were all translated by men. However, since "Ithaka" has become an emotional touchstone for me, a poem I find myself meditating on a great deal, I was inspired to create a personal translation/adaptation of Cavafy's classic for women:

> Pray that your journey be long,
> full of many summer mornings
> when with much pleasure and much joy
> you anchor in harbors never seen before;
> Browse through Phoenician markets,
> to purchase exquisite treasures—
> mother-of-pearl and coral, ebony and amber
> and sensual perfumes of all kinds—
> as much as you desire.
> Visit many Egyptian cities, content
> to sit at the feet of sages, eager
> and open to receive learning.
>
> Keep Ithaka always in your mind.
> Your arrival there is your destiny.
> But do not hurry the journey at all; be patient.
> Better that it lasts for many years—
> longer than you can even imagine.
> So that finally, when you reach this
> sacred isle, you will be a wise woman,
> abundantly fulfilled by all you have gained along the way;
> no longer expecting Ithaka to make you wealthy,
> no longer needing Ithaka to make you rich.
>
> Ithaka offered you the profound journey,
> the chance to discover the woman you have always been.
> Without Ithaka as your inspiration, you
> never would have set out in search of Wholeness.
>
> And should you find her poor, Ithaka did not deceive you.
> Authentic as you have become, full of wisdom,

beauty and grace, enriched and enlightened by all you have 'experienced
You will finally understand what all of life's Ithakas truly mean.

DECEMBER 31

Pray the Journey Is Long

*The world is round and the place which may seem like the end may
also be only the beginning.*
— IVY BAKER PRIEST

Life as a journey. Life as safari. Life as a pilgrimage. Life as a garden. Life
as the highest art.

Pathfinders. Prospectors. Pioneers. Detectives. Explorers. Archaeologists.
Pilgrims. Poets. Sojourners. Gardeners. Artists of the Everyday.

Women of Spirit. Women of substance. Women with style. Women who
have lived the questions. Women ready to embrace the answers. Women
who look great in hats. That's why we wear so many different ones.

Seekers of the Sacred in the ordinary. Real Life. The Mystical in the madness. The Holy Mysteries of the mundane.

Seekers of Love. Passion. Wholeness.

Authenticity.

Where are we headed?

We're headed Home.

Ithaka.

But before we arrive, there are vast worlds awaiting exploration. Worlds
within. Worlds without. Earth. Heaven.

Heaven on earth.

Sometimes the terrain is rocky and the slopes steep. Sometimes the jun-
gle is thick and its interior very dark. Sometimes the water is deep and the
waves extremely rough.

Do you see now why we need some variety in our approaches?

How will we know when we get there?

You'll know.

It's that simple. Real things are.

Are we there yet?

Not quite.

But it's taking too long.

Often it seems that way. Chronologically we're at the end of the year but
the beginning of the journey. Not to worry. We'll have all the time we need
in *kairos* to find ourselves.

Here's where we must part company. At least for a little while. I've got some discoveries I need to make on my own. And so do you.

But you won't be alone. Someone who loves you unconditionally is at the helm. Divine Love sustains you, surrounds you, enfolds you, protects you. Go in peace. You're as ready as you ever will be; well equipped for the adventures awaiting. Divine Substance—which is your only Reality—provides abundantly. But you must ask. Ask for help, supply, guidance, Grace. Ask for the Power to be switched on. Ask to catch the Flow. Ask to soar.

Ask. Ask. Ask.

Ask for a respite from all your crises. Surrender suffering, sorrow, pain. Surrender expectations. Ask to be surprised by joy.

Give thanks. Wait. Watch what happens. Get excited. Open your arms as wide as you can to receive all the miracles with your name on them.

Never forget that all you have is all you need.

Simple Abundance is a creative and practical path, full of joyful simplicities waiting to be revealed in the small moments. But don't forget, the path is a spiral. If you get stuck, look out at the wider vista and see how far you've traveled. For the parts of the journey when only the far horizon is in sight, Simple Abundance becomes a *caravel* of contentment—a small but sturdy vessel, strong enough to withstand storms. Her triangular sails have been spiritually designed to take advantage of winds blowing from either side of real life—the shadows and the Light.

Let's see. Do you have everything? Get out your treasure map. Think of your illustrated discovery journal as your ship's logbook. Your wise and loving heart is your compass to determine the latitude and longitude of longing. Check it every day. Trust it to keep you steady and on the mark. Love will not fail you.

Believe. Believe in yourself. Believe in the One who believes in You. All things are possible to she who believes.

Blessings on your courage.

Navigate by the stars. Search the Heavens for yours. Follow it. Keep on the lookout for soulful markers. They surround you. The Soul's awakening is gratitude. The Soul's essence is simplicity. The Soul's serenity is order. The Soul's serenity is harmony. The Soul's passion is beauty. The Soul's purpose is joy.

Pray your journey be a long one. Savor the stops along the way. They make the search marvelous. Meaningful. Memorable. Find and honor your own pace. There are still so many harbors to be seen for the first time. You're headed for someplace you've never been before. Keep your thoughts held high. Let personal passions stir your mind, body, and spirit.

Set your course for Authentica. Legend has it that once you reach her shores, you'll not leave the same woman. For if you find this sacred isle, you will remember what you have always known. You will discover the woman you have always been. No longer will you see things as they are. You will see things as you are. Through the parting of the mists where doubt and faith meet, you will see *the authentic self is the Soul made visible.*

Godspeed.

Joyful Simplicities for December

➳ Really deck the halls. Spread holiday cheer throughout your entire home with seasonal decorations, no matter what holiday you celebrate. Evergreens, beautiful flowering plants, candles, tiny lights, and natural decorations don't have to be associated with any one holiday unless you make them so. When you make a special effort to create beauty in your home, you set the stage for festivity, an authentic quality of Hanukkah, Winter Solstice, Christmas, and Kwanzaa.

➳ Dip into the simply abundant treasury of seasonal stories. Read O. Henry's *Gift of the Magi* before you start your Christmas shopping. Enjoy *A Christmas Carol* as a serial story over a couple of weeks. But don't stop there! Many wonderful writers have given us holiday word gifts over the last century. My favorite anthology is *A Christmas Treasury*, edited by Jack Newcombe.

➳ To every month there is a sale, and you'll find a savvy strategy for gift shopping throughout the year (and it works!) in *365 Ways to Prepare for Christmas* by David E. Monn, with Marilyn J. Appleberg.

➳ Delicious food is each winter holiday's gift. Enjoy potato latkes, Christmas pudding, sugarplums, eggnog, wassail, spicy creole shrimp. You don't have to bake to enjoy Christmas cookies. Start thinking about calories on January 2. Forget about fruitcake. Think about Black Cake. "There is fruitcake, and there is Black Cake, which is to fruitcake what the Brahms piano quartets are to Muzak," Laurie Colwin tells us. She'll tell you how to make one in *Home Cooking*.

➳ Hold a Christmas classic-film fest. Besides familiar favorites, there are many more marvelous movies you probably aren't familiar with that celebrate Christmas as the star or the subplot. You'll find a list of them in *The Great American Christmas Almanac* by Irena Chalmers and Friends.

➳ Frederic and Mary Ann Brussat, directors of the Cultural Information Service, write and publish a newsletter dedicated to identifying the spiritual dimensions of Real Life that can be found buried in contemporary books, films, videos, audio, television, and radio programs. They're also the authors of the delightful *100 Ways to Keep Your Soul Alive: Living Deeply and Fully Every Day*. For more information on their newsletter, write: Cultural Information Service, P.O. Box 786, Madison Square Station, New York, New York 10159.

➳ Fulfill the holiday dreams of a child who isn't yours.

➳ Share your blessings with a shelter for women or the homeless.

➳ Prepare a Nativity Tray.

➳ Find your star. Follow its Light. If you really want a star you can call your own, you can have one. Each day new stars are discovered in the heavens. The International Star Registry will name one after you, a dream, or a loved one as a memorial. (Contact the International Star Registry, 34523 Wilson Road, Ingleside, Illinois 60041; 1-800-282-3333).

⊰ Michael Podesta's inspirational calligraphy art is exquisite. For a catalog of his prints, write Michael Podesta Graphic Design, 8847 Eclipse Drive, Suffolk, Virginia 23433; 804-238-3595.

⊰ If you would like information on obtaining a signed, limited edition print of the Simple Abundance tree by Margaret Chodos-Irvine, featured on the cover and throughout this book, please write her, enclosing a self-addressed stamped envelope: 311 First Avenue South, #306, Seattle, WA 98104.

⊰ Look back on the aspirations you wrote on January 1. Don't be discouraged if you haven't achieved them. It's the reaching for them that's important. Make a new list. Carry whatever's still meaningful to you over to the New Year's list. Now confide your new dreams to a close friend, who will act as your witness.

⊰ Before we can welcome in the New Year, we need to put the Old Year's unfinished business—mistakes, regrets, shortcomings, and disappointments behind us. Here's how: write down on small slips of paper whatever you'd like to forget, then place the slips of paper in a small cardboard box. Next, with ceremony, wrap the box in black or very dark paper, sealing in the sorrow and hard luck. Say, "Good riddance," and toss the box into the fireplace to burn away the past. If you don't have a fireplace, toss the bad memories from the past into the trash where they belong. Keep only the good.

⊰ Chill something bubbly. Honor the Old Year with a farewell toast, welcome the New Year within. Offer thanks. Celebrate how far you've come, how much you've learned, and the glorious woman you Really are.

Happy New Year!

WITH THANKS
AND APPRECIATION

A longing fulfilled is sweet to the soul.
—BOOK OF PROVERBS 13:19

During the long time it took to realize the dream of this book, a close circle of family, friends, creative colleagues, and "unseen hands" assisted me and nurtured *Simple Abundance* as if it were their own. I want to acknowledge the love, support, time, creative energy, emotion, guidance, inspiration, and faith so generously given me as I followed my bliss.

With all my heart I thank God for entrusting me with *Simple Abundance* and rejoice in the countless contributions that made its completion possible. Among my many blessings was being led to Liv Blumer at Warner Books. Her generosity, thoughtfulness, passion, intelligence, wit, and warmth made our creative collaboration a joy. Liv's devotion to this book and respect for my work moved me deeply, and her elegant grace is evident on every page. A special note of heartfelt affection goes to Caryn Karmatz, who also superbly edited portions of this book, and always responded to my requests and concerns with cheerful élan and much appreciated kindness. From the very beginning it was apparent to me that Liv and Caryn really loved *Simple Abundance*, confirming what Victorian philosopher John Ruskin said about the harmony that results "when love and skill work together."

Grateful thanks to my other benefactors at Warner: Managing Editor Harvey-Jane Kowal, Production Editor Anna Forgione, and Copy Chief

Ann Schwartz. A private nod to a copy editor extraordinaire, Ann Armstrong Craig, for perpetuating the illusion that I have command of the English language. Kudos go to the Warner design team, headed by Executive Art Director Diane Luger, with assistance from Thom Whatley, for turning a dream into a beautiful book. Margaret Chodos-Irvine designed the cover art, which gives me a thrill every time I look at it. Finally, a word of thanks and appreciation to the many creative people working behind the scenes on my behalf, especially Publicity Director Emi Battaglia and her talented team; Julie Saltman, Hannah Simon, and everyone in subsidiary rights; Patrick Jennings in special sales; and the sales reps whose energetic enthusiasm sent *Simple Abundance* into the world with more than a wing and a prayer.

Many others blessed me enormously, and to all I express my deepest thanks: to Dona Cooper for the creative brainstorming that always kept true north in focus; to Dawne and Tom Winter for the gift of breathing space by inviting our family to share simply abundant holiday dinners and summer respites; to Barbara Mathias for almost daily doses of encouragement, empathy and editorial jump-starting; to Zoe Kosmidou for the enormous help with the Greek translation of "Ithaka" that made my adaptation possible; to Frances Bernstein for her translation of the hymn to Vesta; to Jeri Metz for herbal insights; to Carolyn Starks for lifting my spirits while I was divining the book; to Linda Frey for keeping me sane while I was writing it; to Annie for everything; to my wonderful sister, Maureen Crean, for laughing and crying with me in all the right places when I read her the work-in-progress, and for pushing me past my comfort zone; and to my great brothers, Pat Crean and Sean Crean, for never allowing me the luxury of doubting whether I could finish this enormous undertaking.

Special thanks to Jack Voelker, Director of Special Studies at The Chautauqua Institution, Chautauqua, New York, for giving me the opportunity to teach Simple Abundance for the first time in a workshop setting; and to the women who attended those early workshops and urged me to continue.

The love and support of my husband, Ed Sharp, gave me the time, space and freedom to write. He magnanimously kept the home fires burning for two years in between negotiating contracts, reading city council minutes, and driving the car pool while I had this out-of-body experience. Thank you, sweetheart. It's good to be back.

Although this was the book I was born to write, sadly my mother and father—Dru and Pat Crean—are not here to read it. May *Simple Abundance* be a loving remembrance. And, yes, Mother, "while" does have an "h" in it.

But my greatest debt is expressed in my dedication. This book could not have been written without my agent and dear friend, Chris Tomasino. Her unconditional faith in me and her deep and fervent belief that women needed to read what I needed to write made *Simple Abundance* possible. She was the first to read my drafts in monthly installments, and her vision of what this book could be stretched and sustained me. Her steadfast support gave me the courage to take the creative risks necessary to hear my authentic voice after two decades of writing. I learned to soar on these pages because I knew Chris was always holding the net.

My daughter, Katie, was eight when I conceived this dream and will turn thirteen just as the dream comes true. For over four years—a third of her life—she graciously accepted the overwhelming presence of "The Book" in her daily round with great humor, patience, and consideration. She assisted me in many mundane and mystical ways—from finding quotes to making savvy editorial suggestions to keeping the faith when mine faltered. But writing this book meant many personal sacrifices for my family, especially Katie. Only Heaven and I know the depth and breadth of her contribution.

More than the world can possibly understand, *Simple Abundance* is as much Chris's and Katie's book as it is mine. I only pray that they can read the love and gratitude in my heart between every line.

SARAH BAN BREATHNACH's work celebrates quiet joys, simple pleasures, and everyday epiphanies. She is the author of *Mrs. Sharp's Traditions: Nostalgic Suggestions for Re-creating the Family Celebrations and Seasonal Pastimes of the Victorian Home* (published in paperback as *Victorian Family Celebrations*) and *The Victorian Nursery Companion*. She has written a nationally syndicated column as a member of *The Washington Post Writers Group*, and her feature articles have been syndicated by *The Los Angeles Times Syndicate*. She also teaches Simple Abundance workshops to help women reorder their life priorities.

Sarah Ban Breathnach is the founder of the Simple Abundance Charitable Trust, a nonprofit bridge group between charitable causes and the public, dedicated to increasing awareness that "doing good" and "living the good life" are soul mates.

SARAH BAN BREATHNACH would like to hear from you. If you're interested in receiving information on a forthcoming SIMPLE ABUNDANCE newsletter, please write, enclosing a #10 self-addressed, stamped envelope.

If your favorite charity would like information on participating in the Simple Abundance Benefactors Program, please ask them to contact:

SIMPLE ABUNDANCE
P.O. Box 5870
Takoma Park, Maryland 20913-5870

Sarah Ban Breathnach is available for lectures and workshops based on this book. Details will be sent upon request.

BIBLIOGRAPHY

I am a part of all I have read.

—JOHN KIERAN

My sources for the quotes have been many and varied. Collecting the pithy and the profound has been an absorbing pastime for over twenty years, and I gather them from many sources: books, magazine articles, reviews, newspaper features, radio interviews, television broadcasts, plays, and films. My favorite collections of quotations are: *The Beacon Book of Quotations by Women*, compiled by Rosalie Maggio (Boston: Beacon Press, 1992); *Bartlett's Familiar Quotations*, Sixteenth Edition, edited by Justin Kaplan (Boston: Little, Brown and Company, 1992); and *The Columbia Dictionary of Quotations*, compiled by Robert Andrews (New York: Columbia University Press, 1993).

Ackerman, Diane. *A Natural History of the Senses.* New York: Random House, 1990.

Anthony, Evelyn. *The Avenue of the Dead.* New York: Coward, McCann & Geoghegan, 1982.

Antin, Mary. *The Promised Land.* Boston: Houghton Mifflin, 1969.

Armstrong, Karen. *The History of God: The 4,000-year Quest of Judaism, Christianity and Islam.* New York: Alfred A. Knopf, 1993.

Austen, Jane. *Mansfield Park.* New York: Oxford University Press, 1990.

Baldwin, Christina. *Life's Companion: Journal Writing as a Spiritual Quest.* New York: Bantam, 1991.

Beattie, Melody. *The Language of Letting Go.* New York: Hazelden/Harper & Row, 1990.

————. *Gratitude: Affirming the Good Things in Life.* New York: Hazelden/Ballantine Books, 1992.

Beeton, Isabella. *The Book of Household Management.* London: 1861.

Bender, Sue. *Plain and Simple: A Woman's Journey to the Amish.* New York: HarperSanFrancisco/HarperCollins, 1989.

Bennett, Arnold. *How to Live on Twenty-Four Hours A Day.* London: 1910; Plainview, New York: Books for Libraries Press, 1975.

Berenbaum, Rose Levy. *The Cake Bible.* New York: William Morrow and Company, Inc., 1988.

Berwick, Ann. *Holistic Aromatherapy: Balance the Body and Soul with Essential Oils.* St. Paul, Minnesota: Llewellyn, 1994.

Black, Penny. *The Book of Potpourri.* New York: Simon & Schuster, 1989.

Bolen, Jean Shinoda. *Goddesses in Everywoman.* New York: Harper & Row, 1985.

Borysenko, Joan. *Minding the Body, Mending the Mind.* New York: Addison-Wesley, 1987.

———. *Guilt Is the Teacher, Love Is the Lesson.* New York: Warner Books, 1990.

———. *Fire in the Soul: A New Psychology of Spiritual Optimism.* New York: Warner Books, 1993.

———. *Pocketful of Miracles: Prayers, Meditations, and Affirmations to Nurture Your Spirit Every Day of the Year.* New York: Warner Books, 1994.

Breathnach, Sarah Ban. *Mrs. Sharp's Traditions: Nostalgic Suggestions for Re-Creating the Family Celebrations and Seasonal Pastimes of the Victorian Home.* New York: Simon & Schuster, 1990. (Published in paperback as *Victorian Family Celebrations.* New York: Fireside/Simon & Schuster, 1992.)

———. *The Victorian Nursery Companion.* New York: Simon & Schuster, 1992.

Brontë, Emily. *Wuthering Heights: Complete Authoritative Text with Biographical and Historical Contexts.* Boston: Bedford Books, 1992.

Brussat, Frederic, and Mary Ann Brussat, editors. *100 Ways to Keep Your Soul Alive.* New York: HarperSanFrancisco, 1994

Buchman, Christina, and Celina Speigel, editors. *Out of the Garden: Women Writers on the Bible.* New York: Fawcett Columbine, 1994.

Budapest, Zsuzsanna. *The Grandmother of Time: A Woman's Book of Celebrations, Spells and Sacred Objects for Every Month of the Year.* New York: Harper & Row, 1989.

Burnett, Frances Hodgson. *The Secret Garden.* New York: Frederick A. Stokes, 1911.

Burnham, Sophy. *A Book of Angels.* New York: Ballantine, 1990.

Caddy, Eileen. *Opening Doors Within.* Forres, Scotland: The Findhorn Press, 1987.

Cantwell, Mary. "The Mauv-ing of America." *New York Times Magazine*, March 17, 1991.

Cameron, Julia. *The Artist's Way: A Spiritual Path to Higher Creativity.* New York: Jeremy P. Tarcher/Perigee Books/Putnam Publishing Group, 1992.

Carter, Mary Randolph. *American Junk.* New York: Viking Studio Books, 1994.

Chalmers, Irena. *The Great American Christmas Almanac.* New York: Viking Studio Books, 1988.

Clampitt, Amy. *The Kingfisher.* New York: Alfred A. Knopf, 1983.

Clason, George S. *The Richest Man in Babylon.* New York: Hawthorn Books, Inc. 1955; New York: Bantam, 1976.

Clurman, Carol. "Family vs. Career: A Woman on the Road to Power Takes a U-Turn." *USA–Weekend*, December 2–4, 1994.

Colwin, Laurie. *Home Cooking: A Writer in the Kitchen.* New York: Alfred A. Knopf, 1988.

———. *More Home Cooking: A Writer Returns to the Kitchen.* New York: HarperCollins, 1993.

Conran, Shirley. *Superwoman: For Every Woman Who Hates Housework.* New York: Crown Publishers, 1978.

Conwell, Russell H. *Acres of Diamonds.* New York and London: Harper & Brothers, 1915.

Cooper, Dona. *Writing Great Screenplays for Film and TV.* New York: Prentice Hall, 1994.

Coupland, Ken. "Is There a Doctor for the House?" *New Age Journal*, November/December, 1991.

Csikszentmihalyi, Mihaly. *Flow: The Psychology of Optimal Experience.* New York: Harper & Row, 1990.

Damrosch, Barbara. *The Garden Primer.* New York: Workman Publishing, 1988.

Davidson, Diane Mott. *Catering to Nobody.* New York: St. Martin's Press, 1990.

———. *Cereal Murders.* New York: Bantam, 1993.

———. *Dying for Chocolate.* New York: Bantam, 1992.

Davis, Bette. *The Lonely Life.* New York: Putnam, 1962.

Deval, Jacqueline. *Reckless Appetite: A Culinary Romance.* Hopewell, New Jersey: Ecco Books, 1993.

de Wolfe, Elsie. *The House in Good Taste.* New York: The Century Company, 1913.

Dickinson, Emily. *Emily Dickinson: Selected Letters*, edited by Thomas H. Johnson. Cambridge, Massachusetts: The Belknap Press of Harvard University Press, 1985.

Dillard, Annie. *Pilgrim at Tinker Creek.* New York: Harper & Row, 1974.

———. *The Writing Life.* New York: Harper & Row, 1989.

Dominguez, Joe and Vicki Robin. *Your Money or Your Life.* New York: Viking, 1992.

du Maurier, Daphne. *Rebecca.* New York: Doubleday, Doran and Company, 1938.

Eco, Umberto. *The Name of the Rose.* San Diego: Harcourt Brace Jovanovich, 1983.

Eliot, George. *The Mill on the Floss.* New York and Chicago: Scott Foresman & Company, 1920.

Eliot, T.S. *Collected Poems 1909–1962*. New York: Harcourt Brace Jovanovich, 1963.

Emerson, Ralph Waldo. *The Best of Ralph Waldo Emerson*. New York: Walter J. Black, Inc., 1941.

————. *Self-Reliance: The Wisdom of Ralph Waldo Emerson as Inspiration for Daily Living* (selected and with an introduction by Richard Whelan). New York: Bell Tower, 1991.

Engelbreit, Mary. *Mary Engelbreit's Home Companion: The Mary Engelbreit Look and How to Get It*. Kansas City: Andrews and McMeel, 1994.

Esquivel, Laura. *Like Water for Chocolate*. New York: Doubleday, 1992.

Estes, Clarissa Pinkola. *Women Who Run with the Wolves*. New York: Ballantine Books, 1992.

Fields, Rick, with Peggy Taylor, Rex Weyler, and Rich Ingrasci. *Chop Wood, Carry Water: A Guide to Finding Spiritual Fulfillment in Everyday Life*. New York: Jeremy P. Tarcher/Perigee/Putnam, 1984.

Ferguson, Sheila. *Soul Food: Classic Cuisine from the Deep South*. London and New York: Weidenfeld & Nicholson, 1989.

Fernea, Elizabeth Warnock, editor. *Women and Family in the Middle East: New Voices of Change*. Austin, Texas: University of Texas Press, 1985.

Ferrucci, Piero. *Inevitable Grace*. New York: Jeremy P. Tarcher/Putnam Books, 1990.

Field, Joanna. *A Life of One's Own*. London: Chatto & Windus, 1936; Los Angeles: J. P. Tarcher, 1981.

Fisher, M.F.K. *How to Cook a Wolf*. New York: Duell, Sloan and Pearce, 1942.

Fitzgerald, Sally, editor. *The Habit of Being: Letters of Flannery O'Connor*. New York: Farrar, Straus, and Giroux, 1979.

Foster, Patricia, Editor. *Minding the Body: Women Writers on Body and Soul*. New York: Doubleday, 1994.

Fox, Emmet. *Power Through Constructive Thinking*. New York: HarperCollins, 1989.

Fox, Matthew. *The Reinvention of Work: A New Vision of Livelihood for Our Time*. New York: HarperCollins, 1994.

Fraser, Kennedy. *The Fashionable Mind*. Boston: David R. Godine, 1985.

Freeman, Eileen Elias. *Touched by Angels*. New York: Warner Books, 1993.

————. *Angelic Healing: Working with Your Angels to Heal Your Life*. New York: Warner Books, 1994.

Geddes-Brown, Leslie. *The Floral Home*. New York: Crown, 1992.

Gibson, Cynthia. *A Botanical Touch*. New York: Viking Studio Books, 1993.

Glaspell, Susan. *The Visioning*. New York: Frederick A. Stokes, 1911.

Godden, Rumer. *A House with Four Rooms*. New York: William Morrow and Company, Inc., 1989.

Goldberg, Natalie. *Writing Down the Bones: Freeing the Writer Within*. Boston: Shambhala, 1986.

————. *Wild Mind: Living the Writer's Life*. New York: Bantam, 1990.

Graham, Abbie. *Ceremonials of Common Days*. New York: The Womans Press, 1923.

Green, Harvey. *The Light of the Home: An Intimate View of the Lives of Women in Victorian America*. New York: Pantheon Books, 1983.

Guest, Edgar A. *Collected Verse of Edgar A. Guest*. Chicago: Reilly & Lee Co., 1934.

Hampton, Mark. *Mark Hampton on Decorating*. New York: Condé Nast Books/Random House, 1989.

Hancock, Emily. *The Girl Within*. New York: Fawcett Columbine, 1989.

————. "Growing Up Female." *New Woman*, May, 1993.

Hanh, Thich Nhat. *The Miracle of Mindfulness: A Manual on Meditation*. Boston: Beacon Press, 1987.

Hepner, Harry. *The Best Things in Life*. New York: B. C. Forbes & Sons, 1953.

Hill, Napoleon. *Think and Grow Rich*. New York: Fawcett Crest, 1963.

Hillier, Malcolm. *The Book of Container Gardening*. New York: Simon and Schuster, 1991.

Holland, Barbara. *Endangered Pleasures*. Boston: Little, Brown and Company, 1995.

Holmes, Marjorie. *I've Got to Talk to Somebody, God*. New York: Doubleday, 1968.

Holt, Geraldene. *The Gourmet Garden*. Boston: Bullfinch Press Books/Little, Brown, 1990.

Huxley, Judith. *Table for Eight*. New York: William Morrow and Company, 1984.

Hyatt, Carole, and Linda Gottlieb. *When Smart People Fail: Rebuilding Yourself for Success*. New York: Penguin Books, 1988.

Irion, Mary Jean. *Yes, World: A Mosaic of Meditation*. New York: R. W. Baron, 1970.

James, William. *The Principles of Psychology*. New York: Henry Holt & Co., 1890; Cambridge, Mass: Harvard University Press, 1983.

Johnston, Mireille. *The French Family Feast*. New York: Simon & Schuster, 1988.

Kelly, Marcia, and Jack Kelly. *One Hundred Graces*. New York: Bell Tower, 1992.

Kornfield, Jack. *A Path with Heart: A Guide Through the Perils and Promises of Spiritual Life*. New York: Bantam, 1993.

Kosinski, Jerzy. *Being There*. New York: Harcourt Brace Jovanovich, 1971.

Kripke, Pamela. "Create Your Own Decorator's Notebook." *Mary Emmerling's Country Magazine*, Premiere issue; August, 1993.

Kron, Joan. *Home-Psych: The Social Psychology of Home and Decoration*. New York: Clarkson N. Potter, 1983.

Kushner, Harold. *Who Needs God?* New York: Summit Books, 1989.

————. *To Life! A Celebration of Jewish Being and Thinking*. New York: Warner Books, 1993.

Johnson, Samuel. *Samuel Johnson / Oxford Authors*. Oxford / New York: Oxford University Press, 1984.

Lamott, Anne. *Bird by Bird: Some Instructions on Writing and Life*. New York and San Francisco: Pantheon Books, 1994.

Lawrence, Brother. *Practicing the Presence of God*. Wheaton, Illinois: Harold Shaw, 1991.

L'Engle, Madeleine. *Walking on Water: Reflections on Faith and Art*. Wheaton, Illinois: Harold Shaw, 1980.

————. *A Circle of Quiet*. New York: Farrar, Straus and Giroux, 1972.

————. *The Irrational Season*. New York: The Seabury Press, 1979.

Lewis, C.S. *Miracles*. New York: Macmillan, 1947.

Lindbergh, Anne Morrow. *Gift from the Sea*. New York: Pantheon Books, 1955.

Magoun, F. Alexander. *Living a Happy Life*. New York: Harper & Brothers, 1960.

Martin, Tovah. *The Essence of Paradise: Fragrant Plants for Indoor Gardens*. Boston: Little, Brown, 1991.

May, Rollo. *The Courage to Create*. New York: W. W. Norton, 1975.

McCall, Anne Bryan. *The Larger Vision*. New York: Dodd, Mead & Company, 1919.

McGinley, Phyllis. *Saint-Watching*. New York: Viking, 1969.

Merker, Hannah. *Listening*. New York: HarperCollins, 1994.

Miller, Ronald S., and The Editors of *New Age Journal*. *As Above, So Below: Paths to Spiritual Renewal in Daily Life*. Los Angeles: Jeremy P. Tarcher, 1992.

Mitchell, Stephen. *Tao Te Ching, A New English Version*. New York: Harper & Row, 1988.

Monn, David E. *365 Ways to Prepare for Christmas*. New York: HarperCollins, 1993.

Moore, Thomas. *Care of the Soul: A Guide for Cultivating Depth and Sacredness in Everyday Life*. New York: HarperCollins, 1992.

————. *Soul Mates: Honoring the Mysteries of Love and Relationship*. New York: HarperCollins, 1994.

Morris, Mary. "Hello, This Is Your Destiny." *New Woman*, February, 1993.

Moss, Charlotte. *A Passion for Detail*. New York: Doubleday, 1991.

Murphy, Joseph. *The Power of Your Subconscious Mind*. New York: Bantam Books, 1982.

Nearing, Helen. *Loving and Leaving the Good Life*. Post Mills, Vermont: Chelsea Green, 1992.

————. *Simple Food for the Good Life: An Alternative Cook Book*. New York: Delacorte Press / Eleanor Friede, 1980.

Nearing, Scott, and Helen Nearing. *The Good Life: How to Live Sanely and Simply in a Troubled World*. New York: Schocken Books, 1970.

————. *Continuing the Good Life: Half a Century of Homesteading*. New York: Shocken Books, 1979.

Needleman, Jacob. *Money and the Meaning of Life*. New York: Doubleday / Currency Books, 1991.

Nelson, Gertrud Mueller. *To Dance with God*. New York / Mahwah: Paulist Press, 1986.

Newcombe, Jack, editor. *A Christmas Treasury*. New York: Viking, 1982.

Norris, Gunilla. *Being Home*. New York: Bell Tower, 1991.

O'Connor, Elizabeth. *Eighth Day of Creation: Gifts and Creativity*. Waco, Texas: Word Books, 1971.

Ohrbach, Barbara Milo. *The Scented Room*. New York: Clarkson N. Potter, 1986.

————. *Simply Flowers*. New York: Clarkson N. Potter, 1992.

Olsen, Tillie. *Silences*. New York: Seymour Lawrence / Delacorte Press, 1978.

————. *Tell Me a Riddle*. New York: Seymour Lawrence / Delacorte Press, 1979.

Pascale, Richard Tanner. "Zen and the Art of Management." *Harvard Business Review*, March / April, 1978.

Peck, M. Scott. *The Road Less Traveled*. New York: Simon & Schuster, 1978.

————. *Further Along the Road Less Traveled*. New York: Simon & Schuster, 1993.

Perenyi, Eleanor. *Green Thoughts: A Writer in the Garden.* New York: Vintage Books, 1983.

Phipps, Diana. *Affordable Splendor.* New York: Random House, 1981.

Ponder, Catherine. *The Prosperity Secrets of the Ages.* Marina del Ray, California: DeVross & Company, 1954.

————. *Open Your Mind to Prosperity.* Marina del Ray, California: DeVross & Company, 1971.

Porter, Eleanor Hodgman. *Pollyanna.* Boston: The Page Company, 1913.

Post, Emily. *The Personality of a House.* New York and London: Funk & Wagnalls, 1948.

Priestly, J.B. *Delight.* London: Heinemann, 1949.

Radner, Gilda. *It's Always Something.* New York: Simon & Schuster, 1989.

Raynolds, Robert. *In Praise of Gratitude: An Invitation to Trust Life.* New York: Harper & Brothers, 1961.

Redfield, James. *The Celestine Prophecy.* New York: Warner Books, 1993.

Ripperger, Henrietta. *A Home of Your Own and How to Run It.* New York: Simon & Schuster, 1940.

Rilke, Rainer Maria. *Letters to a Young Poet.* New York: W. W. Norton, 1934.

Robbins, John, and Ann Mortifee. *In Search of Balance.* Tiburn, California: H J Kramer Inc., 1991.

Roesch, Diana K. "Body Language." *Lear's,* February, 1994.

Roman, Sanaya, and Duane Packer. *Creating Money.* Tiburn, California: H J Kramer, Inc., 1988.

Rossbach, Sarah. *Feng Shui: The Chinese Art of Placement.* New York: Dutton, 1983.

————. *Interior Design with Feng Shui.* New York: Dutton, 1987.

Sacks, Oliver. *Awakenings.* New York: Summit Books, 1987.

Sangster, Margaret E. *Ideal Home Life.* New York: The University Society, Inc., 1910.

Saltzman, Amy. *Downshifting: Reinventing Success on a Slower Track.* New York: HarperCollins, 1991.

Sarton, May. *Plant Dreaming Deep.* New York: W. W. Norton, 1968.

————. *Journal of a Solitude.* New York: Norton, 1973.

Seal, Mark. "Laura Esquivel's Healing Journey." *New Age Journal,* May/June, 1994.

Seuss, Dr. *Oh, the Places You'll Go!* New York: Random House, 1990.

Shain, Merle. *Hearts That We Broke Long Ago.* New York: Bantam, 1983.

————. *Courage My Love: A Book to Light an Honest Path.* New York: Bantam, 1989.

Sheehy, Gail. *Pathfinders.* New York: William Morrow, 1981.

————. *New Passages: Mapping Your Life Across Time.* New York: Random House, 1995.

————. "The Flaming Fifties." *Vanity Fair,* October, 1993.

Sher, Barbara, with Annie Gottlieb. *Wishcraft: How to Get What You Really Want.* New York: Viking Press, 1979.

Sher, Barbara, with Barbara Smith. *I Could Do Anything If I Only Knew What It Was.* New York: Delacorte Press, 1994.

Shi, David E. *In Search of the Simple Life.* Layton, Utah: Peregrine Smith/Gibbs M. Smith, Inc., 1986.

Shinn, Florence Scovel. *The Wisdom of Florence Scovel Shinn.* (Includes four complete books: *The Game of Life and How to Play It*; *The Power of the Spoken Word*; *Your Word Is Your Wand*; *The Secret of Success.*) New York: Fireside/Simon & Schuster, 1989.

Siegel, Alan B. *Dreams That Can Change Your Life.* Los Angeles: J. P. Tarcher, 1990.

Sinetar, Marsha. *Do What You Love and the Money Will Follow.* New York/Mahwah: Paulist Press, 1987.

————. *Reel Time: Spiritual Growth Through Film.* Ligouri, Missouri: Triumph Books, 1993.

Starhawk. *The Spiral Dance.* New York: Harper & Row, 1979.

Steindl-Rast, Brother David. *Gratefulness, the Heart of Prayer: An Approach to Life in Fullness.* New York/Ramsey, New Jersey: Paulist Press, 1984.

Steinem, Gloria. *Revolution from Within: A Book of Self-Esteem.* Boston: Little, Brown and Company, 1992.

Stern, Jane and Michael. *Square Meals.* New York: Alfred A. Knopf, Inc., 1984.

Stern, Janet, editor. *The Writer on Her Work.* New York: W. W. Norton, 1980.

Stoddard, Alexandra. *Daring to Be Yourself.* New York: Doubleday, 1990.

————. *Creating a Beautiful Home.* New York: William Morrow, 1992.

Taylor, Terry Lynn. *Messengers of Light: The Angels' Guide to Spiritual Growth.* Tiburon, California: H J Kramer Inc., 1990.

————. *Guardians of Hope: The Angels' Guide to Personal Growth.* Tiburon, California: H J Kramer Inc., 1992.

————. *Creating with the Angels.* Tiburon, California: H J Kramer Inc., 1993.

Terkel, Studs. *Working: People Talk about What They Do All Day and How They Feel about What They Do.* New York: Pantheon Books, 1974.

Thoreau, Henry David. *Walden and Other Writings of Henry David Thoreau.* New York: Modern Library, 1992.

Thurman, Judith. *Isak Dinesen: The Life of a Storyteller.* New York: St. Martin's Press, 1982.

Tisserand, Robert B. *The Art of Aromatherapy.* New York: Inner Traditions International, 1977.

Tudor, Tasha, and Richard Brown. *The Private World of Tasha Tudor.* Boston: Little, Brown, 1992.

Uchida, Yoshiko. *A Jar of Dreams.* New York: Antheneum, 1981.

Underhill, Evelyn. *Mysticism.* New York: World Publishing, 1955.

van Amringe, Judyth. *Home Art: Creating Romance and Magic with Everyday Objects.* Boston: Bulfinch Press/Little, Brown, 1994.

Wasserstein, Wendy. *Uncommon Women and Others.* New York: Dramatists' Play Service, 1987.

———. "The Me I'd Like to Be." *New Woman,* December, 1994.

Watts, Alan W. *The Way of Zen.* New York: Random House, 1965.

White, Katharine S. *Onward and Upward in the Garden.* Edited by E.B. White. New York: Farrar, Straus and Giroux, 1979.

Wickham, Cynthia. *House Plants through the Year.* London: William Collins Sons & Co. Ltd., 1985.

Williams, Margery. *The Velveteen Rabbit, or How Toys Become Real.* Garden City, New York: Doubleday, 1960.

Williamson, Marianne. *A Return to Love: Reflections on the Principles of a Course in Miracles.* New York: HarperCollins, 1992.

———. *A Woman's Worth.* New York: Random House, 1993.

Witty, Helen. *Fancy Pantry.* New York: Workman Publishing, 1986.

Wolfe, Thomas. *Look Homeward, Angel.* New York: Charles Scribner, 1957.

Wolfman, Peri, and Charles Gold. *The Perfect Setting.* New York: Harry N. Abrams, Inc., 1985.

Woolf, Virginia. *A Room of One's Own.* New York: Harcourt Brace Jovanovich, 1929.